Gavin

Aristocrat, social renegade, shark-hunter, adventurer, racing-driver, traveller, naturalist, poet and painter, Gavin Maxwell was also one of the most popular authors of wildlife books in the twentieth century.

Never had the simple life been pursued by so complicated a character. Grandson of the Duke of Northumberland, Maxwell never knew his father (killed in battle in 1914, the year of his birth). His childhood was spent at the isolated Scottish ancestral home of Elrig, and after his wartime experience training SOE agents in survival techniques in the remoter parts of Scotland he set up a shark-hunting enterprise on the Hebridean isle of Soay – the subject of his first book, *Harpoon at a Venture*.

It was the explorer Wilfred Thesiger who introduced Maxwell to otters in the Tigris Marshes of Iraq. *Ring of Bright Water*, his classic account of life with otters at his inaccessible Highland refuge by the sea brought him worldwide fame as an outstandingly gifted writer and a latter-day eccentric in the grand manner.

This is the first full-length biography of Gavin Maxwell – a magnificent and moving *tour de force*, as evocative of the places and creatures in Maxwell's life as of the man himself.

Douglas Botting is a writer whose previous books reflect his interest in travel, exploration and wild places. He has accompanied expeditions to Socotra (Yemen), the Sahara, the Amazon and Arctic Siberia, and was an exploration film-maker for the BBC's 'World About Us'. He became a full-time writer with the publication of his highly praised biography of the German explorer-naturalist Alexander von Humboldt, *Humboldt and the Cosmos*. Subsequently he has written several travel books and a bestselling investigative history, *Nazi Gold* (with Ian Sayer). He first met Gavin Maxwell after the tragic death of Maxwell's first otter, Mij. He was at Sandaig during the writing of *Ring of Bright Water* and spent a winter there with Maxwell's otters during their owner's absence abroad.

BY THE SAME AUTHOR

Island of the Dragon's Blood
One Chilly Siberian Morning
Humboldt and the Cosmos
Rio de Janeiro
Wilderness Europe
Wild Britain
In the Ruins of the Reich
Nazi Gold (with Ian Sayer)
America's Secret Army
Hitler's Last General: The Case Against Wilhelm Mohnke

From Helen. Dec 1996.

DOUGLAS BOTTING

GAVIN MAXWELL

The Life of the Man Who Wrote
Ring of Bright Water

HarperCollins*Publishers*

IN MEMORIAM
BESSIE DOUGLAS BOTTING (NÉE CRUSE)
1910–1990

HarperCollins*Publishers*
77–85 Fulham Palace Road,
Hammersmith, London W6 8JB

This paperback edition 1994
1 3 5 7 9 8 6 4 2

First published in Great Britain by
HarperCollins*Publishers* 1993

ISBN 0 586 07109 1

Set in Linotron Bembo by
Rowland Phototypesetting Ltd
Bury St Edmunds, Suffolk

Printed in Great Britain by
HarperCollinsManufacturing Glasgow

CONTENTS

ILLUSTRATIONS

Unless otherwise indicated, photographs are from Gavin Maxwell Enterprises.

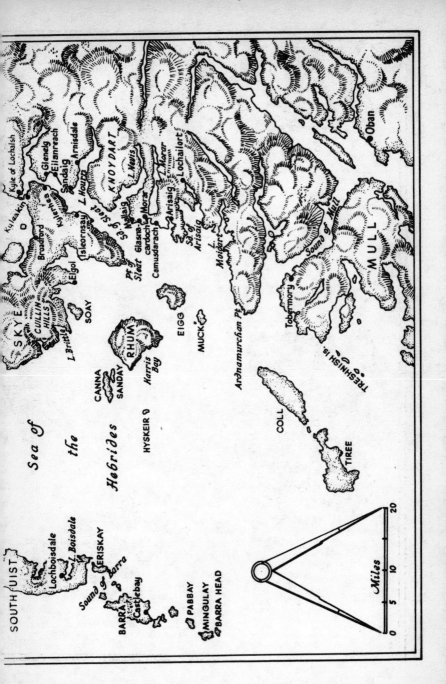

PREFACE

THE SEA IN THE LITTLE BAY is still tonight and a full moon casts a wan pallor over the Sound and the hills of Skye. A driftwood fire crackles in the hearth of the croft on the beach, and through the open window I can hear all the sounds and ghosts of the night – the *kraak* of a solitary heron stalking fish in the moonlight at the edge of the shore, a seal singing softly in the bay, the plaintive, child-like voice rising and falling like a lullaby in the dark.

It was on just such a night that I first arrived in this tiny paradise in the company of the unusual man who is the protagonist in the saga which follows. There have been many changes – natural, ecological, man-made – during the intervening years. A tall dark conifer forest now covers the once bare hills. The encircling burn, the ring of bright water, runs along a different course, and the dunes and the foreshore follow a different configuration. Sand martins no longer nest in the sandbanks above the burn, and far fewer seabirds congregate on the islands in the bay. The rowan tree – the source of so much myth and conflict in years gone by – finally died this summer, overwhelmed by the Norwegian fir planted beside it. Camusfeàrna itself is now a venue for fans and tourists who find their way through the woods to savour its peace and seek its pervasive magic; they leave votive offerings on the cairn that marks the grave of Edal the otter and on the great granite block that covers the spot where Gavin Maxwell's ashes were laid to rest, the same spot where he wrote his classic account of life with otters at Camusfeàrna, *Ring of Bright Water*.

There are otters still at Camusfeàrna, descendants of the wild otters that once kept Gavin Maxwell uneasy company at the long-gone house – I saw tell-tale signs of them this afternoon, in the tumble of rocks out at Otter Island. And the place has not lost its ability to surprise and delight. The moment I stepped out of the croft this morning a brilliant rainbow sprang up between the waterfall and the mouth of the burn, and a skein of seven whooper swans in perfect V-formation came honking low beneath the exact centre of the rainbow's arc – an effect so stunningly theatrical that I thought for a moment Gavin's spirit had returned to Camusfeàrna especially to lay on a good show for me.

But the shadow that darkened Gavin Maxwell's later life reaches even to the present. Plans are afoot to destroy his last retreat on Kyleakin Island, along with the wild otters and eiders that have colonised the place since his death, by laying the controversial Skye Bridge right across the middle of it. Soon the only testimony to this remarkable man's life will be the memorial rock with its life-size bronze otter overlooking Luce Bay, near Gavin's birthplace in his beloved Galloway.

Gavin Maxwell was to otters what Joy Adamson was to lions, Dian Fossey to gorillas, Jane Goodall to chimpanzees and Grey Owl to beavers. *Ring of Bright Water* was one of the twentieth century's most popular wildlife books (top of the US bestseller lists for a year, over two million sold worldwide, and still in print), and was habitually bracketed with Thoreau's *Walden*, Gilbert White's *Natural History of Selborne* and Henry Williamson's *Tarka the Otter*. The book gained its author a huge following as a guru of the wilds among a whole generation, especially in Europe and America, where he was ranked with John Burroughs, W.H. Hudson and Gerald Durrell as one of the finest nature writers of the last hundred years. The *New York Herald-Tribune* acclaimed it as 'one of the outstanding wildlife books of all time', and *The Times* described its author as 'a man of action who writes like a poet'. It was largely thanks to Maxwell and his book that the world began to take notice of the delightful species that was its subject, and to initiate measures to protect it from the depredations that threatened to destroy it. Today the otter is a protected species, and is making a comeback in Britain.

But never had the simple life been pursued by so complicated a character. Maxwell had come into contact with otters purely by chance, and his many schemes and adventures took him round many other bends in the river – travel, war, shark-hunting, portrait-painting, espionage, poetry and journalism. This is the first full-length biography to tell the whole story of Gavin Maxwell's extraordinarily picaresque and ultimately tragic life. Though there have been a number of previous attempts, all fell at the first hurdle of the family and the literary estate. My own redeeming virtues seemed to be that I had known Maxwell during the last twelve years of his life – an essential advantage, it was felt, in unravelling the paradoxical and contradictory personality of this highly complex man – and had conducted a long interview with him about his life and work shortly before his death (the starting point of this present biography).

Among the many complexities in the general mix was the matter of Maxwell's homosexuality. Readers who view modern biography as a kind of voyeurs' bazaar may be disappointed that I have felt unable to pursue this aspect to the last drop and tittle of detail. There are various reasons. One is my personal respect for the persons involved (of whom there are relatively few). Another is a stricture laid down by Gavin Maxwell's literary trustees that the matter should be aired only in a general way, with no reference to specifics. One accidental result of this, perhaps, has been to give Maxwell's heterosexual involvements a disproportionate emphasis in his life. Though inveterate witch-hunters may ransack these pages for clues to identities, they will be disappointed. Friends of Gavin Maxwell who appear in this book are just that – friends, or colleagues, whether they are accountants, animal keepers, fellow expeditionaries or shark-hunters. Or for that matter biographers.

I knew Gavin well. I liked him (not everybody did), I enjoyed his company and conversation and judged him to be a truly remarkable man, a troubled spirit and genius *manqué*, an outstandingly gifted descriptive writer, a latter-day eccentric in the grand manner whose life was spent on a kind of knightly quest to achieve an ideal life and find an ideal Avalon. In a word, I looked on him as a friend I admired, for all his patent flaws.

This biography could not have been written without the help of a host of people who knew Gavin Maxwell at almost every stage of his life. A full list of acknowledgements is given at the end of the book, but I would like to give special thanks here to the following select little band, who helped me above and beyond the call of duty: Michael Cuddy, Anthony Dickins, Richard Frere (and his book *Maxwell's Ghost*), Lavinia Hankinson, Peter Janson-Smith, Constance McNab, Terence Nutkins, Raef Payne, Kathleen Raine (and her reminiscences, poems and book *The Lion's Mouth*) and Jimmy Watt. I am grateful to Time-Life Books for permission to make use of my book *Wilderness Europe* in the writing of passages of

Chapter 20 and the Epilogue of this biography; to Gavin Maxwell Enterprises Ltd for permission to quote extracts from *God Protect Me from My Friends* © 1956, 1972 Gavin Maxwell Enterprises Ltd, *The House of Elrig* © 1965 Gavin Maxwell Enterprises Ltd, and *The Ten Pains of Death* © 1959 Gavin Maxwell Enterprises Ltd; to Penguin Books Ltd for permission to reproduce extracts from *Ring of Bright Water* (first published by Longman Green, 1960, Penguin Books, 1974) © 1960 Gavin Maxwell, *Harpoon at a Venture* (first published by Rupert Hart-Davis, 1952, Penguin Books, 1984) © 1952 the Estate of Gavin Maxwell, *The Rocks Remain* (first published by Longman Green, 1963, Penguin Books, 1974) © the Estate of Gavin Maxwell, 1963, and *A Reed Shaken by the Wind* (first published by Longman Green, 1957, Penguin Books, 1983) © 1957 Gavin Maxwell. I am also grateful to the Authors' Foundation (Society of Authors) and to Andrew and Margaret Hewson (John Johnson Agency) for their valuable financial support during the extensive period in which this book was written, to Katie Rigge for translations from Italian, to Dominic Cooper for the invaluable interviews he conducted in the West Highlands, to John and Viv Burton for their unstinting encouragement and advice, and to Duff Hart-Davis for his enthusiasm about writing this biography in the first place.

DOUGLAS BOTTING
Camusfeàrna
9 October 1992

I am going a long way
To the island-valley of Avilion;
Where falls not hail, or rain, or any snow,
Nor ever wind blows loudly; but it lies
Deep-meadow'd, happy, fair with orchard lawns
And bowery hollows crown'd with summer sea,
Where I will heal my grievous wound.

TENNYSON, *Morte d'Arthur*

PROLOGUE

Encounter with a Guru

A riddle wrapped in a mystery inside an enigma
WINSTON CHURCHILL

The first time I met Gavin Maxwell – poet, painter, shark-hunter, naturalist, traveller, secret agent and aristocratic opter-out – was a shock. 'Come round for a drink,' he had said over the phone. 'Say, about tea time? Take the bus up the King's Road. Get off just before the World's End and double back. The square is on your left, between the road and the river. Paultons Square. Number 9.'

I found the house without difficulty, a tall, narrow-fronted terrace house in a large, tree-filled square on the furthest frontier of fashionable Chelsea. There were two bell pushes by the front door: the lower one was labelled 'G. Maxwell', the upper one 'K. Raine'. I pushed the lower one and waited. Nobody came, and after a minute or two I went back to the pavement and leaned over the railings to try and peer through the front window. Behind the net curtain I could make out nothing but a brightly lit glass fishtank standing waterless and fishless on the windowsill. Inside the tank I could see the outline of what I took to be a large stuffed lizard, a sort of dragon in miniature, about a foot and a half long, with a tawny coloured, scaly skin. As I stared transfixed at this Jurassic apparition I saw that it was not stuffed after all but very much alive, for suddenly a long tongue like a snake's flickered out of its mouth, snatched at an insect that looked like a grasshopper, then just as suddenly retracted. My attention was instantly distracted from this startling reptile by a flash of iridescent wings and a frantic fluttering of brilliant electric-blue and green feathers in the upper window pane. Some kind of tropical bird, wings beating furiously like a humming bird, hovered momentarily behind the glass, then swooped away and was lost from view in the darkness of the room's interior.

At least the house was inhabited, I decided; no one could stray for long from a menagerie as exotic as this. I went back to the door, rang the upper bell and waited again. After a minute or two the door was pulled fractionally ajar. A keen, wary face appeared cautiously from around the door, eyeing me guardedly with a shy half-smile as I stood there. Gavin Maxwell was forty-three then, in the autumn of 1957, but to me he looked far older, with a face lean and lined and wrinkled as though he had spent a lifetime in the desert. His pale blue eyes stared at me quizzically from under a mop of flaxen hair.

'Gavin Maxwell?' I asked. 'I'm sorry I'm late. If I *am* late. I must have pushed the wrong bell.'

'You're *not* late,' he answered. 'You're *early*.' He spoke with a carefully modulated deepish tenor voice, enunciating his words positively, even authoritatively.

'I heard the doorbell the first time,' he went on. 'I was just checking you out through my binoculars from the other end of the room. Come in and have a whisky. After all, it *is* tea time.'

He ushered me in. The sitting room ran the whole width of the house from front to back. It was clearly no ordinary sitting room. It was ornate, baroque, even eccentric. Partly this was due to the creatures that inhabited it – the dozen or so tropical tanager birds that fluttered freely around the furniture, the giant Saharan monitor lizard I had already seen skulking in its glass case by the window. Partly it was the opulence of the furnishings – the antique aqua-marine tapestry hanging from one wall, the magnificent ormolu clock, the tall lampstand of clear fluted glass, the gilded mirror and luxurious velvet curtains. Partly also it was the eclectic assortment of weaponry that was dotted about the room – the chrome-nickel whaling harpoons and curved Arab daggers with jewelled hilts that hung from the walls, and the brace of expensive-looking hunting guns that stood in a corner. A portrait in oils of an attractive, long-haired blonde young woman, painted by Maxwell himself, hung above a mantelpiece. With an expression of faint sensual bemusement she stared across the room towards a life-size ancient Roman terracotta phallus on top of the bookcase opposite.

When Maxwell went out of the room to fetch water for the whisky I cast a quick eye over the titles in the bookcase. They were a random collection. Some were foreign editions of his own works – one about his shark-hunting venture, another about a Sicilian

outlaw and bandit, a third about his travels in the Iraq marshes.
Travel books by other authors rubbed covers with volumes on
zoology and ornithology, works by Freud on psychoanalysis and
Havelock Ellis on the psychology of sex, a book about Salvador
Dali, a book by Salvador Dali, and various specialist works including an illustrated monograph on the anatomy of the female human
pudenda and a police textbook on forensic medicine and murder
in all its forms. When Maxwell came back into the room he said:
'I had to sell most of my books when I was virtually bankrupted
after my shark-hunting business failed. I lost almost everything,
my inheritance, the lot. This is all that's left.'

He sat me down, poured me half a pint of Scotch, opened the
drawer of an escritoire, took out a small, ivory-handled pistol and
without a word clapped it to my right temple and pulled the trigger.

'You blinked!' he cried, laying the pistol down. 'You're quite
obviously *not* a born killer.'

The pistol, a .32 Colt semi-automatic engraved with his name,
had been a gift from the Norwegian Resistance when he was in
Special Forces during the war. This and the other implements of
death in the room contrasted oddly with the animals that lived
there.

'I've always kept animals,' Maxwell told me as he fed a live locust
(specially delivered from Harrods' pet department) to the monitor
lizard. 'Till this spring I had an otter I'd brought back from the
Iraq marshes. Then it was killed by a roadmender in Scotland. I
had a ring-tailed lemur as well until recently. But one day it bit
me through my tibial artery and I nearly bled to death. I lost two
pints of blood all over the floor before I got a tourniquet on to stop
the flow.'

Maxwell, I soon discovered, was more accident-prone than any
human being I had met. He was for ever being wrapped round
lamp-posts, shipwrecked on reefs, attacked by wild animals, half
blinded by sandstorms, struck low by diseases unknown to science,
robbed by Arabs, cheated by crooks, betrayed by friends. In fact,
in almost every way he was quite unlike any other person I had
ever encountered. He lived alone and was an avowed neurotic.
He chain-smoked and was rarely without an enormous glass of
well-watered whisky in his hand. He was far fiercer than I had
expected of an author whom a reviewer had described as 'a man
of action who writes like a poet'. Of medium height and wiry

build, he held himself taut and erect as if squaring up to an imminent assault. His look was fierce and his speech, too, was fiercely authoritative, even aggressive, with great emphasis on amplifier words like '*fantastic*' and '*absolutely*', and sudden dramatic shifts from humour and laughter to anger and depressive gloom.

His conversation was original and wide-ranging and his personality highly engaging. He was clearly endowed with considerable physical and nervous energy, a keen analytical intelligence, boundless curiosity and a restless creative drive, the masterwork of which was the high drama of his own chaotic life – for he existed, as far as I could see, in a whirl of wild hopes and plans and tragic episodes largely of his own creating.

This whirl of high drama tended to involve anyone who happened to be in the vicinity. When I casually told him that an Oxford friend of mine who had joined the Foreign Office (and was later to become Governor of Hong Kong) had recently asked me if I was interested in applying for the job of private tutor to the Crown Prince of Nepal, Gavin's instantaneous and exaggerated histrionics knew no bounds. 'That job cannot *possibly* be what it seems!' he pronounced, looking gravely alarmed. 'If I were you I wouldn't touch it with a barge pole. Were you given a telephone number to ring?' I gave him the number of an office in Whitehall. Gavin looked at it and whistled through his teeth. 'I thought as much,' he said. 'Do you have the extension?' I gave him that too. Gavin picked up the phone and dialled the number. When it answered he gave me a conspiratorial confirming wink and brusquely asked the operator for the extension. When the extension answered he slammed the phone down as if he had just received an electric shock and shouted across the room: 'Just what I thought! If you go after that job in Kathmandu you'll be getting into deeper water than you ever dreamed of. It's up to you, but don't say I didn't warn you.' Only much later, when I had got the measure of Gavin's propensity to conjure drama and danger out of thin air, did I realise that the course of my life had been shunted from one branch line to another.

Gavin was the first real writer I had ever met, and he shared my own enthusiasm for travel and wild places. It was this which had led me to contact him. In my last year at Oxford I was Chairman of the Oxford University Exploration Club, and was looking for interesting guest speakers who differed from the explorer stereotypes – the burly, booted pemmican-eaters and craggy, glacial crampon men. One Sunday in November 1957 I read in the *Sunday Times* a long, highly favourable review of a book called *A Reed Shaken by the Wind*, by a writer I had not heard of before called Gavin Maxwell, about a journey through the Tigris marshes with the renowned Arabian explorer Wilfred Thesiger. 'As the title suggests,' the review began, 'he is a man on a quest; and he even gives us a hint that this is a *voyage d'oubli* . . . The moving quality of the prose is the expression of a sensibility delicate and troubled, humorous and observant, with which it is a pleasure to converse and which overlays a tough and stoical core. For such disturbed personalities the marshes become a symbol . . .' I read the book, was impressed by the brilliance of the narrative and intrigued by the enigmatic persona of the writer, and wrote at once inviting him to come to Oxford to lecture about his travels.

Maxwell replied by telephone. Was I, he demanded sternly, the Douglas Botting who had just returned from an expedition to Socotra (an unexplored island in the Arabian Sea)? I said I was. 'Have you written a book about it?' he asked. I said I had. 'Then I'd like to have a look at it, if it's all the same with you.' I brought the manuscript on my first visit to Maxwell's flat. Later he wrote me a note: 'Let me say at once that you are a born writer in the true sense and will be wasting your time in the future doing anything else.' So the die was cast.

Maxwell's lecture to the University Exploration Club at St Edmund Hall was captivating and often hilarious. At dinner afterwards we were joined by my predecessor as Chairman of the Club, a rugged ex-Marine Commando whose nose had been broken in a bottle fight in a Maltese dockside bar, and who now appeared wearing a Stetson and despatch rider's boots and a heavily plastered arm in a sling. It was clear that Maxwell warmed to this kind of company, and when my friend told him he had broken his arm in Somaliland while trying a high-speed turn on a racing camel, Maxwell leaned across to me and whispered, 'Now that's what I call a *real* explorer.' By the time coffee came Maxwell had formed an idea. 'Why don't I go on a dangerous expedition and get lost,' he suggested to me, 'and you come out and look for me? If you find me I can write a book about the journey. But if you don't find me *you* can write a book about the search.'

He was only half joking, and when I next met him he had developed the idea. We should pool our talents and organise a major expedition – through the Berber country of the Atlas Mountains of Morocco, for example, or among the Nilotic tribes of the Sudd in the southern Sudan. It was clear that he saw his contact with the Exploration Club, and myself in particular, as a means of making use of our practical knowledge and expertise in mounting expeditions to far-away places for his own purposes. The success of his book on the Iraq marshes meant he was virtually bound to be commissioned to write another travel book, but he was not himself a very practical person, and was not entirely clear how to set up complicated forays of this sort on his own account. Perhaps I could help, he suggested; perhaps I could even make the film of the expedition while he wrote the book. But first, perhaps, I might like to accompany him on a less ambitious journey.

'I've got a little lighthouse-keeper's cottage by the sea up in the Scottish Highlands,' he told me. 'I haven't been there for a year. Not since my otter Mijbil was killed. I couldn't bear to go back alone. You'd enjoy it. It's miles from anywhere and you could bring your textbooks.' So began my association with that loveliest and most tragic of Shangri-Las – the tiny wilderness that was to become renowned throughout the world as Camusfeàrna, the Bay of Alders.

We drove up in Gavin's vintage Bentley roadster at the start of my Easter vacation of 1958. There were no motorways then and it took two long days to reach the West Highland coast. Little by little as the miles sped by I began to learn more about the curiously dramatic personality at the wheel. He drove sensationally fast, like a racing driver, with much squealing of tyres and restless changing up and down through the gears. When I commented on this he told me he had once been an amateur racing driver – but *only* when he was crossed in love, he said, and *only* after he had downed half a bottle of Scotch before the start, 'Otherwise I'd have been scared out of my wits!' He told me the psychologist and writer Elias Canetti (who later won the Nobel Prize for Literature) once remonstrated with him for his reckless speeding. '"Givin, Givin,"' Gavin said, gleefully mimicking Canetti's pronounced Central European accent, '"do you really have to identify with a motor car in this way? I mean, when the car goes fast, do you feel fast? When it goes slow, do you feel slow? When it breaks down, do you feel broken down?" And I told him: "Yes, all those things."'

At Scotch Corner Gavin pulled in for a fill-up of petrol and whisky. When I told him I would prefer a beer he remonstrated with me. 'My dear Douglas, you can't *possibly* drink that plebeian stuff. You *must* have a whisky!' All games except chess and canasta were also plebeian in the Gavin canon, I discovered. It was not until we reached Northumberland and turned off the main road to the small coastal town of Alnwick that I discovered why.

'I thought I'd show you my grandfather's house,' he explained. 'It's only just down the road.'

We roared up to the great gates of a medieval stone pile with curtain walls and battlements and round towers and a great keep. This was Alnwick Castle, the ancestral home of the Dukes of Northumberland.

'I used to stay here when I was little,' Gavin told me. 'I didn't like it much. I once said to my mother: "When are we going to get out of this tight place?" She was the daughter of the Duke of Northumberland. This was his castle – my grandfather's castle, the seventh Duke's. Now it's my uncle's, the ninth Duke's.'

By and large, Gavin wore his exalted status lightly – though he could make use of it if he chose to pull rank or impress, or if an accent or a social mannerism pained him. Though he was born an aristocrat, his political leanings at the time I first met him were towards the more radical left. He was much preoccupied with furthering social reform among the Sicilian poor, and even appeared on the same public platforms as such committed left-wingers as Victor Gollancz, the socialist publisher, and Fenner Brockway, the radical Labour M.P. But he *was* a snob of a particular kind. He could not abide fools, and loathed the human pack and all herd-like behaviour. He was not a true loner, but he hated groups and could never have travelled on an expedition comprising more than two people.

We crossed into Scotland and stopped over in Edinburgh. Gavin had a commission from an industrial journal called *Steel* to do a photo-feature on a magnificent brand-new steel bridge across the Firth of Forth. But the journal's editor had been badly misinformed. Though we went up the river one way and down the river the other we could find no such structure – it had not even been started. Rather than leave empty-handed we decided to photograph the old nineteenth-century bridge over the Forth, and spent a perilous afternoon clambering precariously over its ageing girders high above the swirling river. Not until we spotted policemen climbing after us among the girders of the bridge's intricate tracery of ochre-red ironwork, and heard them hailing us to come down, did we descend to earth again.

At dinner in the grand old North British Hotel that evening Gavin was highly elated about this escapade, but as the meal progressed and the wine flowed his mood darkened, and when a band started playing and couples began to dance his mood grew positively black and he sat staring furiously ahead of him with his hands clenched together under his chin in a characteristic gesture of outrage. Was it the fact that men and women were dancing together that so affronted him, participating together in a collective tribal ritual such as he, a lifelong and irremediable outsider, could never join? Or was it simply the drink?

'Douglas, one thing you must understand,' he confessed over another double whisky, 'I am no saint.' He was, it seemed, a homosexual, though not entirely so, for women had featured in his life from time to time. It took me a few moments to take this in. There was clearly no question that the implications of this revelation could involve me in any way, but it was obviously crucial to an understanding of his complex and rebellious nature and the alienation which characterised his life. Though he enjoyed female company, and had loved several women in his time, his inclinations were more strongly Grecian in nature, he explained, and he was romantically in love with youth and beauty. 'More *Death in Venice* than *Antony and Cleopatra*, if you see what I mean. You may not approve. But you'll have to accept me for what I am.' What he was, as I gradually discovered, was a troubled and tempestuous but often hilarious terrier of a man, a flawed genius whose obvious faults of character were redeemed by a rare generosity of spirit, an undimmed utopian vision of life and nature, and a stoical courage that was undaunted even in the face of ultimate adversity.

Gavin took the slow road to Sandaig. We thundered along a narrow twisting track that wound between mountains and over moorland to the west coast and the haunts of his wartime and sharking days – Arisaig, Morar, Mallaig. On the way we stopped at the houses of old friends and relatives, ex-commandos and harpoon-gunners, taking a wee dram here and a wee dram there, till the drams put end to end must have occupied the best part of a bottle and the road seemed to grow more tortuous than ever. Fortunately it ended at Mallaig, the brash, bustling, frontier-style

West Highland fishing port that had been Gavin's sharking base in the post-war years. From here, on a wild wet morning in early April 1958, we set sail aboard the island steamer bound for the Small Isles of the Inner Hebrides. I had never been this far north in Britain before, and the sights and sounds of this wild corner of Scotland were like a foreign land to me. Though Gavin had travelled these parts time and again in previous years, his enthusiasm was unabated. He was an ideal travelling companion, informed, inquisitive, even rapturous about the wild world that encircled us.

After an hour or two of butting the heavy Atlantic swell the steamer drew in beneath a great, hump-backed island called Rhum, where Gavin had hunted the basking shark a decade before. On such a storm-tossed day the impression of Rhum from the sea was daunting. Huge cliffs girt the island's wild coast; volcanic mountains, pyramidal and black, rose straight from the sea; an extraordinary turreted Gothic edifice, an incongruous dark sandstone red in colour, stood four-square on the shore. As the ship hove-to – Rhum was still privately owned then and we were forbidden to land – a flurry of gannets hurtled around us like flying crucifixes and floating 'rafts' of Manx shearwaters rose and fell in the sea like flotsam. Gavin had a fund of knowledge, historical and zoological, about the island. By Rhum, and its black peaks, Norse names and oceanic birds, by this whirl of sea and weather and far and ever-changing horizons, I was spellbound, as Gavin himself had been years before. Then the ship's siren echoed between the crags, the anchor was hauled in and the steamer pointed north-west into a heaving, rain-swept sea.

We disembarked at Canna, the most westerly and most beautiful of the Small Isles. The laird of Canna, the scholar and naturalist John Lorne Campbell (an etymologist and collector of Gaelic folk lore and a dedicated lepidopterist who tagged migrating butterflies like birds), was an old friend of Gavin's, and it was at his home, Canna House, a comfortable old mansion overlooking the harbour approaches, that we stayed during our few days on the island. It was on Canna that Gavin's mind began to turn to the subject of his next book. During a long walk along the high cliff's edge of grassy, rabbity Compass Hill in a blustering gale he argued the pros and cons of the various alternatives. One was a biography of Toussaint L'Ouverture, the mad black tyrant-emperor of eighteenth-century Haiti. I thought this an interesting but rather

arcane topic. The other possibility, Gavin told me between booming gusts of wind, was a book about his West Highland home at
Sandaig, our ultimate destination. 'I've written a little outline about
it. Perhaps you'd like to read it when we get back and tell me what
you think.'

The thousand-word document was not so much an outline as a
sample of text. I remember it as one of the most brilliantly written
evocations of place I have ever read, conjuring up in a few lines a
magic world of light and sky and water, an enchanted patch of
earth and the miraculous grace and freedom of the wild creatures
that inhabited it. It described an unforgettable episode of natural
prodigality and death Gavin had observed on a late summer evening
in Sandaig Bay some five years previously. The twin sons of the
local peat-digger had brought a bulky packet of letters down to
Gavin's house by the sea, and he was reading the letters in the twilit
kitchen when he heard the boys shouting from the shore.

He went out into the low evening light. The boys were standing
in the sea, their figures silhouetted against the pale, glassy water.
'They were shouting and dancing and scooping up the water with
their hands, and all the time as they moved there shot up from the
surface around them a glittering spray of small gold and silver fish,
so dense and brilliant as to blur the outline of the human torsos. It
was as though the boys were central figures of a strangely lit Roman
fountain, and when they bent to the surface with cupped hands a
new jet of sparks flew upward where their hands submerged, and
fell back in dazzling cascade.'

Gavin went down to the sea, and so dense was the mass of fugitive
fish fry in the shallows – driven there by predators further out in the
bay – that it was like wading in silver treacle. The scene was so extraordinary and the sense of fun so infectious that soon Gavin too was
shouting and laughing and scooping and scattering new fountains of
bright metallic chips. 'We were fish-drunk, fish-crazy, fish-happy in
that shining orange bubble of air and water . . .'

The whole passage was an ecstatic celebratory paean to place and
the natural world, but I little thought that in a year or two's time
it would form part of a modern nature classic that would transform
its author into a guru of the wilds for a whole generation of readers.
'I've come up with two possible titles,' Gavin told me after I'd
finished reading the piece. 'One of them is based on an invocation
Wilfred Thesiger taught me when we were in the Iraq marshes.

Whenever the Arabian bedouin see a raven, a bird of ill-omen, in the desert, they try and avert the omen by calling out: "Raven, seek thy brother!" The other title is based on lines from a poem written by a friend of mine, the poet Kathleen Raine:

> He has married me with a ring, a ring of bright water
> Whose ripples travel from the heart of the sea . . .

Gavin said he was inclined to use the raven image for his title; what did I think? I told him I thought it was too harsh and too black for what he had in mind. But a ring of bright water was a beautiful and evocative image. 'It has to be *Ring of Bright Water*,' I said. 'There's no other possibility.' 'All right, chum,' Gavin grunted. 'Anything you say, chum. Wouldn't you say? Or wouldn't you?'

I at last saw Sandaig late at night under a clear and brilliantly starlit Hebridean sky. From Glenelg on the Sound of Sleat a single-track road ran along a hillside to Tormor and a lone corrugated-roofed house that stood like an eyrie between the mountain and the sea – the home of Gavin's long-standing friends Mary and John Donald MacLeod, the local road-foreman and peat-digger, a canny and thoughtful old Highlander and an authority on the English classics. From Tormor the only way down to Sandaig was on foot, a mile and a half of slipping and stumbling over peat bogs and down precipitous rocky paths. Gavin had been dreading this final stage of his return to Sandaig and all the painful reminders he would encounter there of his beloved otter, Mijbil, who had been killed somewhere along the Tormor road almost exactly a year before. In the event, he put a brave face on it. We had had a few drams at Tormor before setting off and Gavin was in uproarious good humour as we plunged into the darkness. We had not gone far when he hit on a device that successfully took his mind off darker thoughts till we were near the bottom. This was the McBotting song, a soused improvisation on the infinite Gaelic permutations of my very un-Gaelic name of Botting, intoned like human bagpipe music to the approximate tune of a Highland reel.

'O McBotty, McBottlich, McBottock,' he sang,

> 'O BotFiddich, BotLachlan, BotLoch,
> O BotTavish, BotDonald, BotGregor,
> O McBotWatt, McBotIntosh, McBot . . .'

From time to time Gavin's tone-deaf pibroch was cut off in mid-drone, and the sudden silence was followed by a violent thump and a forcible exhalation of breath as he plunged from one level of the hillside to a lower one without any visible step in between. Then, amid much hysterical mirth, the dirge would begin from a different and more distant part of the darkness, and recede ever more downward and seaward below me.

'O McBotNot, McBotsIt, McBotsHisname . . .'

At a natural platform halfway down the view suddenly opened out, the world wanly illuminated by the gleam of a full, cut-glass moon. The darkened bulk of Skye lay to the right, and the pallid surface of an ocean bathed in moonshine seemed to stretch to the edge of vision. Apart from the murmur of a distant waterfall there was an unearthly quiet all around, and in the dead centre of this eerily phantasmagoric nightscape a distant lighthouse winked its beam every seven seconds. We carried on down. On the left the roar of the waterfall grew louder. We crossed a torrential burn on two parallel wires. Then on a flat patch of turf the outline of a house loomed against the moonlit sky – an abandoned lighthouse-keeper's cottage, two up, two down, with no electricity, water, drainage or indeed anything at all. 'You drink the water higher up the burn,' Gavin explained, 'and do big jobs lower down the burn. No toilet paper, please. Dangle from the branch of a tree and use a smooth pebble dipped in water like the Arabs do.' As we stood before the house, staring as if mesmerised at the sea silver and shimmering beyond, Gavin turned to me and said:

'Welcome to my Island Valley of Avalon.'

He turned the key in the door, then paused a moment.

'Do you know Tennyson's poem about Avalon? Well – this is where I come to heal my grievous wound. I know every dune and hollow and rock and twist and turn of the shore here like the back of my hand. Every stick and stone and fern and flower holds some memory for me. This is where my soul comes home to, Douglas. And this is where I shall leave my heart and bones.'

We went in. The flickering candlelight revealed a kind of dark wooden-panelled peasant cave festooned with all the paraphernalia of the sea – fish baskets and glass lobster floats, ropes, flippers and sou'westers, brass barometers and multifarious shells and relics cast

up by the waves. Much of the furniture was improvised from fish
boxes Gavin had beachcombed from the tideline. One chair had
been fashioned out of a wooden whaling barrel; another was a
passenger seat from a Dakota salvaged from an aeroplane junkyard
somewhere. A Primus stove stood on a fish box by the window,
and on a stone slab beneath the mantelpiece were inscribed the
words '*Non fatuum huc persecutus ignem*' (It is no will-o'-the-wisp
that I have followed here). After a year abandoned the house was
chill and dank as a tomb. We tried to light a fire but the driftwood
only spluttered and fumed in the ancient range-fire, filling the
candlelit gloom of the kitchen-parlour with an eye-watering blue
haze.

We spent two weeks at Sandaig. The sea was a few yards distant,
and a seal in the bay watched every move we made. On the left a
snow-capped mountain towered more than three thousand feet
above the house. When the weather was fine we walked out to the
small islands at low tide to search the rocks for the holts of the
native wild otters, snuffling with our noses close to the ground to
catch a whiff of fresh spraint above the spray line; or we collected
stones and scallop shells covered in the strange hieroglyphics of the
serpulid tube worm; or scavenged the high-tide line of the long
west-facing beaches for the flotsam washed up by the prevailing
wind and tide – practical everyday objects like fish boxes and hot
water bottles, or on occasion the enigmatic memento of some
unfathomable sea drama, such as a sail with the words 'NOT YET'
scrawled on it, and two brooms lashed together in the form of a
cross. When the weather was foul we stayed in the house in a hot
paraffin-fume fug of oil lamps and pressure heaters and toiled at
our respective deadlines – myself on my English studies for my
impending Finals, Gavin on the manuscript of his latest book, a
portrait of life in a poor Sicilian village, told largely in the inhabitants' own words, which was published the following year under
the title *The Ten Pains of Death*.

It became evident during my stay that I had not been invited to
Sandaig simply to keep Gavin company in this lonely spot. It
seemed I was also on probation in some kind of way. I suspected
that Gavin was using this trip to weigh up my capabilities as a
potential expeditionary on some joint venture in the future and to
decide whether I was compatible company in isolated circumstances
such as these. As his friend Kathleen Raine was to write later: 'He

had the gift of making us all his slaves. It came naturally to Gavin to initiate adventure, and to assign the parts to those who gladly joined him.' I was required to converse, to joke, to amuse, above all to sing (though he was tone-deaf he had a particular fondness for Greek bouzouki music and the Portuguese *fado*). I had to read poetry aloud (mostly Yeats) and comment meaningfully about it. I had to tackle questions on anything from the nature of God to the relative merits of the Ferrari and Model-T Ford. I had to ferry rucksack-loads of goods over the hills and forage for wild food around the bay as if I was on a survival exercise. I had to deliver an impromptu disquisition on the likely purpose and date of an ancient Pictish broch in the vicinity. I was expected to hold my drink and my tongue, comment intelligently on his manuscript, react sympathetically to his tales of lost loves and sexual misadventures, and be accepted by his friends – from peat-diggers and deckhands to local lairds and gentry. The fine details of social etiquette were important to him. 'You take sherry, Douglas,' he explained one day, 'just as you take tea. No indefinite article, you see. Don't ask me why. *But* – you have *a* whisky or *a* brandy. Definitely an indefinite article job, wouldn't you say?' My handwriting was analysed for clues to my personality, and so was my physiognomy. 'Do you have a temper?' he asked me one day. 'Do you ever fly off the handle, blow your top, run amok, raise Cain, boil over? Do you ever, dear Douglas, chew carpets or *foam at the mouth*? No? You have flared nostrils, you see. And flared nostrils suggest a hot temper.'

It seems that I passed the test, for on several evenings Gavin sat whisky in hand before the driftwood fire and rhapsodised on the great explorations we might undertake in some of the wildest and most far-flung corners of the planet at some indeterminate date in the future. 'When you have finished your Finals,' he would say, 'you can start the planning. Africa, New Guinea, the Amazon Basin? What does it matter? A true writer can write about anywhere and anything . . .'

The routine of the Gavin day was invariable. A huge and very late breakfast of black pudding, white pudding, bacon, sausage, egg, tomato and potato hash was fried up over the Primus stove in the kitchen parlour. Not long afterwards the first whisky and water of the day was poured out. There was nothing else to eat until late in the evening. By then Gavin would have finished the day's writing and read it aloud for my comments. Then, endlessly chain-smoking cigarettes he stored in the sporran he wore over his kilt, his whisky glass on the desk in front of him, he would hold forth. In the oil-lamp gloom of his pitch-pine panelled study, with the waterfall roaring in spate in the wild dark outside, he spoke with a lucidity and authority that compelled my attention.

'One of the primary symptoms of our civilisation is a search for our mammalian roots, for no social convention can destroy their validity or necessity. That is why there are now so many more books about animal relations than human ones . . .'

The whisky seemed to act as a lubricant for Gavin's mental processes and he ranged far and wide over a multiplicity of subjects, for he loved to inquire and discover almost as much as he loved to converse. Sometimes on these occasions I scribbled down the tumble of axioms, admonitions, confessions and musings about life and death, nature and art that poured out.

At times his reflections would stem from his private life, though in what context was never entirely clear. 'I have always found,' he would declare, 'that what you want and cannot have you can only have when you no longer want it . . .' Sometimes more extraneous activities would dominate his mind. 'Every journey must be to some extent a journey of the spirit, a voyage of self-discovery . . .' he would muse, and continue disconcertingly, 'What every secret agent wants is power – the power of knowing that nobody knows the power that he has . . .' On other occasions literary matters engaged his attention: 'I used to write poetry, but the poems I wrote were exercises in nostalgia, and no good poetry can be written out of nostalgia alone . . . Perhaps explorers who want to write their own records should be sent on a course first – nothing really tough, but to include the rescue of a perilously dangling preposition, the simple bridging of a yawning caesura, above all the avoidance of verbal wind-crust . . .' Once he had warmed to his theme nothing but total profundity, nothing less than God and the Universe, was good enough as a subject for his probing speculation: 'Why can't one admire the greatness of Christ's teaching without having to believe that he was God?' he would ask. 'He never said he was.'

And so it poured out, night after night, as we picked periwinkles out of their shells with a pin, or chewed limpets and garlic on toast, or boiled up an improvised goo called 'Maxwell's Bean Feast', a stomach-lining concoction which Gavin had invented in rural

Sicily while researching the life and death of the notorious
bandit Salvatore Giuliano. Sometimes he gossiped about friends
and acquaintances: Augustus John, the ornithologist Peter Scott,
Wilfred Thesiger, Kathleen Raine ('the most beautiful woman of
her generation at Cambridge'), Elias Canetti, the Sicilian social
reformer Danilo Dolci, Princess Margaret and many others. But
there were times when Gavin chose to reminisce about less salubri-
ous company, and I was regaled with lurid tales from his past –
brawls in Scottish dockside bars, dagger fights in backstreet Tangier
rooms, live sex-shows on the Hamburg Reeperbahn, the low-life
world of the outlaw and the outcast . . . All this, too, was part of
the man's contradictory and complex nature, for the knight errant
who pursued a beatific vision of unattainable freedom and beauty
also suffered from a *nostalgie de la boue*.

So were his violent changes of mood. For days he could remain
in uproarious good humour, imbued with a keen sense of the ridiculous and a driving zest for life, and bubbling with jokes and comic
fantasies and hilarious mimicries of the speech and idiosyncrasies
of his friends. Then one morning he would appear frowning and
dejected and ask: 'Have you ever known despair – I mean, *real*
despair? I have spent the whole night staring at my bedroom wall
in *absolute* despair.' The source of this despair he never explained.
Whatever it was, I had no doubt it lay at the heart of his troubled
personality, and was the mainspring of many of his consequent
actions.

On my last evening at Sandaig before returning south Gavin
gave a clue to the roots of his make-up. As an adult he was generally
perceived to be a kind of romantic hero and cultured tough guy –
an explorer, shark-hunter, man of the wilds. But as a child, he said,
he had been physically delicate and socially isolated. 'I was always
ailing, always being laughed at,' he told me. 'I feel it has been like
this all my life – being too vulnerable, too easily hurt.' Gavin's
alienation from the mass of humankind and his compensatory passion for the wild creatures of nature was the direct consequence of
an upbringing which, though privileged in terms of wealth and
status, was deprived in terms of human relations and emotional
life. He was born into the aristocracy and enjoyed all the perks of
his caste. Yet it seemed somehow appropriate that his own private
rendering of the Latin motto on the Maxwell family's baronial coat
of arms ('*Reviresco*' – 'I shall put forth leaves again') should be

'Don't let the bastards get you down'. For the aristocratic insider grew up to be a radical opter-out; a social renegade so shattered by his own English public-school experience that he later proposed the dismantling of the entire system of education for the young; a Guards officer who was seconded to that most arcane of undercover organisations, the wartime resistance and sabotage agency, Special Operations Executive; the grandson of a duke and the brother of a baronet whose preferred abode was a two-up, two-down light-house keeper's cottage in a West Highland wilderness and whose chosen company were the poor and unsophisticated – the tuna fishermen and rural bandits of Sicily, the reed dwellers of the Tigris, the Berber mountain people of the High Atlas.

Quoting (or misquoting) his favourite book, *Brideshead Revisited*, Gavin bitterly spelled out his present lot. 'I am homeless, childless, loveless, Douglas,' he told me. 'Time for another dram, chum.'

Next morning, we climbed up the sodden hill from Sandaig and in a vaporous kind of saturating Highland rain nosed the Bentley down the narrow track towards the high Mam Ratagan pass and the long road to distant London – and another world.

. . . But sing,
Dream, laugh, move on, be alone, have a choice,
have a watchful eye and a powerful voice,
wear my hat awry, fight for a poem if I like –
and perhaps even die.
Never care about fame or fortune –
or even travel to the moon!
Triumph by chance or my own merit . . .
Refuse to be the clinging ivy
or even the oak or the lime.
Perhaps I'll not get far.
But I'll get there alone.

EDMOND ROSTAND *Cyrano de Bergerac*
(translated by Anthony Burgess)

PART I

THE QUEST FOR AVALON

ONE

The house on the moor

Gavin Maxwell was born on 15 July 1914 in Elrig, the great grey
house his parents had built for themselves on the lonely moorlands
seven miles from the family seat at Monreith, Wigtownshire, in
the Lowlands of Scotland. His father was Colonel Aymer Maxwell,
a product of Eton, Sandhurst and the Grenadier Guards, a Boer
War veteran and heir presumptive to the baronetcy of Monreith,
who had planted rubber in Malaya, bred short-legged labradors,
done a lot of shooting – and not much else. His mother was Lady
Mary Percy, fifth daughter of the seventh Duke of Northumberland, head of one of the noblest families of England (and one of
the biggest coal owners in the land), whose members moved
between their castles and palaces at Alnwick, Kielder, Syon, Albury
and Northumberland House with an almost medieval retinue of
servants. When Gavin's maternal grandfather died, it was his uncle
and godfather, Alan, who succeeded him as eighth Duke of Northumberland. It was from the Percy side of the family that Gavin
inherited the characteristically long, straight, sharp Percy nose; and
from the Maxwell side, probably, that he unwittingly inherited a
genetic disposition to a modified form of what is now called 'bi-
polar illness' a form of clinical manic-depression, that was to exert
a considerable influence on his patterns of behaviour in later adolescent and adult life.

By descent Gavin thus belonged to the aristocratic élite, related
by blood or marriage to other great dukedoms and earldoms of
Scotland and England – the Argylls and Sutherlands, the Norfolks,
Richmonds and Surreys – and through them down the ages to King
James I of Scotland, Harry Hotspur, John of Gaunt, William the
Conqueror, Charlemagne and the Consuls of Imperial Rome.

Through his great aunt, Princess Alice, Duchess of Argyll, he was distantly related to the Royal Family, and he was also related – as twelfth cousin four times removed – to Lord Byron, whom he resembled in many ways.

Gavin was keenly aware of his aristocratic background, and intensely proud of it. It was an essential feature of his personality, without which he would have been a different animal. In adult life he was to use it as a passport to get him wherever he wanted to go, a shield to hide behind, a snub to put down people he disliked. But he was to learn that happiness is not necessarily the product of privilege. For there were other forces at work in his infancy and formative years, and these were to mould him into something quite different from the typical product of his class and generation, creating the misfit and the outcast, the dissenting and mischievous subversive of his later years.

Gavin was persistently and cataclysmically accident-prone throughout his life, so much a prey to misfortune that his life has something of the quality of a Greek tragedy, with Gavin in the role of the sacrificial victim of fate. His first misfortune took place at the very beginning, at the moment of his arrival in this world; his second not long after it. His delivery seems to have been a difficult and prolonged one, leaving him with five strawberry birthmarks stretching down his right inside forearm from the elbow to the wrist ('a symbol of shame before strangers, the most private part of my body') and a delicate and ailing constitution in childhood (according to his mother he had suffered at one time from a serious infection of the spleen). Then, less than three months after he was born, on 9 October 1914, his thirty-seven-year-old father was killed in the first German artillery barrage of the war, barely two or three hours after he had disembarked at Antwerp with the Collingwood Battalion of the Royal Naval Division of which he was commanding officer. His wife was thus left with three young children aged between one and three, and a sickly baby not yet weaned. The implications of this tragedy for Gavin Maxwell's future development were considerable.

The chances of the young widow marrying again were remote, for it was the unwritten rule of the Percy family that the daughters could only marry someone of the same faith as themselves, and this faith – the Irvingite or Catholic Apostolic Church, which believed in the restoration of the Twelve Apostles and the imminence of the Second Coming – had been embraced by only a handful of aristocratic families in the British Isles. Faced with the grief of mourning and the prospect of spending her prime in solitary widowhood, Lady Mary, who had been one of the two noted beauties of her family, rejected her sexuality. In her voice, manner and dress she denied her femininity, striding about the moors in tweeds as her husband might have done had he lived. All her natural instincts for love and affection were lavished on her youngest child, Gavin, who had been her husband's final gift to her, and was the most vulnerable, most needy and most dear human being in her life at the moment when the shock and grief of her husband's death were most acute and unbearable.

'I kept Gavin very much as the child of my anguish,' Lady Mary was to confide in her old age, 'and he stayed in my bedroom until he was eight years old.' Between the forlorn young mother and her ailing child there developed a relationship so close that it was to inflict a permanent imprint on the personality of the child. Many years later, in his middle age and in his cups, Gavin was to admit to a close friend in Tangier that he believed his mother was the cause of all the problems in his life. 'Was she one of those cold, aloof, icily aristocratic mothers of the period?' his friend asked. 'No,' Gavin replied. 'Exactly the opposite, alas. I was suffocated by love.' He was also suffocated – as were his siblings – by the sternly moralistic and dominating persona of his mother.

Frail and ailing, and never knowing a father, Gavin was brought up close to his mother's apron strings, and during the early years of his boyhood he not only slept in her bedroom but in her bed as well. Nothing could ever replace such mother love, and in the years to come life would always seem bereft by comparison. Brought up in a largely female ambience, and lulled by so much unfailing security and affection, it is hardly surprising that the boy grew up dangerously uncarapaced, like a hermit crab without a shell; hardly surprising that the adolescent found it difficult to relate to adult women or resolve the conundrums of his own sexuality; or that the adult was so preoccupied with proving his masculinity and rejecting female values.

But there were substantial compensations to be found in the strange milieu in which he grew up. Chief among them was Elrig itself, built four-square on a hill of heather and bracken. Elrig was to be Gavin's model for his idealised Island Valley of Avalon throughout his life, the Eden from which he was eventually expelled and to which he sought perpetually to return, the Paradise whose essence and myth he recreated in the Camusfeàrna of *Ring of Bright Water*, only to be banished one last time. Strictly speaking Elrig did not become his home until he was four, for during the war years his mother found it too painful to live in what had once been the conjugal home, and chose to reside with her children in various family houses far away in London and the south instead. But in the summer of 1918, with the war and mourning near to their end, she returned to Elrig, and it was Elrig that Gavin was to remember as his true childhood home. His memory of it, his longing and nostalgia for the untrammelled happiness he experienced there, was to haunt him through all the days of his life. More than forty-five years later he would still remember the house with a love undimmed by time – early images of 'big windswept sunny spaces', picnics on the moors, peat-fires in the nursery, the sound of the moaning wind, the smell of bog myrtle crushed in the hand, the acrid tang of hill sheep and the smell and taste of bracken fronds as bitter as almonds.

It was in and around Elrig and the wide unencumbered spaces of rural Galloway that Gavin Maxwell first grew aware of nature and landscape, and first felt the exhilarating freedom of the moors and skies. From his mother he had inherited or acquired an appreciation for natural beauty that was spare, austere and wild – 'an inherent approach of melancholy or nostalgia,' he was to write, 'so that splendour could not be splendid if it were not desolate too.' It was at Elrig too that he discovered the deep, serene happiness of life far from the hue and cry, the baying gabble of the human pack. Gavin grew up as shy as a wild animal within the tiny, closed community of his family. Apart from his brothers Aymer and Eustace and his sister Christian he met no other children. Apart from his mother, occasional relatives, and the servants that tended this reclusive household – a full complement of staff in livery – he met few other human beings. Out at play on the wild moors, barefoot, kilted and armed with slate-headed tomahawks the gamekeeper had made for them, the children explored the world of nature with the intimate proximity of natives of the Amazon rainforest, tunnelling through the high bracken that formed a canopy above their heads, hearts pounding at the thump of a rabbit's foot or sudden animal movement. It was out in the Elrig wilderness, close to the ground and in intimate contact with nature in all its teeming minutiae, that Gavin first learned to observe with a close, objective eye the myriad forms and idiosyncrasies of living things – the intricate pattern of bracken seeds on the undersides of the leaves, the tiny bubbles that made up cuckoo-spit, the sound and colour of insects swarming in the sun. 'Slice through a bracken stem with the keen Stone Age tomahawk and one revealed in the juicy marrow the brown outline of an oak tree; the very tree, our governess assured us, in which Charles II had hidden . . .'

Certain close relatives also played a key role in shaping the young Gavin's interests and ambitions in those early formative years. Closest in terms of geography and chronology (though in no other respect) was his paternal grandfather, Sir Herbert Maxwell, Bart., KT., P.C., F.R.S., seventh Baronet of Monreith, Lord Lieutenant of the County, Grand Old Man of Galloway, and scion of one of the oldest aristocratic families of Scotland. This awesome patriarch had not only pursued a distinguished political career as sometime Secretary of State for Scotland and Lord of the Treasury, but had also achieved academic fame as a man of letters and natural historian. Sir Herbert – a venerable figure whom Gavin knew as 'Gar' and who lived alone in the mouldering family seat at Monreith on the lowlands by the sea overlooking the White Loch of Myrton – was already seventy-three (and had another twenty years to live) when Gavin returned to Elrig at the end of the Great War. The chasm of age was too great to allow any close contact between the young Gavin and his family's most distinguished elder, and in any case visits were few, for his mother cordially disliked the old man, who had turned his back on the family faith and was so financially inept that he had managed to run up an overdraft of £120,000. In the gardens of Monreith Sir Herbert had formed one of the finest collections of flowering shrubs and trees in Britain, and in his leisure hours, when he was not writing his voluminous memoirs and learned articles, he would work at an easel painting the flowers of his garden as a record of the collection he had planted beyond his window. For many years he remained for Gavin a potent model in the fields of writing, painting, natural history and historical enquiry, a model which the growing boy might himself aspire to emulate one day.

A more direct influence and spur to action was Gavin's aunt Lady Muriel Percy, the youngest of his mother's sisters, and familiarly known as Aunty Moo. Unconventional, slightly mannish and inclined to outbursts of irritation, Moo spoke with a pronounced drawl and had the knack of arousing children's interest in new things. She was, in Gavin's estimation, an exceedingly good general naturalist, as well as a serious research zoologist specialising in the denizens of ponds and rock pools. Like Gavin's mother she was also a talented water-colourist and draughtsman, though she concentrated exclusively on illustrating the creatures that interested her. Above all, her enthusiasm for revealing the secret lives of the natural world communicated itself to the Maxwell children 'like mercury filling an empty tube'.

With Aunt Moo's guidance and encouragement Gavin and his siblings would explore the pools of the garden and encircling moorland and learn the slimy mysteries of frogspawn and tadpoles, newts and aquatic insects. Sometimes they would venture further afield, setting off in their mother's 1914 Ford (with uniformed chauffeur, brass lamps and gleaming radiator) on excursions to the sea a few miles away, and bringing back new wonders discovered by Aunt Moo in the sea-pools and tide's edge.

It was Aunt Moo who arranged the unused gun-room of Gavin's father into a biological laboratory – 'a sort of primary school for the study of life' – full of aquaria, vivaria and glass-fronted cages in which spawn hatched, caterpillars pupated, grubs metamorphosed, newts hibernated and the lower forms of animal life were ranged in all their oddity and variety, 'so that we were on nodding terms,' Gavin observed, 'with almost every living thing we could see.' The children became collectors in the classic Victorian mould, each a specialist in his favoured field. Aymer collected beetles, Eustace every kind of insect except beetles, Gavin butterflies, dragonflies and birds' eggs. Because Gavin so worshipped his elder brother Aymer they would often go around together like twins, hunting for Aymer's beetles beneath stones and the undersides of dead animal carcases – a true nether world of nightmare.

But more often Gavin ventured out on to the moor alone in pursuit of his butterfly prey, dressed in a kilt and white cotton sun-hat, and carrying a butterfly-net and killing bottle. Sometimes, down in the marshy hollows of bog myrtle and rushes, he would glimpse a butterfly he had only set eyes on in a book, and once, when a very unusual and spectacular species eluded every swipe of his net, he was forced to resort to prayer. 'Please God,' he prayed aloud, kneeling on the soft sphagnum moss of the boggy hollow, 'let me catch the Dark Green Fritillary.' And God did, 'strengthening an absolute belief that could not be called into question'.

Under Moo's aegis Gavin became a tireless naturalist, illustrator and author – an infantile pre-echo of the professional he was to become. By the age of nine he was compiling illustrated monographs such as 'The Book of Birds with Beautiful Tails' and his more general 'Book of Birds and Animals' – childish pastiches of the genre put together from arcane ornithological fantasies:

The Crested Bird. This is a foreign bird you find his eggs in foreign lands they would be about as big as the biggest persons head if you compaired the sizes.

The Skiping Long Nose. He lives in America like the Mustangs. He has babies almost as big as their mothers. The mothers are only as big as your head.

The Brown Legged Hinda. Does eat chalks and knifes and blue eyes and grass his babies are brown and white.

Gradually the children progressed to an interest in larger creatures. There were goats, bantam cocks, hedgehogs, wild rabbits, owls, a tame jackdaw that was shot by the Duke of Abercorn's butler in the act of stealing a spoon from the Elrig pantry, a whole family of rooks that would perch all over Gavin 'like parasites' wherever he went, and a heron that shone like a beacon in the dark, the phosphorescence of the putrid fish it had eaten glowing eerily through the thin skin of its distended crop.

Gavin began to develop an extraordinary gift with animals that was never to leave him. His cousin Lady Elizabeth Percy (later the Duchess of Hamilton) remembered playing cards with Gavin after tea one day, with a barnyard hen he had tamed sitting on the back of his chair. 'What was so remarkable,' Lady Elizabeth recalled, 'was that he had only made its acquaintance forty-eight hours before. He also had a tame Brown Owl called Andrew which appeared to live in a holly tree and came to him whenever he called. A mouse only had to run across the floor and in no time at all Gavin had befriended it.'

From close relationships with a variety of pets, Gavin not only learned the habits and mental processes of birds and animals, but gained an awareness of the fragility of life. 'All our pets came to what are called bad ends,' he recalled, 'but the end of an animal is bad anyway, like the end of a human being, and through these extinctions we learned a little sympathy, a little understanding and a little compassion.'

There was one other member of the family who was to have a tremendous impact on the youthful Gavin – the formidable figure of his uncle, Lord William Percy, a father-substitute for whom Gavin conceived a deep and lasting admiration, 'a little as a rabbit is fascinated by the antics of a stoat'. Explorer, soldier, secret agent, ornithologist and former Deputy-Governor of Jerusalem, Uncle Willie was, in Gavin's view, 'the perfect Buchan hero', a man of steel who had traversed the greater part of the earth's surface, the length and breadth of Canada and the Siberian Arctic, the whole of the American continents, much of the Middle East and the interior of Africa. He was a crack shot and a first-class field ornithologist, possessed of a keen intellect, hawk-eyed powers of observation and views on conservation far ahead of their time. When Gavin's brother Eustace boasted of having just wiped out a whole nest of carder bees in order to remove the honey, Uncle Willie reprimanded him with the chilling rebuke, 'Then you're a very cruel and destructive little boy, *aren't* you?' This was Gavin's first inkling of the notion of compassion and proportion in man's relation to the natural world, and he felt an all-pervading guilt for the bees that had died in the killing bottle.

Gavin did not just hold his uncle in awe – he adopted his persona and his mannerisms when it suited him. Short, slim and wiry, Uncle Willie was garbed habitually in riding-breeches and belted Norfolk jacket; his voice and gestures were crisp and incisive and his brilliant eyes bored into the object of their gaze 'like the muzzle of a gun'. Uncle Willie, it seemed, knew no other form of conversation than cross-examination – a cross-examination in which the cross-examined was transferred within the first minute from the witness-box to the dock. Rare was the victim who could stand up to the simultaneous fire of the eyes and voice; any resistance was summarily dealt with. To Uncle Willie this was a game, and any temper or tears he caused his opponent were greeted with great and obvious glee. The least weakness in factual knowledge was pounced on, and if ever a return missile landed dangerously near, Uncle Willie would change the whole direction of his argument and suddenly attack from the rear, for it was a military maxim that a weak position should never be reinforced.

Anyone who ever engaged in a lengthy conversation with the adult Gavin Maxwell will recognise that portrait at once. As Gavin grew older and discovered that attack was the best means of defence in his dealings with his fellow man, it was his uncle's fierce and uncompromising directness of delivery – his 'verbal ju-jitsu', as Gavin put it – that was to serve him as a ready-made model.

So Gavin's infancy passed in happy and idyllic intimacy with the world of nature and his own closed family. 'Between the ages of seven and ten, I was wonderfully, gloriously happy,' he once told me. 'This is when I became identified with the countryside, with other living creatures, and with my home at Elrig.' By the age of ten Gavin's unusual upbringing had given him many of the distinctive elements of the man he was to become – he was a creative, venture-some boy who loved nature and the wild countryside, loved to observe and explore, related more to animals than to human beings, painted and drew, wrote and read, and admired the tough persona and adventurous travels of his father manqué, Uncle William Percy.

But the idyll of Gavin's childhood at Elrig was violently shat-tered, as idylls often are, by an event so cataclysmic that he never totally recovered from the trauma, which left him psychologically and emotionally scarred for the rest of his life. For in September 1924, after several years of instruction by private tutors at home, he was despatched to a version of hell – a preparatory school in England, where his formal schooling was to begin.

TWO

Mowgli with a gun

> I went into the woods. They're the safest place. I
> understand animals. Human beings are *dangerous*.
>
> VIETNAM VETERAN (1985)

Gavin had developed into a shy, sensitive, gentle, caring and broadly contented child with an unusually limited experience of contact with human beings of his own (or any other) age. But at his first English prep school – Heddon Court, in Cockfosters, north London – he was plunged into a human jungle peopled by a tribe of savages the like of which he had never known. He had so far met fewer than ten other children in the whole of his life, three of them his own siblings. Now he was thrown among a multitude of boys, most of whom seemed alien and hostile, and so unnerving was this horror that even the simplest action seemed beyond him. From the moment he entered his first classroom Gavin lived in a world of total confusion punctuated by moments of fear and humiliation. 'This was the beginning of the breakdown of my image of what life was,' he confided to me very near the end of his life. 'Going to school in England seemed nothing but a violent disruption, something terrible.'

It was not the lessons that were the boy's problem, for he was as well educated as any of his classmates. His vocabulary and his handwriting were precocious, and he was unusually widely read, having worked his way through all the animal stories of Ernest Thompson Seton by the age of eight, and the works of popular novelists like Baroness Orczy (*The Scarlet Pimpernel*) and Stanley Weyman (*Under the Red Robe*) by the following year. He could recite great swathes of narrative verse by heart, from the *Lyra Heroica* to *The Lays of Ancient Rome*, as well as ten long poems in German (a language he did not understand) which he declaimed with a Swiss accent acquired from a governess who was Swiss.

It was people *en masse* that Gavin could not cope with – the treachery and enmity, the violence and aggression that seemed part and parcel of the human pack as he perceived it. Everywhere he turned he was confronted with images that shocked or terrified. Communal bath night and his first sight of naked human bodies. The stale tobacco smell of a dreaded master's room. The ammonia stench of the urinals. The pain of a 'beaker' (an excruciating tweak of the buttocks) from the school bully, an ugly little pig called Garshawe. A beating with a cricket bat in the headmaster's study. A stand-up face-slapping match with his first mortal enemy, a bat-eared boy called Studley with a face like a clown's mask. Above all, the loneliness – 'I was always mooching about in corridors or empty classrooms, and always alone.'

At the end of the term Gavin was removed from Heddon Court and at the beginning of 1925 sent to St Cyph's, Eastbourne, where Cecil Beaton, George Orwell and Cyril Connolly had been pupils some years before. The new school was dominated by the buxom figure of the headmaster's sadistic wife, but it was his fellow-pupils who dominated Gavin's life. They mocked him because of the birthmarks on his arm, the fact that he couldn't swim or box and because his mother had a title and his uncle and guardian (Sir Eustace Percy) was Minister of Education. It made no difference that he could draw and paint, write fluently, run fast and shoot straight. Such skills made him doubly suspect. His insecurity and alienation crippled his behaviour in the company of adults and contemporaries alike, so that he appeared stupid, gauche and defensive.

Gavin was beyond doubt the odd-boy-out. 'You've got to learn to be like other people,' a senior boy had warned during an evening's prep. It was well-intended advice, but Gavin did not have the means to follow it – and never did follow it, for he was never to become like other people. As an adult he learnt to adjust to his chronic non-alignment with the majority of his fellow humans, but as a boy he suffered torment for it. Photo portraits of the young Gavin reveal the transition in his personality from the relaxed, smiling child of the pre-school years to the uptight, unsmiling schoolboy of twelve or thirteen, biting his upper lip in defensive frustration, the look of the hunted animal in his eyes.

By his second year at St Cyph's Gavin's dull unhappiness had turned to outright misery, and he began to suffer nightmares from which he would awake after screaming at the full pitch of his lungs for up to a quarter of an hour at a time. By now he was highly neurotic, and could hold out no longer. Determined to be removed from St Cyph's, he scribbled a desperate letter to his mother which ended, 'For God's sake take me away from this awful place,' and climbed out of the school at dead of night to post it. Gavin was taken away from St Cyph's in the spring term of 1927, a few months before his thirteenth birthday. He left not in triumph but in a mood of remorse at his apparent failure to succeed.

Gavin returned to the amniotic security of Elrig – and pets, mother-love and the peace and freedom of the open countryside. With his brothers away at Eton and Winchester, Gavin attached himself to the family gamekeeper, Bob Hannam, as he went about his distant traps during those cold bright March days. Hannam was a homespun Yorkshireman, a brilliant mechanic and inventor – he invented the only really effective shotgun silencer Gavin ever saw – with an innate dignity of bearing and courtesy of manner. He lived in a remote, peat-fired cottage on Elrig Loch and went about in an old tweed suit that smelled of dog, stoat, mole, black tobacco, human sweat, peat-smoke and bog-myrtle. From this wise old countryman Gavin acquired an intimate knowledge of wildlife and a pragmatic philosophy which frankly acknowledged the incurable cruelty of nature and the ephemeral nature of all life. At that age Gavin hated to see anything killed – the baiting of a hook with flesh cut from a living fish filled him with horror and tears – and the sights he saw on his rounds of the Elrig estate in Hannam's company (the gin-trapped animals, the strychnined birds) induced a profound revulsion in him. But Hannam reassured him. 'They all come to die,' he would tell the boy, 'there's no mercy in nature, and as like as not their natural deaths'd be worse'n that. The stoat eats the rabbit alive, screaming away for twenty minutes or more, and he'll kill maybe a thousand rabbits in his lifetime . . . Na, na. A man doesn't like to see suffering, but it's there whether he looks at it or not.'

Paradoxically, and with his mother's encouragement and Hannam's expert guidance, Gavin turned his interests from bird-nesting and butterfly-catching to guns and shooting, which before long became as obsessive a passion with him as it had been with his father. He saw no contradiction in loving the creatures he killed, and from now on he was to be accepted by those few friends he found as a sort of 'Mowgli with a gun'.

*   *   *

At the beginning of the summer term Gavin arrived with his mother in the chauffeur-driven family Studebaker to begin a year at his third and final prep school, Hurst Court, overlooking the Sussex downland at Ore, near Hastings. Gavin's mother had chosen the school on the advice of her brother, Sir Eustace Percy, who was not only Minister of Education but the local Member of Parliament as well. For the first time Gavin began a term without shedding tears. The staff accepted the new boy as a challenge, making allowances for the fact that he was known to be a 'difficult' child, and it helped that his brother Eustace (who had preceded him at the school) had won the respect of the boys and the teachers. But it was Hurst Court's headmaster, Dr Vaughan-Evans, a highly decorated pilot of the First World War, who made all the difference for a boy as alienated and anti-authoritarian as Gavin now was. Gavin had nothing to worry about, Vaughan-Evans promised him. There were no ogres at Hurst Court, and everyone was prepared to like him. And he was indeed treated with friendliness by boys and staff alike – a transformation in his experience of human society that was almost bewildering.

To Lady Mary the headmaster wrote reassuringly a week after Gavin's enrolment: 'He appears normal in every way.' One contemporary of Gavin's at Hurst Court was Peter Kemp, a future secret agent and guerrilla fighter, with whom Gavin was to stay in touch for the rest of his life. Kemp remembered Gavin as a tender plant, but a tremendously sympathetic person who found himself in the perfect school environment, for Hurst Court was an easy-going place where beatings were virtually unheard of. Gavin became a fast bowler and captain of the second cricket XI, and in collaboration with the school's head boy he produced a school magazine, *The Overall*, which reflected his own interest in animals and birds and his newly-discovered passion for motor-racing (he had recently watched Sir Henry Birkin lap Brooklands at 140 miles per hour).

Gavin's voice suddenly broke in class one day, plunging to the bass key. This public trumpeting of the onset of puberty generated a flurry of activity amongst his elders. 'The pitcher seems to have gone to the well once too often,' Vaughan-Evans declared, and took him into his study for his first sex talk. Sex was a subject about which Gavin was totally ignorant – the limit of his knowledge seemed to be a belief that babies came into the world via the navel. Dr Vaughan-Evans' explanations and admonitions on this arcane matter added nothing to Gavin's comprehension, and though he realised he was being warned against something, he wasn't sure what. Later his mother gave him a batty and highly misinformative Edwardian sex manual called *What a Young Boy Ought to Know* which pronounced dire warnings concerning 'the private parts' (which were not defined) and 'self-abuse' (any other sexual activity seemed so beyond the pale as to get no mention at all). This clarified nothing. Not that it mattered much, for by his own confession Gavin was to remain sexually inactive for the next three years of his adolescence.

In September 1928, at the end of the summer holidays spent sailing, sketching and lizard-hunting *en famille* in Brittany, Gavin was sent to public school. Again it seems likely that his guardian, Sir Eustace Percy, lent a hand in the choice of school, for instead of following his brother Aymer to Eton, Gavin was sent to Stowe, deep in the lush green countryside of Buckinghamshire. Housed in the fabulous country palace of the extinct Dukes of Buckingham and Chandos, Stowe had been open for less than five years, and unlike Eton and the other heavily academic, highly ritualised, tightly buttoned-up great public schools of that era, it was broadly permissive in attitude, tolerant of the individuality of its pupils, and lacking the complex of meaningless rules and rituals that permeated the daily life of the older institutions. There were no bounds, and boys could go sailing on the ornamental lakes or on expeditions into the great park, conceived on a scale to rival Blenheim Palace.

Presiding over this magnificent and idiosyncratic establishment was its remarkable young headmaster, J.F. Roxburgh, one of the towering figures in the history of the British upper-class educational system, a brilliant eccentric who defied all the usual traditions and conventions of such organisations.

Gavin was still frightened of human beings in numbers, and the numbers at Stowe were very much greater than he had hitherto encountered. His reaction to the implicit danger and threat he perceived in the mass of humanity that swarmed around him was very like that of some combat veterans after their return from battle – he went into the woods and sought solace in nature; the still, over-grown wilderness of Stowe Park, its rank green English jungles dotted with Palladian temples and follies, statues and arches.

It was easy to be alone in such a vast landscape, and Gavin was

indeed alone during his free afternoons and the free time after breakfast every morning, when he took to the thickets of laurel and
rhododendron in preference to the school toilets, which he was far
too shy to use.

In time he made a few close friends among like-minded boys.
Among them was Anthony Dickins, who entered the school on
the same day as Gavin:

He was an elusive boy of my own age with pale blue eyes
and pink lips and cheeks and a certain unusually intense wiry
alertness about him. A strong and independent spirit shone
from his face beneath a head of lank, fair hair. Yet at the same
time he was quiet and gentle. He was an aristocrat to the
fingertips, of the old-fashioned country type. He was more at
home among the bracken when the rabbits were out in the
evening than anywhere else – but there was nothing offen-
sively 'huntin' and shootin'' about him. He was too simple to
be a braggart or a swashbuckler. The amazing amount of mischief and good humour in Gavin's compact little body
attracted me to him – and the twinkle in his eye when he
smiled. We planned to start a magazine together, with some
clever caricatures of the masters drawn by Gavin, but it never
went further than the manuscript copy of the first issue. I
see him now, fleet as Mercury, speeding down the hill to
Buckingham on a Saturday afternoon wrapped in his huge
rabbit gloves, myself following no less speedily but rather
more clumsily, to have a warm tea of poached eggs and sausages at the Grenville Café. On free days when we did not have
to take part in organised games we used to explore Stowe
Park. It was on these explorations that I discovered how intimately he was in contact with birds and animals, and I was
amazed how he seemed to be able actually to communicate
with them.

In the early days at Stowe the boys were encouraged to have pets.
Several kept peacocks, and one even kept a bear. Gavin looked after
the waifs and strays, including a tea-chest full of starving redwings
that had been caught in an early snowfall and were fed on ants'
eggs and mealworms he bought with his pocket money. One boy,
John Nesfield, was constructing an aviary and pigeon loft on some

waste scrubland when he first encountered Gavin. 'A young, rather quiet boy came up and asked if he could help,' Nesfield recalled.

> He told me his name was Maxwell and he expressed a great interest in keeping birds. We soon had some dove house pigeons, blue bars and chequers, and before long we were keeping a jay, a magpie, three jackdaws, an elderly crow, a little owl blind in one eye, and a male kestrel hawk we bought for eight shillings. I found Gavin one of the most interesting friends I have ever had. He was always very well mannered: a gentleman in every sense of the word. We had many walks in the beautiful countryside around Stowe and discussed the future. Gavin did not want to be tied down to a profession like accountancy or the law. He thought he might be able to write and even considered joining the regular army one day.

John Hay, an athletic, outgoing boy a year younger than Gavin, shared Gavin's preoccupation with wild creatures and soon became one of the best friends he ever had at any school – a friend who possessed so many qualities Gavin lacked that he became inordinately proud of his friendship. During Gavin's final term at Stowe he spent long happy summer hours wandering among the lakes and oakwoods of the Stowe wilderness – with the knowledge that he had found a true friend at last and was no longer alone in a cruel and hostile world. 'By the time I left Stowe,' Gavin once told me, 'I'd formed one or two friends, and I was very fond of them. But what I couldn't understand were my enemies. I couldn't understand why they disliked me, why they mocked me. I feel this thing has followed me through life – being much too easily hurt, being unarmoured in some curious way.' Even John Hay had to acknowledge: 'Gavin was just all screwed up.'

When it was not possible to go into the woods physically, during lessons, for instance, Gavin contrived, by means of a vivid imagination and a degree of self-hypnosis, to enter them in spirit – not so much the woods, in fact, as the Elrig countryside which was always for him his childhood Avalon. In his mind's eye he would set off through the gun-room side door, then down the track and out on to the moors or towards the woods: 'The world is full of birds' voices; below me as I climb, the rooks come and go from the elm clump, above me on a hill a curlew trills a steadily ascending scale

"*Wharp—wharp—wharp—wha-a-up—wha—a-up*", a lark is singing at some invisible point overhead. Up from the bracken on to the short, bare heather, springy heather under my young springy feet, up on to the ridge . . . The sea is in sight now, a glittering high horizon; the sense of space is enormous, and holds in it something near to rapture.'

Gavin did not always reach his journey's end in these classroom reveries. For out there on the hill he would hear his name roared in anger and the whole insubstantial structure of his dream of Elrig would dissolve into the chalky present.

'MAXWELL!'

It could be any one of half a dozen masters who stood towering in outrage above the dozing boy. Perhaps his Latin master – 'a little pince-nezed Himmler of a man with mincing voice and industrial-urban clothes' – who would twist his ear and pull his hair and address a few insulting remarks to him.

Not surprisingly, Gavin fared badly at Stowe academically. It was not that he was slow-witted, far from it; he was just not mentally there. His school reports were almost universally dismal. 'He appears utterly incapable of any form of concentration,' went one master's subject report. To his mother, J.F. Roxburgh had been forced to admit: 'I think if you taught Gavin yourself in Form you would understand what his Masters mean when they say that he is lacking in interest and concentration. Gavin's manner suggests the most perfect indifference to what is going on, and he has quite definitely a vein of indolence in him.'

Gavin sank to the bottom of his class and remained there throughout his Stowe career. A biology master and two English masters – Humphrey Playford and C.R. ('Spuggins') Spencer – managed to elicit (as Gavin put it) 'ephemeral sparks from my dour flint', and under Spencer's eccentric and inspirational tutelage Gavin even rose to the top of the form in English for one brief term, having learned by heart most of the poems in *The Golden Treasury*. According to his friend Anthony Dickins, Gavin was a budding writer even then. 'All this time Gavin was sexually virgin, totally inactive in every way,' Dickins believed. 'Hence all his latent sexual energy went into his dreams, daydreams, imaginings, longings, thoughts of his home and surrounding countryside. What he was really doing in these dreams and reveries was *writing* letters and descriptions to himself, even in class, which is why he always came bottom. He was teaching himself "silently" to write. In class I used to watch his lips moving as he told himself a story or described a walk through his home park at Elrig – always day-dreaming, always looking out of the window.'

Much later in life, when Gavin had the opportunity to study the education system with the more objective mind of an enquiring adult, he concluded that part of his problem had been the system itself, which damped down and finally obliterated the untapped creative ability of many of those who were subjected to it. Later still he came to see the problems he had faced as a schoolboy in a more broadly sociological perspective:

All through my life, through school, right up to the time I joined the army, people were always trying to change me. They refused to accept me as I was. One had to conform. This was the main point of the whole of my upbringing. Everything that made you different from anyone else – any idea, any preference, any viewpoint – had to be erased. There was a norm to which everyone had to conform. This left you with two choices. You conformed and you suffered for conforming. Or you said, 'I'm not going to conform, this is suppressing my personality, my potentiality,' and so you broke out, and you suffered for breaking out, because you were shot at as if you were breaking out of a concentration camp, and once you were outside you were hunted too.

THREE

Breakdown

I'm going where the water's deep
And wrecks have sunk before,
And there I'll lay me down and sleep
And be reviled no more.
GAVIN MAXWELL, *'I've Had Enough
of Right and Wrong'* (1931)

15 July 1930 was a day Gavin would never forget. It was, for one thing, his sixteenth birthday. More than that, it was to end in a cataclysm that was to change his life and his attitude to himself and the world for ever.

The day had begun with a promising adventure and no hint of the catastrophe to come. Gavin had planned to climb out of his school house at dawn with a friend, James Ashton, and go rabbit-shooting in the surrounding country, for he had by now taken up shooting in a serious way and was in possession of a prized new .410 shotgun pistol which he had bought from the proceeds of dubious deals in jackdaws, owls and an owl-food composed of crushed beetles and meat scraps. The dawn was grey, the dew sopping, the human world still asleep as the two boys crept out towards the mist-hung lakes. 'A sense of adventure and liberation,' Gavin was to write of that portentous morning; 'in all the world we were the only two awake, the only two hunters . . . I was the young predator in the dim red dawn of man.' At the edge of the sandpit rabbit-warren they shot two rabbits with the new gun, and Gavin showed James – 'expertly and with contempt' – how to gut a rabbit with his roe-horn handled sheath-knife, a skill he had learnt from Hannam, the Elrig gamekeeper.

Then rain began to fall, drenching the boys in a deluge so heavy it seemed almost tropical. Their grey suits were sodden by the time they returned to the school, furtive and breathless, in time for morning assembly.

Morning lessons passed in the usual reveries. Shortly after mid-day Gavin's elder brother, Aymer, and his mother arrived to take him off for a birthday lunch at Brackley. By the time they returned to Stowe Gavin was feeling indefinably ill, with a vague sensation of physical and mental depression, and he felt faintly relieved when his mother and brother left and he was able to clean his gun and sell the rabbits he had shot. In the late afternoon he went to the changing room to change his socks. He took off one sock and at that moment, he was to recall, 'life came to a dead stop'.

'I looked at my foot,' he wrote, 'and thought in a dull repetitive way: "It can't be mine." I took off the other sock and I said the Lord's Prayer to myself and then my baby prayer, over and over again.'

His feet and ankles were covered in dark purple spots and patches, the joints were swollen and aching, and Gavin felt frightened and alone. Two boys came into the changing room and Gavin burst into tears. He ought to go to Matron at once, one of the boys advised him. But Matron could not explain the phenomenon and sent Gavin to the sanatorium to await the school doctor. By the time the doctor arrived the pain had intensified and spread to his stomach, and when Aymer returned later Gavin was so ill that even the presence of his revered brother brought no reassurance. The next morning an ambulance carried the critically ill boy off to a nursing home. 'Of the journey I remember only darkness and pain,' Gavin recalled, 'and the sudden sweet release of morphia.'

At Kiama Nursing Home in Weybridge Gavin lay dreadfully ill, drifting in and out of consciousness. The massive internal bleeding from which he was suffering caused him intense pain and he was given constant doses of morphia to ease him through the long, desperate days and nights. His condition was diagnosed as Henoch's purpura, a rare bleeding disease which in Gavin's case, as his medical report concluded, 'showed certain characteristics of Purpura haemorrhagica, with extensive ecchymosis, haemmorhage from all mucous surfaces and massive excretion of blood from bladder and bowel'. As his condition worsened his moments of consciousness became fewer. During one of these moments he was visited by the eminent Lord Horder, physician to King George V. Lord Horder was short, dark and very formally dressed, and Gavin disliked him on sight. Shaking his head slowly from side to side, Horder picked up Gavin's right arm and remarked to the hospital consultant who was with him: 'Should you come across this condition again, Doctor, it is worth noting that these ecchymoses on the right forearm are diagnostically perhaps the most typical.'

Summoning all the strength that was left in his exhausted body, Gavin exclaimed in the eminent physician's outraged ear: 'Those are birthmarks, you bloody fool.'

The prognosis was grim. Lord Horder was in no doubt that Gavin was dying. The next day a minister of the Apostolic Church arrived in Gavin's darkened room, set out the miniature Communion plate on a table beside his bed and began to give him the Last Sacrament. His mother propped him up a little to receive the wafer and the Communal wine. 'The body of our Lord Jesus Christ, broken for thee,' the minister intoned, 'preserve thy body and soul unto everlasting life . . .' After he had gone Gavin whispered to his mother: 'Mother, am I going to die?' His mother, with her eyes full of tears, replied: 'Only if God wants you.' Recalling this moment in the latter years of his life, Gavin believed that death would have been like taking morphine, and he would 'float away through space and time to Elrig in perpetual spring sunshine'.

Of the following days the hospital medical records note: 'After dangerous prostration and repeated transfusion, crisis was passed on August 5th.' The bleeding stopped, the pain receded, and Gavin began the slow climb to recovery through a protracted, year-long convalescence. In the first few weeks he was helpless and almost totally dependent, for it was feared that the slightest movement would set off the bleeding again. All he could do was lie in his bed and look out through the french windows, enviously watching the birds and butterflies as they flitted about the nursing-home garden. Day by day his frustration at his captivity and the weakness of his frail and treacherous body grew in him. His desire for physical freedom was overwhelming, and he wanted nothing but to run, climb trees, and walk long distances.

In his memoirs of childhood, *The House of Elrig*, written some thirty-five years after the trauma of his adolescent illness, Gavin seems to have accepted the medical diagnosis that it was Henoch's purpura that had nearly killed him. But reflecting on this a few years afterwards he gave me an alternative view which by then he found more convincing:

I believe very strongly that practically every physical ailment of the human body is directly under the control of the human brain, so my view is that this almost fatal illness was really due to *psychological* factors. I had very few friends when I was at Stowe. I spent most of my time alone, and I was completely sexually inactive, due to my upbringing. I think all these factors combined together might today have resulted in a nervous breakdown. But in those days things like nervous breakdowns were unheard of in the class to which I belonged, and in my own family would have been looked upon as shameful. 'I'm afraid he's not quite right in the upper storey,' they'd have muttered, raising their eyebrows. Well, in my case it was not just the 'upper storey', it was all the storeys, the whole block of flats which gave way, and I suffered from a violent internal bleeding disease which today would be classified by part of the medical profession (though not all) like any other psychosomatic illness.

Gavin had more difficulty calculating the consequences of his illness. He acknowledged that he resolved to make himself a tougher, manlier, more physical person, but the true cost of his collapse seems to have escaped him, perhaps because it lay too close to the very heart of his personality to be detected by himself alone. In reality his illness had the effect of ruling a thick line across the course of his life to date. Though he was to advance far beyond it in terms of his intellectual development, emotionally he progressed no further, and remained stuck, like a needle in the groove of a gramophone record, at the age of sixteen, for ever an adolescent in his attitude to the adult world, his sexual relations and his interests and enthusiasms. In this enforced atrophy of his emotional development lies an essential clue to the mystery of his later personality, with all its unpredictable complexities and paradoxes.

On 23 August 1930 Gavin was discharged from the nursing home in Weybridge, and shortly afterwards he was installed in the best bedroom of Lower Northfield, the family's winter home on the outskirts of Albury in Surrey. Here he was cosseted in almost total seclusion from the world. Subsisting on a salt-free diet of champagne and white fish (as it was thought his kidneys might have been affected by his illness), he slowly began to regain his strength and power of movement, and in the company of his sister, Christian, turned to drawing and painting and endless games of chess and cards to help while away the long, sedentary hours of his captivity. He also read whatever books he could get hold of. Many of them were poetry, including A.E. Housman, Siegfried Sassoon, Omar Khayyám (which he learnt by heart in its entirety) and James Thomson's 'The City of Dreadful Night'. He also began to write verse himself, generally in the manner of the poet he had last been reading. It was the sonority in poetry that attracted him, and melancholy and despair.

During these months of confinement at Albury Gavin stumbled, almost by accident, and after more than three years of repressed sexual maturity, on the physical manifestations of the sex drive while luxuriating alone in his bath. Brought up in the shadow of late Victorian sexual prudery, with its dour burden of guilt and shame, Gavin's unexpected spasm of sexual take-off plunged him into an agony of moral confusion. 'A moment later, awareness regained,' he was to write in his adulthood, 'I was trembling in the witch-doctor's world of my indoctrination . . . madness, sin, and fear, fear, fear.' His inhibitions had grown to become a substantial part of his psyche, and their destruction was a process of painful confusion. Agonised with guilt, the convalescent boy became locked in a desperate struggle to control the new-found demon, torn between pleasure and sin. Only after a close study of some rudimentary sex manuals he found in the changing room of the local masseuse (where he went for ultra-violet ray therapy three times a week) did Gavin begin to question his identification of sex with sin – although this revolutionary move left his sense of guilt 'surprisingly intact'.

Towards the end of the year Gavin fell in love for the first time – 'blindingly, helplessly' – with a girl of his own age called Elizabeth whom he met in the Duke of Argyll's great country mansion at Strachur on Loch Fyne, where he was staying with his mother. In *The House of Elrig* he was to recreate the exquisite torment of his unforeseen and hopeless condition: 'It was the more confusing because I could not have said what I wanted of her; the longing, ocean-deep, poignant as a weeping violin, was supremely unconscious of its purpose.' He first set eyes on his unattainable heart's desire in the castle's great drawing room – 'a background contrived for passion' – with its giant potted azalea, Aubusson carpet, chiming clock and enormous chandelier. 'I cried myself to sleep because she was somewhere else, in another room; yet the idea of going to bed with her, which never crossed my mind as a desire, would have been sacrilege. I didn't know that I wanted to.'

Shy, fastidious, romantic, guilt-ridden and confused, it was to be a long time before Gavin was to go to bed with anyone. But thinking about that disturbing encounter after he had returned to Albury, Gavin lit on a comparison which integrated the two strands of his conflicting adolescent desires – his emotional longings and physical ecstasies. A conjunction of the two, he realised, might lead to unimaginable happiness, 'Some time, far away in the future; not this year, not next year; some time, but not never.'

Shortly before Christmas Gavin moved with his mother and sister to Cookes Place, a small house next to the Apostolic Church at the other end of Albury – a south-facing residence which it was hoped would catch the health-enhancing winter sun. In spite of occasional relapses, when the purple stigmata would reappear and he would unexpectedly lose consciousness, Gavin continued to gain strength. On 14 February 1931 his mother reported on his progress in a letter to J.F. Roxburgh, the Headmaster of Stowe. Though he was very much better and his kidneys had sustained no permanent damage, she wrote, he would have to undergo an operation for the removal of his tonsils once the warm weather came in April, so the prospects of his returning to Stowe in the summer were virtually nil. She added: 'He is almost beside himself today with the rapture of what seems to him like a release from prison – in the leave given him by the doctor yesterday to walk where and as much as he likes (within reasonable limits) and to carry a gun. Although the object of the latter will be only vermin, it means much to him – after seven months' severely restricted liberty; his heart was affected for some weeks in the autumn and winter, and he has not been allowed to walk uphill or for more than half an hour to an hour a day.'

In the spring of 1931 Gavin began to attend a crammer in Godalming as a day pupil with a view to sitting for his School Certificate at the end of the year. In the summer he learned to drive his mother's Rover up and down the long drive of the Duke of Northumberland's country mansion at Albury Park, taking over as his mother's chauffeur on his seventeenth birthday and driving her on a long tour of her girlhood friends in castles and country mansions

the length and breadth of England. At first he was shy and tongue-
tied in these grand establishments, but he quickly learned how to
tip and what to give a butler – 'all the little rituals that together
composed the password of the tribe'. He learned the totems and
taboos, and conformed fanatically, for he had no tribe he could call
his own. As he saw it, his family had been disbanded, his school
was a thing of the past, and he was conscious of the need to be
adopted by another tribe quickly. He met few young people of his
own age on this grand tour, but the men warmed to him when
they discovered his passion for shooting and his prowess with a
gun, and it was in this world of plus-fours and dubbined boots,
shotguns and rifles, that he sank temporary tribal roots.

Six months at various health-spots along the south coast of England were followed by a drab winter in out-of-season Bournemouth. By now Gavin was in the full flood and turmoil of
adolescent rebellion. The only people he knew in Bournemouth
were his mother and his tutor – a 'poor old gentle gourmet' who
induced in him a silent and contemptuous fury. His only companion, the only recipient of his affection, was Judy, his bright
little Cocker Spaniel bitch, whom he used to walk in the unspoilt
pinewoods of Ringwood Forest. His mother herself became a
stranger to him, and he fought and quarrelled even with her in his
adolescent struggle for his personal freedom. 'I hated everything
that confined me, and I hated it with a sharp-edged resentment.'

Gavin's immediate aims were now clear. He wished to achieve
freedom and manhood. Above all, he wished to return to Elrig,
his true home. In the spring of 1932 he was judged well enough to
make the long journey to Scotland and to resume his life at a place
far from emergency medical care. This news marked the end of
nearly two years on the sidelines of society, and to celebrate his
release Gavin wrote to his Stowe friend John Hay, asking if he
could join him on holiday at Elrig as his first and very own guest.

Elrig house impressed John Hay with its aura of great state and
privilege. Almost uniquely among the Scottish houses of that time
it had central heating, porridge was served with salt at breakfast,
and the house cigarettes were Egyptian, very long and stamped
impressively with the letter 'M'. Garbed in Gavin's bedraggled old
Harris tweed plus-four suit, John Hay set out each day with his
aristocratic friend to quarter Gavin's home patch. Gavin was to
recall of this time: 'John and I explored the kingdom from which

I had been exiled for so long. The high, wind-whining moorlands of rock and heather, the far hill and sea horizons; and in his company I consolidated a long-lost position. We went to look for an eagle's nest in the Galloway Hills, and as we scrambled up the rain-gleaming rock and scree I asked, because this was important, "John, what do you ordinarily do in the holidays?" He said: "Well, nothing as good as this," and suddenly the rock and the rain and all the gigantic windswept kingdom of Galloway seemed mine to live in, all exile over.'

Much can be explained by Gavin's unusual and chequered boyhood – his romanticism, his unconventionality, his alienation and rebel-liousness, his tastes in books, language and literary style, food and décor; his attitude to money, social classes, sex and mores, courage, nobility and the knightly quest; his reaction against religion, formal education, the parental role and any kind of authority; his passionate pursuit of those things he discovered for himself, like nature, ani-mals and the wilds, painting and poetry; his thirst for freedom and his egocentricity and self-preoccupation, the consequences of childhood isolation. Perhaps by now Gavin had also developed the symptoms of the 'bi-polar illness' which was to shadow him all the rest of his life.

But that boyhood was now over. Ahead lay the years of maturity – and the battle to understand and come to terms with the human world and the cruel and wayward vagaries of time and fate.

FOUR

The Celtic fringe

Fee, Fi, Fo, Fum!
Here sit I till the grouse packs come,
Builded butt with a beachen floor,
Two guns, loader and Labrador;
We'll pick up in the usual run
(Gather 'em galloping, sweep, my son!)
Twenty brace when the drive is done
Fee, Fi, Fo, Fum!

GAVIN MAXWELL,
'Game Book 1932–35'

Shortly after his eighteenth birthday, Gavin took up serious shooting again. 'I was brought up to be a country gentleman, shooting
and fishing,' he told me years later:

> Not hunting, because it didn't exist up there. I loathed fishing,
> but shooting became a passion with me – and, later on, wild-
> fowling, the toughest blood sport in the world. To be out on
> an estuary – out on the salt-marsh and mud-flats of Wigtown
> Bay – completely on one's own in the early hours of the depths
> of winter was hard beyond belief – the conditions were so
> tough you'd think nothing could survive out there at all, least
> of all a human being. These were challenges I deliberately
> sought out. After my illness, after being a weakling for so
> long, I wanted to prove myself physically, I wanted to prove
> I could do macho things, that I was a man of action.

But there was another element in Gavin's passion – the call of
the wild, the siren song of freedom. Out there in the midwinter
wilderness between the land and the sea he would strain his ears
'to hear in the dawn and the dusk the wild music of those voices
that quickened my pulse as I waited shivering in the ooze of some
tidal creek with the eastern horizon aflame.'

Gavin began to shoot game and game birds with obsessive fervour and increasing accuracy on the moorlands and wetlands around Elrig and Monreith, and eventually further afield. Sometimes alone, more often with his elder brother Aymer or various family friends and local chums, he strode the mosses and heather-clad roughs and hills, or lurked about the coverts and the lochs and dams of the Maxwell domains, blazing away at grouse, snipe, pigeon, mallard, teal, shoveller, greyhen, goldeneye, wigeon, greylag, partridge, pheasant, blackgame, woodcock, rabbit, hare, stoat, and even curlew and heron, with inexhaustible enthusiasm.

For the next five years Gavin was to keep a large and elaborate Game Book, as his father had done before him, in which he recorded his sporting adventures in meticulous detail, lavishly illustrated with photos, drawings, poems and elaborate lettering in his own hand, and written in the curious jargon of the shooting aristocracy – what he called 'the priestly, esoteric language and all the passwords' – which he had learned from his father's Game Books. From this ornate compilation it is possible to draw up a tally of slaughter which might seem incomprehensible to people not brought up in the landed gentry's age-old tradition of rural blood sports. In his first season, for example, when he was confined to his home ground, he took part in the shooting of 385 head of game in August and September and a further 621 head in December (including his first goose, a greylag) – a total of more than a thousand birds and animals killed in the course of a few days. The gunfire carried on merrily into the new year, as Gavin duly recorded for 5 and 6 January: 'Good days, but not very many birds. Such as they were, they came beautifully, with hardly a low bird among them. The 5th was a glorious sunny day with slight frost – cock pheasants topping the high trees looked wonderful in the sun . . . The 6th was a good day, but the shooting at the mighty host of rabbits was a trifle ineffectual and the total of 82 does not do justice to their numbers . . . We finished with a terrific bombardment at starlings as they came in to roost, and must have killed a hundred or more.'

Much of Gavin's time during the year following his release back into the normal world was occupied in intensive study with private tutors and crammers in an attempt to catch up with his interrupted education and qualify for Oxford. In the summer of 1933 he was accepted to read Estate Management at Hertford College, and in

October he went up to Oxford for the start of the Michaelmas term.

Neither his college nor his course was his own choice, having been decreed for him by his mother and his guardian, Sir Eustace Percy, and Gavin felt somehow slighted that he had not been sent to Trinity, Cambridge, or Christ Church, Oxford, which were the more usual destinations of young men of his class and background. Hertford College at that time was neither particularly rich nor particularly brilliant. Its only notable luminary in recent years was the novelist Evelyn Waugh, who went down eight years before Gavin came up. He was to describe Hertford as 'a respectable, rather dreary little college', halfway up the University pecking order, with nondescript buildings (Bridge of Sighs apart) and no outstanding members of distinction among either the dons or the undergraduates. Its advantages were a good kitchen and an easygoing atmosphere free from boyish 'college spirit' and rowdy hooliganism. 'It was,' concluded Waugh, 'a tolerant, civilised place in which to lead whatever kind of life appealed to one.' It is likely that Hertford was as carefully chosen to suit Gavin's particular personality and needs as Stowe had been – neither expecting too much from him nor imposing too much on him.

Gavin was not a natural college type, for he had a dread of institutions and organised collectives of all kinds. It is no accident that in the Freshmen's group photograph taken in the main quad he is the only one of the thirty-three sports-jacketed new arrivals who has half-turned aside and is staring aloofly *away* from the camera. The majority of his fellow undergraduates remembered him as a loner who kept very much to himself. He took no part in college sports or other activities, was never seen on the river, never sat down with the college Dining Club, and rarely appeared in the Junior Common Room except to take a brief look at a magazine and depart without exchanging a word with anyone. He struck most of those who knew him as shy, retiring, introspective, almost aloof. 'He had a raffish and well-heeled look about him,' one contemporary remembered, 'that deterred friendship.' Some thought he might have been a bit 'mousy'; others, noting the cloth cap and hacking jacket he habitually wore, assumed he was 'horsey'.

In fact, Gavin did not ride at Oxford, but unusually for undergraduates of that time he did drive his own car – an enormous Bentley coupé with a leather strap round its vast bonnet. This

was not the only monster car at Oxford at that time. Another
undergraduate, a friend by the name of Mike Wills, owned a large
sports car that could do 100 miles per hour on the new Woodstock
Road. Wills liked to demonstrate his motor's prowess by taking
friends out for demonstration runs, and Gavin would find out when
these demonstrations were taking place, lie in wait at a lay-by, then
roar after them and overtake at 113 miles per hour. The Bentley
set Gavin apart from most Hertford men of his age. So did the fact
that he had the college furniture removed from his rooms in the
quaint and ancient block between the Chapel and the Senior
Common Room known as the Cottage and replaced with his own
antique sofa, chairs, carpets and screen culled from the sumptuous
recesses of Elrig and Monreith. When he moved to lodgings at 3
Banbury Road in his second year he took his furniture with him,
and filled such space as was left with a multitude of stuffed geese.

Gavin's interests, like his friends, lay outside the bounds of his
college. 'In those days the various groups within the university
were much more rigidly formed than they are today,' he once told
me. 'But I was so completely non-integrated with my surroundings
that I behaved like a chameleon. I tried to belong to all the different
groups at the same time. I wanted to be everything to everybody.
But you can't do this – you have to put on a uniform of some
kind.' Before long he was to discover the uniform that suited him
best during his Oxford years.

'Looking back with distaste to the brashness of my late adolescence,' he was to recall, 'I perceive that I was an earnest member
of the Celtic fringe, avid for tartan and twilight.' This was not due
to any Scottish nationalistic fervour (for he was, he confessed, 'an
arrant snob', and looked down on this movement as an essentially
plebeian one), but to aristocratic conservatism and nostalgia, and
to what he was later to describe as 'an inherently romantic nature
tinged with melancholy'. The fact that he was not a Highlander
but a Lowland Scot who could neither speak Gaelic nor perform
Highland dances was immaterial; at least he was entitled to wear a
kilt (of shepherd's plaid), and his maternal grandmother had been
a daughter of the Duke of Argyll, MacCallum Mor himself, the
clan chief of the Campbells. In those days he did not question the
established order, and for him the West Highlands meant deer
forests, hereditary chieftains and the romantic life of an indigenous
aristocracy.

It was hardly surprising, therefore, that at Oxford he became a member of a curious clique of assertively un-urban landed gentry, most of them Scots, who affected a way of living and dressing that was quite unsuited to University life in a town like Oxford. They wore tweed shooting suits and heavy, thickly dubbined shooting shoes studded with nails, and wherever they went spaniels or Labrador retrievers trotted at their heels; when they re-assembled in the autumn term their rooms were invariably hung with the heads of the stags they had shot in the Highlands during the summer vacation. Gavin himself looked back with disfavour on the brashness of his late adolescence, and viewed his clique as little better than a species of privileged hiker – 'a striking example of the fact that aristocracy and education were no longer synonymous'.

The degree course in Estate Management for which Gavin had been enrolled may have been appropriate for some of his landed gentry friends, but it was not of the slightest interest to him. Such time as he devoted to academic studies during his first year at Oxford was dedicated to subjects closer to his heart, and instead of attending lectures in his own course at the School of Rural Economy he went to those at the medical and zoological schools, and began to learn to paint at the Ruskin School of Art. The inevitable result was that he failed his preliminary exams at the end of his first year, and was required to sit them again at the end of his second.

The implications were serious – if he failed the preliminary exams a second time he would be sent down in disgrace, and even if he passed he would still be faced with two more years of study before taking his finals, after four years rather than the usual three. But the second year was spent in much the same desultory fashion as the first; Gavin attended the minimum of lectures, and passed the time during the interminable discourses on inorganic chemistry, soil science and the like playing noughts and crosses with fellow undergraduates, emerging from each lecture as ignorant as when he had entered it. By the time the second exams approached neither he nor his fellow examinees were in any better position than they had been before. An emergency conference was convened in an oak-panelled room at The Old Parsonage, and over glasses of brown sherry and Balkan Sobranie cigarettes four of them hatched a plan.

There was only one way to pass the exams, they agreed, and

that was to steal the examination papers from the houses in which they were kept in a series of perfect burglaries. Reprehensible though this might seem, it would spare their parents the distress of having their sons sent down, and it would harm no one, for the exams were not competitive and did not even confer a degree, merely entitled those who passed them to continue their studies at the University. The plan was elaborate and ambitious – to Gavin's consternation it was voted that he should carry out the actual burglaries, since he was the lightest and nimblest of the group, while the others acted as look-outs and decoys. So they set to work. They carried out a reconnaissance. They 'borrowed' two keys and had replicas cut. They acquired masks, gloves and pencil-beam torches. They fitted two of their cars with false number plates. Then, on a moonless night a little less than a week before the exams were due to begin, they struck. In middle-age Gavin was to look back with mild disapproval and bemusement at this escapade of his youth: the palpitating progress up the long drainpipe of the first house he burgled, the signal of a double owl's hoot to alert the get-away car when the work was done, the horror of stumbling on a confederate in a darkened room when he should have been keeping watch outside. Only the Economic History paper, locked away in an uncrackable safe, eluded them. For that exam, therefore, they covered their shirt-cuffs in white paper on which they wrote all the facts they required in microscopic lettering using pale yellow ink, and whenever they needed to look something up they studied their cuffs through high-powered reading spectacles.

'So we passed our preliminaries in this disgraceful manner,' Gavin recalled, 'and we remained at Oxford for a further two years of idleness.' Some passed the time in sexual adventures or a lifestyle of caviar, champagne and debutantes. Gavin, however, remained virgin, and pursued his childhood hobbies of natural history and painting.

He still shot as often as opportunity allowed. Sometimes he organised pigeon shoots with friends like Tony Wills (the future Lord Dulverton and landlord of Sandaig) and Simon Ramsay (today the Earl of Dalhousie), and in the spring he would go off into the countryside to shoot young rooks with his old Stowe friend John Hay (now a member of the Oxford and England rifle teams), returning to Oxford to cook a traditional dish of rook pie in his rooms. By now he was a first-class shot – good enough to be a member of the Oxford University gun team and reckoned by many to be one of the best dozen guns in the country – and throughout his Oxford career he invariably spent both the winter and summer vacations with a gun in his hands in the Highlands. He reported his continuing prowess in his Game Book. 'Some wonderful shooting,' he recorded of a December pheasant shoot at Cairnsmore House, Kirkcudbrightshire. 'I got off 36 cartridges in 14 minutes and killed 27 pheasants and one woodcock. Total for the day: 98 pheasants and three woodcock – 147 cartridges.' A few weeks later he wrote of another shoot on the same ground: 'Enormous number of hares on the low mosses, of which quite as many were missed as killed (94). I had 63 head to my own gun and shot rottenly.' By now he was shooting intensively – '36 days shooting since Aug 12,' he recorded 45 days later: '16 at home and 20 away.'

Not for a good few years was Gavin to sense any paradox in both loving wild animals and killing them. He was born and brought up a predator, he was to argue, and his only concern was to kill as cleanly and efficiently as possible. But in a poem written in 1934 in celebration of his sport he does briefly question – and then justify – the mass slaughter:

> Fee, Fi, Fo, Fum!
> That is the way my pets succumb,
> By the stone and the hundred brace,
> Northern corrie and Southern chase;
> But let guns be oiled and game books inked.
> For here's my view of it put succinct:
> If they didn't succumb they'd be extinct,
> Gone to the dodo dead and dumb,
> If it wasn't for me and my Fee, Fo, Fum!
> Fee, Fi, Fo, Fum!

Gavin was a keen and exotic game cook, digging out ancient country recipes for almost every kind of game, even inedible kinds. An old Stowe friend, Patrick Brodie, remembered dining uneasily at Elrig on greylag geese he had shot with Gavin in Wigtown Bay. Gavin stuffed the geese with red herring and dried them for a week before cooking them, but the result was not a success, and was not improved by a kitchen mix-up whereby the birds were served with chocolate sauce instead of gravy.

By now Gavin was travelling widely to shoot at the grand houses and aristocratic estates of noble-born relatives and well-placed friends in the Scottish Lowlands and Highlands and even across the water in the Irish Republic, where he was Christmas guest at the Annaskaul (County Kerry) home of his friend Douglas Collins, the future head of Gaumont Pictures and founder of Goya, the perfume company. But the huge turreted castle of Inveraray, the ancestral seat of his great-aunt H.R.H. Princess Louise, Duchess of Argyll and her husband the Duke – and the headquarters of the Clan Campbell since the fifteenth century – offered by far the stateliest accommodation and finest hunting on his vacation shooting circuit. At Inveraray Castle and at Strachur on the opposite side of Loch Fyne he passed most of his long vacations, and it was on Inveraray lands that he shot his first stag on 10 September 1935, as he duly recorded in his Game Book: 'The Scaurnoch Wood. *My first stag.* Short stalk, lying shot at about 90 yards, in the wood to the N.W. of Donquhaich rock. Switch. wt: 15.12.'

These shooting days were not exclusively concerned with sporting endeavour, for in part they were the occasion for a seasonal get-together of Britain's pre-war upper-crust, then in the heyday of its privilege and power. The photographs Gavin took of these exclusive shooting parties – the plus-foured, Harris-tweeded gunmen with their kills laid out in rows – depict human types now largely vanished from the British scene. Moustachioed, bandoliered and gaitered, they stand tightly buttoned and tied at the neck in informal military lines-abreast before Bentley and castle doorway, their stern expressions denoting innate breeding and unquestioned authority – a ruling class as yet inviolate. Sometimes Gavin himself appears in these pictures – a slim, melancholy, waif-like figure clad in a checkered hunting suit and wearing a youthful moustache on his not very stiff upper lip. He seems to fit uneasily into these groups of stalwarts – half-hidden at the back, or diminished by perspective at the far end of the line, as if he wishes to conceal his presence among them, or is half-minded to dart away to the nearest covert.

What the photographs do not reveal are Gavin's ordeals at the end of the shooting day. Always shy and unnerved in large social gatherings, but held together by black tie and dinner jacket, he would reluctantly deliver himself to the tortures of trial by sherry in the stately home ante-room, the torment of the formal dinner in the antlered, chandeliered castle dining-hall. This was the price he paid for the freedom of roaming some of the wildest and grandest hunting lands in the world in pursuit of the birds and beasts he loved – and loved to kill.

But Gavin was still essentially an interloper in the Highlands. 'My own yearning for the Highlands was in those days as tormenting as an unconsummated love affair,' he recorded later, 'for no matter how many stags I might kill or feudal castles inhabit I lacked an essential involvement; I was further from them than any immigrated Englishman who planted one potato or raised one stone upon another.'

There was more to Gavin than the image of the simple gun-toting aristocrat and Hibernian romantic might suggest. A completely different dimension to his personality is revealed by his Stowe friend Anthony Dickins, then a music scholar at Corpus Christi, Cambridge, whom Gavin visited unannounced in his college rooms on 20 November 1935. Dickins noted in his diary:

Towards evening the door bursts open and in comes Gavin Maxwell!! God! how my heart races to see him again. I am dumb, completely dumb. He is publishing a volume of poems at Methuens soon [an unrealised ambition]. He is now grown very good-looking – clean-limbed, clear of countenance, as eager and enthusiastic as always, with a great personality and a fire or wind that burns or blows through him catching up his life in ardent fury. He stays about half an hour and then I go to see him off in his immense Bentley on his way to dine at the Pitt Club. He wears a cloak.

But that today Gavin should walk in out of my past still seems like a dream. He is as child-like as he ever was, as simple as ever; with this new thing added. He takes my mind back to long winter evenings in Chatham house-room and afternoons in Stowe grounds. He has much of the true poet in him.

By now the day of reckoning was drawing near, as Gavin approached the end of his University career. But in late April 1937, at the beginning of his last term at Oxford, he contracted a bad bout of jaundice and was left with only six weeks in which to prepare for his final examinations for his Bachelor's degree. In vain he asked to be allowed to retire on the ground of ill-health rather than face certain failure. He was to sit for his degree, he was told, no matter what the outcome might be. So he resigned himself to six weeks' hard work – and somehow managed to scrape through.

FIVE

To the Low Arctic

The strong life that never knows harness;
The wilds where the caribou call;
The freshness, the freedom, the farness –
O God! how I'm stuck on it all.

ROBERT SERVICE,
'The Spell of the Yukon'

Gavin came down from Oxford at the end of June 1937 with a Third Class Degree he did not value and training in a profession he did not respect or intend to pursue. Educated he might be, but he felt lacking in any meaningful qualification to put after his name – essentially an amateur in every sphere.

Almost immediately after taking his degree Gavin was offered the job of private secretary to Sir Archibald Clark-Kerr, then British Ambassador in Iraq. It was, Clark-Kerr told him, a 'back door to the diplomatic service', and Gavin was eager to accept. But his uncle and guardian Lord Eustace Percy, now Minister without Port-folio in Neville Chamberlain's Conservative government, dis-approved of Clark-Kerr's unconventional approach to life and the British Establishment, and strongly urged Gavin to decline. Gavin followed his guardian's advice, and when he told Clark-Kerr of his decision, the Ambassador replied: 'You're making a big mistake. I'm going to the top and I could take you with me.' The following year he was made Ambassador to China; in 1942 Ambassador to the USSR; and in 1946, as Lord Inverchapel of Loch Eck, Ambassa-dor to the United States. Occasionally he wrote to Gavin from his exalted postings abroad. From beleaguered Russia he wrote to assure Gavin that he was as certain the Allies would win the war as he was that he would be a future Ambassador to the United States. He could still get Gavin out of the army and on to his staff if he wanted. But by now Gavin was preoccupied with other things and – 'like a bloody fool' – he again declined.

Having let this opportunity slip by, Gavin cast about for more mundane employment as a temporary tutor, placing an advertisement in the papers which provides a remarkably exact profile of his interests and attributes at this stage of his life:

> Mr Gavin Maxwell, age 23, educated Stowe and Hertford College, Oxford, is seeking a post as holiday companion-tutor to not more than 3 boys of Public School age, period July 25 to September 25 or shorter period. English or Scottish country house, Scottish preferred. Good teacher of shooting with rifle or gun. (Oxford University team for the latter.) Fair and careful shot. Experienced in the training and handling of gun dogs. Thorough knowledge of all game, deer, wild fowl, and natural history. Could act as stalker or puntsman if required. Excellent and careful car driver, all makes, clear licence. Could teach estate management in all branches, English literature, composition and style, and ordinary school subjects. Willing to be useful in any way.
>
> References as to character and capacity from Mr Maxwell's uncle, The Rt. Hon. Lord Eustace Percy, M.P., The Lady Elizabeth Motion, and the Principal of Hertford College, Oxford.

A few weeks later Gavin joined a bizarre little agricultural firm in Hereford called the Sprout Chemical Company, which was partly funded by his brother Aymer and which manufactured a novel (and fairly useless) maize sprouter for the farming industry. 'The Managing Director, who had invented the sprouter, was a comical character called Mr Wallace Turner,' Gavin was to recall, 'and he looked – and sounded – exactly like a frog. "Wonderful prospects, wonderful potential," he croaked at me when I went for my first interview. But when I asked him whether he had sold any of these devices he closed his eyes, put his fingertips together like a bishop, and silently mouthed the word, "No." Well, he gave me the job of what he called "Fieldsman Number One" with the ludicrously grand title of Managing Director for Scotland, which was simply another way of saying I was the commercial traveller in Scotland – a one-man band in a joke organisation. I stuck this for more than a year, but it was very much *not* what I wanted to do, and as I had great difficulty in taking orders from idiots in authority over me, eventually I resigned.'

That was the end of the first and last job Gavin Maxwell ever had in his life. War years apart, he was to be a freelance to the end of his days. By the spring of 1938 he was already contributing occasional freelance articles to *The Field*, the magazine devoted to field sports and country pursuits. But his real ambition was to be an explorer – not as a member of large expeditions (his dislike of groups precluded this even more than his lack of formal scientific qualifications) but as a lone wolf, using a minimum of his small capital to pursue his own interests and travel where he wanted, and returning to write about what he had found and seen. The question was – where to go?

Three main influences contributed to his decision. The first was the residual influence of his boyhood reading – of North American wilderness writers like Jack London (*White Fang* and *The Call of the Wild*) and Ernest Thompson Seton (*Wild Animals I Have Known*, *Wild Animal Ways*). 'The books I loved best when I was a boy were all about the Rockies and the American north-west,' Gavin was to recall, 'and I think that's why, when I broke away and began to travel, I went north rather than south to, say, Arabia or the tropics. I used to fancy myself as someone obsessed with the idea of the far north and all that went with it.' It was a particular book he had come across at one of his prep schools that impelled him to the Arctic – a boys' picture book with a garishly painted polar landscape on the cover, complete with polar bear, fathomless sea, and flaming aurora borealis. 'I was drawn into a majesty of icy desolation and loneliness,' he recalled, 'of limitless space and awful splendour, colder and remoter than the stars, so that my throat tightened and I wanted to cry because it was so beautiful and terrible.'

Another influence was his passion for wildfowl – the essentially northern geese and duck he hunted obsessively, and equally loved and protected. At Monreith he had been building up a unique living collection of the wild geese of the world, starting with the native birds he had wing-tipped on the mud-flats of Wigtown Bay and brought back to Monreith to nurse and tame. The collection grew till it included such exotics as snow geese from North America, bar-headed geese from Tibet and a Cape Barren goose that would walk through the open french windows of the library to squat in front of the fire – 'her delicate dove-grey argus-eyed plumage quivering with contentment'. All these exotic geese fed out on the nearby loch or grazed on the grassy slope below the old castle, and

at the hour of the evening flight, Gavin would recall later, he would
listen to the wings and desolate music of the greylags and the snow
geese from the loch. It was a fair bet that if ever he headed off into
the wilds it would be for reasons connected with these entrancing
creatures, who were for him the very embodiment of the freedom
of the vast skies and far horizons of high latitudes.

The third influence – the essential catalyst – was his friend Peter
Scott, only son of the Antarctic explorer Captain Robert Falcon
Scott. Peter Scott was five years older than Gavin and already an
established and successful painter of wild landscapes and flying
geese. He and Gavin had many interests in common, not least
wildfowl, natural history and painting, and Gavin visited him
sometimes at his lighthouse at Sutton Bridge, Norfolk, where the
Nene runs into the Wash. It was Peter Scott who provided Gavin
with the aim and direction for his first independent travels abroad.
Friends more experienced than Gavin in matters of exploration had
already advised him not to be too ambitious at the start – better,
they said, to begin with a short journey and a limited but attainable
aim. Such an aim was suggested to him by Scott. It was well
established, he told him, that the beautiful little duck known as
Steller's eider had its breeding grounds along the Arctic coast of
Siberia. But did those breeding grounds extend across the border
into Arctic Europe, and specifically into that part of Finnmark
(Norwegian Lapland) adjoining Varanger Fjord, where the Russian
and European Arctic meet – a barren region of cold tundra four
hundred miles north of the Arctic Circle, the most north-easterly
coastline in Europe and the only place in Europe where Steller's
eider could normally be seen? Whether or not they bred there, it
would be worth trying to track down this elusive bird, for it had
never been photographed in the wild.

So off to the Arctic tundra of East Finnmark Gavin went in the
summer of 1938, travelling alone with just £100 in his pocket and
what he could carry on his back. A Norwegian steamer, the *Linga*,
took him from Newcastle to the Norwegian port of Bodö, then
on to Spitzbergen in the High Arctic to pick up fur trappers, and
from there to Bear Island and on to Nordkapp, the most northerly
point of Europe, before carrying on to the small Norwegian settlement of Vadsö on the Varanger Fjord – his final destination. Years
later he was to regale me with the highlights of this first journey
abroad alone:

I thought to myself – this is the life for me, close to nature, testing my physical prowess. But when I arrived at Vadsö at half past three in the morning, after twelve days on board the steamer, it was raining sheets and sheets of rain, and an awful perpetual grey daylight, neither dark nor light, persisted throughout the whole 24 hours, and I thought, 'This is the most depressing place I have ever come to in my life.' I had made prior arrangements to stay in the house of a Norwegian woman, Fru Pedersen, who had once worked as a nursemaid in Newcastle, so I shouldered my heavy rucksack and walked down the gangway on to the pier and wandered through the village in the pouring rain till I found the house. I knocked on the door and after two or three minutes a girl in a nightdress opened it. She stood there talking very rapidly in some foreign language I couldn't understand, but eventually she showed me to a room and said, 'Madam will come soon.' I sat there on the edge of the bed and I waited and waited for hours, looking out of the window at the rain streaming down, but nobody came. Then suddenly I saw a dozen or so of one of the birds I had come all this way to see – Steller's eider – so close I could almost touch them. That cheered me up enormously. And after about four hours madam came at last. She brought me tea, smoked reindeer, an exercise book in which she had written out Lapp phrases for me, she even brought me supplies for the tundra – a whole smoked salmon, two dozen boiled eggs and so on. 'Leave your luggage here,' she told me. 'Come back when you like. Wake us up when you like. I'm going back to bed now.'

So I drank my tea and packed my rucksack with the food she had given me and set off into the tundra. It was sheeting with rain, and after about two miles I walked, literally, on to the nest of another bird – a rare goose, a Lesser Whitefront – which flew away when I arrived. I got my camera out of the rucksack, and sat down and waited for the bird to come back to the nest, and when at last it came back I photographed it – and that proved these birds nested here.

After that I decided it was time to go home – except I had no idea where home was. In that vast, featureless expanse of bare tundra I was quite lost. I wandered around trying to get my bearings, and after a while I saw a man striding across the tundra towards me, and when he came up to me he said (in very curious English): 'Did you know there's been a search party out for you?' No, I replied, I didn't. 'You must never go on to the tundra again alone,' he told me. 'This is very important. Never go on to the tundra alone. Understand?' Then he took me back to Vadsö. The next morning Fru Pedersen produced a pair of Lapp boots with great turned-up toes, and a reindeer skin jacket and reindeer skin trousers and other Lapp garments. 'If you want to live in this country,' she said, 'you do what the Lapps do, wear what the Lapps wear.'

After that I went to see the man who had rescued me. He worked in the mayor's office. 'So you are one of those people,' he said, 'who want to know whether Steller's eider breeds here or not? The Russians were here last year for the same reason. All right then. You go out on to the high tundra, to a district called the Thirteen Lakes, about twenty miles from here. I'll lend you a guide, and when you get there it will be as if you are on the moon.'

So the next morning I set off with the guide, and I was out there, on the moon, among the Lapps, under those brilliantly jewelled night-long Low Arctic sunsets, for many weeks – far, far from anywhere and happier than I had ever been in my life, or ever would be again.

Gavin saw plenty of Steller's eider out by the Thirteen Lakes, and though he could not prove they bred there – in fact they don't – he was able to take a unique series of photographs of them. By now he was living with a Lapp family, and on one memorable occasion he assisted in the breech-delivery of a Lapp baby, a boy whose father named him Gavin.

Gavin was so taken by the strange, desolate world of the East Finnmark tundra that in the early summer of the following year, the last summer before the war, he returned there to collect Lesser Whitefront goslings for his wildfowl collection at Monreith and to study Steller's eider again. From Fru Pedersen's *Hospitzet* at Vadsö, Nord Varanger, Gavin wrote to Peter Scott the day after his arrival:

Well, Peter, I have arrived. Conditions here are Arctic, or nearly so. It is a very late year. In many places the snow is several feet deep; there is ice everywhere. I saw a lot of reindeer higher up, many weird birds of prey, including a hawk owl; but many I did not recognise. One interesting thing about the Lesser Whitefronts – or perhaps you know it – is that they feed on crowberries. The droppings are a deep steel blue, almost ultramarine, full of crowberry seeds, and stained a little with streaks of purple juice. L. Whitefront are pretty tame; they fly round your head, cackling. The noise reminds me of your lighthouse.

On 30 June 1939 Gavin wrote again to Peter Scott from Vadsö with a further report of his ornithological progress in the Far North:

I am bringing you back 3 skins shot in May this year here: one adult ♂, one adult ♀ and one immature ♀. Also 3 eggs, May this year, and some nest down. I am bringing back any- way 2 geese alive, caught as goslings here 2 years ago. But – awful complication – their legs are almost pink, while all the others have vivid orange legs. I have not found any signs of a Steller's nest, but I have taken some very good photographs of them, and today I am going to try and catch some. The country is so vast that a few Steller's nests would be very easy to overlook. I may still catch some goslings if I am lucky; I shall stay here another week anyway.

A few days later Gavin received a telegram from home warning him that war was imminent and advising him to return to Britain immediately to avoid being trapped in Scandinavia for the duration. He sailed on the first available boat and returned to Elrig towards the middle of the month, bringing with him the eggs, down and geese he had collected – and also a few little Lesser Whitefronts which he released among his collection of exotic geese in the grounds of Monreith. 'They would answer to their names,' he was to write later, 'with a shrill clamour that reminded me of the vast tundra and the shine of still lake water under the midnight sun, of the sour tang of reindeer grease and the smell of trout cooking over a camp fire.' Though he had not proved whether or not Steller's eider bred in Varanger Fjord, he had at least brought back more rare photographs of this mysterious bird, and his future life might well have taken this direction had not the war intervened.

Two weeks after returning to Britain Gavin joined a weekend

party at Carlton Towers, the great house of Lord Howard of Glossop, at Goole in Yorkshire. Among the other guests invited by Miles Howard (Lord Howard's son, and the future Duke of Norfolk) was Gavin's favourite modern writer, Evelyn Waugh. In his diary entry for Saturday, 29 July 1939, Waugh recorded the encounter:

> The whole Howard family are together. I never discovered exactly how many, seven or eight of them, each with a Christian name beginning with M. A nice chap called Gavin Maxwell and Maureen Noel [the daughter of the Earl of Gains-borough] were the rest of the party . . . We played 'the game' after dinner. Maxwell, to be civil to me, chose clues from my books which no one recognised.

All talk now was of impending war with Germany. With armed conflict seemingly so certain Gavin was anxious to volunteer for the regiment in which his family had traditionally served, and which his elder brother, Aymer, had already joined – the Scots Guards. As early as September of the previous year Gavin had asked to join the regiment's officer reserve, but had been told there were no vacancies. A few days after the Carlton Towers weekend he was informed that a vacancy had been created by the resignation of a distant relative, Lord Lovat, Chief of Clan Fraser of Lovat, who had left to join the Lovat Scouts and (later) the Commandos. On 21 August the War Office wrote to Gavin at Elrig to confirm that he had been selected and to advise him that he would be required to do thirteen weeks' preliminary training on joining the regiment.

SIX

A call to small arms

Who is the happy warrior? Who is he
That every man in arms should wish to be?
WILLIAM WORDSWORTH, *'The Character
of the Happy Warrior'*

On 2 September 1939, the day after Hitler's invasion of Poland,
Gavin Maxwell joined the Training Battalion of the Scots Guards
at the Guards Depot in Pirbright, Surrey, for the start of a thirteen-
week course of basic infantry training. Three days later he was
gazetted Second-Lieutenant.

Gavin viewed the prospect of active service with both enthusiasm
and trepidation. He was determined to do what was required of
him, and hoped to find some kind of personal fulfilment – adventure, old-fashioned honour, perhaps – in one of the British Army's
élite fighting regiments. But he was well aware that regimental life,
with its emphasis on authority and discipline, communal living and
physical slog, was something to which he might not be ideally
suited, either psychologically or physically.

Basic army training is a shock to the system for anyone joining
from civilian life, and for Gavin it was doubly so, for he was not
physically robust and he did not take kindly to orders from anybody, least of all the martinets of the military machine. Less than
three weeks after joining the army he fell seriously ill with the first
of his many duodenal ulcer attacks and was sent home on sick leave.
He returned on 9 October, and though he was able to complete his
initial training his service with the Scots Guards was to be dogged
by recurring bouts of acute stomach pains.

In February 1940, Gavin was posted as a platoon commander to
Ground Defences at RAF Kenley, and during the spring and early
summer, as the Germans launched their lightning offensive in
Europe, he attended a series of specialist courses at the School of
Tactics back at Pirbright, including a course in sniping, at which

he showed such aptitude that Evelyn Waugh, now a Lieutenant in the Royal Marines, invited him over to Bisley to lecture about it to the troops under his command.

By the time Gavin had completed his courses the war had finally come to Britain. On 10 July the German air force launched its air campaign against the British mainland – the Battle of Britain. Nine days later Gavin was posted to the Scots Guards Holding Battalion in the Tower of London, from which he sallied forth each day (and very often each night) as a member of a detachment of three officers and two hundred men forming a mobile anti-parachute column intended to intercept any German airborne landings in south-east London and its environs. On 7 September, anxious to join one of the Scots Guards fighting battalions, Gavin approached his commanding officer with a request that he be borne in mind for the post of Intelligence Officer in the 1st or 3rd Battalion. 'He is, of course, an expert sniper and camouflageur,' the C.O. noted in an informal memo to his Regimental Adjutant, 'and they could easily send him on a short I.O. course. On the other hand I'm not sure that all the Maxwells have not got an exaggerated idea of their value!'

Gavin had chosen an unfortunate moment to request a transfer, for late in the afternoon of that same day the Germans switched their target from RAF airfields to London itself and sent nearly four hundred bombers and more than six hundred fighters in two waves to attack London's East End, followed by another two hundred bombers after dark. This was the beginning of the London Blitz. Gavin's column became entangled in the air raids on the capital, and all question of a posting was, for the moment, forgotten. By this time the column was stationed in the South Metropolitan Gas Works on the riverside just below the Blackwall Tunnel and opposite East India Dock – within the bullseye, in other words, of the German bombers. During one of the heavy air raids on the London docks that September an incident occurred which was to bring about an unforeseen and radical change in the direction of the whole of Gavin's subsequent life.

It was the third week of the Battle of Britain. An air raid had been in progress all night and Gavin was doing a round of his column's extensive perimeter when he heard a bomb falling almost directly overhead, and dived for the nearest cover. The bomb fell with a gobbling roar but did not explode, and when the All-Clear

sounded about an hour later Gavin went out into the deserted,
dawn-lit streets to look for the bomb-hole. He found it amongst
the gravestones of a churchyard and remembered 'with a sickening
lurch' that the crypt underneath was in use as an air-raid shelter.

I ran down the long winding steps and struggled with the
door. As it burst open under my weight I was hit by a stifling
wave of air so noisome that I retched even at its first impact.
The temperature was that of a Kew hot-house, the stench
indescribable. As I became accustomed to the dim light I saw
that the stone floor was swimming in urine, and between the
packed human forms were piles of excrement and of vomit.
One hundred and twelve people had been in that airless crypt
for seven hours. They were not anxious to be disturbed; abusive voices, thick with sleep, told me to close the doors. I had
just time to open both wide before I was myself sick, helplessly
and endlessly.

He returned to his unit's HQ in the Gas Works so thickly coated
with bomb-blast that he looked like the corpse of the man he had
seen removed from the ruins of the pub on the corner the previous
day. There were two Guardsmen in the shower when he got there
– one of them from a small island in the Outer Hebrides. 'I did not
know it, but I had seen it from the sea, and the name and his soft
speech brought a momentary vision of its low hulk dark against a
harsh Atlantic sunset.'
The image of the Hebrides set Gavin's mind racing, and he told
a fellow officer in the windowless, gaslit mess room: 'I've made a
resolution. If I'm alive when the war's over I'm going to buy an
island in the Hebrides and retire there for life; no aeroplanes, no
bombs, no commanding officer, no rusty dannert wire.'
They spread a map of Scotland on the floor, and in a spirit of
childlike make-believe lay full-length on the floor and worked their
way down through the islands from north to south.

We spoke of Hyskeir, Rona, Canna, Staffa; in my mind were
high-pluming seas bursting upon Atlantic cliffs and booming
thunderously into tunnelled caverns; eider-ducks among the
surf; gannets fishing in deep blue water; and, landward, the
scent of turf smoke.

After an hour there were rings drawn around several islands. I had drawn an extra red ring round the Island of Soay, an island unknown to either of us, below the Cuillin of Skye. We were still playing at make-believe; Soay was my Island Valley of Avalon, and Avalon was all the world away. Presently the sirens sounded, and down the river the guns began again.

On 16 October, Gavin was finally posted to a fighting battalion – the 1st Battalion Scots Guards – first as Weapon Training Officer and then as Liaison Officer with Brigade. At the beginning of 1941 he was promoted to the rank of Lieutenant, but towards the end of the winter his old ailment returned and on 9 March he was admitted to the Royal Masonic Hospital in London with a serious ulcer condition. He remained there for six weeks, and a month's sick leave at Monreith followed, during which he was downgraded to Category C by a Medical Board at Dumfries. Such a low medical grading, meaning home service only, put an end to any hopes he might have had for an illustrious wartime career with the Guards. He returned to London on 21 May, and from the Guards Club in Brook Street, where he had a day or two to spend before learning his new posting, he scribbled a note to the Regimental Adjutant in which he aired his concern about his future:

I have hardly been off training work since the war started, and I am *most* anxious that my re-grading and removal from a service battalion should not result in my returning to training work. There are a great many Intelligence and Liaison jobs for which I should be perfectly fit physically (and I hope mentally) – the only way of life I am supposed to follow being a pretty simple sort of diet and an outdoor life . . . I feel so strongly about it that I think I should really rather become a private in a Labour Battalion than remain for a long time in general training work again!

This heartfelt plea received short shrift from the Regimental Adjutant: 'If you write any more stupid letters,' he replied with typically military bluntness, 'the Lieutenant-Colonel will take you at your word and you *will* find yourself as a private in a Labour Battalion!'

When the Scots Guards service battalions were mobilised for the front, Gavin was not with them. After a month with the Training Battalion back at Pirbright Camp he was posted yet again to the Tower, and in October he returned for a third time to the Training Battalion. The truth was, the Scots Guards did not really know what else to do with him. His physical disability clearly ruled him out of active service, and though he was keen and willing, and came from the right background, he was a prickly character and did not conform to the stereotype of a typical Guards Officers' Mess. Yet his prowess as a marksman and sniper, his expertise in fieldcraft and camouflage, and his excellence as an instructor, ensured that he did not count among the waifs and strays of the Regiment.

The sole surviving photo of him at this low period – an identity card 'mug shot' – reveals a Gavin Maxwell virtually unrecognisable to anyone who knew him in later years. Tightly buttoned up in his army greatcoat, and with his officer's hat jammed firmly down over his head, he stares at the camera with the fiercely fixed glare of the martinet subaltern, his *de rigueur* moustache bristling, but his eyes wary, fugitive and vulnerable-looking. This, one cannot help feeling, is Gavin camouflaged in the guise of the British military establishment. The moustache alone could serve as a metaphor for the singularity of his situation. Many years later he was to recall the bizarre ceremonial this moustache engendered: 'Every morning when you got up, your servant had a pair of tongs warming on a little methylated-spirit stove. Every so often he tested the tongs on a piece of toilet paper, and when the tongs no longer singed the paper he handed them to you and you started to roll up your moustache with the help of the tongs and a comb. You did this regularly every morning, and if you were going on parade in the afternoon you did it in the afternoon as well. Looking back on it, this strikes me as incredible.'

But Gavin did not look back on his days in the Guards as altogether a waste of time. 'In the Brigade of Guards no moment is lost, everything is just right and in its place,' he once told me. 'Now I think this did me a tremendous amount of good. It gave me a tremendous feeling of responsibility. The years I spent in the Scots Guards taught me, I suppose, how to be a freelance – how to manage one's day, how not to waste time, how to plan.'

* * *

There seemed little future for Gavin in the Guards. By the summer of 1941 he was determined to leave the regiment, and at the end of August, after a Medical Board had extended his low medical category for a further twelve months, he made contact with an old friend from Stowe, Captain Alfgar Hesketh-Pritchard, the head of the Czech Section of the Special Operations Executive, better known by its initials SOE.

SOE was an independent secret service, set up on Churchill's instructions in July 1940, shortly after the retreat from Dunkirk and the surrender of France. Its aim was to conduct subversive warfare and (in Churchill's phrase) 'set Europe ablaze', by co-ordinating (and if necessary initiating) subversion and sabotage activities by resistance organisations throughout the occupied nations of Europe (and eventually of the Far East as well). As an unorthodox organisation created to wage war by unorthodox means in unorthodox places, SOE resorted to the services of unor-thodox people, many of whom, as agents in the field, faced terrible dangers – a quarter of the SOE agents sent to France never returned.

There was no formal selection process for SOE in those days, and recruitment was usually by invitation rather than application – often as the result of chance encounter or personal introduction. SOE needed men and women with an extraordinary range of special skills – safe-breakers and demolition experts, linguists and under-cover operators with high motivation and ice-cold courage. At a searching interview at SOE's London headquarters in Baker Street it was noted that Gavin was an outstanding small-arms and fieldcraft expert who had spent over a year as an instructor in sniping and camouflage. There was never any question that he could work as a secret agent himself – his medical condition saw to that – but he might prove invaluable in training SOE agents for their secret work in the field. On 10 September 1941 Hesketh-Pritchard recommended Gavin to SOE, noting that though he had a low medical category he was 'actually perfectly fit if he can stay in the open and does not eat certain foods'. On 5 November Gavin was formally engaged as a Lieutenant Instructor in the SOE training branch; he ceased to be paid from Army funds, receiving quarterly payments from clandestine Foreign Office funds instead.

Training was crucial in the preparation of an agent. At that time trainee agents (who were grouped according to their nationality – British, French, Belgian, Dutch, Danish, Norwegian, Czech,

Polish, Yugoslav, Spanish Republican and even German) first had to pass a stiff preliminary course of basic military and physical training lasting two to four weeks. The successful ones were then put through an even stiffer three-to-five-week para-military course at the Group A Special Training Schools located in various country houses in the Arisaig area on the West Highland coast of Scotland, before going back to England for parachute training at Ringway and a finishing course in clandestine techniques at Beaulieu.

Gavin himself was put through the first two stages of the training course. First he underwent a brief spell of preliminary training at the SOE Special Training School (STS) No 4 at Winterfold, Cranleigh, Surrey, during which it was reported that though he had difficulty keeping up with the other students and had collapsed after twenty minutes' strenuous PT he was 'very keen and interested . . . knows his subjects and lectures well'. This was followed by the tough para-military course at Arisaig (STS 21), at the end of which a medical report recommended that 'he should be fit for an Instructor's post in a few weeks, provided he remains free from abdominal symptoms . . . in his own words he has not felt so well for many months'. His STS 21 report was glowing:

> This officer is a very good lecturer with an easy manner and has obviously had experience of lecturing. He is very good at fieldcraft and quite at home in this type of country . . . He is a good organiser and has a strong personality. The only doubt is regarding his health, but if this is not likely to break down we should like to have him in the area and he is himself keen to be posted here.

At the end of November 1941, Gavin returned to London and for the remainder of the year worked as Alfgar Hesketh-Pritchard's assistant in the Czech Section of SOE, where his main task was to handle the paperwork. Sometimes, however, he would escort Czech agents to Tangmere airfield, near Chichester, where they boarded the aircraft from which they would be parachuted into their Nazi-occupied homeland. Major (later Sir) Peter Wilkinson, the overall chief of the Czech and Polish Sections of SOE, recalled of Gavin's time at the Baker Street headquarters: 'I saw Gavin in London every day while he was there, and I would have lunch with him now and then, though not very often – we were tremendously busy. Alfgar treated Gavin shockingly – he viewed him as a sidekick and bossed him about all over the place. Gavin took it meekly. He was then a very nice, perfectly normal person – not as odd as he later became. He was always a pleasure to be with, always pointing things out, it was impossible not to like him.'

At the end of December Gavin travelled to Monreith to spend Christmas with his mother and his brother Aymer – his last full leave for several years. Despite his intensive military involvement with small arms, he had not lost his love of shooting. 'I had ten days' leave at Christmas and some quite good shooting,' he wrote to Peter Scott. 'My brother and I killed 1,200 head of game at the time shooting alone, and had 246 in one day, which is reasonable enough for two guns anyway.'

Early in January 1942 Gavin took the train north to begin work as an instructor at the para-military training schools in the Arisaig area. With him travelled two tyro instructors who were to become good friends – Matthew Hodgart (later Professor of English at Cambridge) and Edward Renton (a musician and conductor). The para-military schools were centred on eight large houses in and around Arisaig, Morar and Knoydart. The area had been chosen by the operational chief of SOE, General Sir Charles Gubbins, himself a Highlander, who knew this rugged country well. Its advantages were many: the terrain was suitable for the training involved, it was remote and sparsely populated, and it already had a high-security status due to the naval bases and commando training centre in the vicinity. It was also one of the wildest, grandest and most beautiful parts of Britain, with mountains, deer forests and sea lochs inland, and a magnificent coastline that looked across shell-sand beaches and rocks to the rearing cliffs and peaks of the Small Isles of Eigg and Rhum to the west. Gavin was back in the West Highlands – for him it was like coming home.

The para-military course at the Arisaig schools was short, packed and gruelling. Its main elements were physical training, including cross-country marches, swimming and rock-climbing; silent killing and knife work; weapon training; demolition training; map-reading and compass work; fieldcraft; raid tactics (including ambushing and house-clearing); elementary morse; appreciations, planning, reports and orders; schemes and exercises (including all-night schemes, survival training and living off the land); and para-naval training and boat work. It was training which could turn an ordinary mortal into a superman, capable of blowing up a bridge, sinking a ship, or derailing an express train with an overcoat.

In the first few months of 1942 Gavin was a general instructor at the SOE schools in Arisaig, Knoydart and Morar in turn. His superiors were impressed with his abilities. 'His knowledge of fieldcraft and minor tactics is an eye-opener,' went one report. 'His knowledge of weapons is first-class.' In August 1942 he was posted, to his own surprise, as Group Instructor at the Group A Headquarters at Arisaig House with the rank of Captain, and a year later he was made Commandant of STS 24 at Inverie House on Knoydart.

Gavin's specialities were small arms (particularly 'fast and fancy' pistol shooting) and fieldcraft – he was less interested in explosives. The years he had spent in pursuit of deer and wildfowl before the war had given him tremendous expertise in the art of fieldcraft, and since there was no great difference between stalking a game animal and a human target, as far as camouflage and all the other tricks of the art were concerned, Gavin became SOE's star instructor in the military application of fieldcraft. His lectures and practical demonstrations – the nature of night vision, the art of night hearing, how to make use of broken ground, double skylines, a low sun in front of the enemy and a full moon behind him, how to read different kinds of footprints – were a revelation to the student agents who attended them.

In his weapon training sessions Gavin taught how to strip, reassemble, load, fire and maintain a variety of Allied and enemy firearms, in the dark as well as the light; how to shoot on sight at snap targets in the woods and in the streets of SOE's specially constructed mock-up village; how to storm a room in which Resistance agents were being interrogated by the Gestapo (always kick the door open, always switch on the light, always select your targets deliberately and shoot them systematically one after the other). It was Gavin who provided the live ammunition firing at the SOE assault course, blazing away with a Bren gun just above the level of the students' heads.

Towards the autumn of 1943 Gavin formed an idea for a new training school at Glasnacardoch Lodge, where student agents, who hitherto had only trained on British and American models, could familiarise themselves with the weapons of all the Resistance organisations of occupied Europe, from his own extensive collection. At the same time he was put in charge of the Wireless Telegraphy Training School at Rhubana Lodge, in Morar, and promoted to the acting rank of Major. 'I said I didn't know how I could possibly do both jobs,' he recalled, 'and I was told: "Just do it!"'

In spite of the gruelling schedule, Gavin's time with SOE was probably one of the happiest in his life. He was involved in important and meaningful work at which he excelled. He enjoyed the security of a loose and congenial organisation which gave him status and freed him from the practical worries of life without sacrificing his independence and essential personality. Above all, perhaps, he was back in the land where he most wished to be – the Scottish West Highland coast. In short, he had found a niche in which he could function.

Gavin found at SOE Arisaig a rather odd collection of people, many of them larger than life. One of them (a Norwegian) was a world champion ski jumper, another (a Russian) a world champion lightweight wrestler; one had been a Fascist at Cambridge and fought for Franco in the Spanish Civil War; another had been a Communist at Cambridge and a member of the Apostles group that had included the Soviet spies Anthony Blunt and Guy Burgess. Two legendary instructors in the early days, known collectively as the 'Heavenly Twins', had been officers in the Shanghai Municipal Police before the war and taught pistol shooting, silent killing and close combat. One, Captain Bill Sykes, looked and spoke like a bishop, but was endowed with enormous hands and fingers with which he taught students how to throttle people. (It was later rumoured that he was the model for a rather sinister character in the James Bond stories.) The other was Captain W.E. ('Desperate Dan') Fairbairn ('Murder made easy, that's me!'), a Black Belt judo master who devised a method of silent killing out of a mixture of ju-jitsu, karate and miscellaneous practices picked up from the villains on the Shanghai waterfront, and taught Resistance students such skills as the Chin Jab, the Bronco Kick, the Japanese Strangle, the Back Break, the Chair and Knife and the Match-Box Attack, along with the use of such silent weapons as the crossbow dart, the spike, the flick-knife, the spring cosh, the garrotte and an alarming-looking dagger of his own invention known as the smatchet.

Tex Geddes, a rugged Newfoundlander and Sergeant Instructor in matters amphibious, used knives to play darts. Wildest amongst the students were the Poles, who fired their revolvers through the ceilings and tossed hand grenades into the mountain streams to catch trout. A few of the SOE personnel were endowed with serious personality disorders. One Quartermaster officer had a serious drink problem, and appeared one morning at breakfast waving a revolver, stark naked and spattered from head to foot in green ink.

Gavin himself, of course, numbered prominently among the eccentrics of the community. He would interrupt students' ping-pong matches by bursting into the games room and blasting the ball in mid-air with a Colt .45, or bemuse them by walking into a room in such a way that he appeared to be walking out.

Dr James MacDougall, an SOE medic who kept an eye on the psychiatric health of the instructors and the trainee agents, believed that Gavin shared with Winston Churchill, the poet Robert Burns and many great artists a personality profile for which he employed the term 'creative psychopath'. A creative psychopath's personality is composed of an entire series – concurrency might be a more exact word – of characteristics that are absolute opposites. They can be simultaneously friendly and unfriendly, truthful and untruthful, bold and fearful, loyal and disloyal, thick-skinned and thin-skinned, considerate and callous, and so on through the entire range of human emotions and attitudes. Such a person, in whom opposing characteristics are perpetually at war with one another, is full of anomalies and can be very unpredictable and difficult to get on with, inspiring affection and loathing in equal measure. According to Dr MacDougall a creative psychopath also tends to lead a disorganised life and to have an inconsistent work record. Overall, a creative psychopath's emotional make-up is more like that of a child than a mature adult; he is unable to sustain an emotion for any length of time, and though he is capable of deep feelings, they are fleeting and transitory. It follows that it is difficult for creative psychopaths to sustain mature relationships, and they tend not to get on well with people. It was Dr MacDougall's view that Gavin was emotionally retarded, almost certainly because his sexual and emotional development had been put on hold at the age of sixteen, when his nearly fatal illness cut him off from all but his mother.

Even among his colleagues in SOE, Gavin was not a figure who could easily be ignored. Though he was slight in stature, he had a presence and a manner – part aristocratic, part shy elfin charm – and a voice of resonant authority that compelled attention. With his full, blond, drooping moustache and his floppy shock of blond hair falling over his high forehead he looked, to at least one of his fellow officers at Arisaig, like Tenniel's illustration of the White Knight in *Through the Looking-Glass*. This image of the eccentric, questing knight was to be evoked by several of those who knew him at different stages of his life.

Though his medical category was still abysmal – the SOE medics had diagnosed an enlarged heart and synovitis of the ankle as well as the usual chronic duodenal ulcer – Gavin was fit enough for most challenges, and could display a toughness of mind and body that astonished instructors and students alike. Hamish Pelham-Burn, a fellow instructor and one of Gavin's closest friends in SOE, recalled one occasion after dinner at Garramor when he and Gavin were drinking whisky with some French Resistance students who were soon to be parachuted into Nazi-occupied territory.

As always, the conversation got round to the question of what they would do if they were caught by the Gestapo. The Frenchmen said they weren't worried, they would just bite on their cyanide capsules. 'Oh no you wouldn't!' retorted Gavin. 'You'd try and survive it. Like this!' He was going to stub out his lighted cigarette on his bare thigh, he told them (he was wearing a kilt), and they could watch his eyes and see what effect it had on him. So he took a puff on his cigarette and then ground out the burning end on his thigh. I watched his face and there was not a flicker of reaction to the pain. It didn't do his thigh much good, but the French were very impressed. He'd made his point – as he always liked to.

In spite of his relative frailty Gavin was a great outdoor man, forager and improviser. The years of stalking and wildfowling out on the hills and estuaries in all weathers had not only hardened him but also given him a hunter's instinct and a predator's awareness of the opportunities for human survival within the natural ecology – something that was generally lost on his more urbanised colleagues. He took full advantage of the natural provender of the hinterland to provide for both the staff and the students – generally in a style far above that to which they were normally accustomed. Dr Hamish Ireland, SOE's first medical officer at Arisaig, remembered Gavin's succulent messing regime well. 'His menus were the most exotic and marvellous dishes of salmon, game and butcher's meat ever set before us. His reign, alas, was short-lived – the Mess got into the red. But we all felt better for having lived off the fat of the land.'

Gavin's aptitude for living off the land was not entirely an epicurean pursuit. For the students it could be a matter of survival. He taught them how to collect mussels and limpets off the rocks in the inter-tidal zone and eat them raw when there was no alternative; by way of demonstrating the potential for survival using the most improbable by-products of the available wildlife, he killed a seal, removed the blubber, strained the seal oil through blotting paper, and drank it. Once he took a squad of student agents on a survival course in the hills. Before setting out Gavin told them he would personally eat any bird they brought him, to demonstrate what good meat there was to be had. His hope was that someone would bring him a tasty grouse, but the best they could come up with was a jackdaw, which he ate with as much relish as he could muster. He even incorporated basic butchery into his SOE lectures, starting with the warm carcase of a deer – a shocking experience for some of his more fastidious trainee agents.

Though some of Gavin's fellow officers at SOE found him rather strange and moody, and were inclined to tease him when they found him writing poems under a rhododendron bush, most were fond of him. He was not universally popular, however. Derek Leach, a lawyer in civilian life, was Chief Instructor at Meoble. He first met Gavin when he came over to Meoble as a training officer in 1943, and had mixed views about him. 'He was a bit of a loner,' he recalled. 'He didn't pull social rank, but he was offhand, unpunctual and somewhat egotistical – he'd interrupt you in mid-sentence and go on to his own thing.' Dr MacDougall remembered: 'When he was good he was very, very good, but when he was bad . . . well!' He added: 'All healthy relationships are based on ambivalent attitudes, but I believe Gavin inspired markedly ambivalent reactions – in friends and foes alike.'

David Tree Parsons, for example, the Commandant at Inverie, didn't take to Gavin at all when he first met him in November 1943, noting in his diary: 'I found Maxwell highly-strung, spoilt, eccentric and intolerant. He told me he had written five, as yet unpublished, books.' Before long, though, they were the best of friends, mainly because of their mutual love of nature and the great outdoors.

SOE's confidential reports on Gavin reflect some ambivalence. 'Quite a cheerful person,' went one, 'but rather self-centred.' 'An excitable temperament,' went another, 'and egotistical to a degree.' A third declared: 'He is, I think, too inclined to create problems for himself and to worry over them. Although temperamental, he has a pleasant and likable personality.'

Dr Hamish Ireland, Gavin's medical officer during his first year at Arisaig, recalled: 'He must have been a bit spoiled at one stage in his life. He was quite temperamental, a bit "agin the government", and he reacted childishly if he was reprimanded by a senior officer.' Gavin did not get on very well with the Colonels. 'I was very much my own man in SOE,' he once told me. 'I was almost a freelance, in a way, and commanded my own establishments fairly early on. I didn't get on with my superiors. Some of them had got there simply by influence and were very objectionable and unpleasant people. But one or two of them did say to me, "Well, your job is to get on with your job, so we won't meddle and pry," and with those I got on extremely well.' To avoid being billeted with the Colonels at Arisaig House, Gavin moved out and lived on his own in a little old-fashioned two-up and two-down lodge on a hill near Glasnacardoch – a highly irregular arrangement by military standards.

Gavin's conflict with higher authority led to many difficulties with his commanding officer, Colonel Jimmy Young, who was in charge of the whole area command. Young, a former tea planter from Ceylon, was a personality in his own right – 'a great wencher, a great drinker, a great character, but not a great brain'. According to Hamish Pelham-Burn, he once did a parachute jump wearing a kilt with nothing underneath, but was so overweight that he broke both legs on landing. Colonel Young was sorely tried by the antics of the more wayward and eccentric of the officers under his command, and was constantly engaged in a 'passage of arms' with Gavin. He took a dim view of Gavin's non-military style of dress – cream shirt and yellow Texan scarf under his battledress top, family kilt instead of regulation army-issue one – and spluttered with outrage when Gavin asked him for compassionate leave after receiving a telegram from his mother at Monreith telling him his flamingos had flown out to sea. 'I was recommended for court martial twice,' Gavin once told me, 'both times on rather flimsy pretexts. Once was when I left a British officer, who was going to be dropped into Yugoslavia, alone in a room at my weapon training establishment. After half an hour I heard a loud bang and when I went in I found he had shot his thumb off. I was recommended for court martial on the grounds of gross negligence, but it was never proceeded with.'

For all his flaws, Gavin inspired genuine affection and loyalty among those in SOE who took to his mercurial personality. 'He had a delicious sense of humour,' recalled his old school friend Peter Kemp. 'He could be very funny and he told very funny stories. He used to mimic me wickedly – he was a very good mimic and he mimicked everybody.' Matthew Hodgart found a lot in Gavin he admired:

> He was very witty, very entertaining, very well-bred; and though he could be irritable and prickly, he was usually great fun to be with and cheered people up a lot. And he was a very gifted fellow, highly skilled at a variety of things. He was a terrific shot, a fine naturalist, and an excellent draughtsman; and later it turned out he was a wonderful descriptive writer as well. We had a lot of things in common. Both of us had had a father who had been killed by a German shell in the First World War. Both of us were products of Oxbridge. Academically I was much his superior. He was not a great scholar, and I am not sure if he had a first-class mind or not. Nor was he very literary-minded in those days, and I don't ever recall talking about English literature with him. But he was socially much my superior. He knew the world in a way I didn't. He was also quite the most neurotic person I have ever met in my life. He was very fond of Captain Michael Bolitho, an intelligent young officer from the Scots Guards who was an SOE instructor at Garramor. When Bolitho was killed in action in Algeria, Gavin cracked up – he was absolutely devastated and began drinking heavily. There was never any shortage of whisky in the Highlands during the war. We used to drink like fish in the evenings after the day's work and talk about everything under the sun. Looking back, that's what it was all about – being young and alive in the most beautiful place in the world.

A number of Gavin's friends at Arisaig were sent on special operations. Derek Leach and Edward Renton were dropped behind

German lines in Italy, Matthew Hodgart was sent on a clandestine mission into Algeria, Peter Kemp was dropped into Albania and Alfgar Hesketh-Pritchard lost his life with the partisans on the Yugoslav–Austrian border. Gavin himself doubted if he could have coped with field operations. 'On one occasion we had a small batch of German trainee agents arrive for their para-military training,' he once told me. 'They were going to be parachuted into Germany itself. I found this amazing – it seemed an absolutely suicidal thing to do. And I remember thinking at the time that I personally lacked the cold-blooded courage to do something like that – I don't think I could ever have gone off on special ops behind enemy lines. I'd have been much too afraid.'* Gavin's colleagues in SOE doubted this. 'Of course he had the guts,' said Peter Kemp. 'But he was totally medically unfit for the job.' Others agreed, but added they thought he might have been temperamentally too excitable and too nice. 'He was too bloody kind,' Tex Geddes considered:

> I mean, if he and I had gone on an op, and I'd broken my leg, he would never have left me. But if he had broken *his* leg, I'd have buggered off and left him for sure – which would have been the right thing to do according to our training and instructions. He was a very fine bloke, an excellent fellow. His outstanding qualities were honesty and integrity, I would say. He was a bloody loyal bloke and he'd never let anyone down. Never. Not even when they deserved it. For example, we had a basket of a ration sergeant who was cheating the Mess Fund – and that is an unpardonable sin in the army. I was for cutting his balls off, but Gavin wouldn't have it. He said to me: 'That fellow's a sergeant. If we take his stripes away it won't be him that we'll be punishing but his wife. Her sergeant's allowance will be cut but it won't make any difference to him at all. I've visited the glasshouse at Aldershot and I swore that I'd never put anybody in there if it was in my power to avoid it. Now it *is* in my power to avoid it –

---

* After the war Gavin wrote a novel centred around these agents, all of whom went to their deaths. He showed me the manuscript but never allowed me to read it. 'It's no bloody good,' he told me. 'I can't write novels because I can't structure stories properly.' The manuscript was later destroyed in the fire that burned down his house in Scotland.

so I'll just pay the bloody bill myself!' A hundred-odd pounds
it was. He was very irritating in things like that. He had no
sense of the value of money – money didn't mean anything
to him, it was just something that his mother gave him. I
remember having a pair of sealskin gloves and he wanted them
and offered me a lot of money for them. He irritated me like
bloody hell for thinking that everyone had a price and he could
buy anything if he had enough money to pay for it. But against
that he would sit down and make tea in a tin hat like the rest
of us.

Gavin was greatly respected as a teacher by his Resistance students,
and was given a nickel-plated, ivory-handled .32 Colt semi-
automatic by a Norwegian student as a token of gratitude when he
was Commandant at the Rhubana STS towards the end of 1943 –
the same pistol with which he pretended to shoot me in the head
when I first encountered him in London fourteen years later. Few
agents ever returned from enemy Europe to record their view of
the practical value of Gavin's courses. One exception was Peter
Kemp, who remembered him as a tremendous teacher. Another
was Suzanne Warren (a cover name).

Suzanne was a courageous, attractive, twenty-two-year-old
Frenchwoman who arrived for para-military training at SOE Arisaig in June 1944. For the first three years of the German occupation
of her country she had worked for a Paris-based network which
had helped Allied escapees to evade capture and return to England.
But in January 1943 she was arrested by the Gestapo and for two
months subjected to brutal interrogation. When it became clear she
would not talk, she was sent to a hostage prison at Castres, from
which she escaped during a mass breakout the following September. After several months in hiding in a monastery guest house,
she joined another Resistance network as a courier and escort travelling to and from Paris. Eventually orders came from London
instructing her and a number of other Resistance personnel to
embark for England, and in April 1944 she was picked up on the
Brittany coast by Royal Navy gunboat and brought to Dartmouth
carrying important secret papers. Some weeks later, after recovering her health and strength, she was sent up to Arisaig as a
member of the last intake of European Resistance students to be
trained at the Arisaig schools before the end of the war. This intake

included a thirty-four-year-old agent of the OSS (Office of Strategic Services, the American equivalent of SOE) by the name of André Charisse, whom Suzanne was later to marry, thus becoming the sister-in-law of the future Hollywood film star Cyd Charisse.

'Gavin reminded me of Byron,' she recalled, 'but a nicer man than Byron. He was one of the few people in my life who were like shining stars – something really special.'

> I was at SOE Arisaig all through July of that glorious summer. I used to go out with Gavin in his lobster boat and explore the coves and islands along the coast, and the seals would follow us and the birds swoop around us, and it was all so beautiful and wonderful after the nightmare of the Gestapo. I got to know Gavin very well in that short time. He was a marvellous person, a gifted leader, and I grew very fond of him. He never pulled rank on us and treated us all as his equals. We were an unruly mob of different nationalities but he never used a rod of iron, he was not a run-of-the-mill officer, he didn't go by the book. He was a rebel, like me. He exercised leadership by the sheer force of his personality. And he created such a happy atmosphere that there was no resentfulness, no rebellion, even though we were all confined and cooped up and couldn't go anywhere. I don't like people telling me what to do, but *he* could, and I didn't resist it. He made you feel you were part of a team, so he got far more out of us. He wasn't soft – we had to work damn hard. But he could be very kind and considerate. Once, when we were practising grenade throwing, one of the students – an Englishwoman called Joan – pulled the pin out of the grenade, then felt faint and was in danger of dropping the grenade and blowing them both up. But Gavin calmed her and helped her and gently got her to throw the grenade over the wall.
>
> There was always a bit of sexual tension in Gavin's company. He didn't flirt with me – after all, I had met André by then – but I knew he liked me. He was a very striking, romantic personality. I didn't know then that he was the grandson of a Duke, and the darker side of his nature he kept hidden.

There was precious little free time at SOE Arisaig, either for the instructors or their students. The relentless pressures of the war, the deadly serious business of preparing the Resistance agents for their imminent ordeal behind Nazi lines in the shortest possible time, meant that weeks and months went by without a break, and as the momentum for the Second Front and the liberation of Europe gathered pace, so the pressure on SOE mounted. By the autumn of 1943 Gavin was not only Commandant of STS 24 at Knoydart (and subsequently Commandant of STS 22 at Rhubana) but also Chief Instructor at his Foreign Weapons School at STS 22a at Glasnacardoch.

But sometimes on a weekend, during the long northern summer days, he was able to slip away on his motorbike for an hour or two's birdwatching, or take his lobster boat, the *Gannet*, out for a trip among the bays and islets of that glorious Arisaig coast, or stalk deer among the wild hills overlooking Loch Morar. And now and then on a Sunday evening he would meet up with some of his SOE officer friends at the Morar Hotel, or venture further afield to his favourite watering-hole at Lochailort, in the Commando training area, to down a few drams and exchange a few words and sing a few songs at an impromptu carousel or *ceilidh* at the Lochailort Inn, run by his hugely larger-than-life friend Uilleamena MacRae. An eccentric, warm-hearted, striking-looking, Lewis-born woman in her early forties, with a Bonnie Prince Charlie hairstyle and a big, swishing Inverness cape, Uilleamena had once had a Hollywood screen test before the war, and ran her wartime inn like a private home for her friends and her horde of pets. Gavin was especially fond of her, and recognised in her a kindred spirit and life-force to whom he instantly and instinctively related.

It was Uilleamena who, not long before her untimely death after the war, was to sell Gavin the furniture (fairly awful furniture at a fairly outrageous price) with which he furnished his retreat at Sandaig – the Camusfeàrna of *Ring of Bright Water*.

Leisure time was so rare in SOE that a year and a half were to pass after Gavin's arrival at Arisaig before he had an opportunity to visit the tiny island of Soay – his 'Island Valley of Avalon' beneath the Cuillins of Skye – to which his mind had once turned during the London Blitz in the early days of the war.

SOE had two yachts at its disposal in the West Highlands. One was a luxury yacht of eighty tons called the *Orca*, which was used almost exclusively for entertaining the Colonels in Mallaig Harbour. The other was the *Risor*, a forty-ton Norwegian lifeboat converted into a small varnished yacht, with bottles of champagne stowed in the bilges as ballast. The *Risor* had originally been requisitioned by SOE to run secret agents to and from Norway, but was used most of the time to give SOE students amphibious training in the Mallaig area. Gavin had made friends with the yacht's commanding officer and original owner, Tommy Martin, and on the first day of his summer leave in 1943 he persuaded Martin to take him across to Soay. It was to be one of the most momentous excursions Gavin ever made – his second stepping-stone to adventure – and its repercussions would be felt to his dying days.

They sailed from Mallaig on a blue, hot morning when there was not the faintest breath of wind and the whole length of Sleat was mirrored in a still sea dotted with resting birds. In a little over an hour they rounded the point of Sleat and headed due north for Soay through the long, oily swell of the Hebridean seas, the island barely separable from the long bulk of the Cuillin hills as they soared, peak upon peak, across the eight miles of sea from Sleat to Skye.

'We crept cautiously into Camus na Gall, Soay's east bay,' Gavin was to write of his first landfall at the island, 'the leadsman calling soundings from the bows. The yacht's captain, a stranger to northern waters, had the navigational guide in his hand, a long bleat of warnings that makes one wonder at any stranger sailing the Hebrides without a pilot. At "By the mark, five," he gave the order to let go, and the anchor rattled out noisily into the stillness.' Though there was smoke coming from the dozen or so cottages above the high-water mark, no one appeared as the visitors rowed to the shore.

And so Gavin stepped ashore at last on the island he had called his Avalon, and for two hours of that hot, breathless July day was free to explore its diminutive microcosm of moorland, glens and lochs. Climbing to the top of a round purple hill, he looked down over the western end of the island and saw the Sea of the Hebrides stretching beyond, with all its islands spread dim and blue upon the horizon.

'I made my way down through a wood of oaks to a small bay on the Soay Sound. The sun was hot on the red, sea-smooth rock. Six feet below me the tide lapped, a vivid intense blue, with the transparency of white sand and sea-tangle two fathoms down. From everywhere on the island the Cuillin seemed towering and imminent, three thousand feet of bitter black rock rising stark and hostile out of the sea.' The island seemed pervaded by an immense stillness, the only sounds the low lapping of the tide, the humming of the bees in the heather, the champing jaws of the cattle cropping the rushes.

Gavin returned to Camus na Gall, and as he was rowed back to the yacht one of the crew began to relate some of the island's troubles: its inadequate communications and transport, its decreasing population, and the absence of state support. There was a lot of feuding between the inhabitants, he told Gavin, which inclined them to think that a resident landlord would do the place some good.

Not long after this first visit to Soay, Gavin decided to buy the island, if he could do so at a figure that would give him the equivalent of a small rate of interest from rentals and feu-duties on his invested capital. He entered into protracted negotiations with the island's owner, Flora Macleod, and a year later completed the purchase for the sum of £900, which he paid for with a loan from his mother. With the island came the salmon-fishing rights of its coast, a commercial bag-net fishing which had for some years been leased to a Scottish commercial salmon fishery. But Gavin made a blunder during his negotiations for the island which, in retrospect, was a worrying omen for his future business enterprise. By an oversight, the commercial salmon fishery's lease had been renewed for a further eight years, with the result that he was deprived of the only substantial commercial returns that could ordinarily be derived from the island. From the purely financial point of view he had bought a pig in a poke. He could see no way of developing or improving the island or the welfare of its inhabitants, except by introducing new industry – which, in the Hebridean islands, had already defeated far richer men and mightier organisations than Gavin could ever aspire to emulate. He was now the owner of his Island Valley of Avalon – and also, as he was soon to acknowledge, 'of all its troubles, internecine feuds, frustrations, and problems'.

SEVEN

Harpoon

Dear God be good to me;
The sea is so wide
And my boat is so small
BRETON FISHERMAN'S PRAYER

By the late summer of 1944 the work of SOE was as good as over.
After the Allied invasion of Europe the role of the Resistance was
replaced by the regular forces of the liberating armies, and though
SOE's training schools in Britain were still kept fully staffed there
was little for the instructors to do. Gavin, like the rest of his colleagues, found himself increasingly idle and free to spend the hot,
still summer days as he chose. While others chafed at not being
allowed home to see their wives and families, Gavin for his part
wanted nothing more than to be where he was. 'Those brazen days
I spent in my boat,' he was to write, 'exploring the coast and the
islands from Mull to the narrows of Skye, slipping imperceptibly
back into a world I had almost forgotten, dream-like and shining.
I used to visit the seal-rocks and spend hours watching the seals;
sit among the burrows of a puffin colony and see the birds come
and go, unafraid, from their nests; fish for conger eels by moonlight; catch mackerel and lobsters.' It was during this halcyon period
of unexpected leisure that Gavin first set eyes on a creature with
which his future was to be intricately embroiled:

We were returning from Glenelg; it was late afternoon, the
sky paling and the hills turning to deep plum, their edges sharp
and hard, as though cut from cardboard. We were about a
mile off Isle Ornsay Lighthouse, heading southward over a
still, pale sea, when I noticed something breaking the surface
thirty yards from the boat. At first it was no more than a
ripple with a dark centre. The centre became a small triangle,
black and shiny, with a slight forward movement, leaving a

light wake in the still water. The triangle grew until I was looking at a huge fin, a yard high and as long at the base. It seemed monstrous, this great black sail, the only visible thing upon limitless miles of pallid water. A few seconds later the notched tip of a second fin appeared some twenty feet astern of the first, moving in a leisurely way from side to side.

When Gavin realised the two fins belonged to the same creature he was overwhelmed by excitement and fear. The sheer bulk of the first basking shark he had ever seen clear and entire was unbelievable – like a creature from a pre-historic world, and longer than a London bus. At a distance of only five yards Gavin could look down on a vast barrel of a body that seemed to get steadily wider towards the distant head. A wondrous deep-sea monster, its gigantically distended gills were the widest part of its body, and its mouth was held so wide open that a child could have walked right into it without stooping. Mounted in the bows of the *Gannet* was a Breda light machine-gun which Gavin carried in the boat to shoot up drifting mines and – fantastical though it may sound – to engage any German U-boat that came his way. (U-boats had been sighted as near as Eigg, and Gavin believed that a small launch armed with a gun could not only knock out the submarine's periscope but command the bridge as well once the vessel had surfaced.)

'Try him with the gun, Major,' suggested Gavin's assistant on board – a very fat but enormously strong local man by the name of 'Foxy' Gillies.

Gavin circled the shark and approached it from behind, drawing so close that the boat almost scraped its side. Into the monster's huge expanse of flank Gavin then fired a full thirty rounds point-blank in a single burst.

'A great undulating movement seemed to surge through him,' Gavin was to write, 'and near the stern of the boat his tail shot clear of the water. Its width was a man's height; it lashed away from the boat and returned, missing Foxy's head by inches, to land with a tremendous slam upon the gunwale of the stern cockpit. It swung backward and hit the sea, flinging up a fountain of water that drenched us to the skin.' Gavin closed in on the creature six times and with the last burst despatched him, as he thought, for good. But when Foxy tried to make the shark fast with the boathook, it was torn from his hands as the shark, all too evidently alive, dived in a boil of white water. Not for some time did the hook reappear, shooting ten feet out of the sea as though hurled back in derision from the deep.

Gavin's curiosity was aroused by this encounter, and he tried to find out more about the gigantic creature. The basking shark got its name, it seemed, from its habit of 'basking' near the surface of the sea, but it was also known to the local fishermen by other names – as sailfish (because of the shape of its dorsal fin), or sunfish (because it was most usually seen on sunny days), or *muldoan* (from Muldoanich, an island in the Barra group where it was common), or by the Gaelic name of *cearbhan*. The basking shark was the biggest fish in European waters (up to 36 feet 6 inches), and the second-biggest in the world – only the Pacific whale-shark (up to 41 feet 6 inches) was bigger. And yet, remarkably, almost nothing was known about it. From the local herring fishermen Gavin gleaned a few facts based on first-hand observation, but these begged more questions than they answered.

It seemed the basking shark, *Cetorhinus maximus*, had not been common in Hebridean waters before the 1930s, but since then it had increased steadily in numbers. As far as could be judged, they were seasonal, migratory creatures – possibly migrating south to north and back again, or perhaps from deep to shallow water in summer, followed by a return to their deep over-wintering grounds in autumn. In March they might be spotted off the Irish coast, having arrived from no one knew where, or gathered together in huge congregations in the open Atlantic south of Barra Head; then in the last week of April they would arrive among the Hebridean islands, returning in the autumn before disappearing from human ken in September at the latest.

No one knew where or how the basking shark passed the winter. It seemed no one even knew what it ate, or whether its young were hatched from eggs or born alive. It was generally assumed by the fishermen that it fed on herring, because it was usually found where the herring shoals were (in fact it is a plankton feeder), and they complained loudly at the havoc the creature inflicted on their her-ring nets, and the danger its huge and powerful body posed to small boats. It was known that the basking shark's liver contained large quantities of valuable oil, and that in times past the people of the islands used to harpoon them from massed formations of small boats in order to extract a winter's supply of lamp-oil from them.

There was almost no scientific data, and few if any specimens had ever been examined by a qualified marine biologist – the rare carcases that were ever washed ashore were simply hailed as sea monsters, and that was that. In sum, Gavin discovered, the basking shark, for all its huge, unignorable bulk and regular sightings on the surface of the sea, remained a mysterious enigma – an almost total blank in the lexicon of the world's natural history.

Gavin was fired to discover more, and this led him to acquire two traditional barbless, spear-shaped whaling harpoons, with which he hoped to secure a basking shark should he ever encounter one again. It was not until mid-September 1944, when he took his first leave for nearly two and a half years, that the chance arose. It was now late in the basking shark season. Gavin was out in the *Gannet* with Foxy Gillies and a friend by the name of John Winter, an international sailing-dinghy champion, and his wife and brother-in-law, when they encountered a shoal of some half dozen of the creatures in a little bay at the Point of Sleat, the most southerly point of Skye.

'*Major, Major, sharks!*' cried Foxy at the tiller. They turned the boat into the bay and suddenly a great fin surfaced almost alongside, barely a yard from where Foxy, the strongest of the three men, stood ready to push home the boathook with the harpoon lashed to its end. With all his strength he drove it down into the water, pushing on the shaft for a final thrust into the side of the shark.

'Got him this time,' yelled Foxy. 'Right in the bugger this time!'

A fountain of spray shot up from the sea as the shark's tail lashed down on the water with several violent slaps, and then the rope attached to the end of the harpoon-shaft began to whip out at a tremendous speed from the coil in the hold as the shark dived down. Then the rope stopped running and went slack. As Gavin began tentatively to haul it in, it was whisked from his hands as though attached to an express train, skinning his palms. After the second dive the rope again went slack, and cautiously Gavin again began to haul it in. But only the harpoon came up. The shark must have dived straight to the bottom and then rolled on the harpoon and worked it free. Of the boathook there was no sign, but the harpoon looked like a corkscrew which had been bent double and then crushed in a vice.

'Ach, to hell!' exclaimed Foxy angrily. 'The harpoon was no good. I would have been better putting salt on his tail.'

On the way home Gavin and John Winter busied themselves with measurements and calculations for the design of a better harpoon. It was then, as Gavin was to recall later, that an idea was born. 'A firm determination to catch a shark was growing in me,' he was to write; 'it seemed a challenge. And then, quite suddenly – without, I think, any conscious build-up – I thought that here was the industry for Soay, the occupation I required, new and utterly absorbing.'

The time was ripe. It was clear that before long the war would be over, and Gavin needed to turn his mind to post-war employment. In October orders came for the SOE training establishments at Arisaig to be closed down. Gavin put his unique collection of foreign small arms into two metal trunks, loaded them on his lobster-boat and took them out to sea, where he dropped them overboard. It was the end of his war. In SOE he had spent his time among congenial people who liked and respected him, living a secure, regular and purposeful life, working at the things he could do best in the area he loved most in the world. Now he was returning to the doubts and uncertainties of private life.

At the beginning of November 1944 he was formally posted back to the Scots Guards, and entitled to remuneration from Army funds again. But rather than return to the dull routine of barrack service in London, he arranged to have himself excused on medical grounds, persuading an old friend of his, 'Doc' Rattray, the much-liked but chronically alcoholic local doctor at Mallaig, to write a note to Regimental Headquarters diagnosing an apparently serious medical condition.

On 8 November Gavin attended an Army Medical Board at Inverness and was pronounced to be Category E (permanently unfit for any form of military service). He would be invalided out of the Army and would relinquish his commission with effect from 24 February 1945, with the honorary rank of Major. In the meantime he donned civilian clothes, quit his little SOE billet near Glasnacardoch, and took up residence at the congenial and idiosyncratic family home of his cousins the Shaw Stewarts, at Morar Lodge, a mile or two down the road to the south.

Tucked away inside a rhododendron jungle overlooking the loch, Morar Lodge had been built by the Lovat family in the 1870s as a three-bedroomed, no-bathroomed summer holiday home for their

children, and had later been extended to include an extraordinary
wooden annexe that housed a laboratory full of ancient micro-
scopes, rats and junk. The house had escaped being requisitioned
by SOE and remained throughout the war a haven not only for
human waifs like Gavin (who now lived in the dining room), but
for a bizarre multitude of stray animals of all kinds.

'In fiction, perhaps, old Mrs Knox's house as described in *The
Experiences of an Irish R.M.* approached it most nearly,' wrote
Gavin; 'its atmosphere of comfort, kindness, mingled squalor and
riches, but, above all, its animals. The house and its environs were
inhabited, by invitation, by an infinitely greater number of animals
than of humans, and against their amiable but ruthless depredations had accumulated an elaboration of uncouth barricades and
defences.'

A large floating population of dogs, including Gavin's own
young springer spaniel, Jonnie, occupied the downstairs rooms,
and the noise of their disagreements, amours, and outraged protestations as they were stepped upon by some unwitting guest was
one of the characteristic sounds of the house. At bedtime the armchairs had to be piled with books to keep the horde of dogs off
during the night. Two grey cats, one perpetually pregnant, and a
scrawny, disabled black pullet named Angusina which lived in the
drawing room completed the indoor population, but outside lurked
a more extensive and unpredictable menagerie, including a vast
black sow called Minnie, against whom many of the trip-wires
and booby-traps had been constructed. But meals were interrupted
so often by Minnie's successful penetration of these outer defences
that they were abandoned at last and the veranda became her siesta
place, and her vast sleeping carcase was occasionally used as a convenient seat by the younger members of the family.

Many odd specimens and egregious breeds of sheep and cattle,
turkeys and geese, gave the place the air of an agricultural zoo, and
two animals of Gavin's own were later added to the collection: a
Shetland ewe that had fallen into Mallaig Harbour during transport
of the flock to Soay, and a cantankerous Great Black-Backed Gull
which he had taken when young from a rock in the Outer Hebrides.
'Only one obvious animal was missing from the house,' Gavin
wrote, 'but there was evidence of its existence in the past, for on
a shelf in the bathroom there stood for a long time a bottle labelled
in faded ink "Lotion for donkey's eyes – *I think*."'

At Morar Lodge Gavin busied himself with a preliminary investigation of the commercial possibilities of a basking-shark fishery,
and from there, a few days after failing his medical board, he wrote
to Major Archibald Pearson, Regimental Adjutant at the Scots
Guards, to explain his absence from soldiering duties in distant
London:

> I am very sorry to think that I shan't be with the Regiment
> again, but I think I should be pretty useless, as after 3 years I
> remember just about as much about Regimental soldiering as
> about my pre-natal life.
>
>   I am living up here for a time, as I am starting a commercial
> shark-fishing station for extraction of oil. The work will have
> to be done with drifters and trawlers which I am buying now,
> and most of them require some conversion before they can be
> fitted with the whaling harpoon guns. I seem to be as busy as
> I was in my job, tho' I visualised this as a period of ease and
> idleness! I wish I was better at working out the commercial
> side of things – the finance, I mean.

So the White Knight embarked on his great quest – and the serious
business of tilting with harpoons at the monsters of the deep.

To fund his new enterprise – Isle of Soay Shark Fisheries – Gavin
persuaded his mother to advance him as working capital a sum of
£11,000 (a vast figure in 1945) set aside for him in her will and due
on her death. This represented the sole funding of his company
until he persuaded nine friends (among them his ex-SOE friend
Hamish Pelham-Burn, the Antarctic traveller and ornithologist
Niall Rankin, and the Cambridge classical scholar and future headmaster of Westminster School, Walter Hamilton) to contribute
loans of £500 each.

Uppermost in Gavin's mind was the commercial success of the
venture; but it is doubtful that this was the innermost thing in
his soul. Kathleen Raine once remarked: 'Making money was not
Gavin's line of country. Making money was quite incidental to
Gavin the knight. It was the wild adventure – he was Captain Ahab
after the white whale, after Moby-Dick. And you can't win against
the white whale.'

Practically speaking, Gavin saw himself as a sea-going version of the elephant hunter in the African bush. Liver oil was the basking shark's ivory. The huge liver could account for up to a quarter of the body weight of the basking shark, and its 160 gallons of oil comprised three-quarters of the liver's weight. A major component of the oil was a terpenoid hydrocarbon called squalene, which was in great demand in the post-war margarine industry (and is still of value today in the cosmetic, health food and aviation industries). An average basking shark produced just under half a ton of oil. In 1945 this oil could be sold for £50 a ton; by 1947 the price had more than doubled.

Provided he could keep overheads down, Gavin's plan to concentrate on the oil was commercially sensible. But he was in a desperate hurry to get the venture started, and as a result made some serious errors.

The first and most obvious of these was the boat he bought to serve as his main catcher. The *Dove* was a forty-five-year-old drifter from the Stornoway fishing fleet for which he paid £1000 without ever having set eyes on her. When he finally saw the vessel he intended to carry the main burden of his sharking enterprise (with his own *Gannet* in support), he quickly realised his mistake. 'She was in roughly the condition one might expect of Noah's ark were it thrown up by some subterranean upheaval,' he wrote later, 'nor would the engines have made one marvel at Noah's mechanical genius.' Only one engine was in working order, the timbers were rotten, the galley was deep in filth and the whole boat was so overrun with rats that sixty were caught in the first two days. For three months the *Dove* lay in Mallaig Harbour undergoing repairs which only served to reveal more of her terminal decay.

The qualities of Gavin's crew compensated for the wretchedness of the vessel. His very first employee in the sharking venture was Tex Geddes, the Newfoundlander from SOE Arisaig, for whom Gavin had formed the greatest respect. Tex was in his late twenties, and had all the attributes Gavin most admired in a man – above all a wild and colourful past. Expelled from school as unmanageable at the age of twelve, he had worked as a lumberjack, rum-runner, boxer and knife-thrower before joining a Scottish regiment shortly before the war. An expert boat-handler and able harpoon-gunner, he was to prove a staunch companion in the ordeals and adventures to come.

Bruce Watt was the next to join. An ex-Merchant Navy engineer officer of Gavin's own age, he was as teetotal as Tex and Gavin were not, and as solid and commonsensical as they were volatile and impetuous. He was to serve most ably as Gavin's skipper. Foxy Gillies and a deckhand and a cook made up the rest of the crew for that first 1945 season.

While the small factory on Soay for extracting the shark liver oil and processing the fish meal was still under construction, Gavin busied himself with trial and experiment at sea. For all concerned, shark fishing was virgin territory. There was no more crucial or contentious aspect of the business than the design of the harpoon and the gun to fire it. Here Gavin made a second blunder. If he had gone to Norway to see at first-hand the harpoons and harpoon guns the experienced Norwegians used on their whaling ships, he would have saved himself a lot of trouble and expense. Instead, he started to design his own harpoons and guns from scratch. His first harpoons – ancient, spear-shaped specimens, intended for whaling – proved quite useless, for they were crushed by the sheer power of the basking shark's body. Subsequent modifications were of varying merit, as were the early models for a custom-built harpoon gun.

In the first sea trials with the newly-designed harpoon and gun the crew fired a total of fourteen shots at sharks and five at killer whales, and every time the equipment malfunctioned. Not a single harpoon struck home. They fared no better with hand harpoons they had designed themselves. Off the isle of Rhum they came across a large basking shark with its huge fin standing high out of the sea. Peering down, Gavin saw the great brown bulk of the shark a few feet beneath the surface, and stood poised and ready in the bow with the hand harpoon, waiting for Tex to give the word to strike.

'*Let him have it!*' yelled Tex. Both Gavin and Tex drove down with all their strength and the harpoons entered deep into the shark's back. For a moment nothing happened. Then the shark crash-dived in a shower of spray. The rope ran out at a terrific speed, and the shark began to tow the *Gannet* slowly ahead. They steered an erratic course, but at the end of four hours they were not more than two miles from where they had started. At about five in the afternoon they tried to haul the fish up, but after an hour's pulling the shark had only six fathoms of rope left, and they could not gain an inch. 'It was like trying to pull a house,' Gavin recalled. 'It was a dead-

lock; we had not the strength to pull him in, and he could not tear
the harpoons from his back.' The strain was terrific; something had
to give, and in the event it was one of the harpoon shafts – the
inch-and-a-half-thick steel snapped off short at the body of the
shark. The second harpoon pulled out as soon as it took the single
strain.

They had not gone a mile before they spied another shark travelling slowly westward, its fin rolling in the increasing swell. Gavin
struck with the only harpoon left. The harpoon made fast and the
shark began to tow them towards the south-west – into the gathering dusk and an approaching storm. Rhum was blotted out and the
darkness became inky.

After an hour the breeze began to stiffen and it became very
cold; then with the night and the breaking seas came the most
beautiful of all the sea's jewels: the phosphorescence of *nocti-
luca*. Each breaking wave glowed with pale opalescent fire, ·
and when the water slapped against the boat's sides they were
left sparkling with a thousand tiny lights.

I crawled up the foredeck to feel the position of the rope;
it led ahead at an angle of forty-five degrees, and from it
streamed a trail of phosphorus which told me that our speed
was increasing. We were heading west nor'west, and making
about five knots into a rising sea. Except for the sound of the
breaking water, the night was very quiet. We sailed into a
dream sea in the dark and the eerie phosphorescence, towed
by the wounded shark far below in the dark water.

The boat was being towed steadily seaward in a rising wind when
Gavin turned in, rolled up in his duffel coat on the floor of the
hold. At two in the morning he roused himself to find that they
were now in a heavy sea, the breaking phosphorescence stretching
away on all sides to the very limit of vision. 'There was a distant
undercurrent of sound, deeper and heavier than the nearby breakers,
which at first I could not place. Then through it came an unmistak-
able call, thin and buffeted by the wind, but sweetly familiar, the
calling of curlews – curlews that meant rock and reef.'

Bruce gave the inevitable order. They must free themselves from
the shark at once. Gavin crawled up the foredeck and felt the rope;
it stretched out at an acute angle, and thirty yards ahead was a little

boil of phosphorescence in the water. The boat was being pulled
rapidly due west; the shark was swimming almost on the surface,
and it was impossible to pull the harpoon out. The only way to
free themselves was to cut the rope. Bruce chopped it through with
an axe, seven and a half hours after Gavin had planted the harpoon.
They had lost the fish, and Gavin felt seasick for the first time in
his life.

Though the sharking venture's proper arena was the sea, much of
Gavin's time was necessarily spent on the land – not on Soay (where
he never resided, though he was the island's laird) but at the shark
boats' home base at Mallaig, then a raw working fishing port,
where the weather, and the life, could always turn a little wild, like
a West Highland Klondike. In his tiny office in Mallaig Gavin
wrestled with the bureaucracy that threatened to strangle his enterprise at birth.

The season for hunting the basking shark was brief. The giant
fish rarely appeared in Hebridean waters before the beginning of
May. They spent the best part of the summer in the Hebrides,
cruising to and fro in search of plankton drifts off the islands, then
for no understood reason disappeared for a month in late July,
reappearing in greatly reduced numbers in the second week of
August to spend another six weeks or so in these waters before
vanishing again.

The west-facing shores of the islands were littered with the flotsam of five years of war and scores of torpedoed convoys, with
ships' rafts, RAF dinghies, lifebelts, fuel tanks, bales of raw rubber
and timber everywhere, and nowhere thicker than along Harris
Bay, on Rhum. Here Gavin sent the *Dove* to salvage beams and
spars for the Soay factory jetty whenever there were no sharks
about. When it became clear that the factory would not be ready
till September, Gavin decided to write off the 1945 summer as a
purely experimental season.

One day in August, in the midst of these preparatory chores, the
crew had their first kill. Driving into Mallaig from Morar one
morning, Gavin spied from the hill above the harbour a large shoal
of basking shark some six miles out. It was midday before the
Gannet was ready to put to sea, with two teenage boys on board
– Gavin's Morar hostess's son, Jackie Shaw Stewart, and a school-
friend of his from England by the name of Raef Payne. By the time

they had reached the spot many of the shark had vanished from view, but they managed to locate a likely quarry and made a perfect approach from astern. At point-blank range Gavin fired the harpoon gun and scored a palpable hit. He could see the shark a fathom or two down in clear water, the harpoon shaft sticking out of its side and a dark plume of blood trailing from it like smoke. Tex saw the great fish, too, and gave a war-cry of triumph: 'He feels it! He feels it!'

For four hours sharkers and shark engaged in a herculean tug of war. At the end of that time the rope was still as vertical as a telegraph pole, the shark three hundred feet down in the green dusk of the sea. Gavin lay flat on the deck and peered down into the dim water. He could see the rope stretching down, and then, at the extreme limit of vision, something that resembled a giant punkah swinging rhythmically to and fro. This was the tail of the shark, some six feet wide, and so powerful that when it came clear of the surface it beat the water with such force that the sea exploded like a fountain.

At length, late in the afternoon, they managed to slip a noose around the lunging creature and make the tail fast to the stern. The shark was theirs. Jubilantly they set sail for Mallaig, towing their prize at less than a mile an hour across a white, oily calm. It was near dusk when they reached Mallaig. Word had gone round that a shark was coming in, and a crowd some fifteen hundred strong thronged the pier to watch. It was evident that the shark was still very much alive, for time and again it tried to bore down to the harbour bottom. It was also evident that it was inordinately heavy, for the steam winch was unable to lift the creature out of the water, and the sharkers had to seek the assistance of a nearby boom ship equipped with massive cranes. The crowds grew denser as the rope was transferred to a giant crane under the glare of searchlights.

The crane began to winch the fish up, and as it was slowly hauled clear of the water its monstrous girth was revealed to the excited crowd.

'Oh, wha'a crayture!'

'You wouldn' believe it!'

'It canna be a fish!'

When twenty feet of the shark was clear of the water there was a snapping sound, and the crane stopped lifting. For a moment there was silence, then a terrific crack and a tearing noise as the shark's body snapped in two at the tail and fell into the oily water of the harbour, followed a second later by the severed tail and a groan from the watching crowd.

The shark was recovered next day and served as shark steak at Morar Lodge, where it was pronounced tasteless.

The first, experimental, season ended in October 1945, and Gavin stood back to reflect on what he had learned and consider his options. He had solved a few teething problems and gained some experience in the practical difficulties of catching basking shark on a commercial basis. He had also reinforced a fatal decision.

From the outset Gavin had believed that the basking shark's only real value lay in its precious liver oil. But his commercial advisers, a big firm of Glasgow fish marketeers who had little concept of the handling problems presented by such a gigantic fish, whose head alone could weigh a ton, felt it was a shocking waste to take the oil and abandon the rest of the massive carcase, every scrap of which they felt had some market potential somewhere. Unwisely, Gavin agreed that during the 1946 season his enterprise would attempt to process and market no fewer than a dozen different products from the basking shark – liver oil, liver residue, glue from the membranes, shagreen from the skin, frozen flesh and salted flesh, fish meal, dried fins, bone manure, plankton, stomach contents and glandular products.

The implications of this decision were substantial. For a start, the factory, not the ships, would form the nerve-centre of the venture; the factory on Soay would have to be extended and a replacement found for the unseaworthy *Dove*. All this would cost money which Gavin had not got. To work the whole of the basking shark's carcase required a factory ship like those whalers used. It was to take several years of hardship and tribulation for Gavin to prove to his own satisfaction that he had been right all along.

The winter of 1945–46 was a period of endless frustration and delays. In an attempt to find something profitable for the Soay factory to do during the long off-season in the shark-fishing year, which lasted at least eight months from October to May, Gavin investigated the possibilities of peat drying, seaweed drying, stone quarrying and a lobster pond, but none of these island resources looked remotely profitable, and in any case the half-built factory was flattened and then bodily removed by a 120 mile per hour hurricane in February, and had to be rebuilt. 'The early months of that year were a nightmare,' Gavin recorded, 'a dream in which one runs but does not move.' Factory, boats, catching equipment – all suffered one delay after another.

The replacement boat for the *Dove*, an ex-Admiralty Harbour Defence Motor Launch that Gavin bought for £4000 and renamed the *Sea Leopard*, did not arrive at Mallaig until 20 April 1946, but her *élan* made up for her tardiness. 'Lying among the fishing boats she was like a greyhound among bulldogs,' Gavin wrote, 'seventy feet long, sleek and graceful, and with Admiralty written in every line of her.' The large engine room amidships contained two powerful, gleaming 160 horsepower diesel engines; crew quarters were for'ard of it and the after-part of the ship accommodated an officers' ward room as finely fitted as an expensive yacht.

This small saloon, measuring ten foot by ten, Gavin took over as his home and office, and within a few days he had furnished it with a carpet, a filing cabinet, a typewriter, a sofa and a mahogany bookcase full of technical works on ballistics, navigation, biology and whale fisheries, along with a score or so of tattered paperback novels (seven of them by Evelyn Waugh) and several literary works, including T.S. Eliot's *Four Quartets*, William Empson's *Seven Types of Ambiguity* and Cyril Connolly's *Enemies of Promise*.

By the last week of April Gavin had got together everything and everyone he thought he needed for his first full season as a working fishery. The modified and refurbished harpooning equipment had arrived from the gunsmith in Birmingham – twenty harpoons for the breech-loading Oerlikon gun on the *Sea Leopard* (the main catching ship) and another twenty for the old-fashioned muzzle-loading whaling gun on the refitted *Gannet*. A new crew had been assembled, with Dan MacGillivray, a Skye man who had worked on sailing schooners and on an Australian sheep station, replacing Foxy Gillies as mate. An engineer, a deckhand and a cook made up the rest of the more or less regular crew, with Tex Geddes and the deckhand taking over the *Gannet* whenever she was cast off from the *Sea Leopard*.

Only the arrival in Mallaig Harbour of Tony Watkins, brother of the polar explorer Gino Watkins, and his small fleet of ring-net shark boats and a steam drifter factory-ship spoiled Gavin's departure. Watkins had hunted basking shark in these waters for three seasons before the war, and there was much he knew about the business that Gavin didn't. Of his first meeting with Gavin, in his cabin on the *Sea Leopard*, he recalled: 'Seated at a table was a fair-haired, sharp-featured man of about my own age. He greeted me, I thought, with more than a touch of hostility. "What I came for is this," I explained, disconcerted by the atmosphere. "As you know, I only use the livers. Perhaps we can do a deal over my carcases. That is, of course, if you produce fish-meal at your factory . . ."'

Gavin resented Watkins' intrusion into what he regarded as his home territory. 'Well,' Watkins told him, 'if there aren't enough sharks in the sea for both of us, we might as well both give up.'

'Neither trusted the other an inch,' Gavin wrote, 'and for all the season our crews vied with each other in the magnificence of their lies, forgotten failures and multiplied successes.'

Watkins was the first to sail out of Mallaig. Gavin's little fleet followed on 7 May, the *Sea Leopard*'s bow proudly breasting the rolling Atlantic swell, the salt tang sharp in the air as they headed for Soay and the west-facing coast of Skye for the start of their first professional sharking season.

EIGHT

'Muldoan!'

The dragon-green, the luminous,
the dark, the serpent-haunted sea.
JAMES ELROY FLECKER,
'The Gates of Damascus'

The arena in which Gavin sought gladiatorial combat with his giant fish – the Hebridean Sea and the great range of the Hebridean islands – is one of the most unpredictable and unforgiving seas in the world. It is also one of the most sublimely beautiful, and Gavin's latent painter's eye and poet's perception watched it and listened to it enthralled. 'The sea and the open sky, the sharks and whales and seabirds, were the *Sea Leopard*'s background,' he wrote, 'and my own diary, when I had leisure to write it, is concerned with each almost equally.'

There was the mist furling to reveal the early sun covering the whole sea with light; the pure savagery of the Hebridean sunsets, the whole dome of the sky a fierce blood-red to every point of the compass, and a wild disorder of purple streamers reflected in an almost unrippled sea; and the brief midsummer nights, when the hills were black and sharp against an apple-green sky, the darkening blue pricked by the hesitant light of the western constellations, the brief two-hour dark burning with the brilliance of the stars and the Aurora flickering in the north as bright as winter.

Then there were the birds – the peregrine falcons on the great dark lighthouse rock of Uishenish in South Uist; the rock pigeons catapulting out of the sea-caves deep in the rock; and the fulmars, the most consummately skilful of all the seabirds, skimming, climbing, turning and diving in intricate patterns of aerial ballet above the giant cliffs of Moonen Bay. 'Birds occupy the eye a great deal when one is continuously at sea in Hebridean waters,' Gavin recalled. 'They were my first love in childhood, and filled many long empty days on the *Sea Leopard* when there seemed to be no sharks in the sea, and I would grow tired of the heat and tobacco smoke of the fo'c'sle or of working through accounts and business correspondence in my cabin. The minute actions of birds, the intimate realisation of separate sentient life, have always held for me an almost magic fascination.'

The Hebridean Sea itself is not only beautiful but awesome, and the more Gavin saw of it the more he came to respect it. The *Sea Leopard* was often storm-bound in small ports and sheltered anchorages during the summer of 1946. Once, anchored off the small island of Barra, Gavin was astounded to see the vast and orderly ranks of the lead-grey, thirty-foot Atlantic rollers smash into the west-facing shore and bury a whole three-hundred-foot cliff in a fountain of white spray. The wind was mad and irresistible, the sheer noise of the sea stupefying. 'I was beginning to be afraid of the sea,' Gavin was to write; 'that is to say, my landsman's fear of it was just beginning to be tinged with a seaman's fear, and with a faint, very incomplete concept of its almost illimitable power.'

This fear was justified when Tex Geddes almost met his death in a wild sea and raging southerly gale near Loch Hourn in the Sound of Sleat early in June. He was finally snatched with a boathook from the trough of a big wave and hauled on to the *Sea Leopard*'s deck.

But Gavin's skipper, Bruce Watt, was too experienced and canny a seaman ever to wantonly imperil his ship in those treacherous waters, and the shark-hunters' lot was generally not so much danger and disaster as the dour discomfort that besets every fisherman's life in northern seas – the chill damp, the saturating, insinuating rain, the ceaseless and exhausting wallowing of the hull, the unfriendly hours and sleepless nights. To this litany of inescapable woes had to be added the state of Gavin's own health. All through the shark-fishing time he suffered from bouts of acute pain in the duodenum, for which the treatment was bismuth and belladonna, fish and milk. Sometimes the spasms would go on for several days, and then Gavin wouldn't want to see anybody. 'He was bad-tempered sometimes,' Tex Geddes recalled. 'Well, we were all bad-tempered. But you see he had a hell of a bad gut – duodenal ulcer – and I'd have to feed him on sago and cut out bacon and eggs and things like that, and he'd get bad-tempered over that, though you could hardly blame him. Sometimes, when the buzzer went on the boat to signal a shark sighting, he found he couldn't straighten up, he'd be doubled up with pain, so he'd pour half a bottle of whisky into himself and *then* he'd straighten up!'

Gavin had plenty of reason for nursing an ulcer. He could not disguise the anxiety that the business side of his venture was causing him. The Oerlikon gun on the *Sea Leopard* had proved useless, and the steel of some of the harpoons was too soft, so that the barbs bent and the harpoons pulled out. That left only the muzzle-loading gun on the *Gannet* to catch enough sharks to pay overheads of £160 a week and a full crew and factory staff – and even that gun misfired constantly. As early as 17 May Gavin wrote in his diary:

> We have been at work for ten days, the first ten days of what was to have been our first trading season, and every day has revealed more of our ignorance and the inadequacy of our equipment. We should be at school, if there were a school to teach this new trade, not trying to earn money. Every day, almost every hour, teaches us a new lesson, but at a cost we cannot pay. I do not think our capital can carry us beyond this season. We must capitalise in experience every failure and disappointment – nothing now can prevent this summer being full of both.

The workforce at the Soay factory was one cause for concern. Most of them were Soay men who could find no better job, a disaffected, malingering, feckless lot; and the imported labour from Skye, Gavin noted, 'only swelled the numbers as dummy figures upon castle battlements did in the Middle Ages'. There were times, too, when his crew grew bored and discontented. Late one evening in June, after two tedious days confined to harbour, one of the crew came to his cabin to voice some private complaint. Gavin knew the man and liked him; foolishly he offered him some rum, and very soon the man grew heated, then angry, then homicidal. When Gavin, reverting to a Scots Guards officer's manner, told him to get out and come back when he was sober, the crewman pulled out a sheath-knife.

'You're not in the bloody Guards now,' he said. 'Take your eyes off me, and I'll stap this through your guts.'

With some difficulty, and the help of a second bottle of rum, Gavin managed to placate his guest, and at about three in the morning the man dozed off. Taking the knife from him, Gavin lugged him up on deck. 'I plumped him down on the poop deck, and seated myself beside him, staring foolishly at the moon and thinking what a wonderful night it was and what a wonderful life it was. You must have been able to smell the rum a quarter of a mile away.'

Gavin's irascibility was tempered by his considerateness, and on the whole he was liked by his crew, for reasons which had nothing to do with his engaging eccentricity or the generous bonus he paid for each shark harpooned. Tex Geddes recalled a typical incident:

> He was a bloody loyal bloke. I remember one occasion when his uncle, Lord William Percy, arrived at Mallaig to spend a weekend shark-fishing on the *Sea Leopard*. Gavin asked me to go with him to the station to meet his uncle, and of course the uncle got the idea that I was the wee man that picked up the cases, and I told him to jump over the moon, I'm carrying no bugger's case – I'd carry no man's bloody case, not even the King's. Well, the old fellow was hopping mad, and Gavin's problem was – who was he going to be loyal to, his uncle or me? Well, he chose me, and he picked up the case and carried it himself.

Gavin had developed a whole network of spies to look out for sharks from one end of the Hebrides to the other. Mostly they were the lighthouse keepers who kept lonely vigil on the top of the islands' soaring cliffs all the way from Barra Head to the Butt of Lewis, with whom Gavin communicated by loudhailer or elaborate hand and arm signals like a racecourse tick-tack man. Friendly ring-net fishers too would sometimes give him a tip about the location of the shark shoals when they saw them, for they had no love for the *muldoan* that destroyed their nets. In those years the basking shark kept to a fairly regular pattern of movement. In May they would be off the west coast of Skye in the Inner Hebrides, then in June they would move across the Minch to the Outer Hebrides, cruising slowly north from Barra Sound up the east coast of South Uist to Scalpay Island in Harris and beyond. But even though their course was roughly known, their exact whereabouts was always a matter of speculation, and Gavin could search for days without sighting so much as a single fin, then find himself in the middle of a vast concourse of the creatures.

An abundance of sharks did not necessarily result in a surfeit of kills. Twice off the Skye coast Gavin came on a sea full of the giant fish, only to be frustrated by a misfiring gun, damp powder, and the difficulty of getting a clear aim and a steady shot from a surging deck in a confused and choppy sea. One of the biggest shoals he ever encountered was in Loch Scavaig, Skye, in May, every fish showing its tail-fin and dorsal high above the surface, the whole mass progressing leisurely into the loch like leviathans strolling in a park. Gavin peered over the side of the *Gannet* and was astounded at what he saw: 'Down there in the clear water they were packed as tight as sardines, each barely allowing swimming room to the next, layer upon layer of them, huge grey shapes like herds of submerged elephants, the furthest down dim and indistinct in the sea. A memory came back to me from childhood – Mowgli and the elephants' dance, and the drawing of the great heaving mass of backs in the jungle clearing . . . I thought, "This is a shoal of fish – *fish*."'

Large congregations such as this were the exception rather than the norm, and may have been due to the existence of a sea 'front' where clear ocean water met turbid inshore water and produced a high concentration of the plankton on which the sharks liked to browse. Possibly, too, the concentration of individuals along these 'fronts' enabled the sharks to form breeding shoals, though whether such shoals represented discrete population groups or random concentrations of individuals roaming gipsy-like round the coasts of Europe was a matter of speculation.

The size of a shark might make it an easier target, but not necessarily an easier catch. The biggest basking shark Gavin ever encountered was a vast and solitary individual halfway between Lochboisdale in South Uist and Castlebay in Barra in July. The shark's dorsal fin was much higher and thicker than any Gavin had ever seen, and its tail measured at least ten feet across instead of the usual seven. When Gavin fired the shark dived at a tremendous speed, and a thin trickle of smoke rose from the three-inch-thick rope as it raced through the metal fair-lead, the manila almost catching fire. The rope, which had a seven-ton breaking strain, snapped off at its tie-ring when the shark was still some ten fathoms from the bottom.

In his diary entry for 9 July 1946 Gavin tried to work out his own reactions to a question he felt must present itself to every averagely sensitive person who kills great creatures – the question of pain and its offspring, cruelty, a subject which, as a man who loved wild creatures and yet slaughtered them wholesale, troubled a part of him deeply. 'All this harpooning has its unpleasant side,' he wrote. 'If a warm-blooded animal were concerned, and more especially if it were a land animal, ninety-nine people out of a hundred (of whom I should be one) would hold it to be unthinkable cruelty. Yet is one justified, because this monstrous bulk of flesh and muscle is cold-blooded and directed by a brain which could almost be enclosed in a match-box, in assuming that the experience undergone by the shark is so widely different from our own?'

The biological purpose of pain, Gavin was sure, was to act as a deterrent to self-destruction on the part of the animal that felt it. What was less clear was the exact degree of pain animals at different evolutionary levels were capable of experiencing, though Gavin was convinced (and no doubt reassured) that this had nothing to do with size.

The size of the animal involved is completely unimportant, and one who is moved to pity by the sight of a stranded thirty-foot shark suffocating on a beach should be moved a thousand times more by the sight of a thousand herring suffocating in the hold of a fishing boat; or one who is revolted by the idea of a ten-pound steel harpoon in a thirty-foot shark should be equally revolted by an inch hook in the jaw of a salmon. And perhaps both these facts can be brought into fair proportion only by the realisation that at every moment in the sea millions and millions of fish are being pulled into bloody pieces by millions and millions of other fish.

Perhaps for a true comparison between shark pain and human pain, Gavin argued, one should look at the theoretical difference between sentience and consciousness – the ability to feel as opposed to the ability to translate it into experience. The problems of pain were complex, he acknowledged, but they were crystal clear by comparison with those of cruelty – 'indifference to, or delight in, another's pain' – virtually the exclusive preserve, he thought, of the human species.

Hunting the basking shark was an unpredictable business, but by the middle of the 1946 season Gavin and his crew had worked out an efficient *modus operandi* for the run-up to a target shark. A shark's black, sail-like dorsal fin could show over the surface up to two or three miles away, and though once or twice a year the sharks might collect in great shoals, two or three fins was the most the catchers were likely to spy in an average day. As soon as a fin was sighted Tex Geddes would yell '*Muldoan!*' and the ship's buzzer would screech the alarm. The buzzer was just above Gavin's bunk, and if he was asleep it would scream so shrill and urgent in his ear that he would be out of his bunk and up the companionway before he was fully conscious or properly dressed, or even dressed at all. As he ran up the *Sea Leopard*'s deck towards the harpoon gun in the bows a man would pass him a harpoon-stick, wad and powder charge through the wheelhouse window, and eventually the crew became so practised that within three minutes of the alarm going off every man would be at his station and Gavin behind the gun and ready to fire.

The tension on board at these times was terrific. The boat would move to within four hundred yards of the shark and then drop down to half-speed. At a hundred yards the engines would be throttled down to a soft purr. At forty yards both engines would be cut and the boat would drift forward, rolling with each wave and rapid turn on the helm as it came up on its quarry from astern. Though the target was large and slow-moving, it was surprisingly difficult to track. One moment the shark would appear with the whole dorsal fin clear of the surface, the next it would be totally submerged, changing course each time it dived and reappearing on an opposite parallel course on the wrong side of the boat. To Gavin it often seemed the sharks had a precise sense of the manoeuvrability of the boat and the range of its gun, for time after time they would suddenly change course at the last moment or slowly dive at exactly the distance that made a miss a mathematical probability. In his diary entry for 9 July 1946 Gavin recorded:

I killed one fish today that I did not expect to hit . . . He was submerging rapidly when I fired, aiming at the base of the edge-on dorsal fin, but as the water cleared I could see the great fish a fathom down, swimming away from the boat with blood pouring in a dark stream from a white-edged hole in his back where the steel trace entered it. He made off slowly, almost as if unconscious of the deadly wound; the eye could follow him far under the surface, a vast grey shadow with glints of white.

Gavin and his crew were pioneers who had no corpus of acquired knowledge on which to base their actions; every day produced its crop of new experiences, its unforeseen surprises, and the shark-fishers advanced with many a backward step, learning the hard way by trial and error. For Gavin, as the owner and business head of the venture, this was a painful and costly way of proceeding. In the first two months of the 1946 season he was operating at a loss because too many sharks were either missed outright or lost after they had been harpooned, and too many days were wasted taking successful catches back to the factory on Soay. In July the strike rate went up when Gavin came across a sea full of sharks off South Uist, and for a week or two the shark-hunters went desperately short of sleep as they hunted by day and towed their catches back to Soay by night, returning to the killing grounds in the early hours of the next morning.

Gavin fished for another two months, but he had had the best of the season. For a month the wind never moderated and the sea was too rough to tell whether there were shark in it or not. During that period the average catch was only two sharks a week, and even that proved more than the Soay factory could handle. Fewer than seventy-five sharks were caught during the entire season. Financially, the running loss was not too disastrous, but the enterprise showed a hefty capital deficit, and though every hunt was still an adventure, fears of failure and bankruptcy became daily more oppressive.

Inevitably the story of one man's bid to found a new industry on a tiny Hebridean island by wrestling with the monsters of the deep attracted considerable media interest. Many press reports were wildly, even comically wide of the mark. But there was one notably well-informed exception. Late in July 1946 *Picture Post*, the mass-circulation news picture weekly, sent a twenty-nine-year-old red-haired, buck-teethed, freelance journalist, John Hillaby, and a staff photographer, Raymond Kleboe, to do a feature story about Gavin's shark-hunting venture in the Hebrides.

It proved to be a remarkable adventure. Gavin sent the *Gannet* to pick Hillaby and Kleboe up from the railhead at Mallaig on the morning of their arrival; but it was blowing a gale and the party were storm-bound in harbour throughout the morning, whiling the time away with the help of a bottle of Scotch thoughtfully sent over by Gavin from Soay. 'We drank and we drank and we drank,' Hillaby recalled,

> and eventually Gavin's boatman said, 'Ach, hell, let's get out!' So about two in the afternoon, in an extraordinarily pissed state, we struck out. I don't think I've been in worse seas in my life. There was a huge tide-rip going across between Skye and Soay and we were tossed about all over the place. My photographer became very seasick but I stuck it out and eventually we beached on Soay at some time in the night – goodness knows when, I had so many drams inside me by this time that I had no idea of the time. And the chap at the helm said to his mate: 'Jock, hold the wheel. If God got us across the Sound of Sleat, I'll do the rest myself.'

Next morning all was quiet, and John Hillaby met Gavin Maxwell for the first time. 'The intricacies of Maxwell's character would exercise anyone's powers,' Hillaby was to recall. 'An aristocrat, a naturalist, a bisexualist, a bit of a buccaneer – he was a *very* complex character.'

> There was serious manic-depression there, and though I didn't find him a particularly magnetic personality, he was very deep. He could become absolutely tyrannical towards his crew – but they revered him, because on the other side of the coin there was also his niceness, his generosity, his humanity. He was very extravagant with money and the *Sea Leopard* was littered with expensive gear – Leica cameras, Shetland jackets, oil paintings, Gobelin tapestries rotting with sea water on the walls of his luxuriously appointed cabin in the fo'c's'le, mahogany bookshelves full of a hundred or more rare editions, mostly about the Hebrides (Lee's *Sea Monsters Unmasked*, Pennant's *Tour in Scotland 1769*, Boswell's *Tour to the Hebrides*). And he tended to flash rank and put on a heavy aristocratic act. I was a very unsophisticated sort of person, the son of a bourgeois family from Leeds, a hard-up freelance journalist who didn't know his arse from his elbow, and when he found out I was just a lowly ex-Gunner in the war he would take

every opportunity to remind me that he had been an officer in the Guards.

At first he was very aloof, very off-hand with me – or else he was highly combative, always challenging everything I said, and petulant if I disagreed with him. I had to find some sort of equality with Maxwell in the time I was with him, keep my end up with this curious, presumptuous aristocrat, living this piratical sort of life, telling these stories, doing these things. I had to fight to do it – it wasn't easy. But eventually I found a rapport with him through natural history. We were taking a walk round the island when suddenly I heard a strange bird cry.

'That's a sea eagle,' I said.

'Oh,' he said, 'so you're an *ornithologist*, are you? There may be a pair nesting at the end of Skye – but we don't want that talked about.'

I wasn't really an ornithologist, but I was good on recognition and very good on voices – a dickybird-ologist. Maxwell realised I knew seabird noises and this was our rapport. Then another bird went up.

'Good God,' I exclaimed. 'That's a rock pipit.'

'Oh, you *do* know your birds,' he said.

Then I quoted a line from Virgil: 'Happy is the man who understands his surroundings.' That transformed him – because he was a bit of a cultural snob himself.

'Oh,' he said, 'and you're a wandering *scholar*, too!'

'This is a strange island,' I went on. 'Are we on the schist basalt of Skye or what?' Maxwell was a bit peeved by this, because he thought I knew a bit more about something than he did.

'Well, I'm not a *geologist*,' he replied. 'I'm fundamentally a *naturalist*.'

I think he was really at heart a poet, but he was a talented naturalist, quite erudite, and brimming over with curiosity. His grandfather, Sir Herbert, was a great naturalist, and I got the impression that Maxwell was constantly trying to keep up with him, and always trying to justify himself to me. Kleboe, my photographer, a working-class lad and a very nice person, got on very badly in this company and didn't understand what we were talking about half the time. But my own relationship

with Maxwell intrigued me enormously – I never knew where
I was with him, and he was never sure what I knew and what
I didn't know. This was what in physics they call a tensile
relationship – the gravitational forces that keep the planets
apart and in their order. So we were for ever skating sus-
piciously around each other, though in due course we became
friends of a kind, and on Christian-name terms. I remember
thinking, 'Stick close to this man, you may be able to learn
something from him,' and I would have many long talks with
him about everything under the sun. Usually we ended up
cracking a bottle of whisky. He rarely talked about himself,
but he was very boastful about his lineage, though never boastful about his achievements.

Hillaby was fascinated by the industrial end of the shark-fishing
business – the Soay factory, where the carcases were cut up with
saws, axes and knives. Spine-covered, elephantine hide was removed using armoured gloves, the liver cut out and put in the
oil-extraction plant, the flesh cubed and put into the ice-house or
pickling tank for export abroad (mainly for starving Germans in
British-occupied Germany), the fins, tail and head thrown into glue
tanks, and most of the rest put into the fish-meal plant. The gigantic
cartilaginous vertebrae were strewn about the 'boneyard' behind
the factory to be dried for bulk shipment for manure.

Part of the factory's problem was due to the sheer weight and
bulk of the sharks. The liver alone could weigh three-quarters of
a ton, the head a ton, and the flesh a ton and a half. The bogie-truck
would capsize under its five-ton load and tip the giant fish back
into the shallows. One false incision could release half a ton of
glutinous tomato-red plankton mash over the unfortunate factory
hand who made the erring cut. John Hillaby recalled:

At the shark harbour I stopped and watched the men cutting
up the carcases and extracting the livers. They threw the guts
into the water and this attracted a lot of conger eels which fed
on the guts and grew to an enormous size. Conger eels are
foul things like barrage balloons – not slim and eel-like but
fat and pig-like. I could look down into the clear water and
see them congregating on the bottom – a monster about twelve
foot long among them. 'Heavens!' I thought. 'These are the

most dangerous waters in the world. Don't fall in there –
they'll bite your arse off.'

Shortly after his arrival Hillaby boarded the *Sea Leopard* in Soay
East Harbour and put out to sea for a sharking cruise. It had been
a very bad season so far, and few sizeable shark had been harpooned,
with the result that Gavin was running out of money and
borrowing heavily from his mother to keep the enterprise afloat.
The crew seemed somewhat agitated, and Hillaby got the feeling
that their wages had not been paid. He was also aware of an underlying battle of wills between Gavin and his skipper, Bruce Watt.
'Bruce was worried about Gavin's attitude towards boats and his
tendency to take unnecessary risks,' Hillaby recalled:

> Bruce Watt was a very steady, rather dour man, and he knew
> the limitations of the boat and was not prepared to take risks
> with it, but Gavin was all for derring-do. There were not
> infrequent arguments between them about whether the *Sea
> Leopard* could get into such and such a harbour or whether it
> had enough fuel to reach some island or other. Sometimes
> Bruce got so frustrated he would say to Gavin: 'All right then
> – *you* take the wheel.' And then there'd be all hell to pay. In
> some of those tiny harbours there was barely room to
> manoeuvre and Gavin would charge in – reverse-forward-
> reverse-forward – and then BANG! – he'd crash into the jetty
> so hard he'd almost shake the end off the boat. He was pos-
> sessed by the *idea*, you see – and the boat *had* to fulfil it.
>
> It was a strange, piratical sort of voyage. All the time I was
> on board we never got a decent shot, never caught a shark
> worthy of the name, and Gavin was always having violent
> arguments with his mercurial harpoon-gunner, Tex Geddes.
> Then he began to get a bit buccaneer. He was obsessed with
> the orca, the killer whale, which he regarded as the most
> terrible creature of the sea, the very embodiment of evil. So
> one day, when we overhauled some small shoals of orca, he
> started banging away at them with his old-fashioned, muzzle-
> loading, converted Sven-Fyne whale harpoon-gun in the bows.
> Another day he got so fed up with catching no shark that he
> struck out for Rockall, way out in the North Atlantic, miles
> from anywhere. We never got there, of course – the boat had

nothing like the range – but on the way we got into a whole
sea full of pilot whales leaping this way and that – a fabulous
sight. There was always something to look at. Schools of
small whales called Risso's grampus would signal danger by
slapping their tails on the water like a volley of champagne
corks going off. And when the sea was calm Gavin could
summon up families of cheery dolphins by lowering a bucket
full of pebbles into the water and waggling it about.

The arrival of the *Sea Leopard* was treated like a gala event
by the girls living on some of these remote little Hebridean
islands, and there'd be six or eight of these avid, forlorn young
females lining up on the quay waving madly to Maxwell's
lusty crew, waiting for them to come ashore and jolly roger
them in the bushes. The whole crew would go ashore and
disappear into the dark with the girls. Only Bruce and Gavin
would stay on board – Gavin in his cabin, working his way
through a bottle of Scotch, waiting for his crew to come back.

Many of the eccentrics of the isles were his chums. One day
he said to me: 'I'm going to introduce you to two of the most
interesting people I know in the Inner Isles.' So we went ashore
at Canna to have dinner at the grand house of the bonnet-laird
of the isle and his wife – friends of Gavin by the name of John
Lorne Campbell, a Gaelic scholar and lepidopterist, and his
wife Margaret. It was a remarkable dinner. There was a tremendous tradition of ancient ceremonial, and a tremendous
amount of whisky consumed – especially by Gavin, who was
always popping up to give Gaelic toasts, though he didn't
know any Gaelic. The wife had 'the sight' and with hazel twigs
and salt she exorcised boggarts and banshees that plagued their
sheep and cattle. And there was a lot of talk about sea monsters, sprites, pixies and things like that.

At the end of our allotted week Gavin asked me to stay on
for another week and I only left when a friend of his, a rather
handsome youth to whom he seemed completely devoted,
joined the boat. For me the entire shark-boat episode had been
an amazing period of almost undiluted derring-do – and an
illuminating experience that influenced me enormously. It
showed me what other worlds there were out there, and taught
me that one has to make a decision between merely earning a
living and experiencing the things life has to offer.

Early in August 1946 Gavin attended an Army Medical Board in Inverness. He did not rejoin the shark boats when he returned, but concentrated his attention on the venture's embattled finances. He was still confident that basking-shark fishing was commercially viable, but he was only too aware that his version of it was no more than (as he put it) 'an experimental project already in debt and struggling on insufficient capital'. Recapitalisation was urgently needed to pay off the capital debt and operating losses, though this would almost certainly mean selling it to an individual or firm who would then take a controlling interest in the company.

Armed with his prospectuses and balance sheets Gavin traversed the length and breadth of the country looking for a wealthy backer. Eventually, after his boats had returned to Mallaig on 17 September at the end of the 1946 season, he found one. The Duke of Hamilton had married Gavin's cousin Lady Elizabeth Percy, and had many interests in the Hebrides; he agreed to buy Gavin's Isle of Soay Shark Fisheries – lock, stock and all its barrels – for £13,550, and re-register it as a tiny subsidiary of the parent company under the new name of Island of Soay Shark Fisheries Ltd. At a stroke Gavin's debts were all paid off. But the price was high, for he would now hunt for shark not as the owner of the venture but as its employee. He ceased to be the laird of Soay, losing the Island Valley of Avalon of which he had dreamed amongst the bombs and debris of the London Blitz, and lost too his boats and gear and every penny of his original capital. He was now the managing director of the new company, with a nominal salary and a share of the profits, and though he still had high hopes for the future he was aghast when he learned that the board of the new company had decreed he should work the 1947 season with the same boats and the same gear – and for the same useless multiplicity of by-products.

In the autumn of 1946, while he was wrestling with the problems of his shark-fishing business, Gavin disposed of the whole of his private collection of fifty wildfowl at Monreith – the last and largest such collection, he claimed, to have survived the war in Europe. The recipient was his ornithologist and conservationist friend Peter Scott, who had just established his Wildfowl Trust at Slimbridge on the edge of the Severn mudflats in Gloucestershire.

Quite why Gavin parted with his precious collection is not clear. Nor is it clear whether he sold them to Scott or donated them.

Scott paid over £700 for birds in the first year of setting up the Wildfowl Trust, though it seems Gavin's birds were merely 'on indefinite loan'. Whatever the deal, Gavin Maxwell's birds formed the nucleus of the collection at Slimbridge, which was to become one of the world's premier wildfowl stations.

To look after the new birds Peter Scott had appointed John Yelland, later Curator of Birds at London Zoo, and the two of them travelled to Monreith to collect the birds. Because their pen at Slimbridge was not ready the new arrivals were kept in a bungalow for the night – the snow geese in one bedroom, the little Ross's geese in the other, the quarrelsome upland geese in the larder and the emperor geese in the kitchen. A few pairs of birds from Peter Scott's Norfolk days were added to Gavin's nucleus, including a pair of Lesser Whitefronts Gavin had brought back from Finnmark just before the outbreak of war.

Only a few greylags were now left at Monreith, but before long they too were to find a new home, and this time it would be Gavin's own – a new, more permanent Avalon.

On 23 January 1947 Gavin gave a lecture about the habits and distribution of basking shark and his own shark fishery in the Hebrides to a learned audience of zoologists at the Linnaean Society in London. After the lecture two of Britain's most eminent zoologists – Dr Harrison Matthews, then Scientific Director of the Zoological Society of London, and Dr H.W. Parker, of the British Museum (Natural History) – asked him about the research opportunities provided by his sharking venture. Very little was then known about the anatomy and biology of this mysterious species, for the only specimens to have been examined were a few badly decomposed corpses that had been washed ashore, and none had ever been properly dissected by a qualified scientist. Gavin's fishery provided a unique chance to study the basking shark at close quarters, and the two zoologists went up to Soay in May to investigate the anatomy, biology and reproductive system of sharks caught by Gavin in the surrounding waters.

Harrison Matthews recalled:

Our lab was just a little shed, but most of our work was out on the slipway where the carcases were hauled up. It was an enormous help to be able to use the machinery Gavin had

installed for cutting up the sharks, because these creatures were
not easy things to dissect – some of the organs were so big
and heavy we could barely handle them, and if your scalpel
slipped and you punctured the stomach you could release half
a ton of semi-digested plankton all over your dissection. And
often the carcase was not dead in the usual sense. It's actually
quite difficult to kill a basking shark. Its brain is incredibly
tiny, no bigger than the brain of a small dogfish, so you could
hold it in one hand quite easily. In practice this means that
even if you fire a twelve-bore through its head at point-blank
range you won't kill it; and you can sever the brain from the
spinal column and all the usual organs go on working – existence without awareness. So when I first cut a male shark's
clasper off – its sexual organ, which is a yard long and eight
inches thick – the nerves were stimulated and the thing flew
up and hit me in the face. And even after the flesh had been
cut up in cubes it continued to twitch most disconcertingly.
This also meant, of course, that basking sharks had relatively
little sensitivity to pain. Though Gavin enjoyed hunting these
sharks, he was very conscience-stricken about the pain he
might be inflicting on them. But he needn't have worried –
sticking a harpoon in them didn't make much difference, not
like killing a whale or a seal, which could be very cruel.

On the whole Gavin was not a happy person when we were
with him. We had plenty of fun with him, but it was against
a background of melancholy, and he was very worried that
the project wasn't working out. And it was a hopeless venture,
really. As a commercial enterprise I think the idea was flawed
from the start – the overheads were huge but the season was
only three months long, so that for three-quarters of the year
there was nothing to do and no money coming in. It has been
suggested that what Gavin should really have gone after was
the insulin in the basking shark's pancreas, which would have
been worth a fortune. But this wouldn't have been possible.
The pancreas in the basking shark is not a solid discrete organ
but distributed throughout the body, so there's no exact place
you can extract it from.

The *Sea Leopard* sailed out of Mallaig for the start of the new
sharking season on 5 May 1947. Apart from Bruce Watt, who

would stay on till mid-season, the entire crew was new. For more than a thousand miles they scoured the coasts of the Inner and Outer Hebrides without a sight of a basking shark's fin. Then, halfway between Barra and Canna, they came across the biggest shoal Gavin had ever seen, fifty-five dorsal fins in sight on the surface at the same time, and down below in the green ocean water an almost continuous layer containing many more shark, a great herd of antediluvian monsters moving steadily along in the depths of the sea. For three days and nights they followed this vast north-ward-moving shoal, even shooting by searchlight long after it was dark, towing the carcases back to Soay five at a time and never tying up or dropping anchor in all that time. Gavin and his crew were averaging only two hours' sleep in the twenty-four and almost dropping from exhaustion. Then a thick mist came down and they turned for home. It was an eerie voyage, as Gavin wrote to Raef Payne during the voyage back :

> The mist, right down to the surface, was moving and twisting and reforming, and out of it would appear again and again those great slippery fins, ahead, astern, and on both sides. Heaven knows how many sharks we could have killed if we hadn't had to think about towing them home; we should certainly never have had to wait for a shot after reloading. There was enough money round about us to make us all rich for life and we couldn't touch it.
>
> Next week – if we haven't lost the shoal. This year, next year, sometime . . .

Next week they were out after the shoal again, now far out in the middle of the Minch; but wild unseasonal gales hampered the pursuit, they lost the shoal and by the time they caught up with it again it was off Barra Head. 'We found the big shoal again at four-thirty this morning,' Gavin wrote in a letter from on board the *Sea Leopard*, 'but they wouldn't remain steady on the surface, and we never got a shot. For sheer temper-trying I know nothing quite as powerful as being among a lot of sharks that won't allow themselves to be shot at.'

Once again they intercepted the shoal, now further north off Scalpay in Harris, and for the first time Gavin achieved the kind of results he had dreamed of when he first conceived the idea of a shark-fishing industry three years before. For eighteen days he hunted the great shoal, harpooning a total of nearly fifty sharks – a third of the number he felt could have been taken if time had not been wasted in towing the carcases to Soay or beaching them on the nearest shore at Scalpay to extract the liver oil *in situ* rather than waste time towing them back to the factory. The beaches soon became a terrible sight, the sea crimson for hundreds of yards – 'a true sea of blood', Gavin called it. When a shark's belly was cut open a tremendous weight of liver and entrails would be released. 'One had to jump aside to avoid that ponderous slithery mass as it came rumbling out like an avalanche,' Gavin wrote. 'Once I was not quick enough in avoiding it, and was knocked flat on my back and enveloped by it, struggling free drenched in oil and blood, with a feeling almost of horror.'

With the price of the oil having risen to £135 per ton, that one haul represented a gross revenue of £2500 for the livers alone. By the time the first board meeting of the new company was convened Gavin had killed eighty-three sharks, and the future looked bright – so bright that a bold promise was made of a factory ship and a spotter aircraft for the following season.

All seemed well – and yet all was not. The fate of the pickle-tank on Soay could be read as a metaphor for the insidious canker at the heart of the enterprise. The salt solution in the tank had not been strong enough, and the sixteen tons of shark flesh it contained had turned rotten. When Gavin lifted the tank's hatch he was greeted with a wave of suffocating ammonia that knocked him back like a fist. After he had got his breath back and his choking and spitting had died down, he lifted the hatch again, steeling himself to peer down into the dark nightmare of the fifteen-foot-deep tank. He wrote: 'To say that the surface was crawling would be an under-statement . . . It was alive, heaving, seething, an obscene sea such as Brueghel might have conceived, alive as the sanctuary of Beelzebub himself, with a million million grubs, twisting, turning, writhing . . . Those million million grubs would become a million million flies; my mind's eye saw the island darkened with them as with a swarm of locusts, Avalon eclipsed by the Prince of Flies whom I had summoned up.' Not even a hefty dose of paraffin or quicklime could entirely still the grubs.

More dire news followed. The *Sea Leopard* was found to have dry rot throughout her shark-scarred hull, which was to be sold for firewood, and Gavin's efforts to replace her with a factory ship that could extract the shark oil at sea came to nothing. As the weeks crept by and meeting after meeting of the company board came to no firm decision about future plans, Gavin began to realise that the whole venture was tottering – receding and dissolving through indecision, lack of will and growing lack of interest on the part of the parent company. 'I seemed to detect,' he wrote of that deeply frustrating time, 'that strange agitation that moves among the high leaves of a great tree as the saw bites into the heart of the trunk.'

In March 1948 two small boats were bought to join Gavin's old *Gannet*, but Gavin was never to go to sea in them. He was still nominal managing director of the Island of Soay Shark Fisheries Ltd, but his thoughts began to turn more and more to the possibility of resignation. He had already moved all his possessions from his cabin on the doomed *Sea Leopard*, and though his faith in the idea he had conceived in 1944 was unshaken, he knew in his heart that he would have no active part to play in it ever again. The taste of failure was bitter, but he would never lose his vivid memories of the bold adventure. Four years later, and almost within sight of Soay, he was to write an elegiac requiem to those strange Hebridean years when he was laird of his very own Avalon, and hunted the great shark in pursuit of a dream:

> When I think of Soay . . . I remember it on those glorious summer days when a smooth blue sea lapped the red rock of the island shore and the cuckoos called continuously from the birch-woods; or the bright winter mornings when the Cuillins were snow-covered, hard, intricate and brittle as carved ivory; I remember it with nostalgia for something beautiful and lost, the Island Valley of Avalon to which there can be no true return, no sudden spring.

Or can there, could there?

To those who know Gavin Maxwell as a key figure in the development of the animal protection and conservation movement, the violence and slaughter of the sharking venture must present a shocking and dismaying paradox. But the enterprise, stemming from Gavin's inner drive, found expression at a time when public opinion imposed no moral constraints on it (big-game hunting was still

approved and whale hunting condoned). Gavin himself felt few
inhibiting qualms. He was simply doing what he had hitherto done
best – hunting wild animals with a gun, and finding a tough-guy
masculine role for himself (hunting the second-biggest fish in the
world could be made to fit this scenario, even if it was a poor,
harmless, lumbering monster that browsed on plankton like a cow).

Gavin felt, moreover, a need to prove himself, to achieve something of note as a man of action, for his war had been non-
combative, unlike his dashing warrior relatives Lord Lovat (the
commando leader), and Colonel David Stirling (the founder of the
SAS). Harpooning the basking shark was not a fair fight, but in
the context of drably austere post-war Britain, and the need to find
a vocation or at least a living after six years of war, the project
could be justified as an attempt to harvest the bounty of nature
and provide a living for an impoverished, backward Hebridean
community on a small, neglected island.

The sharking episode provided perhaps the most involving and
purposeful period of Gavin's life – and eventually, in a roundabout
way, the springboard for the career upon which his reputation rests.
But this was achieved at the cost of his inheritance and much bitter
heartache and disappointment, and the final failure left him stranded
as a kind of upper-class down-and-out.

With the advantage of hindsight it is clear that the project was
bound to fail in the long term. The intrinsic nature of the quarry
was against it. Elusive and unreliable, the basking shark's appear-
ances and disappearances were subject to cycles that are still not
fully understood. For eight months of the year it vanishes, no one
is sure where; and after a decade or two in one body of water it
may disappear altogether, only to reappear decades later. The fish
is slow to grow and reproduce, and could not survive sustained
modern industrial fishing for long before its population was annihil-
ated, and the industry with it.

Today, though large shoals of these great fish are still seen off
the Isle of Man and the south-west peninsula of England, and a
lone shark-hunter called Howard MacCrindle carries on Gavin's
tradition in the area of the Clyde, the basking shark is a rarity in
the Hebrides. But the reason is not, as some have claimed, the
depredations inflicted on the species by Gavin in the 1940s, which
were minimal in terms of the basking shark population of those
years. Norwegian whalers (who have killed more than seventy

thousand of the creatures in the forty or so years since Gavin gave up) certainly have had a hand in it, but other factors may also be in part to blame – changes in sea temperatures, plankton distribution or migration patterns – global factors over which Gavin and his little band of marine Don Quixotes had no influence whatever.

One day, perhaps, the basking shark will become a protected species – once it has been proved that it is endangered, for even now next to nothing is known for certain about its population, migration or reproduction.

As for Gavin, he seems to have undergone a sea-change. Perhaps in contrition for his ravages among the shark shoals, perhaps in acknowledgement of the fact that his love for wild creatures was now stronger than his urge to kill them, he rarely hunted wild animals again except perhaps on a few special occasions.

NINE

An artist's life

I put no end to
The life that led me,
The friends to lend to,
The bard who bled me.
Every bad penny
Finds its own robber,
My beds were many
And my cheques rubber.
DOM MORAES,
'Song' in Poems (1960)

By the spring of 1948 Gavin had turned his back on the sharks and
the sea, the Hebridean arena of his long struggle and final defeat,
and bade farewell to the Shaw Stewarts and their exuberant menagerie at Morar Lodge. As a temporary lodging he moved into the
factor's house at his brother Aymer's baronial seat at Monreith.
Not long afterwards he installed himself – complete with his loudly
snoring springer spaniel, Jonnie, and loudly roaring 3½-litre Bentley
roadster – in a flat in a wing of Glenapp Castle, a Scottish baronial
pile near Ballantrae on the Firth of Clyde, which was then the home
of the shipping magnate Lord Inchcape.

Though Gavin was still receiving his Soay Shark Fisheries salary,
he was to all intents and purposes completely broke – 'not two
halfpennies to rub together' he wrote. Yet he contrived to live in
some splendour. 'This room is rather fine,' he wrote to Raef Payne,
who had been out in the shark-boats several times and was now
an undergraduate at Cambridge. 'I have succumbed to the obvious
temptation of making it more so, and have transformed it by my
last purchase – some lovely panels of French First Empire damask,
which now drape the walls in very pale salmon pink. The room is
really lovely now. Rough sketch appended.'

The sketch portrayed all four sides of Gavin's resplendent castle room in the form of an extended panorama. Gold carved-wood eagles spread their heraldic wings above the doors. Precious china plates and a Wedgwood plaque surrounded by ornamental gilt moulding surmounted a wide recessed bookcase. A marble statue of naked wrestlers, dating from 450 B.C., was proudly displayed beneath one of the new pink damask panels, and a heavy inlaid Florentine table stood before a twelve-foot window, draped with crimson damask curtains, which looked out over the castle grounds towards the distant sea. Dominating the room was a large portrait of a distant ancestor, the fourth Duke of Argyll, which had come up for auction ('attributed to Gainsborough') following the death of its owner, Gavin's aunt by marriage Princess Louise. 'The picture is not beautiful,' Gavin reported, 'but fine in a heavy and competent way – if it's a copy it's a damn good one, and if original (which I much doubt) worth a lot. I bought it for £25, *and* nine magnificent carved wood frames for a total of £6.10. Just about the first good buy I have ever made. The finest of these I have made into a mirror, which is hanging over the fireplace, a really beautiful piece of elaborate carving, circa 1740.'

To anyone not accustomed to the wildly divergent polarities of Gavin's personality, the transition from rugged deep-sea sharker to urbane interior designer and denizen of a baronial stately home would have seemed improbable. But at Glenapp he was simply returning to the panoply of his high-born background. Here, after the rigours of his sharking years, Gavin lived not only in style, but in comfort. 'I am looked after by a charming and quite lovely child,' he wrote to Raef Payne in early June, 'who looks about fourteen but I believe (incredibly) to be twenty or more. I have started two portraits of her, and for someone more competent than I she would make the most perfect (though perhaps rather childish) model for a madonna. Her reign of a month here has been heaven – she dotes on me and anticipates my every need. Alas, she is supposed to go and be trained to be a doctor or theatre nurse or something soon, and I can think of no remedy but marrying her, which is perhaps a little drastic – though *one* might fare much worse, I don't suppose *she* could!'

Sharking was no more than a casual, distant concern now. Though he sometimes drove up to Mallaig to cast an eye on things, Gavin never went to sea any more, and had virtually no control over sharking operations. At the end of June 1948 he was advised that if he did not resign from the company it would be liquidated and then reformed, in order to remove as shareholders his ten friends who had invested £500 each in the enterprise. They would receive no more than two shillings and fourpence in the pound. This was an option Gavin could not tolerate, and on 12 July he resigned as managing director of the Island of Soay Shark Fisheries. In due course the company was wound up, the factory demolished, the boats and the island sold, and the population evacuated.

'A remarkable fact stands out from a welter of confusion,' he wrote to Raef Payne on 26 July:

> I HAVE LEFT MY JOB. Provocation to do so became *very* great indeed, and after chewing it over for forty-eight hours I wrote off. Reactions at present:
>
> 1. Fear my resignation will be accepted
> 2. Fear my resignation will not be accepted
> 3. Faith in self as great artist
> 4. Lack of ditto.
>
> See, I will lose
>
> (a) the only fixed income I have
> (b) my seaman's ration book
> (c) my typewriter
> (d) security from labour direction.
>
> But, I will gain
>
> (a) FREEDOM
> (b) (Can't fill this in)
>
> So what. Anyway, 'tis done. Now I feel I really am a struggling artist.

Gavin was more hurt than his chirpy tone would suggest, for he felt an overwhelming sense of failure. He had personally lost £11,000 (worth more than fifteen times that amount by 1992 values) – 'all the money I shall ever have, as it was secured by a total advance on my mother's will'. All he had left was his Bentley, £250 worth of personal possessions, and the unprofitable salmon-fishing

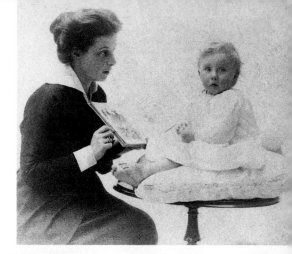

Gavin Maxwell with his mother, Lady Mary, in 1915.

Above: Aged twelve and wearing the persecuted look of the unhappy schoolboy.

Left: Gavin Maxwell aged ten, with jackdaw pets at Elrig.

To winds blowing cold from quartz and ling
And grouse in the morning challenging
To the lodge and the glen wild roses — when shall we come there
   again?
      Harebells, horizon seas,
      Blossom-powdered bees,
And grass of Parnassus opening white
And the low burn singing through the night
      Jar tides and redshanks flying
      Curlews from wet moor crying
To the hills and the curlew crying — Shall we ever come there again?

The house of Elrig, childhood home of the Maxwell family, with youthful poem in praise of the house inscribed by Gavin Maxwell in his Game Book.

Gavin Maxwell beside his first Bentley and a 'bag' of birds from a day's shooting. Galloway, Christmas 1932.

Above: Gavin Maxwell in the uniform of a Scots Guards subaltern, on joining SOE in November 1942.

Right: Gavin's brothers, Eustace (left) and Sir Aymer. Galloway, 1933

Below: On board his lobster-boat, the *Gannet*, Gavin takes a pot at a basking shark with a Breda machine-gun off the Isle of Eigg during a break from SOE duties, September 1944.

Top: Making a basking shark fast to the *Gannet* after a long struggle in the Minch. Summer 1946.

Middle: The East Harbour on the Isle of Soay, where Gavin Maxwell was to build his sharking base. Behind are the hills of Skye.

Left: Gavin reloading his muzzle-loading harpoon gun. Summer 1946.

Left: On the bridge of the *Sea Leopard* during the 1946 sharking season.

Middle: Gavin Maxwell (centre) with a basking shark waiting to be cut up at the Soay factory in the summer of 1946.

Bottom: The cartilagenous vertebrae of processed sharks laid out to dry in the factory 'boneyard' on Soay.

Top left: Peter Scott. Drawing by Gavin Maxwell, 1946.

Top right: Raef Payne. Drawing by Gavin Maxwell, 1946.

Left: Tambimuttu. Painting by Gavin Maxwell, 1949.

Below: Tambimuttu, Kathleen Raine and Gavin Maxwell photographed at their first meeting in the garden at Paultons Square, August 1949.

Above: Racing the 3½-litre Bentley at Silverstone in the summer of 1949.

Right: Clement Glock working on a set at the Royal Opera House, Covent Garden, c.1949.

The burn and the bay – the twin components of the ring at Sandaig (Camusfeàrna).

rights on Soay. He had also invested the prime of his young manhood in the four years of the venture. Now, a few days short of
his thirty-fourth birthday, he found himself stranded, with large
debts and no occupation. Circumstances compelled him to earn a
living, an activity for which he was almost totally inexperienced
and temperamentally unsuited. With the vision of his future in
ruins, he was now to perform a somersault in his career and lifestyle
as radical as the metamorphosis in his habitat.

At school and university he had displayed a talent for drawing –
mostly birds and animals and country scenes. He had acquired some
desultory knowledge of painting at the Ruskin School of Art
while he was at Oxford, and in 1946 he had taken a little instruction in human portraiture from talented friends like Peter
Scott, and had tried his hand at sketching the heads of friends
and relatives.

As the shark fishing began to wind down in failure and penury,
the idea occurred to Gavin that, with his wide network of well-
placed and well-heeled friends and relatives, he might be able to
put his talent to good use by setting up as a portrait painter of the
rich and famous. At Monreith the idea hardened into a resolve
when he met a fifty-one-year-old Australian painter and sculptor
by the name of Colin Colahan, who had been commissioned to
paint a portrait of his brother, Sir Aymer, for a substantial fee.
Colahan painted in the manner of Velàzquez, placing the easel next
to the sitter, viewing him from the other end of the room, then
rushing up to the easel to paint. This method required a large
room, which was one reason why Gavin moved into the vast flat
at Glenapp Castle. It was here that he set about transforming himself, with all his habitual energy and optimism, from a shark-hunter
into a society portrait-painter.

His first subject was his landlady, Lady Inchcape, seated with
flowers in her hand and a mirror on the wall reflecting the sea and
the gannet island of Ailsa Craig. 'Although it is not at all a good
painting,' Gavin reported, 'it is quite like her and is liked by her
husband, and I hope to sting him a full hundred guineas for it with
luck.' Other portraits followed in quick succession – portraits of
locals and neighbours, old comrades from SOE, and his brother
Eustace ('very bold, modelled, unkind, and generally satisfactory
– probably the best painting I have done').

He did not find it easy. 'I'm getting better,' he wrote at this time,

'but find that I can only paint with confidence and un-niggle when
I don't care a damn what the sitter thinks of it – women especially
make me go all KEEP-IT-BEAUTIFULLY-SOFT. But I'm making
progress.' He tended to lose interest once he had done the head,
and found it hard to finish a picture. He had difficulty managing
backgrounds and making two eyes a real pair, and disliked using
mirrors. On the rare occasion he tackled a female nude he found
himself unable to resolve the sexual confusion that ensued – a confusion all the more acute in that his body appeared to react in direct
disobedience to the messages sent by his mind. 'I've painted another
nude,' he wrote after one such session: 'Huge woman, great fids
of flesh, creases, all tits and buttocks and things. I think she expected
me to seduce her (judging mainly by assumed postures). But honestly, how can one view with desire these mountains of flesh, these
voluminous folds? Why can't there be *less* of them? Promise of
pneumatic bliss was never a strong attraction for me, alas. But talk
of lighthouses! I had to increase the shadows under the tits second
by second. How fortunate that women are otherwise made more
discreetly than men.'

Sometimes he abandoned human beings and indoor work and
took to the hills. One day, revisiting Soay, he decided to take
advantage of the glorious summer weather to paint some landscapes
of Skye. 'Itching to paint,' he recorded, 'Found marvellous scene
– unloaded canvas, etc, etc – no easel. Buckets of blood. Walked a
mile from road and erected vast and moon-eclipsing cone of peat.
First touch of brush – whole thing collapsed. Stuck canvas upright
in ground and lay on stomach. After five minutes canvas fell.
Started again. Clegs began to bite. Couldn't get away from canvas
to look at it. Began to rain. Upset turpentine. Finally in general
struggle walked on canvas. Dangerous smouldering of temper. Ce
n'est pas gai.'

Commissions were few in those early days, distractions frequent.
Visitors tended to have a deranging effect, but some were more
distracting than others. One such was the wife of a Harley Street
surgeon who had taken a short let on another flat in the castle with
her husband and children.

She is forty, looks and behaves exactly like a tart, has a figure
young for her age and a face fifteen years older. Well, I have
practically been raped by her – *not* a nice sensation. The second

time I met her she came up to my flat to have a drink, and insisted first on showing me a mole so high up on the inside of the thigh as to leave little to the imagination, and second, having explained to me that her youngest son was born by Caesarean section, tried to show me the scar. Next day she came up here with both sons, and stayed (with both of them) till 4.30 a.m. Despite desperate resistance she practically undressed me, at last said, well anyway kiss me goodnight, after which I spent minutes, but minutes, trying to disengage her tongue from my uvula or epiglottis. Now I daren't be alone with her for a second.

At the end of September Gavin took three weeks' holiday away from Glenapp, staying with various friends in the West Highlands in order to stalk deer and walk the hills and breathe deeply of the clear, cool, autumnal West Coast air. The trip was to prove crucial in the future course of his career and reputation.

His first destination was the grand old Highland house of a long-standing friend called Mrs Tew, who lived at Conaglen in the wildly rugged region of Ardgour, Argyll. Conaglen was un-believably beautiful, and quite unlike anything he had seen in the rest of Scotland. The house was on the sea, and the glen ran up for fourteen miles inland behind it. A small, shallow river ran down the glen over huge grey slabs of stone, in half a dozen places developing into quite considerable falls, with high hills on either side.

My God, the colours! On Thursday I stalked at the head of the glen, and rode the fourteen miles up on a pony. Listen. The river pure cobalt, with raw sienna stones showing under it, and the whitest of white foam at every little waterfall and blue-grey slabs of smooth rock at the sides. The reds and yellows – every one in the Materia Pictoria. The ferns pure chrome yellow coming down to the cobalt water, the bracken an indian red behind it – then the wild cherry trees, turned every colour from chrome yellow to vermilion, and rowans with scarlet berries between them. Every colour was almost literally dazzling, and all in lovely great defined patches and blocks. Behind all this the turning oakwoods and the hills rising bare with deep purple shadows above the trees. Says I

to myself, if Sunday is a fine day I'll spend all of it up here
painting like a stoat (or something).

I went on and duly ascended a gigantic mountain – views
stupendous, over seventy miles in all directions – and killed
two stags and tittupped home again in the twilight.

Next day Gavin set out for the hills again, and after a long walk
of sixteen miles and a climb to the top of the highest mountain in
Ardgour, returned so impassioned by the beauty and the solitude
of the natural world all around him that he was like a man in a
mescalin trance. 'Where vegetation is sparse and the ground
covered only by a thin layer of granite chips,' he wrote,

> where you can see the sea nearly a hundred miles away, where
> everything is blue and yellow and one is incredibly high up,
> it is like a big dose of benzedrine. The ears stick forward
> juttily, the nose beaks craggily, the toes spring sorbo-
> rubberly, sweat dries icily. Where would the drab world be
> without mountains to stand on top of, without the distant sea
> to look at, without the crushed and drying myrtle leaves in
> the pocket? Perhaps you think I exaggerate? I have, I admit,
> a certain tendency to rhetoric. But what I do feel is this: THE
> WORLD IS STILL YOUNG AND BEAUTIFUL – so young and
> beautiful I could eat it. My mind is crammed with things I
> THINK ARE BEAUTIFUL. I'm glad I was born onto this earth
> and not a Martian or something dim . . . My day was very
> wonderful, and I was all alone, and I just wished I could go
> on looking at everything for ever and ever and never come
> down to where one can't see so far or feel so supercharged.

Gavin's route next took him further north along the West Highland
coast, through Glen Shiel and over Mam Ratagan to the sleepy and
reclusive village of Glenelg on the Narrows of Skye. A little beyond
Glenelg lay Eilanreach – 'a lovely place, on the sea, approached by
eighty miles of barely passable dirt road, amid positively Alpine
scenery'. Here Tony Wills, head of the Wills tobacco empire and
a friend from Oxford days, kept a Victorian shooting lodge from
which the huge estate he had recently acquired in the area was
administered. Gavin hoped to collect a commission to paint Wills'
wife and children and to spend a few days stalking deer on the

slopes of Beinn Sgritheall, but he was laid low by a virulent cold, contracted no doubt after his drenching in Conaglen, and for most of the time he was confined to the house, fretful and ailing and complaining loudly.

One Sunday morning, as his stay at Eilanreach drew to its sneezy, stuffy end, Gavin casually hinted to his host that he was minded to find another *pied-à-terre* in the Highlands, now that the sharking venture was over. Tony Wills mentioned that a shepherd's-cum-lighthouse keeper's cottage on his estate had recently become vacant, the lighthouse having been converted to automatic operation. 'It's right on the sea and there's no road to it,' he said. 'There's been no one there for a long time, and I'd never get the estate people to live in it now.' If Gavin did not mind its remoteness and inconvenience, its total lack of all mod cons, he would be happy to rent it to him for a pound a year, on condition that he kept it in repair and did not let it fall into ruins.

Tuesday, 13 October 1948 was to prove a day of destiny in Gavin's life. Coaxing his Bentley out of Eilanreach, he drove up the single-lane track that led southwards to the road's end at Arnisdale on Loch Hourn, climbing steadily higher over the steep deer moor, with the sea and the hills of Skye stretched out majestically on his right, till he came to a lonely green house roofed in corrugated iron at a place called Tormor, near a point where a burn starting high on the flanks of Ben Sgriol began its descent towards the sea below. Here he parked his car and followed the course of the burn as it plunged down between the walls of a steep wooded ravine. He could hear the roar of a waterfall tumbling between the rock walls of a narrow chasm, and climbing out of the ravine he reached a small bluff of heather and bracken where a steepening track levelled out before its final drop to the shore.

He paused here and drew a deep breath. A vast and marvellous panorama of sea and mountains stretched away before him. Immediately beneath him lay a small house in a little patch of heaven at the edge of the sea. Filled with an intense, impatient excitement, he half fell, half flew down the track, stony now in its final descent, crossed the swiftly-flowing burn and found himself standing alone, breathless in Avalon. That evening he wrote to Raef Payne:

NEWS – hold your breath! I have rented a cottage – an idyll, something out of a dream!

No road, approachable only by boat, nearest human habitation two miles. Stands on little white shell sand beach, on green turf with river flowing round it, sea within fifty yards of the door. Absolute paradise, everything one could possibly want in a tiny compass. A reef on which the sea breaks, an automatic lighthouse, and six little islands, also with green turf and white sand. Faces across to Skye with hills rising steeply behind it. House in excellent repair, only been empty three months. Two biggish rooms downstairs and ditto upstairs. I intend to furnish it and spend a few weeks there every summer, painting the sea and lying in the sun and planting roses and revelling in privacy.

The name of this place was Sandaig, and it was to be Gavin's true Island Valley of Avalon for most of the rest of his life.

For the moment, though, Sandaig lay in the future. Gavin had begun to perceive that he was getting nowhere closeted alone with an easel in a remote castle in Scotland. He needed more stimulus, a more painterly ambience; he needed, above all, professional instruction if he was to progress at all. On his return from the West Highlands, therefore, he flew to London for a preliminary meeting with Colin Colahan, who enjoyed considerable respect as a teacher, armed with two paintings by which Colahan could judge his potential. Gavin reported to Raef Payne on their meeting: 'Criticism frank (devastatingly so!) but v.v. encouraging. I felt I had learnt more in one day than in the whole of the past year, and came away alternating between great hope and despair.'

Colahan told Gavin that he had not studied the faces in his pictures as a whole but as the sum of parts, and that he was too obsessed with getting a likeness and searching for details which one wouldn't normally see. But for all its faults, his work showed competence and power, and Colahan was interested enough to give him further instruction. 'He then proceeded to paint me, with a running commentary and a huge mirror in which I could see every action. Forty-five minutes' work – quite brilliant! He is quite the most conceited man I have ever met – but how justifiably and charmingly so.'

Gavin returned to Glenapp with revived enthusiasm about his artistic future – and some misgivings about his artistic past. Looking

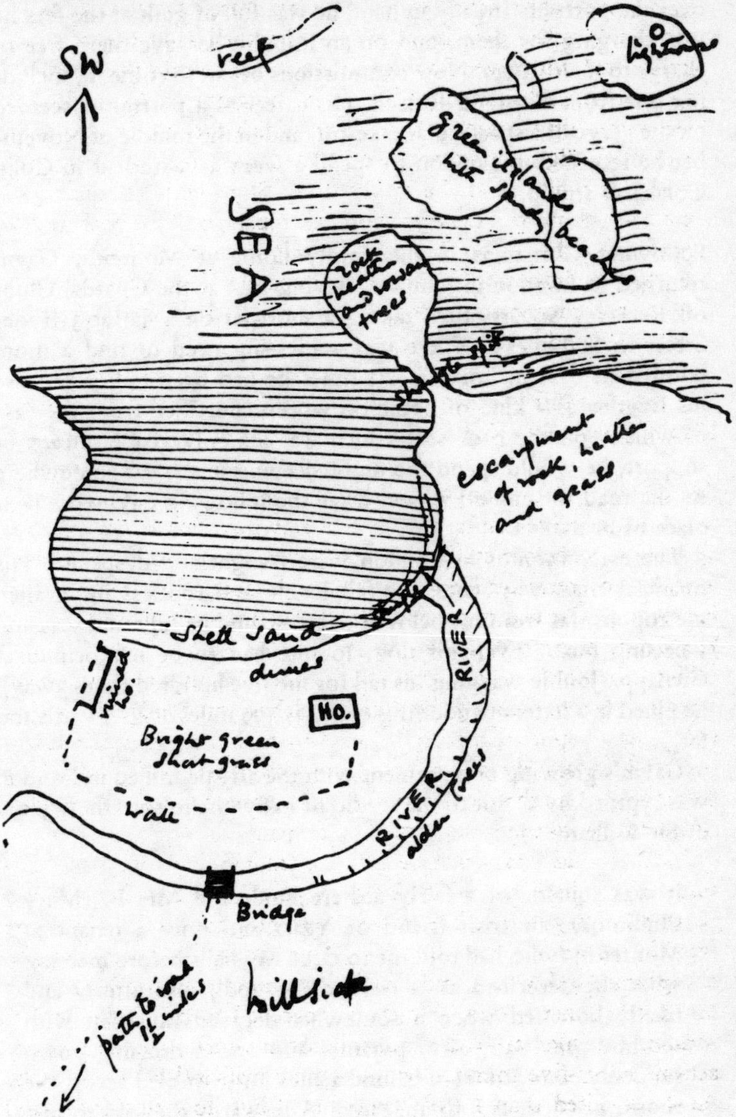

SW

reef

lighthouse

green hill and dark heather

SEA

soft heath and bracken trees

slopes off

escarpment of rock, heather and grass

Shell sand dunes

wreck

HO.

RIVER

Bright green short grass

Wall

RIVER (new)

older

Bridge

path to road 1/2 miles

hillside

over the portraits already in hand he was full of guilt at the fees he was charging for them, and on an impulse he gave them free of charge to their sitters. New commissions began to come in, including one from Bertrand Russell. His career as a portraitist seemed on the verge of a spectacular take-off, and in the middle of November he returned to London to spend a week as a student in Colin Colahan's studio.

Following Christmas in the family home at Monreith, Gavin returned to London in January, staying first at the Guards' Club, off Berkeley Square, then taking a short let on a flat at 3 Ryder Street in St James's. There was a pressing need to find a more permanent base in London. At times he had been obliged to use his Bentley as a kind of home on wheels. Fortified from the case of whisky on the back seat which was his only visible means of support, he would spend the night sleeping in the car somewhere on the road, or just off it, and drive the following day to his next place of rest.

The early months in London were fraught and desperate. His financial crisis was acute. He felt lonely and rootless in an alien metropolis, far from his beloved Scotland and its hills and seas and wheeling birds. Even his dog, Jonnie, had to be left behind at Glenapp. 'Jonnie wagging his tail for me five hundred miles away,' he pined in a letter at about this time, 'is 499 miles 1759½ yards too far.'

Gavin's growing bemusement with the artistic milieu in London was typified by a visit to the studio of Lady Nicholson, the widow of Sir William:

It was squalor of a fairly austere kind, and Mrs P. [Mary Phillimore, an Irish friend of Yeats and now a tenant at Monreith] (who had told me to clean my nails before meeting what she described as 'a *real* lady' – god!) was utterly and finally horrified when a somewhat decayed musician with scrubby grey hair, dirty pyjamas and a torn dressing gown suddenly emerged from behind a curtain, shambled across the room, belched, and disappeared. Afterwards she said to me: 'Gav'n, is there *any* studio in London that hasn't a piece of *garbage* like that lying around?' I told her that if there was I hadn't yet seen one.

Gavin was presented with a totally different face of the art world, however, when he attended a Boat Race party at the riverside home of the artist Julian Trevelyan, in Hammersmith. 'The party was fun,' he enthused, 'hundreds of people but hardly a face that wasn't striking in some way and hardly a name unfamiliar. What a collection, but Gosh they're all geniuses, and I do feel flattered when they're nice to me.'

But Gavin was becoming disillusioned with the artistic life, and particularly with the depressing realisation that his own endeavours were not progressing as he had hoped. This knowledge spelt the end of the confidence and enthusiasm that had buoyed him along in the early days. In the autumn he cancelled an exhibition of his paintings in Cambridge. 'I find I can no longer produce even a likeness,' he wrote, 'much less a decent painting . . . My Gawd, I'm a bad painter. I shall never dare to face Colahan again.' But commissions and sitters continued to turn up, including his old ex-SOE friend, the conductor Edward Renton, the concert pianist Louis Kentner and his wife Griselda, and others.

The recipient of most of Gavin's letters was Raef Payne, the English friend of Jackie Shaw Stewart whom Gavin had first met at Morar Lodge. Raef was himself a good enough painter to have thought seriously about pursuing an artistic career, and he shared many of Gavin's other interests. Gradually Gavin came to realise that this was no ordinary friendship.

Sexually, as in a number of other ways, Gavin was a late developer. By his own admission his knowledge of sexual matters at school had been zero, and for three years after the onset of puberty he had remained sexually inactive, emerging from this hormonal torpor into a state of adolescent confusion and embarrassment made all the more acute by the difficulties he encountered in working out his real sexual polarity. The course of his sexual evolution in those early years is difficult to chart. It seems his first romantic infatuation was with the aristocratic beauty called Elizabeth he met at Strachur when he was sixteen, but he appears to have had difficulty translating this impulse into an active relationship, still less a steady heterosexual state. A Freudian interpretation would have it that Gavin's sexual orientation was virtually decided for him by the circumstances of his early childhood – no father, and a suffocatingly adoring mother in whose bed he slept till he was eight years old.

By the middle of the war, when he was in his late twenties, it seems Gavin had come to terms with his predominantly homosexual nature, and admitted as much to one of his closest friends in SOE, Matthew Hodgart.

In those years homosexuality was against the law in Britain, and since Gavin was a shy, fastidious, romantic and guilt-ridden young man, he had suppressed his sexual emotions – he had not, indeed, felt able even to attempt a deep relationship with another human being. Now his intense friendship with Raef became such a dominant element in his life that he could no longer escape or conceal it. When Raef realised the nature of Gavin's feelings, his response was one of bewilderment and some alarm, though he was sympathetic enough not to reject a friendship which had become such a good one, and which continued to grow through the interests and sense of humour they had in common. Nor was it in any sense an exploitative affair on the part of the older man; while Gavin finally accepted the nature of his own feelings, he was scrupulously careful not to let them put a strain on the relationship. Or so it was at first.

To Gavin, for whom loneliness was almost a way of life, this friendship was a tremendous source of comfort and strength. But until he came down from Scotland to live in London on a permanent basis early in 1949 the liaison had been of necessity an intermittent, long-distance one, and the longest period the two men had spent in each other's company was two weeks. It was this, perhaps, that had enabled the relationship to develop so happily, with only occasional meetings, but regular and lively correspondence. When Gavin began to spend more time in London, Raef began to feel oppressed by the demands being made on him. In the spring of 1949 (Raef was now at Cambridge) the matter came to a crisis, and he told Gavin he could cope with it no longer; for both their sakes the relationship must end.

This was more than Gavin could take. The fracture left him orphaned, so to speak, privately alone and stranded among a multitude of strangers. By the time he found his London *pied-à-terre* – a studio flat with a gallery and dry rot throughout the woodwork at 8 Avonmore Road, Olympia – Gavin was in the middle of an acute breakdown. A chronic neurotic at the best of times, he finally gave way to the combined weight of the sharking failure, the hand-to-mouth existence of a tyro painter, the financial crisis, the end of the friendship – and just about everything else.

'I appear to be in a somewhat mentally feeble state,' he wrote during this period, 'owing to too much hard work, too many bad paintings, bad poems, efforts to organise, dust, dirt, expired ration cards . . . Oh mists that will not part, oh dove that finds no resting place, oh feet without lendals, pots without croon . . . With my fal-de-ro and di-de-dum-de, with my bottle of rum my throat speaks every human tongue.'

Though Gavin did not know it – perhaps never knew it – he was by now almost certainly suffering from 'bi-polar illness'. Though it seems he only suffered from the affliction in a modified form, its symptoms were sufficiently marked to bewilder and confuse anyone who happened to be in his company at the time of their occurrence. Gavin would experience intensely buoyant periods characterised by boundless creativity, optimism and omniscience, a feeling that all things were possible, a sense of being at one with the cosmos, of containing the whole of the human condition within himself. For days and weeks there would be an endless stream of random but often profound *pensées* (often embracing concepts as huge as God and the Universe), wisecracking good humour and bubbling enthusiasms. But these would be followed by collapses into utter despair, self-absorption and misdirected paranoia.

In this dark night of the soul Gavin's stream of letters dried up, his work faltered, he began to drink heavily and take sleeping pills. His thoughts even began to dwell on suicide. To help relieve his distress, he sought the advice of a psychiatrist, Dr Ellis Stungo – 'a wise man and a very understanding one' – who had a practice in Harley Street. When Gavin said he was feeling suicidal, Dr Stungo told him: 'The best thing to do if you feel like killing yourself is to go off and do something really dangerous.' Soon afterwards Gavin rang John Hillaby, who recalled:

He said he wanted to say goodbye. Why, I asked, was he going abroad? No, he said, his fortune teller had told him he was going to die in a racing crash and as he was racing his Bentley at Brooklands the next day he thought he would like to say goodbye to a few old friends. By this time I had got used to Gavin saying things totally beyond my comprehension, so I said, Oh yes, well, goodbye then. I couldn't think of anything else to say. But about three weeks later I bumped into

him again and I said, I thought you were dead? Oh, he said,
I didn't race, the car developed a fault and wouldn't go.

In fact by mid-summer the suicidal mood had passed. Dr Stungo
had got in touch with Raef Payne and by dint of wise counselling
had brought about a reconciliation between him and Gavin. The
friendship was resumed, but on Gavin's part at a less intense emotional pitch, and in time it settled into a deep and abiding affection
that enriched both their lives.

Gavin began to rebuild his life with the help of his latest enthusiasm, and at the beginning of July he entered his Bentley for the
races to be held at Silverstone later that month. 'My race is only
for 3½ and 4¼ Bentleys,' he reported, 'and I'm relying on leaving
the field at the start and having the corners to myself, as I don't
fancy being one of a huge pack cornering at 90 m.p.h. Up is what
the wind will be in any case.' A phone call from the Silverstone
race secretary soon demolished this plan. 'Not sufficient entries in
the 3½–4¼ Bentley class – now I have to race against a mixture of
Mercedes, Bugatti, Maserati and Lord knows what. *Much* more
wind-up-putting, and no sure hope of getting away from the pack
early on in the race. Buckets of blood.'

Gavin proved to be a dramatic racing driver, but he was inclined
to forget that in order to win you have to finish. On the eve of the
race he was awake all night with worry, tossing and turning and
chain-smoking through the early hours; and in the morning he
consumed half a bottle of Scotch in preparation for the looming
ordeal. His huge 3½-litre Rolls Bentley had a fine turn of speed and
a light aluminium body by Corsica, but it was no match for the
likes of Maserati, and at the start Gavin chose to take the lead, as
his best and only hope of winning the race. At the drop of the
starter's flag he roared off down the straight, his goggled, hawk-like
face peering intently ahead, gloved hands clutching the wheel
tightly as he approached the first, dreaded corner. When he reached
it he over-braked, span round in front of the rest of the pack, and
was forced to retire when the stewards gave him the black flag.

This failure did not weaken his determination, but he fared little
better in other races. At Goodwood – 'the course difficult and
frightening; no straights, only something like a circle full of outrageous kinks, all banked the wrong way, on which 100 m.p.h.
felt like tight-rope walking' – he nearly came to grief in practice

and was forced to retire with fuel starvation in the actual race. 'I went, and returned, alone and uncheered,' he recorded. Time trials were more his forte. In the Bentley Drivers' Club time trials at Silverstone he won two pewter tankards for the standing half-mile (32.89 seconds) and flying quarter-mile (eleven seconds). And at the Firle hill trials he totally forgot his worries in the exhilaration of the occasion.

I had the Bentley tuned for two days before the event, and when I set off for Eastbourne she was going as never before, and leash of greyhounds slipping thong was what she was like most. I spent the night in a rose-trellised hotel in Lewes, and on to Firle at 8.30 in the morning – a marvellous morning of early sunshine and heavy dew. Chalk downs, blue sky, and big white cumulus; sea, and shipping in the Channel.

Firle Hill itself turned out to be a lovely place – skirting a big chalk ridge of the downs, and a merry throng of cars of all makes and colours at the foot. There were eighty-six cars competing, including quite a lot of famous ones – three of the official Lagonda racing team, Pitts' supercharged 4¼ Bentley, Hutton's Bugatti, and many others familiar by name or sight. From the moment I saw this assembled horde, the hosts of Midian, the Philistines, I didn't hope to do more than not disgrace myself, and quite expected to be killed and eaten at the end of the day.

Judge therefore of my amazement and delight to make the (I think) sixth fastest climb of the day, and (I think) fastest time of any unsupercharged car. AND I absolutely squashed Hay's much vaunted and Rolls-sponsored 4¼ Bentley which had been winning things all over the world this year. And, which made my day, I got a cheer when I drove down the hill again, and some very nice and kind remarks from the commentator. And in the chalk pit I picked up a lot of Salvador-Dali shaped flints coated with chalk, as edible as anything I've ever combed from a beach in the past. So altogether it was a good day.

TEN

The man of light

> The power that wheels the eagle's wing
> And darts the silver herring shoal
> Strikes from my rock a mountain spring
> That has no knowledge of its goal
> But only of its will to sing.
>
> GAVIN MAXWELL, *'Poem from
> a Sequence'* (1951)

Gavin's venture into motor racing broadly coincided with another point of departure in his life. His Stowe friend Anthony Dickins, by now a gifted pianist and chess player, had come to London to renew old friendships, and Gavin was one friend he sought out. Another was an extraordinary half-genius, half-bohemian called James Meary Tambimuttu – known as Tambi to his friends, and Tuttifrutti to his enemies.

A descendant of the royal house of Jaffna in Ceylon, Tambimuttu had first come to London in 1938 in pursuit of a beautiful Kandyan dancer called Miriam. When she eluded him, he stayed on, drifting to the area around Fitzroy Square and the Fitzroy Tavern on which he later claimed to have bestowed the name of Fitzrovia – a name which today signifies not so much a place as a legendary era and way of life long gone. Fitzrovia in those days rivalled Chelsea as an artistic and intellectual quarter of London. Its inhabitants included such figures as Dylan Thomas and Augustus John, together with a wild and noisy sub-stratum of drunks, sensualists, bohemians, eccentrics and aspiring literati. Prince among them was Tambi. 'Tambi's blue-black hair was bobbed, and curled at the corners,' recalled Julian Maclaren-Ross in his *Memoirs of the Forties*; 'his extraordinary hands, with fingers that bent right back, apparently boneless like a lemur's, only longer, flickered mesmerically as he talked in rapid tones with an accent that on the wireless sounded Welsh, white teeth and eyeballs flashing meantime in the dusk of his face.' Almost every night Tambimuttu led an invasion of Fitzrovian pub-crawlers into Soho, where the pubs stayed open half an hour longer. Dan Davin, in his book *Closing Time*, describes one such invasion: 'Tambimuttu came and went with his train of girls and poets, a comet rather than a star, black-rimmed finger-nails gesturing, a wild, dark and crafty eye.' It was in an attic room in Fitzrovia, where one of W.H. Auden's boyfriends was throwing a party, that Anthony Dickins first met Tambimuttu, shortly after his arrival in London, and together they went on to found the influential magazine *Poetry London*, the first issue of which came out just before the outbreak of the war.

Whatever else one made of him, there is no doubt that Tambi-muttu was a gifted if erratic poetry impresario, with an almost infal-lible nose for sniffing out poetic talent. The works of many poets of promise and quality first saw the light of day in the pages of his *Poetry London*; and there were few poets in London who were not known to him. When Anthony Dickins introduced Gavin to him in the sum-mer of 1949, Tambi (who was a year younger than Gavin) at once perceived in him a rare talent of some kind and took him under his wing, encouraging him to write poems and working out ways of advancing his career as a portrait painter. The thing to do, he told Gavin, was to hold an exhibition of paintings of the rich and famous as a bait for future custom, and he promised to introduce him to potential sitters, among them the poet Kathleen Raine.

When Tambimuttu brought Gavin to her house at 9 Paultons Square, Chelsea, in August 1949, Kathleen Raine was forty-one years of age – six years older than Gavin. Once described as the most beautiful woman of her generation at Cambridge (where she had read biology), she had been twice married and was now the handsome mother of two young children, a Research Fellow of Girton College, Cambridge, an acknowledged authority on Wil-liam Blake, and the author of three books of intense, rhapsodic, and often mystical and metaphysical poetry, much of it inspired by her sense of the sacred she saw as permeating nature, which had placed her in the front rank of contemporary English poets. There were many things this gifted and unusual woman had in common with Gavin Maxwell – and many things she did not. The extent of the gulf between them she was to explore during their tumultuous and often painful future relationship.

Kathleen showed very little interest in Gavin at that first meeting, or he in her. She was highly suspicious of any friends Tambi brought round to meet her, for experience had shown they could be princes or beggars, poets or drug addicts. 'Yet Tambi was right in discerning, in Gavin, a vein of genius,' she was to write in the third and final volume of her autobiography, *The Lion's Mouth*. Tambi bustled the two of them into the garden and photographed them – 'like a reluctant Adam and Eve' – under a pear tree. And there the matter might have ended had not Kathleen, as Gavin was about to leave, mentioned that she had just returned from Northumberland, and thus made the fatal connection.

Northumberland, where her grandfather had been a schoolteacher, was Kathleen's paradise, the land of her childhood, 'an inviolate sanctuary of imaginative solitude' to which she always yearned to return. It turned out that Gavin's grandfather, the Duke of Northumberland, had owned the salmon waters where Kathleen's grandfather had fished, and her mother had sat behind Gavin's mother at church, admiring her coils of shining hair. 'Gavin was native of my paradise,' she wrote. 'It was as if he came from Eden itself.'

That evening they met again, this time without Tambi present. They showed each other their childhood photographs, swapped reminiscences of their common northern past. 'Above all it was in nature,' she recalled, 'in the wild world above the frontiers of the human, where he and I alike had found our escape and joy. I found in him what I had found in no other person, a knowledge which had always been mine: not a scientist's knowledge of nature (though he was a naturalist of some distinction) but a knowledge by participation, the knowledge nature has of itself.'

It was Gavin's knowledge of nature, not his painting (which she thought conventional) or his poetry (which from her own Olympian height she deemed the work of a gifted amateur), that Kathleen believed was the source of Gavin's genius. 'For him, as for me, such knowledge of nature was less a branch of learning than an experience of imagination,' she reflected. 'This secret knowledge of nature was Gavin's gift, as poetry was mine . . . As my vision of poetry stemmed from a vision of nature, so was his participation in nature a kind of poetry.'

But this alone did not account for the extraordinary impact of Gavin's arrival on Kathleen's life; nor did the common bond of Northumberland; nor the joy of being in his company – 'the best person in the world to laugh with at the happy comedy of life'. There was something else – something that made the encounter for Kathleen inevitable and transcendental. Recalling her impression of Gavin on the day of their first meeting, Kathleen wrote: 'He was like some blind bird . . . its restless energy a torment to itself for want of sight. It was as if those lids that cover the eyes of nestlings covered the eyes of his spirit.' A few days later they met again for lunch, and Kathleen saw that this time Gavin's eyes were no longer hidden but were looking at her, holding her own eyes in a long gaze as if testing her. It was then, she was to write, she saw who he was. 'What drew me to him was nothing bodily, but rather the radiance his presence had for me always.' He would always be for her, as she put it, 'the man of light'.

It was her meeting with Gavin that enabled Kathleen to redis-cover her true, childhood self. In Gavin she believed she had found her soul mate, her true love in a sense above and beyond the merely romantic or carnal – something more to do with poetry than per-sonal fulfilment. It was as if he were part of herself, as if 'one consciousness' lived in them both. She had not been looking for a lover, nor could the poet in Kathleen ever satisfactorily marry, any more than the homosexual in Gavin (though she had been married in the past, and he was to marry in the future). She was prepared to sacrifice sexual desire to this higher love, abjure physical involve-ment, since Gavin had warned her at the outset that he could never desire her in any erotic way. 'But it was he who sought me out, he who seemed to need me,' Kathleen wrote later, 'for at that time I was strong, he was weak; I was happy, he wretched; my life had achieved some sort of stability, his was in ruins.' Kathleen felt deeply sorry for Gavin. She wanted to help and console him, and believed she possessed some sort of magical power to achieve 'strange and beautiful miracles' to that end. 'I saw him as a little brother,' she was to remember years later. 'He was not really tough, though he tried to give that impression. He was so femininely sensitive, so vulnerable, so childlike, that I saw him as a child – the *puer Aeternus*, the eternal child, the vision of nature, the world in all its fullness of beauty before adolescence. Looking back, I think my attitude to Gavin was rather condescending – unduly so.'

One of the 'strange and beautiful miracles' that occurred between them had to do with the poem of the Tree. A few days after her first meeting with Gavin, Kathleen had a vision, a kind of waking dream, of a may tree or a rowan (a mountain ash). The tree was covered in white blossom, a blackbird was perched among its branches, and a boy of about twelve was asleep at its foot. Tree, flower, fruit and bird, the very flow of life into and through the tree, was in the mind of the sleeper at the tree's foot – 'his dream raising the tree and its flowers continually into being'.

This powerful vision was inextricably associated in Kathleen's mind with her chance meeting with Gavin, as if his arrival and the vision of the Tree belonged to the same order of reality, outer and inner worlds miraculously coinciding, Heaven-sent. Shortly afterwards Kathleen departed for Cumberland, where she wrote, among other poems, her 'Northumberland Sequence' (published in her fourth collection of poems, *The Year One*, in 1952). The fifth part of the sequence described her vision of the Tree:

> The sleeper at the rowan's foot
> Dreams the darkness at the root,
> Dreams the flow that ascends the vein
> And fills with world the dreamer's brain . . .

While Kathleen was away Gavin had also been writing poetry, and he sent her some of the fruits of his labour. 'Had a long letter from Kathleen from somewhere in Cumberland,' he wrote to a friend in November, 'approving wildly of the opening stanza of the third part of my island saga. This for some reason enthused her no end – I can't think why, as it was written in my head in a taxi between Leicester Square and the studio.'

When Kathleen returned to London she showed Gavin her poem. 'Everyone will think I copied my poem from yours,' he said, and indeed the resemblance was extraordinary – not in the language or metre but in the sequence of images, which was virtually identical. Miles away from her, Gavin had, by some fantastic alchemy, written a poem which described her vision of the Tree, though in his there was no sleeper and the blackbird was an ousel.

Kathleen had an explanation. The place they had both described, she believed, was one of the archetypal objects of visionary knowledge – the archetype of Eden. 'I thought we had been greatly blessed,' she wrote, 'in meeting on that holy ground, by the Tree of Life.' Together they shared the mystery, the same vision of paradise. Gavin was part of Kathleen's Eden, its only other inhabitant. That bond, she felt, was indissoluble. Only one element of the Eden myth did she neglect to apply to them – the Fall.

For the moment, however, all was calm. Gavin did not love Kathleen in the way she loved him – indeed, he did not really love her at all. But he had enormous respect for her intellectual accomplishments, and was happy to sit at her feet, humble and anxious to learn, like an acolyte before a master. He also seems to have genuinely believed that Kathleen had special powers, magical powers perhaps, that set her apart from other people; he told me so several times. Thus it was to Kathleen that he turned for intervention to save the life of his pet bird, a golden-breasted fruit-sucker called Psuckah (pronounced 'sucker'), who had unaccountably fallen ill. 'Psuckah was moribund and infinitely pathetic,' Gavin recalled. 'I was distraught, and having phoned every bird expert in the country and administered medicine from a fountain pen, an atavistic superstition took charge and I rang up Kathleen, told her Psuckah was dying and she must employ all her occult powers. She said she would bind a spell and he would recover quickly, very quickly – and he did, apparently miraculously, in half an hour.'

Kathleen's timely spell, it seems, did not end with the ailing bird's medical recovery, but led directly to what Gavin described as the marvellous and unaccountable Metamorphosis of Psuckah. Until then the bird had behaved as one born dumb. But no longer – as Gavin recounted:

Twenty Years of Uproar is the way I should describe it. On Friday morning, having breakfasted lightly on two worms and a grape, he took a firm stance on the easel, tried a few tuning-in notes, then sang a variety of light numbers for twenty minutes. These varied from Gilbert and Sullivan to sentimental Victorian love songs. He then polished his beak and ate half a pear. At noon he awoke, bubbled slightly, and started again with greater feeling and volume, pausing to suck a grape every now and then when his throat got dry. On Saturday, the same breakfast, then after a little temperamental screeching, he settled down and sang in a low melodious voice for nearly forty minutes. And at intervals all day. The same yesterday and this morning – the morning immediately after breakfast is when there is the greatest flow of inspiration – the songs are really beautiful and with a great deal of form. The stance is also interesting – maximum size, as for sleep, with head on one side. He sings beautifully into the telephone, and I've relayed him with complete success to Kathleen, once for an uninterrupted quarter of an hour.

Magic apart, Gavin was shrewd enough to realise that Kathleen, with her wide circle of artistic and literary friends, could help enormously to advance his own career. 'Kathleen Raine, who has become a friend, came here to sit this morning and stayed to talk instead,' he wrote to Raef Payne:

> She is a fascinating person – but a discouraging person. She has the same geographical kind of background as I have (Northumbrian actually) and has the same love of mountains and the sea. Depressingly, she says I shall always feel discouraged and unproductive here, and that good work (creatively) is rare in people away from their roots.
>
> About the poets and writers she says: 'You have seen most of them now; there is no more to it than that, no glamour; just a lot of people bickering and arguing and trying to find new names for things, and then, with very few exceptions, either giving it up and wondering what it was all about or trying fitfully and going steadily downhill.'
>
> So that's all very encouraging, isn't it? I do seem to have met a lot of these people now, but for the most part I can't remember t'other from which. They seem only to share one main characteristic – a defiance of convention, or rather, a disregard of mores, particularly sexual mores. Many of them seem to live in great squalor, or nebulously at someone else's expense.

Gavin's reactions to the antics of the literary and artistic world were on the whole tolerant, if not exactly adulatory. Of the poet David Gascoyne he wrote: 'I like him enormously – he comes here quite often now, sometimes to sit, but since I have scrapped his portrait he just comes and sits down and either jabbers fascinatingly or stares in front of him in dead silence.' Of Arthur Waley, the oriental scholar and translator of Chinese classical poetry, he reported: 'He does seem a very odd person. He arrived at dinner early, left very late, and I don't think he opened his mouth once the whole time except to put food in it. When taxed by his hostess with this he said he had an insatiable curiosity about other people's lives, and was never tired of listening. He lives with a woman called Beryl de Zut (which is a nice touch).'

Roy Campbell, the South African-born poet (and occasional bull-fighter), whose poetry Gavin had long admired, was cast in a very different mould. 'Roy was a terrible brute, a freak of nature,' Gavin told me years later. 'He was all that is best and worst in a predator. He was like an animal himself in that he was entirely emotional and the question of reason never entered his arguments at all. But there was nothing phoney in Roy – there was something admirable in him.' In the autumn of 1949 Gavin reported:

> The Talk of the Town at the moment is Roy Campbell, who is now becoming like one of his own bulls, and slogging people more or less indiscriminately. The day before yesterday he got into an argument with a poet called Geoffrey Grigson, and proceeded to slap his face resoundingly. Finding this had no apparent effect, he repeated the process backhand with his knuckles. This was in a pub called the *George* in Mortimer Street. I arrived just after the slapping, R.C. still flushed with fulfilment. Now he's evidently found out it's the form of expression he really wanted all his life, cuz yesterday he got in a couple of smashing forehand drives on Louis MacNeice.

A few nights later Campbell turned up at Gavin's studio. 'He was very sober,' Gavin recalled, 'and accompanied by his wife, with whom he wants to be painted. He occupied most of the time by long and detailed descriptions of his assaults upon Stephen Spender, Geoffrey Grigson and Louis MacNeice. Who, I wonder, will the next victim be? – *NO!*'

But the most perplexing of Gavin's poet friends was Tambi-muttu. Gavin tolerated this wayward spirit with affectionate bemusement, though his patience was sometimes exhausted by his drinking, which was heavy even by Gavin's standards, and his late hours. 'Tambi has been hell undiluted,' he wrote in November. 'He came here at 2 a.m. two nights ago, stayed till 5.30 a.m. and drank an entire bottle of gin. I tried new tactics and lost my temper. An act – but it seemed to work.' Tambi was at this time preparing to return to Ceylon, and was in a state of continuous tumult which sorely tried the patience of his most forgiving friends. 'I'm in the middle of one of the stomach attacks which I thought I'd shaken off for good,' Gavin wrote, 'possibly brought on by the preparations for Tambi's departure. Words fail me – purgatory, the beaches of Dunkirk . . .'

At about this time, Gavin met Clement (short for Clemency) Glock, a slight acquaintance of Kathleen Raine's. She was the head of the scene-painting studio at the Royal Opera House, Covent Garden, a striking thirty-four-year-old woman with a marvellous head surmounted, like Brünhilde, by a veritable *casque d'or* of tumbling blond hair. Twice married – previously to the literary critic John Davenport, and currently to the music critic and Head of Music at the BBC, William Glock – Clement created waves around her wherever she went. Through his friendship with this dazzling woman, Gavin stepped into yet another, even more (for him) arcane artistic circle – the world of the London theatre and ballet. It was not a world in which he felt instinctively at home.

At the first night of Richard Strauss's *Salome* at the Royal Opera House he was moved by the music and stunned by the scenery but almost prostrated with mirth by the figure of Salome herself – 'a little dumpy figure with a huge round stomach doing a strip-tease dance'. Clement took him afterwards to a party given by the producer, Peter Brook, in the Royal Box. Gavin reported: 'dull, but lots of champagne and small things to eat. Clement looked quite unbelievably staggering in regal dress of black and red shot satin with a ruff of Elizabethan height, looking more femininely lovely than I should have imagined possible, and making all these people in their Schiaparelli models and four-hour face preparations look very silly. Arresting is the word that springs to mind in that connection. What a woman.'

Clement Glock was one of the few women with whom Gavin was able to form a normal, strong, emotional and sexual relationship. To what extent he loved her is difficult to say; but he certainly admired and coveted her. One night he took her to dinner at the London house of his friends Edward and Lavinia Renton. 'I'd always liked him very much,' Lavinia Renton recalled. 'I found him fascinating, unusual, very amusing, very eccentric, very screwy, very much a law unto himself and most undependable – one never knew whether he'd turn up for dinner or not. This par-

ticular evening he rang up and said he was sorry, he couldn't come
to dinner because he was seeing Clement Glock that evening. So
we said, why don't you bring her? And he said, no, he couldn't
do that, she'd got a husband, William. Well, we said, Edward's a
musician and William's a musician, so why don't you all come? So
they did. William arrived first and then a very long time later Gavin
drove up in his enormous Bentley and out of it jumped Clement
– bohemian, barefoot, and looking terribly dirty and unwashed. It
was a very funny and peculiar evening indeed. Clement and William
sat at opposite ends of the dining table hurling verbal hand-grenades
at each other all through dinner, and between the two of them
sat Gavin, totally pissed, sinking lower and lower in his chair in
embarrassment, till his face was almost literally in the soup.'

Around Christmas 1949 Clement went up to Monreith with
Gavin to discuss with Aymer the possibility of painting some
murals for the library. Some kind of romantic triangle seems to
have developed, and Aymer swept Clement off to Paris and checked
in at the Ritz for a weekend *à deux* with her. Gavin was mortified.
Before departing for France, Aymer had telephoned him at Rayn-
ham Hall, the Norfolk home of Gavin's friends the Marquess and
Marchioness of Townshend, who had commissioned him to paint
portraits of their children. Gavin wrote:

> Aymer virtually presented me with a pleasant little ultimatum
> – either I would have nothing more to do with this object of
> mutual attraction or he would have nothing more to do with
> me . . . and Clement had said that it wasn't a question of her
> dropping Aymer or dropping me, but that if she had to drop
> either she would drop both. So hadn't I better just swallow
> my nasty medicine and not make a fuss about it? I couldn't
> think of very much to say – an inner voice kept crying 'Why
> can't Aymer find a Clement and an object of his own – why
> must it be *my* Clement and *my* object?' I don't know what to
> do. How can I be so fond of Aymer, so grateful for all he has
> done and does for me, and so deeply resentful in my inner
> heart of any intrusion by him into my private life?

On his return from Paris, Aymer announced that he intended to
marry Clement, and even broached the subject with her husband,
William. 'Everything makes nonsense to me,' Gavin wrote on

hearing the news, 'most of all perhaps that apart from sleeping together I am expected to keep up the spoony kissing-and-petting relationship with Clement that had existed up till now. I feel even more that this morning London is an empty and desolate waste. It's only just borne in upon me how much of my time I have been spending with Clement and how extremely fond of her I had become.'

In the end, neither Gavin nor his brother was destined to enjoy Clement's company for long. Her husband soon left her for another woman, she drifted away, began another affair, became a Roman Catholic, and in her fortieth year died of a sudden brain haemorrhage. Her death was a terrible shock to Gavin. Before she soared out of his orbit, however, she bequeathed him one last favour, and introduced him to a new sitter, a brilliant and attractive young chess genius from the Continent by the name of Tomas, who with his untidy mop of blond hair bore an uncanny resemblance to her. The idea was that Tomas would be the model for the 'dreamer at the rowan's foot' in a picture Gavin would paint for Kathleen to illustrate her poem. In due course Gavin was to become as involved with Tomas as he had been with Clement, thus redoubling Kathleen's jealous torment.

Tomas and his family had come to England as refugees some years before the outbreak of the war, and with Gavin's support he went on to study mathematics at Oxford. His analysis of Gavin's complex personality in the early 1950s was penetrating and incisive:

Gavin cut a very romantic, adventurous figure in society, but this was only one side of him, for in reality he was two different people – the respectable public figure (the aristocratic painter, author, ex-Guards officer and member of learned societies) and the less respectable private one (the homosexual, the outlaw, the fearful, repressed, inhibited inner man). So though he was not a schizophrenic he often behaved like one – he separated his personality into two distinct parts and led two compartmentalised lives. Like everybody who has an unresolved emotional problem he was a role player. He always had to express himself as a duality – a personality in conflict in all areas. In front of his friends, for example, he could ham it up histrionically, but he was really a very inhibited person by nature. And though he was genuinely drawn to people from outside his class – I mean to working-class people (because he couldn't stand middle-class, suburban values) – he was very class-conscious, very aware of his background as an aristocrat, having been brought up embedded in the system, and he was anxious to protect his social reputation among his peers. For example, when he took me to the Guards Club for lunch he was afraid my accent would give my non-aristocratic background away and lead his toppy friends to believe that he was associating with someone from an inferior class. So he told me he would make out I was an Albanian prince and asked me to speak in a foreign accent so as to bolster up the disguise.

This division of his personality was crippling for him. It meant he could never experience what life was really about, never experience true joy – except perhaps on some of his explorations abroad – because only wholly integrated people can experience that. Gavin was too fearful to live in his essence, so he lived in his ideal; and, like many people in conflict, he lived as he wished to be, and not as he was. He faced life seeking rather than being – for only an integrated person can *be* – and in this sense he was a genuinely romantic figure, like a knight on a quest. The immense emotional deprivation he suffered as the result of his childhood upbringing and his public-school education meant he had to externalise his life, over-compensate. Every aspect of his outside life was role play (the Major in the Highlands, the Guards officer at the Guards Club) and many of his activities (like his studies of foreign cultures) were over-compensation. And the externalisation of his emotional life led to a mistrust of relationships with adults, so that he only felt safe in the animal world, the natural world, and would be more heartbroken at the death of a favourite animal than of his best friend. His own emotions affected him as a writer, made him less than the great writer he might have been, for there was a mixture of cruelty and sentimentality in him, of repressed violence.

All this was the product of his sexual dilemma, which was at the heart of his depressive problem. For he was sexually quite confused and inhibited, and far too fastidious to be promiscuous – I mean, he was already past the halfway point in the Biblical span of his life when I met him, yet I was only the second boy friend he had ever known. This was why he was so interested in the study of psychology and why he was so attracted to Freudianism, with its narrow concentration on sexual conflict as the source of psychic breakdown. But his Freudianism was really just a flirtation; he wasn't committed to it, it gave him no satisfaction, just some sort of explanation for his inexplicable motives, which so perplexed and depressed him. But Gavin should have been a Jungian rather than a Freudian. Jungianism was far more universal and creative, more tuned to a human being's spiritual needs. Gavin's search in nature was a genuine search for a spiritual life. To Gavin nature provided a spiritual outlet and held for him a mysticism which some people see as a spiritual need. But he was not a guru himself, he was more passive than active – he *thought* through nature rather than *was* a mystic. I remember lots of conversations with Gavin which indicated that he was evolving from Freudianism to a more power-orientated psychology – not Adlerian, more Canettian. Perhaps that was the direction he was going – looking for power in personal relations, power to form and mould young people.

He tried this with me. I was a complete fantasy of his. He wished to mould me, dog-train me, correct my English and try and improve me socially and culturally; but I recognised that and I wouldn't have it. As far as I am concerned he could be very pleasant, charming and generous; but was not a wholly integrated human being, and this prevented him from becoming the great man he might have been.

Before long Gavin's secret life came to the attention of Kathleen Raine. Her suspicions were first aroused when she visited his studio flat in Avonmore Road one evening and found a pair of woman's gloves left there the previous evening by another visitor – Clement. Wounded and dismayed, Kathleen fled the premises, then scribbled Gavin a letter – 'bitter, reproachful, and in places almost venomous – 1000 words long':

She is the fury that hell holds no other like, and I don't think that anything in the world that I could do could make her any happier except to fall in love with her – and as I can't do that, this terrifying mixture of love and hatred will follow me directly or indirectly for a long time. If I am friendly to her, I am accused of triviality; if I act more warmly than I feel, of insincerity; if I accept her offers of help with my work, of exploitation – there's nothing I can do or say that can be more than momentarily acceptable. How are we expected to find women other than frightening and bewildering when their emotions are stirred?

Eventually, in the early spring of 1950, Kathleen was apprised of the whole truth. Gavin reported her reaction:

Kathleen has been erupting with unprecedented violence, and for forty-eight hours had the inhabitants of the surrounding countryside in a state of near-panic. She rang me up in a terrible state at 8 o'clock on Monday morning to tell me that Sonia Orwell [widow of George Orwell, who had died a few weeks earlier] had spent the previous evening with her and had told her

(a) the truth about myself and Clement
(b) my real attitude to herself (Kathleen)
(c) much else

– and when asked where all this information came from had replied that Sonia had had lunch with Canetti and that he had told her all this.

Elias Canetti was a key figure in the world in which Gavin and Kathleen moved at this time. Then in his mid-forties, a Bulgarian Jew thrown out of Austria by the Nazis before the war, Canetti was a formidably talented European intellectual, the author of a classic novel, *Auto da Fé*, and a philosopher-psychologist whose main preoccupation was the question of power and its manifestation in the crowd (as mass hysteria and crowd solidarity). He was to receive the Nobel Prize for Literature in 1981. Kathleen was not alone in considering Canetti to be the most learned and the most intelligent person she had ever met, endowed with the wisdom of Socrates and a mixture of insight and compassion which gave him a genius for understanding human beings and the human condition. Canetti was a guru to many, including Gavin and Kathleen, and they would come to him for advice about all their emotional, psychological and sexual problems, which he would discuss with them with a confidentiality that was absolute.* Both Gavin and Kathleen sought Canetti's advice in the storm that now raged, as Gavin recorded immediately after:

> I did an hour's rather frantic telephoning before Kathleen arrived in a terrible state here – she was obviously suicidal and her sanity in real danger, of which Canetti had warned me. I expect you can imagine what the morning was like. It ended, after she had left in the greatest grief and bitterness, by her returning a quarter of an hour later to make a reconciliation of the least desirable and most passionate kind. During the course of the next two days, during which I felt as if I was in the process of being run over by a steam roller, both she and I had long separate talks with Canetti – who, being a wise and discerning man, pointed out that Kathleen's sanity was more important than my having an easy life, and outlined my most desirable course of action; then, moving us like puppets, did the same for Kathleen. The upshot is as good as can be expected in the midst of these raging passions – a surface reconciliation between her and Clement, and a determination on everyone's part (for how long, I wonder?) to make everything as easy as possible for everyone else.
>
> Canetti told me that this is a real near-hallucination with Kathleen, that she is a sort of goddess who must never be opposed or spurned, and that in her mind it is a necessary myth without which she would disintegrate. So she suffers more than the average person of strong emotional nature who loves someone without return – because it is an unthinkable sort of blasphemy that a goddess's love for a mortal would be unrequited.
>
> Canetti handled her extraordinarily cleverly, telling her that it would be an indignity for her to love anyone sexually, and that the only possible relationship between the goddess and the mortal was one of calm bounty. This must have appeared

---

* So absolute that he declined to talk to me about Gavin at all, telling me: 'He spoke to me about himself – I never had any permission from him to pass on what he said.'

to her as a very acceptable way out, because when I took her down to David Jones's [painter and poet, author of *In Parenthesis* and *Anabasis*] studio at Harrow, she explained to me that she had come to realise that the only reason she was in love with me was because it could never be returned, and would therefore always be bound to remain on the astral plane in which she lived.

Alas, the more I live the more I must reject Jung and accept Freud – all else seems ultimately to lead to the wildest fantasies of self-deception.

Kathleen was only temporarily placated. There were more storms, recriminations and reconciliations, more fervent pleas, urgent letters and anguished phone calls. 'When she is not hysterical she is just miserable,' Gavin noted in the early summer of 1950, 'and she is never far from tears. How terribly much responsibility is forced into one's hands, and how unfit the hands are to cope.' Time and again, both parties resorted to their mutual counsellor, the ever patient, ever thoughtful Elias Canetti. To Kathleen, Canetti spelled out the obvious – that there was another side to Gavin from the one she chose to see. There was, for example, his homosexuality, which she could never bring herself to approve or condone. There was his lack of commitment to the inner ground of imagination, to the life of the spirit – a yawning gulf between them. There was the possibility that Gavin was simply making use of her to further his own ends. There was his streak of cruelty, which co-existed with his kindness and generosity. 'Poor old Kathleen,' he once taunted her, reducing her to tears, 'you look like a fat squaw.' Once, at Paultons Square, a great spider crawled out from beneath her chair, and Gavin cried out, with a look of dismay on his face, 'A *spider*, Kathleen!' The implication was clear: the spider was the female devourer – and so, for Gavin, was Kathleen. 'I really do think Gavin was afraid of me,' she recalled. 'I couldn't believe it. At the time it was unimaginable to me that he should fear me. But I was so aware of my own suffering that it never occurred to me that I was making Gavin suffer.'

Canetti told Kathleen bluntly that Gavin did not love her. More, he did not really like her poetry. These warnings fell on deaf ears. For her, the 'real' Gavin remained the 'man of light' who could do no evil. With the help of the immortal powers, she told Canetti, she could rescue Gavin from the abyss. To which Canetti replied, with the utmost gravity: 'For you, Gavin *is* the abyss.'

Kathleen the spider: Gavin the abyss. They were an odd, doomed, tragically warring couple. Only once did Kathleen pass a night with Gavin, and even then only in a state of carnal innocence, as she later described it: 'He had been desperately wretched and asked me if I would stay; on the understanding, of course, that there should be no sexual contact between us. And to that I gladly agreed. Yet to me that act was binding as no marriage had ever bound me . . . Every night of my life, since then, I have spent alone.'

ELEVEN

The house by the sea

To be only my original self – to be the thing that is
the strongest urge in my depth – that is to lay all that
down and laugh at it and walk on a mountain alone –
really alone in a wild place. And not want to meet a
soul. And that is really true and it is the urge and the
flame and it needs no fanning.

ELIZABETH SMART, *Necessary Secrets:
The Journals of Elizabeth Smart* (1991)

Gavin had first come to stay at Sandaig, his lighthouse-keeper's
cottage on the remote and almost inaccessible Highland coast of
Wester Ross, one cloudless, bracing day in early April 1949. With a
rucksack bouncing and jingling on his back and his springer spaniel,
Jonnie, trotting in front of him, he once again picked his way down
the course of the burn towards the sea. Even at a distance, he noted,
the empty house 'wore that strange look that comes to dwellings
after long neglect . . . that secretive expression that is in some way
akin to a girl's face during her first pregnancy'. Crossing a wooden
bridge over the burn, he passed a small rowan tree on his left, went
up to the house and turned the key in the door. 'There was not a
stick of furniture in the house,' he was to write later; 'there was
no water and no lighting, and the air inside struck chill as a mor-
tuary, but to me it was Xanadu.' There was more space inside than
he remembered, with a parlour and a kitchen-living-room on the
ground floor, a scullery at the back, and two bedrooms and a landing upstairs. The entire house was panelled with the dark-varnished
pitch-pine typical of Highland houses at the turn of the century.

Gavin had brought with him no more than the bare essentials
for survival on that first visit – a bedding roll, a Primus stove and
a little fuel, some candles and tins of food. That night he slept
in the empty kitchen with his head cushioned on Jonnie's fleecy
black-and-white flank, listening to the unfamiliar sounds of this

unfamiliar place – the soft thump of rabbits' feet among the dunes at the back, the squeak of hunting bats, the piping of oyster-catchers at the sea's edge, the muffled roar of the waterfall, ceaselessly tumbling into the pool at the head of the burn's last encircling run to the sea.

When he went down to the burn to fetch water next morning, five stags stood and watched him from a primrose bank. In those days, before they were kept out by a forestry fence, these stags spent every winter low down along the Sandaig burn. 'They were in some way important to me,' Gavin recalled, 'as were the big footprints of the wildcats in the soft sand at the burn's edge, the harsh cry of the ravens, and the round seals' heads in the bay below the house.' For these creatures – and the goats and the black-faced sheep and the black Highland cattle that cropped the turf around the house and beyond the burn – were his neighbours. Such was the start of his great adventure – and the laying-claim to his Island Valley of Avalon.

Gavin's shark-fishing years had taught him that along the west-facing beaches of the West Highland coast one could find all sorts of objects that could be put to household use, and a large proportion of his early days at Sandaig was spent scouring the sea-wrack for whatever he could find washed up by the sea. Fish-boxes served as seats and tables and storage containers; fish-baskets as repositories for firewood, waste-paper and laundry; barrel tops as chopping blocks; rubber hot-water bottles as table mats and – well, hot-water bottles; planks as shelves, whisky bottles as water decanters, glass floats as ornaments, and so on to the limits of ingenuity. When it became clear that the flotsam and jetsam of the sea could not provide all that the house required, Gavin purchased from his old wartime friend, Uilleamena MacRae at Lochailort, a small load of basic items – two small chests, two kitchen tables, a bed, three kitchen chairs, and a threadbare Brussels carpet – 'really frightful furniture' – which had to be shipped in by sea at outrageous cost. Finally, in its rudimentary way, the house was habitable, smoke issued from the chimney, meals were eaten at a proper table, Gavin wrote at a proper desk and slept in a proper bed, and Avalon was occupied.

Life in Avalon was a special kind of existence – but it was never an easy one, nor was it meant to be. The West Highlands are the rainiest part of Britain, and it could, if it chose, rain for weeks on end, a deeply saturating and unremitting downpour; or it could rain violently in spasms, as a long succession of brief south-westerly squalls swept in from the ocean and lashed the house with driving horizontal rain as hard and sharp as tin-tacks. It was always a battle to keep firewood and clothing dry, and if the meths and paraffin ran out it could take up to an hour to coax a kettle to boil on a spluttering wet wood fire.

Sometimes the practical difficulties of life seemed so great that Gavin would rather creep back to bed than go downstairs and try to solve them. The livestock that grazed haphazardly around the house, for example, proved ever alert to an open door. Sometimes the goats – 'their cynical, yellow, predatory eyes bright with an ancient, egotistical wisdom' – would break in to plunder the kitchen and the last of the precious supply of loaves. Once Gavin returned to find a pregnant cow stuck tight halfway up the stairs, unable either to go up or down. It took an hour to heave the creature down and out of the house, even longer to clear up the 'positively Augean litter of dung' with which she had plastered the stairs.

Before long Gavin had explored every inch of his territory. It was the waterfall rather than the house that was the soul of Sandaig, he decided. 'If there is anywhere in the world to which some part of me may return when I am dead,' he was to write, 'it will be there.' It was not the highest of the waterfalls that marked the precipitous passage of the burn from the high ground down to the sea, but it was the most magical and mysterious. 'It emerges frothing from that unseen darkness,' Gavin wrote, 'to fall like a tumbling cascade of brilliants into a deep rounded cauldron enclosed by rock walls on three sides, black water in whorled black rock, with the fleecy white spume ringing the blackness of the pool . . . The sun reaches the waterfall for only a short time in the afternoon; it forms a rainbow over the leaping spray, and at the top of the burn between the boulders it gives to the smooth-flowing water the look of spun green glass.' Its voice was always with him, day and night. He fell asleep to it, dreamed with it, woke to it. It changed with the season, from the full-throated roar of winter to the hushed crooning of parched high summer. In spring it was alive with birdsong and bedecked with massed clusters of yellow primroses and wild blue hyacinths; in autumn it glowed with the bright red berries of the rowan trees jutting from the cracks and fissures of the rock chasm. It was here that Gavin would sometimes sit, and sometimes write, and very infrequently – for even at the

height of summer the waterfall was snow water and its tiny drops
scalded the naked skin like ice – bathe.

If the waterfall was the soul of Sandaig, Gavin felt, it was the
encircling burn and the wide-spreading sea that gave it its essential
character. The burn was Sandaig's sole source of fresh water and
essential means of survival. The sea was an immense stage where
the scene and the dramatis personae changed constantly according
to the time of day and the season of the year. From Sandaig one
could watch the violent squalls sweep in from the sea and the lurid
sunsets burn and die over Skye, and the great sea creatures – whales,
porpoises and basking shark – pass up and down the sound on their
summer procession.

So Gavin pitched his camp and planted his flag in his new Highland home. Yet for many years it was to be no more than a part-time
paradise, a temporary retreat to which he periodically withdrew
for up to three months of the year to live closer to nature or to
escape from more urgent preoccupations elsewhere.

In May 1950 Gavin allowed Kathleen to stay at Sandaig for the first
time, while he remained in London; after a few days she was joined
by her friend Winifred Nicholson. The place acted like a balm on
Kathleen. 'She's brimmingly happy,' Gavin noted with satisfaction,
'to the point of almost slipping out of this world.' She planted
herbs by the door, tended the rose on the wall, brought home the
natural treasures of the place – scallop-shells, mussel-pearls, wood
carved by the waves – and sat with her back against the rowan tree
that grew by the house, staring up into the boundless blue windy
sky. 'What a miracle,' she was to write of her thoughts then, 'what
unimaginable blessedness to be here and now at the place on earth
I most desire to be; by Gavin's rowan.'

Later she wrote: 'Living in his house, seeing his sky over me,
the spaces of his sea, those near hills and far mountains which were
the regions of his imagination . . . I lived like Psyche in the house
of love, alone yet not alone. In the pool of his waterfall I bathed,
on his beaches I gathered shells and stones written with the strange
language of the sea.' It was as if, in Gavin's absence, he wished her
to experience his world for him, or so she felt. 'I saw for him,
touched and smelled and heard all for him, as if every wheeling
bird, every radiance of sun or moon on water, every sound of
wind or sea or waterfall I was hearing and seeing and touching

and knowing for him; or for both of us, perhaps; for the "one consciousness". I felt it my task to enrich and transmute for him his world into poetry.'

This she did. Sandaig was the inspiration of many of her poems – most notably, perhaps, 'The Marriage of Psyche' in her collection *The Year One*. The poem, which was actually written at Sandaig, was in two parts. The first stanza of the second part, 'The Ring', contains the phrase with which Gavin Maxwell's name was to be inextricably associated:

> He has married me with a ring, a ring of bright water
> Whose ripples travel from the heart of the sea,
> He has married me with a ring of light, the glitter
> Broadcast on the swift river . . .

The calm that Kathleen brought back to London did not last long. A series of contretemps, each more furious than the last, escalated the conflict in her relationship with Gavin. The most lethal occurred during the winter, when Gavin, Sandaig-bound, gave Kathleen a lift in his Bentley as far as Winifred Nicholson's house in Cumberland. It was dark and snowing heavily by the time they reached Greta Bridge, and though they were still some way from their destination they decided it would be prudent to spend the night at the local hotel before resuming their journey in the morning. In a letter to a friend Gavin described the catastrophic dinner that ensued:

> Up to date K. and I had been getting on quite nicely with each other; but after dinner she seized the opportunity to show me a brand new diary, the last entry being only twenty-four hours old, consisting of a detailed analysis of my sexual impulses. To do her justice the analyses were mainly admiration, but the fact that she was keeping such a diary after having given her solemn word that she wouldn't put me in a rage which I found difficult to conceal. Anyway, when I went to bed she came as far as the door of my room imploring me to kiss her goodnight, in plain hearing of two servants, and just wouldn't go away. All appallingly awkward and embarrassing. Eventually I had to leave my room and only return to it after she'd gone. After that she apparently sat up all night writing a gigantic letter to me which she delivered at breakfast.

The next morning Kathleen was still terribly upset and distressed. That night she had had a dream about Sandaig. She dreamed that the house and its rowan tree were barred to her by a high wooden palisade, and the beauty of the place was all destroyed. Perhaps the palisade was a symbol for her of the wall built around Eden after the Fall. Certainly a great rift had now opened up between her and the object of her love. For Kathleen her diary was a record of things that were sacred to her, the raw material for poetry; to Gavin it represented a dangerous indiscretion and a betrayal of trust. Some years later, following an even deeper estrangement from Gavin, she hurled all her diaries into the waters of the River Eden, in Cumberland.

Those drowned diaries had presaged the beginning of the Fall. Nothing could be quite the same again between Gavin and Kathleen. The direction of Gavin's life was already changing, and he was beginning to move outwards and away from London life and London people.

After more than three years of wrestling with his painting, he had finally abandoned all hope of achieving any great skill or distinction as a portrait painter, and felt increasingly guilty at charging high fees from the few people who commissioned their portraits from him. During this period his financial predicament had, if anything, grown more acute. 'I am living from hand to mouth and from day to day,' he recorded in mid-1950. 'An hour's letter writing a day keeps the more pressing creditors quiet.' Gavin's disintegration was observed by his friend Stanley Peters, an interior designer: 'He was drinking heavily – easily a bottle of Scotch a day. When he was sober he could be highly amusing, but when he got drunk he could turn into a savage. And by now he was really living in a shit house – he'd even eat caviar out of a toothpaste-squeezer.'

To make ends meet Gavin was forced to sell, bit by bit, his books, his clothes, his furniture, even his bed, so that eventually all that was left in his studio flat was a mattress, three hard chairs and some empty bookshelves. Some while later he was even obliged to part with his pride and joy, his magnificent 3½-litre Bentley, buying in its place a modest but curious Hotchkiss – he would never stoop to owning a run-of-the-mill mass-production vehicle – an unusual and unreliable oddity that looked and sometimes behaved like a large green grasshopper. Only an annual allowance from his brother Aymer kept him functioning – together with a munificent birthday present of a year's rent on his studio, also from Aymer.

But money problems, Gavin believed – speaking with a certain loftiness as the brother of a baronet and the grandson of a duke – were not the real problems of life, merely tiresome conundrums. The true threats to happiness and fulfilment lay elsewhere. In his thirty-seventh year, for example, he had no real home – no place to which he could truly give that name, no real mate, no family of his own. The idea of Elrig as his home had faded imperceptibly during the war years, and finally died when his mother left it. 'It was never the same after we left Elrig – that really was a home and it has always been odd to think of strangers in all the rooms.' Nor did he belong in any real sense to a community, for he worked and had his being as an aristocrat amongst the bourgeoisie, and felt himself a pariah in conventional society, and at odds with his own aristocratic kith and kin, whose inherited wealth he could not emulate and whose stiff, old-fashioned mores he could not share, mocking them from afar while at the same time half wishing he could be at one with them.

As for his own immediate family, his relationship with them was a complex and increasingly detached one. He remained fond of his mother and saw her frequently once he (and she) had moved to London; and she continued to darn his socks in her flat in Eaton Place until he was well into his forties. He had little rapport with his unmarried sister, Christian, and seldom saw her even when she moved into a studio not far from his own in London; for him she remained 'that odd Bolshevik painter', and he would tease her when she went on protest marches, asking her: 'Why don't you go and live in Russia?' He did not have much in common with his brother Eustace either, a gentleman farmer whose talents diversified in a number of practical directions (he later turned out to be a first-class film cameraman, and invented a successful 'car-wash' for double-decker buses), and the only one of the siblings to produce children (a daughter, Diana, and a son, Michael, who was eventually to inherit the family title). But Eustace was straightforward and commonsensical, in a way that neither Gavin nor Aymer could ever be, and Gavin for his part regarded him as a figure of fun and treated him unkindly at times.

It was with Aymer that Gavin formed the closest family relation-

ship. Throughout his life Gavin continued to view his eldest brother
with a volatile mixture of envy and admiration, rivalry and respect.
Aymer had inherited the Maxwell baronetcy in 1937 on the death
of his aged grandfather, Sir Herbert Maxwell, and used a portion
of his inheritance to 'bank' Gavin after the failure of the shark-
fishing venture. Raef Payne, who knew them both, was a keen
observer of the complicated dynamics of the brothers' relationship:

> They were *very* close, yet (in adult life at least) often at odds.
> They shared the jokes and mimicries and the whole mythology
> of childhood – and of course, as they came to recognise (quite
> when I wouldn't know), they shared sexual inclinations *and*
> Clement Glock. And they were always trying to emulate and
> outdo each other. When Aymer did up Monreith grandly,
> Gavin had to acquire a palatial flat in Glenapp Castle and do
> it up even more grandly. When Gavin became an 'artist'
> (painter/poet), Aymer became a film script-writer and pro-
> ducer, and shot a feature film called *Another Sun* on location
> in Morocco in the early 1950s. Possibly Aymer's eventual
> withdrawal to the Greek island of Euboea was his answer to
> Gavin's 'Avalon' at Sandaig. Gavin used to speak of Aymer
> with resentment sometimes (Aymer had all the money and
> Gavin was for a time largely dependent on him, though often
> grumbling that Aymer was so mean), yet also with affection
> and regard, and when they were together they were often like
> children, helpless with giggles.

Yet, well into adulthood Gavin felt it desperately necessary to live
as apart from his family – even from Aymer – as he could, and
anyone who lumped him together with his siblings was in for a
shock. To a woman friend who once made just such an unforgiv-
able gaffe he sent a scorching reproof:

> You must never say 'the whole Maxwell clan'. It's about the
> most goading thing you can say to me. All my childhood it
> was 'Aymer-and-you', and after I grew up it was 'You-and-
> Aymer' or 'you Maxwells'. I don't identify myself with my
> family, and perhaps least of all with Aymer, and I hate being
> grouped with him either in approbation or derogation. When

you've done as much as I have to get free from the bracketing,
by leading a quite separate and very different life, it's more
than galling to find it all in vain . . . An ungracious remark,
and one which I hope you will repent.

As for Aymer, his view of Gavin was in some ways a mirror-image
of Gavin's view of him. Aymer was always deferring to Gavin's
superior gifts. He was a talented, sensitive, creative man in his own
right, and even embarked on a literary career himself following his
venture into films. He started writing before Gavin, but when he
heard that Gavin was writing a book he tore his own up; and when
his translation of a Montherlant play was not staged he turned his
back on the arts and lived on his investments, a rather sad and
disillusioned intellectual *manqué* who never fulfilled his potential. 'I
envy you very much your literary career,' he was to write some
years later when Gavin was rich and famous, 'not so much for the
fame and laurels but for the fact of having something to do worth
doing.'

Now, immured among the sooty streets of London in the depths
of dull despair, human society itself and the mire of human relationships grew intolerable to Gavin, and he dreamed again of his Island
Valley of Avalon. 'Oh take me away, take me away to an island,'
he yearned on one such occasion, 'I'm sick of this jungle.' He was
a misfit in the metropolis, he realised. He could no longer abide
dressing up in a dinner jacket to dine in other people's houses, and
sometimes when he did so he arrived the worse for whisky and sat
speechless at table. It was at Monreith in late November 1950 that
he saw his predicament with blinding clarity, and realised that perhaps he had driven himself into a cul de sac.

It is glorious here – frost and bright sunshine and the old
disturbing sounds of wildfowl wings in the dusk that make
me feel that I have forsworn a whole life that was perhaps the
only possible one. I think we should not be taught to see
beyond the limited worlds (islands?) into which each of us is
born. I think my world was really that of birds and animals,
and the realisation that it was a limited world, a stage on
the journey, should not have made me want to leave it. I
think I only understand people or love them when I see

them translated into the terms of an unhappy animal species, with difficulties opposed to all their activities and aspirations. I know I'm an animal, and rather a messy one, but I can only like myself as that. If I have a soul it is perpetual and not subject to my endorsement or self-hatred; the best thing it does is to love other people and use me in complicated or uncomplicated ways to express it. And if that love is a placation for guilt, does it matter?

I went for a walk in the woods today – all these thousands of birds, some going to roost, some feeding, some being killed by hawks – why should that Psuckah that died last week mean *anything*, or why should I stand miserably before one blackbird, sleek on a great festoon of berries, that I took to be glutted and stupefied and then realised was blinded and bleeding?

Oh how much we need the fish the fox the toad and the larks to give us back what men take away.

The London years had matured and deepened him, and also saddened him. Now they were exhausted. But ahead lay new horizons and a new career.

TWELVE

Writing man

I have grown up, hand on the primal bone,
Making the poem, taking the word from the stream,
Fighting the sand for speech, fighting the stone.
                DOM MORAES, 'Autobiography', in
                            A Beginning (1957)

Increasingly it was now the pen rather than the paint-brush through which Gavin was to channel the flow of his creative energy. He never had any formal education in English literature, and by his own confession he had neither seen nor read any Shakespeare, and precious little else from the standard works had crossed his path – no Milton, no Pope, no Jane Austen or even Charles Dickens. But at school he had learned to write lucidly and precisely, and with his mother's encouragement during the protracted convalescence following his serious illness in late adolescence he had become impassioned by lyric poetry, especially romantic high Victorian.

Writing had always come naturally to him, and even during the hurly-burly of the shark-fishing days he had found time to write at least two extended short stories and begun at least two novels, of which only fragments survive. In his apprentice period as a portrait painter he had read voraciously and haphazardly, and spent long evenings copying out his favourite passages from writers as wide-ranging as Thomas Mann and Kenneth Grahame, Descartes and T.E. Lawrence. From such eclectic studies he ingested many of the fundamentals of the prose writer's art – rhythm, narrative pace, paragraph structure, diction and dialogue.

Later, in London, he had taken to rereading the works of Evelyn Waugh, his favourite modern prose writer and the one who influenced him most, during lonely meals at the 'dead cow house' (as he called the cheap Cypriot restaurant near his studio at Olympia). From Waugh he learned a number of tricks of the trade – how to handle the semi-colon, for example, particularly in building up long extended sentences made up of layers of subordinate clauses; and how to enliven dull but necessary passages by writing them in blank verse disguised as prose, the regular beat of the subliminal iambic pentameter carrying the reader through with the minimum of effort. Conversely, he was to incorporate some of his early verse in the form of prose in his later books, a notable example being his description of the wild swans on Skye in *Ring of Bright Water*. But it was poetry that was Gavin's first and last love, and he became excited by prose only when it came near to the domain of poetry, more especially the kind of poetry he himself preferred – romantic, introspective, melancholy, nature mystical. He had already acquired a taste for more recent poets such as Hopkins and Yeats, and under Kathleen Raine's tutelage he began to renew his interest in the works of contemporary poets, including William Empson, Louis MacNeice, David Gascoyne and George Barker.

On 28 January 1950 the *New Statesman* published the first of Gavin's poems to appear in print – indeed the first writing of any kind to be published under his own name, as his pre-war journalism had been unsigned. Entitled 'Poem from a Sequence', this was actually the 'Rowan Tree' poem that had so amazed Kathleen Raine by its inexplicable similarity to her own 'Rowan Tree' poem in her 'Northumberland Sequence'. It had found its way into the hands of the Literary Editor of the *New Statesman*, Janet Adam-Smith, at a private London dinner also attended by the eminent poet and art critic Herbert Read, and by Gavin himself, shortly before Christmas 1949. Gavin reported of the occasion:

Unfortunately I was just a little tiddly. However, no one seems to have noticed anything except a rather marked silence during the latter part of the evening . . . After I'd gone Kathleen handed over to Janet Adam-Smith the revised version of 'the power that wheels the eagle's wing', and two days later I got a letter from her which made me feel so conceited that I can't, no simply can't, resist quoting it. 'You say you are diffident, an amateur; I can only say that, as a hardened reader and chooser of poetry, I haven't for a long time met a poem that I was so sure I liked straight away, and so sure I would like in six months' time.' That letter kept me buzzing the remaining couple of days I was in London.

Janet Adam-Smith was Gavin's crucial guide through the London literary maze. She took to him at once. 'In appearance he struck one as so slight,' she remembered. 'But he had a look of breeding, a touch of *hauteur* in his looks and manners, the *hauteur* that goes with great diffidence. He was so diffident that he would walk out of any social gathering he did not feel at ease in.'

Gavin's literary friends applauded him warmly after the poem's publication, and Roy Campbell, a literary editor in his own right, said that he would like to publish Gavin's next poetic work. Emboldened by this reception, Gavin submitted a second poem, 'The Caves of Mingulay', which was published in the *New Statesman* on 15 July 1950, and several other poems, including 'Island Poem' and 'The Scapegoat', were published in the same magazine over the next couple of years. Gavin began to feel that he was being taken seriously in an unfamiliar world.

But as he had no money, and as few people can make a living by writing poetry, his mind began to turn more and more to the sharking adventure that was now behind him. Here, he realised, was a ready-made subject for a book that was waiting to be written – a book it would be better to write now than in the dim future. He had always known he would write a book one day. 'I had envisaged it as a projection of what I considered to be my more serious interests,' he recalled, '– a learned contribution to the study of animal behaviour, perhaps; or, as that interest had led inevitably to the study of human behaviour, a novel that should amaze by its insight and penetration.'

But the combination of chance and necessity changed all that. With the encouragement of friends like Kathleen Raine and an ex-SOE comrade, Simon Ramsay, Earl of Dalhousie, he repaired to Sandaig in the summer of 1950, and there, in the familiar surroundings of mountain and sea, he began to work out a synopsis for a book about the Soay venture. When it was finished he took it to the writer and poet John Pudney, who was a director of Evans, the only large publishing firm Gavin knew, confident that he would publish the book if anybody would. But he would not, and explained at some length why such a book would not sell. Deeply despondent, Gavin returned to Sandaig, and being virtually penniless he devoted himself to gathering shellfish and snaring rabbits for food, dreaming of what he might have done with his inheritance if he had not lost it in the shark fishery.

The condemned synopsis, meanwhile, lay crumpled and stained

in a drawer – at first a reproach, and then a challenge. The stimulus that was to push the idea a stage further was as bitter as it was unexpected. Gavin had been searching the shore below the house for some piece of flotsam that could be conveniently turned into a bread board when he spied the projecting edge of a barrel top – white, smooth and sea-worn – half-buried in the sand. He pulled it from the shingle and read the letters 'I.S.S.F.' – Island of Soay Shark Fisheries. 'It had all the nostalgia of a *carnet de bal* tied with faded ribbon; it brought so many half-forgotten scenes so vividly to my mind that I began the book the next day.'

Scribbling away with his fountain pen at the rickety kitchen table in the pitch-pine panelled kitchen-living-room at Sandaig, Gavin began to cover ream after ream of foolscap writing paper in a neat hand as he turned his *Sea Leopard* diary and his undimmed memories of Hebridean seascapes and sharking derring-do into the diamond-hard images of a superlative narrative. When he needed a change of scene or a word of encouragement or advice, he would visit his former shipmates in the neighbourhood, including his ex-harpoon-gunner, Tex Geddes, who was then living near Mallaig. 'Gavin came to stay at my home at Glasnacardoch Lodge,' Tex recalled. 'Dammit, he was almost living there. He complained that he was broke, so I told him I was broke too, but his broke and my broke were two entirely different things. Well, using my typewriter and my paper and my coffee he wrote some of *Harpoon at a Venture* in Glasnacardoch Lodge. In fact, *we* wrote *Harpoon*. He didn't know he could write and he found it a hell of a chore. But he got three chapters written and then he went off to London to try and get a contract for it.'

This time Gavin was lucky. He showed his manuscript to Janet Adam-Smith, who recommended that he take it forthwith to a sympathetic publisher who ran an enterprising new publishing house of his own. 'I went to see Rupert Hart-Davis yesterday afternoon,' Gavin wrote to Raef Payne at the end of November 1950. 'It was all very like a dream, and everything exactly the opposite of how I would imagine publishers behave. They have, to cut a long story short, accepted the book without demur, and are sending me tomorrow a contract – and an advance of £100. Cor – the fools! . . . Someone pinch me.' Gavin knew he had committed himself to a year's hard labour. 'Immediately,' he recalled, 'I began to doubt the future of the finished work: the dread of failure that lies like a coiled worm at the heart of all who are ambitious. But when during that week I spoke to others about this fear, they said, in effect, "Don't worry . . . Just write it."'

So Gavin settled down to write, sometimes at Sandaig, sometimes at the houses of friends, sometimes in his studio flat in London. Still unsure of his literary talent, he would enlist the nearest available friend to comment and advise. 'He would ring me up at all hours of the day or night,' Kathleen Raine recalled, 'and ask me to go over and help with the latest couple of pages he'd been working on. He used to read them out to me and I'd say, Oh it's terribly good – and it was, he had a gift. Then he'd bite his pencil and prowl up and down and say, "What shall I write next, Kathleen?"' She was still sufficiently Tambi's 'great poet', she reckoned, for her criticism to be valuable to him. But writing, she perceived, was not Gavin's true *métier* – merely a means to an end. Years later she was to enlarge on this theme:

He had a wonderful gift for vivid descriptive writing. But this was secondary to his real gift – his gift of actually living his imaginative life in action. Yes, he was literate, he could write very well, but I would never rate Gavin as primarily a writer but as primarily the man who did these things, a man of action. He was a highly imaginative, deeply sensitive person who lived his inner adventure by means of his outer adventures – that was his form of self-expression. To him the imaginative achievement was the living of it, not the writing about it. And making money was not Gavin's line of country. Making money was quite incidental to Gavin the knight. It was the wild adventure – he was Captain Ahab after the white whale. But you can't win against the white whale. For all the people who read him he represented their heart's desire – they would love to have lived that life, had those adventures, sailed round Soay, hunted the great creatures of the deep as he had done. But Gavin's first book (like all the ones that followed) wasn't about his inner quest, it was about what he chose to make a story of, what he chose to present to his public, the mask he presented to the world. He saw the world with an observant eye, he had the gift of mimicry, he could tell a funny anecdote and describe people and their funny ways and idiosyncrasies. But he saw all this from the outside, not the inside. The inner life was what he chose to pour out late at night after a bottle of whisky, and it was very different – not what he chose to put in his books.

Gavin was unprepared for the sheer slog of book writing. 'Pressure, pressure . . .' he wrote to a friend in May 1951. 'I have been working like a nigger (averaging nearly 2000 words a day) but I can't seem to catch up with my target in chapters, and all letters lie unanswered.' By now his work-in-progress had been tracked down by Gwenda David, a London-based talent scout for the big American publishing firm of Viking Press, and as a result Gavin had recently signed a contract for a US edition. Gwenda David soon became another of his confidantes and literary coaches, and before long was as much the mesmerised target of Gavin's routine of midnight calls for attendance and salvation, both professional and personal, as Kathleen Raine:

> Gavin would ring me up at three or four in the morning and say, 'If you're not round here within half an hour I'll kill myself.' So I'd get up and get dressed and ring for a cab and then I'd go round to his flat and find him drunk and lonely and needing someone to talk to, and I'd sit with him and he'd talk to me over a bottle of whisky about everything under the sun till morning came. He made very great demands on people. He could be wonderful, horrid, funny, bitchy, nasty and nice – all those things. But I liked him enormously. I was fascinated by him, by his beautiful voice and those sunken, cold blue eyes, and I was attracted by the life he led – the loneliness of his life and the way he would just go off into the hills whenever he felt like it. He was a very tormented soul and he drove like a maniac. Once when he was driving madly along like a rocket I asked him whether he preferred men or women, and he thought about that for a long time and then said: 'I'd rather not answer that.' He'd been going out with Clement Glock before then, and now he was going out with a youth called Tomas, whom Clement had introduced to him. He was a very mixed-up man.

By the late autumn of 1951 the text of Gavin's shark book was written – a vivid and impulsive medley of taut physical adventure, sudden riotous fun, poetry, metaphysics, marine biology, boyish nostalgia, gaucherie and hard-learned wisdom about human life.

Even before it was published *Harpoon at a Venture* was being acclaimed as one of the year's outstanding books. 'I don't think I like being on the verge of fame or infamy or whatever it is,' Gavin wrote to Raef Payne in the week before publication. 'Yesterday I was interviewed by three newspapers, and at the end of the time my hands were trembling like leaves and thin trickles of smoke coming out of my ears. (I was asked what two novels since the war had made the most impression on me, so I said *Auto da Fé* and *Father Goose*). Come on boys, let's form a square and pick up sides.'

Harpoon at a Venture was published in Britain on 26 May 1952, to universal critical acclaim. *The Times* hailed Gavin as 'a man of action who writes like a poet' – praise to which he was to cling for the rest of his writing life. Comparing it with *Robinson Crusoe*, Louis MacNeice wrote in the *New Statesman*: 'The book is pregnant with symbols and, unlike many other pioneers, he is deeply aware of the symbolism.'

The reviewers on the influential BBC radio programme 'The Critics' were unstinting in their praise of the poetry, the vivid and memorable imagery, the beauty and the horror of a magnificent adventure story written by 'a really master writer'. But they went beyond the printed page and singled out the personality of the author behind it as well – the first, but by no means the last, hint of the cult of the personality with which Gavin's readers were to greet this and his subsequent writings: 'He has the zest, the courage, the uncalculating enthusiasm and generosity, above all the panache of the non-professional, the highly intelligent inexpert. He's a youthful version of the White Knight . . . a highly sympathetic and attractive character in a world of glum and narrow experts, and the White Knight's spirit is a noble and a chivalrous one. It is as an exposition of an adventure of the spirit that *Harpoon at a Venture* is most worth reading, most exciting. We respond to an individual who tries to beat the lot.' *Harpoon* was selected as a Book Society Choice, and as the *Daily Mail* Book of the Month.

In September 1952 the book was published by Viking in the United States under the abbreviated title *Harpoon Venture*, and foreign-language editions appeared in various European countries. The book's reception was as rapturous abroad as it had been at home. 'A great dream safe between the covers of this book', wrote the *New York World Telegram*: 'Not since I discovered Conrad have I felt the poetry and terror of the sea as I did in reading this.' And in Paris the periodical *Carrefour* declared: '*Voilà un écrivain.*'

Few new authors can ever have got off to a more spectacular start. In Britain the first edition of 25,000 copies quickly sold out, and the book was reprinted. But with his first royalty statement not due for another six months, there was little immediate reward in prospect for Gavin, who was as broke as ever. This struck him as an unfair anomaly, and reinforced his view of publishers as authority figures to be harried and suborned – exactly as his superior officers in the army had been. Rupert Hart-Davis was the first publisher to be on the receiving end of Gavin Maxwell's authorial importunity, as he was wearily to recall: 'In all my years of publishing, Gavin Maxwell was one of the most tiresome authors I ever had to deal with. He used to ring up every day, asking how many copies of *Harpoon at a Venture* had been sold the previous day. This I could tell him, but when he asked how much they represented in royalties, and could he call for the money in cash, it became a daily nuisance. He used to arrive in an enormous car which he had great difficulty in parking. I asked him why he used such a huge car in London and he said: "It gives me a feeling of power."'

There was one unexpected development following the publication of *Harpoon at a Venture*. Another shark hunter, P. FitzGerald O'Connor, had written a book about his own sharking venture, and in an attempt to debunk *Harpoon* he had conspired with Gavin's former rival Tony Watkins to persuade some of Gavin's old shipmates to bring an injunction against it. Gavin sued him for libel. Among the key prosecution witnesses was Tex Geddes, Gavin's former harpoon-gunner, who recalled:

I was on Soay when the matter came to litigation and had to come down to the Law Courts in London for the trial. Gavin's counsel was Gerald Gardiner Q.C., who later became Lord Chancellor. O'Connor had Melford Stevenson, who became a judge. Melford Stevenson was able to bully Gavin, who was a bit more gentle than me, but I was a plain-speaking fisherman, so we had a hell of a carry-on. I told Melford Stevenson he didn't know a thing about sharks and couldn't even tell his arse from his elbow. I had the court in uproar. When Melford

Stevenson suggested I was a liar I told him I'd take his trousers down and wallop him if he said that again in court. I'm sure Mr Justice Slade enjoyed himself enormously.

Anyway, some letters were produced in court which proved beyond doubt that O'Connor had been involved in a conspiracy with Watkins against Gavin and his book, and Mr Justice Slade read one out which said: 'We will have to debunk this bastard somehow.' At this point Gavin's mother stepped in and told Gavin she wasn't going to have the family name dragged through the mud. So Gavin announced that he would stop the case if O'Connor wrote a letter of apology to *The Times*. And he did. And that's how the case was settled.

Abandoning his faltering career as a society portrait-painter, Gavin now set up shop as a full-time author. Almost immediately he was confronted with the problem of what to write next. He had used up the one ready-made real-life story he had in him, and he began to cast around for a new idea. He remembered a great-great-great aunt who had run away and married a 'shady Sicilian', and decided to set off on an exploratory foray round Sicily in search of her story. Rupert Hart-Davis was less than enthusiastic. 'Maxwell asked me if I would give him £500 as an advance against his next book. I asked him why he wanted what was in those days such a large sum, and he said that he needed to buy a Jeep to go and look for his aunt in Sicily. This seemed such a dubious assignment that I told him I couldn't tie up so much money in it.' Undaunted, Gavin approached the small Catholic firm of Burns & Oates, publishers to the Holy See, and persuaded them to advance the money he needed for the project. In the autumn of 1952, knowing little about Sicily and not a word of Italian, he set off in a Land Rover he had 'borrowed' from the Monreith farm estate, taking with him a research assistant by the name of Mark Harwood, a talented linguist.

No record remains of Gavin's first trip to the deeply divided and Mafia-dominated island that was to preoccupy him for more than a decade to come. What is known is that he failed to discover any trace of his wayward ancestor, but stumbled instead on an infinitely more violent and intriguing tale, centring on the dramatic life and mysterious death of the legendary secessionist leader and bandit hero Salvatore Giuliano, who had been betrayed and killed only two years previously.

Giuliano was a good-looking, charismatic, ruthless and violent idealist from the hill village of Montelepre in Sicily's desperately poor north-west. He was only twenty-seven at the time of his death, but his seven-year campaign of banditry and guerrilla warfare against the carabinieri had already gained him world-wide notoriety and the veneration of the Sicilian poor, who saw him as a latter-day Robin Hood and supporter of their cause. In 1950 Giuliano was finally hunted down and shot in circumstances of great mystery; and though it was almost certainly the collusion of the police and corrupt local leaders with the all-powerful Sicilian Mafia that brought about his death, somehow it turned out that it was his trusted cousin and co-chieftain, Gaspare Pisciotta, then serving a life sentence for murder in Palermo, who was suspected of killing him.

It was a sensational story, and contained many elements that appealed to Gavin's taste for exotic high drama: the archetypal romantic hero who takes on the world and falls from eminence through the treachery of those he trusts – an allegory, almost, of the way Gavin saw himself and the pattern of his own life. He returned to England convinced he had found a winner, and began to prepare himself for his challenging new task – a difficult, possibly dangerous investigative assignment behind the lines, so to speak, of the feudal, closed and treacherous society of the Sicilians.

THIRTEEN

The Sicilians

> To wait for one who never comes,
> To lie in bed and not to sleep,
> To serve well and not to please,
> To have a horse that will not go,
> To be sick and lack the cure,
> To be a prisoner without hope,
> To lose the way when you would journey,
> To stand at a door that none will open,
> To have a friend who would betray you,
> These are the ten pains of death.
>
> GIOVANNI FLORIO, *Second Fruits* (1591)

Through 1953 and into 1954 Gavin's time was largely occupied in unravelling Giuliano's extraordinary story in Sicily. Tomas accompanied him on his first trip back to the island, which was mainly spent in tracking down people connected with the story. Later, as he began to integrate himself into the local society around Giuliano's home village of Montelepre, he began to rely heavily on the intelligence services of a bright and able young barber's apprentice by the name of Giuseppe M., who with Gavin's support and encouragement was to rise to become a radical political leader in Sicily's capital city of Palermo some years later. Gavin operated on a shoe-string during these long Sicilian summers spent in investigative research. He drove a battered Land Rover, lived in a tiny tent outside the crumbling walls of the town cemetery where Giuliano lay buried, and subsisted on a diet of bread, cheese and tomatoes, and the windy concoction known as 'Maxwell's Bean Feast' (a brew-up of canned baked beans, canned Italian tomatoes, Italian sausage, Parmesan cheese and garlic).

It was desperately hot in Sicily in August 1953, and during the heat of the day there was no shade anywhere. Inside Gavin's tent it was hellish – cramped, stifling, full of flies and ants. Outside was no better, for he was an object of fascination to a crowd of local rubbernecks who came to stare at the strange *Inglese*, talk to him, and smoke his English cigarettes. They would even follow him into his tent to watch him. The only place where Gavin could find shelter from the heat – and some respite from the people – was in the tomb in which Salvatore Giuliano lay at rest in a white marble sarcophagus.

After a while Gavin moved to a more congenial site, pitching camp on a terrace overlooking the town, where there was shade beneath the olive trees and prickly pears. The people still came to stare at him, but now they brought figs and grapes as presents. Gavin could cope with these small informal groups, and with the confidential conversations with people close to the story he was writing. It was the Sicilian crowds – the alien herd of which he could never become a part – which unnerved him, especially in the streets of Castellamare del Golfo, the sirocco-dusted little waterside town some twenty miles across the plain from Montelepre, where he pitched a new camp above a Saracen fort overlooking the harbour. 'I was the rifler of the tomb,' he was to write. 'I felt the vengeance of its guardians upon me.' It was not so bad in the daytime when he could hide behind his dark glasses; but after dark, he wrote, 'I glanced unarmoured and vulnerable from stare to stare; the curious, the hostile, and the blank'.

Gradually, as he moved from one informant to another, Gavin began to feel confident that he had got the scattered pieces of his strange story into a coherent picture. But, just when he thought he had solved the major mysteries, he met a man who had inside information about the death of Giuliano, and realised to his dismay that the account he had laboriously pieced together was founded on sand.

Where on earth did the truth lie, Gavin wondered? And who would reveal it to him? Perhaps the simplest thing would be to go to Palermo and put a direct question to Giuliano's cousin Gaspare Pisciotta, who was serving a life sentence in the prison there. But even inside the prison Pisciotta was heavily guarded, and no meeting was possible without the written authority of the Italian Minister of Justice. Five months later Pisciotta was dead, poisoned by a massive dose of strychnine smuggled into his cell with his medicine – murdered to keep his mouth shut at his impending trial for the murder of Giuliano. Gavin was at an impasse. To the essential question – who killed Giuliano? – he would have to add another –

who killed Pisciotta? Did an elusive high-ranking figure give the orders and lurk behind the puzzles that bedevilled the story? Gavin would have to come back to Sicily and begin all over again.

All this was a time-consuming and tortuous business, and as the months passed by his publishers, Burns & Oates, grew more and more insistent that Gavin either deliver the book he had promised them or pay back the money they had advanced him. Early in 1954 the dispute came to a head. In desperation, Gavin decided it was time he put his literary career on a more stable footing. His first step was to acquire a literary agent, and his choice fell on Graham Watson, a partner in the leading London agency of Curtis Brown. On 15 March 1954 Watson approached Mark Longman, chairman of the publishers Longmans, Green & Co, with an urgent proposition. His author, Gavin Maxwell, wished to change publishers. If Longmans agreed to advance £1000, Maxwell would pay off Burns & Oates and place his new book at Longmans' disposal, along with an option on all his future books.

A few days later Gavin met Mark Longman for the first time. Longman was a discerning and accommodating publisher who was patiently building up an outstanding list of highly talented but often quirky authors, and he was used to dealing with awkward individualists like Gavin. 'I spent the morning with him,' Longman noted in a memo to his fellow directors, 'and the material which he has gathered turns out to be even more interesting and exciting than I had imagined. I have no doubt at all that Maxwell will produce a thoroughly good book with a very considerable sales potential. The *Giuliano* book is not only extremely exciting but also interesting and important politically. I at once informed Graham Watson that we wanted to go ahead.' So began a long and fruitful partnership that was to endure for the remainder of Gavin's career.

Not long afterwards, in the early summer of 1954, Gavin was introduced to Princess Margaret by a mutual friend, Robin McEwen, a talented artist as well as a brilliant lawyer and future heir to one of Scotland's leading Catholic baronetcies, who had been his junior counsel during the O'Connor libel case. 'She was a marvellous woman,' one of Gavin's closest friends recalled, 'and very much a catch. Gavin really quite fancied her, in fact I'd go as far as to say he was almost in love with her, or so Elias Canetti claimed. But he only went out with her three times, and it was never more than an utterly formal, totally innocent romance.' On the first occasion Gavin escorted the Princess to the theatre (*Hippo Dancing*, starring Robert Morley) with Robin McEwen and his fiancée Brigid. At the end of the evening they all went to Clarence House, where Princess Margaret played the piano and sang, and then repaired to Gavin's studio flat, where they sang 'Ye Banks and Braes' and other songs into the early hours. Not long afterwards Gavin went with her to a ball, and even danced with her – the first time he'd danced with anyone since his youth, and the last. Kathleen Raine was perplexed by this turn of events: 'I told myself that this might well have been in order to please or simply impress his mother, who would have seen such a match as altogether appropriate for her son, as of course in respect of birth it could have been.' But Kathleen need not have worried. One night Gavin took the Princess to a little Sicilian restaurant in Kensington Church Street called Chez Ciccio, and afterwards he took her back to Buckingham Palace, where he said goodbye to her and never saw her again.

Gavin returned to his manuscript; by 15 July he had written all but three chapters, and in August he returned to Sicily to enquire into the murder of Gaspare Pisciotta. Gradually, as his eyes were opened to the widespread iniquities and injustices of Sicilian society, he began to penetrate the obfuscation and half-truths, the binding code of silence – *omertà* – surrounding his subject. During the third week of his stay Gavin perceived a sudden mysterious change in the situation. Typescripts of police documents came into his hands, along with records of confessions, cross-examinations and conversations between prisoners. Most importantly, his contacts began to talk freely about the deaths of Giuliano and Pisciotta – and it seemed none of them believed the latter was responsible for the former's death. All this new material meant he would have to rewrite his manuscript, though paradoxically the essence of the story – its moral – remained the same. 'It remains a tale of treachery and betrayal,' he wrote, 'the tale of a few young men who were pampered, deceived, and finally murdered, for political ends that their education had not fitted them to understand.'

Gavin wrote in his diary: 'Tomorrow I am leaving the island. I do not feel that I am leaving a race of criminals, but that as a stranger I have understood a very little the reactions of a bitterly ill-used people who resort to violence in the face of age-old injustice; that as a stranger, too, I shall not quickly forget the surviving dignity and generosity of friends whom I am proud to have made.'

He could hazard the name of Giuliano's murderer, he reckoned. He had been obsessed with the problem for a long time, lived with it, dreamed of it, woken with it. But it was no longer important. 'What is important,' Gavin wrote, 'is that Giuliano lived the myth contained in his epitaph, that his "proud inspiring phantoms" were great enough to destroy him. To many in Sicily he will remain the King asleep in the mountains.'

In September 1954 Gavin finally finished the book. Its American publishers, Harper & Row, were reported as 'getting behind it in a big way'.

Even as he was putting the finishing touches to his biography of Giuliano, Gavin was urgently casting about for ideas for his next book, and in September he came across an article in the *Journal of the Royal Geographical Society*, of which he was a Fellow, which excited his interest greatly. Entitled 'The Marshmen of Southern Iraq', it was written by Wilfred Thesiger, the last of the great old-style explorers, famous for his pioneering camel journeys across the Empty Quarter of Southern Arabia, one of the world's most formidable deserts. For the last five years Thesiger had spent a few months of each year exploring the hitherto unexplored marshlands and lagoons of the Tigris and Euphrates rivers of Southern Iraq – a wild, watery wasteland inhabited by a primitive and little-studied people known as the Marsh Arabs, or Ma'dan.

'The Ma'dan,' wrote Thesiger,

have acquired an evil name. The aristocratic tribes despise them for their dubious lineage, and willingly impute to them every sort of perfidy and wickedness, while the townsmen fear them, shun them and readily believe all that they hear against them. Among the British, too, their reputation is bad, a legacy from the First World War when from the shelter of the marshes they murdered and looted both sides indiscriminately as opportunity offered . . . Hard and primitive, their way of life has endured for centuries, but in the next few years the marshes will be drained and the marshmen as I have known them will disappear to be merged into the stereotype pattern of the modern world – more comfortable, perhaps, but certainly less free and less picturesque. Like many others, I regret the forces which are inexorably suburbanising the untamed places and turning tribesmen into corner boys.

Here, Gavin realised, was exactly what he had been searching for – a hidden, almost unknown and as yet unspoilt world, peopled by a lost and forgotten tribe about whom no one had ever written a book before. To penetrate the frontiers of such a land, and to live and function among such a people on his own account was beyond his personal capability – he lacked the knowledge and the resources, above all the language. But if he could persuade Thesiger to take him on his next expedition into the marshes, then the gates of that treacherous and comfortless paradise would be open to him. He wrote to Thesiger, who was staying at his mother's house in Chelsea, and arranged to meet him for lunch at the Guards Club in a few days' time. It was to prove a fruitful encounter between two highly unusual and basically eccentric men, neither of whom were ever entirely at home among the metropolitan conventions of polite European society.

Gavin knew of Wilfred Thesiger as the last of the great Arabian travellers in the classic style. Born in Addis Ababa, son of the British Minister in Abyssinia, he had been brought up by an Ethiopian foster-mother and came to feel himself in many ways more 'native' than 'European'. At Oxford he was a boxer and explorer, making a remarkable journey through the wild Danakil country of Abyssinia while still an undergraduate. In the Second World War he won a DSO in the SAS and Sudan Defence Force and after the war made an historic double crossing of the great Empty Quarter of Saudi Arabia by camel and on foot. Since then he had explored most of the remoter parts of the Near and Middle East, and there were few men alive who knew more about the tribal Arabs. All this he accomplished not for honours or career advancement, still less for money; he did it because he loved it, and loved the tribal peoples amongst whom he travelled.

Thesiger was a year older than Gavin, and a good few inches taller. His appearance at their first meeting was every bit as lean and autocratic and rugged-looking as Gavin had expected. What he had not bargained for was Thesiger's sartorial disguise – the bowler hat, the hard white collar and Eton tie, the shiny patent-leather shoes and tightly rolled umbrella – the armour and emblems of a City stockbroker or establishment functionary that belied the ex-guerrilla fighter and wilderness traveller within.

Thesiger was sympathetic to Gavin's ambition to travel in the marshes, but dubious about whether he was physically resilient enough to put up with all the discomforts such travel entailed. 'You seem to have led a fairly rough life,' he warned Gavin, 'but this would be a bit different from anything you've had before.' He would have to sleep on the bare ground, because there was not a mattress of any sort to be found anywhere in the marshes; he would have to endure the onslaught of armies of fleas, which drove even the Marsh Arabs half crazy; and he would be confronted with a vast multitude of diseases, nearly all of them infectious.

When Gavin professed indifference to hardship and an absolute determination to go to the marshes, Thesiger tried one more tack. A great deal of every day would be spent sitting cross-legged in the bottom of a canoe, and most of every evening sitting cross-legged in a marshman's hut. 'Can you sit cross-legged?' he asked. Gavin couldn't, but assured Thesiger he would try.

Thesiger recalled of that first meeting:

I realised that he had never really travelled in his life – at least not what I'd call travelling. He'd done his shark fishing, but that wasn't really travelling. And he'd been round Sicily, but that wasn't really travelling either. He was very proud of showing me a review which said he was 'a man of action who wrote like a poet' – but to call him a traveller was nonsense in my definition of the term. I also realised that Gavin couldn't get on in the marshes by himself. He couldn't speak Arabic, and even if he found an Arab in Basra who spoke English and could interpret for him, such a person would be totally out of sympathy with the Marsh Arabs and would have looked on them as animals. So as he was determined to go I said, OK, you can come along.

Everything was arranged – or so it seemed. But Gavin was unable to obtain the necessary visas from the Iraqi government, including the all-important permit to visit tribal areas, and eventually Thesiger had to leave without him. Gavin was left twiddling his thumbs in London, with no clear idea of what to do or where to go. In this aimless void he distracted himself with a new toy – a

second-hand, supercharged 3-litre Grand Prix Maserati of pre-war
vintage, converted from a single-seater racer into a two-seater roadster a few years previously, and one of the fastest road cars in the
world. This terrifying monster could get up to 150 miles per hour,
though rarely for long and seldom without breaking some vital
and expensive component in the process.

To keep this exotic folly on the road Gavin urgently needed to
raise funds of some kind, and at the end of November 1954 he
thrashed out a deal with Graham Watson and Longmans Green,
whereby Longmans would buy options on his next two books and
advance £350 against a third, a novel – a new departure in Gavin's
literary career. 'He did a draft of a novel some years ago,' Longmans
reported, 'but has not submitted it anywhere and wants to rewrite
it. It is a true situation in which all those concerned are now dead,
so the author says.' Longmans were also persuaded by Gavin's
arguments that, even though his Giuliano book had only just gone
off to the printers, there was a second, spin-off book to be written
about Sicily to take the place of the abortive Iraq project, and they
agreed to advance £1000 for a book about the violent and bloody
tonnaras, the so-called 'chambers of death', the labyrinth of nets in
which the Sicilian fishermen, in crews of up to fifty, trapped and
killed the tonna, the great tunny fish of the Mediterranean, during
their seasonal migration.

To begin research on this new project Gavin set off for Sicily
again in May 1955, writing to Raef Payne on the thirteenth:

> I am still in Palermo, because my beautiful car [a locally pur-
> chased Fiat of 1930 vintage] broke down, not once but five
> times, each time immobile on the road miles from home. No
> car that I have ever owned, driven or dreamed of has had so
> many maladies, or such a power of invention of ever-fresh
> reasons for coming to a complete standstill. Repairs and over-
> hauls have so far cost considerably more than the car is worth.
> She is worth a chapter in the book, but would need careful
> handling to avoid reading like an article in Punch. I myself
> have been in bed for three days with one of my well-known
> spastic stomach attacks, but I hope that both the car and I will
> be ready to go to Castellammare tomorrow. I can't say life is
> particularly bright; I long for someone to talk to without
> fumbling around in little known genders and constructions.

Gavin had decided that the best place in which to base himself for the *tonnara* season was Scopello, a few miles down the coast from Castellammare del Golfo. Not only was it one of the most beautiful places he had ever seen, but it was one of the most ancient and certainly the most isolated of all the *tonnara* along the Sicilian coast, without even so much as a road to it. A motorable track stopped short at a half-deserted village of scarecrow houses called Scopello di Sopra, and from there a stony path skirted the cliffs in a precipitate one-in-four descent to the sea five hundred feet below – a sea of purple and blue and peacock green lapping a coastline of jagged cliffs and great cactus-topped rock towers (or *faraglioni*) like pinnacled islands. It was down this track that Gavin stumbled and fell, into a world of thistle thickets and a wilderness of flowers, brilliant butterflies, gigantic bees and fat, foot-long green lizards, darting snakes and wheeling kites; everywhere the air was heavy with the sweetness of aromatic leaves and clangorous with the lazy thudding of distant, deep-toned cattle bells.

The principal buildings in the tiny, seasonal settlement of Scopello were a square pink villa known as the *palazzo*, where one of the owning syndicate of the *tonnara* lived during the summer; a barracks inhabited by the *tonnara* crew; a few long low houses and storerooms; and a ruined Saracen tower high on a rock above the *palazzo*. Gavin had barely reached flat ground after his descent from the cliff top, and was wondering which way to turn, when the custodian of the *palazzo* stepped out of the shadow of an arch. 'He was,' wrote Gavin, 'a man of vast girth, with the face of a good-humoured villain, and the rolling foot-splayed walk of a Turkish *pasha*. Most of his teeth were missing, and during all the time I was at Scopello I found him largely incomprehensible.' It was this custodian, Roberto, who showed Gavin a room where he could stay – a square white bedroom, utterly devoid of furniture, at the top of a dazzling whitewashed building high on a rock. After having his luggage sent down on the back of a mule, Gavin moved into this room, which was to be his home for many weeks to come.

The only family living permanently in Scopello, apart from Roberto's at the *palazzo*, was Alberto Galante's in the cottage beyond the barracks. Here Gavin took his meals and talked with the *tonnara* crew when they came in to gossip and drink wine in their off-duty hours. Alberto looked after the stored fishing gear during the winter and worked as a member of the crew during the tuna months. The most remarkable member of his family was his mother, known as *la nonna*, who was then in her late sixties, though she looked a hundred. All day she would sit among the clucking hens in the cool of the cobble-floored kitchen, telling her beads and coughing and praying and from time to time farting thunderously. '*La nonna* was frail and weary,' Gavin was to record, 'but she would exhibit a terrifying energy in making me understand her stories, shouting and gesticulating until she was satisfied that I had taken everything in.'

On 23 May Gavin wrote to Mark Longman to report on his progress so far – not an easy task, for the absence of a table and chair in his sparse quarters made typing a challenge:

> I am at Scopello, round which the book is to be based; the fishing has started three days ago. A bloody business by any standards (sharks hadn't prepared me) but a spectacle indeed. This is the most beautiful place in the world; unnumbered flowers and bright insects under a sun like a burning-glass; utterly isolated and without any road to it. A cluster of rock towers jutting out of the sea at the foot of a mile of steep vineyards, olives and brilliant flowers. I think you'll get a good book.

After two more weeks at Scopello, however, it was clear that things were not working out as planned. It was the worst tunny season for many years, and few fish entered the huge trap that the crew manned night and day – only a swordfish, some big blue mackerel and the flying fish that soared in rainbow parabolas to land in the scuppers of the encircling boats. Gavin penned a note to Mark Longman to warn him of the turn of events:

> I feel I ought to let you have some news. Some aspects are, I'm afraid, discouraging. The fact is that this tuna fishing season has been a complete flop. Weeks go by with only an odd fish being taken here and there. I myself have been at the *tonnara* (Scopello) for more than three weeks; there have been only three days on which any tuna were taken, and then only very few. I selected Scopello as the place on which to base the book because of its isolation and its extreme beauty; I must admit that after this long period of inactivity, always either

entirely alone or in the company of the whole crew of the *tonnara* (50), I am heartily sick of both . . . They say this is the worst season in living memory, and with the amount of money that is being lost daily I doubt whether the *tonnara* will go on working for more than another ten days or so. I think I shall stay in Sicily for several weeks after that, mainly in the hope of accumulating more writable material and to see the tuna festa at Favinniana – that is if they hold it this year; the cheers for St Peter after the taking of two or three puny fish have already become ragged and rebellious.

What this really boils down to is that the book will have to change its character in order to survive; it can no longer be a book solely about tuna fishing, but will have to be more or less a personal journal embracing other subjects, with the *tonnara* of Scopello as the thread to hold everything together.

Here, then, is the germ of the idea which was to bear fruit in 1959 in Gavin's disturbing and impassioned account of the lives of the Sicilian poor, *The Ten Pains of Death*. He had already begun to jot down the personal stories that members of the *tonnara* crew confided to him during their days of enforced idleness at Scopello – stories that for the most part revolved around their four abiding preoccupations of sex, money, politics and religion. Gavin conceived the idea of writing a book composed entirely of autobiographies told to him by members of the Scopello *tonnara*; but he soon realised that a series of exclusively male self-portraits from one occupation would be too limited in scope, and that to do justice to his theme he should collect stories from the broader catchment area of the villages dotted about the hills and plains of western Sicily.

Meanwhile he hung on in Scopello through the rest of that abysmal tunny season, as the sun grew hotter and the earth cracked and gaped and the flowers faded and died. So oppressive was the heat of the sun that increasingly the *tonnara* crew were all forced into the shade and thus into greater privacy, and this enabled them to speak more freely to Gavin about their lives and thoughts. 'It was like the Arabian nights,' he reported later; 'there were not a thousand and one, but if there had been they would not have become wearying, for I was learning more and more about human beings.' One of the many things he learned during those *conversazioni* in the heat of the day was the fact that most members of the *tonnara* crew had a criminal record, for grinding poverty had made thieves of them all, or nearly all; in Castellammare 80 per cent of the adult male population had been convicted of criminal offences, from petty theft to murder, at one time or another. 'When the babies cry we steal for them' was a sentence Gavin came to hear very often. 'There is at the heart of their attitude,' he wrote, 'the sullen violence of the oppressed, who, because Sicily also contains rich men, are bitterly conscious of their under-privilege.'

Sometimes, tiring of his confinement at Scopello, Gavin would venture forth into the hinterland – usually to his old haunt at Castellammare, where he had a few friends with whom he could pass the time of day. Often on these trips he would take the country bus, an instructive window into the chaotic heart of everyday Sicilian life, but sometimes he would set off in his treacherous Fiat. The Fiat had developed the embarrassing vice of hooting spontaneously at the sight of a policeman, and on one occasion even loosed off a wheel at one. In a vehicle as idiosyncratic as this it was impossible to tell whether even the shortest journey would be successfully completed.

In the hope that one day the tuna shoals would appear in all the teeming abundance of previous years, Gavin remained at Scopello until the end of the season in early July, when the entire trap was dismantled and taken ashore. The season had been such a fiasco that the festival on which he had been hoping to write a complete chapter was abandoned, and on 21 July he left Sicily. After three days in Rome he returned almost empty-handed to London on the evening of 25 July.

During Gavin's absence abroad the manuscript of his book about Giuliano, entitled *God Protect Me from My Friends*, had been set in galley-proofs. Mark Longman warned the proof-reader: 'Gavin Maxwell is a most awkward person and very stubborn . . . I have a great admiration for him as a writer, although I certainly wish he was a little easier as a person.' This admonition proved all too well founded. Two days after Gavin's return to London his publishers sent him the galleys, together with editorial comments and illustrations for captioning. Gavin's riposte to the editorial comments was scathing. The trouble was that after three years' work on the book he had almost lost interest in it. He could not be bothered to correct the proofs, and ill-advisedly ignored his publisher's libel lawyer's qualms about certain passages, especially one describing the alleged involvement of one Prince Alliata, a member of the Italian Parliament in Rome, in a massacre of Communists at a May Day rally in Sicily in 1947, and another accusing Bernardo Matarella, a minister in the Italian Government, of being an influential member of the Sicilian Mafia.

Within a day or two, Gavin left London on a lengthy round of visits to friends and relatives in the north. 'Gavin has decided to go away again,' a weary Mark Longman advised Harper & Row, 'and therefore cannot correct his proofs or do his captions . . . This book must surely be one of the most tiresome ever and I shall hardly believe my eyes if and when we actually receive some bound copies.' There seemed nothing for it but to put the book back to the following year. 'But it will be good when it is done,' he added encouragingly, 'and all the trouble is worthwhile.' Harpers were not so sure. The delay, they warned, was now verging on the catastrophic. 'If it is delayed yet again in the US it will have appeared in three catalogues and been carried by Harper's salesmen three times.'

Gavin, meanwhile, continued his tour of the grand houses and remote seats of Northumberland and the Scottish Highlands. All thoughts of his book were driven from his mind by a more overriding concern. His springer spaniel Jonnie had fallen ill with pneumonia in the spring of 1954 at Tormor, the house at Upper Sandaig where he lived in the care of the road foreman and keeper of the Sandaig light's wife, Mary MacLeod, who was Gavin's nearest neighbour. He survived that illness, but he was an old dog now, and a few months later he was diagnosed as suffering from cancer; by the winter the vet on Skye was recommending that he be operated on at once. Gavin drove him to the surgery and helped hold the rubber mask over his dog's face as the anaesthetic was administered.

For an hour or so Gavin wandered up and down the Skye shore. The grey, leaden sky and bitter wind from the sea matched his mood of sorrow and foreboding. Jonnie had been his constant companion since his army days twelve years before, and he recalled with a pang how he had taught him to retrieve and quarter the ground for game, and had used his fleecy flank as a pillow in open boats. There had always been an effusive welcome from Jonnie whenever Gavin returned to Sandaig. But now?

Jonnie survived the operation, and for another six months enjoyed an active life at Sandaig. But in the late summer of 1955 the cancer came back, and this time it was inoperable. With a heavy heart Gavin agreed to Jonnie being put down. On 30 August he wrote to Raef Payne from the house of a friend, the film actor and ornithologist James Robertson-Justice, at North Kessock in Ross-shire, announcing the sad news. 'In answer to a letter from Mrs MacLeod I felt I had to sign his death warrant. I felt a traitor to him and a double traitor in not feeling able to be there when it happened, but I thought that in the state of emotional depression that I was in I could only make things more difficult for everyone by being there.'

Jonnie died in Mary's arms. 'Yesterday I drove over to see her,' Gavin wrote. 'I thought her looking terribly ill and worn out and hated to go and leave her. Having Jonnie had meant more to her than even I had understood; she says she doesn't know what to do with herself from the time she gets up in the morning. She asked me whether now that Jonnie was dead I was ever going to come back to Sandaig, so I said of course I was, and I hope to God I wasn't telling a lie but am a little afraid that I was. I shall be back in London in about a week and don't suppose I shall be away from it for long for many months – or at least until my new book is written. I've no money, and have been put on a weekly salary by Longmans until mid-Jan.'

But by November, having finally attended to the proofs of his Giuliano book, Gavin was back in the north again. He found Sandaig a lonely place without an animal companion – especially as Jonnie's death had coincided with the traumatic and bitter break-up of his relationship with Tomas. In a mood of deep despair and rootlessness he moved on to Monreith. There he announced that he planned to try for the Iraq marshes again, and two weeks later Mark Longman applied to the Iraqi Embassy for a visa on his behalf.

In January 1956 Gavin was back in London and being treated again for depression by his psychiatrist, Dr Stungo. He met Wilfred Thesiger several times in London during January, but by now his commitments seemed so interminable that there appeared to be little chance he could leave the country before April. On 23 January, Thesiger's last free evening before he left for the marshes a week later, Gavin met the explorer for dinner one last time.

This would be his final journey to the marshes, Thesiger told him. After that he was going to spend the summer among the pastoral tribes. Gavin could join him there if he wanted – though life wasn't so different there as it was in the marshes.

Gavin leapt at the opportunity, and the two men parted with an agreement to meet in Basra on 2 April. But when Gavin returned home his mind was so restless that he could not sleep. The cause of his sleepless discontent, he realised, was the fact that while Thesiger was going to the marshes for the last time, he himself would be staying behind in London. He was passing up an opportunity which could never be repeated. By four o'clock in the morning he had made up his mind, and he rang Thesiger as early as he dared.

'Wilfred,' he said when his call was finally answered, 'if I can get visas, can I come with you on Monday?'

Thesiger agreed. Gavin was to bring nothing but two shirts, two pairs of trousers, one pair of shoes, a jacket, a razor and an old Leica Mk. III camera, and they would meet for dinner on the evening of their flight to Baghdad. A day or two later Longmans sent each of them a contract – to Gavin for a book about his prospective travels through the Marshes of Iraq (which was to become *A Reed Shaken By The Wind*), and to Thesiger for a book about his past explorations of the Empty Quarter of Arabia (*Arabian Sands*). Thus it was that late in the evening of 30 January 1956 the future authors of two of the finest works on Arabian travel in the English language sat side by side as their plane droned over the wastes of the Syrian desert en route to Baghdad.

Looking down from a height of five thousand feet, Gavin stared fascinated as the sun dipped towards the dim and smoky horizon. 'Every now and again,' he wrote, 'I could make out specks whose shadows were longer than themselves, long rows of moving specks that were the camel caravans of the nomads. They and the clusters of black tents were the only signs of life in all the desert. As I looked down at them I became conscious of an emotion, an unease, and I shrugged it off, but it returned, demanding attention. I took it and looked at it and turned it over, as it were, and recognised it with surprise, even bewilderment. I was feeling afraid.'

FOURTEEN

Into the great marshes

What went ye out into the wilderness to see? A reed
shaken with the wind?
The Gospel According to St Matthew

They did not tarry long in Baghdad. Armed with letters of introduction to the governors of the provinces through which they
would travel, they took the night train to Basra, the great port on
the Persian Gulf, and after a few days hired a taxi, loaded it with
medicine chests, and drove for an hour to a village of date-
cultivators at the edge of the marshes, where Thesiger's crew of
marshmen and his canoe awaited their arrival.

To the north the marshes stretched over two thousand square
miles of flatland crossed, drained and fed by the Tigris and
Euphrates rivers. In the central area lay the permanent marshes,
which were the travellers' principal destination; to the east and west
were the semi-permanent marshes, subject to seasonal flooding.
The Iraq marshes were one of the world's great unspoiled wetlands,
and until Thesiger 'discovered' them six years previously this
watery wilderness had been one of the unexplored territories nearest
to the civilised world, the heart of the marshes virtually unknown
to the world at large. The marsh people, the Ma'dan – a name
which defines a way of life rather than a tribe – had little contact
with the outside world and maintained an existence unchanged
since pre-Christian times, extracting a living from the reeds and
the water and dwelling in reed huts that sat on the water like a fleet
of boats at anchor in a calm sea. It was a world of stillness, as
Thesiger put it, that had never known an engine.

Thesiger's canoe was a *tarada* or war canoe, an aristocrat among
the craft of the marshes, and so expensive that few other than
sheikhs could afford one. Thirty-six feet long but less than three
and a half feet at its widest beam, the *tarada*'s slender curving prow
rose five feet from the water, enabling the craft to force a passage

through the thickest reed beds, while its shallow draft enabled it
to float in ankle-deep water. Only in the deeper water of the open
lakes, where storms could brew up out of nowhere, was the canoe
less than master of its element, for a sudden gust could send it to
the bottom like a stone (a characteristic which gave Gavin some
food for thought, for though he had spent much of his life on water
he could not swim a stroke).

Four crewmen – Amara, Sabeti, Hassan and Kathia, all marshmen known to Thesiger – were ready and waiting at the water's
edge. The *tarada* was loaded, and on a morning as cool and grey
as an English autumn the two Britons stepped on board. The
canoe turned out into the Euphrates, left the main river at Huwair
and headed north for Ramla, the last of the dry-land villages before
the great marsh. The journey of exploration through an almost
unknown region and among an almost unknown people had begun.

It was cold and blowing hard when they left Huwair – no colour
anywhere, and the grey sky, unbroken by a single hill or tree, as
immense as a sky viewed from a small boat far out at sea. 'It was
in some way a terrible landscape,' Gavin wrote of that tentative
first encounter, 'utterly without human sympathy, more desolate
and inimical than the sea itself . . . Here in the limitless stubble of
pale bulrush one felt that no sheltering ship could sail nor human
foot walk, and there seemed no refuge for any creature whose blood
was warm.' Ahead, very far away, he could see a few dark specks
that marked the last of the palm groves before the edge of the
permanent marsh. 'The earth seemed flat as a plate, and stretched
away for ever before us, vast, desolate and pallid.' The wind tore
a chorus of strange sounds from the sedge stems – 'groans and
whistles, bleats and croaks, and loud crude sounds of flatulence; if
the devils of Hieronymus Bosch could speak from the canvas this
would be the babel of their tongues, these the derisive notes of the
trumpets at their backsides.'

Gavin had been given the position of honour in the stern of the
tarada. Though this provided him with the maximum leg-room,
the ordeal of sitting cross-legged for hours on end left his lower
limbs agonised, and every bone and muscle from the waist down
ached and creaked. The relief of getting out of the canoe at a halt
was usually short-lived, for within a minute or two he would be
required to sit cross-legged again on the floor of some Marsh Arab's
reed house, and the agony would begin all over again. It was

Thesiger's immutable rule always to travel like a native of the country, and the party carried none of the usual paraphernalia of an expedition – no tents, camp beds, camping-gas cookers, tinned food or the like, nothing but their guns, cameras and minimal personal kit. For food and shelter they relied entirely on the hospitality of the Marsh Arabs and such edible fowl as they could shoot for themselves from time to time.

Arab hospitality to strangers is obligatory and unstinted, but it is bound up with a system of etiquette and a code of behaviour which the stranger neglects at his peril. Part of Gavin's painful process of adaptation to a primitive ambience and an alien society was to come to terms with this code, from the elementary rules (never use the left hand, which is considered unclean, for anything but unclean things, always enter a house barefoot, always place your right hand over your heart after shaking hands, belch after eating by all means but never – ever – break wind) to the elaborate rituals of Arab greetings and the free-for-all of the communal Arab meal. For Gavin, dining among the Marsh Arabs was a tricky business. The *pièce de résistance* was invariably a monolithic mound of rice surrounded by bowls of gravy, mutton, chicken and sometimes a whole boiled sheep's head, and the only utensil was one's right hand. Gavin found that sitting cross-legged put the communal rice pile a disconcertingly long way off, and by the time his hand had reached his mouth there was very little rice attached to it, so he had to resort to cheating, pouring gravy over the rice to turn it into an adhesive ball that could not disintegrate and fall to the ground.

After the communal dinner came the long communal conversation – a double penance, for Gavin was obliged to remain cross-legged, while his ignorance of Arabic prevented him from joining in the conversation, a source of accumulating frustration throughout the journey. Nights were spent in spartan discomfort on the floor of the reed house with all valuables distributed beneath and about the body – for the Ma'dan are notorious thieves – while guard dogs howled and the wind scurried through the gaps in the reed walls. Mornings were occupied with Thesiger's surgery for the sick and ailing – his return for the hospitality of the night before.

Gavin was full of admiration for Thesiger's competence. The marshmen were riddled with diseases – dysentery, yaws, ringworm, bilharzia, the list was endless. For three hours Thesiger would inject and stitch and anoint and hand out pills from his large medicine chests, and at the end of the session he would perform surgical circumcisions, which the marsh people found vastly preferable to the barbarous work of the professional circumcisers of the marshes. Gavin recorded in his diary:

> The number of people with only one eye.
> "   "   dog bites.
> "   "   pig gores.
> "   "   miscellaneous but
> "   "   horrifying ills.
>
> Four noseless faces . . .

His view became a kaleidoscope of cataracted eyes, suppurating boil-craters, patches of angry rash on brown skins, wounds, and swollen genitals.

So varied and infectious were the diseases of the marshes that Gavin was amazed that neither he nor Thesiger succumbed to any of them. Gavin was, however, the victim of a persistent assault by fleas and lice that attacked him in droves at night, and since it was the custom to sit barefoot in the *tarada* as if in a reed hut his feet were soon a mass of mosquito bites that never cleared. Thesiger, by contrast, was able to cover his feet by a mere flick of the skirt of his Arab *dish-dasha*, and as the weeks went by Gavin began to rue the fact that all he had to wear were the hopelessly inadequate European clothes he had brought from London. In fact, he did once attempt to dress as 'one of the people', as Thesiger recalled: 'Before we set off for the marshes he asked me if I could get him a long Arab-style shirt and a loincloth like the Arabs wore. I said, "No, you'd look ridiculous if you dressed like the Arabs and couldn't speak a word of their language." Well, one day we left him at a sheikh's house in the marshes and when we got back we found him dressed up like a sheikh! He had persuaded the sheikh to lend him the clothes, but instead of wearing the shirt long he had tied it up like a kilt, and my Arabs said, "If Gavin is going to travel around dressed up like that, we're not going with him."'

Gavin had set off into the unknown full of enthusiasm for the enterprise and the strange world of the marshes. Even at the end, despite all the discomforts and difficulties, when he had learned so much and saw the marshes plain, he was able to declare: 'I could have made the marshes my home.' The marshes displayed a savage pristine beauty unspoiled by urban and industrial change. They also presented a fiercely barbaric exterior world which balanced his own warring interior, and provided a refuge where a man could be lost to the world and all its pressures and hurts and disappointments. Gavin was for the most part positively happy in the midst of the empty waters and choking reed beds of the true marshes. But the nearer the party came to dry or cultivated land the more disenchanted he became. Once, halfway through their wanderings, when they touched on the big town of Amara on the lake region's northern edge, Gavin's disenchantment turned to anathema at the sight of yellowish brick and corrugated iron, peeling enamel advertisements for Western products, dirt and refuse. Everything, after the wide clean skies and astringent life of the marshes, seemed to him shoddy, mean and ugly.

The leisurely progress of the *tarada* as it was paddled through the lagoons and labyrinthine waterways gave Gavin ample time to observe and record; what he saw and heard he jotted down in his pocket notebook as it happened. In essence his work was that of a reporter; but very often his reportage began to sing with the authentic voice of poetry. For Gavin even the reeds were a perpetual object of wonder, the landscape as weird as a Lost World. Birds were everywhere, at every level of the air, in primordial abundance and every shape of God's creation, darting low over the water with glittering glint of electric green, then soaring up to show the dazzling copper sheen beneath their wings, 'as though a rainbow had suddenly come to pieces'.

But it was not just the visual imagery of the marshes that enthralled him. At dusk their aural dimension would come into its own with the tumultuous chorus of the frogs. 'Those million million voices,' Gavin recorded, 'could turn the great marsh desert into a cauldron of sound seeming more limitless than the falling horizons themselves.'

It was the nights that were most special for Gavin. 'I remember nights that were hopping with fleas,' he wrote, 'but I remember, too, the proud curving silhouettes of the canoes and their reflections on moon-whitened water, the moon gliding through troubled cloud and the women wailing for the dead; the fresh wind blowing through the house all night with the smell of rain upon it; the night sounds and sweet breath of the buffaloes at the end of the house. I used to wake in the night and take in these sights and sounds with a curious intimacy, like memories of childhood, as though they were things once known and forgotten.'

But Gavin began to grow weary that, amongst all these prodigal and unbounded symbols of natural freedom, he should find his own personal freedom severely trammelled. The rigid formula of the host–guest relationship was almost unrelieved, and in Gavin's case it seemed a double host–guest relationship, in that he was the guest of a guest. In time he began to grow bored with the long wearisome evenings passed in conversation in which he could not take part. He continued to show a lively interest in every aspect of the reed dwellers' culture – from their boat- and house-building to their water-buffalo economy, their pig shoots and war dances and erotic dances – but he had difficulty relating to the Arabs on an individual basis, and they to him. 'Part of the trouble was that he was never able to get on terms with the Marsh Arabs,' Thesiger recalled. 'It wasn't language – language doesn't stop one relating to that extent. He just couldn't get on net with them. They felt he wasn't really interested in them, only in himself – and more interested in the birds and the otters than in the Ma'dan.'

Gavin had difficulty relating to Thesiger himself, for this magisterially authoritarian, masterfully competent old-style explorer was in complete control in a world he knew and understood as if it was his own, and Gavin could only tag along, never quite sure what he was doing or what was going on. To Gavin, Thesiger was an awesome figure, tough as nails, never at a loss. To Thesiger, by contrast, Gavin seemed a curiously impractical person, always falling down or losing things or dropping his camera lenses in the water or breaking his nose with his spear-gun. Once, when it seemed they were likely to be stranded for the night, Thesiger gave Gavin two shotgun cartridges and told him to go off and shoot as many coot in a row for supper as he could. His reputation among the Ma'dan depended on how many he shot. 'God help you if you miss!' Thesiger warned him. 'They're all watching.'

Gavin shot five coot with the two shots, and the crew were impressed. So was Thesiger, who looked 'like a scoutmaster whose most oafish pupil had tied an accomplished and esoteric knot'.

Later that day Gavin shot a duck, then failed to hit a single bird out of a flock of thirty or forty coots when the canoe tilted as he let fly with both barrels.

'That little duck won't go far among seven people, will it?' Thesiger remonstrated with him. 'Your name's mud among these boys now.'

As the journey drew toward its final weeks morale began to wilt. For a few days Gavin felt giddy and feverish, and Thesiger too was unwell and lost his voice. Gavin began to harbour grievances, to marshal trivial complaints against his companion. Thesiger was among friends and Gavin was among strangers, and he felt isolated, neglected and frustrated. Thesiger recalled:

> One day he was looking very sulky in the canoe and I said, 'Oh Gavin – what's wrong now?' And he said, 'Well, if you can't see what's wrong what's the use of my trying to explain it to you?' I said it might help if he did. So he said, 'Well, if I was your guest in Scotland you might be expected to take a bit more trouble over me than you are here!' 'But you're not my guest,' I told him, 'and this isn't an expedition with a leader and a member, but two free individuals.' So then he sulked a bit. He was quite a neurotic person, but on the whole he was affable enough and we got on pretty well considering, apart from a few *contretemps* when he was unable to cope.

All this came to a head one day near the Persian frontier when Thesiger gave Gavin six cartridges and sent him into the marshes to shoot duck for supper. Gavin jumped at the chance to be on his own, stretch his legs and enjoy a modicum of personal freedom for the first time in weeks. It was an area of canals and dykes in seasonally flooded marsh – water up to his knees, soft clinging clay, burnt reed stubble and treacherous potholes of buffalo footprints underfoot. In this bare marshscape Gavin could see only one possible bit of cover, an eighteen-inch-high lump of earth about 250 yards away. He began to make towards it, and when he was some fifty yards away he saw another lump, and recognised it as a very large wild boar which was moving in his direction.

Gavin understood his situation only too well. The boars of the Iraq marshes are huge and savage, and among the marshmen they take a terrible toll of deaths and injuries with their formidable slashing tusks. 'My heart came into my mouth,' Gavin recalled; 'the boar was charging me, and we were all alone, he and I, two little dark specks out in the glittering waste of water.' Gavin's spirits were momentarily raised when he remembered he had a gun, then almost instantly dashed when he realised his ammunition consisted solely of duck shot, useless against a charging boar. He remembered Thesiger's instructions for just such a contingency – wait till he's almost on you, then shoot between the eyes and fall on your belly so he can't get your guts.

From Gavin's perspective the boar seemed all shoulders and head, like a bull, and was throwing a white splash of water all around him. Feeling sick with fright Gavin brought the gun up to his shoulders and aimed between the boar's eyes. It took him all his self-control not to fire at fifteen yards; at two or three yards he pulled the trigger, and at that split second the boar veered at the edge of a ditch and was hit not between the eyes but behind the shoulder, right over the heart. The enraged creature careered away from Gavin, and from the distant *tarada* he could hear an encouraging yell from his English companion which sounded like: 'You bloody fool!'

Gavin sloshed back through the mud to the *tarada*. Thesiger was in terrific good humour and the canoemen were chattering with excitement, and welcomed him back like a long-lost brother.

'What a man!' cried Thesiger. 'Here he is, charged by a boar from an unprecedented distance, absolutely no right to be alive at all – and then, when he's safe, he has to go and *fire* at it with No. 5 shot! You really *are* a bloody fool! Well, well! Do you know I became quite fond of you when I saw you were going to be killed? I realised I should definitely miss you when you'd gone . . . Extraordinary fellow – quite mad . . .'

Gavin's encounter with the wild boar changed his outlook. 'Perhaps it was because I no longer felt myself to be so perfect a cypher; at last one living thing in all this alien waste of water and sky had really taken notice of me, had thought me important enough to be worthy of destruction. It gave me some ecological status, as it were, even to be the target of a charging pig.'

Gavin's standing as so much dead baggage on the trip, with no freedom of movement and no responsibility or essential involvement, had been profoundly irksome to him. Almost the only act of free will he could perform was to light a cigarette; even to go for a walk was impossible, either because there was no land to walk on, or because savage guard dogs deterred the attempt. He was reduced to the level of a child, he realised, with all a child's resentment and frustration. The long evenings spent studying a circle of forty firelit Ma'dan faces because he could not understand what they said lost its charm when he realised that each of the forty faces was studying his own. The wild boar, his brush with death, had changed all that. Now he was the object of a flattering interest. At last he was somebody. The journey continued in a less occluded spirit.

At the village of Dibin Gavin had come across one of the most splendid creatures he had ever seen, an eagle owl with gold and orange plumage and vast eyes that burned with an intense orange glow. He agreed to pay the woman of the *mudhif* (reed house) three dinar for the eagle owl if it was still in good condition when he came back to Dibin in two or three weeks' time. But on his return he found the once-glorious bird so starved it had almost no flesh on it. Its feathers were coated with slime and filth, its tail had been pulled out, and one eye was inflamed and partially closed. 'I was angry for the humiliation of something beautiful and savage,' Gavin was to write, 'angry as I would be for these people themselves when they became humiliated by the soiling contact of our modern civilisation.' The great carnivorous bird had been forcibly fed on slabs of doughy Arab bread and a mush of pulped dates. Gavin recalled: 'It died a few hours later, bedraggled and contorted. Poor humiliated eagle of the silent glittering night, wings clipped, tail pulled out, stuffed with bread and dates until it died squalidly on the ground, stained with its own excrement, in a dim corner of its captor's dwelling, one great orange eye still open and staring out at the stars.'

Gavin brooded over the owl. He was angry and upset that he had lost a little outlet for his restless and frustrated energy, a living creature to care for and protect. He sat in the reed hut silently fuming while the conversation flowed around him until his ears caught two of the few Arabic words he knew – '*celb mai*', meaning water-dog, or otter. He was suddenly alert, the eagle owl momentarily forgotten. He had already become faintly otter-conscious during his time in the marshes, and had learned that the Marsh Arabs recognised four distinct types of otter – 'common', 'black', 'red' and 'white'. At Abusakhair, about five miles west of the Persian frontier, on 29 February he was shown four otter skins, two of which appeared to be of the 'black otter' type and the others 'common otters'. He bought one of each type to take back to England with him, but his mind had begun to turn to the possibility of acquiring a live otter, and he had asked Thesiger if he could enquire about getting an otter cub among the Ma'dan.

'What was that about otters?' he asked Thesiger.

'I think we've got you that otter cub you said you wanted,' Thesiger replied. 'This fellow comes from that village half a mile away. He says he's had one for about ten days. Very small and sucks milk from a bottle. Do you want it?' Gavin was cautiously excited. It sounded exactly what he wanted.

The man got up and went out, and Gavin watched his canoe glide away silently over the starry water into the dark. After half an hour or so he came back, entered the hut and put the otter cub down on Gavin's knee as he sat cross-legged in the firelight. The cub was a female, the size of a small kitten or a squirrel, with a stiff, tapering tail the length of a pencil. The creature looked up at Gavin, chittered gently at him and wobbled a little on his knees, for she was still unsteady on her legs. Then she rolled over on her back, revealing a round furry tummy and the soles of four tiny webbed feet, and exhaling a strange musty odour that Gavin found wholly agreeable. Gavin bought her for five dinar, the price to include the teat and the precious bottle – bottles being rare items in the marshes – from which she drank.

Gavin named her Chahala, after a tributary of the Euphrates down which they had paddled the day before. He cut a collar from the strap of his field-glasses and tied a six-foot string to it so that she could not wander away and be lost. Then he slipped her inside his shirt and she snuggled down into the warmth and darkness of a security she had not known since she was taken from her mother. From that moment Chahala accepted Gavin as her foster-parent, and never once showed fear of anyone or anything. When she was awake she would peer out from the top of his pullover like a baby kangaroo, or scuttle along at his heels whenever there was somewhere dry to walk on (for she hated getting her feet wet). She played like a kitten and answered to her name. When she grew tired she would give a bird-like chirp and paw at Gavin's legs until he bent down, then she would dive head first into the friendly warmth and darkness of his pullover and fall asleep at once, head down and pointed tail sticking out of the pullover top. At night

Chahala slept inside Gavin's sleeping bag, usually lying on her back with her feet in the air inside the crook of Gavin's armpit. Gavin slept fitfully, trying not to sink into too deep a sleep for fear of rolling over and crushing the tiny otter with his body. Sometimes in her sleep Chahala would utter a wild desolate little cry – three poignant, falling notes, resembling the syllables that made up her name. Often she would wake in the night, and would clamber out of the sleeping bag to relieve herself on the bare earth between the reed columns in the furthest corner of the *mudhif*. When she returned she would clamber on to Gavin's shoulder and chitter quietly for her bottle, then hold it between her paws as she sucked it lying on her back, till she fell asleep again with the teat still in her mouth.

Gavin's Arab companions called Chahala his daughter, and would ask him when he had last given her suck. This was ironic, for on the evening after leaving Dibin a discussion took place between Gavin and Thesiger about weaning Chahala. Both felt that the otter cub was old enough to eat something more substantial than the buffalo milk which had been her fare till now. This view seemed confirmed when Gavin tried to introduce a few drops of blood into the otter's milk from a couple of sparrows that had been caught for her; the moment she smelt the scent of the meat she snatched at the carcases with savage greed and was evidently furious when they were taken from her. 'Finish with milk,' Amara said. 'She is grown up now.'

And so it seemed. Gavin gave Chahala the chopped-up meat from the breasts of the two sparrows, and she wolfed them down and looked for more. From now on the young otter would be fed with such meat as could be found for her, mostly bird flesh.

The next night was bitterly cold, and for Gavin, who was obliged to leave his sleeping bag open to allow Chahala to come and go as she pleased, it was the most acutely uncomfortable of the journey. Unable to sleep, he lay shivering on the floor of the *sarifa* (guest house) of a local sheikh, listening to the jackals howling in the night while an icy wind tore through the gaps in the reed walls. As he lay there, fretful and anxious, his mind began to wander and ramble, and he tried to divine some reason why he was here, on the banks of this strange river, at a place whose name he did not even know. His musings, when he wrote them down, encompassed not just the journey but his whole meandering life; indeed, the one was but a reflection of the other. Nowhere did he make a more honest statement of his view of the course his life had taken – the puzzle of the quest whose goal he could not fathom:

> I must be here for some purpose, I thought, for those who wake at night in desert and jungle to see the stars at strange slants in the sky have some goal before them, some enemy to conquer before returning home. The lines that·drew them here would form some plan on paper, a firm design that showed the growth and aim of their endeavour, a geometry that expressed the journey of their lives. I tried to see my own like this and saw it as a doodle on a scrap of paper beside a tele-phone, formless, full of heraldic flourishes and ignoble retreat, with here and there a random line running far out on to the blank page; and at the end of one of these I lay now listening to the jackals skirling at the moon. What went ye forth for to see? A reed shaken by the wind?

Now, as the two-month journey drew towards its end, his perspective changed radically. At the beginning – goggle-eyed, his senses finely tuned and alive – he had seen the marshes as a glittering land of beauty and wonder, and he had looked and heard and touched and smelt and tasted with the uncritical enthusiasm of a child. Gradually his mood had passed to irritation and frustration, but now it had shifted again. He was a man too rawly sensitive to survive long without experiencing pain, and now he perceived the canker beneath the mask, the cruelty and violence, the widespread and innumerable manifestations of pain and horror and dying that characterised the life of both man and nature in the marshes – and not just in the marshes, perhaps, but in the very system of God's creation itself. 'How very heavy must be the heart of the Creator,' he thought as he contemplated the sheer prodigality of destruction all around him.

The awareness of suffering, compassion for those who suffered, whether animal or man – these had not suddenly and spontaneously generated in Gavin's mind since he arrived in the marshes. They had existed at one level or another of his consciousness since child-hood; but it does seem that it was in the marshes, and more especi-ally in those last days following the death of the eagle owl and the acquisition of the otter cub, somewhere between the Chahala and the Agra rivers of the Eastern Marshes of Iraq, that Gavin came to see these things more clearly than he had seen them before. This new clarity of perception embodied a philosophical shift that was to lead, step by step, to the ardent conservationist of future years.

But there was one more life to pay in this endless sequence of small and helpless deaths, and this death was to hurt Gavin above all others.

Gavin now had only one more night left in the marshes. It was a bitterly cold night again, and a keen wind – 'as chill as the tinkle of icicles' – rustled the dry reeds of the hut. Chahala was restless throughout the night, and Gavin grew impatient with her; but in the morning, when he took her to a spit of dry land at the edge of the village for a walk, he realised that she was very ill. She was unable to move and lay on the ground looking up at him in a helpless and pathetic way, and when he picked her up she wished only to regain the warm security inside his pullover.

They paddled for an hour through the flower-choked waterways of a green, shallow marsh, and at the next island village they stopped. It was clear to Gavin when they landed that Chahala was dying. She was very weak now, and in the reed house she lay on her tummy in obvious distress, breathing fast. Gavin could think of nothing but castor oil to give her, but it had little effect. For two hours he sat with his otter cub, feeling helpless and hopeless, and then they were off again, with Chahala stretched out restlessly on the floor of the canoe beneath the shade of a little awning Gavin had rigged with a handkerchief stretched across his knees. He was to write with moving poignancy of the bitter moments that ensued:

Once she called faintly, the little wild lonely cry that would come from her as she slept, and a few seconds after that I saw a shiver run through her body. I put my hand on her and felt the strange rigidity that comes in the instant following death; then she became limp under my touch.

'She's dead,' I said. I said it in Arabic, so that the boys would stop paddling.

Thesiger said, 'Are you sure?' and the boys stared unbeliev-ingly. 'Quite dead?' they asked it again and again. I handed her to Thesiger, the body drooped from his hands like a minia-ture fur stole. 'Yes,' he said, 'she's dead.' He threw the body into the water, and it landed in a brilliant carpet of white and golden flowers and floated on its back with the webbed paws at its sides, as she had been used to sleep when she was alive.

'Come on,' said Thesiger, 'Ru-hu, Ru-hu!' but the boys sat motionless, staring at the small corpse and at me, and Thesiger grew angry with them before they would move. Amara kept on looking back from the bows until at last we rounded the corner of a green reed-bed and she was out of sight.

The sun shone on the white flowers, the blue kingfishers glinted low over them and the eagles wheeled overhead in the blue sky, but all of these seemed less living for me than Chahala was dead. I told myself that she was only one of thousands like her in the marshes, that are speared with the five-pointed trident, or shot, or taken as cubs to die slowly in more callous captivity, but she was dead and I was desolate. The fault lay with whoever, perhaps more than a million years ago, had first taken the wild dog cub that clung to the body of its dead dam, and I wondered whether he too had in that half-animal brain been driven by the motives that in me were conscious.

The precise cause of Chahala's death was never known, but Gavin bitterly reproached himself for it for a long time afterwards. At first he thought he had killed her by feeding her raw meat before she was properly weaned. Later it occurred to him that perhaps the heron she had eaten had ingested the digitalis poison which the Marsh Arabs used to drug fish, and it was that which had killed her. It is also possible that Chahala may simply have died as a result of drinking too much buffalo milk.

That evening the party returned to the Tigris, halting at a holy spot called Ezra's Tomb, much visited by Muslim pilgrims. The local sheikh was away, but he had a European-style guest house in which Gavin and Thesiger could stay. Here Gavin finally gave way to the grief and desolation that had gripped him all day since Chahala died. 'Gavin had hysterics,' Thesiger recalled, 'there's no other way to describe it, and he went on about how he'd never forgive himself, he'd killed the little animal that trusted him, and so on. "I'd wanted something on which to lavish my affections," he said, "and I'd found it and through sheer stupidity I killed it." He was sobbing away and the tears were streaming down his face. It was just as well we were not in a public guest house in front of a lot of other people. It seemed to me extraordinary. I could have understood it if it was to do with a human being he was very fond of, but it amazed me that it was over an otter we'd had with us for less than a week. I've never shared Gavin's sentiments about animals. Personally I think if people go to extremes where animals become more important than human beings then they ought to be locked up.'

FIFTEEN

Mijbil in Basra

Does not take root like the badger. Wanders, cries;
Gallops along land he no longer belongs to;
Re-enters the water by melting.

TED HUGHES, '*An Otter*'

The journey was over. In spite of all the hardships and tribulations he had endured, Gavin was to look back on his sojourn in the marshes as one of the happiest periods in his life. He dreaded the prospect of returning to nothing and no one in England, and he was grateful when Thesiger suggested that perhaps he should stay on in Iraq and join him on another foray into the marshes, and later, perhaps, spend the early part of the summer with him wandering on horseback among the pastoral tribes to the north. It was arranged that they would return to Basra to collect their mail and write a few letters and then set off again two or three days later. On 29 March 1956 they drove the sixty miles south to Basra and checked in as guests at the resplendent old British Consulate-General on the banks of the Shatt al Arab.

Gavin's mail had not arrived, and he decided to hang on in Basra till it did. He wrote to Raef Payne in England telling him of his intentions:

I am staying on here . . . I have a burning but rather hopeless purpose in doing so; I had a tame baby otter which gave me all its heart and I gave all mine in return and it died yesterday. She was the size of a squirrel and fed from a bottle, slept in my sleeping bag at night and inside my shirt in the daytime. She knew her name and would come running to it, and was more affectionate than any dog. I killed her by allowing her to eat meat too soon, and I am desolate and full of self-reproach. My heart weeps for that curious little otter and I'm very very sad. Now I feel that I shall never be content until I get another, but it's getting late in the year to get them at the right age. If I fail to get another now, I'm coming back specially in Feb next year just for that.

With an otter for company, Gavin explained, he felt he could forgo all the travails of human love and affection. Clearly, at that moment he saw an otter as the solution to the principal problems of his life – a comfort in his solitude, a cure for heartache. This extraordinary conclusion was to have profound consequences for his future life and career. His provisional plan was to leave Basra as soon as he had received his mail from England, catch up with Thesiger in the marshes and stay with him till he found another otter. This might keep him in Iraq for up to a month. It says a great deal for Gavin's determination, or perhaps desperation, that he was prepared to put up once again with the many discomforts and torments of the marshes to achieve his goal. But he hoped this might not be necessary. 'If I have the luck to get an otter earlier,' he wrote, 'I shall come straight back.'

After nearly two months in the wilderness Gavin seemed curiously disorientated and inarticulate, as though the endless hours of Arabic had deprived him of his customary command over his own language. He himself seemed aware of this. 'Sorry this is a really dull and laborious letter,' he concluded apologetically, 'but you know the moods when ideas and words just don't come and string themselves together. I'll leave it open till Monday, April 2nd, in case I think of anything worth saying.'

On Sunday Gavin was invited by the Crown Prince of Iraq's game warden, Robert Angorly, a British-educated Christian Iraqi, to a duck shoot on the Crown Prince's fabulous marshes. There Gavin sat at the Crown Prince's exposed and prominent shooting-butt with his feet in six inches of water – 'the cynosure of every bird's eye in the place' – until after five hours he was rescued from his indignity. On Tuesday he added a postscript to his letter: 'Have now received all my mail from England, and am pushing off again the day after tomorrow.'

Gavin never did return to the marshes. After finishing his letter he went out to post it. He was away for several hours, and when he returned to his room in the Consulate-General he was surprised to find two Marsh Arabs squatting on the floor. One of them was Hasan, a member of Thesiger's *tarada* crew; the other was a stranger. Beside them was a sack that squirmed now and then. The Arabs handed Gavin a note. It was from Thesiger: 'Here is your otter, a male and weaned . . . It is the one I originally heard of, but the sheikhs were after it, so I said it was dead. Give Ajram a letter to me saying it has arrived safely – he has taken Kathia's place.'

Gavin had barely finished reading the note than another stranger appeared in the doorway; a tall, rugged-looking Englishman by the name of Gavin Young. He was an experienced Arabian traveller (and a future journalist, war reporter and author of distinction) who had accompanied Thesiger in the marshes a few years previously, and had returned on several subsequent occasions by himself – the only other European to have explored the marshes in recent times.

Young had just returned to Basra for a short visit after two years wandering in south-western Arabia for the Desert Locust Survey, and his first call was to the British Consulate-General. There he was surprised to see through a doorway two Marsh Arab friends, Ajram and Hasan, who jumped up when they saw him and ran forward to greet him with broad grins on their faces. Behind them was a slim Briton with long blond hair, who was deeply preoccupied in wrestling on the tiled floor with a sack that seemed to have a life of its own. Presently he looked up and smiled. 'Please excuse me,' he said. 'My name's Gavin Maxwell. I see you know these two. They've just brought me this down from the marshes. Stand clear a second. There's something very interesting in this bag and it's coming out.'

Gavin untied the sack, and out of it stepped a small otter quite unlike any he had ever seen before – a creature like a small medievally-conceived dragon, with short, close fur like a chocolate-brown mole and a black button-nose like a koala bear. The animal shook itself, and Gavin picked it up and began stroking it and talking to it soothingly. So Mijbil (named after a tubby sheikh he had encountered in the marshes) entered Gavin's life, and suddenly he had a *raison d'être*, something on which to lavish his affection. Mijbil, familiarly known as Mij, was to become in a sense Gavin's home and destiny, and there was to be no more talk about wandering among the pastoral tribes. Now his life began an entirely new phase, characterised by what he was to call 'a thraldom to otters, an otter fixation'.

When Gavin Young caught up with Wilfred Thesiger in the

marshes he asked him about this unusual man he had met playing
with an otter in the Consulate-General in Basra. 'Wilfred told me
what a curious person he was, and how neurotic and disturbed,'
he recalled.

Wilfred had formed a not terribly high opinion of Gavin, he
found him too squeamish and sentimental – though later he
came to quite like Gavin as human company, and recognised
he was a serious ornithologist, even if he was, by Wilfred's
Olympian standards, an indifferent explorer. Wilfred's Marsh
Arabs were enigmatic about Gavin, too, and confused by his
temperament. Gavin was a moody person, easily moved to
tears or fury, and he was a nervous, sensitive man with a very
shy manner, always flashing a quick grin or a laugh or an
angry look, and the Arabs complained they couldn't get on
his wavelength. In his ideal life-plan Gavin might have quite
liked to have been someone like Wilfred Thesiger. But in Wilfred Gavin encountered the archetypal hardened Victorian
explorer, making serious maps, studying languages, collecting
plants and insects, living exactly as the natives did with no
concessions to comfort whatsoever. That sort of life required
tremendous organisation and serious intent and Gavin found
it too hot a pace to serve as a model he could aspire to. Gavin
the man expected something more romantic than that.

Gavin stayed on in Basra with his new-found animal companion.
For the first twenty-four hours Mijbil kept himself aloof, sleeping
on the floor as far as possible from Gavin's bed. The main problem
was food. The patient and hospitable Consul-General, Mark Kerr-
Pears, sent out a servant to buy fish in the market, but Gavin was
advised by Robert Angorly that the fish the servant had bought
had been caught with the use of digitalis poison, and would be
dangerous for a small otter to eat. Angorly offered to procure fresh
fish that had been caught with nets, and every day thereafter he
brought half a dozen small red fish from the Tigris for Mijbil to
eat.

For a fortnight Gavin and his otter stayed on at the Consulate-
General. Most of this time was spent in getting to know each other.
On the second night Mijbil came on to Gavin's bed in the small
hours and slept in the crook of his knees until the servant brought

tea in the morning. From then on the young otter began to take
an interest in his surroundings and to accept Gavin in a relationship
of dependence. Very soon Mijbil discovered the thrills of a modern
bathroom and a bath full of sloshing water. Once, when he escaped
from Gavin's room, Gavin spotted him scuttling down the corridor
to the bathroom, and when he caught up with him was amazed to
see that the otter had already discovered how to manipulate the
chromium taps with his paws to produce a full flow of water –
evidence of a higher level of intelligence than Gavin had previously
guessed. Gavin was astonished at Mijbil's aptitude for play and the
virtuoso dexterity with which he could juggle small objects,
lying on his back and rolling two or more marbles between the
palms of his paws for minutes on end.

He began to learn an otter's ways and an otter's language. Mijbil,
he discovered, uttered a wide range of sounds, each sound convey-
ing a different meaning. The simplest was the call note – a short,
anxious, penetrating call between a whistle and a chirp. Then there
was the query – a 'Hah!' uttered as a loud, harsh whisper – which
Mijbil made if he entered a room and wanted to know if there was
anyone there. Another distinct sound was a musical bubbling call
interspersed with chirps, signifying excitement and anticipated fun,
as when waiting for a walk or a bath; while a high, snarling, screaming wail was an unequivocal indication of anger, though this was
rarely followed by anything more significant than a nip. But
Mijbil's main means of vocal communication was the chirp, in all
its numerous permutations, from a continuous chitter to the single
querulous note. Gavin found him an extraordinarily intelligent,
excitable, affectionate, good-humoured and engaging companion,
of whom he was to become fonder than almost any human being.

Gavin's plan was to take Mijbil back to Britain with him and install
him eventually in the watery world of his Highland home at Sandaig. In those days there were no controls on the importation of
endangered species, so his problems were practical rather than legal.
Even so, he dreaded the prospect of escorting the inquisitive and
irrepressible Mijbil to Britain by air. A Trans-World flight was
booked to Paris, and an Air France connection of dubious certainty
from Paris to London that evening. Trans-World required that Mij
should be carried as personal baggage in a box not more than eighteen inches square. Since he was just over a foot long at the time,

with a tail measuring another foot in length, this posed a problem, which was never properly solved. A zinc-lined box was constructed with two compartments, one for sleeping, the other a lavatory. To accustom Mijbil to it, Gavin put him in the box an hour before he was due to leave the Consulate-General for the airport, and left him there while he went away for a hurried meal.

When he returned he found a horrific sight. Blood was trickling from the airholes and the hinges of the lid, and inside lay an exhausted, bloodstained Mij, his mouth, nose and paws scratched and torn in his efforts to tear his way through the zinc lining of the hated cage. It was after nine in the evening before Gavin had removed the last of the jagged metal from inside the box, and there were only ten minutes left before the flight. Forcing the otter back into his torture chamber, Gavin slammed the lid down and jumped into the waiting car. By the time they reached the airport, after a nightmare drive, Mij had torn one of the hinges of the lid clean out of the wood, and Gavin knew that before long he would break out completely.

Desperately late, harassed and dishevelled, Gavin boarded the waiting plane. The other passengers were already seated and stared oddly at the late arrival as he searched for his seat, clutching a briefcase stuffed with old newspapers and stale fish, and a shattered wooden box from which issued diabolical menagerie noises. Gavin took his place next to a *soigneé* and elegantly dressed middle-aged American woman, laid the box with the otter at his feet and the briefcase with the fish on his lap, and fastened his safety belt.

Within a few minutes the plane was flying westwards over the marshes that had been Mijbil's home, their dark waters glinting in the moonlight. Next stop was Cairo. Gavin took the newspapers out of his briefcase and laid them at his feet. Next he took out the fish and rang for the air hostess. A little shrilly, and none too coherently, he asked her if she could keep his fish in a cool-box. The hostess – 'the very queen of her kind' – took the ill-wrapped fish 'as though I were travelling royalty depositing a jewel case with her for safe keeping'. Perhaps, she suggested to Gavin, his pet might feel happier sitting on his knee. Gratefully, Gavin bent down and opened the lid.

Mijbil shot out like a rocket and disappeared at high speed down the aisle. Gavin heard a commotion behind him, shrieks and squawks from his fellow passengers and a woman standing on her

seat crying out, 'A rat! A rat!' He rose from his seat and set off in
hot pursuit towards the back of the plane, and tried to catch the
fugitive otter with a flying tackle, only to find himself clutching
an Indian lady's foot, with his face covered in curry. It was the
curry that persuaded his fellow passengers that it was a clown rather
than a lunatic they had in their midst. Gavin returned to his seat
while the turmoil of flight and pursuit passed up and down the
aircraft behind him. Then he heard at his feet a distressed chitter
of recognition, and Mij jumped up on to his knee.

'In all the strange world of the aircraft I was the only familiar
thing to be found, and in that first spontaneous return was sown
the seed of the absolute trust that he accorded me for the rest of
his life,' Gavin wrote. For an hour or two Mij slept peacefully on
Gavin's knees, and whenever he grew restless Gavin rang for fish
and water. But as they were nearing Cairo the otter sprang into a
frenzy of intense activity. First he tore the newspapers at Gavin's
feet into shreds, then shovelled out all the fine wood-shavings in
his box, with all four paws working in a frenzy. Finally, he turned
his attention to the travel bag of the American lady in the seat next
to Gavin, unzipping it without a moment's thought and throwing
the contents in a chaotic heap on the cabin floor. Fortunately the
woman was asleep, and Gavin was able to cram the articles back
into her bag before she woke at Cairo.

It was in rain-drenched Paris that Gavin's troubles really began.
Mijbil had to be nailed back in his coffin-like box for the transfer
to Orly airport on the other side of the city. Worse, airline regulations for the flight to London required that he would have to fly
as freight in the cargo hold of the aircraft. Worse still, the plane
diverted to Amsterdam, and it seemed the luggage of the London-
bound passengers was either lost or left behind in Paris. By now
Gavin had not slept for thirty-six hours, and he was fractious and
overwrought. In such a state of mind he could be a fearsome proposition for anyone who earned his wrath, and he threatened to sue
Air France and to broadcast their inefficiency throughout the world
if his precious animal was not found.

Eventually it was announced that the London-bound baggage
was on board a British aircraft which was about to take off. Gavin's
great fear now was that Mijbil would succumb to travel shock, a
kind of voluntary death that kills many wild animals in transit.
When he took a look inside the cargo hold of the waiting aircraft,

he saw Mijbil's box in a corner, but from it there issued not a sound.

In the early hours of the next morning they arrived at last in London, where Gavin was confronted by a Customs officer every bit as cantankerous and bellicose as himself. The official scrutinised Gavin's list of the purchases he had made in Iraq – two uncured otter skins, a Marsh Arab's dagger, three cushion covers woven by the Beni Lam tribe, and a live otter.

'You have with you a live otter?' the official demanded.

'I doubt very much whether he is still alive,' Gavin replied, 'but he was when he was in Paris.'

'If the animal is dead,' the official intoned drily, 'there will be no duty payable on the uncured skin; if it is alive it is, of course, subject to the quarantine regulations.'

Gavin vehemently objected. He had checked this out himself in Iraq, he said. There were no quarantine regulations applicable to the otter. Since he had now cleared his luggage, he proposed to leave with it, and if the Customs officer tried to detain him he would hold him legally responsible for the death of a valuable animal.

The battle might have gone on for ever had not the Customs officer been relieved by a more conciliatory colleague. Within three minutes Mijbil's box and the rest of Gavin's baggage had been loaded into a waiting hire-car and they were speeding through the darkened streets towards the studio at Avonmore Road and the completion of a horrendous journey. From inside the box Gavin was gratified to hear faint chittering sounds and the rustle of wood shavings that indicated Mijbil was still alive. He had probably survived the journey from Paris by going into the self-protective trance-like state by which many wild animals attempt to escape the unbearable reality of adverse circumstances – 'back, for all one may know, among the familiar scenes of his Tigris swamps, or perhaps in a negative, imageless world where the medulla had taken over respiration and the forebrain rested in a state bordering upon catalepsy'.

When they reached the studio flat and Gavin closed the door behind them, he experienced a moment of deep satisfaction. In spite of everything, he had brought back a live otter cub from Iraq to London. He prised open the lid of the box, and Mijbil climbed out to greet him with frenzied affection.

SIXTEEN

Mijbil in London

I think I could turn and live with animals . . .
I stand and look at them long and long.
They do not sweat and whine about their condition,
They do not lie awake in the dark and weep for their sins,
They do not make me sick discussing their duty to God . . .
WALT WHITMAN, *Song of Myself*

Mij was tired after his long ordeal – but not that tired. He had not been out of his box for a minute before he began to explore his new home with alarming enthusiasm, and the moment Gavin went into the kitchen to find food for him he heard the first crash of breaking china in the room behind him. It was blindingly clear that Gavin's cluttered studio-flat would require considerable modification if it was to contain the two of them in any kind of harmony. Living with an otter, Gavin realised, was going to be a demanding and full-time business. Quite apart from their tireless inquisitiveness and exuberance, otters that had been reared by human beings required almost constant human company, affection and play. Without them they quickly became unhappy and tiresome. For the first few weeks in London, therefore, Gavin was preoccupied with making his home otter-proof – 'like a cross between a monkey-house and a furniture repository' – while creating for Mij an environment in which he felt secure and at ease. Routine, he knew, was the key, for as soon as routine was broken a new element came into play – the fear of the unknown which is basic to the behaviour of all animals, including man.

One day Gavin was given a salutary reminder that Mijbil was essentially a wild animal and not – no matter how much he enjoyed playing with rubber balls and marbles – a conventional pet. Mij had been catching eels in the bath, and brought one in to eat in the studio. Gavin knew that it is folly to deprive a wild animal of its prey, but when Mij decided to take the half-eaten eel up to Gavin's bed in the gallery, he decided enough was enough. Putting on three pairs of gloves – the outer pair well-padded flying gauntlets – he caught up with Mij halfway up the stairs and bent down to pick up the eel. Mij emitted a high humming noise that should have served as a warning to Gavin, and as he lifted the eel Mij bit him just once, and let go. The canines of the otter's upper and lower jaws had passed clean through the gloves and the tissue and bones of Gavin's hand and met in the middle with an audible crunch. Two bones were broken. Mijbil rolled on his back, squirming with apology.

Sometimes Gavin took Mij out into the streets of London for a walk on a lead. The reactions of passers-by were many and various. None, it seemed, had ever set eyes on an otter before, and their guesses as to the animal's identity were often far from the mark. Otters belong to a group of animals called Mustelids that includes the badger, marten, mink, mongoose, polecat, weasel and stoat; astuter Londoners rang the changes on these species, and threw in beaver, bear cub, baby seal, squirrel, newt, walrus, and even brontosaurus for good measure; none, it seemed, ever guessed otter. One day Gavin was assailed by a navvy digging a hole in the street, who spoke for all when he called out: ''Ere, mister – what's that supposed to be?'

It was a good question. Mijbil was an otter, Gavin knew that much; but what kind of otter? The scant scientific literature available indicated that the only known otter species in the Iraq marshes was the Persian sub-species of the common Eurasian otter, *Lutra lutra*. Gavin's first otter, the tiny Chahala, clearly belonged to this species; Mijbil, Gavin was sure, did not. Mij's fur was shorter, sleeker and darker, the colour of plain chocolate; and the underside of his tail was flat like a ruler, unlike those of Chahala and other European otters. Of the two otter skins Gavin had brought back from the Marshes, one resembled Chahala, the other Mij. Gavin was puzzled, and phoned the British Museum (Natural History). That afternoon an expert taxonomist from the Zoology Department, Robert Hayman, came round to look at Mij and the otter skins. He, too, was puzzled, and took the two skins away with him in order to compare them with others in the Museum's collection. In due course Gavin was summoned to the Museum and shown cabinets full of otter skins from all over Asia – all of them sub-species of *Lutrogale perspicillata*, the Indian smooth-coated otter that ranged all over eastern Asia from India and Burma through Indo-China to Sumatra and Borneo, though none had ever been recorded west of Sind, in India, and none resembled either Mij or the darker of Gavin's two skins in colour. It was Robert Hayman's opinion that Mij must belong to a race of otter hitherto unknown to science, and he proposed that he should be designated after his owner and bear Gavin's name – *Lutrogale perspicillata maxwelli*.

Gavin was inordinately proud to have joined the ranks of those who had had exotic creatures named after them – Steller's eider, Humboldt's woolly monkey, Meinertzhagen's forest hog, Grant's gazelle, Père David's deer – and felt, in some measure, that he now wore the halo of creator. 'I had realised a far-off childish fantasy,' he wrote later, 'and there was a Maxwell's otter . . . So Mij and all his race became *Lutrogale perspicillata maxwelli*.'

To have a species named after you is indeed a kind of immortality – though among professional scientific naturalists, who regard new species as two a penny, it is generally considered the hallmark of the amateur to glory in the fact. On his death-bed Gavin was to declare the discovery of Maxwell's otter to be the greatest achievement of his life and his most abiding monument. Only one person dissented from this judgement, and that was the man who had actually found Mijbil – Wilfred Thesiger. 'I found this otter at the tumulus village of Daub, some twelve miles north-west of Ezra's Tomb,' he told me. 'Gavin wasn't there at the time so I sent the otter to him in Basra. He'd had no hand in getting it and frankly I found it rather odd when he had it named after himself – if it was going to be named after anybody it should have been named after me. Gavin owed everything to his trip with me in the marshes. The marshes gave him the otter, the otter gave him *Ring of Bright Water*, and without that he would never have been heard of again.'

It was the spring of 1956. As best he could, given the incessant and distracting demands of his young otter, Gavin began to pick up the threads of his professional life. His first concern was for his second book, *God Protect Me from My Friends*, which had finally been published in the month preceding his return from Iraq. Its critical reception was almost universally enthusiastic. Bernard Levin wrote in the periodical *Truth*: 'It is one of the most beautifully and brilliantly written books, and one of the most exciting, that I have had in my hands for many years. Mr Maxwell's prose has the strength and the cool clarity of a fine sapphire.' Mervyn Jones in *Tribune* called Gavin a 'beautiful, beautiful writer'. Though few reviewers were able to comment knowledgeably on the subject matter, most agreed that the book made an exciting, engrossing and moving documentary thriller that took the lid off modern Sicily and all its troubles as no previous book had done.

But in spite of the glowing reviews, the book proved difficult to move in the bookshops, and Longmans reported: 'The booksellers insist there is no interest whatsoever in Giuliano.' The situation was much the same in America, where the book was published under the title *Bandit. God Protect Me from My Friends* was destined to be a *succès d'estime* and no more. In many ways it was the least satisfactory of Gavin Maxwell's *oeuvre* – in part, perhaps, because it never really got to the bottom of the mystery surrounding Giuliano's life and death, and in part because of all Gavin's books this one bore least the stamp of his personality. A film company did take out an option on the book, but this fell through; and though Francesco Rosi's powerful, documentary-style movie *Salvatore Giuliano* (1962) would appear to be loosely based on Gavin's researches, he received no acknowledgement in the credits and not a penny in his pocket.

Of more pressing concern was Gavin's next book – the journey through the marshes. At first he had thought this would be the easiest book in the world to write; but by the time he got back to London he had begun to have second thoughts, so much so that he warned Longmans that he feared he did not have enough material for a book at all. Only slowly, and in a desultory fashion, did the book that was to become a travel classic take shape.

Gavin had read widely in the field of travel literature and had given a great deal of thought to the genre before setting out to write a travel book of his own. He was to present the fruits of his studies in a lecture on 'The Technique of Travel Books' to the National Book League in London on 6 December 1960 – a lecture that was important not only for what it revealed about his attitudes towards his own craft, but also for the insight it provided into his approach to his book about his travels in Iraq, *A Reed Shaken by the Wind*.

Writers of travel books fell into two main groups, in Gavin's view. The first group consisted of travellers who wrote; the second of writers who travelled. It was the latter category which interested him most:

> A travel writer must, in fact, be a writer who travels and not a traveller who writes, and he must have some feeling or thought to communicate, something beyond observable or recordable fact; for him each journey must be to some extent a journey of the spirit, a journey of self-discovery. That, besides how to build an igloo or throw a boomerang, is what he has to communicate, and if he does so he has succeeded . . . The travel writer's work should remain the presentation (and implicitly interpretation) of his sensory perceptions, and this necessarily involves selection and compression in exactly the same degree as in fiction writing. Once this necessity is granted the whole conception of an exact narrative becomes unimportant, at least on a literary plane as opposed to the transcript records of an expedition. We then begin to deal with the true material of literature, which is truth as opposed to fact.
>
> Truth and fact *may* be related, but they are more often apparently opposed, and a collection of facts, no matter how conscientious, does not constitute truth unless by accident. The writer must state an imaginative besides a factual truth, and if he travels in company the imaginative truth will inevitably be questioned by his companions, who cannot be expected to see anything with his eye. Here the writer who travels alone is at an enormous advantage. He is untrammelled, he can compress and select without question provided he retains a certain basic integrity. He can also convey situations by reported dialogue, whose factuality is always dubious. I have never been in this fortunate position since I began to write. I have been afraid of the slightest rearrangement of anything that has happened to me, the slightest shift of emphasis that might be interpreted by ever-present witnesses as distortion of fact for my own ends.

It was with such precepts in mind that Gavin began to turn the raw material of his travels into the brilliant cinematographic imagery of his finished book. 'In its preparation I enjoyed peculiar advantages not often accorded to voyagers in primitive places,' he recorded. 'Spending long weeks squatting during the daylight hours in a leisurely-paddled war canoe, with the priceless blessing of an introductory companion who was not by nature garrulous, I was at liberty to set down any thought or impression that occurred to me while the image was still fresh and unconfused. I carried a small notebook and biro pen in the breast pocket of my shirt and the published form of *A Reed Shaken by the Wind* was little more than the dateless transcripts of the diaries I had kept during two months of travel with Wilfred Thesiger in the great marshes of Southern Iraq.' When he showed an early portion of his manuscript to Gavin Young, now back in London, Young was bowled over by the dazzling virtuosity of the writing, and realised that Wilfred Thesiger was in for a shock.*

Thesiger met up with Gavin in London later in the year. Their reunion took place at dinner at the London home of the formidable Colonel Richard Meinertzhagen, a soldier and traveller of the old school, a mighty African hunter and ornithologist, a world authority on the birds of Arabia and the discoverer of the forest hog that bears his name – and an outspoken judge of a man's character. Meinertzhagen was an old friend of Gavin's Uncle Willie Percy, an explorer and naturalist from the same mould, and Gavin had met him once before the war, when his uncle had warned him: 'I wouldn't say things like that in front of him if I was you – *he's killed men with his bare hands.*'

Meinertzhagen noted of the dinner in his diary:

---

* The water-Garden of Eden Gavin had explored did not remain for ever as he brilliantly encapsulated it in his book. In 1958 a revolution took place in Iraq which in time was to bring to power a dictator of extreme cruelty by the name of Saddam Hussein. During the Iraq–Iran War of the 1980s the marshes were bombarded with chemical weapons on Saddam's orders in an attempt to exterminate deserters from the Iraqi army who had sought sanctuary there and the Marsh Arabs who had given them shelter; and in the aftermath of the Gulf War of 1991 thousands of Iraqi Shias – 250,000, according to diplomats and opposition sources – fled into the watery, disease-ridden labyrinth of the marshes, only to be encircled and bombed by Saddam's forces in a wilderness holocaust without precedent. In May 1992 Saddam Hussein launched a new and perhaps final offensive against Shia refugees in the marshes, using heavy artillery, helicopter gunships and amphibious assault vessels, and by the spring of 1993 two-thirds of the marshes had been torched, drained and poisoned. Gavin Maxwell's 'Lost World' – a world Wilfred Thesiger once claimed had never heard the sound of an engine – is no more.

I like Wilfred but I would not travel with him for untold gold. He is accustomed to have his own way and cannot stand contradiction or even views different from his own; he is inclined to shout down and trample on any obstruction or difference of opinion. But he is able and in many ways likeable.

Gavin is a vastly different person, amenable, enthusiastic, has much charm, but an adventurer who has never settled down. He has lots of ability but cannot tackle anything really worth doing. He has recently travelled with Wilfred and says he will never do so again; he wants to return to the Euphrates marshes but lacks money. Gavin is good company and there is something about him which appeals to me, but I cannot help feeling that he is near approaching what is termed a 'rotter'. He is remarkably like Willy Percy in both looks and character but he has none of Willy's bad characteristics whilst having most of his good ones.

Gavin hated keeping Mijbil cooped up in the confines of his London flat, and longed to introduce him to the wide, watery freedom of Sandaig. 'I felt I could no longer wait to see Mij playing,' he was to write, 'as I visualised him, under the waterfall, or free about the burn and the island beaches.' At last, not quite a month after his return from Iraq, he was free to set off. So began a new era in his life, and the realisation, for a while, of the idyll of his dreams.

PART II

AVALON FOUND

SEVENTEEN

The bay of alders

And others – others go further still and move outside
humanity altogether. A place, as well as a person, may
catch the glow. Don't you see that all this leads to comfort in the end? It is part of the battle against sameness.
E. M. FORSTER, *Howards End*

Gavin and Mij set off for the north in May 1956. Gavin had booked
a first-class overnight sleeper for the two of them, and since he did
not want Mij ever to be confined in a box again he bought a dog
ticket for him and put him on a lead like a poodle.

Perhaps oddly for an animal that until a few weeks before had
known no other world but the wilderness of the marshes of Iraq,
Mij adored trains and everything to do with them – the hissing
engines, the shouting porters, the jostling crowds, the rumbling
luggage trolleys, the bustle and confusion. But paradise for Mij
was the sleeping car with its wonderful panoply of Western technology – its hot and cold water taps, its light switches, its attendants'
button. He had no sooner entered the sleeping compartment than
he discovered the wash basin and in an instant had curled up in it,
his rubbery form fitting its shape 'as an apple fits a dumpling', his
agile paws fidgeting feverishly with the shiny chromium tap like a
manic midget safebreaker.

The train roared north through the English summer twilight as
Mij explored, fingered, pushed, pulled, pressed, twisted, opened,
closed and chewed every object and fitting in the sleeping car that
excited his restless curiosity. By the time they were in the Midlands
there remained only one item untested – a short length of chain
which disappeared mysteriously into a metal tube high up above
the luggage rack. By standing on a pile of luggage Mij was able to
reach the cord while Gavin was staring absent-mindedly through
the window, and by the time Gavin spotted what he was up to Mij
had already seized it firmly between his teeth and braced his paws

against the carriage wall preparatory to giving the cord a hard tug that would have brought the express train to a juddering halt. There was only one thing to do. Mij was very ticklish around the ribs, and Gavin began to tickle him furiously. With a foolish grin Mij let go and began to squirm violently. The situation was saved; the train roared on, and Gavin took to his bed in relief. When the attendant brought tea next morning he found Gavin asleep and the otter flat on his back in the bed with his head on the pillow and his arms outside the bedclothes. The attendant stared at Mij, then asked: 'Was it tea for one, or two, sir?'

The plan was to stay at the family home at Monreith so that Mij could be given a partial but supervised measure of freedom before achieving total liberty at Sandaig. It was at Monreith, with its streams and loch and farm mill dams, that Mij was able to return to a watery world for the first time since he left the Iraq marshes. This was the first opportunity Gavin had had to watch Mij at large in his natural element, and he could only stand in wonder at the extraordinary swimming prowess which the otter now displayed. At the beginning, fearing that the call of freedom would be too strong for him, Gavin only let Mij swim at the end of a long fishing line. But after a week, worried that the line might snag underwater, Gavin let Mij swim free, wearing a close-fitting harness to which a lead could be attached in emergency.

To Raef Payne Gavin wrote excitedly on 4 June: 'Report on Mijbil. Beyond wildest expectations; comes for long walks like a dog, swims free and untrammelled both in lochs and in the sea, returning to a whistle (sometimes the 141st whistle). On land he never goes more than a few yards from one's feet – in water up to 100 yards, but always tries to keep one in view.'

For both man and otter those weeks at Monreith were a halcyon time. Gavin was later to describe that marvellous shared adventure: 'The time of getting to know a wild animal on terms, as it were, of mutual esteem, was wholly fascinating to me, and our long daily walks by stream and hedgerow, moorland and loch, were a source of perpetual delight. Though it remained difficult to lure him from some enticing piece of open water, he was otherwise no more trouble than a dog, and infinitely more interesting to watch.'

Following Mij's routes led Gavin into his native otter's world – 'a world of deep-cut streams between high, rooty banks where the leaves in the undergrowth met overhead; of unguessed alleys and tunnels in reedbeds by a loch's edge; of mossy culverts and marsh-marigolds; of islands tangled with fallen trees among whose roots were earthy excavations and a whisper of the wind in the willows.'

And yet . . . and yet . . . Some troubled sense of rootlessness and despair seems to have seized Gavin by the throat even now. It was as if he had realised – as he was bound to realise – that an animal companion was no more than that, and could not be the final answer he sought. Gavin was alone at Monreith, and he found the old house, once so grand and fine, depressingly run-down and neglected. Crippling estate duties had largely impoverished his elder brother, Sir Aymer. Nettles and ivy were rampant everywhere, windows broken, pigeons nesting in the rooms. On 20 June Gavin wrote to Raef again: 'This place alone is in the long run as bad or worse than any place alone. If I hadn't got Mij I think I'd spend the summer in some auberge on the continent . . . I want to go and start a new life in a new land and make new friends.'

By late summer he was installed with Mij at Sandaig. It was flaming Mediterranean weather when they got there. The wild roses of the north blazed deeply pink against the royal blue of sea and sky; the yellow flag irises bloomed brightly along the burn and the foreshore; the white shell-sand beaches of the islands dazzled the eyes. On 14 September Gavin wrote to Raef: 'Mij lives free with the door open, and comes and goes from the sea or the burn as he likes. It's been glorious weather for most of the time – too good for any work – and only tonight it's blowing a full gale and battering rain. Mij is asleep on his back in the chair you made.'

It was the beginning of the idyll. Avalon found. A story that reached back for years – but did not have much longer to run.

When Gavin first set eyes on Sandaig in the autumn of 1948, looking down from a bare hillside over the intricate scatter of islands and skerries and the deep, delicious lostness and tranquillity of the place, he thought of it as a paradise found, 'something out of a dream.' And so it remained while it stayed in the form in which he discovered it. Sandaig for a long time was a kind of frontier post, 'a fortress,' he wrote later, 'from which to essay raid and foray, an embattled position behind whose walls one may retire to lick one's wounds and plan fresh journeys to further horizons.'

For the best part of ten years Sandaig was a place upon which

no human ambitions were allowed to impinge. Throughout that
time it remained without a road or transport to it, without any
modern conveniences of any kind, and with rudimentary furniture
constructed largely from what was cast up by the sea on to the
beaches nearby. Nor was there much intrusion by man. Few local
people ever came down to the place, apart from the lighthouse
assistant who made periodic visits to the automatic light on the
furthest of the small islands. No casual tourists or passers-by
visited, for none even guessed at the existence of this out-of-the-
way haven, which was invisible from the single-lane road that
traversed the hillside one and a half miles inland.

Unless the visitor arrived at Sandaig by sea, there was no way
of avoiding the long, steep and arduous slog over the peat moors
from Tormor, the green corrugated-iron roofed house that stood
alone in a wilderness of mountain and peat-bog on the lonely road
that ran above the sea between Glenelg and Arnisdale on Loch
Hourn. Tormor was the home of John Donald MacLeod, the local
road foreman and keeper of the Sandaig light, his wife Mary and
their three young sons, who were Gavin's nearest neighbours. Both
were remarkable people. Mary had an extraordinary affinity with
animals, and could talk to them and command their attention and
affection in a quite uncanny way. Wild deer running on the hill
would stop and approach at her call, birds would follow her when
she was out walking and alight at her feet, bees would cover her
and not sting, and the wildest of horses would allow her to ride
them bareback. John Donald was a very different kind of person.
'I have no objection to animals,' he once told me, 'as long as they
are in their place – which is under my heel.' He hated God, Chris-
tians, the British Empire, the Royal Family and D.H. Lawrence,
in that order. He was a congenial, wise and erudite old Highlander
and had read most of the English classics and many works on
astronomy, evolutionary theory and English history. Conscious
that he had had no formal education and lived far from the haunts
of conventional culture and high society, he would preface any
remark with the apology, 'Oh, you wi' not be wanting to listen to
the bletherings of an old prole like me, but I have had a thought,
a very foolish thought . . .' Such were Gavin's nearest neighbours
and friends of many years – his link with the rest of human kind
and an unfailing source of comfort and encouragement, hot baths,
scone teas, canasta, ceilidhs and bagpipe music.

In fine weather the walk down the rugged track that began at Tormor was always an adventure. But at night, or in driving wind and rain, with a loaded rucksack on one's back and only a tenuous foot-track over rough and treacherous ground to guide you, the final stage of the journey to the tiny enclosed paradise of Sandaig resembled some fiendish commando exercise. On one occasion Gavin was forced to crawl on his hands and knees to avoid being swept away like a leaf in the gale; on another, trying to climb up to Tormor in a blizzard, he stumbled on a stag sheltering from the driving snow behind a rock shelter, and when it ran off he gratefully took its place under the rock, the smell of the stag pungent in his nostrils.

A sojourn at Sandaig in those days was not lightly undertaken. Kyle of Lochalsh, the nearest town with more than one shop, was some thirty to forty miles away by road. Supplies from Kyle reached Sandaig along the same complicated sea and land route that brought human visitors; but unlike the human visitors, the supplies – paraffin, potatoes, matches, sausages and virtually every essential that could not be gathered from the natural surroundings of Sandaig itself – had to be humped down the hill-track in a bulky and often exceedingly heavy rucksack. Orders for further provisions had to follow the same route in reverse, and were subject to unpredictable improvisation. Once, after sending an SOS for methylated spirits for the Primus stove, Gavin received in return a squidgy package and a note which read: 'Sorry no methylated spirits but am sending two pounds of sausages instead.'

In the early years, more from necessity than choice, Gavin attempted to live a life of at least partial self-sufficiency at Sandaig. Before myxomatosis wiped them out, rabbits were plentiful in the warren in the sand dunes behind the house, and Gavin could shoot them from the back scullery window. At other times he would forage the sea-shore for edible shellfish, the cockles, mussels, limpets and periwinkles that thrived there, or lower a lobster-pot below the tide line around the islands to catch not only lobsters but the big edible crabs that frequented the weedy jungle of the sea-bed. Each season brought its own harvest. In early summer there were gulls' eggs to collect out on the bird islands, and for a few weeks in high summer mackerel could be caught in abundance with darrow-lines. Very rarely salmon and sea trout came into the lower reaches of the burn, though Gavin seldom succeeded in landing any. Autumn brought one last wild culinary treat for the Sandaig table – the huge shiny brown mushroom known as *Bolitus edulis*, which grew among the tangle of alder woods higher up the burn, and was the only kind of fungus which Gavin knew to be non-poisonous and worth the trouble to look for.

When eventually Gavin's account of life at Sandaig brought him fame and fortune as a champion of animals and the wild, a number of his readers were dismayed that he killed rabbits and gathered birds' eggs and cockles for food, and wrote to him to protest. Aware of the paradox, Gavin defended himself strenuously:

Some of these people totally failed to realise that when any-body lives under the conditions that I lived under at Sandaig, then you are part of the ecology and there will be times when you must kill for your food. I have letters from all over the world written in sometimes violent and hysterical terms ask-ing me how I can condone this, that or the other – why do I catch fish, for example, or shoot rabbits, and isn't it horrible? I could show you letters from people who happily feed pro-cessed whale or cow meat to their pet cats and dogs, and people who won't use leather goods, and yet drink milk and don't stop to think what happens to the bull calves that are born to dairy herds, and so on. I have a letter from a woman who wants to breed vegetarian lions and another from a Swedish spinster who will kill nothing – she even ushers flies out of the house, and the fact that she is ushering her flies out to die of cold is perhaps less significant than the fact that she has never lived as I have in countries where flies literally kill children.

The nearer you are to some status in a local ecology the more you can understand the relationship between any one species – including your own – and other species. In a place like this you become part of the ecology and the nearer you can get back to an animal status the better. It's a dangerous thing to be quoted on, but I am prepared to be quoted as saying this: 'I am a predator by nature and by instinct and I keep my predatory instincts under control and I kill in the same way as an otter or a tiger or almost any other animal would kill.'

Communications were as tenuous as the transport system at Sandaig. The mail followed the same frontier-style supply line, and an exchange of letters could take a week. Telegrams were speedier, but each telegram required a heroic safari – twelve miles by bike, three miles on foot – on the part of the Glenelg postmaster, and was not always worth the cost in human endeavour. The first telegram ever delivered to Gavin at Sandaig, for example, was brought by the exhausted postmaster on a blazing summer day, when the hills shimmered in the heat-haze and the cattle stood knee-deep in the motionless sea to escape the torment of the summer flies. It conveyed the message: 'Many happy returns of the day.' The nearest telephone was a public call box in Glenelg, over six miles away by land. Because of the surrounding mountains television reception was impossible at Sandaig, and for many years even the radio was virtually inaudible, emitting (as Gavin put it) 'a furtive whisper, mouse-squeak reminders of far-off human frenzy'.

This same isolation was both the cause of all the practical difficulties of daily life at Sandaig and the source of its immense attraction. For with it came a sense of absolute liberation from the cares of the world and all the ordinary nagging frets of man; a liberation not only from external pressures but from internal rules as well, and with that a regression to an earlier life-style, to the intensity, the absorption, the sense of discovery and fun that characterise childhood. In an environment that was entirely natural, with hardly a man-made object within sight or earshot, Gavin was intensely aware of the spiritual and emotional metamorphosis that Sandaig brought about in those that lived there, and wrote later: 'To be quite alone where there are no other human beings is sharply exhilarating; it is as though some pressure had suddenly been lifted, allowing an intense awareness of one's surroundings, a sharpening of the senses, and an intimate recognition of the teeming sub-human life around one . . . as though life were suddenly stripped of inessentials such as worries about money and small egotistical ambitions and one was left facing an ultimate essential.'

It was not simply its isolation, but its location and its myriad combination of natural features within so small a compass – waterfall and burn, sand dunes and sand banks, hills and mountains, sea and islands – that made Sandaig almost unique among the old, disused houses that stood among the wild sea-lochs of the West Highlands. Cut off from the world by the peat bogs and moorland hills, and made almost an island by the encircling burn and the sea, Sandaig was set in the infinitely grander context of the sea and a wondrous, uplifting prospect down the sound to the isles of Eigg and Rhum – a confined microcosm on the edge of a nearly infinite macrocosm. It was the sea and its littoral that gave Sandaig its extra dimension and special meaning, as Gavin perceived: 'There is a perpetual mystery and excitement in living on the seashore, which is in part a return to childhood and in part because for all of us the sea's edge remains the edge of the unknown; the child sees the bright shells, the vivid weeds and red sea-anemones of the rock pools with wonder and the child's eye for minutiae; the adult who retains wonder brings to his gaze some partial knowledge which can but increase it, and he brings, too, the eye of association and of symbolism, so that at the edge of the ocean he stands at the brink of his own unconscious.'

The sea at Sandaig was a constant source of wonder and surprise. The beaches, especially the small beaches and sand bars of the Sandaig islands, were a treasure house of shells of bewildering variety and colour, from tiny fan-shells to great scallops, and out on the islands the shell sand and coral beaches were blindingly white under the sun.

One natural feature that Sandaig notably lacked was a safe anchorage, so for many years Gavin had no boat there, remaining oddly land-bound. Eventually he bought a little nine-foot flat-bottomed pram, and this was followed by a succession of ever bigger and more seaworthy craft. His horizon was vastly extended, and through the long summer days he was able to voyage and fish and explore the islands and bays and the deep chasm of Loch Hourn to the south, and even to reach the nearest shop at Glenelg without the long slog up to the road at Tormor. Above all he was able to become part of the pelagic life of his environment, where before he had only been a watcher on the shore.

Sometimes dramas of extraordinary power and prodigality were enacted in the waters that encircled Sandaig. Gavin described one of the most miraculous of these in a letter he wrote to Raef Payne, then just embarking on a career as classics master at Eton, at the beginning of September 1952:

One evening millions and millions of herring fry of about three inches got jammed in the bay, so thick one had to force one's legs through them to move, and Tomas and Roderick [the MacLeods' eldest son] 'bathed' in them in the sunset, throwing up bucketfuls of little silver fish with their hands and going quite mad with excitement. When they waded thigh-deep the fish shot up out of the water to shoulder height, so that they were like figures each standing in the middle of a fountain. Wonderfully beautiful . . .

This incident was to form the basis of the synopsis of *Ring of Bright Water* which Gavin showed me on Canna and which was later incorporated, almost word for word, into the book itself, where it featured as one of its most celebrated episodes.

No less fantastical as a spectacle, but far more awesome in its numbers and mysterious in its mechanism, was the annual mass migration of the elvers up the Sandaig burn. They arrived each spring to seek the upper reaches of the rivers and streams where they could feed and mature before embarking on the return journey to their spawning grounds in the Sargasso Sea. By the time the thin, steel-blue, three-inch eel fry reached the burn they had spent two years crossing the breadth of the Atlantic Ocean; and yet despite the extreme length of the journey and the apocalyptic toll taken by a multiplicity of predators every inch of the way, they arrived at Sandaig in their teeming billions, an unbroken mass of wriggling forms inches thick, driven by an overpowering instinct ever upwards against the current of the stream, up the vertical rock face of the first waterfall, up the eighty-foot second fall and then the third fall above that, till a few of them, millions out of billions, reached the mountainside where the burn had its source. So powerful was this upward urge that Gavin had found the diminutive, transparent bodies of a few of the most determined individuals as high as two thousand feet above the level of the sea from which they had arrived in such bewildering numbers.

So the years rolled on and the seasons passed at Sandaig, and summers gave way to autumn, with the stags roaring on Skye and the wild geese calling high overhead as they flew out of the north, and the bracken and the berries turning red and scarlet on the hills all around, and the first frosts of winter turning the ground to iron, and the burn running to spate and the waterfall roaring, and the storms howling in from the sea and beating about the lonely house. And after every winter came another spring and promise again of a season of wonders on land and sea in and around the ring of bright water.

Gavin had always had his springer spaniel Jonnie with him since he had first started coming to Sandaig. After Jonnie's death in the summer of 1955 he had vowed never to have another dog, but he found Sandaig a lonely place without one, and after a while he began to cast about for a different species of pet – a badger was one idea – though none that he could think of seemed quite right. Oddly, an otter had never come into consideration. Throughout all the years he had been visiting Sandaig he had never set eyes on a wild native otter, nor had one made its presence known to him there. Otters he regarded as hopelessly non-domesticable; the call of the wild was too powerful an instinct in such a creature, he felt, for it to make a pet that could happily relate to man. It was therefore a curious turn of fate that less than six months after Jonnie's death he should return to Sandaig bringing not just an otter, but an otter all the way from the waters of the Tigris and Euphrates that bore his name.

With his arrival at Sandaig in June 1956 the house became Mij's holt; from the house he ventured forth in total freedom during the day and to it he returned to sleep at night. Mij slept in Gavin's bed, curled in the crook of Gavin's knee, and woke punctually every morning at eight-twenty, waking Gavin at the same moment by nuzzling his face and neck with long, thin squeaks of pleasure and affection. If Gavin did not rise at once, Mij bullied him till he did, removing the bedclothes with a violent tug of his teeth and leaving Gavin naked and shivering on the bed. 'Otters usually get their own way,' he was to write; 'they are not dogs, and they co-exist with humans rather than being owned by them.'

Mij's next objective was a tour of the ring of bright water, the three-quarter circle formed by the burn and the sea, starting with the eel-box by the bridge and proceeding down the freshwater burn in pursuit of fish and eels till he reached the saltwater world of the bay and the islands. As the weeks went by he stayed out longer and longer on these excursions, so that in time Gavin would not begin to worry until he had been gone for half a day. When Mij did return, carrying home with him half a gallon of water in his fur, he would always try and dry himself by rubbing himself vigorously all over the sofa or bed blankets, or preferably all over Gavin.

Living with an otter, Gavin found, was a wrong-way-round sort of business. If you played ball with an otter, for example, it was usually the otter that threw the ball and the human being that fetched it.

It was in the sea that Mij came into his own. When Gavin rowed out in a little dinghy he had the use of Mij would swim out alongside into the deep, crystal-clear waters of the bay. 'I would watch him,' Gavin wrote, 'as he dived down, down, down through fathom after fathom to explore the gaudy sea forests at the bottom with their flowered shell glades and mysterious, shadowed caverns.' Mij could walk on the bottom without buoyancy and stay down for at least six minutes searching for fish and crustacea without coming up for air. Only on the surface did he seem clumsy in water, dog-paddling laboriously like any land animal; but even then he could display enviable prowess, as in the violent seas whipped up by the equinoctial gales, when he would hurl himself like a torpedo through the roaring walls of the breakers, seemingly invulnerable to the monstrous weight and momentum of the waves. 'He would swim through wave after wave,' Gavin wrote, 'until the black dot of his head was lost among the distant white manes, and more than once I thought that some wild urge to seek new lands had seized him and that he would go on swimming into the Sea of the Hebrides and that I should not see him again.'

Mij's absences grew longer as the summer passed. Once, after he had been missing for nine hours, Gavin found him trapped on a narrow ledge high up the cliff of the dark, dank ravine beyond the lowest waterfall, the wild and sinister region which Mij made his special haunt. Gavin was only able to rescue him with great difficulty by lowering himself on a rope attached to the feebly-rooted stump of a tree at the top of the cliff. Then one night Mij did not come home at all. Gavin referred briefly to the incident in a letter he wrote on 23 September 1956: 'Mij was lost all day yesterday, and I was grieving his death when he turned up with his harness broken, having obviously been caught like Absalom, tho' where I can't imagine as we searched for miles. Very harrowing.'

He was later to write this incident up in a long narrative extrapolation of the basic facts. Quite apart from the power and brilliance of Gavin's prose, this extended passage contains his clearest statement on his relationship to animals in general and Mij in particular.

He had left Mij, he wrote, in the early morning at the burn side eating his eels, and began to be uneasy when he had not returned by mid-afternoon. He had been working hard at his book (*A Reed Shaken by the Wind*), and it was a shock to realise that he had been writing for some six hours. He went out and called for Mij down the burn and along the beach, and when he did not find him he went again to the ravine above the falls. But there was no trace of him anywhere, though he explored the whole dark length of it right to the high falls, which he knew that even Mij could not pass. He left the burn then, and went out to the nearer islands; it was low tide and there were exposed stretches and bars of soft white sand, and in the sand he saw the footprints of an otter leading out to the far lighthouse island, though whether they were the foot-prints of Mij he could not tell. All that evening he searched and called, and when dusk came and Mij still did not return he began to despair, for until now his otter had always come back by sundown.

It was a cloudy night with a freshening wind and a big moon that swam muzzily through black rags of vapour. By eleven o'clock it was blowing strong to gale from the south, and on the windward side of the islands a heavy sea was beginning to pile up; enough, Gavin thought, for Mij to lose his bearings if he were trying to make his way homeward through it. He put a light in each window of the house, left the doors open, and dozed fitfully in front of the kitchen fire. By three o'clock in the morning there was the first faint paling of dawn, and he went out to get the boat, for by now he was convinced that Mij was on the lighthouse island.

But the dinghy was soon half swamped in a beam sea and nar-rowly avoided being wrecked on the black cusps and molars of the foam-lashed rocks and skerries around the islands. Gavin, who could not swim a stroke, rowed well out to avoid the reefs, only to be confronted by one of his recurring nightmares – his zoological obsession and true *bête noire*, the Killer whale: 'The Killer broke the surface no more than twenty yards to the north of me, a big bull whose sabre fin seemed to tower a man's height out of the water; and, probably by chance, he turned straight for me. My nerves were strung and tensed; I swung and rowed for the nearest island as though man were a Killer's only prey. I reached the tern island, and the birds rose screaming around me in a dancing canopy of ghostly wings, and I sat down on the rock in the dim windy dawn and felt as desolate as an abandoned child.'

With considerable difficulty Gavin struggled off the island in his waterlogged boat and regained the house at nine in the morning. All that day until four o'clock in the afternoon he wandered and called, and with every hour grew the realisation of how much his animal companion had come to signify to him. 'I resented it,' he wrote, 'I resented my dependence upon this subhuman presence and companionship, resented the void that his absence was going to leave at Sandaig.'

In this mood of reasserted human independence Gavin began to remove the remaining evidence of Mij's past existence, taking away first his drinking bowl and then his half-full bowl of rice and egg. While he was thus occupied he thought he heard a muffled sound like the hoarsely whispered 'Hah!' that Mij used when he interrogated an empty room. Gavin went to the front door to look out but, as before, there was nothing there; he returned through the kitchen-parlour and suddenly stopped, for there on the floor in front of him was a large, wet footprint; and then he heard the sound again:

'*Hah!*'

And there was Mij, soaking wet, his harness broken, bouncing and leaping about him like an excited puppy. He must have been caught by his harness for a day or more, Gavin realised – and then he realised something else. 'I knew by that time that Mij meant more to me than most human beings of my acquaintance, that I should miss his physical presence more than theirs, and I was not ashamed of it. In the penultimate [*sic*] analysis, perhaps, I knew that Mij trusted me more utterly than did any of my own kind.'

In July 1956 an incident occurred at Sandaig which, rightly or wrongly, has been considered to have played a significant, indeed catastrophic part in the course of Gavin's subsequent life. It took place during the visit of Kathleen Raine.

Kathleen had been staying at Sandaig alone, looking after Mij while Gavin was away. She was one of only three people in the world to whom Mij extended his whole-hearted affection, the other two being Gavin himself and Mary MacLeod. Her mere presence could send the young otter into ecstasy, and while he was rumbustious and possessive in her company, she for her part established a strange, deep bond with him and accepted his exuberant horseplay without complaint. Mij, she perceived, was the bond that united herself and Gavin, and was equally attached to them both. Mij slept curled up in her bed, as he did with Gavin, and each morning would call her to follow him as he bounded over the grass to the burn. Such time as was not taken up with Mij she devoted to prettifying the house. 'Like some shrine I tended Gavin's house,' she recorded later, 'happy to scatter, as I thought, fairy-gold for him to find; shells and stones from the shore, things I had made or done for him.' Kathleen had stayed on longer than planned, and was at the house when Gavin arrived late one evening with the English friend he had first met in Basra, Gavin Young. Gavin, it seems, was outraged to find Kathleen still in residence at Sandaig and told her, very brusquely, to leave immediately. Kathleen was deeply hurt and angry. There was a violent altercation outside the house.

'May God forgive you!' Kathleen cried.

'He will,' Gavin snarled in reply.

Gavin Young was highly embarrassed. 'It was a very odd, dramatic, storm-ridden evening, all blasted trees,' he told me. 'And there were these figures shouting at each other and Kathleen Raine pointing her fingers very dramatically. I didn't know what was happening.' Years later Kathleen recalled: 'I was so wretched. I had been thrown out of the place I most wanted to be. Instead of welcoming me and saying, "Well, do stay for supper," I was just thrust out of the door. I felt I had sown Sandaig with invisible treasures – but he couldn't get me out of the door fast enough.'

Kathleen left, and toiled up the hill in the gathering stormy dark, sobbing, torn apart. Eventually she arrived at Tormor, where she proposed to stay the night with Mary and John Donald MacLeod, but she was so distraught that she could not settle, and after a while she left and made her way down the track that led for a mile and a half over the moor and peat bogs to Sandaig. The house was quiet, there were no lights in the windows, and a fitful gale blew in from the sea. There, halfway between the bridge over the burn and the house, stood the rowan tree. Beside herself with anguish and weeping aloud, she laid her hands on the trunk and called upon the tree for justice.

'Let Gavin suffer, in this place, as I am suffering now!' she cried.

She was calling for the loosing of the lightning from the magic tree. To Kathleen this was not so much a curse as 'a desperate heart's cry for truth'.

Just what events, if any, were brought about by that curse is a matter for a later stage of this story. More than a decade was to pass before Gavin began to take the implications on board, and by then, it is true, he had suffered many terrible blows. The first of these was not long in falling.

Gavin and Mij left Sandaig on 6 October 1956, travelling by car to Inverness to catch the night sleeper to London. Mij seemed to accept without question the transformation of his life from a wild state to the circumscribed condition of a domestic animal. At the station hotel he lapped milk from a saucer while Gavin took tea; he boarded the train as though he had done so every day of his life; and he quickly settled back into his old surroundings in the studio flat in Avonmore Road. Nothing, indeed, seemed able to diminish the intense and boundless *joie de vivre* of this extraordinary animal. He took his eels in the bath as he had done in the ever-changing, free-flowing Sandaig burn; he walked the London streets on a lead as contentedly as a dog; and he greatly enjoyed shopping at Harrods. One day Gavin took him to buy a toy at a novelty shop nearby, where he was given the choice between an india-rubber mackerel that wheezed or a chocolate éclair made of plastic. Mij chose the éclair and trotted happily home holding it between his jaws. As they passed the door of the pub on the corner a swaying figure emerged, saw Mij, and exclaimed 'Good God!' To which a voice behind him shouted, 'You've got 'em again, Bill – you've got 'em again!'

So Mij settled down to London life for the winter, demonstrating in the metropolis the same charmed life and invulnerability to physical injury that had preserved him from the stormy seas and jagged rocks of the West Highlands. Once he fell from the gallery of Gavin's flat to the parquet floor below, landing as if he had dropped on to a feather bed; once he caught his head in a slamming door and walked away without a murmur of complaint; on another occasion he chewed a razor blade into tiny fragments without suffering so much as a scratch. But London was hardly an ideal environment for such a creature, and as the weeks went by Mij became an increasingly difficult tie for Gavin, whose writing required that he should travel away from home from time to time.

In desperation Gavin tried to board Mij in the sanatorium of the London Zoo, where he displayed total indifference to lions and tigers and other predatory beasts, but cowered in fear before the aviaries containing the eagles and other great birds of prey that were an otter's only natural enemy in the Iraq marshes. The zoo proved no place for Mij, however. Alone in his cage he at first wailed piteously and dug till his feet bled at the iron and cement that enclosed him. Then he turned his back on the world, burrowing far into the sleeve of the sheepskin coat Gavin had left behind for him, and refusing all food and attention. Within a couple of days he had sunk into a coma that would have led inexorably to self-willed death.

Advised that he should return from his travels at once if he wanted to see his otter alive again, Gavin hurtled through the fog of the East Midlands in his Grand Prix Maserati at speeds of up to 145 miles per hour, till a sudden rending sound brought the car to an abrupt halt, the cockpit filled with blue smoke and the rear-view mirror showed a thin black trail of oil stretching away down the road behind. Abandoning the car, Gavin dashed for the nearest railway station, jumping on to the last possible train as it was moving out of the station. He arrived at the zoo just before it closed for the day. Mij lay motionless deep inside the sheepskin coat. He had fouled his bed and his fur stank like an ill-kept ferret. When Gavin put his head inside the coat and touched the otter's face, Mij awoke as from a trance and emerged to race around his cage and greet his saviour with a frenzy of joy.

Only on one other occasion did Mij ever go back to the zoo. Gavin obtained the zoo's permission to erect at the back of the Aquarium a large glass tank which he had hired for the day at the prodigious cost of ten shillings a minute, and asked the painter Michael Ayrton to come and make drawings of Mij as he cavorted underwater in pursuit of goldfish. An underwater view of an otter in action was a rarity in those days, and Gavin was unprepared for the virtuosity that he saw through the transparent walls of the tank: 'His speed was bewildering, his grace breathtaking; he was boneless, mercurial, sinuous, wonderful. I thought of a trapeze artist, of a ballet dancer, of a bird or an aircraft in aerobatics, but in all of these I was comparing him to lesser grandeurs; he was an otter in his own element, and he was the most beautiful thing in nature I had ever seen.'

The problem of what to do with Mij whenever he went away continued to dog Gavin. He advertised in the papers for a temporary home, but none of the forty replies he received offered a satisfactory solution. He approached retired zoo keepers, but none seemed keen to turn their hand to their old job again, no matter how temporarily. Among his friends and contacts in the zoological world Gavin put out an urgent plea to find him, by hook or by crook, a full-time otter-keeper. But by the time one was found and engaged it was too late.

EIGHTEEN

The death of Mij

Who sees with equal eye, as God of all,
A hero perish, or a sparrow fall,
Atoms or systems into ruin hurled,
And now a bubble burst, and now a world.
ALEXANDER POPE, *An Essay on Man*

The new year of 1957 found Gavin and Mij holed up in Avonmore Road while Gavin frantically tried to finish the overdue manuscript of *A Reed Shaken by the Wind*. He was once more penniless, and Mark Longman agreed yet again to help him out. By the end of January the book was critically late, and Mark Longman noted: 'Gavin Maxwell must deliver 40,000 words within the next week if we are to achieve publication in the autumn.' As soon as a chapter was written Gavin would ring his typist, a teenage girl by the name of Beryl Borders, who had typed his previous book, to come and collect it. She would pick up the manuscript from Gavin's flat the same evening, take it back to her foster-father's office in the Inner Temple and type till two or three in the morning, then walk all the way home to Streatham when she had finished. By dint of such Stakhanovite labours on the part of author and typist alike Gavin was able to deliver six chapters by the end of the week. A month later he delivered several more, and a covering note which read: 'Apologies for this scrawl; I have writer's cramp and my secretary is ill (so is my charlady, and I also have incipient housemaid's knee and otter-keeper's head).'

Time was so short that Longmans were forced to set the text piecemeal in galley as it came in. 'Gavin is our most difficult author,' his editor advised the production manager. 'The MS, although incomplete, is to go straight into galley. I'm sorry we have to do it this way but this book has involved negotiations of the utmost difficulty.' Toiling away by day and night, sustained by tall glasses of well-watered whisky, a limitless supply of cigarettes and Beryl Borders' selfless toil, Gavin finally completed the manuscript of *Reed* on 18 March. With an ebullient and endlessly demanding otter for company it is extraordinary that he was able to put one word after another at all.

Gavin's plan now was to spend the spring and summer alone with Mij at Sandaig – indeed, without an otter-keeper or otter-kennel to look after Mij, he had no alternative, no matter how much he may have wanted to resume his travels abroad. Shortly before finishing *Reed* he had put forward the idea of doing a light-hearted book about Mij called *Otter Nonsense*. This was to be a short book, only 30,000 words or so, but it was to be profusely illustrated with photos and Michael Ayrton's drawings of Mij swimming in the glass tank at the London Zoo. Longmans liked the idea, paid out an advance and fixed a delivery date for the end of June 1957.

Gavin hoped to be able to write *Otter Nonsense* at Sandaig without any distractions other than those provided by his subject. But first he needed a fortnight's freedom from Mij's incessant demands so that he could put his affairs in London in order before his departure. He therefore arranged for Kathleen Raine, with whom he was again reconciled, to take Mij up to Sandaig during the Easter holidays, two weeks ahead of his own arrival there, and on 6 April 1957 he drove Kathleen and her otter charge to Euston station to catch the night sleeper to the north. Under the astonished gaze of the other passengers, Gavin walked Mij on his lead down the platform to his sleeping compartment, followed by Kathleen carrying Mij's special travelling basket containing his chocolate éclair and other toys, his cod-liver oil and unpolished rice, his spare harnesses and leads. Gavin stayed long enough to watch Mij settle down and curl up in the wash basin, then, as the guard's whistle blew, bade them both goodbye. Next day, from the Scottish terminus at Mallaig, Kathleen and Mij continued to Sandaig by sea in Bruce Watt's boat.

Never had Sandaig seemed more beautiful to Kathleen than it did then, nor had she ever felt a stronger sense of coming home. The poignant beauty of early spring was all around her – the scent of young birch leaves in the air, the song of the green linnet among the alders, the primroses, anemones and golden saxifrage blooming brightly among the green, sheltered banks. At her side, at the edge of the sea or along the burn, bounded the irrepressible young animal companion she loved so much. 'Never had I been so happy,' she was to write; 'every hour of every day was filled with beauty.'

Each day as she walked with Mij around the Sandaig hinterland Kathleen realised more and more clearly that Mij was essentially a wild animal, and that his bond to her was one of personal affection and no more. Each day she grew more and more anxious about the hazards inherent in these walks, for Mij, roaming free, could go where she could not – up cliffs, past waterfalls, round rocky headlands at high tide. Sometimes he did not answer her call, and sometimes he gave her the slip completely, so that she returned to the house alone, only to find him already there, curled up under the blanket on her bed. Once he was out all night, and though he eventually came back of his own accord, the danger signs were there to see. Mijbil was showing dangerous signs of independence. Kathleen prayed that he might remain unharmed until she could hand him over to Gavin safe and well. She tried to undo the curse she had made at the rowan tree the previous year, asking the tree to forget her past anger.

Kathleen was perhaps unwise to have ignored Gavin's instruction and allowed Mij to run free, without his specially designed harness and the lead that could be attached to it in an emergency. But she felt the harness was more a danger than a safeguard; she feared Mij might get snagged on some tangle of wire, or caught up underwater and drowned. Three days before Gavin was due to arrive, she had second thoughts and tried to put the harness on, but Mij wriggled too vigorously and nipped too hard for her to be able to complete the task. On 14 April Mij wandered again, this time a great distance, for he was seen at the village of Arnisdale, eight miles south of Sandaig by sea, but recognised for what he was and left unmolested to return home in his own good time.

Kathleen also disregarded another of Gavin's instructions – not to take Mij north up the shore of the Sound of Sleat, for in that direction lay the village of Glenelg, and people, and potential danger. But on 15 April, the day before Gavin was due to set off from London, Kathleen made a fateful misjudgement. Every day during her stay she had taken Mij south down the shore; but that last day when she came to the mouth of the burn she turned north. The tide was in and Mij ran into the sea as he always did. This time, however, instead of swimming about along the edge of the tide, exploring the shallows and hunting among the in-shore weeds and rocks, he swam directly out to sea, suddenly wild, and deaf to Kathleen's urgent calls. She stumbled along the boulder beach in the direction of the cavern known as Joe's Cave, trying to follow her charge, but she could no longer see his little black head in the water, and after much frantic searching along the shore she realised that she had lost him and turned back alone towards the house.

Mij, meanwhile, had regained the shore at some point further to the north and continued his explorations inland as far as Glenelg. There he was seen by a man in his hen run, who would have shot him had he not observed that the otter was not the slightest bit interested in his chickens and correctly judged it was probably the tame one that was reputed to belong to 'the Major'. Late in the day, with the light beginning to fade, Mij turned back for home. Lolloping along the ditch at the side of the road, he had just reached a sharp bend where a little churchyard stood between the road and the sea at Glenelg when a lorry drew up alongside him and the driver got out. Mij stopped and waited as the man, a roadmender from Glenelg, went to fetch something from the back of the lorry, and was still waiting when the man came back. Mij had never had any reason to fear or distrust human beings.

'That night,' Kathleen wrote, 'I could not sleep; I hoped against hope that in the morning I would hear Mij whistling again at the door, left open for him. I lay in anguish, listening to a storm the like of which I seemed never to have heard, the wind full of lamenting voices as the ragged cloud flew over the moon from the south west as the gale raged. Anger and grief were in the wind; and though I did not know it, all was over, Eden lost, its gates closed against me for ever.' In the morning she continued her search, even after she heard that an otter had been killed by a workman on the road.

Gavin had received advance warning of a problem at Sandaig before he left London by car with Raef Payne on 16 April. Having finished reading the proofs of *Reed* in a last desperate late-night scramble, he was packed and ready to leave when he received a worrying phone call from the factor at Eilanreach Estate. There was a rumour going about that an otter had been killed in the vicinity and that Mij was missing. He could not confirm that the dead otter was Mij, because it was said that the otter in question had been so mangy that the man who had killed it had not thought it worth keeping the skin. There was no other information.

Gavin arrived at Glenelg with Raef the following afternoon. Asking everyone he met in the village and along the shore, he had heard conflicting tales as to what had happened. But he did not believe the stories he was told. He knew in his bones that Mij was dead. He just wanted to know who had killed him and why. In the village he was told that the roadmender had been driving past the church when he had seen an otter by the road and had killed it. The skin was in bad condition, and the man, who in his subsequent account Gavin gave the name of 'Big Angus', had thrown it away. His next step was to pay a visit to Big Angus's house. The man was not at home, but his family stuck to the authorised version. Yes, an otter had been killed, but the skin had been so mangy that it had been thrown away. When Big Angus himself arrived home he confirmed what his family had said. He had seen an otter on the road and had stopped his lorry and gone to the back to fetch a pick-head, with which he smashed the creature's head in. 'It was very old and skinny,' he assured Gavin. 'I threw the carcase in the river. I don't remember where.' He resisted all Gavin's efforts to persuade him to tell the whole truth and spare Gavin the anguish of waiting in vain day after day at Sandaig for Mij's return. Later a local informant told him the true story.

He had seen the body of the otter on the lorry when it stopped in the village – a perfect specimen except the head, which was bashed in. It was obvious it wasn't a wild otter, and the story Big Angus put about was 'just a pack of lies'.

Mij had been with Gavin for a year and a day on the night he had left London. 'I hope he was killed quickly,' he wrote later, 'but I wish he had had one chance to use his teeth on his killer.'

The fate of Mijbil caused some commotion in Glenelg, and is remembered still. Big Angus is still alive as I write, and he has received much calumny over the years as the killer of Mij. He was portrayed both in Gavin's book and in the film based on it as a thoroughgoing brute – the quasi-mythological evil-doer of his era. In reality Big Angus was a decent man, and both his family and the community to which he belonged at Glenelg strongly resented what they saw as his character-assassination at Gavin Maxwell's hands, pointing out that otters were widely considered vermin then and that the death of Mij was simply a case of 'the wrong otter in the wrong place'.

★   ★   ★

While Raef took the car on to Tormor, Gavin – much dejected and forlorn – continued on the final sad stage of the journey to Sandaig by boat. Kathleen was waiting on the beach to meet him.

'The day cleared in the afternoon and the wind dropped,' she recalled; 'and against the empty horizon I saw at last Gavin's boat nearing the shore. It slowly grew and grew, like a death-ship in a dream; and at last the dinghy was lowered that brought him to the strand. He already knew; and, bowed with a single grief, we sat side by side beside the dark brown waters of the empty burn, where no animal companion delighted us with his greeting.' Neither Gavin nor she had yet realised that Mij's death had ended a world; nor that the very grief they shared was to divide them.

Kathleen was beside herself with grief and remorse, and wept bitterly. Gavin did his best to comfort her. He was himself partly to blame for what had happened, he told her; he did not blame her, he was not angry, she should not cry, what was done was done and that was an end of it. But she was inconsolable and would allow no one, not even (or especially) Gavin, to relieve her of her burden of guilt. Gavin was a lonely man, she knew, and all his love had been bestowed on Mij. 'To Gavin and to me, he was more than an animal; a creature of Paradise, a part of ourselves. In him I loved Gavin; in his love, a part of Gavin loved me, and Gavin through him accepted a part of my love.' And now it was over. Her beloved Sandaig could never again be Eden for her. The gates of Paradise were closed.

Looking back on that deathly, now distant event, Kathleen once told me: 'It all boils down to Mij, doesn't it, and my losing him. Gavin's quest was for perfect human love. But really it was Mij that was perfect love; Mij was an angel. Mij would have gone eventually, given his propensity for straying, but it was I who was the instrument – I was the instrument for evil in Gavin's life. Yet I had meant so intensely to be only the instrument for good. This is something that bewildered and embittered me for many years.'

From Sandaig Gavin wrote to Mark Longman to tell him the news:

I'm so very sorry to be once more in the position of letting you down; it seems to be becoming a habit and I feel guilty. The otter's death has upset the programme for the moment, but I assure you that I *will* write the book – it's only that it seems a bit grizzly to sit down and do it straightaway. I know that to mind about an animal so much must seem quite insane to you, but if you remember that I live alone and had this creature with me night and day for a year as, for most of the time, my only companion, you may be able to excuse if not understand.

There was nothing to keep either Kathleen or Gavin at Sandaig now – indeed, it would have been impossible to stay – and after a day or two they went their separate ways. On 22 April Gavin's London typist Beryl Borders and her foster-father (and future husband) Jim Borders took Gavin and Raef from Sandaig to Mallaig on a sailing boat they had chartered from Bruce Watt. From Mallaig Gavin went on to Canna to stay with his friends the Campbells, who did their best to comfort him and cheer him up. But there was a vast hollow in his life now, and a deep despair. On 27 April 1957 he left Canna and returned to the south. It was a year before he could bear to return.

NINETEEN

Writer at work

No one but a blockhead ever wrote, except for money.
SAMUEL JOHNSON

London was lonely and suffocating and Gavin was desolate. 'I mourned for my fallen sparrow,' he was to write. 'I could not deny to myself how much I had been affected by the death of one wild animal.'

Mark Longman had now had an opportunity to read the complete text of *A Reed Shaken by the Wind* and hoped to jolly Gavin up with words of praise. 'I have read every word of the galleys,' he wrote on 30 April, 'and let me say at once that I find the complete work just as impressive as the admirable portions I saw before you left. You have done a splendid job and I congratulate you.'

Wilfred Thesiger, however, was harder to please. He did not like the way Gavin had portrayed him on their expedition in the marshes, and said so. 'I can see nothing in these galleys,' Longman assured Thesiger, 'which redounds to your discredit – indeed you emerge with flying colours, perhaps a little stern, but that, after all, was your role as leader of the party.' But Thesiger was not placated. From the retreat where he was writing his classic of Arabian exploration, *Arabian Sands*, he scribbled a riposte, demanding that certain passages be excised from Gavin's text, if only because Arab propaganda could make political capital out of them. He added: 'I think Gavin's treatment of me remains ungracious and ungenerous . . . I am fed up with my own book which is bloody. Boring and hopelessly put together.'

Gavin agreed to the cuts and Thesiger was content. A week later, on 18 May 1957, Gavin left London for Sicily, for one last try to gather material for his faltering work on the *tonnaras*. Sicily provided a timely distraction from his private grief, even if it did no more than substitute one kind of penance for another. In a letter to Raef Payne on 11 June he described his life in unenviable terms:

Life here is undiluted hell. I've been pretty continuously on the move, as it's practically impossible to get a bed anywhere. At the moment I'm staying in a youth hostel about ten miles from Palermo; it is full of fat Germans and northern Italians, none of them under fifty. They wear clackety wooden *sabots* and play the gramophone day and night. Add to that a sirocco that seems to come out of a furnace, swarms of flies, and a general feeling of malaise, and you have a pretty good recipe for hell. I can't imagine what I'm doing here, but also can't imagine what I should be doing in England. The world is still terribly otterless, and in general I feel a greater lack of purpose or direction than I ever remember.

I find myself very well known in Sicily, and the Palermo bookshops still display rows and rows of the book [*God Protect Me from My Friends*] in the windows. Hardly a day passes without a local press comment of some sort or a lecture on 'the Scottish journalist Maxwell'. The atmosphere is usually equivocal and uncomfortable.

The summer months passed slowly under the scorching Sicilian sun, and there were times when Gavin's much-mourned otter companion and even Sandaig itself seemed like the figments of some half-forgotten dream. By the beginning of July he was installed after a fashion in his old haunt at Castellammare, the poor fishing village not far from the *tonnara* where every summer the tuna fishermen took their seasonal toll in the chambers of death. But the Giuliano affair had begun to catch up with him, darkening the present and threatening the future. On 1 July he reported to Raef Payne:

Here not all is fun and games; far from it indeed. An atmosphere began to develop when the friends of a certain politician mentioned in my book began to try to persuade him to bring a libel action. Whether or not he will I don't know, but some unpleasant things have been happening, for these friends are *mafiosi*. The first symptom was a note in my car, saying: 'Englischmann go home, you sayed too much someone going to kill you soon.' To which I replied in a moment of bravado by another note left on the car at the same place – saying, in effect, go ahead. Nothing happened, but after that I was conscious of being followed from time to time. Then, as a result of an article published in *L'ora* – an interview with me – the police have become actively interested in where I got certain information and assume in fact that it came from the gentleman whose address I'm using here. So they are going to try and make life very difficult for him, because he is already a little non grata in the same quarters as I am. Meanwhile he has warned me to be careful of what I eat(!) and not to accept drinks or coffee from strangers. I eat in the evening at his house, and in the daytime bread and cheese where I am living – part of the castle (but the wrong part) now converted into an as yet unfinished house for the lighthouse keeper. Workmen are still working on it, and any form of privacy is impossible. Also they sing unmelodiously all day.

All this is a *very* strange feeling; frankly, I'm scared stiff, and would come home but for (a) leaving a friend in the lurch, and (b) loss of face. As an addition to a repertoire of experienced sensations this is one I could have done without. Paranoia rampant. And Lord how Sicilians can stare! When a street is full of several hundred of them and they all stare it is quite something.

My ticket home is booked for the 20th, and I should arrive in London that evening (if still alive). My plans beyond that date are uncertain, except in as far as I shall move house within a week of arrival, and then take stock.

Having failed once again to obtain the material he needed for his tuna-fishing book, Gavin returned to London. Shortly afterwards he moved from Avonmore Road, his London base for almost a decade, to Kathleen Raine's larger and more up-market house at 9 Paultons Square, Chelsea. It was here, some eight years previously, that he had been brought by Tambimuttu for the first meeting with Kathleen that had, in some measure, led to the start of his literary career. Kathleen's children were grown up now and she no longer needed the whole of a property that occupied four floors. So she rented the ground floor and basement (and a small bedroom on the first floor) to Gavin, thus providing him with a stylish through-sitting-room, two bedrooms, a dining room and the run of the small garden – more commodious accommodation than he had ever enjoyed anywhere away from his own family home.

Kathleen kept a small flat at the top of the house, and thus remained in contact with Gavin whenever she was not in Cambridge (she had a Research Fellowship at Girton College). Gradually she came to realise that their relationship was irremediably shattered. It was not the curse on the rowan tree or even the death of Mij that had caused this, she realised, but her pride in not accepting his forgiveness. 'To see Gavin now was to weep,' she was to write; 'not a few tears, but streaming rivers of tears that would not stop, that I could no more control than the waters of a swollen burn. And that no man can bear.'

One night she was sitting with him in the room that was now his, talking sadly (as she put it) 'like Adam and Eve after the Fall', when Gavin asked her to share his bed with him, as once before. 'And I did not do so. Sadly, slowly, I climbed the stairs to my lonely bed, leaving him to his own. Knowing that I could no longer, now, give him either help or comfort.'

All might still have been well, or at least bearable, but for a fatal evening they spent in the fashionable buttery of the Berkeley Hotel in Knightsbridge. For some reason – it might have been whisky – Gavin used the occasion to destroy Kathleen once and for all. He catalogued all her faults as he saw them (including her dress and her physical appearance), and every one of her mistakes. 'His words had come up from the depths,' she recalled, 'the fiery pits and deserts which lie far beyond our everyday selves.' By the time he had finished she was so distraught and wept so bitterly that Gavin was concerned for her safety, and after delivering her to the house of one of her friends he telephoned their mutual guru, Elias Canetti, and warned him, 'If Kathleen has killed herself, I shall never forgive her.'

Gavin had closed his life against her. Now he presented merely an external and social mask. And eventually, somehow or other, he took over the rest of the house from her. One day he invited her back to admire his alterations and furniture, but it was all too much and she wept again. 'I sat alone in a corner of the Blue Cockatoo restaurant,' she wrote, 'where there were candles on the tables, and dark shadows, and tried to regain command of myself before returning by a late train to Cambridge. Gavin had rid himself of me.'

Too late, perhaps, Kathleen had discovered that Gavin was driven by a daemon fuelled by his deep anger about people. At times it seemed he had infringed so many of the norms of human relationships and crossed so many forbidden frontiers in his own inner world that the integrity of his persona had been destroyed.

Not long after Gavin moved into 9 Paultons Square (for which his mother agreed to pay the rent), he began to enquire about a daily help to clean and tidy and cook his lunch for him. Mrs Lamm, who lived nearby, saw his advertisement on a board outside a tobacconists: 'Daily help needed one and a half to two hours, for Author and Traveller, away quite a lot.'

'What struck me most of all when I first met him,' Mrs Lamm recalled, 'was his friendliness, kindliness and politeness, not forgetting his sense of humour. He was very charming and natural. I felt at ease and very friendly towards him. I wanted to look after him so much. "Can you cook?" he asked.

'"Well, yes," I said, "I can cook all right to suit my husband and son."

'"Can you cook *sausages*?"

'I felt like laughing but I could see that he was serious. I thought to myself, this is going to be easy – I could do that standing on my head. Before I left him he asked me if I liked animals. "Yes," I said, "I am very fond of animals." Another thing he said was: "I suppose you want a Hoover." And that was the beginning of the most exciting, amusing, nerve-racking, alarming and interesting time I have ever experienced.'

It was not the kind of household Mrs Lamm was used to. Gavin was so preoccupied and absent-minded that sometimes he forgot to pay her wages. But within a fortnight of her starting he had given her a substantial pay rise, and when her husband fell ill he readily volunteered an open-ended loan to tide them over. Then there were the animals. Gavin shared his quarters with a succession of strange and wonderful birds and beasts, not all of which were entirely adjusted to human society.

Fortunately, perhaps, Mrs Lamm arrived too late on the scene to be exposed to the unsociable habits of the earlier animal occupants of the house. The first was a ring-tailed lemur called Kiko, formerly the pet of the writer and critic, Cyril Connolly. Gavin bought Kiko in Harrods' pet department for the colossal sum of £75 (more than £1000 today). She was a beautiful creature, a little larger than a cat, with soft blue-grey fur, a foxy black-and-white face, golden eyes, a huge bushy tail with black-and-white rings, and monkey-like hands with needle-like claws. Beautiful Kiko may have been, but her habits were (Gavin wrote) 'both insanitary and obscene'. Kiko also turned out to be a psychopath. Gavin described the problem: 'She had some deep-seated psychosis that made her about as suitable a pet as a wild-caught leopard. She was a killer, attacking without warning or *casus belli*, and always from behind.' Twice she leapt from a bookcase onto Gavin's shoulder and tried to tear at his eyes with her sharp claws.

In a third attack she switched targets and made for his leg. This time she succeeded. Gavin's tibial artery was slashed, so that it stuck out of his calf like a black cigarette end, spouting blood to a distance of a foot. To his horror, Gavin saw he was standing in a speedily widening puddle of blood. He soaked a handkerchief and tried to apply a tourniquet, but he could not remember where the pressure point was. He looked around wildly for a thread with which to tie off the artery but all the time the blood was pumping out – two pints, he reckoned, had already been lost – and he began to feel faint and shaky. Then suddenly he remembered – the tibial artery surfaced at the groin. He applied the tourniquet, lit a cigarette and contemplated the mess – and Kiko's future. Since lemurs shared a common ancestor with man, he concluded, they might perhaps have to be chosen as carefully as human friends. Kiko would have to go; and go she did, to Chester Zoo and the company of her own kind.

Next came a nameless bush baby, as acrobatic as the unlamented lemur but far less homicidal. Alas, this wide-eyed creature soon proved to be a crashing bore. His habits were (as Gavin put it) 'solitary and embarrassing', and being largely nocturnal he would nightly shatter the sleeping jungle of Chelsea – and Gavin's dreams – with blood-curdling shrieks. The bush baby, too, was soon moved on. By the time Mrs Lamm arrived on the scene an altogether more docile menagerie had taken over No. 9.

There was Prodnose, for instance, a Brazilian hangnest, and Kali, Gavin's mynah bird, who used to wolf whistle and make the most revolting noises, like an old man coughing and spitting, in imitation of his former owner, a retired and not very healthy zoo keeper. Kali soon learned to copy Mrs Lamm's laugh, and when she was dusting or making the bed he would land on her back – 'like a

large bag of flour dropping on me' – and chatter and laugh away
demonically. Kali also had a remarkable musical talent which was
only discovered when he was boarded out with Gavin's old school
friend Anthony Dickins, a concert pianist, during one of Gavin's
absences abroad. Dickins recalled:

> When it came to my studio and heard me playing classical
> music all day, it was at first simply an attentive listener. Then
> it felt emboldened to try a little itself – a few squawks and
> shrieks and grunts, totally unrelated to anything I had played.
> It soon gained confidence, however, and by the second week
> was making the most eerie and startling attempts to accom-
> pany me whenever I played the piano. Scales, arpeggios and
> trills were its special favourites and soon it was squawking
> and shrieking in upward and downward glissandos from basso
> profundo to sopranissimo with delirious joy. Kali's virtuoso
> performances bore no relationship at all in tone, register,
> rhythm, volume or sequence to what I had been playing, but
> the enthusiasm was fantastic. I would say that Kali was an
> accomplished and highly original 'modernistic' composer, far
> in advance of Peter Maxwell Davies or Humphrey Searle.

Then there was Violet, Mrs Lamm's favourite among the thirteen
brilliant tropical birds – the iridescent South American tanagers –
that fluttered at liberty about the ground-floor sitting-room, feeding from fruit suspended from branches and glittering like jewels
in the light of the concealed spotlights about the room. Two tortoises and Rawni, the taciturn and usually motionless Saharan
lizard, made up the complement of pets in the early days.

The lizard was a delicate creature, requiring such a high ambient
temperature that Gavin had to train three electric fires on it even
in summer – much to the discomfiture of the lodger in the room
above, a barrister by the name of Anthony Lincoln. In its natural
habitat the lizard was bathed in morning dew which kept its skin
from cracking in the Saharan sun, and when Gavin moved up to
Sandaig he asked Anthony Lincoln if he could get up at dawn to
sprinkle water on his pet's back. 'OK,' said the barrister. 'And what
do I feed it on?' 'Oh, locusts,' Gavin told him. 'And where on
earth do I find those?' 'Oh, Harrods.' Sometimes Mrs Lamm would
be asked to feed the lizard with live locusts that were kept in a tin,

and as often as not they escaped, whizzing around the room, she complained, 'like aeroplanes'. Much larger creatures were to come and go at No. 9 in due course. Mrs Lamm fed and tidied up after them all, irrespective of their shape, size, species, genus or proclivities.

Mrs Lamm could never be sure what she would find when she went into the house. Once she came across a whole deer's head – antlers, fur, eyes and all – boiling away in her largest saucepan. 'My goodness, I thought, I suppose that's how they cook up at Sandaig. I knew they did do things up there in the quickest possible way. For instance, one day I was lighting the fire in the Bird Room when the Major walked in. Seeing I was having a little difficulty in getting it to go, he said: "We usually sling a gallon of paraffin on when we're at Sandaig if it won't start."'

One day she went into the dining room and was confronted by Gavin's mother. 'My son says you're the best charlady he's ever had,' said Lady Mary. 'The best *housekeeper*, Mother,' Gavin corrected her.

'The Major was very fond of his mother,' remembered Mrs Lamm. 'He often had her to tea at No. 9 when he was there. He used to ask me to make sure the silver was looking nice because his mother was coming to tea. She loved the crispy noodles that came from the Good Earth Chinese Restaurant in the King's Road.'

But the curious ménage at No. 9 was not really where Gavin's heart was, Mrs Lamm realised. 'He loved all things of nature, birds, animals and flowers. That's why he loved Scotland so much, I'm sure. He felt free and happy to live with nature in all its aspects; and that was the only time he was really happy. He wasn't a misery when he was in London – far from it. I actually heard him singing, once. A short sharp Scottish dirge, I suppose. It proved one thing to me at any rate – he couldn't sing. His enthusiasm for some things was childlike at times, specially if he had got a bargain at the Hammersmith Market or Portobello Road. I was very fond of him and looked upon him as a son and cared for him as best I could. I cooked quite a lot of things for him, but I can never ever remember cooking sausages.'

In the period after Gavin's move to Paultons Square his preoccupations were many and varied and often he seemed to be doing a great many things at once. The period between the autumn of 1957 and the spring of 1959 was chaotic and incoherent, and characterised by two distinct aims – the ever-urgent need to earn a living as an author, and the no less desperate striving for some still centre of peace and security in his personal life. He had no money to speak of and no one and nothing that he wished to love or be loved by. He changed literary agents at this critical juncture, abandoning Graham Watson for Peter Janson-Smith, who had recently left Curtis Brown to set up on his own. Graham Watson was not entirely sorry to see Gavin go, for though he admired his 'blazing talent' he didn't much care for him as a man, particularly his 'endless importunate demands for money' to cope with his expensive tastes. 'The telephone would ring in my office,' Watson was to write in his autobiography: '"Gavin here. I'm in a garage near Inverness. My supercharger has blown. It's going to cost £150 to repair. I need the cash before my cheque bounces. See if Mark will provide. I'm coming down by sleeper and we'll meet for lunch tomorrow." I would duly report at the luncheon rendezvous to find the impoverished Gavin driving up in a Daimler, temporarily hired to replace his Alvis.'

In October 1957 Gavin's book about the Iraq marshes, *A Reed Shaken by the Wind*, was published in Britain. Not long afterwards it came out in America (under the title *People of the Reeds*) and later in a number of foreign-language editions. The reviews were enthusiastic and did much to advance Gavin's literary reputation. Harold Nicolson wrote in the *Observer*: 'Mr Maxwell must possess strong nerves and a romantic soul. He has a gift of visual memory and a gift of language. It is a delight when books of travel are written as well as this.' Cyril Connolly, reviewing the book in the *Sunday Times* (the review which first prompted me to contact Gavin in late November 1957), saw the author as 'a man on a quest' and described his journey with Thesiger as 'a *voyage d'oubli*, a modern version of big-game hunting in Africa, in which roughing it is part of the cure'. In Connolly's opinion, *Reed* was 'one of the best travel books in years', and he praised 'the moving quality of his prose which is the expression of a sensibility delicate and troubled, humorous and observant', and predicted that one day Gavin would 'like Achilles shed his present hair-shirt for some act of creative assertion'. The UK hardback sales were modestly encouraging, but the book was mainly a *succès d'estime*, winning the Heinemann Award of the Royal Society of Literature and eventually establishing itself as a modern travel classic – and a brilliant exercise in literary cinephotography.

Gavin now began to cast about for new ideas. He had already received publishers' advances for three books still under contract – a novel, the book about tuna-fishing in Sicily, and *Otter Nonsense*. But the money had long ago been spent, and it was most unlikely that the books would ever be written. Gavin found life as precarious as any other freelance author, for he had no source of income other than what his mother and his elder brother cared to dispense to him. Though he was a writer of proven ability, he had not yet found a regular public. His publishers nurtured him to an admirable degree, humouring him, cajoling him, guiding him, accommodating his repeated requests for loans and advances against advances, for Gavin had star quality as well as literary potential. This was why they put up with him, for he was far and away the most difficult author in their stable.

There was one thing Longmans could not help Gavin with, however, and that was an *idea*. Now and for the rest of his working life he was constantly hunting about for the next idea, fretting about what to write next, tormented with the thought that nothing would turn up and he would never write another book again. Abandoning the book about the *tonnara*, he now proposed in its place a book based on the lives – the sociological case histories – of the fishermen and other inhabitants of Castellammare del Golfo whom he had come to know while working on the tuna project. He had already received from his friend and assistant Giuseppe M. the raw material of many of the case histories. These were based on long, intensely intimate interviews with a variety of Giuseppe's neighbours, the poor and the desperate of western Sicily. Longmans agreed in principle to the idea of the book. This marked the start of his next published work, *The Ten Pains of Death*, which was to preoccupy him throughout most of 1958.

But though Sicily was at the top of his working agenda, Gavin's mind was never far from his much-mourned otter and the peace and loveliness of his Sandaig refuge. As the traumatic year following the otter's death drew to its end, he began to realise that Mij, and what Mij meant to him, required a more substantial memorial than the lightweight bauble of *Otter Nonsense*. Sandaig and his life at the sea's edge, he saw, was not merely the background to an otter's antics, but the integral component of a much bigger and infinitely more urgent story about himself and what he stood for and cherished above all things.

He was therefore immediately receptive to an idea put forward at a meeting attended by George (later Lord) Hardinge, Mark Longman and Peter Janson-Smith – though not by Gavin himself – early in the new year of 1958. Gavin had been looking for a big advance for a new book about an expedition to Assam or Siam, a venture which his publishers regarded as both vague and expensive. A cheaper, more feasible, and possibly more profitable alternative, suggested by Hardinge, might be for Gavin to write a book about the remote corner of the Scottish West Highland coast where he lived and the part played by the otter in his life there.

Mark Longman was greatly in favour of the proposal, firstly because it would not entail spending a large part of the advance on travel, and secondly because in his view Gavin could make an excellent job of it. 'If anybody can make a proper portrait of a remote part of Scotland, he can,' Longman told a colleague, 'and it is the sort of book that could sell really well.' A few days later Gavin wrote a short essay indicating the way in which he intended to treat the subject and giving some idea of its scope. This essay – the famous silver-herring-fry scene – fired Longman's enthusiasm still further, and on 4 March 1958 Gavin signed a contract for a book about Sandaig, as yet untitled, for a total advance of £1250. He would write the story – the vision – of Sandaig; the otter would be a part of that vision, the free spirit, the star creature among all the many wild creatures that inhabited that Paradise. A world bestseller was in the making. Out of the puny ashes of *Otter Nonsense* would arise the vibrant and shining phoenix of *Ring of Bright Water*, the book that would transform Gavin Maxwell's life – and the lives of otters, too, in Britain and around the world.

In April, almost a year to the day since the death of Mij, Gavin returned to Sandaig in the Bentley saloon he had bought on the strength of his latest book advance. I went with him. I have described already the discussion we had on Compass Hill, Canna, about the embryonic Sandaig book. The visit did bring keenly home to him how empty the place seemed without Mij. 'He had filled the landscape so completely,' he was to write, 'had made so much his own every square yard of the ring of bright water I loved, that it seemed, after he had gone from it, hollow and insufficient.'

From that moment he determined to find a replacement otter as soon as possible, so that there would always be an otter at Sandaig for as long as the house was his. Together that spring we explored the boulder-strewn littoral of Otter Island, one of the chain of tiny islands in Sandaig Bay where otters had bred in past years, crawling about on our hands and knees in our search for tell-tale otter spraint (droppings) and signs of inhabited otter holts in the warren of low little caves and tunnels amongst the rocks; but there seemed to be no evidence of otters in the Sandaig area, and for the moment Gavin abandoned the idea of finding Mij's successor so close to home.

Most of the time he was at Sandaig Gavin was working on *The Ten Pains of Death*, and in the early summer he returned to Castellammare, to collect more autobiographies of the destitute and oppressed inhabitants of that poverty-stricken little town and tales of the violent and medieval society in which they lived and loved and died. At midsummer he was back at Sandaig, working still on his gallery of Sicilian lives, and he remained there till the end of the year. By then he had obtained able assistance in translating the raw Sicilian of his source material from Pat Fulwell, who had recently graduated in Italian from Oxford.

He had also made repeated efforts to find another otter, and had even built a large glass water tank in the garden at Paultons Square and acquired the services of an otter-keeper in expectation of an otter's imminent arrival. The otter-keeper, Jimmy Watt, was a remarkable young man who was just leaving school. He had considerable practical gifts and personal qualities, an instinctive natural feeling for animals, and an unquenchable love of boats and the sea and the wild places of the Scottish Highlands. Jimmy was destined to play a large part in the story of Sandaig, and to become like a son to Gavin and, eventually, his heir. For the moment, however, he was otterless, for all Gavin's efforts to acquire an otter through the summer and early autumn of 1958 proved fruitless. In Iraq the Crown Prince's chief game warden, Robert Angorly, had obtained a succession of young otter cubs from the Marsh Arabs on Gavin's behalf, but all except one had died within a few days of arrival in Basra, and plans to despatch the sole surviving otter by air to London were brutally interrupted by the Iraqi Revolution, the murder of the king and the imprisonment of Angorly himself. Attempts to acquire an Indian clawless otter through a dealer and a Malay otter from an English zoo were just as abortive.

Yet Sandaig was not all frustration and literary grind. At the end of September Gavin wrote to me:

This has been, so far, a very remarkable stay at Sandaig, outstanding among all I can remember, except for the year I had the otter up here. For six weeks the sun shone every day and it was gloriously technicoloured. During that time I was mentally in your place of filming, and I had many very felicitous ideas, which I should, for a small consideration, be prepared coyly to disclose to you. The addition of a second and very much larger dinghy extended our range vastly, and such things as going by boat to Glenelg or down to Knoydart became a matter of everyday occurrence. I even started enquiries about buying the *Gannet* back, which has been located in some fishing village on the west coast of Skye. But they wanted three times the amount I paid for her fifteen years ago. No doubt her association with me contributed – like a french letter once used by Napoleon.

A few weeks later, the repercussions Gavin had feared might arise from the publication of the Italian edition of his first Sicilian book, *God Protect Me from My Friends*, finally materialised. The book had been published in Italy in 1957 under the title *Dagli amici mi guardi iddio* – the exact Sicilian equivalent of the English title – and had been serialised on the front page of the prestigious Italian national newspaper *Il Tempo*. The first Gavin heard of impending trouble was at the beginning of March 1958. On 5 March the *Daily Express* carried the story:

AUTHOR FRIEND OF PRINCESS SUED FOR LIBEL

Author Gavin Maxwell, adventure-loving friend and escort of Princess Margaret, is being sued for libel by Italy's Minister of Posts and Telegraphs. Sicilian-born Bernardo Mattarella claims he was libelled in Maxwell's book 'God Protect Me from My Friends', the story of Sicilian bandit Giuliano. He alleged that Maxwell wrote that Matarella had contact with British and American special operations in Sicily before the Allied invasion; that he quoted Left Wing newspaper reports that he was a member of the Mafia, the secret society which

ran Western Sicily; and that Matarella's name occurred frequently in the trial of Giuliano's band.

Mr Maxwell said last night: 'I will defend the action.'

Mr Maxwell, 43-year-old ex-Guards officer, is a cousin of
the Duke of Northumberland. Besides being an author, he is
a poet, painter, shark-hunter, lecturer and part-time hermit.

Longmans immediately set out to assess the situation and imple-
ment a damage-limitation exercise. When Gavin's defence lawyer
returned from Milan he advised them that the case – a *criminal* libel
action – was being brought purely as a result of an internal political
squabble. Mattarella, a native of Castellammare del Golfo, simply
wished to clear his name before the forthcoming elections in Italy.
That he actually *was* a member of the Mafia, as Gavin had alleged,
there seemed no doubt – plenty of information from various private
sources confirmed this. It followed that it was almost certainly the
Mafia that had pushed Mattarella into bringing the case to court.
Since the Mafia was a secret society, Mattarella could not allow
open accusations that he was a member to go unchallenged. The
situation was complicated by the fact that Gavin's Italian publisher,
Giangiacomo Feltrinelli, was one of Italy's leading Communists,
and only too happy to stir up bad publicity for someone like Mattarella. He had decided to fight the case in a big way, engaging Piero
Terni, a leading Italian barrister, for his own defence and the most
eminent lawyer in Italy, Professor Cesare Degli Occhi, a Member
of Parliament, for Gavin's. The case would come up in October,
and Gavin was advised not to attend for fear that the Mafia might
bypass the legal process and exact their own kind of summary
justice. In any case, Gavin knew enough of the horrors of Italian
prisons not to risk setting foot on Italian soil if he could possibly
help it. Piero Terni was sure there was nothing to worry about. It
was most unlikely, he claimed, that the case would go against the
defendants.

It was something of a shock, therefore, when the court, after a
trial that was front-page news in Italy, found Gavin guilty of criminal libel. His co-defendant, Feltrinelli, was dismissed from the case
after persuading the court he had not actually read the book. Gavin
was fined £3000 and sentenced to eight months imprisonment *in
absentia*. Since he actually had the money in Italy at the time of the
trial, he lost the lot. But in spite of the fact that he had been found

guilty of a criminal offence, Gavin could not be extradited, and he only had to make sure he did not set foot on Italian soil again, or on an Italian aircraft or ship, to avoid arrest.

Towards the end of 1958, the Italian Government declared an amnesty for political prisoners, and Gavin felt free to return once more to Sicily. He had heard that the home of Giuseppe, his friend and collaborator, had been burgled and all his possessions (including his precious books) stolen. So at the end of December he returned to Sicily on a four-day visit (crossing by boat from Tunis where he was staying at the time) to give Giuseppe such help as he could. Aware that there were enemies more dangerous than the law in that lawless land, he took care to disguise himself with a beard and dark glasses.

The disguise was not as impenetrable as he had hoped. At a trattoria, an old haunt, he was approached by two carabinieri. 'Il Capitano Inglese, il Maxwell?' said one of them. He ordered Gavin to roll up his sleeve. Under the heading 'Distinguishing Marks' Gavin's passport mentioned five large strawberry marks on his right forearm. Gavin was promptly handcuffed. 'You're making fools of yourselves,' he told the carabinieri. He was under amnesty, and there were no charges against him. One of the carabinieri went away to check, leaving Gavin under the watchful eye of the other. Twenty minutes later the carabinieri returned and unlocked the handcuffs. 'The English could never take a joke,' he said. Gavin was not amused. 'I don't like Sicilian jokes,' he replied. It wasn't the police Gavin had to worry about, he was told – it was *them*, the Mafia. He was advised to leave, and quickly.

Gavin never returned to Sicily. He continued to maintain a lively correspondence with Giuseppe and to make a regular allowance towards the cost of his medical training at the university; but he had completed his work on *The Ten Pains of Death*, and Sicily, which had been a second home for almost seven years, was now an episode in his life that was over and done with. Ahead lay other horizons and other adventures – and, always, the peace and security of his Highland sanctuary.

TWENTY

The ring and the book

For only out of solitude or strife
Are born the sons of valour and delight.
ROY CAMPBELL, *'Choosing a Mast'*

In the second week of April 1959 Gavin returned to Sandaig for a
prolonged stay. He had two aims in mind. One was to write *Ring
of Bright Water*. The other was to try and rear a young otter in his
own home. Within a few days of his arrival in the north, by quite
the oddest of coincidences, he suddenly found himself in a position
to do both.

On 19 April 1959, having opened up Sandaig after its winter
shut-down, Gavin and Jimmy Watt drove to Kyle of Lochalsh to
meet the train bringing Raef Payne, who was making a short visit.
The train duly arrived, but instead of taking the road back to
Sandaig straight away the three of them decided to call in at the
Lochalsh Hotel for a wee dram and a leisurely natter.

They were sitting in the sun-lounge of the hotel overlooking the
sea when the hall porter came running over to them.

'Mr Maxwell!' he called. 'Mr Maxwell! Come quick to the door
and tell me what's this strange beast outside – quick!'

Whether as the result of clairvoyance or intuitive deduction, both
Gavin and Raef were absolutely certain what it was they were about
to see. They ran to the door. A man, a woman and two foreign
girls were walking past the hotel, making for a car parked near the
jetty. Behind them, lolloping along at their heels, was a large, sleek
otter of a species Gavin had never seen before, with a silvery head
and a white throat and chest. He took one look at this apparition
and then, with Raef and Jimmy in hot pursuit, bolted out of the
hotel door and down the steps, still clutching his glass of whisky
and feeling as if he was struggling in a dream. He quickly caught up
with the otter and its human companions and breathlessly addressed

them, jabbering wildly and incoherently about Mij and Mij's death and how he had been looking for another otter.

The name of the otter that had so fortuitously crossed Gavin's path was Edal; and her owners were Dr Malcolm and Paula Macdonald, on leave from Nigeria. From them Gavin learned that Edal had been found by two African fishermen on the banks of the Benin River and taken to a nearby market where Paula Macdonald had bought her for a pound. That was the previous August, when the young otter was about one month old. With loving care she was hand-reared on a bottle, then brought to London at the end of the Macdonalds' tour of duty, and from there to the West Highlands and the Lochalsh Hotel and the miraculous chance encounter with Gavin by the hotel steps. In six weeks' time they were due to return to Africa, and were desperate to find a suitable home for Edal before they left. They had thought of a zoo – but perhaps Gavin could help? She was house-trained, they told him, and came and went as she pleased; and she liked ice cream and pastries and playing with matches. And she was irresistible.

A week later Edal and her owners came to Sandaig for an afternoon to check the suitability of her prospective new home, and discovered for themselves that Sandaig was an otter's paradise. Determined not to repeat the mistakes that had led to the death of Mij, Gavin set to work to get everything ready for the new arrival in the ten days before Edal was due to return. To the Macdonalds he sent an otter harness that had been specially designed for Mij; and with Jimmy Watt's help he enclosed the house with a fence and dug a pool to which he piped water from the waterfall. Finally, on 9 May 1959, the Macdonalds brought their otter to Sandaig. Three days later they left her behind, stealing silently away while she slept, with her familiar toys and towel and Paula's jersey beside her on the sofa, to reassure her when she woke.

Once more there was an otter at Sandaig – an otter that was destined to become one of the most famous living animals in the world.

Gavin started writing the Sandaig book, as it was still provisionally known, a few days after Edal's arrival. 'I put very little work into the book,' he was to claim later, 'and wrote it mostly in a leisurely way as I sunbathed. This was the first book I had ever been on schedule with.' His guests saw it differently. John McEwen, the

sixteen-year-old brother of Gavin's close friend Robin, stayed at
Sandaig while Gavin was writing *Ring*, and recalled that Gavin
worked like a true professional:

> Gavin was extremely disciplined and retired upstairs for a full
> working day while we rampaged around with Edal and the
> five greylag geese. We pestered him to accompany us on some
> of our outings, especially when we took the outboard motor
> across the Sound to Skye, but Gavin always held firm. He was
> very good natured with guests and very kind to the young. He
> was most amused, for instance, when I succeeded in beguiling
> the greylags into the front parlour. The greylags were almost
> as much a feature of the place as Edal – full grown and
> unpinioned birds but completely tame. One of their most
> endearing habits was to come and settle alongside the boat
> when we were out to sea.
>
> I suppose the house was quite unsalubrious. Once, when
> we were all playing Monopoly in the evening, a splat of some-
> thing unpleasant [Edal's excrement] hit the board, having
> dripped through from the rafters upstairs. When it rained,
> which it did quite a lot – 'the Sound of Sleat is on the roof'
> was one standing joke – we amused ourselves by drawing the
> otter using the new felt-tip pens. Some of my drawings
> appeared in the book as end-papers for which Gavin paid me
> a very decent professional rate of £50. This was typical of the
> encouragement he gave the young.

If there were no guests to get out of the way of, Gavin wrote sitting
at the desk in his study-bedroom on the ground floor of the house,
with a view through the small sash window to the hill above the
house. It was a room like an exotic cabin. Pinned on the pitch-pine
panelled wall opposite the desk was a *Life* magazine centrefold
reproduction of a highly sensuous nude by Modigliani. Lower
down was another nude by the same painter, pinned into a picture
frame. Hanging on the same wall were three glass lobster-pot floats,
an old brass sea-captain's telescope, a whale vertebra from Lapland,
and a peculiar antler shaped like a dead man's hand. A single bed
stood against the wall, with a fish barrel beside it, and a deerskin
on the floor. By another wall stood a sideboard that was so warped
it must have been immersed in the sea once, with books on it, and

some lamps with lampshades decorated with fern leaves and wild flowers dried and pressed by Kathleen Raine. Nailed on the wall above the sideboard hung an elaborately patterned camel-wool blanket of Arab origin, from the middle of which stuck a candle-holder in the form of a Viking shield. On the mantelpiece above the small Victorian fireplace rested a big model yacht, a present to Jimmy from his father, and next to it hung some kilts in the tartan of the Maxwell clan. By the window stood the large wooden desk with a typewriter on it (used only for typing letters and reviews, never books). The window looked out over a small grass field and patch of flower-strewn boggy ground to the hillside beyond and to the burn – the ring of bright water – on the left. In summer, when the window was open, the room filled with the songs of the birds and the distant, lulling murmur of the waterfall nearby.

Sometimes, when the weather was particularly fine, Gavin would retreat to the waterfall and write seated on a rock overlooking the pool – a cool, quiet, out-of-the-way spot. Indoors or out, he was rarely without a cigarette in his hand and a long, well-watered whisky at his side, and he worked steadily through the day without a break until by six or seven in the evening he felt he had reached a natural break or done enough for the day. He wrote fluently and without hesitation, with few pauses for thought and no hold-ups to research facts. It was as though the entire book was already written in his head, and all he had to do was carry out the purely mechanical operation of transferring it on to the paper in front of him. Later he was to explain his method of composition:

When I have planned a book, I write it quickly. If I stop writing without knowing what I am going on to say the next morning, I may stop for weeks. But if I stop and know what I am going to say next, I can go straight ahead despite all distractions. I can't write on a typewriter. I write with a foun-tain pen on foolscap pages and I leave the left-hand page blank. This large wonderful blank page tempts me to add to it and concentrate on alterations. I don't have any fixed periods for writing but when I am getting pushed by my publisher I may write up to fourteen hours a day, after which I get sores on my elbows. Writing is always hard work to me. I would much rather be a painter. I was a bad painter but I loved it.

In fact, Gavin positively disliked having to write for a living. Writing was 'blood and tears, toil and sweat', and writing a book indoors when the sun was shining outside was 'like being shut up inside a prison'. He once wrote: 'I do not consider myself to be a writer by nature, only to have a desire for expression which has been channelised into literature. In fact I loathe the process of writing.' In a letter he wrote to me a few months after finishing *Ring* he explained why: 'It *is* a hell of a job, and one I wish more and more I wasn't so committed to. Always, always, always working against time, turning out stuff less good than it might be because of time and money.'

Possibly *Ring* was an exception. He was writing about what he loved best, in the place he loved best. To safeguard the anonymity of that place he coined for it the Gaelic name of Camusfeàrna – 'The Bay of Alders' – a name that does not exist on any map. That summer was a tranquil and contented time for him. The Sandaig in which he wrote coincided momentarily and completely with the Camusfeàrna of idyll and myth about which he wrote. The house and its environs were as enchanting as the day he first set eyes on the place. There were no gates, no road, no electricity, no phone, no intrusion of any kind from beyond the magic circle of the ring and Avalon's natural, age-old defences of sea and mountain. Life in Avalon was bucolic, clockless and other-worldly – detached in space and suspended in time. Meals were still served off a frying pan on a Primus stove; at night the light came from the yellow glow of candles and oil lamps which created a mysterious and enchanted atmosphere, like a peasant cave in the hills, or a log cabin buried deep in the wilderness.

To George Hardinge, his editor, Gavin wrote encouragingly from Sandaig at the end of May: 'The Sandaig book – Ring of Bright Water – is progressing steadily, but of course not as fast as I had hoped. As a matter of fact I think it's going to be rather a good book, and might be a breadwinner. I hope you are *really* going to town on illustrations.'

Though Gavin was deeply preoccupied with his book, he did contrive to entertain the few visitors who managed to straggle down to Sandaig during that summer and early autumn. Mostly they were old friends he knew would fit in – Peter Scott, the painter Michael Ayrton and his wife Elizabeth, Robin McEwen and his wife Brigid and brother John, the actor and ornithologist James

Robertson Justice, the falconer Phillip Glasier, the novelist Eric Linklater and his wife Marjorie, and a few others. In the last week of July I arrived at Sandaig to make a short film about Edal, the first otter I had ever encountered. Gavin was standing in the kitchen-parlour with his arms folded looking very baronial and pleased with himself when I entered the house.

'Guess what I've found,' he exclaimed, stepping to one side to reveal a large, silvery-grey animal squirming on a rug in front of the range fireplace. 'Edal, this is Douglas,' he said, picking the otter up by its tail. 'Douglas, this is Edal, also known as Snoo. Snoo is a very clever young lady. She can do things you can't do.'

For example, with her shark-sharp teeth and man-trap jaws, Snoo could bite my ankles, and did so frequently in a relatively gentle, exploratory kind of way, so that I was forced to sit on the kitchen table with my legs crossed under me out of harm's way.

I spent much of my time at Sandaig filming Edal's marvellous aquatic acrobatics as she explored the burns and pools around her new home, hunted for gobies and butter-fish in the shallows along the shore, dived and swam, or ran through the bracken, or stood on her hind legs to peer about for her human friends, or played with objects that caught her fancy – seashells, seaweed, dabs, marbles, ping-pong balls. The most remarkable thing about Edal was the dexterity of the monkey-like hands of her forepaws. Prehensile, unwebbed and without nails, her fingers were nearly as mobile as a human being's, and with them she was able to peel an egg, roll a marble, pick a pocket, dribble a ball. But like all young otters she was liable to bouts of mischievous destructiveness, and inside the house every table and shelf had to be raised out of her reach, which increased week by week till by August she was nearly fifty inches long and some forty pounds in weight.

Edal was not the only animal inhabitant of the human outpost at Sandaig. Five greylag goslings had been brought to Sandaig that year, descendants of greylags that Gavin had shot and wounded in his pre-war wildfowling days in Wigtown Bay and then introduced into his collection of wildfowl at Monreith. 'Perhaps it was from some obscure part of the guilt under which, unrecognised, we labour so often, that I wanted these birds to fly free and unafraid about Camusfeàrna,' he was to write, 'wanted to hear in the dawn and the dusk the wild music of those voices that long ago used to

quicken my pulse . . .' The young geese were tame and fond of
human company, but just as Edal had to be taught to swim, so
they had to be taught to fly, once their wing feathers were long
enough for flight. This was achieved when Jimmy Watt had the
bright idea of running in front of them, wildly flapping his arms,
until one day the goslings, running behind him and copying his
actions, found themselves airborne – much to their consternation,
since they had received no precise instructions from Jimmy as to
how to come in to land again. Soon, of course, they were expert
fliers, and ranged far and wide, till one evening they failed to return
to the house at nightfall and Gavin feared they had gone for ever.
But out on the islands next day he saw, half a mile to the north,
the long, unhurried beat of goose wings against the sky, and
recognised – 'with an absurd surge of joy' – his missing greylags.
He called to them and they checked and spiralled down to alight
on the sand at his feet. 'It never ceased to give me delight,' he
wrote, 'this power to summon wild geese from the heavens as they
passed, seemingly steady as a constellation upon their course, or to
call them from the house when the sun was dipping behind the
hills of Skye, to hear far off their answering clangour, and see the
silhouette of their wings beating in from the sea against the sunset
sky.' He gained more pleasure from these humble greylags than he
ever had from his collection of exotic wildfowl.

There were other creatures, waifs and strays, that came and went
at Sandaig that summer – a Slavonian grebe that mistakenly landed
by Edal's pool and could not clear the fences to take off again; an
injured herring gull; a water rail found unaccountably squatting in
the hearth of a house in Glenelg; and more memorably a wildcat
kitten that Gavin found swimming in the sea off the islands and
kept for one traumatic week in his bedroom. During that week
the wildcat – 'an image of primordial ferocity' – systematically
destroyed Gavin's room and much of its contents, while Gavin
himself, with some reluctance, was obliged to shoot a turnstone,
a shag, a curlew and an oyster catcher in order to feed the creature.
The ordeal was only ended when the beast was taken away in the
charge of a wildcat lover from the south called Willie Kingham
with a penchant for insuperable challenges.

Gavin meanwhile laboured away at his manuscript in his study-
bedroom, sustained by a diet of whisky and black pudding. Every
evening he read aloud what he had written that day and asked for

my comments. One day, when the weather was bad and I was confined indoors, Gavin sat me down with a glass of whisky and brought me the whole of what he had written so far of *Ring of Bright Water*, which was then about three-quarters finished. 'I'd be glad of your comments, chum,' he said. 'But take your time. No hurry. What I'd like is a *considered* opinion.'

The manuscript was contained in four or five foolscap barristers' case books (by the end there were six). For the most part it was written in a beautiful flowing hand, with remarkably few corrections, using a fountain pen filled with sepia-brown ink. This same ink ('Ink?' commented Jimmy Watt. 'That's *blood*!') seems to have brought the book to the verge of disaster. Gavin was well into Chapter Eight (in volume four of the manuscript) and was describing Mij's encounter with a dog in the streets of London – 'their eyes rolled sideways with what appeared to me to be a wild surmise' – when it seems that Edal clambered on to his desk and knocked over the ink bottle, spilling the contents over the first two volumes as well as over the one in which Gavin was writing; the otter then paddled in the pool of spilt ink and walked across the open page of the manuscript, leaving sepia-brown footprints from bottom left to top right of the page.

That accident apart, the manuscript was immaculate. Only occasionally did the fine handwriting lapse into untidiness, usually when Gavin was writing out of doors by the waterfall. On such occasions his handwriting became small, cramped and rushed-looking, and drops of water from the waterfall (and very likely from Edal) splashed on the paper and made the ink run. In only one section of the narrative did the events of the story itself seem to have affected Gavin's hand. This was in the chapter describing the death of Mij, which he seems to have written with great haste and urgency under considerable emotional pressure in a small, slanting, tightly controlled, racing hand.

Otherwise the manuscript was astonishingly free of corrections, almost like a fair copy, and for long passages Gavin had evidently written exactly as he thought, with no break or hesitation in the transmission of thoughts and images from brain to hand. One or two sections of manuscript had clearly been copied out from other documents. The herring-fry sequence was one such – it was almost word for word the same as the typewritten sample he had showed me on the Isle of Canna some fifteen months before.

The description of the wild swans on Soay was another – a copy of one of Gavin's early poems, transcribed as prose.

So, while the summer rain streamed down upon Camusfeàrna and its little world, I sat in the pitch-pine panelled kitchen-living-room, and began to read – 'I sit in a pitch-pine panelled kitchen-living-room, with an otter asleep upon its back among the cushions on the sofa . . .'

I was fatally hooked. The magic incantation beguiled me as it was later to beguile a million other readers. I read on while the rain eased and the sun broke through the mists and the outdoors called. Outside were the same mist-hung mountains and the same greylag geese sweeping past the window that now were conjured up on the pages in front of me. What I was reading was not simply an animal story or an autobiographical adventure or even an escapist dream, but an impassioned, utopian celebration of freedom and the wonder and oneness of life, written not by a scientific naturalist but by a nature mystic and romantic poet. It was exquisite; a master-piece of its kind, a classic in a very small, select genre. All day I read, till Gavin emerged from his study with the day's latest sepia-brown offering of idyll and adventure.

'Well?' he asked. 'What do you think? Is it awful?'

I considered the occasion important enough to bring all my heavy, recently graduated Eng. Lit. critical apparatus to bear. It was, I told him, beautifully written, often passionate, always enchanting, frequently comical, a wonderful read. 'But,' I added, 'it is deeply flawed.'

It was not one book but two, I went on. Or at best one book split into two distinct and separate parts – the first half a wonderful evocation of Camusfeàrna and the Robinson Crusoe life there, the second half a diverting entertainment about the joys and tribulations of living with pet otters.

'What I suggest,' I told him, 'is that you rewrite the entire manu-script and integrate the two halves to form a single unified text.'

Gavin, who had been scribbling away for three months, stared at me blankly.

'OK, chum,' he shrugged. 'Time for another dram.'

Wisely, he ignored my advice.

Gavin was not totally desk-bound. Sometimes he would sally forth along the sea's edge to explore the caves and the islands and the beachcombing potential of the high-tide line; and sometimes he would put out to sea. On one such excursion we had put out in the dinghy in the still of the summer evening to cast darrow lines for mackerel, and were drifting well out in the Sound in the direction of Knoydart, when we had a visitor. Swimming slowly and making little more than one knot through the water, it appeared from behind and entered the extreme right-hand edge of my field of view, overhauling us barely an inch or two below the surface of the sea and no more than a foot away from the side of the dinghy. The new arrival was the length of a London bus.

This was the first time I had ever seen a basking shark. The colossal grey-brown bulk and uncannily silent, irresistibly buoyant passage of the creature barely an arm's length away froze me to my seat. I hardly dared breathe or turn my head. Only my eyeballs moved; they watched the tip of the shark's nose slide forward above the surface, followed more than a boat's length later by the black, plastic-looking, triangular dorsal fin, standing a good two feet out of the water. The great fish slid silently forward, taking with it several fathoms of darrow lines, mere gossamer on such a vast and leathery back, until the tip of the flickering tail – describing arcs and parabolas and figures-of-eight like a skater on ice – drew level with where I sat.

It was the tail that I feared most. Simple mathematics told me that this giant fish, some thirty feet long and weighing perhaps five or six tons, could with a single lash of its seven-foot, half-ton tail easily capsize a boat a quarter of its length and a fraction of its weight. I was well aware that basking sharks are not carnivorous animals and graze only on plankton; but in the moment of sudden, unexpected close contact with great animals, reason deserts even the most hard-headed human being.

The shark's tail slid along the clinker-built hull of the dinghy with a delicate caress, then flicked away and was drawn in the wake of the dorsal fin towards the open sea, before changing direction and approaching us again. Now I had a clear view of the creature's vast mouth, held open to feed on a surface stratum of plankton. Staring into that spongey vortex, peering down that seemingly bottomless black throat, I experienced a curious sense of vertigo, as Jonah must have done before he was drawn into the belly of the Leviathan. Then, as the dorsal fin drew alongside, the shark dived. There was a slow stirring of its tapering afterquarters, a leisurely flick of the tail, and the fin slid under the water like a submarine's conning tower. I peered down into the clear green ocean and watched our visitor sink soundlessly and recede into the gloom of the deep water. For a second or two its monstrous outline seemed to pulse on the furthest limit of visibility, and then it vanished in the darkness, leaving us alone on a long, oily Atlantic swell dotted with resting gulls.

For Gavin the encounter was like a confrontation with his past. For me it raised an uncomfortable conundrum. Only the day before I had read in the manuscript of *Ring of Bright Water* a passage about the hunter of leviathan and 'the most brutal and agonising death in his armoury, the harpoon buried deep in the living flesh'. Might not the reader of *Ring of Bright Water*, I asked him, be confused when he or she discovered that the man who loved otters and all the other wild creatures of Camusfeàrna was the very same man who for four years had hunted the great fish, inflicting on it that 'most brutal and agonising death'? Gavin gave this question some thought, bringing up the darrow line hand over hand as he did so.

It was an understandable paradox, he said, but there were various things to be said. In the first place, a cartilaginous fish like the basking shark, which has a minute brain in relation to its huge body, didn't feel pain in anything like the degree felt by a highly evolved mammal like the whale, which has a much more developed nervous system. This doesn't condone his killing the basking shark, but it did diminish the brutality of the act, as some people might see it.

The second point was this. He had never pretended that he hadn't hunted various kinds of animals and birds at some time in his life. 'I was born a predator,' he said. 'I think you were too, but I was conditioned to be one by my upbringing much more than you were. I have shot game, wildfowl, wild boar, deer and other creatures. I did this because that was what people of my class and generation did, and because as a weakly boy I wanted to prove myself. But I learned to be a crack shot and to kill cleanly and not to wound or maim. And I shot within the rules. I shot rabbits for food, for example, and I shot deer because they had to be culled for the sake of the herds. Another point is this: people grow and change. Today, in the main, I *don't* like killing animals. I'm not ashamed of the fact that I hunted basking sharks for a living some years ago, but I wouldn't do it now. But I would still maintain that the love and respect I've always had for animals, even in my shooting and killing days, has never excluded my right to kill them whenever I have been forced to exist in a predatory role within the ecology. But some forms of hunting I have never condoned. And though I may once have harpooned the shark that has just this minute dived beneath this boat, I would oppose to my dying day the hunting and trapping of the other creature you referred to – I mean the otter.'

So the summer passed. Little by little the evenings began to shorten and the days to grow cooler with approaching autumn. The sand martins left the banks of the burn to return to Africa, and there were no more basking shark to be seen in the Sound. That last golden summer had flowered and faded before Gavin reached the end of *Ring of Bright Water*. Finally, on 16 October 1959, he came to the closing paragraph. It was, had he realised it, his farewell to Sandaig as he had known it, and to himself as he had been. Neither would ever be the same again. For soon Avalon would be destroyed by the very book he had just completed and all that it brought in its train.

'It is October,' Gavin wrote,

and I have been for six unbroken months at Camusfeàrna. The stags are roaring on the slopes of Skye across the Sound, and yesterday the wild swans passed flying southwards low over a lead-grey sea. The ring of tide-wrack round the bay is piled with fallen leaves borne down the burn, and before a chill wind they are blown racing and scurrying up the sands. The summer, with its wild roses and smooth blue seas lapping white island beaches, is over; the flower of the heather is dead and the scarlet rowan berries fallen. Beyond are the brief twilit days of winter, when the waterfall will thunder white over flat rocks whose surface was too hot to bear under summer suns, and the cold, salt-wet wind will rattle the windows and moan in the chimney. This year I shall not be there to see and hear these things; home is for me as yet a fortress from which to essay raid and foray, an embattled position behind whose walls one may retire to lick new wounds and plan fresh journeys to farther horizons. Yet while there is time there is certainty of return.

TWENTY-ONE

To the High Atlas

Oh that I were
Where I would be,
Then would I be
Where I am not;
But where I am
There I must be,
And where I would be
I can not.

NURSERY RHYME

In September 1959, shortly before Gavin finished *Ring of Bright Water*, his second Sicilian book, *The Ten Pains of Death*, was published in Britain. The work had never endeared itself to his publishers and their initial reaction to the manuscript had been downbeat. The critics saw the book differently. The Book Society judged it 'the most haunting book of 1959'. William Golding, a future winner of the Nobel Prize for Literature, gave the book a dazzling review. John Connell in the London *Evening Standard* pronounced Gavin Maxwell to be 'one of the most remarkable and original of the post-war generation of writers'. His study of the poor and suffering of Sicily was sensitive, humane and written with intense compassion, he wrote, and with love and understanding untinged with sentimentality. 'Its deeper merits make it impossible to ignore or forget the book.'

Inevitably Gavin's book was bracketed with the Sicilian social worker and anti-Mafia campaigner Danilo Dolci's account of the island's poverty, *To Feed the Hungry*, which was published at about the same time. 'Dolci is a reformer who writes,' Wayland Young pointed out in the *Observer*; 'Gavin Maxwell is a writer whose skill and conscience turn the reader's mind to reform.' Other critics compared Gavin's work with an earlier exposé of poverty and degradation in Italy, Morris West's bestseller about the slums of

Naples, *Children of the Sun*. Morris West himself wrote in *The Tablet* in Australia:

> The facts of *The Ten Pains of Death* are, for me at least, beyond controversy. They are too brutal for fiction, too patent for disproof. Mr Maxwell's presentation has the authentic flavour of a tape-recording made on the spot by a trained observer and a skilled commentator. No one who has felt in his own body or soul any of the daily crucifixions of poverty can doubt the truth of the account or the integrity of the narrator. The book is built of a series of vivid portraits and landscapes set down as nearly as possible in the idiom and dialect of rural Sicily. The sum of them is a Goya-esque canvas at once a caricature of human dignity and a condemnation of the conditions which have produced it. Such books as Maxwell's do us all a service. They affirm the unity of the human family. They affirm the right of the strong and the enlightened to speak loudly and clearly for the silent, the ignorant and the dispossessed.

Gavin was a man moved both by fear of and compassion for the human race. In *Ten Pains* he was able to give his compassion free rein. In that sense it is the best book he ever wrote, for in his life in general he was unable to express the compassion he felt. As a work of sociological revelation and moral outrage *Ten Pains* ranks with Oscar Lewis's *Children of Sanchez*, George Orwell's *Road to Wigan Pier* and Henry Mayhew's *London Labour and the London Poor*. Gavin himself always took particular pride in *Ten Pains*, and a few years later he told *Life* magazine: 'It is the only good book I have written and it was not written by me. I received so much help with this book that in fact I only wrote seven of the biographies. Those that I collected myself were mostly about old people who had lost all their teeth and were virtually unable to speak.'

Despite the book's critical success, it sold only modestly, though it remained in print for a decade. As Morris West had predicted: 'There are few tangible rewards for the writer whose works expose the major miseries of mankind . . . As an honest scribe he will expect no more, being convinced that the truth has a life of its own which may lie apparently barren for a hundred years until it strikes root in the heart of man.'

The Ten Pains of Death presented a damning picture of the Catholic Church in Sicily and an unforgiving criticism of some of the
provincial clergy. The Church emerged as an overt organ of political manipulation; and in combination Church and State were portrayed as either utterly indifferent to the fate of the poor or as
exploiters of them, employing ugly techniques of terror and torture
to keep them in their oppressed condition of conformity, so that
even sexual activity – in a society where sex was almost the only
liberation from the horrors of daily reality – was subject to ferocious
religious and social sanctions. Gavin had been a non-believer since
his late adolescence, and years of living among the poor and
oppressed of feudal Sicily had done nothing to improve his opinion
of the clergy. But he had not set out to write an anti-clerical book,
nor had he chosen the subjects of the autobiographies for their
anti-clericism. Of the thirteen autobiographies, four were from
ardent Catholics, including a priest and a nun. The rest were from
a cross-section of the population of Castellammare, who knew little
of religion beyond its external forms.

But Gavin's criticism of the Catholic Church in Sicily – and by
implication of Catholicism in general – upset some of his readers,
including a few of his own friends and acquaintances. Marjorie
Linklater was one, and after reading the book she wrote to Gavin,
defending the Faith and those that served it. This led to a correspondence – conducted on Gavin's side from among the souks and
kasbahs of Mohammedan North Africa – from which emerged his
first and only formal statement as to his religious beliefs, or lack
of them. From the Hôtel Royale in Rabat, Morocco he wrote on
20 January 1960 to defend himself against Marjorie Linklater's praise
of his book as a whole and her criticism of the religious standpoint
contained in it:

> I don't deserve the credit; it was my friends who wrote the
> book, not I. Surely the narrators [of the autobiographies] are
> objects of compassion because we *all* are? I am of course not
> a Catholic; I believe in no conceptual religion; and I think that
> the only sin is the conscious harming of others, or indifference
> to their suffering. Conceptualised religion – certainly any form
> of orthodox Christianity – lends, I think, to both these things.
> So of course I don't believe in salvation of souls by ritual
> procedure . . . As for the rest, I think one receives intimate

confidence only by giving it; you couldn't do this in your County Home, and beyond that we are of course all terrified of betrayal among ourselves – the confessional seal had after all to be established to overcome this dread. (In the book, notice how much less the practising Catholics talked about themselves – they didn't need to because they had other confessors. Doesn't this lead inevitably to obscurantism?)

As for who is damned – all, you say; I say none. If you believe (as I don't) in an all-merciful deity, how can you believe that people are damned because of their environmental training? And damned to what?

From the Hôtel Café de France in the Place Djemma el Fna, Marrakesh, Gavin enlarged on his theme in a second letter dated 9 February:

I am utterly convinced that *all* forms of ritual are specifically designed to kill thought, destroy true contemplation, initiate the solidarity of a group and provoke intolerance of other groups. More incidentally and fortuitously, they do, of course, provide comfort of a sort to the illiterate masses of the few great religions. There is, I should have thought, only one close parallel to religious ritual – military ritual (under which category I include the pageantry of the throne, which is of entirely military origin); and I invite you to consider the purpose of ritual in the management of troops. Contained in that paragraph are (somewhat tacitly) all my views on ritual worship!

As for not being a Christian – can one not recognise the greatness of Christ's teaching without believing that he was God? He never said he was. Why this desire to conceptualise a deity? – for the process is necessarily circumscribing, limiting and (if the deity were sentient) impertinent. If God is Good, that is an equation and can be reversed; if God is in heaven and the kingdom of heaven is within you, then God is part of the human (and, to my mind, the animal) entity.

And to return for a second to the Gospels – if Joseph was no physical relation to Christ, why is Joseph's ancestry traced to the line of David? Does this not suggest that the virgin birth was an arrière, very arrière, pensée? And even then it took the Church another two thousand years to find out that the Virgin herself had no human father! – and left no human remains! Is not our universe full enough of wonder and mystery, true wonder and mystery, without creating these fairy tales? I feel that for many they serve only to confuse and obscure, and because all our perception is necessarily a mosaic of symbolism, they obscure more than the point at issue. But while it is clear that the desire to worship is innate (and this is explicable only in terms of a species which has in the rapidity of its evolution outrun its security) it is also clear that the instinct is animistic, leading to the polytheistic attitude visible in the multiplication of saints in the R.C. Church and 'marabouism' in Islam. But while orthodox Islam condemns 'marabouism' the Roman Church exalts the multiplicity, and in its home country it has certainly restored a goddess as supreme in the hierarchy. In the Mediterranean the name of the Virgin is much more potent than that of Christ. (Woman, what have I to do with thee?)

But enough of this – we must talk of it sometime, though I shall no more shake you than you will shake me! I'm sorry about this rather incoherent letter; the drums in the Djemma are a little distracting!

Gavin had arrived at this dazzlingly exotic Place Djemma el Fna, beneath the snow-capped Atlas Mountains of Morocco, by a lengthy and circuitous chain of circumstances. For a long time now he had wanted to tackle another travel book to capitalise on the success of *A Reed Shaken by the Wind*. As early as August 1957, before *Reed* had even been published, he had mooted to his publishers the possibility of going to Siam or Assam to gather material for another book. But he was never very competent in practical matters and found it difficult to set up expeditions to faraway countries where he had no experience and no contacts. This is where I evidently proved useful to him. At our first meeting at the end of 1957 he learned that I had already undertaken expeditions in Africa and southern Arabia and was planning another among the aboriginal tribes of central India. Clearly his hope was that he could harness such expertise as I could provide to organise his own expeditions. I have no doubt that the main reason he asked me to accompany him to Sandaig the following spring was to assess my competence and compatibility under roughly expedition conditions. Afterwards he asked me if I could plan two trips – one among the Nilotic tribes of the southern Sudan, the other a mule trek across the High Atlas Mountains – which we could undertake jointly, he to write a book and me to make a television film about each foray.

Planning for the Sudan expedition, which for some esoteric reason became known as 'La Mission Maxwell au Soudan', posed considerable technical problems, not least that of travelling and surviving in the uncomfortable and unhealthy swamps of the Sudd – a kind of hell-hole African version of the marshes of Iraq.

One day we drove to Surrey in Gavin's Maserati to seek the advice of a Missionary Bishop who had worked among one of the Nilotic tribes we hoped to visit – the Dinka – and had compiled a Dinka phrase book. This was the most terrifying car ride I had ever experienced. On short stretches of open road Gavin got up to nearly 150 miles per hour. At such speeds the vehicles ahead of us became subject to a curious optical illusion: instead of us catching up with them, they appeared to fly backwards towards us at breakneck speed. Only by the frequent and violent application of the Maserati's brakes, it seemed, did Gavin prevent these flying vehicles from hurtling backwards into us. On the return journey I thought it would be a good idea to occupy Gavin's mind with conversation, and began to read from the Dinka phrase book various handy expressions of everyday Dinka life in the days of empire.

'Tonight we will set out by moonlight,' I yelled over the noise of the slipstream. 'I want ten strong men to carry my boxes. Mind the hyenas don't eat the donkeys. If you do that again I will shoot you. When he said this, he died . . .'

While I recited these phrases Gavin remained totally silent. One glance told me why. His face was contorted, his torso was hunched; and he gripped the steering wheel as if rigor mortis had set in. When he finally gave way to loud guffaws of laughter, his eyes were full of tears and the lorries were flying backwards faster than ever as we thundered through the leafy lanes of rural Surrey at very nearly the speed of light.

We never did get an opportunity to try out our Dinka phrases on the tall, naked Nilotics of the Sudd of the Sudan. A few weeks after the car ride I received an invitation from the University of Ghana to join an archaeological expedition around Lake Chad in the southern Sahara, and disappeared from the scene for several months. One day in the middle of the African bush a native messenger rode up to our camp on horseback, and from his leather satchel produced a small folded piece of paper. It was a telegram from Gavin, addressed to Lt. Botting, Residency, Bornu, which read: 'Moroccan co-operation superlative. Return soonest. Gavin.'

This referred to the second expedition I tried to plan for Gavin – a long trek with pack animals across the High Atlas in the depths of winter along what was known as the 'explorers' route'. Gavin had first visited Morocco with his brother Aymer early in 1952 and had reported ecstatically on its 'splendours and horrors'. He had always planned to return, perhaps even to live there, but somehow had never managed to. Then, in June 1959, when he was halfway through *Ring of Bright Water*, he contracted with Longmans to write a travel book about Morocco, though the substance of the book was not yet known. He had received the first instalment of the advance while I was at Sandaig filming Edal, and now asked me if I would like to join him on his Moroccan travels – the arrangement being (as with the moribund Sudan project) that he would write the book and I would make the television film. He also suggested that the itinerary should be planned by me.

When I returned to London, therefore, I installed myself in Paultons Square and began to make plans. Gavin's criteria were simple: our route should lie away from the roads and among the kasbahs, the age-old fortified villages of the Berber tribesmen of the Atlas Mountains. The technical problems were minor compared with those posed by the ill-fated *Mission Maxwell*, and by the end of September I had drawn up preliminary plans for a two-hundred-mile trek by mule or donkey through the remote heart of the High Atlas. Because of Gavin's schedule this had to be a winter journey, when the mountains were under deep snow; but we dismissed this formidable obstacle as a mere inconvenience. What scuppered the project was money. On receiving my detailed plans for the expedition Gavin wrote from Sandaig: 'I am facing the worst financial crisis of my life, which is saying something. To try to get me out of it my agent is going to try and sell me lock, stock and barrel to another publisher. At the moment I have *no* money to go to Morocco. I would estimate expenditure per person as £529. And I've missed out mule fodder. GAWD! . . . What I wouldn't give to have all these problems settled and be already in Morocco.'

I stayed at Paultons Square during the ensuing winter, working on alternative plans to sail a Foochow pole-junk from Hong Kong to the Thames, and keeping an eye on the house and Edal, who was wintering in London in the care of Jimmy Watt. Edal had taken over the back basement bedroom of the house, with access to a glass-sided water-tank in the garden. She never failed to impress female visitors with her intelligence and extraordinary dexterity, for she could open a woman's handbag no matter what kind of fastener secured it, and unscrew, unzip, unbutton, unclasp, uncap or undo any container inside. Sometimes I took Edal for a walk through the Chelsea streets, where she caused great astonishment, not to say commotion, among pedestrians and motorists alike.

Gavin, meanwhile, had set off for North Africa on a reconnaissance of his own, driving down through France and Spain with his friend Gavin Young, who had taken a reporting job in Tunis. Gavin Young recalled: 'He was a marvellous person to travel with – he had a tremendous sense of humour, a quick brain and a devouring interest in people and places. But he also had some kind of appalling devil in him which sometimes made him a formidably difficult person to be with.'

In Tunis, Gavin was particularly intrigued by Gavin Young's contacts with members of the rebel Algerian army, which had been fighting France for Algerian independence for years and had a force of about fifteen thousand men encamped inside the Tunisia–Algeria frontier, 'very earnest, serious-minded young men who remind one of particularly solemn and studious undergraduates'. Perhaps it was the presence of these unusual men, and the whiff of war and revolution and behind-the-lines adventure that went with them, that helped turn Gavin's head at the outset of his sojourn in Africa. Gavin Young noticed his guest's firm grip on unreality at once:

Gavin was a fantasist. I can't think of anyone who was more fascinated by the unreal world. The fantasy side of him was like a blood clot moving across his eye. It was a tremendous handicap and diminished him in the eyes of anyone standing around. Without it he might have been a very great man. As it is, it took up an inordinate amount of his time and energy, diverted him from what he should be doing. It intruded less at Sandaig, much more when he was abroad and off his own turf. In North Africa he did not see things as they were but as he wanted them to be, and if they weren't like that he tried to make them like that, or believed that they *had* been like that, or would create a great drama so that life could live up to his fantasy expectations. He was always exaggerating the danger and sinisterness of places. He expected North Africa to be like an adventure movie or spy thriller, with mayhem and political murder everywhere. On his first morning he came back from shopping at lunchtime and said: 'Gavin, you realise the house is surrounded and you're being watched on all sides?' So I said to him: 'Gavin, I've lived here for months and I know this can't be true.' And it wasn't true. The fantasist side of him would take over at the most inconvenient moments. It was as though the straight, competent Dr Jekyll side of him was suddenly overridden by the incompetent, fact-ignoring, reality-shunning Mr Hyde side – and that was when everything went haywire for him.

After spending Christmas on the island of Djerba and the New Year in the desert oasis of Gafsa, Gavin flew alone to Morocco on 12 January with a letter of introduction to Gavin Young's friend Margaret Pope, a remarkable Englishwoman who ran the Overseas Service of Radio Morocco in Rabat. Margaret Pope was then in her early forties and something of a legend among the freedom fighters of the old French and British colonial empires in Palestine, India, North Africa and the Middle East, many of whom were her friends and fellow campaigners in the struggle for liberation and independence. Her friendship with most of the Arab nationalist leaders in North Africa made her a thorn in the side of the French colonial authorities and earned her the sobriquet of 'the uncrowned Queen of the Arabs' in the French popular press. By the time she took over foreign broadcasting in Morocco after independence there were few influential people she did not know and few important doors she could not open. Gavin came to form a great respect and regard for her and was soon an habitué of her crowded apartment in the Place Lavigerie in Rabat.

It was through Margaret Pope that Gavin first got wind of the story he had been looking for – the exotic and horrifying story of the Glaoui of Marrakesh, the Lords of the Atlas, whose extraordinary reign had come to an end only five years before.

In the course of the half-century ending in 1955, it seemed, two warrior brothers of an obscure Berber tribe from the Atlas Mountains succeeded, one after the other, in deposing two Sultans of Morocco – supreme temporal and spiritual leaders of their people – and placing pretenders on the throne. These two brothers, Madani and T'hami el Glaoui, enjoyed a medieval splendour of pomp and power, and riches beside which the fortunes of Western millionaires must seem as dross. Madani, the first of the brothers to depose a Sultan, died within a few years of realising his ambition. But some years later the cruel and rapacious T'hami became Pasha of Marrakesh, and after ruling all Southern Morocco from his 'Palace of the Thousand and One Nights' he succeeded, by violence and intrigue, in dethroning the Sultan, Mohammed Ben Youssef V, in 1953, putting in his place a pitiable seventy-year-old puppet. When in 1955 mass demonstrations and massacre forced the French to restore the rightful Sultan, the independence of Morocco followed as inevitably as spring succeeds winter.

T'hami died within a few weeks of the restoration of the Sultan he had deposed; he wanted to die, because he had no more to live for. Now both the Palace of the Thousand and One Nights and the great fortress of Telouet in the Atlas Mountains stood empty and silent. The drama of the swift rise and fall of the house of Glaoua, set against the fantastic backcloth of southern Morocco and the snow-covered Atlas, was to be the subject of Gavin's book.

It was one thing to have an idea; it was another to find one's way through the labyrinth to the secret at its heart. The recent history of the Glaoui was a matter of great sensitivity in Morocco at that time, and the government was only too anxious to forget the whole episode. The facts of the matter were largely locked away in the inner recesses of the Royal Court, or in the memories of the surviving members of the Glaoui family, and it was not easy for a prying investigator from the West to gain access to them. Unfortunately, Gavin had chosen the wrong moment to try. The Chief of Press Services at the Royal Palace in Rabat, His Excellency Moulay Ahmed el Alaoui, a friend and colleague of Margaret Pope and a cousin of the King, was away on a tour of the Middle East and the Holy Cities with the Sultan and his Court. The officials who were left behind in Rabat were unwilling to help without Palace approval, or to arrange an approach to the Glaoui's sons until the way had been paved by the Palace.

'I'm having every possible kind of difficulty and obstruction in

my work,' Gavin complained. For the moment, he found time
weighing heavily on his hands in the capital. From the Hôtel Royale
he wrote to Jimmy Watt on 20 January 1960:

Life here is rather hell. I live between interviews with ministers
of that and this and the palace and my empty hotel bedroom.
Dinner with the Minister of Bubble-blowing, drinks with the
Minister of Crossword Puzzles, endless research in the national
library; but this empty room seems the core of my life and I
am VERY LONELY. I've given several broadcasts on Radio
Morocco but apart from these one is terribly lonely and only
one man in ten speaks anything but Arabic. I spend part of
my time wandering about the Medina (old Arab walled town),
where one is back again in the seventeenth century, but one
is a stranger and remains LONELY . . .

> I wish I was back in Paultons Square
> I wish I was there, was there, was there,
> I wish I was back with otti-tot
> And eels and mess and J.M. Watt.

> Without my explorer friend Botting
> I'm getting less keen on globe-trotting;
> J'aime poco Morocco
> Or Sicilian barocco;
> I'd rather be otting
> At home
> At home
> I'd rather be otting at home.

Enter a long train of camels, on the last of which is seated,
facing backwards, Thesiger.
Thesiger: I see nothing.
All camels: Nor do we.
Thesiger: Then this must be the Empty Quarter!
(Starts writing). (£10,000).
The sun sets. Curtain.
I must go and get something to eat. Hugs and kisses for Edal,
and regards to all.

On 31 January, after nearly three weeks of desultory delving in Rabat, Gavin headed south for the capital of the Glaoui's former kingdom, Marrakesh. If Rabat held the bare bones of the story, Marrakesh and the mountains that towered above it held the living flesh – the dramatic backgrounds and the haunting scenes of the crimes, and all the emotion and high romance. Gavin was instantly more at home in Marrakesh, which conformed exactly to his expectations of the exotic. Installed within the Medina, the old walled city, he wrote to Jimmy Watt on the day of his arrival:

I'm so relieved to have left Rabat that this seems like paradise even though I am alone. This is really one of the most fabulous cities left in the world, and hasn't changed much since I last saw it five years ago – in fact so far as one can tell it hasn't really changed since it was built in the year 1200. At least this square, on the edge of which I live, hasn't changed since those days. It's called the Djemma el Fna, and at any given moment it contains some seven or eight thousand people forming groups round acrobats, dancers, snake-charmers, performing ostriches, apes, story-tellers, musicians, clowns, etc, etc. The people who come to watch are the same as they've always been – people from the mountains (fantastic snow peaks fourteen thousand feet high which form the whole of one horizon), people from the desert, people from the plains and the cedar forests – just people in fantastic numbers who come here for entertainment and pleasure, parking their camels and donkeys and mules and letting themselves enter into the spirit of the thing. The noise is deafening, the drums so loud and urgent – drums and cymbals clashing and pitch flares burning and this fantastic crowd . . . Everything except the bicycles belongs to the middle ages – and an Arabian Night middle ages at that.

I've had to stop this letter, because it's now evening – only 9 p.m. but already so cold that the only thing to do is to get into bed and pile all one's coats and things on it and curl up in a ball. While the sun is up it's too hot to wear a jacket with any comfort, but as soon as the sun goes down the chill of the snows lying on those gigantic mountains creeps down into the town and becomes paralysing. In the square men pressed up against their camels for warmth. I haven't got a camel, unfortunately. Must get one.

By the next evening the crowds in the Djemma had swollen to
between twelve and fifteen thousand people, and round a group of
Sudanese dancers Gavin counted a ring of 872 persons – 'and that
ring is touching all the other rings'. The whole atmosphere made
him restless and unsettled, as he explained in a letter he wrote to
me that night:

> But *how* to concentrate in these surroundings QUARK. I've
> been on the wagon for some time, which means one drinks
> too much coffee, which means one gets headaches and doesn't
> sleep, which means etc etc etc. YOU KNOW. Here one can't
> be bored and just gets restless and ineffectual, feeling that this
> ought to be the jumping off point, not the end of a journey.
> So as a form of displacement behaviour I remove my beard,
> and then think how silly my face looks without it. Like my
> book – long and silly . . .
>
> The stars have come out very bright, and the drumming
> has reached a crescendo and smells of mixed spices waft in at
> the window mingled with all the other smells that make a
> Medina in the olfactory sense. Outside is an enormous and
> shapeless old Berber with a long white beard on a camel so
> big that it looks into the window. It's a bull and it's blowing
> that extraordinary red balloon out of its mouth every ten
> seconds. A boy is leaning against its flank, playing a *genberi*(?)
> and singing, but there's so much din that I can't hear his voice.
> These drums seem somehow to inflate one from inside so that
> one feels ready to burst for no known reason.
>
> I looked at the Atlas with crimson sun on the snows from
> my rooftop this evening, and wondered how we ever thought
> we would cross them in winter! They look like the Himalayas.
> When and if we do go we will need complete Alpine equip-
> ment. I see it all much more plainly now. And sometime we
> *must* do it together.

From his base in Marrakesh Gavin planned to explore by car the
principal locations of his story – the great kasbahs and palaces of
the Glaoui kingdom in the High Atlas. As interpreter and guide he
hired an intelligent and trustworthy young Berber guide named
Ahmed who, in addition to his native Berber, spoke Arabic and
French, and was both literate and artistic (most of the drawings in

Gavin's book were done by him). Early in February they drove out towards the snowy mountains beyond the city, and climbed higher and higher into a bare wintry world where the air was thin and shrill and the sky as blue and as clear as ice. Gavin's objective on that first reconnaissance was the great castle at Telouet – the now abandoned and crumbling fortress capital of the Lords of the Atlas, and the hub of his story.

The castle stood at an altitude of more than eight thousand feet in the High Atlas Mountains, circled by the giant peaks of the Central Massif, all of them rising to more than ten thousand feet, and bearing in their rocks all the colours of the rainbow. A torrential river, the Oued Mellah, flowed away through a valley of salt below the castle, where vultures soared above the high rock spires that clustered before the face of a nearby precipice. The great mass of the kasbah of Telouet was ill-ordered and ill-planned but majestic in its complex ramifications and lack of symmetry. Empty now, its towers were the nesting sites of storks, and vultures, ravens and kites wheeled above the castle's green-tiled roofs. It was a haunting, eerie, magnetic place, this great fortress high up in the heart of the Glaoui's former fiefdom, and Gavin's first exploration of it reaffirmed his enthusiasm for his new-found story.

When the Sultan and his Court returned to Rabat, full approval for the project was granted and Gavin went back to the capital for interviews. 'The return of the Court from Syria and Egypt,' he wrote to me, 'has caught me up in a whirlwind of officialdom which I regret, but which is necessary for my book. I have to talk with Personages, which is after all what I have asked to do, but my thoughts go back like homing pigeons to the mountains.' But Gavin's return visit to Rabat coincided with the test firing of a French atomic bomb in the Sahara, and his appointments were again curtailed. He made further appointments for interviews with Palace officials and key players in the story – including the doctors who had attended the Glaoui's deathbed – for the first week in March. But on 1 March something happened which forced him to put off his interviews for a third time.

He was sitting writing in his small and shabby room in the *medina* in Marrakesh at about eleven-thirty at night, bent low over the table (for the single electric lightbulb gave little light), and had just written 'Hadj Abdullah ou Bihi, grand caid of the Haha, was sent for to the Sultan's palace, where he was given the choice of a cup of poisoned tea or starvation to death while publicly exhibited in an iron . . .' when he was interrupted by a violent shake of his chair. He looked over his shoulder, and as he did so the whole room shuddered, the tiled floor seemed to slope up towards him, and his pen and some small change slid off the table. A second later there was a second shudder, followed by a similar sensation of vibration and tilting. Mystified, Gavin concluded he had been the victim of a hallucination, and carried on writing. Not until he went out the next morning did he begin to have an inkling of what might have happened.

The city was alive with rumours, which before long were confirmed. The seaside resort town of Agadir, on the Atlantic coast of Morocco, had been razed by a violent earthquake which had caused great loss of life – the dead, by the time the final tally was made, amounted to more than ten thousand, nearly a third of the population. A friend of Gavin's, a French photographer by the name of René Bertrand, who had been to the scene of the disaster, told him: 'The limbs of the dead stick out of the ground as if they were waving to you. It is a place of horror, I tell you, horror.' To make matters worse, the shade temperature in Agadir after the earthquake shot up to an unseasonal 105 degrees, and before long the stench of putrescence extended for three miles around the town and the hard-pressed rescue workers had to wear gas-masks to continue their nearly impossible task amongst the rubble. Driven above ground by the destruction of the sewers where they lived, rats swarmed about the ruins, while the dogs and cats fed upon the human corpses. Over all hung a humming cloud of flies.

Gavin returned from Marrakesh to Rabat, where, at Margaret Pope's flat, he finally met the Chief of Press Services at the Royal Palace – Moulay Ahmed El Alaoui, the cousin of the King. Moulay Ahmed was like a human dynamo, Gavin observed, doing a hundred jobs at once in a hundred places at once. Moreover he had the ear of the King, so that his duties had many ramifications beyond the title of his job. The King's cousin took a liking to Gavin, sympathised with his project, and offered to help. But any official interviews were out of the question. The earthquake had seen to that. He himself was taking the King and his entourage to Agadir the next day, along with the foreign diplomats and the press corps. Perhaps Gavin would like to join them?

The next day – Sunday, 6 March 1960 – Gavin set out for the

scene of the catastrophe. The party flew there in two planes, one for the King, his ministers and the foreign ambassadors, the other for the press attachés and international press. From Agadir airport they proceeded in convoy, first the royal cars, then the ambassadors in one bus, followed by the press in another. Masked figures sprayed the vehicles as they entered the death town. To Gavin Agadir looked as if it had been levelled by an air raid. Large areas were now no more than fine dust, but wherever there was more substantial rubble rescue workers were still digging and bulldozers moving amid the debris 'with the infinite slowness of a dream'. 'There was no halt on this weird tour of a city so newly dead,' wrote Gavin; 'again the cars reached the road-block, were sprayed by dim, masked figures, and moved out into the world of the living. For me the nearest parallel in my experience was emerging from the suffocation of drowning . . .'

That evening Gavin was back in Rabat. Though the earthquake, following so hard on the heels of the atomic explosion, had wrecked the formal advancement of his project − a petty setback, he knew, compared with the death and suffering he had just witnessed − his contact with Moulay Ahmed had turned up information about two rich sources of future material. The first was the existence in Marrakesh of ex-Princess Madani Glaoui, one of the few living people in possession of all the facts. She professed to have lived for years in fear of her life, threatened by Glaoui and French alike, and had been personally present at poisonings and other outrages. She would only talk on production of a letter signed by the Sultan or the Chef du Protocol, however, and that could not be produced on this first visit. The second discovery was the existence of a collection of specialist books, the Collection du Pac, in the Bibliothèque Municipale in Rabat, which promised to be a treasure trove of historical information within the public domain.

Gavin returned to London on 7 March, laden with Moroccan rugs, blankets, amethysts, flutes, stringed instruments, ceramics and leather ware. Shortly afterwards he wrote to his publishers: 'It is impossible to complete this work without a further visit. I think the whole subject has greater possibilities than any I have yet tackled or indeed thought of. But time is needed, and in estimating the length of a visit full consideration must be given to the infinite procrastination of Moors.'

To me he wrote: 'I am inspired to write to you to the effect that

you MUST keep Xmas–1st March free next winter for the projected Atlas journey. This because I have been so deeply struck by
my brief excursions into the mountains, and because I've found
what I thought would be so difficult – to wit someone who speaks
all three languages fluently. So the main hurdle of language surmounted, we MUST do the trip, and nothing must stand in the
way. You'd agree if you'd seen the mountains and the mountains'
kasbahs – it's a country that it's impossible to exaggerate pic-
torially.'

Sadly, I never did travel on an expedition with Gavin Maxwell.
Though *The Lords of the Atlas* was to become a classic historical
work, Gavin never wrote another travel book, in the strict definition of the term, to follow his masterly *A Reed Shaken by the
Wind*.

TWENTY-TWO

Avalon besieged

What would the world be, once bereft
Of wet and wildness? Let them be left
O let them be left, wildness and wet;
Long live the weeds and the wilderness yet.
GERARD MANLEY HOPKINS, *'Inversnaid'*

Gavin returned to London to find trouble and near-tragedy awaiting him. In the week before his return the house in Paultons Square had caught fire and his otter had fallen sick. The primary cause of the fire was a faulty oil heater, which in the small hours of the night had developed an excessive flame; one of Gavin's tropical tanager birds had flown into the flame and with its wings alight had flitted about the room setting the curtains and anything else that was combustible on fire; the smoke had killed all the rest of the birds, and by the time the fire brigade arrived, the room was virtually burned out. I was still living in the house at the time, and if I had not *heard* the fire – a lightning-like crackling sound across the floor of my bedroom in the early hours of the morning – the whole house might have gone up in flames, and myself and Jimmy and Edal with it.

I left the house the morning after the fire to fly to west Africa, where I was due to begin filming in a Nigerian leper colony. In the few days between my departure and Gavin's return Edal succumbed to Shigella dysentery, and for a fortnight was too ill to eat solid food – so ill, in fact, that her life for a few days hung by a thread. By the middle of April, however, she was fully recovered and fit enough to take part in a BBC television magazine programme featuring the Chelsea author and his exotic pet. A few days later she returned with Jimmy Watt to Sandaig, travelling by first-class sleeper on a dog-ticket that described her, for the benefit of any suspicious railway official who might feel inclined to check, as an 'Illyrian poodle'. But just before Edal left London an extraordinary coincidence had taken place that ensured she would not be the only African otter living at Sandaig that summer.

Gavin received a telephone call from a Mr and Mrs Del Davin, who were on leave from Sierra Leone and had brought with them a male otter cub they had acquired unweaned in Africa and reared on a bottle. The name of the otter was Teko, after a veterinary station of that name in his native country, and they were looking for a home for him in Britain before they returned to Africa. They had seen Gavin and Edal on television – would he be interested in taking in Teko too?

Presently they were at Gavin's door, and from the back of their car produced a ball of chocolate-coloured fur that uncoiled to reveal a small, tubby otter cub noisily sucking three fingers of its right hand. Despite superficial differences in colour, shape and size, Teko was apparently the same species as Edal – an African clawless otter (*Aonyx capensis*) of the type found throughout Africa south of the Sahara. Teko seemed a thoroughly domesticated and friendly creature, and Gavin coveted him desperately. Already in his mind's eye he saw the two otters gambolling together under the waterfall at Camusfeàrna and porpoising after each other in the blue waters of Sandaig Bay. Perhaps one day there would even be cubs – a whole family of African otters roaming about his Highland home. 'It seemed to be the beginning of just such another summer idyll as the last,' he was to write of this time. 'But there was to be no idyll, then or thereafter, for I had left the calm reaches of the river.'

The first sign of trouble in store came when the Davins brought their otter cub to Sandaig a fortnight or so after Gavin had returned there. In the field in front of the house an attempt was made to introduce the new arrival to the incumbent otter. But Edal no sooner caught a whiff of Teko's scent than she uttered a shriek of rage and would have made a dash at him and done her utmost to kill him had Gavin not restrained her on her lead. Repeated efforts to bring the two otters together ended in failure. 'Edal screamed and remained screaming,' Gavin noted in his Sandaig diary on 5 May. 'Half hour's walk sounded like souls in purgatory. Teko frightened, screamed back once or twice, then silent.' Otters are territorial animals, and Edal's jealousy and possessiveness generated in her an implacable and terrifying hatred of the creature she saw as her rival. A high, screaming wail greeted Teko's every appearance. Once she did manage to get near enough to Teko to catch him by his tail, which she bit and worried as if she were killing a rat. She would kill him if she could.

To complicate the picture even more, a *third* otter had arrived at Sandaig. Mossy, a female Scottish otter cub, had been caught by a local gamekeeper's terriers and brought to Sandaig the day before Teko's first visit. Unlike Edal and Teko she was a truly wild animal and had already been weaned. This made her very difficult for Gavin to care for, especially as she was seriously injured about the jaw. Mossy's life was a short and sad one, and Gavin's Sandaig diary traces the outline of her desperate struggle for survival.

4 May Mossy liberated at night with assortment of food. Cried all night – I imagined because of lost liberty.

5 May Mossy's food shovelled all over floor but little if any eaten. 10 a.m. tried her with bottle. There seemed a token gesture of sucking, but no intake. At 1.30 tried again – this time swallowed perhaps a dessert spoon; injury to jaw now plain as double compound fracture. Fed three-hourly. I slept in same room, she escaped three times, each time pen rebuilt.

6 May Vet arrived 4.30. Doubted plastic surgery possible, suggested possibility healing with false joint, gave Terramyacin tube with fine nozzle to squirt between bone ends three times daily. Fed Mossy three-hourly – now taking two fluid ounces at each feed.

9 May V. short of sleep and nearly exhausted. Slept on floor in my room with Mossy loose. V. active all night – no sleep possible. Mossy climbed everything. Reconfined at 5.30 – after which she scrabbled and dug. V. nocturnal.

10 May Mossy weighed – 3 lbs.

11 May Mossy very active all night, lost fear of me on floor. Managed somehow to tug at my hair. In the dawn a great crying of gulls on the grass outside caused her terror, and the sight of their wings passing the window even more so. They sat on the chimney stack and the chimney acted as an amplifier to their voices.

Mossy established a lavatory behind the door and returned to it four times during the night. Besides her whistle call note, indistinguishable from any of the otters I've heard, she has a whimper like a puppy and a cluck that may precede or turn

into it. Tremendous proclivity for climbing – tried writing
table legs, wall, etc.

12 May Another bad night. Mossy v. active – managed first
to climb on the writing table (went through motions of attacking my ankles when recaptured and put on the floor) and then,
inexplicably, into the clothes basket, where she was located at
6 a.m. feed.

16 May Message arrives – Mossy for operation Inverness
Wed.

18 May Mossy to Inverness with P.C. [Dr Peter Crowcroft,
research zoologist, visiting Sandaig to collect live mice and
voles] Operation performed; Mossy died post operational
shock at Glenelg.

Mossy buried at foot of rowan tree.

Mossy's death was perhaps preferable to a life with a major deform-
ity that would have made hunting and eating in the wild a losing
struggle. 'To a wild animal perfection is necessary,' the London
Zoo pathologist, Oliver Jones, consoled Gavin. 'Man is not so
fussy.'

A week after Mossy died the Davins decided that Sandaig was
the only home in which they could confidently leave Teko. Since
Edal's hatred of the interloper was seemingly permanent and
insuperable, the only answer was for the two animals to inhabit
separate quarters and lead separate lives. With only a few days to
go before Teko's return Gavin and Jimmy worked from dawn to
midnight for two days running to build an otter-proof stockade
around the house and separate paddocks for each of the otters, and
an old lean-to outhouse-cum-coalshed at one side of the house was
converted into living quarters for Teko and a pool was dug for him
at the back. On 26 May 1960 the new otter arrived to take up
permanent residence at Sandaig. He was then only eight months
old but growing rapidly (Edal was a year and nine months old, but
always smaller and slenderer).

Teko settled into his otter paradise at once, revelling in the tumbling wonder of the falls and the adventure playground of the sea's
edge. From the Davins Gavin had acquired a personality profile of
his new acquisition. Teko's favourite foods were sponge cake,
tinned pilchards and Dublin Bay prawns. He had a phobia about
extremely tall human beings but loved music, especially classical

music, which always soothed him and even sent him off to sleep.
Like Edal he liked shiny toys and was especially fond of a celluloid
man that floated in water. His favourite game was 'matador', in
which he played the part of the bull and a towel served as the cape.
When he slept on a human bed he liked to rest his head on the
pillow. After a swim he expected to be dried. He had to be taught
to swim by Del Davin and was still frightened of deep water and
the open sea. When he was roaming about on land he made a strange
panting, laughing noise which seemed peculiar to him alone. 'He
is the most fascinating little animal I have ever known,' Mary Davin
told Gavin. 'Such a happy little chap.'

For the first few nights Gavin slept on a camp bed in the coalshed
to keep Teko company. But nights with Teko were as disturbed
as they had been with Mossy. After exploring the contours of
Gavin's face with his hands and prodding the various orifices of his
head with his fingers, Teko would squirm into Gavin's sleeping
bag and so pass the night, though not always in sleep. Some nights
he would go to his pool every quarter of an hour and soak everything on his return. One morning Gavin woke up to find the lining
of the sleeping bag chewed to pieces, his nose, mouth, ears and
eyes blocked with kapok, and Teko lying on his back and wriggling
violently with his mouth wide open – the luterine equivalent of a
loud and prolonged belly laugh. After that Gavin decided to leave
Teko to his own devices at night.

So began a life with otters – almost a full-time job in its own
right. Edal and Teko had to be taken for walks separately, fed
separately, played with and cared for separately. Edal was furiously
jealous and resentful if either of her keepers took Teko out, and
every stratagem for reconciliation between the two otters proved
fruitless. A six-inch square hole had been cut in the wooden wall
of Teko's enclosure and covered with a double mesh of wire netting
so the two animals could see and smell each other but inflict no
damage. All day Edal would stand at this hole and utter an almost
continuous scream of rage – a shriek so ear-splitting and unearthly
that Gavin was forced to close the hole for the sake of the sanity
of Sandaig's human inhabitants.

With the advent of *two* otters at Sandaig the whole polarity of
Gavin's life underwent a distinct (and, as it proved, irreversible)
shift. Though he kept Paultons Square on, it was no longer to be
his home base but merely a *pied à terre* in London; from now on

his life was to be centred on Sandaig. 'From the concept of a four-roomed cottage standing unfenced on a green sward, the sheep grazing to the door, and neither water nor electric power in the house, things had to change,' Gavin commented a few years later. 'I had to be practical. Camusfeàrna became not a place for fairweather holidays, but a home of permanent residence – through the terrifying storms of winter and the weeks of blanketing snow without transport for fuel. It was rather like maintaining an Antarctic weather station, and we had to avail ourselves of every modern invention we could.'

But ironically – and tragically, too – the moment Gavin decided to settle in his Avalon, Avalon itself began to disintegrate bit by bit, both as a concept and as a reality.

First came the telephone, the destroyer of all illusion and peace of mind. If Sandaig was where he was going to live and work, Gavin decided, he had to have communications, he had to be plugged into the world, with all its distractions and alarums. For a mere five pounds – the same charge as for connecting a house in a suburban street – the post office were prepared to join Sandaig to the nearest phone line, one and a half miles away over the hills. All through the early spring the telephone engineers dynamited holes into which to plant the telephone poles. On 11 April 1960 the big bell over the front door rang to announce the first incoming telephone call. Less than three months later, and at a cost two hundred times that of the telephone, electricity arrived at the house through a cable strung between poles that strode over the same one and a half miles of dynamited moorland. Gone was the Robinson Crusoe charm of candlelight and paraffin heaters; in their place, infinitely more convenient but infinitely more prosaic, came electric light and an electric cooker, electric heaters and an electric mains radio.

Until now the essential virtue of Camusfeàrna's Avalon had been that it was not of this world. Now there was no escape, no refuge, just the struggle to lead the serious everyday life of a professional author and otter-keeper in a corner of Britain that was no longer a never-never land, merely at times extraordinarily inconvenient and expensive – and, as often as not, crowded and full of commotion. For in addition to Jimmy Watt and Gavin himself and a ceaseless host of visitors, a second member of staff arrived in July to relieve Gavin of the need to attend to one or other of the otters himself every single day (since one person could not look after both). The new arrival was Terry Nutkins, an able, sensible and cheerful fourteen-year-old London schoolboy who had a passionate interest in animals (and was later to find fame as a presenter of animal programmes on television). Terry had taken to helping the keepers look after the elephants at London Zoo during the evenings and at weekends, and jumped at the chance of coming up to Sandaig to act as Teko's keeper during his school holidays. Sandaig was changing not only its character but its purpose. It was not so much a hermitage now as a community; the house was no longer Gavin's refuge but his home, and its human and animal inhabitants his family.

There is no evidence in the early years of change that Gavin regretted the metamorphosis he was bringing about. Occasional visitors and entrenched romantics may have rued the passing of something unique and precious – but they did not have to live there during weeks of rain and gales, when the fire would not light and clothes would not dry and there was nothing to eat but what you could gather from the sea or carry on your back over the hills in the windy dark.

Telephone communication and electric power were just a beginning. The simple shepherd-cum-lighthouse-keeper's cottage that had stood untrammelled on the edge of the sea and the wilderness like a symbol of freedom now began to sprout its own symbols of restriction and incarceration. The elaborate system of fences and double gates around the house was the very antithesis of what Camusfeàrna had once stood for. Some years previously Kathleen Raine had dreamed that the house and the rowan tree were barred to her by a high palisade of wooden palings – 'a fit symbol of the wall built about the first Eden after the Fall'. So when she returned to Sandaig that summer – her first visit since the death of Mij, and her last – it was a shock for her to find the house enclosed by just such a palisade as she had dreamed of, and she seemed to be repelled by an intangible negative force, as if the death she felt she had caused still hung there – 'or some greater evil to come'.

Through much of that summer chaos seemed never very far away at Sandaig. Gavin appeared unable to keep up with his commitments, and complained of having to write up to twenty letters a day, seventeen in one morning. 'It must be difficult for you to realise what it is like to keep a house like this going,' he wrote to

a friend. 'This is a house of crisis. There is no peace until one gets
into bed at night, and then one is too tired even to read.' He was
besieged by a steady stream of visitors, for Gavin, though he was
not a ready mixer, was not a true loner either, and did not like to
be deprived of human company for long. Life was made more
complicated by the web and mire of human relationships, for several women seemed to be contending jealously for his affections.

One of them was Princess Constanza de Mazirevich, aged about
forty, daughter of a former Hungarian Ambassador at the Court
of St James, and known to her friends by her married name,
Constance McNab. Constance's life had been a cosmopolitan and
adventurous one. Eventually, in a roundabout way, she had arrived
in London from Argentina with next to no money and a young
son to educate, and had found accommodation as a paying guest
in the house of Lord Patrick Kinross, the author of books about
Turkey and Latin America. There, at a party in 1958, she met Gavin
for the first time.

Constance was an attractive, energetic Central European intellectual with an active mind and soul. A Hellenophile and classical
scholar, she wrote poems and painted pictures, and had written a
fine book about T.S. Eliot's poetry. She was quick to perceive in
Gavin a wayward genius, a troubled spirit, and a knight errant on
a quest, and she found him unusual and intriguing. Gavin for his
part was impeccably charming and agreeable on their first encounter. 'He spoke with a very beautiful voice,' she recalled:

> He was tremendously alive, in top gear, and he talked always
> about fascinating things. He had a good looking, rather cruel
> face, with a high dome of a forehead full of creative thoughts,
> and a wiry, emaciated sort of body that moved like a woman's
> but was also attractive to women. I don't agree with Kathleen
> Raine that Gavin's eyes were so blue. His eyes were mostly
> cold, sometimes turned in, sometimes expressive, but not
> especially spiritual or beautiful. In this country fair men often
> have these eyes. No, I think it was a general impression of
> this thoughtful head – and great breeding. He inspired in me
> a mixture of admiration, pity, fascination, mental stimulation.

Before very long she was hooked. 'If he had asked me to marry
him,' she told me many years later, 'I would have felt absolute

delight, then fear, then second thoughts. I wouldn't have been able to resist.'

In the middle of June Constance arrived for the first of two visits to Sandaig that summer. 'I am afraid you won't enjoy yourself,' Gavin had warned her. 'If you come here you will find it just like living in a cave – and not a clean cave either. Be prepared for SQUALOR.' Constance was not prepared. She was amazed at how down-at-heel the place was after two months of continuous habitation. There were fish baskets full of dirty clothes and sheets over the fireplace, pots and pans piled up thick with grease, windowsills covered in dead flies. The ambassador's daughter made herself useful. She took the laundry down to the burn and left it to soak for twenty-four hours weighed down with stones; she took the pans to the stream as well and scoured them with sand and grit. But she felt she was at Sandaig only on sufferance. 'That is my loo stone,' Gavin had told her shortly after she arrived, pointing to a prominent stone in the middle of the burn towards its mouth. 'I don't know where you are going to go – you'll have to find your own stone.' Once Gavin dismissed her for a whole day, telling her: 'There are days when one has to be alone.' She found it a strange life. 'Gavin and Jimmy ate abominably,' she recalled. 'They had a huge breakfast, then nothing till late at night.'

One day, when the weekly box of live eels that were the otters' staple food failed to arrive from a London fishmonger, Constance was sent off with Jimmy Watt and John Donald MacLeod to 'raid' the tiny cluster of islands in the vicinity of Sandaig for seabirds' eggs. They returned with nearly four hundred – a disastrous haul for the gull colonies that nested on them, but Gavin was unrepentant about living off the local ecology in order to survive.

So the summer days passed. Constance passed the time talking and painting and writing poems. One of the poems she wrote at Sandaig was explicitly erotic, in reaction to Kathleen Raine's Platonic love poetry inspired by Gavin. 'I showed it to him in the kitchen-parlour. We were sitting by the fire, and when he read it he really sat up and became interested.'

One night Constance had a dream. 'I dreamt I saw a wood with a path with grass and flowers growing beside it, but it was not sunny, it was overcast, and at the back was a lovely country house, and by the path there was a priapic statue or garden god, and I went up to it and I felt indescribable pity and lust, and I embraced it and put my arm around it and said "It will be all right," and this white marble face had closed eyes, as if it was asleep, but now it opened its eyes and the blood came up into its head and it shuddered and shook itself and then it went back to sleep. It was so beautiful – I told Gavin about it, because it was about him, I knew.'

Constance's dream prompted a reply from Gavin:

I have nothing to offer you, Constance; please understand that it's not really my fault. And please realise that I'm not the garden god, only a worn-out human being who would like to be more practically useful in any way, but my potentiality is very limited – and always will be.

Like me, your emotions are too active; in the end too destructive (self-destructive), and of this we must be free. Both of us have responsibilities that we must not drop, and your torment that I understand so well (and in other directions share) is something one must set aside and not allow to occupy twenty-four hours in the day. You understand? – on one level I am faithful to people who are so mistaken as to love me, but in the end I have little to give you but an image of your own creation; my preoccupations will always be elsewhere except in emergency, and it would not be fair on my side to pretend otherwise. I think you should look elsewhere for what you seek in me, because there will be no completion, no real fusion at a human level. I do not inhabit your world, nor you mine – nor can either of us effect the transposition. Don't you agree that it is better to understand this? We each live in rarefied atmospheres, which because of their intensity cannot touch except momentarily, and to hope for anything more will always be a disappointment on both sides. You look for a perception beyond my capability, I look for a rationality and knowledge beyond yours. In many ways you remain a child, with a child's wisdom, and in so far as that is true I shall always be an obstacle in your life, always destructive.

Before long Constance felt she was *de trop*, not just at Sandaig but in Gavin's life in general. She left Sandaig in early July, but returned in September. Though she was never destined to be Gavin's lover, she got to know him well enough to form a perceptive insight into his complex personality:

> He was a knight on a knightly quest – or an ego trip. He was at complete loggerheads with his society and his times – with machinery, with mediocrity, with mass-produced vulgarity. He needed adventure and excitement and he lifted everything up to a very high plane of adventure and romance. Even his friends had to be extreme, way-out, romantic people, and whenever he could, whenever there was a glimmer of justification, he would resurrect their old aristocratic titles. There was no middle way for Gavin. 'People are only tolerable,' he once told me, 'at the top and the bottom of society. In the middle they are simply suburban.' His ideal, his life value, was almost medieval, like the troubadour's life, but in the end it came to nothing because it was *pas tout à fait sérieux*. It was a luxury to be like that in the mundane modern world and I wish there were more people who lived as imaginatively as he did.
>
> Gavin needed the fuel of admiration because something was missing in him which he much regretted. His mirror image, his Narcissus reflection, was Icarus who soared towards the sun, then plunged to earth when the wax that held his wings on melted. He couldn't bear the ordinary everyday, so he was always creating dramas which could not be sustained; and in every drama that he created he was the main protagonist, the star lead. One of his dramas was to push women to the limits of their self-control and watch them explode. So every day you got up wondering what the drama of the day would be.
>
> What was the object of his quest? It was the development of awareness – of nature, surroundings, people, everything – a lifetime's search. His quest was to become a more complete man and overcome his own limitations – to become more than he was. It was a drive for perfection. In this he had something in common with Parsifal and the legend of the Holy Grail – and though he was anti-Church this does not mean he was not looking for spiritual perfection. But with his temperament he could not have achieved wisdom or sanctity. Part of his quest was to find a perfect love. But perfect love is not part of this world and causes only unhappiness – it would have left

him in mid-air, not soaring like Icarus but circling like a condor. Perhaps the ultimate goal of his quest could have been something like Peter Scott's Wildfowl Trust at Slimbridge. This would have given him tremendous satisfaction and made him a less tormented person.

All questers are partly mad, but he was a knight on a quest who could not go the whole way – so in his Island Valley of Avalon he lived as a hermit not looking for God or revelation but seeking refuge from man, escaping the fear of death in a death-like solitude. In some ways he resembled Lawrence of Arabia. Lawrence was a greater man, but he had the same element of romanticism. But Lawrence achieved a serenity which Gavin didn't have time to achieve. Some people – who naturally did not become Gavin's friends – saw none of this. I had an Irish friend who saw through Gavin, as she thought. She just saw this little man who was full of vanity, and she looked at me in pity. But she was not an artistic person and she could not see his creative virtues – or his essential nobility.

Gavin's background was crucial. His class underwent a great trauma after two world wars. Their customary pursuits of hunting, shooting and fishing now seem repugnant to the classless urban young. Part of Gavin's awareness process was awakening to the loss and destruction of the environment. In his life there came a moment, he told me, when he shot a bird while he was out shooting and he looked at that bird and his consciousness took in the suffering of another creature. Then one day he was out shooting in the Iraq Marshes, he told me, and he realised this was not right, and that's when he decided to protect nature and not destroy it. From then on he loved all wild creatures and was content to observe them without killing them.

Again, there was an undercurrent of great *désarroi*. From being an aristocrat, brought up in the oldest British traditions – land, farming, country pursuits – he had to back away from the class into which he was born. This is because he was essentially an outsider. He was not conventional landed gentry. He did not share their mindless traditions. So he felt not only an outsider as far as the aristocratic pack was concerned but superior to them as well. And in any case he felt excluded because of his sexuality and his financial status – he couldn't afford to recreate the aristocratic milieu into which he was born on a book or two a year, or return their lavish hospitality.

As for his sexuality – he was a very loving person but he couldn't really love women, even though they often longed for his love. His was a troubadour love – something that has now vanished from the permissive society of today. The Apostolic Church in which he was brought up taught that sex was hellfire and homosexuality was wicked. Much of the time he had to sublimate or repress his sexuality, and though he was very sensitive, kind and generous to his golden youths, they offered no long term solution to his problems and he was often in despair. Once he told me he got so desperate that he rang up four women he knew, telling himself that the first one who was in and answered the phone he would marry; but not one of them answered the phone, so he got drunk and pondered suicide instead.

Gavin grew restless under Constance's shrewd and intensive – and adoring – probing. 'Please realise I'm not as good or rare a product as you think,' he advised her. He rejected her claims to intuitive understanding of his opaque psyche. 'Solomon asked for powers in a particular sequence,' he told her, 'being wise enough to know that it is the only sequence! (1) Knowledge; (2) Wisdom; (3) Understanding – knowing that the last two are not attainable without the first. It has often struck me that the female of the species seems to think it possible to jump straight to the third without the work necessary to achieve the first! Intuitive understanding can only exist sporadically and is apt to fail one at critical moments.'

At the beginning of August, at Gavin's invitation, Kathleen Raine visited Sandaig for the first time since the death of Mij, staying at Tormor as the guest of Mary MacLeod, a good friend despite the difference in the lives they led. Kathleen had been having a hard time during the last year or two, for with the loss of the house in Paultons Square she was virtually homeless, and almost penniless too, and her gift for poetry seemed to have deserted her. 'I am terrified of my future,' she wrote to Gavin before her visit, 'when I stop walking on the tightrope and look down into the abyss all around. The thread is poetry – the only true guide I have ever had. It is that or nothing for me.' The prospect of returning to her lost Paradise and the company of the man she still loved greatly revived her spirits, and she began writing poems again, sending the hand-written drafts to Gavin on an almost daily basis for his comments. But the excitement she felt about her visit was tempered by caution, the memory of past heartbreaks. 'I want nothing but to avoid any further disasters either for myself or you,' she wrote shortly before her arrival, 'and don't want to travel hundreds of miles just in order to cause or undergo one.'

Kathleen's visit did not get off to the best start. At supper on the first evening she confessed in passing that a few years ago she had cursed Gavin on the rowan tree that stood outside the house. Gavin was aghast when he heard this, for part of him genuinely believed she possessed occult powers. He was still upset the next morning, and when his friends Eric and Marjorie Linklater and their two young sons arrived to picnic on a sandy slope overlooking the house, Gavin came over to talk to them about it, as Marjorie Linklater recalled:

Gavin emerged from the house, and walked across the sand and up the slope to where we sat. He seemed distraught. 'I am having a terrible time,' he told us. 'Kathleen Raine is here. She wants me to marry her. Of course it is out of the question. The awful thing is, she has put a curse on me.' He pointed towards the rowan tree but we couldn't see it. 'There she stood,' he said, 'and cursed me.' He went on to talk about the potency of such a spell. He explained that she had special powers, that she was in fact a witch. We attempted to dispel such superstitious fears but Gavin left us soon, deep in gloom. Shortly after, another figure came out of the house. None of us had met Kathleen Raine, so we had no idea who this cheerful, friendly lady could be who now approached us. She was of course none other than Kathleen. Sitting on the sand and gladly accepting a share in our picnic she chattered away with the utmost cordiality and enthusiasm for Sandaig. We might have been having tea on the lawn of an English vicarage and she the vicar's worthy wife. No word of conflict and certainly no reference to rowan trees.

The matter of the curse was quickly forgotten, however, swept aside by a more pressing emergency that overwhelmed the little community at Sandaig on the following day. For the second time in six months Edal fell seriously ill. The illness began with a septic tooth which led rapidly to an infection of the brain. 'In twenty-four hours,' Gavin wrote, 'she became a mad, savage, half-paralysed but unapproachable creature, recognising no one, as dangerous as a wounded leopard yet to me as pathetic as a child mortally sick. I can still see her crazed head weaving in search of something to attack, her useless hindquarters dragging behind her before she would collapse in a twitching rigor.'

Gavin immediately arranged to have the tooth extracted by a vet in Inverness, eighty miles away. It was not an easy journey. After no more than a mile or two the crazed otter suddenly flew at Jimmy Watt's hands, attacking them again and again with such ferocity that he would have suffered terrible injuries if he had not been wearing thick protective gloves. At the vets' Edal seemed to take an intolerable time to lose consciousness in the improvised anaesthetic chamber into which she had been lowered, wailing all the time like a wounded hare, a cry Gavin found so piteous that his hands trembled and a cold sweat broke out on his forehead. To make matters worse, the operation proved impossible to perform. Two vets working together on the limp animal on the operating table were unable to remove the septic molar, for it seemed the roots of the tooth were planted deep in the skull and were virtually immovable. Seeing her lying there with a mouth full of blood and her fur fouled with excreta, Gavin felt there was little chance that Edal could recover.

No sooner had Edal been brought back to Sandaig than a violent quarrel broke out between Gavin and Kathleen. When she first came down to the house from Tormor there had been a reconciliation of sorts between them. 'We will never doubt one another again,' he told her as he walked her to the bridge over the burn. 'Never, never.'

'Never, never,' Kathleen had replied.

Yet almost immediately they quarrelled again, as bitterly and explosively as before. Mary MacLeod was the unwilling witness. Gavin had asked Kathleen to come for a week, she said, but Kathleen seemed to have formed the idea she would stay indefinitely, which did not please Gavin, who had other guests to look after and was in any case deeply preoccupied with Edal's fight for life and sanity. Mary MacLeod wrote to a friend:

> On Sunday night Kathleen went down to Sandaig to cook supper for Gavin and Jimmy. As they had just got back with Edal from the vets in Inverness, I felt she would be a nuisance if she went. I pleaded with her not to go down but she wouldn't listen to me – she must help Gavin. She came back in tears – she wasn't going to see, speak or write to Gavin ever again. He had been monstrous to her and she was going in the morning. Of course she didn't go, expecting him to send for her. On Tuesday when I rang him to ask about Edal he said they had had a dreadful row. She blamed him for her having to leave Paultons Square and kept rubbing this in until in desperation he told her she could have Paultons Square back if it meant so much to her. Then of course she didn't want it. He told her there wasn't any point in them meeting again as they couldn't meet without fighting. She stayed on hoping he would send for her and in the end he wrote her a note.

The note was blunt (and in its draft form covered in a mosaic of demented doodles). Gavin told Kathleen:

> I feel that as things are in this house you would be doing the best for all of us by going on to Canna. I think we must recognise that we cannot be here together without friction and that the experiment was in fact a mistake. My own mind is much preoccupied just now and I have already said all that I can say. I am very sorry that your visit has not ended more happily, but I really do think it should end now . . .
>
> Edal is still alive but the chances are less than slender. Don't judge my frailties too ruthlessly. If I were a greater man I should have more patience with yours, but I have yours to put up with as well . . .

Gavin's note was a shock for Kathleen. 'For once she didn't even cry,' Mary MacLeod recorded, 'but I was heart-sore for her. Day and night I had to listen to her side of it – then to Gavin's when I phoned about Edal. I'm terribly sorry for them both, but Gavin should never have asked her to come up, as he knows how funny she can be.'

Eventually, after offering a prayer for Edal, Kathleen left Sandaig, never to return. But she was not utterly downcast, and from
London she wrote to Mary MacLeod on 13 August: 'I am still glad
I came in spite of all, and feel that now the haunting grief of the
last two years is over. There are otters again at Sandaig and the
burn flows on and Sgriol still stands in its loneliness and peace, and
all else seems petty and momentary in comparison. Grief in excess
can be an indulgence of selfishness, as I now see, and I shall put
grief from me from now on.'

Not long afterwards she wrote a farewell poem, entitled 'Envoi'.

> What has want to give plenty but knowledge of
>   its own riches untold?
> I found you wretched, and miserable, and poor,
>   and blind, and naked,
> And lent you, for a while, the golden kingdom I
>   in you beheld.

Meanwhile, Gavin's worst fears over Edal seemed realised. The
poor creature now appeared wholly mad. She stumbled out into
the garden and toppled over on her side, kicking and twitching as
if in her death convulsions. Then she dragged herself into the sitting
room, where she sat on a chair, screaming and gnashing her teeth
at the least sign of movement in the room. Gavin was all for putting
her out of her misery. He telephoned the London Zoo pathologist,
Oliver Jones, for a second opinion; assessing the situation as best
he could at a distance of six hundred miles from the patient, Jones
suggested the best thing might be to shoot Edal at once. When he
heard this Gavin telephoned me at Paultons Square and asked me
to send his gun up to him by the fastest possible means. Shortly
afterwards, somewhere in the house at Sandaig, he found a pistol
and a single round of ammunition. It was at this point that he got
in touch with Donald MacLennan, the young local vet – 'local' by
West Highland standards, for he had to travel fifty miles by road
and ferry from Broadford on Skye to get to Sandaig.

This was the first time MacLennan had encountered Gavin and
his otters. 'He was absolutely fantastic – not just with otters but
with all animals,' MacLennan recalled. 'He seemed to me to have
this extra sense. He spoke to them in a language unintelligible to
me. He was definitely a most remarkable man. But a strange man.

He could be very difficult. He was the kind of man anyone could have fallen out with very easily. And I would say he was an unhappy man. One would think from what he was doing, from the tremendous pleasure he was getting from it, that his life at Sandaig should have been wonderful. But he was not happy in himself.'

MacLennan felt there was the faintest chance that massive injections of antibiotics (2 cc of chloromycetin) over a five-day period might bring Edal round. If it failed, she would pass into a coma and quietly die. It was a chance worth taking.

It was not easy to inject such an animal, even in her pitiable condition, and the operation was fraught with great physical danger. Only by binding Edal to a chair at three points was it possible to get near her with a hypodermic, and even then she would lash her body like a wounded snake. On 12 August Gavin noted in his diary: 'Last injection, thank God . . . Edal little changed.'

A few days later Gavin's brother Eustace arrived to make a film about Sandaig and the ring of bright water (a film, alas, now lost). For the fortnight he was there Edal lay lethargic and wasting away in her room, her star role in the film taken over by her ebullient understudy, Teko, who laughed and clowned and dived and swam with irrepressible gusto in front of the camera. On the day the film was finished Gavin detected the first definite sign of improvement in Edal. When he went into her room he found her curled up on her bed in the corner with only her head protruding from the blankets, and he sensed there was something different in her appearance. As he approached her, Edal gave him a whimper of recognition and affection, and he knew that mentally at least she was now back to normal.

But her recovery was a lengthy process. When a BBC television camera team (under Alasdair Milne, future Director-General of the BBC) arrived on 12 September to shoot a short film about Gavin and his life with otters, it was again Teko who stole the show, while Edal remained confined to her quarters, still partly paralysed, and subsisting on a scanty fare of omelettes and rice. For Milne, the assignment at Sandaig was 'unforgettable'. So it was for his cockney cameraman Slim Hewitt, whose smart city shoes proved no match for Sandaig's bogs, and his ankles no match for Teko, who 'relentlessly pursued him for two days', Milne recalled, 'nipping his ankles and chirruping with delight'.

TWENTY-THREE

Ring of Bright Water

When one finds a natural style, one is amazed and delighted, for where one expected to find an author, one discovers a man.

BLAISE PASCAL, *Pensées*

The same day that Alasdair Milne and his BBC crew turned up at Sandaig, *Ring of Bright Water* was published. Gavin's Sandaig diary makes absolutely no mention of the fact. Indeed, he gives the impression that the publication of the book that was to transform his life was a matter of no consequence whatsoever – as, at that moment, far away in Sandaig, it may not have been.

Within a week or so of receiving the manuscript of *Ring*, Gavin's publishers had begun to develop their initial thinking on how to handle it. That they had a bestseller on their hands they had no doubt. George Hardinge, the editor at Longmans originally responsible for grooming *Ring* for bestsellerdom, asked Mark Longman: 'What would you like done about *Ring of Bright Water*? You told me you thought it wonderfully good . . . perfect as it stands. This looks like being a case where we ought to decide on an initial printing of fifteen or twenty thousand and really try to put Gavin on the map.' Mark Longman agreed, and eventually put up the first print order to twenty-five thousand, and decided to mastermind the publication and promotion of the book himself. The picture content, it was decided, should be lavish, and in addition to Gavin's photographs, taken over a period of years, there were thirty-seven drawings by Peter Scott and others by Michael Ayrton, Robin and John McEwen and Gavin himself.

By the last week of May Gavin was correcting the proofs and feeling pleased with the book. A fortnight later a proof copy caught the eye of Michael Powell, one of Britain's most eminent and innovative film makers, whose films included such classics as *A Matter of Life and Death* and *The Red Shoes*.

Michael Powell had read and admired all Gavin Maxwell's

previous books, and considered him an author of great talent. But it was not until he read *Ring of Bright Water* that he felt impelled to make a film based on one of Gavin's books. The subject appealed to him at once. 'This was the story,' he explained to me some years later, 'of a man who escaped to a kind of desert island in order to try and get away from himself. Impossible, I know – but that's the point, surely. I think he really did believe he had found what you call Avalon. Of course he did. And besides this, he was a real artist.' Powell wrote to Gavin to offer a film option on the book straight away, and shortly afterwards met him and Edal at Paultons Square. 'He had a very bad temper,' Powell recalled, 'and flew off the handle at almost any question or remark I made. I didn't mind. I liked that. As a matter of fact, I liked him. I thought, "Well, you're going to be a bastard to work with if you're going to be alongside me all the time." But I'd handled difficult people before.'

Powell's concept of the film of *Ring of Bright Water* was a far cry from the family-entertainment film that was eventually made some years later. The book could either be treated as a kind of fairy tale, a nature idyll, Powell felt, or as a novel centring on the relationship between the man, the boy and the otter. He chose the latter concept. 'It would have to be highly personal,' he told me shortly before his death. 'The problem was how to handle it. It was a fascinating thing to try and work out the simplest way to do it. Eventually I decided the only way to deal with the relationship between the man and the boy would be to tell it from the boy's point of view. I was fascinated by it – I saw it as a real novel, but a very lyrical one, almost a "Prospero and Ariel" story. For me the otter would have been of less interest – simply something rich and strange as in *The Tempest*.'

Powell was working at Shepperton Studios, just outside London, at that time, and wanted to make *Ring of Bright Water* with British Lion, a small group that included the prolific British film producers Sidney Gilliat and Frank Launder. He was sure that if the company would put up half the money he could find the rest. Powell himself wrote a fifteen-page treatment with which to try and raise money, and commissioned Gavin's friend Eric Linklater to write an outline script (which did not satisfy him, though it contained some good ideas). By now he had decided the film should be shot on location at the ring of bright water itself; and in retrospect he felt the film star Laurence Harvey might have made a good stab at playing

Gavin on screen. Gavin himself had misgivings about the Michael Powell version from the outset. He was anxious to ensure that if the story was to be told from the point of view of Jimmy Watt, the boy's part should be played by Jimmy himself, and wrote to Marjorie Linklater asking her to urge Eric to bring Michael Powell round to this way of thinking: 'I *know* it's no use Powell wanting to introduce strange children as the otter's owners. The only person (other than myself) who can control Edal and with whom she'll behave naturally is the boy Jimmy Watt who looks after her always; and I'm convinced the only way to make a satisfactory film will be to star him. If Eric will be on my side about this all will be well.'

Then came trouble. This was a period of slump in the British film industry, and Powell had a reputation for extravagance. He had not bothered to explain to his partners the ideas he had for *Ring of Bright Water*, and they, seeing it as 'just one of Micky's ideas for a nature film', were not prepared to go on with it. Nor, it seems, was Gavin. The reason he gave me for opposing the Michael Powell version was his fear that Powell would introduce the sadistic element he had found so shocking in his recent *Peeping Tom*, and perhaps inflict cruelty on the otters, if only to get his shots. But probably the real reason was that he had got wind of Powell's ideas for the story-line, and recoiled in horror from the prospect of his private life and relationships being explored by a famous and uncompromising director of fictional films. 'A pity,' Michael Powell commented, 'because I understood and liked Gavin very much, and it would have made a moving and interesting story.'

Powell met Gavin one last time a few months later, when he spent a night at Sandaig trying to persuade him to change his mind about the film. He arrived uninvited just as darkness was falling one mid-November evening, with an old friend and colleague from the cinema world, Bill Paton, the two of them crouching under an empty 3½-cwt plastic otter-pool that was being ferried from Kyle on top of a small motorboat. At the house the visitors found a coal fire burning in the living-room grate and Gavin cleaning mussels in the sink.

'There's *moules marinières* for dinner. Did you bring whisky?'
'Yes.'
'Then you're welcome.'
Powell found Gavin 'an attractive, passionate and lonely and

gifted man' who had 'infinite patience for animals and children; none for men and women'. Over dinner, with Edal playing marbles in her room above their heads and Teko whistling in his hutch outside, Powell learned that Gavin had no patience for his proposed film of *Ring of Bright Water* either. He recalled: 'As I listened to Gavin, my heart sank. Out came the excuses: the otters were getting unmanageable, Jimmy didn't want to be a film star, the estate didn't want the film made, and would injunct us if we made it . . . I could see that it was serious, and that he had worked himself into a state about it.'

After dinner Powell went to look at Edal, who was to be the animal star of his proposed film. He noted in his journal:

> Gavin came up and opened the door, and she ran up and kissed him ecstatically, and stared at me, purring, turning at intervals for another bout of kissing. She looked just as wonderful as I remembered her. Occasionally she uttered a high-pitched growl in my direction. But that could mean anything. She seemed quite tame to me, although Gavin swore she was dangerous. Gavin would swear to anything to keep his privacy. We went on arguing and talking till one o'clock in the morning.

At eight the next morning Gavin woke his guests by banging on the wooden ceiling of the room below with a walking stick, and when Powell and Paton came down they had to make their own breakfasts. 'It was becoming more and more clear that we were most unwelcome guests,' Powell recalled. 'I signalled to Bill and we packed up and got out, leaving Gavin most of the whisky. Jimmy was nowhere to be seen. We took the rough road up the burn.

'"What way now?" asked Bill, who had uttered perhaps twenty-two words during the entire visit.

'"South," I said.'

Powell never met Gavin again.

'Gavin Maxwell was keen enough to work for a salary on the film before the book was published,' he told me years later, 'but its enormous success since then, only equalled by *Born Free*, had made him rich and lazy!' To Gavin's relief, but to the intense regret of Michael Powell and his many admirers in the film world, the

Powell film of *Ring of Bright Water* was never made. 'I told Walt Disney that the rights were available,' he recalled, 'and he took over the option from me.'

With two months to go before publication *Ring* showed every indication of becoming a spectacular success. James Fisher gave it an excellent pre-publication review in *The Bookman*, the journal of the British book trade, calling it 'a small masterpiece by a strong writer of simple fine English' and predicting that 'all who read it will see life from a different angle and in different colours'. The Book Society made it their Non-Fiction Choice of the Month. The *Daily Mail* published a serialisation of the book which attracted great interest. By the beginning of August the Longmans publicity machine was gearing up for publication with prospectuses, showcards and booksellers' displays all over Britain. From Sandaig Gavin reported that the biggest bookstore in Glasgow 'had placed an order for more copies of this book than they had done for any other except Winston Churchill's Memoirs'.

It was in the midst of all this excitement that Edal, one of the stars of the show, had fallen dangerously ill. Perhaps as a result of the strain of Edal's fight against death, Gavin grew increasingly impatient and short-tempered with the book and film people in London. When the publicity department at Longman's made a nonsense of the otter graphics Gavin complained bitterly about 'such disasters as upside-down otters suspended in mid-air like Baroque cherubs and a standing otter with claws like a giant panda with reptilian eyes'. He didn't even know the publication date, he complained, signing off with a parting shot: 'You chose the better part, to work in a publishing house rather than to write in the workhouse!'

By the time *Ring of Bright Water* was published on 12 September 1960 Gavin was richer and more famous than he had ever been in his life, and it was clear that in the ensuing months he would grow richer and more famous still. The reviews were almost universally ecstatic on both sides of the Atlantic. The *Sunday Times*' doyen reviewer, Raymond Mortimer, wrote: 'Besides imagination, sharpness of eye and profound feeling for nature, he has a rare command of language.' It was poetry, the Americans declared, the most beautiful tribute to nature in the English language since W.H. Hudson's *Green Mansions*. 'I must recommend it with all my might,' wrote Gerald Durrell in the *New York Times*. 'Buy it if you have to hock your watch,' exclaimed the *Chicago Tribune*.

Ring of Bright Water struck a chord deep in the soul not only of the reviewers, but of a large swathe of the public. It was a book of its time, if not of all time, and met a yearning in the heart of urbanised, industrialised man, creating not readers but fans, who could retreat into its world. Predating the revolutionary changes of the sixties, it appealed to many trapped in the old post-war system, who seized on it as depicting an alternative ideal way of life and an escape option. The universal appeal for the rebellious young, the caged clerk and the captive housewife was the *idea* of Gavin – the wilderness man, the wild animals' friend, the strider of horizons, burster of cages, symbol of liberty. *Ring of Bright Water* was one of those works that roused a perception of a different way of life and blazed a trail for the alternative life-style movement and for the conservation and whole-earth movements that followed in the sixties. This in turn served to confirm the validity of Gavin's vision – the desire for personal freedom, for a renunciation of the values of urban life and of materialism for its own sake; the longing to relate more closely to the natural world and its wild places and wild creatures and to live a life that was somehow more meaningful and closer to the needs of the spirit and of the heart of man. Gavin had stated his message clearly enough at the very front of the book. Discussing what he believed Camusfeàrna stood for, he wrote:

> These places are symbols. Symbols, for me and for many, of freedom, whether it be from the prison of over-dense communities and the close confines of human relationships, from the less complex incarceration of office walls and hours, or simply freedom from the forgotten world of childhood, of the individual or the race. For I am convinced that man has suffered in his separation from the soil and from other living creatures of the world; the evolution of his intellect has outrun his needs as an animal, and as yet he must still, for security, look long at some portion of the earth as it was before he tampered with it.

In the first month after publication Gavin reported: 'I am getting a steady fan mail, which is encouraging, but there's no hope of answering them.' Before long the flow had become a torrent.

Eventually Gavin calculated that the total number of fan letters generated by *Ring of Bright Water* reached fourteen thousand.

Some of these letters were from relatives and friends. Elias Canetti's wife, Vera, wrote to tell Gavin that Kathleen Raine had been much upset by the section in the book that dealt with the death of Mij and advised him that she would need consoling. '*Your book is the love story of the century*!!' Vera Canetti wrote. 'Miss Raine is in the next room . . . You will be kind, Gavin, and write to her . . . PLEASE PLEASE!' But the vast majority of letters were of course from total strangers. These letters, many of them moving and heartfelt, ranged from far and wide – from Colombia to Australia and the USSR, from Norway to the southernmost tip of Africa. They came from readers of all ages, occupations and levels of society – from an ailing child of five to an eighty-five-year-old Boer War veteran, from a US Air Force Colonel and a British submarine captain, from scientists, diplomats, teachers, farmers, clerks, housewives and factory workers, from lonely women and idealistic youths, from schoolgirls in Bechuanaland who preferred *Ring* to *Lolita*, from a Russian woman who kept an otter in a Leningrad flat. Many of the letters expressed a profound yearning and nostalgia for a paradise from which they felt barred. An old lady in Salem, Oregon wrote: 'For the multitude of us who cannot – or will not – pursue the desires of the secret heart, it is a delight to be admitted to your world, not only because it is one which I will never know, but because I see my own world in a fresh dimension . . . Through the pages of your book, I feel nostalgia for the shore I never saw and the creatures that I will never know.'

From a commuter in California: 'As one of the many who live and work in the large city, I find myself hungering more and more for the peace and contentment of hills and trees and ocean. As you say, if one is really living, one needs the reassurance that comes from contact with the earth and nature, as it was before the advent of freeways . . . Life is certainly no dream, but one needs a dream to live. Thank you for giving my life-dream a name – Camusfeàrna.'

From a Scots-born woman in Massachusetts: 'Your *Ring of Bright Water* is the only book in my lifetime I have kept beside my bed. I pick it up for a little while before I fall asleep so I can return to Camusfeàrna and pick the primroses beside your waterfall.'

A woman at University College, Dublin, wrote: 'I can only compare the book to a breath of warm fresh air blowing through the dark stale channels of an age of false values. It is like a world above the world that lifts up the heart and sets the mind free in the harsh confinement of the city. I keep one copy at home beside my bed and another in the drawer of my office desk.'

A woman in Somerset went even further, and kept the book by her at all times: 'It has been my constant companion. I carry it with me always and it has never failed to comfort me. I think the first and last paragraphs are the most beautiful and moving words I have ever read.'

A few readers saw in *Ring* the expression of a deeper underlying spirituality. A woman in Kingston-upon-Thames wrote: 'I really think this is in some sort an expression of the love of God. It seems to me important, like a spring of water in a dry place. The twentieth century seems to me a very dry place.'

An elderly Hungarian refugee living in Liechtenstein also saw in the book an affirmation of true values and wrote to a friend: 'I am absolutely fascinated by this author. Gavin creates an atmosphere which I consider unique. Our allies in the USA say "TIME IS MONEY", trying to label TIME with the highest value at their disposal. That TIME is ever so much more than MONEY they cannot grasp. In this book a man *has* time, and makes use of it, and *lives* his life and manages to return to the values of life. And he achieves this not through Aristotelian or other logical philosophy, or through Rousseau-shepherdism-sentimentality! Nothing faked about this author! He should be happy, though I do not think he is.'

To every reader who wrote to him Gavin was eventually able to send a reply. To some he sent a follow-up Christmas card. This was the first time in his professional life that he had had a public, and he was determined to nurture it. But he was completely taken by surprise by the response to the book. He was destined to become a prophet of the wilds to a whole generation – a public image he did not seek and could neither sustain nor enjoy. Years later he gave what he thought were the reasons for the book's mass popularity:

I do think the urge to live a life away from the mass of human-ity probably accounts for the phenomenal popularity of *Ring of Bright Water*. I've had fan letters from readers in every conti-nent and most of the literate countries of the world and they all express the same sentiment – this was the life they wanted

Sandaig, showing the ring of bright water, as it was at the time of Gavin Maxwell's first stay in the spring of 1950.

With a young gull on Gull Island, Sandaig, during Gavin's first exploration of his West Highland retreat, 1950.

Left: Salvatore Giuliano, the so-called Robin Hood of Sicily, at the time of his armed campaign in 1949.

Below: Ma'dan boatmen in the reed channels of the Iraq marshes, during the explorations of Gavin Maxwell and Wilfred Thesiger in the winter of 1956.

Above: Wilfred Thesiger in the *tarada*, or war canoe, in which he and Gavin travelled in the marshes.

Right: The only photo of Gavin in the marshes – and the only photo of his first, short-lived, baby otter, Chahala.

Above: Mijbil asleep on the studio floor at Avonmore Road after his arrival in London.

Left: Mijbil on the steps of the Maxwell family seat at Monreith, Galloway, in the summer of 1956.

Above: Mij in the Sandaig burn.

Right: Kathleen Raine with Mij, autumn 1956.

Below: The pine-panelled kitchen-living-room at Sandaig in its heyday. Left to right: Kenneth Alpin, Gavin Maxwell, Jimmy Watt.

Above: Jimmy Watt and the greylag geese on a shell-sand beach on the Sandaig Islands.

Left: Edal roaming free at the high waterfall at Camusfeàrna, 1960.

Below: Edal emulating the Modigliani nude.

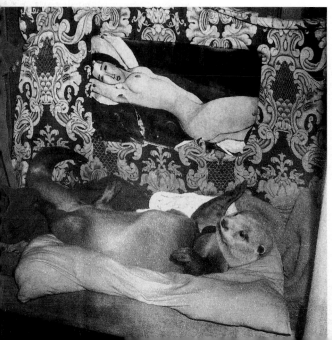

Above: A rare informal portrait, snapped by Gavin's niece Magda Stirling in an off-guard moment in the summer of 1960.

Right: In front of the house at Sandaig, summer 1961.

Below: Gavin with Edal, Sandaig, 1960.

Gavin at his writing desk, Sandaig, 1963.

to lead. Some wanted to live in this kind of environment, some wanted to have this kind of relationship with animals, some wanted both. But hardly any of them seemed to understand what such a life is really like. For example, all these letters ascribed to me a degree of understanding and a degree of knowledge which I haven't got. An enormous number of them appeared to think that I could walk up to a tiger, put my hand in its mouth, and not get bitten, which is simply not true.

But really the dream of a simple life is a dream of life without responsibility. I think that the vast majority of people believe it to be possible, but I have never found it possible, except for brief periods. The stumbling block for me has always been animals. Now in the days before I ever had any otters at all I used to go to Sandaig for up to two months under very, very primitive conditions and I enjoyed it enormously. I had no responsibility. I had no telephone. I was really opting out of responsibility – reliving my nostalgia for my childhood, which was a time when I had no responsibility.

Meanwhile the sales soared. By the end of the third week *Ring* was into its third printing, bringing the hardback total in the UK to fifty thousand, and paper was being made for a fourth printing of twenty thousand more copies. By November the printers were reporting that they had run off so many copies that the type was wearing out and would only stand another twenty thousand copies before they would have to cast a new type. The largest bookshop in Scotland reported that *Ring of Bright Water* was 'our best seller of all time'. In America, where it was the Book of the Month and *Reader's Digest* selection, hardback sales reached sixty-five thousand after only a few weeks. A year after publication hardback sales in Britain topped 120,000 and in America the book had been in the top ten bestseller list for forty-three consecutive weeks. Probably only *Born Free*, Joy Adamson's story of Elsa the lioness, and the unexpurgated paperback edition of *Lady Chatterley's Lover* outsold *Ring of Bright Water* in its year of publication. Eventually sales of English-language editions were to exceed a million copies, and apart from the Bible and Winston Churchill's war memoirs the book became the English-speaking world's biggest bestseller since the Second World War. 'Frankly, I was amazed at the success of *Ring of Bright Water*,' Gavin told *Life* magazine. 'I feel the success was an accident. Maybe it was the singleness of approach to a simple and quite genuine subject.'

And the money rolled in. In the first six months the book earned Gavin around £15,000, the equivalent of about £160,000 in today's terms. In the following six months it earned roughly the same again.

Gavin was now not only rich but famous. To the press he was a celebrity – a bestselling author and former escort of Princess Margaret. To the public he was something else. In so far as he had had a public image before *Ring* was published it was that of the classic British travelling and adventuring eccentric of *Harpoon at a Venture* and *A Reed Shaken by the Wind*, or the committed investigative reporter of *God Protect Me from My Friends* and *The Ten Pains of Death*. Now, as a member of a small but distinctive group of Utopian nature writers, wild men of the woods, visionary recluses, nature mystics and Franciscan animal lovers, he had a new image – an image that was never to leave him, no matter what he did or wrote in the future. *Ring of Bright Water* had its distant origins in Gavin's childhood reading of the wildlife books of Ernest Thompson Seton; as a celebration of place it was to rank with Henry Thoreau's *Walden* and Gilbert White's *Natural History of Selborne*; and Gavin himself was to be bracketed with John Burroughs, W.H. Hudson and Gerald Durrell as one of the finest nature writers of the last hundred years – a romantic saga writer who wrote with a poet's gift for language, a painter's eye for the visual world, and a natural historian's precise and intimate observation of the natural world in all its forms. As Grey Owl was associated in the popular mind with beavers, Joy and George Adamson with lions, and (later) Dian Fossey with gorillas, so Gavin Maxwell became inextricably associated with Mij, Edal and Teko; now and for evermore he would be Gavin Maxwell the otter man.

Inevitably such a label led to comparisons with a distinguished writer of a previous generation: Henry Williamson, author of the perennial bestselling nature saga *Tarka the Otter*, first published in 1927. Both books had a profound influence on public awareness of otters; but whereas *Tarka* was the fictional biography of a wild otter red in tooth and claw, *Ring* was the non-fictional story of a relationship between a human being and otters as accessible friends. Not surprisingly, perhaps, Henry Williamson and Gavin did not get on well on the one occasion they met for lunch in a London restaurant. Professional jealousy and personal antipathy were probably at the heart of the matter, but Williamson did become fed up with people saying to him, 'Ah, just read your book *Ring of Bright Water* – terrific.'

Like most popular images, Gavin's projected only part of the truth. He was an infinitely more complex and versatile human being than the simplistic image of a guru of the wilds would suggest – indeed, never had the simple life been pursued by so complicated a character. Some were later to claim that he was bogus – not a real wilderness man at all but a kind of dilettante eco-tourist with expensive tastes for elegance and ease. Wildlife author Mike Tomkies, who was inspired to emulate Gavin's example and live a wilderness life in the West Highlands after reading a tattered copy of *Ring* he had found on a Canadian rubbish dump, viewed Gavin Maxwell as a 'great, great writer but a wilderness fool'. Certainly, although Gavin had often faced solitude, privation and the rigours of nature with courage and fortitude, he was too impractical to rough it for long periods, and saw little point in discomfort for discomfort's sake. Essentially he was an artist rather than a rugged outdoor man, and *Ring of Bright Water* was more a work of the imagination than a documentary – not in the sense that it was fiction but in the sense that, like the best works of literary creativity, it selected, compressed and transposed pieces of his experience into a work of truth rather than a simple catalogue of facts.

For the moment Gavin's new persona suited him, however. It gave him a professional springboard, an entrée to the bestseller lists and a new-found freedom from penury. It also projected him almost overnight into the front rank of conservationists and popular natural historians. Yet at the time he wrote his book Gavin was only dimly aware of contemporary conservation issues; and though *Ring* profoundly influenced its readers' views regarding man's relationship with the natural world and its wild places, and particularly man's relationship with the other living creatures of the planet, it did so by intuitive emotional persuasion rather than objective conservationist reasoning. As a naturalist Gavin really belonged to the nineteenth-century amateur tradition, and was in no sense a modern scientific specialist. His otters remained firmly part of his private life, not the subjects of any scientific or breeding research programme; and though at one time or another he toyed with applying for a research grant from the Nature Conservancy, or forming an Otter Society for those who had kept otters or had some specialised knowledge about them, he soon let these projects drop. His friend Peter Crowcroft, then Head of the Mammal Section at the British Museum (Natural History) in London, was unequivocal about this: 'Professionally, on the zoological side, Gavin was really a non-person. He had no objectivity whatsoever, and that was part of his charm, of course. His rapport with his otters was remarkable and he did care about them. But his perspective was *completely* anthropomorphic (not that I condemn that out of hand); so I don't think you can say Gavin contributed to *knowledge* of otters. But his was the finest *promotion* for otters there has ever been.'

With the publication of *Ring of Bright Water* Gavin's life would never be the same again.

Ring was published with Gavin safely out of the spotlight in distant Sandaig. As the booksellers sold out and the summer drew into autumn, Gavin's mind turned increasingly to his impending return to Morocco, where he planned to continue his researches into the history of the Lords of the Atlas and his exploration of southern Morocco.

He was not looking forward to his travels in North Africa. After more than six continuous months at Sandaig he was out of sorts with himself and the world and not in the best physical shape. 'You are right that I am ill,' he wrote to Constance McNab towards the end of October. 'I don't know how or why, but I do know that Africa will be no cure.' He had just received a letter from Ahmed, his young Berber companion and guide in Marrakesh, announcing that he had been taken to Holland by a rich Dutchman so that he could pursue his education in Amsterdam, and he would not therefore be waiting for Gavin in Morocco. Gavin was distressed and weary and showing all the signs of the depression that was to darken his forthcoming winter in North Africa. 'I am quite powerless to do anything for anyone,' he wrote to Constance, 'nor do I want anyone to do anything for me. C'est la fin de l'été (et puis bon soir?). I am sorry not to be more coherent, but this has hit me hard. And I'm *tired*.'

By now Edal had substantially, though not completely, recovered from her illness. Slowly she had regained the use of her limbs, and by early October she was fit enough to go out of the house, and by the end of the month to go to her pool. But then an incident occurred which in hindsight was even more serious than it appeared at the time – Edal attacked a stranger. The victim was Margaret Pope, who was on a visit to Britain with the entourage of Prince Moulay Hassan, the heir to the Moroccan throne. She had not been at Sandaig a minute before Gavin suggested she take a look at the otters.

Edal was in an upstairs bedroom, so Margaret Pope took off her galoshes and followed Gavin upstairs to the landing. Gavin opened Edal's door and called her name. In a trice the still ailing otter shot out of the room like a tigress, seized Margaret's bare foot and bit through it so violently that Gavin had to use all his strength to force Edal's jaws open and release the foot. There was pandemonium on the landing and blood on the stairs as Margaret ran out of the house. Down on the beach she bathed her injured foot in the sea while Gavin did his best to staunch the flow of blood. Margaret knew that Edal was still recovering from cerebral meningitis, but when the foot began to swell Gavin told her not to worry, it wasn't infected, and gave her a bottle of whisky to drink during the night to keep her spirits up. 'He was terribly apologetic,' Margaret Pope recalled. 'He had this anthropomorphic idea that Edal had attacked me because she was jealous of me. What a lot of nonsense! I've handled wild animals in Africa, but only when they were babies – the moment they grow up they bite you!'

Gavin begged Margaret Pope not to tell anyone how she had been injured – it would result in the most terrible adverse publicity for his book. So she told the doctors who attended her at the hospital that she had been paddling in Loch Ness when she was bitten by a strange creature. The medics were puzzled. Bitten by a strange creature in *Loch Ness*? They could not make it out. Perhaps she had been shot, they suggested. Or attacked by something nasty in Africa? Even three months later the foot was still swollen, but at Sandaig no one was yet unduly concerned, for Edal's unprovoked attack was still thought to have been a freak, one-off aberration, no more.

Worry about leaving Jimmy and the two otters on their own at Sandaig during the long, hard, dark months of a northern winter added to Gavin's many anxieties at the year's end. Finally he hit on a fortuitous solution. At this time I was looking for a remote and rent-free hideaway in which to write a book of my own during

the winter. If I would care to come up and act *in loco parentis* till
the following spring, Gavin suggested, Sandaig was at my disposal,
rent-free and all found. So the die was cast. Ahead lay a haywire
winter for us both – for Gavin in distant Africa, for myself in a
wintry Camusfeàrna buried deep in northern night.

A few days before he left for the south Gavin found Edal in her
room playing with a new toy she had found somewhere in the
house. It was the round of pistol ammunition with which he had
planned to put an end to her life three months before.

TWENTY-FOUR

The Haywire Winter

I have tidings for you;
the stag bells;
winter pours;
summer has gone;

Wind is high and cold;
the sun is low;
its course is short;
the sea runs strongly . . .

Cold has seized
the wings of birds;
Season of ice.
These are my tidings.

'Summer Has Gone' (*Early Irish
Lyrics*, Oxford 1956)

Late in October, when the geese in long arrow-headed skeins were passing high overhead on their way to winter quarters in the south, I arrived at Sandaig. It was to be mid-April before I saw shops or traffic again, or human faces in groups greater than three.

Sandaig had never been permanently inhabited for the entire length of a winter before – not in Gavin's time, at any rate. Living a normal life at such a remote place presented peculiar difficulties. Partly this was due to the extremes of winter weather, partly to the sheer practical problems of daily life, which took up an inordinate amount of one's time. But the difficulties were infinitely compounded by the presence of two large, essentially wild, immensely precious, African otters, whose needs and whims and playful and sometimes destructive animal instincts made them a full-time occupation for their human carers.

Before departing for Morocco, Gavin made it quite clear to me that he regarded these two creatures – apart from his personal feelings towards them – as his lifeline and livelihood. After all, Edal was fast becoming the world's most famous living animal next to Elsa the lioness, the heroine of Joy Adamson's *Born Free*. The health and well-being of the otters, both mental and physical, were therefore to be given an overriding priority during his absence from Sandaig that winter. Though I still harboured the illusion that I had come to Sandaig to enjoy rent-free peace and quiet in which to write a book, Gavin saw my sojourn more as some guarantee that his precious otters would still be alive and well on his return.

At this time Edal was still as skinny as a rat after her illness, and weighed only seventeen pounds. Though she had begun eating eels shortly after I arrived at Sandaig, she was not eating enough to build up her strength, and in a week might not consume more than three eels, a few omelettes and some milk. But she was still a very pretty animal and had not lost her wits or her dexterity. If her omelette was too hot for her taste, for example, she would pick it up in one hand, carry it over to her drinking bowl, and plunge it in the water to cool it down.

Teko, by contrast, was already more than double Edal's weight, though he was only half her age. Each week he put on another pound, so that he seemed to be turning into a big brown bear before our very eyes. This was hardly surprising, for he ate voraciously and indiscriminately, and apart from his normal ration of thirteen eels a day he would consume whatever else he could scavenge, including mushrooms, seaweed and old bread. Whenever he was hungry and wanted feeding, he would whistle; and if no one paid any attention he would scream. He was a hefty, round, bouncy clown of a creature with a comical face and a nose like a rubber door-stop; and he ran sideways like a crab with his mouth open. He was also inordinately affectionate and indefatigably energetic.

Both otters were incorrigibly mischievous. One day I would find Teko with his head in a pot of paint or in the process of devouring the foam rubber of the fish-box sofa in the kitchen-parlour, the next I would find Edal strumming my guitar with the fingers of one hand while systematically dismantling the sounding board with the other. Both were particularly attracted to the ankles of human beings, especially strangers. The sharp pinpricks of otter teeth on thinly fleshed human bone were not so much an act of aggression as a way of getting to know a newcomer by the most direct possible means. Most strangers found being affectionately gnawed by an otter with teeth like a piranha's and jaws like a sprung bear-trap to be a novel and amusing experience for the first minute or two, a wearing one thereafter. The best refuge was the top of the dining table, which had been specially raised to provide a sanctuary from Camusfeàrna's four-legged denizens.

Living with otters, however, proved a delight as well as a trial. I had never associated with semi-wild animals in a state of such prolonged intimacy before, and I found the experience instructive. I learned to speak to them in a quiet, reassuring voice, to avoid sudden movements in their presence, to react gently and patiently when provoked by them, to try to understand their language and empathise with their way of thinking and range of needs, psychological as well as physical (including the need to play, to explore, to relate, to be themselves and to be accepted as themselves), above all perhaps to recognise their tremendous dependence on a regular, familiar, unfailing routine.

The ailing and unpredictable Edal was more Jimmy's charge than mine, though she accepted me happily enough, for she had known me almost from the very beginning of her life in Britain. Teko was largely my responsibility, however, and became during those winter months the closest animal companion I have ever known – an animal I still look back to, after many years, with nostalgia and deep affection. From this relationship I learned one final lesson – that once an animal has come to accept you as a friend, anger, neglect or treachery are beyond its comprehension.

On 17 December 1960, nearly six weeks after his departure from Sandaig, Gavin finally set off for North Africa in his brand new Land Rover, the first of his lavish purchases from the profits generated by the success of *Ring of Bright Water*, with a small Union Jack and the word 'Britannia' sign-painted in large Arabic letters on the back and sides.

Gavin's route took him by easy stages through France and Spain to Gibraltar, and thence south down the coast road of Morocco to the capital city, Rabat, and the ever-tumultuous apartment of Margaret Pope in the Place Lavigerie. He had barely had time to settle down and get his bearings, however, than circumstances dictated that he should fly back to England again. When I spoke to him on the telephone on New Year's Eve he was cryptic about his plans.

'I've had to come back to London to get a visa to go to Algeria,' he told me. 'I couldn't get one in Morocco. I'm also trying to fix up commissions for articles from the *Spectator* and *London Illustrated News*. But they're just my cover, really. I can't say any more on the phone. But I'm sure you know what I mean, Douglas. So wish me luck.'

Gavin left me in no doubt that he was going to Algeria on a secret mission of some kind. Since Algeria at that time was torn by a singularly intense and bloody war of independence, it had to be assumed that such a mission was not without its dangers. I could only guess that he was acting as an agent for some intelligence organisation or other. Only many years later did I learn from Margaret Pope the exact nature and purpose of his visit to Algeria.

Margaret Pope did not simply run a broadcasting department in Morocco. Her sparsely furnished and chaotic apartment in Rabat, with its avalanches of books and papers and its twelve-foot-long mattresses ranged against the walls, designed to accommodate all comers at all times, was a junction and clearing-house for revolutionary partisans and representatives of unliberated or imperfectly liberated countries from all over Africa. 'Such men,' Gavin confessed, 'live in an atmosphere into which I am drawn as inexorably as a fly into the maw of an insect-eating plant, an atmosphere of intrigue and sudden death. In Africa, they warn me, a British author at large is a suspect figure. They advise me to inspect my car for bombs every morning; at this, while my more habitual proficiencies flag, I have become quick and unforgetful.'

All this was grist to the mill for Gavin, for no one ever grew up with a more deeply ingrained urge to be involved in high drama and great adventure – an urge complicated by an irresistible tendency to see a drama where there was none, or create one where he could not see one. Gavin's English friends in North Africa perceived this only too clearly. 'Gavin was an acute observer of certain things but not of political "situations",' Margaret Pope noted, 'and in any case all his observations in my opinion were always subject to certain moods and even powerful emotive factors which at times amounted to hallucinations and very curious deviations of judgement. He was what one used to call a "tortured soul" and I understood that – but he was always fighting against that and inventing reasons for not facing certain facts. I often had arguments with him about this tendency.'

For such a personality there was no more fruitful place to be sucked into the vortex of radical Third World politics and the anti-colonial struggle than Margaret Pope's hospitable headquarters in the capital city of a country only recently liberated from the colonial yoke.

Among the activists who frequented Margaret Pope's flat were various high-ranking members of the Algerian FLN, or National Liberation Front, which had been fighting a long and savage war against the French. At this time the situation in Algeria had reached a critical stage. The French were not only fighting against the FLN but amongst each other, with the French Army split in two, one half siding with the French settlers, the *colons*, the other siding with General de Gaulle's government in France. What the outcome would be and where this would leave the FLN was unclear. 'The situation was so confused,' Margaret Pope recalled, 'that some of my FLN friends asked me to get some independent observers to fly over and report on the situation. I knew Gavin was not really sufficiently briefed on the Algerian question and I was doubtful if he could digest much of what he might observe. But at least he sympathised with the FLN and there was no doubt he would do the best he could. Anyway, he agreed to go and I did my best to put him in the picture.'

Gavin left London a second time on 8 January 1961, picked up a connecting flight from Casablanca to Algiers, and checked in at the Hotel Aletti, a renowned watering hole and meeting place in the centre of the city, next to the Préfecture. No doubt many of *Ring of Bright Water*'s huge army of fans, fondly imagining their guru cosily ensconced with his wild creatures far from the cares of man, would have been greatly alarmed had they learned of his sudden metamorphosis from a latter-day St Francis into an alternative James Bond. Gavin's overt reason for visiting Algeria – the one listed in his visa application to the Algerian authorities – was to write some magazine articles about the new oilfields that had been opened up in the Algerian Sahara. These were dramatic enough in their own right, as Gavin wrote to Jimmy on his return:

I went down to Hassi Messaoud, the principal oilfield in the Sahara, which is really extraordinary. One flies there in a very old and leaky DC4 (the heating was stuck full on when we

went down in the morning and stuck full off when we returned
in icy starlight – the first was an oven, the second a fridge)
over about three hundred miles of desert and suddenly Hassi
Messaoud is THERE with the desert stretching away for hundreds of miles on all sides. One can see the perpetual flames .
of the burning gas and the great columns of black smoke from
nearly a hundred miles away. They have made an artificial
oasis, with trees and flowers and swimming pools and bars
and jukeboxes and, of course, many million pounds' worth
of machinery. In the sunset I drove across the desert itself for
twenty miles to a lesser oilfield; when the sun got low everything was in shadow except the tops of the dunes we were
passing among, and they were vermilion. I've never seen a
sunset like it – the whole sky was tiger striped with every
shade of red on the palette.

The rest of Gavin's time in Algeria was less agreeable, as he hinted
in the same letter: 'It was no fun there, needless to say . . . I discovered a microphone in a cunningly concealed position in my
bedroom, and snored and farted at it for a bit to keep it occupied
. . . I also had the slightly traumatic experience of seeing somebody's throat cut at close quarters. So traumatic I don't propose to
write about it now or at any other time. I spent the whole ten days
afterwards thinking it was my turn next . . .'
    In fact he did write about this particular incident later, in a vivid
passage in his book *The Rocks Remain*: 'Darkness on the waterfront
in Algiers; a scuffle and a high bubbling cry. A burst of submachine-
gun close at hand and a window splatters somewhere overhead. I
turn the corner; no one has moved him. He lies there, an elderly
Arab with a beard jutting to the sky. There is more blood than I
would have believed possible; I had not seen a slit throat before. A
group of French parachutists swagger by; one kicks the corpse.'
    The handwritten draft of Gavin's report for the FLN, which I
found among his papers after his death, occupied twenty-four foolscap pages. It would appear to have been written on or about 21
January 1961. In essence it was a detailed profile of the state of the
white business economy and the morale and political opinions of
the middle-class French *colons* of Algeria at a point of grave crisis
in the French–Algerian war – a point at which the French settlers
were having to face up to the possibility that Algeria could become

Algerian (and, worse, Communist). Here and there Gavin writes of the general atmosphere of tension and dread, the feeling of disillusionment and betrayal among some sections of the whites, the air full of plots and rumours and a widespread fear of an impending massacre, of British and American intervention, perhaps, even, of world war and a French nuclear bombardment ('a rumour,' Gavin commented with evident relish, 'unconfirmed *but* uncontradicted'). Though his informants are identified only by initials, Gavin occasionally allows himself an aside at their expense. 'Military Intelligence Captain (bearded) attached Préfecture,' reads one such comment, 'lives at Hotel Aletti, has two Muslim mistresses, one of whom is known to be in the pay of FLN. General impression that French security is crazily bad and that given time any European could find out anything.'

Gavin's recommendations to the FLN (under the heading 'Personal Summary') were trenchant:

> True significance of events is not now but in the future. Action must be now; before delaying tactics allow the situation to become fluid again. Feel that key point is not withdrawal of French Army, but right of address by Ferhat Abbas to all Muslim Algerians, and similar right by French to *pieds noirs*. Both should broadcast to all, of both races. *Now*, not later. In the present psychological situation 90+ per cent of all the Europeans would welcome this – they want to be led, want reassurance. In three months new movements will have formed, new allegiances, thinking will again have become blurred, new *culs de sac* will have taken shape. This is the moment. If it is not done now *it will be too late to prevent the long, final, extensive war which both sides dread*.

Gavin had done what he was asked to do and was anxious to put this troubled country behind him as quickly as possible. Privately, he was in no doubt how he felt about the colonial situation in Algeria and what he believed the final outcome should be. Later he was to write:

> Morning, and the city under lashing rain; all along the waterfront the high waves rolled in, not Mediterranean blue nor nordic grey, but mud brown with dark Algerian sand, and

when the crests curled over and the spume streamed back on the wind it too was brown. A French bar-tender looked out on it and said: 'It is an omen – the brown tide, the Arab tide that will sweep us all away, and unlike this tide it will not recede.' I ordered cognac; he poured two and raised his glass, 'Algérie Française'. He looked to me to respond; I raised my glass vaguely and said, 'Algérie!' What other answer could there be?

On 24 January Gavin returned to Morocco. In Rabat he handed his report over to Margaret Pope, who translated it into French and passed it on to the FLN. 'It was not of much importance in the long run,' she was to comment later, 'but the FLN boys were very grateful for his effort.' Then he drove down to Marrakesh and the decaying comforts of the Hôtel Centrale in the city's old quarter, 'with a sigh of relief', as he put it, 'and farewell, anyway, to microphones and murder'. From Marrakesh he sent me a postcard: 'Returned from Algeria Tuesday night. Hardly reorientated yet. *Not* a healthy country, that! I sent my first press collect telegram from Algiers – *just* like Boot of the *Beast* in *Scoop*; it began "Algeconomy moving crisiswards" and so on for two hundred words. Fun. Life in Africa is strange, don't you agree, or don't you? I do.' He had also got enough material for fifty articles, he said, and had sent one off to the *Spectator* already. 'It's so badly written that I daresay they'll decide not to use it.'

The hotel in which Gavin had chosen to base himself for his winter in North Africa was a curious one for a bestselling author who was richer than he had ever been in his life. 'This hotel has practically fallen to pieces now,' he wrote to Jimmy. 'Last year it had four people: a French manageress, two Arab maids, and an Arab porter. Now the Frenchwoman has left, and the porter (who only speaks Arabic) is the manager. The Arab owners have evidently decided to let it fall down, as the squalor and disrepair have increased a hundredfold. No one seems actually to *live* here except a very scruffy policeman, but there is a lot of coming and going all night and veiled ladies are to be seen leaving rooms early in the morning, so I think I know What Is Going On.'

The hotel lay off one of the narrow alleys that made up the infinite, bewildering complex of alleys of the antique Arab town, the earth-floored passage between the high mud walls full of the smells of spice, ordure, and impregnated dust. Gavin had a room in the *garconnière* (bachelors' annexe), which was somewhat removed from the main body of the hotel.

It was not a restful room, for all the welter of sounds of a teeming, closely confined Arab city poured into it by night and day. At sunset, above the endless plaint of the beggars, Gavin could hear the steady rhythm of drums and cymbals from the main square nearby and then the sudden siren that signalled the end of the Moslem fast of Ramadan for the day: 'The siren shrills high and thin, a violin-bow of sound arched over the wide confines of the fantastic city, and suddenly there is everywhere the smell of food where before the air held only the dry tang of spice. The voices of the beggars are silent; the predominant sound now is of dancers' drums. Turbaned figures eating bowls of thick *harrissa* soup sit huddled on my doorstep, for it is the only free seat above ground-level. The light goes out altogether, and I linger on because I have become one of the alley's ghosts.'

Gavin was often asked why he chose to live in such a shabby place when there were large and comfortable European-style hotels within a mile. In his Moroccan notebook he addressed himself to this point:

> It cannot be for financial reasons, for by my standards I am rich, horribly rich; I have never travelled with so much money before and my questioners know this. I answer with half-truths – that I dislike living in an atmosphere of conducted European tourists, that it is a question of habit, that when I go away for days or weeks I can keep the room and my things in disarray, for it costs so little. But the true reason is that I am one of the hotel's ghosts, for whom these four shabby walls once had meaning, and where I was happy; I linger here savouring an emptiness of whose reality I am unable to convince myself.

Gavin's first priority was to look into the circumstances surrounding the disappearance of his Berber friend, Ahmed, with whom he had hoped to travel in the mountains and the desert south. Ahmed's departure to Holland had hit Gavin hard. It also roused the wildest and most exaggerated suspicions on his part. Had Ahmed gone voluntarily, or had he been taken against his will? Had he betrayed

Gavin's trust, or had he, as Gavin was strongly inclined to believe, been the victim of some dark Israeli plot, or even some sort of brown slave trade? Gavin had barely unpacked his bags before he sallied forth to find out. He gave his version of events in a letter to Jimmy Watt:

> As soon as I got down here I saw Ahmed's father (an old man who can neither read nor write nor speak any language but his own) and realised very quickly that something pretty fishy was going on. Ahmed had been given a passport to go to Germany, not Holland, but his letters (not written by himself) came from a postbox number in Amsterdam. No one knew even the name of the man who took him away, and no one had ever had an address, only this postbox in Holland. So I began to suspect he had been kidnapped. His father wanted him back at once, so I cabled the postbox, and the only reply was 'Ahmed's return impossible. Wolfgang.' (Which is a German not a Dutch name.) I then began to suspect that he was after all in Germany, but that the man who took him had covered his tracks thoroughly by having only a postbox address in Holland. So I got Margaret on it, and she is now informing the Dutch and German Ambassadors and the Moroccan Ministry of Foreign Affairs. And I divide my time between interviewing passport police and sitting by a telephone and talking to Ahmed's father through an interpreter, who I don't think interprets anything I say.

Next day, after looking through three thousand photographs at the passport office in Marrakesh, Gavin found Ahmed's passport form – bearing a different name – and also the dossier, which revealed no name or address for the German or Dutchman who had taken him away. The same day Ahmed's father received a letter in reply to his demand for his son's return which claimed that he had now been sent to England. Gavin wrote:

> I then found in the father's house the only thing ever really written by Ahmed, a postcard from *Germany*. So I came to Rabat and put the whole affair directly in the hands of the Moroccan Chief of Police, who took a serious view of it and handed it over to Interpol, who are now searching three coun-

tries for Ahmed. So I've done all I can. Not, you must admit,
a very happy situation, more especially as I'm so sick with
worry about it all that I can't sleep no matter how many pills
I take.

What with the spying and throat-cutting and kidnapping, Gavin's
inveterate thirst for drama was being slaked to a remarkable degree.
But he was rapidly tiring of it all. The loss of Ahmed was a mortal
blow to his plans, for he was not just his friend and travelling
companion, but his tongue and his ears as well, for he was fluent
in Berber, Arabic, French and English and could arrange visits, fix
introductions, facilitate Gavin's passage through local society, and
tend to the practicalities of camels, mules, water and lodgings off
the beaten track. Without the able Moroccan to guide him the
impractical Scottish author was left stranded and alone, deprived
of the expertise and means of functioning that would have made
his travels possible and his visit to Morocco meaningful. Trapped
in his wretched room in the medina, a prey to mounting anxieties
that gradually overwhelmed him, Gavin grew ever more aimless,
depressed and fearful, till his mental state degenerated into a full-
scale crack-up – the personal paralysis that lay at the heart of what
he was to call the Haywire Winter.

'I don't know when I've enjoyed a journey abroad less than this
one,' he wrote to Jimmy. 'Everything has gone wrong, and everything is in a state of complete chaos. Not the happy carefree life
that no doubt most people think I'm leading! I came across a piece
in *The Times Literary Supplement* about me and Patrick Leigh
Fermor, Peter Fleming and Alan Moorehead in my luggage today,
and managed to raise a sardonic smile at the words, "They feel,
fit, lucky, successful people in a world dominated by the petulant,"
etc. Oh, they *do*, do they, I said to myself . . . Well, the drumming
and dancing and snakecharming and so ON and so FORTH go on
in the square outside, but somehow this year I feel a bit cut off
from it all, and friendless. I'd like to get my work done and come
home.'

Sandaig, meanwhile, was in the grip of the Highland winter. The
snowline crept lower and lower down the flanks of Ben Sgriol.
The pale northern sun climbed less and less each day, and soon it
was so low at noon that my body cast a shadow almost fifty feet

long. Our provisions came by mail boat and mail car to a point on
the road where I could carry them down to the cottage on my
back. But if the sea was rough or the road snowbound, no provisions arrived, and at low tide we would go and dig up cockles
from the sand flats by the islands, or tap limpets off the rocks. In
prolonged wet weather, when Skye was blotted out from view and
the waterfall ran in spate, it was impossible to dry out the driftwood, the only combustible fuel readily available, and the fire spat
and hissed in the primitive range, filling the cottage with acrid blue
smoke. Not all of this smoke, I noted with alarm, emanated from
the range fire itself – some seeped out from behind the pitch-pine
panelling of the kitchen-parlour walls, and where smoke could go,
so too could sparks, or even fire.

Yet there were times when Sandaig seemed the most beautiful
place I had ever known. It is the only place where I have ever
walked from one end of a rainbow to the other. It was not a very
tall rainbow, nor a very long one, for it fitted exactly into the small
field of green cropped turf between the waterfall and the mouth of
the burn; and when I reached the far end it was not a crock of gold
I found but a crocked ram dying on its back, kicking its legs in the
air, as though mortally felled by that arching spectrum of light.

When a high-pressure ridge passed overhead, the skies often had
a brilliant crystalline translucency. At night every star glittered like
frost, Venus pulsed with white light, and Mars hung low over
Hell Loch and winked alternately red, white and green. Sometimes
shooting stars fizzed briefly though the night sky, and once – far
away to the north-west in the direction of Greenland – I saw the
cosmic, gossamer drapes of the Aurora Borealis, the Northern
Lights. In such still, breathless weather, visibility seemed to be
limited only by the curvature of the earth, and sounds, too, carried
over enormous distances. No traffic noise, no sounds of people en
masse muddied the aural environment of Camusfeàrna. From the
water's edge two hundred yards away I could hear an otter scratch
itself. From far out in the bay I could hear the splash of a dolphin
leaping and the snort of a grey seal surfacing to breathe – sounds
as hard as diamonds. On some evenings I could hear the stags
roaring far across the channel among the hills of Skye. The plop
and rattle of every tired wave that slumped on the beach was clear
to me, every heron kraak, every raven croak.

One morning I found the burn frozen over, its rocky boulders sealed together with a patina of bluish ice that was cracked like the glaze of old porcelain. The otters, with their infinite capacity for play, turned the frozen burn into a slide along which they would toboggan on their stomachs for hours on end. Only the great winter storms, which cocooned the house in frothy round balls of spume, damped the otters' spirits, for in such ferocious winds they could only inch along on their bellies, with their legs splayed out like newts.

As week followed week Gavin's love-affair with the Maghreb began to wither; yet he could not bring himself to leave. He was like a sleepwalker, he recalled, or someone in a hypnotic trance, living in an evil dream from which he could not wake. At the beginning of March he wrote to me: 'The recent happenings have put the final spokes in all my wheels; I've rarely if ever felt so low. I've had dysentery on and off for some time, which I've now cured myself of with chloromycetin, but it's left me very run down and what with one thing and another I'm groggy both mentally and physically. I project a book called *The Haywire Winter*.' And a few weeks later: 'I've got some awful 'flu in place of the dysentery and I'm so full of antibiotics I can't 'ardly breave . . .' Added to his depression and mental confusion, his physical debility made it difficult for him to summon up the energy to complete even the basic routine of the day. 'Clinically, I recognised symptoms I had seen in others,' he wrote; 'they were those of multiple division of aim, for I no longer knew why I was there.' In his notebook he added: 'It is hard to admit one has failed in all that one has attempted.'

During this nightmare time, Gavin wrote to Constance McNab, giving expression to his feeling of lostness and despair:

Here it is hot and dusty and everything takes a long time to do . . . I am burnt up, used up, not knowing where my loyalties lie: I am a reed shaken by a wind (or a tree shaken by a tempest?). I have lost a symbol and I cannot find another – or perhaps don't want to. My life during the past two months has been a *bateau ivre* with the gamut of all emotion, despair predominating over incessant work; sleepless nights and apparently efficient days. Some day, if we are ever in the right mood, I'll tell you about it, but it will be only words, because it's incommunicable.

With the letter he enclosed the draft of a poem he had just written which would, he said, 'explain a lot'. The poem was entitled 'Tiz'n Test', after the high, windswept pass of that name that crosses over the High Atlas, and referred to an episode during Gavin's travels the previous winter and to its aftermath in this present winter. It spoke of the solace of human love in the deep dark of a bleak and lonely wasteland, and of the bitter nihilism of subsequent betrayal. The poem was clearly addressed to Ahmed, and written in the depths of despair. The imagery, drawn from the wild world of Tiz'n Test, is striking.

> The darkness and the storm,
> Wind-scream, clang of iron,
> The shuddering walls,
> Crash of falling stone,
> Your warm and living flesh against my own . . .
>
> Sunrise and a ruined inn,
> Far off a jackal's cry;
> Dawn, and the world's age
> A vulture in the sky.
>
> Sleeping, insentient, you became the giver
> Of a brief borrowed world –
> Snowthaw and the blood-red river,
> Windsurge of bird;
> Became the archetypal lover
> Knowing a forgotten world.
>
> These your betrayal takes away for ever:
> World without sin,
> Desert and mountain we explored together;
> Where has it led, that road that neither
> Knew? Only the broken inn?

Not all of Gavin's poetry was expressed in verse form. In their imagery and intensity of emotion, some passages in his book *The Rocks Remain*, in which he was to express his anguished experiences in Morocco during the Haywire Winter, are really poems too. Such passages are not statements of pure documentary fact; but nor are they mere inventions; rather they are extrapolations that start from a basis in fact and from that basis build a structure of thought and emotion that states a poetic truth rather than a documentary one. There is no clearer example of Gavin's prose-poetry – his narrative of extrapolation – than the incident at the salt-marsh at Rabat. Late one evening, while staying at Margaret Pope's flat, Gavin went out for a walk in the salt-marsh at the edge of the city. After an hour or two he returned to the flat. He did not talk about his walk and after a little while he went to bed. Later, in *The Rocks Remain*, he developed this straightforward and relatively brief excursion into a haunting and disturbing narrative – a poetic extrapolation that enabled him to come much nearer to the 'real' truth (about his state of mind) than the literal truth could have done:

> One night I wandered on a salt-marsh; I left the streets of the city in which I was living because without solitude I could not resolve the tangle of my thoughts. When I set out the moon was bright. Before me rose ghostly flocks of flamingos; they wheeled pale but colourless in the moonlight, and alighted always ahead of me, so that their numbers became illimitable and all-enveloping. After a long time the moon was hidden by a cloud and I could no longer follow their flight. The only possible paths were the now unlit causeways, running always at right angles to each other, and I had lost my bearings. In utter darkness I came upon a shack. A figure little darker than the sky was somehow beside me and drew me into the warm darkness of the shelter. A bellows fanned a charcoal brazier, a bearded face thus lit by firelight glanced at me without apparent curiosity. '*Min fdl'k*,' he said. '*Min fdl'k*' (make yourself at home), and leaving the brazier he spread a blanket on the floor. I drank mint tea and then slept; in the cold hour of the dawn I was aware that small children came and laid more coverings upon me. No one asked me any questions . . .

Gavin's hastily scribbled notes recording his unhappy domicile in the medina of Marrakesh, some of which were later published in shortened form in *The Rocks Remain*, include some of his finest, most savagely observed and emotionally disturbed and disturbing travel writing. He stares with unhooded eyes into the very heart of horror, the suffering and degradation of the Third World poor, a mirror image of his own private, privileged hell. Here he comes close to the vision of true, naked reality, uncluttered by romanticism, Christian optimism, or any other brand of wishful thinking. Gavin Maxwell's medina is Joseph Conrad's Congo jungle of the *Heart of Darkness*; it is the dying words of the mad, ailing Kurtz – 'The horror! The horror!' Gavin's Marrakesh home and the back-streets that envelop it are an exotic version of T.S. Eliot's *Waste Land*, holding for him a similar abyss, a similar void, a similar terror of the unknown. 'The essential advantage for a poet,' Eliot had written, 'is not, to have a beautiful world with which to deal; it is to be able to see beneath both beauty and ugliness; to see the boredom, and the horror, and the glory.' Gavin's prose description of the nightmare of Marrakesh as he perceived it during the late winter of 1961 is essentially poetic. The imagery, alternating between pity and horror, emptiness and fear, is the clearly focused, uncompromising imagery of the poet deranged, of the front-line soldier after close-quarter carnage, of the condemned to death and the dying. On previous visits Morocco had seemed to him an inordinately beautiful and wondrous land. Images of glory, however, are few now. Instead he sees: 'Two hooded figures squat in the dust of the alley outside my door slitting the throats of chickens over a small drain; there is a terrible commotion from the dying wings as the knife cuts through each neck. The dust soaks up the blood slowly, cats paw at it petulantly and lick their toes. One evening at the close of Ramadan . . .'

Gavin's world in the medina was inhabited predominantly, if not exclusively, by an army of beggars, whose cries filled both his waking and his sleeping hours, reaching their height towards sundown, when the siren sounded the end of the day's fast. He did not have to stir far to see them. They were beneath his window and outside his door.

Not even in sleep was he spared the horror of the suffering he saw all around him. 'One night,' he wrote in his notebook, 'I woke from a dream to hear the blind beggar's invocation from the street outside, and my own voice saying, "Give me back my eyes." But to whomever these words were addressed, they were no more heard than the beggar's, who asked for so little while I asked for so much. I put an Arab shawl round my shoulders and fumbled my way blindly down the stairs and found the beggar and gave him more, probably, than he had ever received in his life.'

At dawn he would wake, or half-wake, from the tension of his dreams, slip his feet out of bed and remain sitting there for a long time, with his eyes resting unfocused upon some ancient obscene scrawl or a crevice in the crumbling plaster of his cell. Recalling his depressive state, he wrote: 'An Arab friend said to me: "You must go – otherwise you never will. People can die like this, without reason; they turn inward and they are against themselves."'

As the haywire winter dragged on, Gavin's depression deepened. Only his physical removal from the scene could save him from continuing decline. Buried deep in the high mud-walled maze of the medina, Gavin was like a man ensnared. In the daytime the narrow view of the sky above was simply a blue blank; but at night he could snatch a glimpse of wider bounds, of infinity and eternity together, the rectangle of brilliant stars hanging above the clamorous city like a studded belt of diamonds on dark velvet; and here and there he could catch an enfiladed view of a more attainable freedom – the snow-covered mountains of the High Atlas caught in the last rays of the sun as it sank towards the Atlantic, the flights of white egrets homing in over the palms and minarets from the open country beyond the city walls. 'Far to the south were the bright deserts where I longed to be,' he wrote, 'the deserts of shimmering castellated mirage and bounding gazelle, the flowering deserts where from waterless stone *jol* grew the miracle of mauve blossom upon pale thorn.'

Gavin's occasional forays away from his confining cell in the medina did little to ease his distress, for they took him as often as not into a realm of farce and chaos. Sometimes they led him westward to Rabat and the restless haven of Margaret Pope's apartment, seething as ever with the ebb and flow of African ambassadors and revolutionaries. 'He used to come with his horrible animals,' Margaret Pope recalled, 'gigantic lizards and things from the desert. He tied them to my lampstands and tried to feed them flies – dead ones at first, then live ones. Once a lizard bit him, right through the quick of his fingernail, when he tried to force its mouth open to feed a live fly to it. So I took the thing to the kitchen and I was going to cut its head off but Gavin wouldn't let me. "You don't know anything about animals," I scolded him. "You're just *emotionally* involved with them."'

In Margaret Pope's flat Gavin found some distraction in the occupational therapy afforded by the domestic chores to which he and the politicians were assigned – sewing buttons, mending gloves, and other millinery diversions. For a few weeks he took part in a radio programme called 'Answers to your Questions' which was broadcast on Margaret Pope's English-speaking service of Moroccan Radio. Listeners' questions ranged from space travel to speleology, and the answers were provided by experts from UNESCO in Paris and the Science Division of OECD in London. To present these answers in a manner suitable for popular broadcasting, Margaret Pope conceived the idea of casting Gavin in the role of 'Professor Svenski' – 'a miraculous combination of Bronowski, Russell, Huxley, and all the great specialised scientists of the decade'. Speaking with a stateless middle-European accent of the kind he had perfected in SOE during the war, Gavin solemnly held forth on every learned subject under the sun. Only when it was felt that to continue the deception would risk exposure was Gavin's role in the programme discontinued; listeners were told that Professor Svenski had left for Indonesia, while Gavin himself returned to his lonely rented room in Marrakesh.

From time to time there were other distractions. Much to the gratification of his highly developed sense of drama, he was caught up in the excitement of the street demonstrations that followed the death of the King of Morocco, Mohammed V in February 1961 – first in Casablanca and then in Marrakesh, where an armed guard was placed at the door to his quarters in the medina. Once, at the instigation of his official mentor in Morocco, His Excellency Moulay Ahmed el Alaoui, the mercurial Minister of Information, Tourism and Fine Arts, a one-eyed cousin of the late King and intimate of the heir apparent, he accompanied a party of fifty Berber beaters and two English sportsmen, *grands chasseurs* with a special permit to shoot the rare moufflon, the giant wild mountain sheep of the Atlas, on a hunting expedition in the foothills of the southern mountains, where he despatched a running boar with his only shot at three hundred yards.

Gavin's Moroccan notebook contains brief, cryptic references to other incidents and encounters in Morocco during that distracted winter:

The tire aux pigeons
Lady Steele Maitland – Marquise – visit – blank
The duck shoot at Larache
Murder of Ghoulé
The angry bull at Sodom and Gomorrah
Visit by stately negro at night to explain cause

and so on. Since no fuller account was forthcoming later, these episodes must remain for ever enigmatic spoors in the sand.

Soon it would be time for me to leave Sandaig. The spring was coming, the geese were flying back from the south, the sun had reappeared over the hills. Soon the elvers from the Sargasso Sea would swarm up the burn and the sand martins from Africa would nest again in their holes in the bank. If my ears had been more sensitive, or better attuned, I would have heard, above the ceaseless murmur of the falls, the secret bustle of spring, the uncoiling of fern and circulation of sap, the chrysalids stirring and the earth alive.

One March day I stepped out of the dim gloom of the house into a landscape startlingly changed. The sun blazed down, the air was warm, the trees were loud with birdsong, the motionless sea stretched away to the horizon, glittering and blue. I followed Teko on his morning's lolloping course towards the islands and their tiny shell-sand coves and on a sudden impulse ran down the beach, following the line of the otter's footprints across the sand, and leapt into the sea. The water closed over my head like a block of ice. Emerging, I cried out, a primitive shout of triumph and glee, and heard the clamour of the startled gulls on the bird islands and my own voice echo back to me from among the rocks.

That night I rolled myself in a blanket in the sand dunes and lay for a long time listening to the strange, wild cries of the night, staring up at the bright white disc of the full moon in the starlit sky and out across the still, moonlit void of the North Atlantic. I had sunk fragile little roots among these hills and islands. I fell asleep among the dunes at the edge of the great ocean as free as any human being could ever be. Though I did not know it then, I would never be so close to Avalon again.

In Morocco, Gavin realised that the only solution for his helpless condition, for the inertia and depression that held him prisoner, was to leave the country altogether and go home. But time and again he postponed his departure, unable to break away, unable to burst through the barrier which confined him, the nature of which he could not understand. 'I would try sometimes to think of Camusfeàrna in March sunshine, of the waterfall and the budding birches, of primroses among dead bracken, of the soft mountain distances and blue sea, but always the image would dissolve before it was complete. Before it was strong enough to draw me from where I was.'

Finally Gavin wrote home suggesting that Jimmy Watt should come out to Morocco to help him with his return journey. Jimmy arrived in the last week of March, and the hypnotic spell was broken. But the unpredictable twists and turns of the Haywire Winter persisted to the very end, for Gavin's exit from Morocco was both farcical and triumphal, a source of hilarity that belied the tortured months that had gone before. He had booked a passage home on a freighter from Casablanca, but the day he and Jimmy were due to deliver the Land Rover at the docks turned out to be the day that Marshal Tito, the President of Yugoslavia, was to begin a state visit to the city. The road to the port – the processional route – was sealed off by army and police roadblocks and decorated with flags and bunting and lined with great crowds of spectators, including tribesmen trucked down from the hills. All traffic had been diverted and there was not a single vehicle on the broad, mile-long avenue when Gavin drove up to the police point that barred further progress.

As it happened, Moulay Ahmed had furnished him with a number of highly official documents to facilitate his travels around the country, including a government *laissez-passer* and a police *coupe-file* which allowed him, to all intents and purposes, to ignore any police order or regulation that got in his way. Presenting these papers to the officer in charge, Gavin was astonished to be waved through the roadblock. Ahead lay the empty avenue and a great, expectant crowd lining both sides as far as the eye could see. The Land Rover was evidently the first vehicle that had passed along this route all day, and as Gavin swept along it the crowd pressed forward. Some, taking him for an outrider, clapped and raised a ragged cheer. Others, the Berber tribesmen from the hills, mistook Gavin, if not for Tito, then at least for one of his entourage. They burst out drumming and dancing, they sang and swayed to the rhythm of their age-old tribal dances. Thus honoured and acclaimed, Gavin and Jimmy passed through the serried ranks of Arab well-wishers and Berber mountain-men, their faces fixed in discreet smiles, their arms raised nonchalantly in a gesture halfway between a wave and a salute, till they safely reached their journey's end.

The next day they shipped the Land Rover on board a small freighter full of oranges and tortoises and headed home across the Bay of Biscay. Ahead of Gavin lay another year at Camusfeàrna and a new life as a famous author; behind him the Haywire Winter withered and died on the Maghreb shore. 'I have buried the rest of it in the compost heap of my subconscious,' he was to write later, 'and now it only returns to me in the poignancy of dreams, urgent and febrile, in which are implicit the sense of some task unfinished, some goal unattained – sometimes I have thought it was death.'

On 11 April 1961 Gavin arrived back in Britain. From Sandaig I sent him a letter reassuring him that the otters were well and happy, and warning him about the smoke that sometimes emerged from behind the panelling in the kitchen-parlour. From the pathologist at London Zoo I received a letter: 'I was delighted to hear that Edal is now almost normal again. The recovery of this animal is a fantastic success story. I think you should all be extremely proud of the way that you have saved her life.'

A couple of days later, at the end of nearly half a year at Camusfeàrna, I set off on my long journey south. Through the dark days and stormy winds of the Haywire Winter, Avalon and its wild creatures had prevailed. But these had been the final months. With the coming of summer, Avalon was to prevail no more.

PART III

AVALON LOST

TWENTY-FIVE

End of the idyll

I have looked upon these brilliant creatures,
And now my heart is sore.
All's changed since I, hearing at twilight,
The first time on this shore,
The bell beat of their wings above my head,
Trod with a lighter tread.

W.B. YEATS, 'The Wild Swans at Coole'

All through his African winter Gavin had pined for Sandaig in the spring; but six long weeks were to pass before he could return to the peace and seclusion (as he hoped) of his Highland home. First, he had pressing business in the south.

Muttering darkly and fantastically about a Jewish plot, he set off for Holland to sort out once and for all the mystery surrounding the disappearance of Ahmed, but he was obliged to return home empty-handed, and passed the case over to Margaret Pope and a private detective agency (who found Ahmed living contentedly with a Dutch family in a suburb of Amsterdam). Then, as a matter of urgency, he needed a medical examination of his eyes, for he had damaged a cornea and contracted some kind of chronic conjunctivitis in a sandstorm in the Moroccan Sahara. Though there proved to be no serious damage to his sight, his eyes remained red and inflamed, and would swell and weep in strong light, so that from now on he took to wearing black-tinted glasses, which gave him a rather sinister look.

He also needed to put his financial affairs in order. The sudden wealth generated by the worldwide success of *Ring of Bright Water* had put him in the topmost tax bracket (at that time running at a punitive 90 per cent of annual income). On his agent's advice he turned himself into a tax-efficient limited company, Gavin Maxwell Enterprises Ltd, with himself as Chairman, and his agent, his accountant and his trusted friend Raef Payne as directors. To relieve himself of the burden of the routine paperwork he appointed a twenty-one-year-old former management trainee, Michael Cuddy, to look after the day-to-day business of the new company as his London manager. At the same time, to cash in on the popularity of *Ring*, he contracted with his publishers to produce a condensed, lavishly illustrated children's version to be called *The Otters' Tale*. The condensation was soon done and the new book was off his hands before he finally returned to Sandaig on 23 May 1961.

During his troubled sojourn in Morocco Gavin had dreamed of Camusfeàrna as a parched man dreams of an oasis in a waterless desert. But on his return he was dismayed to find that the peace and seclusion for which he had yearned were no more. In *Ring of Bright Water* he had gone to some pains to conceal the true identity and location of Sandaig – fearing, he said, a betrayal of its remoteness and isolation. But with casual prescience he had added: 'It will be easy enough for the curious to discover where I live.'

What he had not foreseen was that the book would be a runaway bestseller, and that with the coming of the first fine weather since its publication hundreds of its readers from both sides of the Atlantic would be up and about along the West Highland coast, searching for clues to Camusfeàrna's whereabouts – a lighthouse on an island, a sandy bay, a burn running into the sea, a view of Skye . . . A trickle of unannounced visitors had already found their way down to the house even in the depths of the winter I had just spent there, some of them from as far away as Texas and Maine. But no one had foreseen the flood brought by the warm days of spring. This wholesale intrusion marked the beginning of a long series of setbacks which would in the end destroy Camusfeàrna and much more besides.

As spring turned to summer and the tourist season reached its height the swarm of visitors who succeeded in cracking the code that concealed Sandaig's location grew so great that the routine of the household was turned topsy-turvy. To deter the invading army Gavin posted warning notices at strategic points along the tracks which led over the hills and down to the house.

All in vain. The fans of *Ring* left their cars and tramped through peat bogs, over hill and down dale, through gates and over fences, until they stood at last at Gavin's door, proud and breathless, and announced: 'Look, we've found you! We've read your book – and how we envy you your way of life!' Those who were deterred by the uncompromising warning of the final signboard – the word PRIVATE in bold red lettering a foot high – merely diverted their approach and took up positions on the slope of the hill, where they sat for hours peering intently through their telescopes and binoculars at all the activity that went on around the house.

Finally, Gavin lost patience. Late one evening, when the incumbents at Sandaig had at last managed to sit down to dinner after a long and bothersome day, Gavin heard a murmur of voices outside and was informed that a party of Americans who had travelled three thousand miles to visit Camusfeàrna would like to come in. This was the last straw. Gavin stormed to the door. If they had indeed travelled three thousand miles to visit a total stranger, he railed, they might have shown more courtesy than to arrive unannounced in the middle of dinner at half past nine in the evening. With barely concealed ill-temper he bade them good evening and slammed the door in their faces.

While Gavin's efforts were directed to repelling invaders by land, he neglected to protect his seaward flank. One day a smart yacht sidled into the bay and dropped anchor. According to Gavin's published version of the incident (in *The Rocks Remain*), one of the men on board settled himself into a seat at the stern with a .22 rifle across his knees while his companions threw bread to the gulls. Whenever a gull alighted on the water to take the bread the man in the stern would shoot it with his rifle – or so it seemed to Gavin watching from the dunes below the house with Jimmy Watt and Terry Nutkins. Gavin soon grew angry at what he believed to be the wanton and destructive killing that was taking place on his domain. After five minutes he asked Jimmy to fetch his .350 Magnum Rigby big-game rifle from the house, and the next time the man appeared to shoot a gull Gavin loosed a single round at the floating corpse on the water. So great was the noise of the gun going off and the large-calibre bullet zipping past the yacht that in a second or two the figures on the deck were scuttling about in a frenzy, and the anchor was weighed and the engine started before Gavin had made up his mind to fire a second shot. (The man who had been firing from the boat later protested that he had not been shooting at gulls, but at empty bottles which he had kept for target practice.)

*   *   *

The public invasion of Sandaig led to another, infinitely more serious incident – one which had ominous implications for the future
of the Sandaig household in its current form. Gavin was not present
on this occasion, nor did he ever refer to it subsequently. It took
place on 6 May, barely three weeks after I had left Sandaig following
my winter stint, and before Gavin had come up from London
after his return from Morocco. In view of the friendly and docile
behaviour of the two otters during the previous six months, I was
dumbfounded to receive a letter from Jimmy which announced:
'All's well except that *Teko* bit a woman visitor yesterday! There
was the most almighty yell from Teko and quick as a flash
this woman was lying on the sofa with her wrist and side of shin
open.'

The woman had arrived the previous evening with her husband,
saying she wished to see the elvers which at that time of the year
swarmed up the Sandaig burn on their spectacular annual
migration. After a visit to the burn she came to the door of the
house and asked if she and her husband could see one of the otters,
claiming that Gavin had said that whenever they were passing they
could come and have a look at his pets. The couple were invited
into the kitchen-parlour and the woman sat on the sofa while Terry
Nutkins went out to fetch Teko, who was considered the friendlier
and more trustworthy of the two animals, from his quarters in
the coalshed where he was sleeping. Terry recalled vividly what
happened next:

Teko jumped on to the woman's lap and started playing
around and sniffing her hair. Then he began to make that
horrible angry wailing sound and I knew something was going
to happen; but before I could get him away from her he
launched into her. It lasted only a few seconds but it was a most
horrific attack. He went for her face first and then worked his
way down her arms and legs. Her calf muscle was ripped to
pieces and I could see the fat coming out of her leg. There
was blood everywhere and the woman was just lying there
hysterical. Well, I made a dive at Teko and picked him up by
the root of his tail and rushed out of the room with him to
his shed. It never occurred to me that I risked being attacked
myself. Teko just lay there on his back with his paws over

his face going 'Wah wah wah!' His white bib was bloodstained and there were bits of flesh and fat round his mouth.

While the woman lay bleeding and screaming on the sofa, Jimmy telephoned Dr Beveridge, the young woman who was now general practitioner at Glenelg, forty minutes away. The boys did the best they could for the victim, wrapping her in bandages and towels and giving her tea and aspirins. When Dr Beveridge finally arrived she stitched the woman up but decided that she should be taken to hospital in Inverness as quickly as possible. The first stage of the journey was to Glenelg, and the quickest – indeed, under the circumstances, the only – way of getting her there was in Gavin's little dinghy. So the woman was carried down to the beach and laid in the bottom of the boat for the second part of her nightmare adventure.

It was getting dark now, a Force 8 was blowing and the sea was roaring into Sandaig Bay. Terry had to stand up to his neck in water holding the boat steady while Jimmy tried to start the outboard. Then they were off, into the teeth of the wind and waves. They rounded the lighthouse island and took course down the sound, rolling and heaving in a big following sea, with the wind howling and the spray breaking into the boat and the woman crying and groaning as she was tossed from side to side. 'It was the worst sea I've ever been on,' Jimmy wrote. 'We couldn't get to Glenelg so we dropped her off at Eilanreach.'

The woman, who had suffered terrible injuries, might have sued Gavin for damages. But she did not. Gavin, who was dismayed when he heard the news, claimed that he had never met the woman and had certainly never given her permission to visit the otters. Whatever the reason, the victim of the attack made no complaint and no word of the incident reached the ears of the public or the press.

But why had Teko, of all creatures, attacked a human being for the first time? Edal's attack on Margaret Pope in the previous summer had been ascribed to the jealousy of a female otter for a female human being. But this could not explain Teko's attack, for Teko was a male, and had hitherto displayed no aggressive feelings whatsoever. Were these one-off attacks, unlikely to recur? There was no way of knowing. Gavin at this stage was an otter pioneer, an explorer in all things luterine. There was no data, no corpus of knowledge on otter behaviour to which he could refer. Perhaps an error of some kind had precipitated Teko's attack, perhaps not. In the meantime the otters would continue to live and be cared for as they had previously – as more or less free and integral members of the Sandaig 'family'.

For the next three months all was well. But early in August, while Gavin was out walking Edal in the company of Jimmy Watt and Caroline Jarvis, an attractive young zoologist who helped edit the *International Zoo Year Book* at London Zoo, Edal, in a sudden unprovoked attack, buried her teeth in Caroline's ankle, fortunately without inflicting permanent injury. Edal's attack, Gavin concluded, was due to an explosion of jealousy. In his view Edal considered herself married to both Jimmy and himself, and this put Caroline in the position of a rival. The consequences were plain. 'Alas, Edal has taken strongly against all females,' he wrote to Constance McNab a few days later, 'and (between you and me and whoever else *has* to know) is no longer to be trusted with them.' But a few weeks later Edal attacked again, with infinitely greater ferocity – and this time the victim was a male.

It was late in the afternoon of Sunday, 27 August 1961. Only Terry Nutkins was in the house. Gavin was in London on business and not due back at Sandaig until the following night. Jimmy Watt was collecting the mail from Tormor and Raef Payne was in the croft near the shore, which he used as a summer holiday home. Terry recalled:

I could hear Edal upstairs scrabbling on the door of her room, something she often used to do, so I went up to play with her, wearing a sweater which had been given to me by Caroline Jarvis. I sat on the side of her bed and Edal jumped up beside me and started to sniff the sweater and make that grunting noise that otters make. I sensed that something was wrong but I couldn't quite put my finger on it. When the noise began to get louder I felt very uneasy and put her down on the floor and stood up. And as I stood up she made a sudden lunge straight for my foot and tore the whole of the front of my Wellington boot off in one go. She was making this high-pitched screaming noise which otters make when they are fighting mad, and tearing into my foot, and I thought: 'Well,

I've got to do something about this – my foot's bleeding, the door's closed, and I'm trapped in here with an enraged otter.'

So I bent down to pick her up and as I did so she got hold of the second finger of my right hand between her jaws and began pulling and chewing it as if it was an eel, and I could feel as well as hear the crunching of the bones. Then she got hold of my thumb and was mangling the whole of my hand in her jaws and I thought: 'I'm never going to get away from this animal!' So I jumped on top of her and pinned her head down with my left hand as I tried to move my right hand out of her mouth. I remembered what Gavin had told me to do if ever the otters got too rough – repeat the words 'softly . . . softly . . . softly' over and over again to them in a gentle, reassuring voice. So that's what I did, trying to stay as calm as possible, and she stopped and just looked at me, so I started to move my hand out of her mouth, and I had just got it out when she started screaming again. So I automatically picked her up and flung her across the room, and as I flung her she twisted round and bit clean through the second finger of my left hand. Well, she landed over on the other side of the room and I made a dive for the door, and just as I slammed the door behind me she was back, trying to get me, screaming her head off.

Dazed and shocked, Terry wandered round the downstairs of the house. His right hand was in a dreadful state, mangled and punctured with teethmarks; the thumb hung half off and the top two joints of the second finger had been chewed through and were simply hanging by a sinew. A slightly smaller proportion of the second finger of his left hand had been bitten off and was attached only by the skin. Holding on to a finger that might otherwise have dropped off, Terry ran over to Raef's croft, a hundred yards away. Aghast, Raef did what he could to help. He wrapped Terry's hands in towels, brewed tea, proffered whisky, and summoned the Glenelg doctor. But the towels didn't stop the bleeding – nor the intense pain that now began to come welling through.

Terry was standing by the door of the croft looking puzzled and lost when Jimmy returned from Tormor. 'His hands were like something out of a horror movie,' Jimmy remembered. 'All red and pulpy and bleeding.' When Dr Beveridge arrived she attempted, by dint of rather desperate kitchen-parlour surgery, to stitch Terry's finger back on again, with Jimmy holding the lamp close to give her a better light. 'It was hopeless – like sewing mince,' Jimmy remembered of that horrendous scene. 'Afterwards I lay in the wet grass, rolled in it, getting wet, trying to get rid of the memory.'

It was clear that Terry needed urgent hospital attention, but the nearest hospital was at Broadford on the Isle of Skye, and there was no ferry across till the morning, so Terry had to stick it out through a long and agonising night. 'The pain was a hundred times greater than if you'd had a car door slam on your fingers,' he remembered. 'By three in the morning I was crying and groaning and screaming because the pain was unbelievable.'

All night long Raef walked Terry up and down in Gavin's study-bedroom, trying to help him get through the night, and when morning came at last he helped him up the track over the hill to Tormor. 'When I got there,' Terry recalled, 'I just collapsed – I couldn't stand it any more. Shock and loss of blood and sheer exhaustion, I suppose.'

That night Gavin returned to Sandaig and heard the news. He caught the first ferry across to Skye the next morning and raced over to Broadford in his new red Mercedes roadster. He was surprised to find Terry sitting up in bed in the hospital ward, signalling wildly with his pyjama top.

'When do I get out of here?' he asked. 'Are you going to take me away? You won't leave me here?'

Gavin sniffed the air. Terry, too, was aware of a peculiar odour around the bed. Gavin sniffed Terry's bandages. At close quarters the smell was overpowering.

'My God!' Gavin exclaimed. 'That's gangrene! Here, smell.'

He lifted Terry's hands to his nose. Terry sniffed and noticed the same horrible, putrescent stench.

'We've got to do something about this,' Gavin said, his voice unsteady, for the implications were clear.

'I could see he was very genuinely shocked and concerned,' Terry recalled. 'Whether this was because it was me who had been attacked or because it was Edal that had done the attacking I'm not sure. It might have been both. I think he was shocked that the creature on which he had relied so much had done such a horrific thing, and wondered whether it would do the same to him.'

Terry was taken to the house of the hospital doctor for an examination. The tops of the two half-severed fingers were only too evidently dead and gangrenous.

'Chop 'em off, doctor,' said Terry. 'That ruddy lot's no good to anyone.'

The doctor went to work. It did not take long. Gavin stared in horror at the two black fingertips lying in the white enamel basin. 'Nothing on earth could ever restore them,' he was to write later. 'In some way they had been more terrible to look at than a corpse.'

The plan now was for Gavin to take Terry back to Sandaig that day, then drive him to Glasgow the following morning for plastic surgery at the Bon Secours Hospital, a private clinic run by nuns. The drive to Glasgow, Terry recalled, was a sensational one.

Gavin drove like a bat out of hell. He loved drama and for him this was real drama. My hands had swollen up like balloons because of the gangrene, and the gangrene had already begun to spread up into my arms. For Gavin the drive to Glasgow was a race against death – he had to get there before the gangrene spread. He drove incredibly fast in the red Mercedes – and incredibly well. No expense was spared with the surgeons. They treated my hands, put skin-grafts over my finger-ends and slung my arms up in slings for six weeks to drain away the gangrene. I was lucky to have both arms left, really. I suppose, all things considered, I was lucky to be alive.

When eventually Terry returned to Sandaig it was put about that his injuries had been caused when the chain of a petrol-driven saw hit a nail in a piece of wood he had been cutting. On no account did Gavin wish the true story to be leaked to the press or reach the ears of the local inhabitants. To Constance McNab he sent an urgent note: 'There has been an otter crisis here, the details of which are *highly* confidential. To save writing it all down I've suggested that Caroline Jarvis explain it to you. It has vastly complicated life here, and while before there were few moments in the day there are now none!'

As Terry's employer and guardian Gavin accepted liability for the injuries Edal had inflicted, and arranged for the sum of £1000 to be paid to Terry as compensation once he had reached the age of twenty-one. At the same time he took steps to prevent Edal from ever attacking a human being again. Gavin felt sure that Edal

had attacked Terry for the simple reason that he had been wearing
Caroline Jarvis's sweater. But such was the ferocity of the attack
and the extent of Terry's injuries that he was reluctantly forced to
accept that Edal could never be allowed to roam free again. From
now on she would have to be kept permanently confined, and
only Jimmy and himself would be allowed to go near her. Gavin's
solution was to have a prefabricated wooden house, thirty feet long
by twelve feet wide, erected at right-angles to the seaward end of
the main house, with direct access to a large fenced-off enclosure
containing two swimming pools and every kind of waterworks
that could be devised. In other words, Edal was henceforth to be
confined like a zoo animal – but in a zoo as large and luxurious as
money could buy.

In a short while the wooden house arrived by sea in half a gale
of wind. Its floating sections were poled ashore like rafts by Gavin
and Jimmy and then hauled painfully up on shore. Once again, just
as on Soay seventeen years before, Gavin was establishing a complex organisation on a hopelessly remote site.

When it was finally erected and furnished in September the
wooden house made an imposing room, with eight large windows
looking out over the sea and the hills, permanent access to the
otter's enclosure, and an infra-red lamp hanging over a bed of
towels on which Edal could dry herself when she came inside. But
the elements make trifles of presumptuous human endeavours, and
the house was no sooner put up than it was almost blown flat in a
violent storm on 15 September. 'Yesterday God in his wrath sent
down a hurricane on Camusfeàrna,' Jimmy wrote to a friend, 'and
the sea boiled like only God can make it boil. The hurricane got
underneath the new house and lifted its floor up about three inches.
In Glenelg lots of trees fell, two boats were smashed and the mail
boat only just made it in. The electricity here went off for nine
hours, the telephone is out of order, all the rowan berries are blown
– and some horrible sheep have eaten all my cabbages.'

The next day Gavin departed for a long weekend at the Sutherland home of his friend James Robertson-Justice, whose other
house guests included Prince Philip, Duke of Edinburgh. On his
return he arranged to have three free-standing swimming-
pools despatched by sea to Sandaig at enormous cost and filled
by polythene piping laid from the waterfall nearby. One of the
smaller pools was partially sunk into the ground in the enclosure

surrounding Teko's little coalshed, for Gavin had decided that preparations should be made for Teko's confinement as well, should it prove necessary at any time in the future. Teko's pool, however, burst the moment it was filled, flooding the house to a depth of six inches with four thousand tons of water. But within a week a replacement pool was delivered by hired launch – the fibreglass tank underneath which Michael Powell and Bill Paton crouched so uncomfortably on their visit to Sandaig.

The calamities of that disastrous summer were not yet at an end. Gavin had recently bought a forty-foot ex-RAF high-speed rescue launch called the *Polar Star*. Though she was twenty-five years old she was capable of a good twenty knots, throwing up a spectacular bow wave which made her, in Gavin's eyes, the highly desirable equivalent at sea of his impressive Mercedes roadster on land. The considerable capital outlay and heavy running costs of such a specialist vessel he justified on the grounds that she would greatly extend the radius of his horizon at Sandaig and dramatically shorten the time taken on sea trips away from home – an important factor with the otters requiring full-time attention every day.

But Gavin had a fatal talent for standing logic on its head, and in the light of subsequent events he was forced to admit that the *Polar Star* was 'one of the many minor follies with which my life has been sprinkled'. Exactly as he had done with the *Dove* in the shark-fishing days, he bought the new boat without having set eyes on her beforehand. 'It is aggravating to repeat a stupid mistake,' he confessed, 'and thus to demonstrate that one is slower to learn than many an animal.' When the boat was finally delivered to Sandaig by sea (having caught fire off the Yorkshire coast and run at full speed into the perilous whirlpools and overfalls of the Corryvreckan off the west of Scotland) Gavin was deeply disappointed at what he saw. 'Everything about her reeked of neglect and indifference,' he reported. 'She had little but speed and a sound hull; for the rest she was dirty, neglected, squalid in appearance inside and out.' It cost him almost as much to replace her engines and transmission and restore her interior woodwork and fittings as it did to buy her; and it cost almost as much again to salvage and repair her after he wrecked her on a reef in Sandaig Bay on practically his first outing.

Returning from Glenelg with Jimmy Watt and Terry Nutkins

late in the evening of 7 October, Gavin ran into heavy rain and
patches of dense grey mist off the Sandaig islands, then discovered
there was no dinghy on the *Polar Star*'s moorings – just a cut end
of rope. He realised that the rope must have been cut by one of
the propellers when he set out earlier in the evening, and that unless
the missing dinghy was found there was no obvious way of getting
ashore again. Judging that the dinghy must have drifted ashore on
the Lighthouse Island, he put Terry ashore to search for it, with
instructions that if it could not be found, Terry was to wait until
low tide at about midnight and then wade across from island to
island until he reached the mainland. There he could collect the
small dinghy and row back – a good two-mile haul – to pick up
Gavin and Jimmy.

By the time Terry, his injured fingers still bandaged after Edal's
attack, scrambled ashore on the Lighthouse Island – an inhospitable,
trackless terrain of weed-covered outcrops, treacherous crevices and
impenetrable scrub – it was pitch dark. For more than an hour the
Polar Star waited at anchor on the north side of the island, but
nothing was seen or heard of Terry. After a while the wind and
sea began to get up and Gavin decided to take the *Polar Star* round
to the south side of the island and anchor in Sandaig Bay, so that
Terry would have a shorter, safer row out to the boat in the worsen-
ing weather. But the blackness of the night was all-enveloping and
the boat's searchlight illuminated nothing but an impenetrable wall
of rain; nudging forward at slow ahead in almost zero visibility,
Gavin had a split-second glimpse of solid rock a few feet from the
bow, and then the boat struck, the bows reared, and the propellers
grated on the granite rock.

In the middle of a black night, a rising wind and an ebbing tide,
the *Polar Star* was hard aground on an island or a reef or any one
of fifty rocks – there was no knowing what or which. Holding the
boat's bow and stern lines, Gavin and Jimmy clambered overboard
to try and explore their surroundings – a perilous operation, for
neither could swim and there was only one life-jacket between them
– but they could feel only weed-covered wet rock shelving steeply
upwards. As the wind rose, the waves came out of the dark and
broke over them and over the boat's starboard quarter, so that she
began to ship green water into the after cockpit, and then to bump
and slam on the rock on which she was fast. It was clear she would
break up if she remained where she was.

Gavin and Jimmy clambered back on board and tried to back her off with the engines, and when she would not move Gavin decided they should go ashore again to lighten her, and then push her off on the crest of a wave, hoping she might drift off and beach on a sand or gravel shore. For a despairing half hour they wrestled with the boat in the slimy seaweed, and then suddenly she was free and drifting away into the night. They watched her go, feeling desolate and forlorn, until soon her mast-light was obscured, and nothing could be seen of boat or land or sea. It was about eleven o'clock now, and almost dead low tide; for all Gavin and Jimmy could tell they might be on a reef which would be submerged when the tide came in again before dawn. All they had salvaged from the *Polar Star* was the boathook.

In fact they were below the gull colony on the south face of the Lighthouse Island. So dark was the night, so rough the terrain and so deep the water they had to wade through as they crossed from island to island that it was nearly one in the morning before they reached Sandaig. Terry came in half an hour later, cheerful but far gone from cold and hypothermia after trying to swim out to the drifting *Polar Star*.

The *Polar Star* was successfully salvaged by Bruce Watt, Gavin's former shark-boat skipper, who was now coxswain of the Mallaig lifeboat and ran several charter vessels of his own. She was found abandoned and aground on a submerged rock ten yards from the main reef in Sandaig Bay, and after being towed back to Mallaig she was found to have buckled propellers, a badly strained keel, deeply chafed planking, and a leaking hull. It was some months before Gavin put to sea in her again – and a little while longer before he felt confident enough to run her on to the rocks a second time.

Terry Nutkins had been in regular employment at Sandaig for only about six months, but in that short time he had probably experienced more adventures and endured more threats to life and limb than any other fifteen-year-old boy in Britain.

When Terry had entered full-time employment at Sandaig in April 1961, Gavin had given the educational authorities a written assurance that he would take over his education himself and personally provide him with a course of instruction for at least three hours a day. This marked the beginning of Gavin's intense interest in the

education of the young, about which he had many unusual theories.
Terry recalled:

> He kept his word, except he didn't teach me what the local
> authorities wanted him to teach but what he thought was best
> for me, which was natural history mainly. So instead of lessons
> in maths or science I got lessons about wildlife and life in
> general and the ways of the world. Gavin was a very good
> teacher because he was interested in encouraging people to
> become involved with life and the world, so in addition to
> natural history he taught me about psychology and sociology
> and such-like, which was not the usual fare for people of my
> age. His instruction in natural history wasn't the foundation
> of my knowledge, but it put me more on the right tracks,
> especially in marine zoology. But in a strange way the otters
> didn't come into it, because Gavin didn't seem to class them
> as animals at all. To him they were part of the family, they
> were special kind of people, creatures he could relate to much
> more closely than he could to a dog, say, or a wild animal,
> or even a human being.

In Terry's view, although Gavin appeared to be a fierce, combative
person, he was in reality gentle and timid, and life in the human world
was frightening to him. Terry felt that Gavin was very unhappy, and
that he couldn't get to grips with people or create relationships with
them. He tried too hard, put too much pressure on people, so that he
seemed overpowering and demanding. Whenever he was in a group
he became guarded and defensive, and sometimes bitterly jealous.
But he didn't like being alone. He might like his own company in his
room at Sandaig, but he always needed the assurance that another
member of the household was on the other side of the door. Terry
remembered that sometimes, when the fire was blazing in the hearth
and the pressure lamp was hissing on the table, Gavin could be totally
relaxed, fascinating company – he'd cook the dinner, drink his
whisky, talk about the shark-fishing days and all the other things he'd
done, laugh and joke into the early hours.

'I grew up very quickly at Sandaig,' Terry recalled:

> When you're as young as I was and you're with someone as
> mentally alert as Gavin was and with as many personal prob-

lems as he had, you grow up very quickly – to cope with such a complex person you have to, you have to learn how to listen, how to deal with the situation. Childhood stopped the moment I got on the train to go up to Sandaig. There was not much play up there. It was work, really – and survival. Life wasn't easy – the isolation, the ruggedness of it, all those rucksacks up and down the hill in the rain. There were days when I was absolutely fed up. I used to look at the ships going by down the Sound of Sleat and the scattered houses far away on Skye, and I'd think: 'They're all with their families and we haven't got anything.' There was an emptiness there, and I used to love it when people came to stay.

But I am grateful to Gavin in many ways. I had a life unlike any other boy in Britain, Jimmy excepted. We climbed three-thousand-foot mountains. We were shipwrecked. We saw wonderful things. We met remarkable people like Peter Scott. And I became a much tougher and more independent man.

If I knew then what I know now about life and how to handle people I think I could have done a lot of good up at Sandaig. I could have helped Gavin, made him happier by being a friend to him, not a bewildered child who didn't understand how an adult mind was working. But then I couldn't cope with his intelligence, nor all those days of gloom and whisky. Gavin was striving for something, I'm not sure what, but whatever it was he never found it, and never could. That was his tragedy.

The days of relative liberty for the still unconfined Teko did not last much longer. Shortly before Christmas 1961, Lavinia Renton, a long-standing, close friend of Gavin's from London, was staying at Sandaig with her two sons. While on a walk to the island beaches with Terry Nutkins, Teko flew into a sudden inexplicable frenzy and attacked Lavinia's younger son, Simon. A month later, when Gavin was in London, Teko attacked a second time, again while on a walk. This time the victim was Jimmy Watt, who was bitten in the calf, shin and foot before he managed to escape by jumping down the sand martin cliff and floundering across to the other side of the burn. On both occasions it was Terry Nutkins, already minus two fingers following Edal's earlier attack, who bravely recovered the manic Teko and led him home.

Gavin decided that Teko, too, would have to be confined. From now on, apart from himself, the only human being who would be allowed near Edal would be Jimmy, and the only person who would be allowed near Teko would be Terry. But a few weeks later, when Gavin was again away from Sandaig, Edal turned on Jimmy, who had tended her since the day she had first arrived, forcing him to seek safety in the rafters of the wooden house while she wailed in fury below. Gavin now had no option but to treat both otters as wild, dangerous and untrustworthy creatures, to be tended like zoo animals without human contact. It was the end of the pioneering experiment in living with pet otters, the end of the dream of an idealised animal friendship that had first formed in Gavin's mind on the banks of the Tigris River in Iraq more than five years before.

Why had the otters, who had never lacked for love and care from their human keepers, and had displayed such intense devotion and affection in return, suddenly turned so savage? In Gavin's opinion the attacks were momentary and instinctive, and carried out within the framework of a heritage in which violence was necessary for survival and reproduction: 'I am convinced that the emotion is basically that which we describe as jealousy,' he was to record. 'The otters sensed that something they had regarded as being their exclusive right was being shared with a stranger . . . I do not believe that any fully adult otter is to be trusted completely with any human other than its acknowledged foster-parents. The emotions are too intense, the degree of affection afforded by the otter too pro-found.'

This may well be true, though it may be only part of the expla-nation. Gavin's repeated absences from Sandaig could not have helped, nor could the consequent confusion over the identity of the otters' foster-parents and the interruptions to their precious daily routine. Terry Nutkins, who witnessed almost all of the otter attacks at Sandaig, and has worked closely with animals ever since, has a somewhat different view to Gavin's:

My experience with otters since those days is that adult otters can undoubtedly be explosive, unreliable, untrustworthy ani-mals. But in the case of Gavin's pet otters there was an extra dimension. Edal and Teko – and Mij, too, for that matter – were subject to unusual pressures. They were humanised otters, kept under unnatural, domestic conditions with the pressures of humans on them all the time. This may have been bearable to them when they were young cubs, but once they had grown up it could well have been too much for them. Otters react to people's feelings, and Gavin heaped all his feelings on his otters. He used to get terribly childish in their company. '*Eeedal, Eeedal!*' he would croon. 'Who's a lovely dog?' He had a very odd look on his face when he rolled around with them on the floor, exchanging saliva with them, blowing in their fur, desperately trying to communicate with them and make them become part of him. I think the jealousy theory may possibly have accounted for Edal's attack on Caroline Jarvis, and for her attack on me when I was wearing Caroline's pullover. But it doesn't account for Teko's attack on the woman visitor whom he tore to bits. I mean, Teko may not have wanted to be woken up and taken out of his hut and brought in and shown to a complete stranger that evening. Maybe she was terrified of him and he sensed it. Maybe he had just reached the age when dog otters become explosive in temper. And he probably had sexual urges by then – the male otter's temper is terribly uncertain during the period of the rut. But who knows? Certainly nobody knew a thing about these animals in those days.

The end of the Camusfeàrna otter idyll, the confinement of those two beautiful and much loved creatures who had once roamed joyful and free in and around Gavin's enchanted sanctuary, was a bitter blow to his private hopes and dreams. He was full of nostalgia and sadness, guilt and grief. When he was later asked by a stranger whether his otters were free or were kept like zoo animals, he couldn't bear to tell the truth. He blamed himself and his own species for the fate that had befallen Edal and Teko, and wrote some years later: 'Both had been conditioned to an unnatural dependence upon humans and their company, and both had been deprived of it because when they became adult they had behaved like wild animals instead of like well brought up Pekingese dogs. If their behaviour had been bewildering to us, ours must have been even more so to them; they had both received life sentences for actions, which by the very hysteria that characterised them, were probably unremembered.'

The full implications of the tragedy were summed up by Terry Nutkins, the young man who had watched it happen:

All this shattered Gavin's world. He had created this false world, with the otters that were his personal security (because human beings certainly weren't), and now it was over. Maybe the death of Mij had marked the beginning of the end. Mij was the first. His happiest days were when he was at Sandaig with Mij – but Mij would have turned savage too one day. I couldn't see a future for Gavin anywhere. Human beings were too threatening for him – they answered back, they were unreliable. But as soon as the otters attacked people they became unreliable too, and he became insecure, the whole of Sandaig became insecure, and disaster followed disaster to total destruction.

TWENTY-SIX

The habitat of marriage

> I sent a letter to my love
> On a sheet of stone.
> She looked down and as she read
> She shook her yellow hair and said
> Now he sleeps alone instead
> Of many a lie in many a bed.
> I sent a letter to my love
> On a sheet of stone.
>
> GEORGE BARKER, *The True*
> *Confession of George Barker*

When I met Gavin again in London in the autumn of 1961 he surprised me by announcing that he was thinking of getting married. His reasons for doing so seemed, by his standards, conventional. 'I want to come in from the cold,' he told me. 'I feel I have reached the age when I should settle down – not settle down, that's the wrong word, it sounds like the *Polar Star* hitting a reef – I mean, introduce some stability into my life.'

I was well aware that Gavin was attractive to women – not just physically, but in his wit and conversation, the romantic aura of his personality, and the warmth and enthusiasm of his companionship – and enjoyed their company. I was also aware that several of his women friends were extremely fond of him, and would be happy to be married to him if they could. But until this moment I had always believed that Gavin was disinclined towards marriage – an institution for which he had hitherto shown scant respect – by his sexuality, temperament and way of life. In this I had underestimated the extent to which he craved to be accepted as a normal member of society and to escape the solitude and insecurity of his bachelor life. Two factors, perhaps, had prompted him to consider matrimony now. For the first time in his life he had the financial means to maintain himself and a wife (whoever she might be) at the level he considered necessary. Secondly, he wished never again to endure the loneliness, the prolonged dark night of the soul, of his traumatic winter in Morocco.

The idea of marriage was not, in fact, entirely new. As long ago as the summer of 1958, when Lavinia Renton, then thirty-four years of age, was holidaying with her two sons in the Dower House at Monreith, Gavin had told her: 'If ever I get round to marrying, you will be the woman I shall ask.' Gavin had known and liked Lavinia since his artist days in London in the late 1940s. An attractive and spirited woman, and a talented pianist and singer of opera and lieder, she was married to Gavin's friend and fellow SOE instructor from wartime days, the conductor Edward Renton. But latterly the marriage had begun to come under strain, and looked likely to break down altogether. Lavinia recalled:

> The idea of marriage was born in Gavin and myself quite separately. On my side, I remember I took my two boys to visit him at his London studio to see Mij and afterwards we all went together to a film; and slap into the middle of my absorption in the film there suddenly flashed into my mind – not as a whimsy idea, but in a strangely definite and calm way – 'One day I shall marry Gavin.' It caused me neither surprise nor emotion – it was simply there, a fact, which seemed both logical and inevitable. I wasn't even separated from Edward, but things were very rocky and broke that autumn. Of this, Gavin knew nothing. What eventually did happen was not a snap whim on our parts, therefore, but something which seemed, in time, bound to happen.

What was it that Gavin admired in Lavinia? She herself could only speculate: 'Gavin knew me for a great many years in various situations; he had opportunities to see me in my home, with my children, with Edward; we had talked often and intimately, and I know from mutual friends that he showed as unwavering a respect and affection towards me as I did towards him. He thought I was a good mother, a good "trouper", a good cook, etc. He built me up into the perfect woman, strong, unemotional (yet he had seen me in rages, and knocked sideways on occasions), entirely capable in a somewhat masculine way, and able to enjoy and cope with the rougher sides of life.'

By the summer of 1961 Gavin's idea had hardened into a resolve. But there was a complication, for recently he had become a close friend of Caroline Jarvis from London Zoo. Gavin was very much drawn to Caroline and she to him. 'We seemed to be a couple of waifs,' he told Lavinia, 'and she has gone through more hard times than you can possibly know.' According to Gavin, Caroline poured out her heart to him, and Gavin for his part sought her company as a confidante with whom he could discuss his innermost hopes and plans. Caroline's passion for wildlife and natural history were close to Gavin's heart; but he had known and respected Lavinia over many years, and her social background was closer to his own – and to the standing and pedigree which he expected of a future wife. Lavinia was the elder daughter of the so-called 'Secretary of Kings', Sir Alan Lascelles, the former Private Secretary to both King George VI and the Queen, and first cousin of the Princess Royal (the late King's sister). Before long Gavin was putting it about (erroneously) that Lavinia was fifteenth in line to the Throne.

It was at Sandaig towards the end of August 1961, shortly after Edal's attack on Terry Nutkins, that Gavin first seriously broached the subject of marriage to Lavinia, who was now separated from Edward. 'I needed the companionship of a husband,' she recollected, 'and I understood him to have reached a point when he wanted a wife for the same reason.' Two months later they met again at Paultons Square and talked about the possibility at greater length. Lavinia recalled:

Gavin thought he could be different from what he believed himself honestly to be. He had the tremendous idea of being a full-blooded heterosexual male and believed that if only he had more of the heterosexual in him we would have an ideal marriage. The touching thing was that he would genuinely have liked to have been different (though he once said he would be awfully dull if he were!). Gavin's decision to marry, I thought, was founded on a clear worked-out knowledge within himself.

He gave me such an immense feeling of security by his warmth and gentleness and apparent confidence in me and belief in me – which all restored in me so much that had been wavering and unhappy, and I felt I could really find the necessary sort of peace and purpose with him. He always seemed to accept without criticism everything about me, and boosted my morale sky-high. I really felt that with Gavin's faith in me my fears could be put behind me and my energies once more go outward to him and others instead of spinning round inside me in such a destructive, completely clogging way. And remembering the vital part my own father played in our childhood I regretted acutely the lack of a male parent in Nicky's and Simon's growing-up years. So to remarry was a step which I felt would be not just for my own happiness or needs, but as much for theirs too. That Gavin would be able to meet the bill in this respect, I never had any doubts.

It was agreed that Lavinia should come up to Sandaig again and see how she felt about the idea of living in such an isolated and unsophisticated place. A few days later Gavin wrote her a note: 'I hope and pray that everything will work out. I know I want to try, if we are really active to all problems that may arise . . . I think when you come up we should make up our mind *finally*, and stick by whatever we decide, against all opinion or advice.'

Lavinia spent ten days or so at Sandaig in mid-November. By the end of her stay she and Gavin had fixed a wedding date for 1 February 1962. 'I was perfectly happy about the prospect of living at Sandaig,' Lavinia recalled. 'I was only too happy to turn my back on London and the music world following the break-up of my marriage.' To Raef Payne at Eton Gavin scribbled off an excited note: 'So Lavinia and I *are* going to be married. Announcement, I think, this week. Thank you for being as kind and understanding as always, and please I want you to be best man. I hope you will share a little of my fondness for her and that my marriage will be no barrier to a friendship that has lasted so long and is so infinitely valuable to me.'

On 23 November a formal announcement of their engagement was printed in the *Scotsman*. Two days later a reporter from the *Daily Mail* turned up uninvited in Bruce Watt's boat, bringing his bagpipes and seven pounds of kippers (an engagement present from Bruce Watt). The reporter's arrival provided the occasion for an impromptu *reiteach*. 'That, for my Sassenach readers, is the Gael's jamboree,' he wrote in his subsequent article, 'which puts the seal on an engagement so firmly that even the wee folk can't bewitch it away.' The whisky flowed, the pipes played, everyone was happy. A day or two later the paper printed a photograph of the smiling couple walking arm in arm along the Sandaig shore beneath a caption which read: 'The Road to Romance on the Isles'.

All seemed to augur well, and Lavinia returned to London confident that she had made the right decision and happy that she was to marry the man she loved. But when her friends heard about the prospective liaison, some of them expressed reservations. One told her: 'Lavinia, if you marry Gavin, he will go to bed with you a few times, but what he is really looking for is a mother-substitute.' Kathleen Raine was greatly affected when Gavin wrote and told her the news. 'I suffered to the extreme limit of my capacity,' she wrote later. 'Death would have been less painful, and infinitely less humiliating.' She was brought up sharp by a friend who tersely reminded her: 'No one, after all, ever imagined Gavin would marry *you*.' She sent Gavin her blessings, believing that marriage might be the best thing for him, and hoped that he would have a family of his own and feel secure at last.

Looking back, Kathleen reflected:

I could have given Gavin what he needed. Not sexually – he never asked me to marry him. Sometimes I wish he had and I could have said: 'Now look, Gavin, don't be afraid, I don't want to marry you. I have my destiny also, and it's not like that.' I truly think I could have remained the kind of friend who wouldn't have betrayed him, who could have talked with him and even opened the gates of another kind of world and other kinds of experience for him. You may not believe it, but I do believe that. I do have gifts of a certain kind which were in some way appropriate to Gavin's needs, as he was to mine. After all, I am a poet, I live in the imagination, I have read all the books – I could have been what Gavin needed if I had not messed it up. I don't blame Gavin, I blame myself. I became too emotional, too obsessive.

Now, in retrospect, I see I deceived myself. I didn't see my true motives for what I was doing. What is called love is so often wanting to be loved rather than loving the other person. Only very wise or very good people can really love. I don't regret all that. What's the point of regretting? I am what I am. I regret that I was what I was. I totally regret it. Of course I do.

Back at Sandaig all was not entirely well. It was late in the year now; the days were short and the house was beset by the rain and gloom of the gathering northern winter. Then the weather turned really bad. Hurricanes blew down the fences, salt from the roaring surf encrusted the windows of the house, the burn rose in spate and uprooted the trees.

Gavin grew as gloomy and troubled as the season. The otter idyll was over, Edal was confined in almost zoo conditions, Gavin's mother was seriously ill and he had quarrelled with Terry Nutkins. Gavin was smitten by a crisis of confidence, and to Lavinia on 18 December he penned an anguished *cri de coeur*: 'No doubt things seem worse because I'm very tired, but I'm in a state of flat depression and at moments near to tears. Worrying is my hobby, but there does seem a lot to worry about at the moment. T. is being almost unbelievably wounding, which I fear shows the feeling of having been hurt and hitting back . . . Well, this is not the sort of letter to send one's future wife for Christmas. So I won't drool on – and only pray that a lot of things will come right that seem to have gone wrong.'

With Christmas approaching, Gavin's morale improved some-what as he busied himself with Christmas presents, the impending wedding in the new year and routine Sandaig chores.

I miss you and find myself also wanting to consult you on hundreds of things. Gawd – I hope I don't have to work as hard as this after we're married – today I've *not only* written thirty-five letters, exercised otters, cooked, telephoned, etc, but have corrected *all* the proofs of *The Otters' Tale*. How's that? Out! Or just about. Has a bridegroom ever been carried up the aisle on a stretcher, I wonder?

I've sent by this post a list of relations to my mother – there seem to be exactly twenty Maxwell side and exactly twenty Percy side up to and including first cousins. I've asked her to explain to you who they are – if it isn't too much for her!

Now, will you please buy yourself something SO FINE for a Christmas present – it's frustrating not to be able to do it myself but you know how it is. I should think up to £100 is *quite safe*. Anyway – GET CRACKING.

Shortly before Christmas Lavinia came up with her two teenage sons, Simon and Nicholas, to spend part of their school holidays there – an experiment in communal family togetherness that was marred only by Teko's unprovoked attack on the younger boy. But afterwards, though there was much to be done in preparation for the wedding, which was to take place in London, Gavin tarried at Sandaig, leaving Lavinia to attend to the many pressing details in London, including the purchase of her own wedding ring. In response to her reproach he scribbled a pleading postcard: 'I long to be with you, but we have years ahead and I have so little left of my old life – and it has been so very precious to me – I NEED these weeks, in a way I can't explain. Please, my darling, understand and help me. Our time is endless but my time is short . . . I'm being pulled into little pieces; give me time to put myself together again.'

On New Year's Eve the snow fell thickly and covered Sandaig in a pristine white mantle two feet thick right down to the sea's edge. It turned intensely cold, so that the burn froze over, followed by the waterfall itself. 'It froze solid,' Gavin wrote, 'still in the form of a waterfall, so that only the lack of movement betrayed its sculptural substance. Giant icicles formed a fringe from the banks of the pool beneath it, icicles more than seven feet long and as thick as a man's arm, and the deep pool itself was solid for more than two feet.'

Those last days of Gavin's old life at Sandaig were fairy-tale days, the hills a crisp, blinding white, the sea blue, the night skies starlit and bare. The fire blazed in the hearth of the kitchen-parlour, still hung with Christmas decorations, and the plantation of young firs on the hillside above the house stood straight and orderly like a regiment of Christmas trees. A toboggan was improvised, to the enormous delight of Teko, not yet locked up and enjoying his last weeks of freedom. Teko would climb on to the toboggan, waiting impatiently for someone to push it down the slope, and as it slowed he would kick ecstatically with his hind legs to keep the contraption in motion.

Gavin had staying with him at Sandaig his Sicilian friend and collaborator Giuseppe, who had played an important role in the research for both of Gavin's Sicily books, especially *The Ten Pains of Death*, which he had in part written. The roads were still blocked with snow when the time came for Giuseppe to leave, and Gavin had no option but to launch the *Polar Star* and take him to the railhead at Kyle by sea. It was an enchanted voyage. 'The winter sun was just up in a bare blue sky,' Gavin recorded, 'and the great white hills all about us were salmon-pink above a smooth enamel sea of beetle-wing blue. The *Polar Star* roared north between the frozen mountains . . . to us on board her the racing boat seemed the only moving thing in a world of ice-cold colour, her speed the direct expression of human exhilaration.' Before Giuseppe came to Sandaig Gavin had warned him that the Scottish Highlands in winter would be wet, windy and dark. Now Giuseppe looked at him and grinned. '*Credo che non conosci bene la Scozia*,' he quipped. 'I think you don't know Scotland very well.'

Torn between his old freedom and his future hoped-for security, Gavin finally prised himself from Sandaig on 19 January 1962, and headed south for the unknown – his wedding and the uncharted territory of married life. Three days after he left, Teko attacked Jimmy Watt – an act of savagery that would soon lead to the confinement of the last of the famous otters and mark the sad end of the Camusfeàrna idyll.

Gavin Maxwell, aged forty-seven, and Lavinia Renton, aged thirty-seven, were married on 1 February 1962. By a cruel coincidence Kathleen Raine happened to pass the end of Paultons Square at the exact moment the hired car arrived outside the house that had once been her home to take the man who had been the love of her life to his wedding. 'The marriage hearse!' she thought, shuddering, as she hurried on. The wedding, a private ceremony held at St Colomba's, the Church of Scotland's Crown Court Church, squeezed between the Fortune Theatre and a post office hard by London's old fruit and vegetable market in Covent Garden, was attended only by family and close friends, including the Earl and Countess of Harewood on Lavinia's side and Gavin's uncle, the Duke of Northumberland, on his. The choir from Jimmy Watts's old school sang Schubert's setting of the twenty-third psalm. The press were waiting when the couple emerged. As the flashbulbs popped, Lavinia beamed and Gavin raised his hand and gave a wan smile. The *Daily Mail* reported of the occasion:

> It was a wedding to be wondered at – if only for the incongruity of the setting. Amid the torn cabbage leaves and crushed fruit littering Covent Garden sat a red Mercedes roadster. It was the bridal car.

Barrow boys pushing loads of crates jostled with Rolls-Royces for parking space and the bride and groom looked as unconventional as the porters who impeded their access to the church. The only thing missing was the otter.

Mr Maxwell's sole concession to convention was a carnation in the buttonhole of his navy-blue lounge suit. But the greatest contrast was for the bride. Her previous wedding in the Chapel Royal at Windsor Castle had all the pomp and splendour of a State occasion. It had been attended by King George VI and all the Royal Family.

The reception was held at Lavinia's parents' home in the Old Stables at Kensington Palace. Gavin's literary agent Peter Janson-Smith recalled: 'The reception was not exactly small, but it was typical of Gavin. There were two separate rooms: one for the aristocracy and the other for "trade" and servants etc. Needless to say, my wife and I were firmly ushered into the "trade" room.' The newly-weds set off for a short pre-honeymoon vacation (their real honeymoon was to be in Morocco in the early spring) at Albury Park in Surrey. Lavinia was wearing a long scarlet shawl that had been given to her as a wedding present, and remarked to Gavin how beautifully it matched the colour of his Mercedes. 'Now darling,' Gavin replied, 'remember we are very unusual and unconventional people. So why don't you let your red scarf fly in the wind as we roar off.' Then he revved up the car and with a squeal of tyres they raced away, Lavinia's scarf streaming behind her.

Albury Park, the great house of Gavin's Northumberland relatives, was currently owned by Gavin's aunt, the Dowager Duchess Helen, widow of the eighth Duke of Northumberland. It was in this massive mid-Victorian pile, surrounded by elegant eighteenth-century parkland, that the couple spent their wedding night. They spent a further two nights at the home of Lady Kersty Hesketh (the sister of Gavin's friend Robin McEwen) at Easton Neston in Northamptonshire, a beautiful late-seventeenth-century country house designed by Hawksmoor like a miniature palace, then returned to Lavinia's home in Carmel Court, Kensington and the ordeal of the great wedding party.

This gigantic bash, held on the evening of 6 February in the First and Second Ballrooms at Claridge's, was Gavin's own idea, and was quite alien to his usual social inclinations. 'It was odd for Gavin to arrange such a thing,' Lavinia commented later, 'in view of his horror of great gatherings. I think it was due to his wish to do the right thing and be the bridegroom – he did try terribly hard at the beginning of the marriage.'

Nearly three hundred people turned up, and the whole lot formed a great queue to shake the hands of the bride and groom, Gavin looking rather odd and formal buttoned up in his grandfather's frock coat with braid lapels. I was not among them, for on that day I was camped under a giant fig tree in the Ngorongoro Crater in Tanzania, waiting to continue the balloon safari that had been planned at Sandaig the year before. In the memory of many who attended the event it remains the grandest and most lavish wedding party they had ever known. No expense was spared, and to help meet the bill Gavin asked for (and got) an advance of £1000 from his publishers against his general account.

The guests were drawn from every corner of Gavin's life, and represented an extraordinary spectrum of professions, interests and classes. 'There was a great *mob* of people and a whole *army* of waiters whizzing around pouring out champagne,' John Hillaby, then Zoological Correspondent of the *Manchester Guardian*, recalled. 'There were various groups. One was an indeterminate group who seemed to be family who I never talked to. Then there were some awful "beatniks" – don't know who they were but they were chums of his – and I thought, "Where am I?" I might have been in the middle of Borneo. Anyway, I wandered round and I found a group of zoologists there and all his chums from the academic world – Dr Harrison Matthews from the sharking days, Dr Parker from the Natural History Museum, people like that. So he had his "beat" life, his intellectual life and his family.'

The ordeal was over. Gavin was a married man. He lived in hope of a transformation of his life, but only up to a point. As he left the Claridge's reception Peter Janson-Smith heard him turn to Lavinia and say: 'Well, I'm going to Sandaig. Where are you going?' The next day he left London and set off alone for the seclusion of his remote and beloved Sandaig. This was not a dereliction of his marital duties, however. Gavin had pressing reasons for returning north. Sandaig was where his home was, and he was still responsible for its complex human and animal ménage. The otter situation had undergone significant changes during his three weeks' absence, and the implications of Teko's attack on Jimmy Watt required urgent attention, as did the acquisition of the second of two wild Scottish otter cubs.

The first of the latest arrivals was an unweaned male cub that had been caught by a gamekeeper on a river bank in the south of Scotland about a week before Christmas. The gamekeeper's first thought was to telephone the author of *Ring of Bright Water*, and a couple of days later the cub was collected by Mary MacLeod and brought down to Sandaig by Gavin, carrying the young animal inside his shirt. To the newcomer, an easy-going but not very bright little creature, Gavin bequeathed the name Mossy, in honour of the cub of the same name whose life he had tried in vain to save a year and a half or so before. A few weeks later, on 28 January, another telephone call came through, this time from the Isle of Skye, to say that a bitch otter in milk had been shot a few days before and now a roadmender had found a tiny unweaned female cub in a ditch nearby. The following day this second otter was brought to Sandaig and was promptly christened Monday, after the day on which she arrived. Monday was younger than Mossy, being little bigger than a large rat; but she was evidently far more intelligent, and possessed of a great deal more confidence and initiative than the older male. By the time Gavin returned to Sandaig Mossy and Monday were sharing Edal's old room upstairs, and here they were destined to remain, living under the carpet for the most part in a state of inseparable infantile togetherness, until Gavin and Lavinia returned from their Moroccan honeymoon in the spring.

At the end of February the newly married couple embarked on a small Dutch cargo boat, the SS *Vrijburgh*, bound for Casablanca. It was a rough voyage, and the little vessel pitched and tossed through the Bay of Biscay's storms and snow squalls, while Gavin's Land Rover strained at its lashings above deck, and Lavinia lay in her bunk below, doped with anti-seasick pills that left her half comatose for much of the voyage. They arrived in Casablanca on 6 March, the day of rest following the end of Ramadan, the Moslem month of fasting, and as the customs office was closed they were not allowed to disembark until the following day.

This infuriated Gavin, Lavinia recalled:

I was asleep on my bunk and he came in and said: 'Darling, you must get up at once and go and see the captain. I've just had a word with him and I told him he's got to let us off. He said there's no way we can get off until tomorrow, so I told him that you're a cousin of the Queen of England. You *must* go and talk to him.' Well, I did, and the captain was absolutely seething. 'I don't care who you are,' he said, 'there's no way I can get you off. You'll have to wait till tomorrow like the rest of us.' We didn't finally disembark till the following evening, and Gavin was adamant: 'I'm not going to spend another night on this bloody boat!' So we checked in at a hotel, the Hotel El Mansour, and Gavin started sending telegrams and ringing up various important personages that he thought were going to welcome him with open arms.

Morocco was Gavin's patch, and he was anxious to impress his new bride as he drove her around the country in his big expedition Land Rover. Money was no object and they stayed at the best hotels – La Tour Hassan in Rabat, the El Maghreb in Marrakesh. 'In Marrakesh we stayed a few more days than we meant to,' remembered Lavinia:

We wandered round and saw various people. One of them was Si Mohammed el-Khizzioui, the Glaoui's former secretary, whose aged mother gave me a lovely old kaftan which had been her wedding dress and the wedding dress of her mother before her. Our plan had been to drive up into the High Atlas Mountains along the beds of the dry wadis; but there was still snow on the high passes and the wadis were streaming with meltwater and quite impassable. So we drove down to the south along the coast, turned east and approached the high passes from the other side. We went to the Glaoui's great tumbledown castle at Telouet and slept on the floor in one of the towers, in one of the few remaining rooms with a roof, and I found some lovely old ceramic tiles in the harem of the castle when I was wandering around and gathered a whole box full. And the next day we hired mules and rode up a wadi for a day to a Berber village and drank mint tea with the headman and his wife and I got very sunburnt and came back with a beetroot nose. It was a good trip. Gavin was a good companion in Morocco and I was very happy. There is no doubt at all that he was as happy as I was. At first he had thought in terms of a *mariage de convenance* between us, but to his surprise it had turned into something much closer on both sides.

The Moroccan honeymoon was the first test of the marriage; the first occasion, in fact, that the couple had been in each other's company non-stop for any length of time. Inevitably, they were to see aspects of each other's personalities that they had not fully appreciated before. Lavinia recalled:

The image he liked to project of himself was of the cool, calm, intrepid explorer, and really he was nothing of the sort. This demonstrated one of the pressures on him that made him behave the strange way he did – he could not bear people to see through him. That's why he put up this terrific barrier to protect himself – the dark glasses, the whisky to boost his morale, the remote islands and out-of-the-way houses, the reluctance to let his friends meet each other in case they talked about him together behind his back. I was an adult living with him as a wife and companion and he knew that I saw things about him which he didn't want to be seen and this put a lot of pressure on him – and on our marriage.

After three weeks in Morocco it became evident to Lavinia that Gavin needed solitude and seclusion as other people needed food and drink, and that her constant presence was at times oppressive to him. So halfway through the honeymoon she returned to England by air – ostensibly to get her sons back to school, but mainly to afford Gavin a few weeks' breathing space in which he could research his book about the Glaoui, the so-called 'Lords of the Atlas', and plunge off into the wilds on his own. From Casablanca on 4 April (by which time Lavinia was already settled in at Sandaig) Gavin sent his considered (and contrite) balance-sheet of their marriage so far:

Well . . . I'm afraid the Moroccan trip had some pretty bad *downs* for you, and I only hope that the *ups* will stick in your mind more – I thought there really were some, even though I have been appalled to realise what unsuitable material I am for a husband and how far short I must fall of any reasonable standards. I feel miserable when I think how often I must have hurt you, and how often my being what I am may hurt you in the future. It seems all wrong to start the first letter to you since God knows when with a lot of self-analysis, but I think all the same that it's a perswective [sic] thing to do, because I found it difficult to say, and my brain is very clear this morning.

Anyway – However deep our feelings towards each other go, and whatever levels those feelings are on, we do at the moment lack wide community of interests. I'm coming to realise that my mind seems to inhabit a world composed of only about four things: Animals, primitive peoples, literature, and painting (perhaps something else should come in here?!) – the first two being based on some knowledge besides a lot of feeling, and the second two on the way I think and look at things – I mean that I see any landscape or scene in thought-terms of paint or words (the latter very often being images from poems long known) – and in all these things we lack a common ground as yet. It will come, but at the moment I think it's an aspect responsible for more of my 'absences' than you always understand. It was basically responsible for my friendship with Caroline Jarvis, and I know you won't mis-understand if I tell you that I do miss that a lot sometimes (besides being upset that I have hurt so deeply someone I was fond of). Because, oddly, I never had many 'animal' friends, and even fewer 'literature' friends. So it's bound to leave a blank.

And all these things will come right in time, *Inshallah*; this is just an apologia and an attempt at explanation (to us both, really) . . .

Sitting at the bar before dinner in walked a man with a desert fox on a lead – gosh how beautiful. Full grown, the size of Mossy when I last saw him, very pale beige, almost off white, with huge dark eyes (Justine's colouring) and a face like this (ears really not exaggerated) –

He had reared it on a bottle two years ago in Southern Algeria, and keeps it just like a dog. He has more than once been offered a million francs for it (by film actresses and such) but says with passion not only would he not part with it for any money but that he would *kill* anyone who touched a hair of its head to harm it. This naturally turned my talk to otters, and I answered with a real childish heart-pang when he asked me whether mine never bit and whether they were free or kept like zoo animals. I lied and felt great big baby tears swelling somewhere inside me . . .

My love to all creatures great and small.

P.S. Pray for no disasters at Sandaig this year – I've counted, last year there were SEVEN major ones! [Five otter attacks, one shipwreck, one house-flood]

One evening Gavin found himself at a villa on the outskirts of Marrakesh that was rented by an American film actor and occupied by a very odd ménage. Gavin wrote to Lavinia, '*All* the ménage were nude, but for a G-string worn by the females – nothing else. The American had broken one of the women's jaw and all her teeth recently and she carried her jaw in a sling rather like her string.' A Siamese fortune teller by the name of Doan Ving Thai was at the house and told Gavin's fortune by the Tarot pack – a fateful prediction: 'I shall always be rich and powerful, but my world is mystic and I'm doomed to live alone for ever and like the Wandering Jew to wander and travel until I die – because, according to the cards,

I look for something (not defined) which doesn't exist. Cor stone the crows – what a husband to have.'

A week later Gavin came across a house for sale in the oasis just outside Marrakesh. Its name was 'Dar el Sebaa' and it was enclosed within a wall and built in the Moorish style with a fabulous view from its tower across the oasis to the great snowy range of the High Atlas. Gavin was enchanted by the place and, swept along by the enthusiasm of another irresistible scheme, wrote to Lavinia to tell her about it: 'Listen – I've put in train enquiries about the purchase of a villa. It would be the best springboard for buying a Kasbah such as Tamdacht [site of a gigantic Berber fortress on the lip of an imposing river gorge] in the mountains. OK with you? Silence but for birdsong, palms, a swimming pool, and flowers everywhere. You like, yes?'

The following week he enlarged on this latest caprice: 'The "villa" isn't a villa in your sense. Stands in about eight acres, in the palm oasis about five km away. They are asking eight millions – I'm told they'd take four (that's about £3000). Schön, nicht? Anyway, it's only an idea . . .'

In reality, for a man of Gavin's temperament and aspirations, it was not at all a bad idea. 'Dar el Sebaa' was a beautiful house in a land he loved, and at a price he could afford. Only the timing was wrong; he had been married just a few weeks, and this was perhaps not the most tactful moment to dream of an exotic *pied-à-terre* in Africa, still less a kasbah in the Atlas. In any case his business advisers disapproved. When, years later, his thoughts turned again to a home in Morocco, he could no longer afford it.

Before leaving Morocco Gavin made one last excursion into the interior mountains – the snow-tipped Moyen Atlas this time – in the company of a friend, the French hotelier André Deschasseaux. From Marrakesh on 11 April he sent an enthusiastic report:

Have just returned from a too brief, wonderful, exhausting but in general FINE excursion – 150 miles from here by road, then seventy miles by piste, and arrived with André at his tiny sawmill, looking like a match box in the mountains – Moyen Atlas, and quite different – pine forests and gigantic chasms, and a great roaring river – all much more like Colorado than Morocco. The sawmills are closed, but there is a mad almost illiterate Spaniard who acts as guardian, in the only building there is, a little wooden shack of two rooms so like a Wild West film one could hardly believe it wasn't a scenario [sic]. In the morning we took mules and went for eleven hours – right round the other side (precipice) of the Cathedral Rock and up the gorge. Stopped in two sub-villages with the result that when we got back at night I was confronted for the first time this year with a surgery – blood poisoning, dysentery, syphilis, gonorrhea, the lot, but especially syphilis in all its stages. I did what I could and shall never know how many people I killed. One man had had clap for *two years* – can you imagine the state? (He had also infected his goats, apparently.) Anyway, I don't think I have ever, anywhere, found anywhere so beautiful or so strange. A huge troop of Barbary apes inhabit a nearby cliff. When André last cut wood there they all lined up to watch, absorbed, for five hours. André fully expects the apes to start exploiting timber themselves now.

On 18 April Gavin sailed from Casablanca for Southampton. Before he embarked he wrote one last letter from Morocco, to Jimmy Watt, giving expression to his anxieties about what he would find at Sandaig when he returned and how he would manage after so many changes. How were the otters now they had been locked up, and how did they react to Lavinia? Were Mossy and Monday really tame, and had they ever seen water? Where was he going to work, given the noise and lack of space?

It seems to me I've got one hell of a lot of writing to do between now and the end of the year, and I can't see *where* or *how* (respectively shortage of space and noise). It would be awful to have to go to London to work. Do you think I should work on the *Polar Star*? – or where?

Our household seems to have magnified so many times that I wonder whether I'll ever have a chance to talk to anybody ever again. Don't forget you're the GRAND VIZIER in the North . . . Whatever wonderful things have been gained by marriage (and they're lots), one loses a lot, and fears to lose more – if you see what I mean – well you can imagine it.

See you very soon – a star on the horizon.

TWENTY-SEVEN

Break-up

There is a relation between the tongue and the harpoon. Both can inflict grievous wounds. The cut of
the lance heals, the cut of the tongue rots.

ROALD AMUNDSEN

Early in May Gavin returned to Sandaig and was reunited with his
wife of three months and with the rest of his complex and
demanding household. He soon found that his anxieties about living
and working in a restructured Sandaig were well-founded. It was
now a far cry from the simple reclusive sanctuary that he had portrayed so lyrically in *Ring of Bright Water*.

The pressure on him was greatly exacerbated by the intense shortage of space at Sandaig and the primitiveness of its amenities (there
were as yet no bathroom or toilet, and the burn or the waterfall
had to serve for both). The house was small, only two rooms
upstairs and two rooms down, and into this had to be squeezed
not only Gavin and Lavinia, but Terry Nutkins and (during the
summer holidays) Lavinia's two sons and any friends and acquaintances who might come to stay. For a short while Gavin and Lavinia
were able to sleep in the relative privacy of the small, one-roomed
croft across the field, which Raef Payne had been renovating over
the last few years as his *pied-à-terre* in the Highlands. Raef had lent
them the croft in his absence, and Gavin had moved in the huge
mahogany double bed honeycombed with drawers he called the
Admiral's bed, which Lavinia found as hard as a sarcophagus. But
when Raef came up for the summer the couple had to move back
to the main house again; and though Jimmy Watt had moved out
into the wooden annexe with Edal, Edal's old room was now occupied by the two new otters, Mossy and Monday, and an enormous
deerhound called Dirk had added to the general confusion and lack
of space.

Gavin had always hated to be alone for more than a day or

two, but he now lurched to the opposite extreme, and instead of unbearable solitude he was confronted with insufferable over-crowding. The tumult of Sandaig's little community threatened not only to torpedo the pursuit of his professional career as a writer but to destabilise his personal, interior existence as well. A typical moment of Sandaig life at about that time is encapsulated in a letter I wrote to my fiancée in London during a visit:

> Outside – sea still, sky blue, sun shining, Skye looming, five boats on the shore. Inside – four otters and a five-foot-long dog asleep on the sofa, Brubeck on the gramophone, three-foot log in the grate, and me drinking one of Gavin's half-gallon measures of Teachers whisky amidst flamingo wings and albatross skins, Arab flutes and shark harpoons, fish baskets, old boots and even older cheeses hanging from the rafters of this fantastic house. Gavin is cooking pheasant in the kitchen and has just spilt *all* the pheasant soup on the floor. Lavinia is holding forth at length about the Almoravides of medieval Morocco. Terry has just turned up with a friend called Herb something-or-other, a writer, with *utterly* bald head, one eye and black beard. Jimmy has rolled up and a huge otter has burst in with a noise like – the simile fails me! Sandaig is impossible to work in. The establishment itself takes up too much time (food, water, wood, fire, otters, supplies, repairs, developments). Gavin wastes – time, nervous energy, equipment, money. The amount of money poured in here is fantastic. Lights and heaters are left on all day – for tax reasons, Gavin confides conspiratorially – and some have been on for three weeks non-stop. Articles ruined by neglect (from Jeeps and lenses to buckets and doormats). Generosity of spirit and pocket will ruin him, but he is one of the most remarkable men I know. G. and L. look well together and I hope it works OK for them.

When Lavinia first took up what was intended to be permanent residence at Sandaig she felt very much the new girl of the house-hold. Above her in seniority stood Gavin, Jimmy, Terry, and even Edal and Teko – all of them old hands about the place. She was also only too aware that she was a woman trying to fit into a long-standing bachelor establishment. For their part, Terry and

Jimmy were delighted to have a woman about the house, someone who could care for them as a mother would. But the demands made on her were considerable. At a purely practical level, there was a prodigious amount of housekeeping to be done. During the holiday months six or seven people slept in the house and it was rare that less than eight people sat down to dinner in the evening. Meanwhile a host of day visitors continued to pour down the hill to the tiny house – Lavinia counted twenty-four on one occasion – and all of them had to be looked after and entertained. 'I am flat out all day long,' she wrote to a friend. 'Constant chores and constant clearing up behind the chaps who are in and out of the house all day long. Everything that goes on Gavin wants to relay back to me and discuss. But that side of life has been for me very happy and full.'

'For the first two or three weeks all went marvellously well,' Lavinia wrote. 'We were extremely friendly, everyone appeared happy, myself certainly, and Gavin appeared so too, and in his most expansive and affectionate moods told me so in no mean terms. He told me several times during that time how peaceful he felt, like never before. He told me over and over that we were going to be married for a very long time and that he loved me more than he had loved any other woman and he could never have married anyone but me.'

Inevitably, the closer Lavinia got to Gavin the more clearly she was able to see the conflicting elements of his contradictory personality:

Gavin's actual brainpower was a very splendid thing which was streets ahead of mine – one could only admire and envy. But he was a huge exaggerator and had a vivid and rapid working imagination about all things; and he was very impetuous, and so swept along by his ideas and so absorbed with the moment that he would pick up a phone or run to the nearest sympathetic ear at any time of the day or night.

I think he was really a loner who needed the stimulus of other people – he was a great conversationalist, he loved to talk, and he was a wonderful companion. But you could talk happily for hours with him and then unwittingly say something and the fat was in the fire and he would explode – he had a very deep insecurity. So then he would start talking about betrayal. There didn't have to be any real grounds for the treachery he suspected – with his vivid imagination he could make them up, and did – huge clouds out of nothing, and the bigger the cloud the bigger the depression.

Sandaig life, meanwhile, bumped along in its usual disaster-ridden fashion – what Gavin called its 'general aura of crisis'. At one time or another the kitchen caught fire; the fridge broke down and the food went rotten; the *Polar Star* flooded almost to bunk level; Teko somehow suffered a terrible wound in his paddock (but recovered); Dirk, the gigantic deerhound, broke a leg in a rabbit hole (and also recovered); and a band of itinerant rats, attracted by the rubbish pits that had been dug in the sand dunes to the rear of the house, invaded first the environs and then the house itself. Far worse, Gavin and Lavinia's marriage came under such a strain that before the long summer was through it had entered a prolonged phase of crisis.

'Now I know that his pendulum swings in an even wider arc than mine,' Lavinia wrote at this time, 'and I take this into account in both the best and worst things he says to me; and that applies in everything he does, or says about anybody, or to anybody about anything else, good and bad. For Gavin I have worried because he says he doesn't sleep very well – and he drinks *far* too much – he says he can't get through the problems of the day without it. The trouble is that with whisky inside him his mood can either be super-sentimental or super-aggressive – and Gavin WORRIES so much more than do most of us and builds fantasies which don't fade away with the sane light of day.'

Gradually, as the weeks passed by and the pressures piled on to the marriage one by one, the early euphoria began to vanish like a will-o'-the-wisp. One source of pressure was Gavin's desire to father a child. 'One of the reasons that I hoped so much to start a baby early on,' Lavinia wrote, 'was that it would give him a release from a sexual life with a woman to which he was not accustomed – something to occupy me, so that he could go abroad about his business, leaving me to get on with the job of producing a cub for him. But there again, I, the Perfect Woman, had let him down by not conceiving . . . One day he told me quite solemnly that he had slept with me 111 times, because he had kept count! I worked this out to mean: Oh what a clever man am I – I've done my bit and if you haven't conceived it's not my fault.'

But it was the problem of Gavin's writing that proved the acutest source of friction. Though he was reviewing for the *Observer*, he had not written a word of any book since he finished *Ring of Bright Water* over two and a half years previously. The wealth that had been generated by his bestseller had for a while obviated his need to write for a living, and as Michael Powell had observed, Gavin had grown 'rich and lazy'. But so prodigious had been his spending during that period of bounty that he had been forced to contract with Longmans to produce a sequel to *Ring*. This book – to which he was to give the title *The Rocks Remain* – was due to be delivered in December 1962, and as the summer wore on and the deadline drew inexorably nearer and not a word was set down on paper, Gavin grew increasingly frustrated and irritable.

He was suffering from classic writer's block. One reason was that he had simply got out of the habit – the regular daily routine of writing. Another was that everything he had ever wanted to say about Camusfeàrna he had already said in *Ring*, so that for its sequel he was left with nothing but crumbs. Yet another reason was that it was practically impossible to find the peace and seclusion in which to write at Sandaig. 'Gavin's office was like Piccadilly Circus,' Terry Nutkins recalled. 'The phone never stopped ringing. He not only had his own complex mind to deal with, but all the other pressures as well, like editors' demands for overdue book reviews and so on.'

But these were not the reasons which Gavin gave for his inability to write. In his view his writer's block was entirely due to Lavinia; as marital tension mounted and scenes and rows multiplied, Gavin became increasingly convinced that the only way to break his block would be to end his marriage. Lavinia wrote to a friend in London:

I think just as much to blame is the pressure, not from me (marriage), but from this cracky set-up which has become such a burden on his shoulders ever since *Ring of Bright Water* brought him so much fame and money. He simply is not capable of running around with this large gang on his shoulders. But I am frightened that marriage (me) will become the scapegoat in his mind, in which case he will retreat further and further from it, however much one part of him may want to make it succeed. I take him to be saying in all ways 'I am

finding my way back to where I was before I was married –
which to me is the most comfortable and productive state for
living and working.'

After only four months the marriage was drifting dangerously
towards the reef. Gavin's emotions, Lavinia came to realise, were
those of an adolescent, their full development arrested somewhere
deep in his distant past. She realised, too, that he feared the give and
take of an adult relationship, however elastic and unconventional,
and was increasingly resentful of the demands such a relationship
made on him.

'With his curious adolescent emotions,' Lavinia was to write, 'he
built me up into a sort of goddess creature, who would not frighten
him or smother him or put pressure on him, or show ordinary
female emotions, of which he is dead scared . . . and as soon as
that happens, he retreats, back to the wall and even further, and
begins to fear and hate and feel persecuted – and he must in some
way destroy at all costs.'

Gavin was a possessive man, Lavinia perceived, and he had
grown jealous of the easy, friendly relationship she had developed
with Jimmy Watt and Terry Nutkins, and with the young otters,
Mossy and Monday. But the deterioration in their relationship was
not entirely a one-way business. Lavinia was a gentle person on
the whole, but she could be very strong-willed when she chose,
admitting to a friend: 'I am perfectly aware that I can be very
hot-tempered and stormy if roused.'

With everyone living in such close proximity in that tiny house,
Jimmy and Terry were reluctant witnesses of the growing marital
discord. 'I liked Lavinia very much,' Terry remembered:

and she was certainly very good to me. Gavin desperately
wanted to become involved with Lavinia but he just couldn't
cope – perhaps he just felt she encroached too much on his
life. There were rows, but it was Gavin who mostly had the
tantrums. There were many days when he would sink to the
depths of depression and gloom for no apparent reason that I
could see; and he would lock himself away in his room, come
out to pick up a book and help himself to a whisky, and then
go back and slam the door again. There were other days when
he was a perfect gentleman, a perfectly charming, normal

man, a contented sort of character, so very pleasant and polite,
making jokes and reading out funny things from the papers.
He had to be handled with kid gloves. You could say the
wrong thing very easily.

By June Lavinia had grown so anxious about the state of the marriage that she had confided her fears to Jimmy, and when she and
Gavin went to stay at Monreith for a few days she had a long talk
with the Maxwell family's local doctor, Gavin Brown, a close
friend of Gavin and Aymer, to whom she wrote later: 'I was worrying then as to whether in *fact* Gavin could cope with marriage;
in fiction, in his dreams, yes – but he fooled himself, and he
fooled me too. He thought I was trying to change him, whereas I
thought he had reached a point of wanting to add something
wider to his life by sharing it and his home with an adult and
a woman . . . neither of which he has ever had to do in his life
before. But inevitably tensions have arisen in both of us, and
both of us have exploded or reacted against each other each in
our own way.'

Gavin was away from Sandaig on Lavinia's birthday at the end
of June, but did his best to try and staunch the breach. 'Darling
Mrs M.,' he wrote, 'I miss you and wish we could spend it together
wet or fine. I'm such a bloody awkward and prickly hedgehog that
sometimes I may make you forget that you are the centre of my
life and I pray that you'll always be so and always be as happy as
it's in my power to make you.'

But by early August the crisis had reached an acute stage, and
the strain was apparent even to casual visitors. When Eric and
Marjorie Linklater came to lunch at about this time they were dismayed by the rigours of Lavinia's everyday life – she even had to
wash the sheets in the burn. 'As we climbed the hill after saying
goodbye,' Marjorie Linklater recalled, 'Eric and I turned for a last
glimpse of the house serenely bathed in the light of the westering
sun. "How sad," I said. "Wendy and the Lost Boys."' Shortly
afterwards, overwhelmed by the conflicts that raged within his
marriage and within himself, Gavin suffered some kind of nervous
collapse and for several days lay prostrate in bed in a profoundly
withdrawn and depressive state. When he was fit enough he took
himself off for a short convalescence in London and Monreith,
advising Lavinia before he departed that in his opinion she should

seek psychiatric help, and perhaps even undergo a course of psycho-analysis, in which he had an inalienable faith.

While Gavin was away, Lavinia confided her innermost anxieties in a series of eloquent and anguished letters written in blood and tears to her physician-cum-confessor in London, Rosamond Bischoff, a gynaecologist and marriage counsellor:

As his wife I am a shield in the sense that his marriage is a front for the outside world ('I am a normal man with a normal wife, even if we are both a bit screwy') but inside our world, our tiny private world, I am to take last place – the corner to which he can retreat and expect comfort *when* he wants it – but out of which I must not come to intrude upon his life, his emotions . . . Gavin has said on one or two occasions how much he wished he was more normal in his woman-relationships, but *au fond* he believes that it will never be so. But he has said many things which are complete opposites, and I never know where the truth lies . . .

He spent years freeing himself from his mother (on the surface, that is), and ten years in freeing himself from Kathleen Raine – and if I am placed into that category in his mind, I haven't a hope in hell, and our relationship is doomed – and I want to believe more than anything that Gavin wants our marriage to work as much as I do.

I know that I love him, and no less than I ever have over the years I have known him . . . If I lose him, I think I shall lose myself for ever. But he must never know how desperately frightened I am by the precariousness of all this for me – I feel it would be an intolerable burden which he is not capable of carrying . . .

I do realise and appreciate what an exceptionally fine, warm-hearted and kind human being he is; it would not only break my heart but be a real tragedy if we fail together.

Lavinia found a niche in the Sandaig ecology, and some solace from her anxieties about her marriage, by assuming responsibility for the welfare of Mossy and Monday, and attempting to hand-rear them. 'Perhaps,' she noted hopefully, 'it will help me to tame my ·

wild-Gavin-animal.' She felt a particular affinity with these shy, semi-wild little creatures, for they had arrived at Sandaig at about the same time as she had, and were thus as junior as she was in the Sandaig hierarchy. It was Lavinia who transported Edal's glass-sided water-tank from the garden of Paultons Square to Mossy and Monday's fenced-off compound in front of the sitting-room window at Sandaig; and it was she who, during Gavin's absence in London, observed the young otters' all-important first efforts at learning to swim.

Monday was the first to take to the water. Standing on the rim of the tank, she dipped her nose in, then her head, and then, losing her balance but clinging desperately with one hand to the side, the whole of her body. Within a few minutes she was totally at home in the water, and hurled herself time and again into the depths of the tank. 'It was the most wonderful spectacle of underwater *joie-de-vivre* I have ever seen,' Lavinia wrote. 'After that initial plunge she appeared to have every movement, every trick of swimming, at her fingertips; she was grace and speed and beauty – a water ballerina.'

Not so the dim and backward Mossy. It took him two whole days to master the art – two days in which he clung for dear life to the side with his back toes while the rest of him fell head-first into the water, but would not let himself go, somersaulting over the cross-bars, kicking with his hind legs and thrashing with his tail. Monday mocked and teased him mercilessly, nipped at his tail and his toes, and finally gave him a great shove – and suddenly he discovered that he could swim. 'They began to evolve endless and intricate games together,' Lavinia wrote, 'water ballets, which started in slow motion and worked up gradually to a long crescendo of movement, until the tank seemed a boiling cauldron and the two gyrating animals appeared to be twenty.'

From the moment the two learned to adapt to their true element they became much more integrated into the Sandaig family; they ceased to be mainly nocturnal and fugitive creatures, and before long were bold enough to feed from Lavinia's hand and even sit on her lap as they did so. But gratifying though this was to Lavinia, and to Gavin too when he returned to Sandaig, it was never far from their thoughts that on the other side of Mossy and Monday's fence lay the sound and scent and lure of the rushing stream and the broad expanse of the sea, and that one day the young cubs might feel impelled to claim these native wilds as their own.

On 12 August Gavin drove north from London and arrived dog-tired at Monreith that evening after a long day's drive. The next day he motored over to his old childhood home at Elrig. By coincidence the house was occupied at that moment by an old friend of Lavinia's – the daughter-in-law of the house's new owners – who greeted Gavin warmly and offered him her sympathy for his recent illness. This infuriated Gavin. Someone, he reckoned, had been talking about him behind his back – a cardinal sin in his canon – and he quickly convinced himself that it must have been Lavinia (though it was more likely to have been his brother Aymer). He returned to Monreith in a rage, downed a few whiskies which only served to enrage him still more, then picked up the telephone.

'He has just rung me,' Lavinia recorded,

in a COLD FURY . . . From what I can gather over the telephone, Witty sympathised with him over being ill. What has hurt – and made me very angry – is that his next words were: 'What have YOU said to her?'

This gets down to one of the deep troubles which has hurt me a great deal – this suspicion in him that I am betraying him, the lack of trust. This has GOT to be put right somehow in his mind. I have known for a long time how he inverts things. He takes what someone else has said and makes it come as if from himself; likewise he will transfer to another person some feeling or thought which he doesn't like. Which is why it is often so difficult to get consistency from him, except on his intellectual level. Unless we can trust and believe in each other, implicitly and without questioning, we will never have the essentials of a marriage – part of the inviolable core in the relationship between husband and wife.

Oh dear – now we have to meet tomorrow with this suspicion in his mind. I shall take a tranquilliser – and I hope he arrives at our rendezvous without a lot of whisky inside him! I want peace with Gavin more than anything but it is desperately hard when the slightest thing sends him scampering back into his burrow – just like a wild animal.

I realised this morning that to be wife to Gavin is a very
precarious position indeed.

And so it proved. Life at Sandaig went on as unpredictably as
before. Gavin doodled at his desk but could still get nowhere with
his book. Lavinia busied herself with the household and the young
otter cubs and the continuing stream of visitors. Two blazing rows
punctuated the uneasy truce during the ensuing weeks. The first
flared up on 27 August, when Gavin suggested that Lavinia's son
Simon should accompany Lavinia and himself on a three-day outing
to attend the ceremonial commissioning of the Royal Navy submarine H.M.S. *Otter* (whose commander was a great fan of *Ring
of Bright Water*), despite the fact that Lavinia had been looking forward to being alone with Gavin for a change. 'I broke down and
lost the truce,' she recalled. 'Being as exhausted as I was, I had no
reserve left to keep my head. I felt hit by a huge stone of resentment
and general despair.'

The second row was the consequence of the exhaustion and claus-
trophobia engendered by Sandaig life – and by Gavin's remorseless
probing and manipulating of moods and motives.

'What I find very difficult to deal with in any situation with
Gavin,' Lavinia wrote to Rosamond Bischoff in September, 'is his
eternal interpreting of everything on a psychological basis. I know
it fascinates him and that his insight and knowledge of people gives
him a sense of wisdom and power. But one cannot live day by
day on that level, and molehills are made into mountains when he
searches into the slightest change of expression, tone of voice or
mood in me or any of us, and finds in it a deep psychological
disturbance! So when he is angry he tells me I am destructive, a
"killer" bent on destroying people, and that I am jealous and batty
and hysterical, a "Jekyll and Hyde" character. It was exactly this
sort of thing that led to our second set-to.'

Exhausted after a long, tiring day which had ended with providing supper for nine hungry males, Lavinia was lying on the sofa
having a nightcap when Gavin sat down beside her and asked what
was bothering her. Nothing, she said, she was just whacked and
needed to go to bed. But Gavin went on and on remorselessly till
Lavinia cracked:

In the end I was driven to such a pitch of exasperation that I really blazed and hurled my glass on the floor. Now he may not throw things as I do occasionally when driven to fury – and he says he simply can't understand what makes me throw things; but he, without raising his voice, can goad one with his words and hate with his eyes and be intensely hurtful; and if he is frightened by the quirks in my personality, I am equally frightened by his passion for playing 'chess' with all of us.

For Gavin was a great 'chess-player' with people, Lavinia observed. 'He is a mystifier, a spinner of webs, weaver of phantasies, a commander of situations. All part of his very fertile imagination, which makes him the poet, the good raconteur, the humorist, the writer, and many other things besides. It is superb when it is turned outward, to outside people and situations; it can be very tricky and dangerous if it is turned inward to a relationship like ours.' As Lavinia pointed out to Rosamond Bischoff:

To quote Eric Linklater (who knows and admires and loves him dearly): 'Gavin is a near-genius . . . Gavin can twist anyone round his little finger.' I have all too often seen how he can convince the unsuspecting that black is white! The other day he admitted to me that he does feel himself a God-like power – 'even though,' he said with a wry smile, 'I know very well that I am not.' Well, everyone knows that genius is a form of madness . . . But finger-twisting is *not* a good thing in a husband–wife relationship. Gavin has never been so intimately associated with an adult before, and it shatters his impregnable position of power.

In Lavinia's view, Gavin's picture of what their marriage should be was: 'He is he, Gavin Maxwell, and to be that he must be free to be able to write, paint, come and go when he wants, be a "power" to his dependants and a wise man to his friends, who come to him singly with their problems (women flock to him, as we know, and he hypnotises them and lashes them with his words – isn't it true that women nearly always fall in love with their psychiatrists?).'

It was when it came to the emotional needs of the two that the problems began. In Lavinia's view Gavin was torn between making a success of bringing a woman into his life and having to give up his freedom to live as he chose. 'Gavin is a Gentleman par excellence,' she wrote. 'He has a very deep code of honour and behaviour, whilst at the same time he is a complete law unto himself. He is trying to do the right thing by me, and at the same time *must* do the right thing by himself – and there, I think, is much, if not all, of the rub.'

Lavinia was in no doubt that Gavin needed her as a nanny, mother and friend – but not really as someone to sleep with. Because emotionally Gavin was still an adolescent, Lavinia maintained, he could relate more instinctively to adolescents than to an adult woman, and for this reason was probably closer to his stepsons than he was to their mother.

On 16 September Lavinia returned to London in order to get her sons back to school for the start of the new term. By now she was ill with worry and physically and mentally exhausted; she was edgy and nervous and had lost over a stone in weight in the last few weeks. While she was in London she consulted Rosamond Bischoff about her problems, and on 24 September Gavin wrote a letter to Dr Bischoff in which he outlined Lavinia's 'case' as he saw it. Lavinia reacted with deep, defensive suspicion of Gavin's interpretation of her predicament and told Rosamond Bischoff so in forthright terms:

I am positive it is fatal for me to become his 'case'. I am not afraid of qualified, objective judgement and advice, but I am afraid of his because he is clearly the last person who can be objective and constructive. For me the whole situation is worse than a nightmare – it is a very live hell at times, and I am afraid of not only losing Gavin, but of losing myself as well. The baby I need to give birth to is *myself* – alone – not with Gavin playing the role of doctor, anaesthetist, father *and* mother with 100% labour pains! . . . I know you wish I wasn't going up to Scotland this week – but it is important for *me* to be at home with Gavin – but I don't want him to feel that a tottering wife is coming up on the verge of hysteria (as I admittedly have been for the last two days). Please do one thing for me; after I leave to drive north, will you telephone him – and *no matter* how low you think I am – please tell him that I am fine and in good spirits and very much looking forward to getting HOME – (and I PROMISE that when I arrive at Sandaig I will be all these things).

At Sandaig, meanwhile, the weather was at its wildest, with lashing rain and winds up to Storm Force 10. The water supply was washed away, and the *Polar Star* lost its moorings out by the islands. Then, on 21 September, a remarkable thing happened – salmon appeared in the Sandaig burn for the first time. They were spotted by Gavin's local handyman, Alan MacDiarmaid, who was building a new prefabricated wing at the house's seaward end. Gavin wrote to his stepson Nick: 'In half an hour he caught three big fish by *very* unconventional means. First he tickled a sea trout of four pounds. Then he hoicked out a six-pound grilse [young salmon] with his bare hands, and then, with a snare wire over the tail, another of five pounds. Although Alan was born in this house he had only once in his life seen one salmon in the burn. He thinks that if we could get the sporting rights of the burn we could dam it in two places and make two really good salmon pools.'

At half-past six on the morning of 28 September Lavinia left London in her Mini-Cooper and headed north. It was a journey of 625 miles and normally took two days, but the roads were so empty and Lavinia made such good time that by eight in the evening she was at Glenelg and by nine, after more than fourteen hours on the road, she was at Sandaig. Lavinia recalled:

I got the usual affectionate welcome from Gavin, and he said: 'Come into my room, you deserve a drink.' So we had a drink – he'd had a few already – and then we had another drink and then I said to him: 'Gavin, I'm absolutely licked. I *must* have something to eat, and then I really will have to go to bed.' But he said: 'No no no no no. Just one more drink.' And then he got that tight look over his face, and suddenly, out of the blue, he said: 'Lavinia, I want a divorce.'

'*What*?' I said. 'What on earth are you talking about?'

'Yes,' he said, 'I've been thinking – I just can't go on with this marriage.'

So we started arguing and getting cross and upset, and as I'd had no food inside me all day I was really getting rather sloshed too. Then he handed me this bloody document he'd written and forced me to read it, a kind of profit and loss account of our marriage, with all my pros listed in a short list on one side and all my cons listed in a much longer list on the other, all methodically numbered and marked with a date and time and all serving to prove his marriage was a mistake.

'Look, Gavin,' I said, 'I've *got* to go to bed! We can talk about this in the morning, but right now I'm going to bed!'

So I went wearily up the stairs to the spare room and got into bed. There were two single beds in that room and mine was the far one nearest the window. The other bed by the door had an enormous pile of woollen socks on it – the mending for all the males in the household. I was feeling very upset and nervy, and I lay in bed and thought: 'Oh my God – what's going to happen now?' And then suddenly there was a loud bang like a gun going off in the room below. 'Oh my God!' I thought again, fearing the worst. So I quickly put a dressing gown on and went downstairs. Gavin's room was full of cordite fumes, and there, sitting stark naked on the edge of the bed and clutching a pistol, was Gavin.

'What the bloody hell do you think you're doing?' I shouted.

'I saw a rat,' he said, slurring his words.

'There's never been a rat in your room,' I said. 'They're behind the skirting board. So don't be stupid and scare me like that!'

I went back up the stairs and put out the light and got into bed quickly and pulled the clothes over my head, because I knew what was going to happen next. And sure enough, a few moments later came a PLONK PLONK PLONK as Gavin's heavy footsteps came up the stairs, and he threw open the door – BANG! – and he turned on the light and there he was, with a great big Arab djellabah slung round him, standing there like Lawrence of Arabia or the Lord of the Atlas, swaying about with the gun in his hand.

'Oh Gavin!' I yelled. '*Go to bed!*'

And at that moment his eyes rolled upwards into the top of his head and he slumped on to the bed with all the socks on it and passed out. So I got up again and went and lifted his legs on to the bed and then I went back to my own bed and lay there absolutely trembling, half asleep and half awake, till eventually there was a tremendous crash and Gavin rolled off the bed on to the floor, with all the socks tumbling down on top of him. And there he lay until the break of day.

This was really the watershed of the marriage; there could be no retracing of steps, only a relentless descent. But there was precious little perception of the fact in the note Gavin scribbled to Nick a day or two later:

Lavinia arrived in one piece and in good form on Friday evening after having done the whole 625 miles from London in one day, at some average speed that doesn't bear thinking about. Arrived just in time to eat the last of the salmon. Today we're all in a flap – your grandparents are coming over to lunch, and we are fussing about getting the inside and outside of the house reasonably tidy before they arrive.

Gavin had always felt an honest fear and respect for Lavinia's father and mother and wished that all should appear to be well at Sandaig while they were there. But as soon as they had gone the in-fighting began all over again.

In October the marriage entered another stage of disintegration. Gavin rang up Dr Beveridge at Glenelg and told her that Lavinia was mentally disturbed, and should be put in an asylum. But when Dr Beveridge arrived Lavinia announced that she was not the slightest bit batty, and had no intention of allowing herself to be put away.

A few days later a woman reporter and two photographers from *Home* magazine arrived looking for a scoop – a peep inside the Camusfeàrna retreat of *Ring of Bright Water* fame. Gavin and Lavinia presented a united front of domestic harmony and bliss. The reporter's account of her visit was so riddled with ironies that under normal circumstances it would have left even Gavin and Lavinia speechless with laughter:

Having clanged the ship's bell to announce my arrival, I bent down to lean my umbrella against the enclosure which housed one of the otters, and immediately a small, perfectly formed black hand darted through a gap in the fence and grabbed my shoes.

The appearance of Gavin Maxwell, tall, slim and kilted, rescued me from the tug of war. Maxwell's is the austere face of the intellectual who fasts and meditates. It is only when he removes the dark glasses which he wears constantly – a cornea weakened by a desert sandstorm – that one sees his are the aloof, unvanquished eyes of a wild animal . . .

Mrs Maxwell is a *mondaine* who has thrown her Paris models away without a backward glance. Her charming narrow face, that of the ladies of the Court of Elizabeth the First, is alight with the joy of living. She cooks, cleans, washes, darns and helps with the otters. She told me that she had lost a stone and a half since living at Camusfeàrna, and remembering the walk across the hills, I was not surprised.

The reporter explored the house, peeped at the otters, then sat down to a lavish luncheon of prosciutto, roast grouse and venison. In spite of the restricted space in the kitchen, she noted, Gavin and his wife did not seem to get in one another's way. 'This, I suspected, was a team which could accomplish almost any exploit to which it set its mind.'

Then it was time to go. Halfway up the hillside the reporter paused and looked down. All was quiet and still. 'In its ring of bright water,' she concluded with ill-founded optimism, 'Camusfeàrna was settling down to a long and peaceful night.'

TWENTY-EIGHT

Finale

Selfish? Yes, selfish. The selfishness of a square peg in
a round hole.

FR. ROLFE ('BARON CORVO')

There now began a piecemeal – though not final – retreat from the
conjugal home. As soon as he could arrange it, Gavin left Sandaig
for his London house in Paultons Square. At the end of October
Lavinia too returned to London and took up residence in her own
house in Carmel Court, so that effectively the couple now had not
only separate beds, but separate houses as well. When Gavin heard
that Lavinia was in London he left Paultons Square for a secret
address, scribbling her a hasty note of explanation: 'I disappeared
because I was too tired to be of use to anyone, but you have never
been out of my thoughts . . . At this actual moment what we both
need is rest, both of us, and that's why I haven't told anyone where
I am. But I telephone Rosamond for news of you several times a
day . . . Bless you and get well *soon*.'

Early in November, Lavinia – lonely, exhausted, but still protest-
ing her love for Gavin, still fighting to preserve their marriage –
arranged to enter a private nursing home in Hampstead for a short
period of recuperation and care. Before she went she wrote a letter
to Rosamond Bischoff, a copy of which she also sent to Gavin.
She was patently neither mad nor suicidal, as Gavin claimed, but
she was at the lowest ebb of her life. Her fears were not for herself
but for her sons and her elderly parents. She had now removed
herself from Sandaig for a long period so that Gavin could get to
grips with his writing and work out a new modus vivendi. Her
affection and regard for him had not diminished. He remained, she
wrote, 'unchanged, unchangeable', and added: 'My love for this
funny human animal is simply because HE IS WHAT HE IS.'

Lavinia remained in the nursing home under heavy sedation for
a few days. Several times a day Gavin would ring the nursing home

from his secret address to ask how she was, but he never spoke to Lavinia direct or came to see her, and towards the end of her stay she felt impelled to scribble a furious note of protest to him: 'From the way you are behaving now, it appears your one object is to break up our marriage – and me. You go into hiding – you do not consider whether a gesture to me of either telephoning or visiting me (with bodyguards if you like) wouldn't help mend the breach . . . Why must everything *always* be what *you* want? Try to learn about give-and-take – do something sometimes which would make the other person happy – or do you hate your wife so much you want her made more and more miserable and destroyed?'

On 10 November Lavinia left the nursing home and went to stay at her parents' home in Kensington Palace. Two days later her parents, alarmed by their daughter's condition but not yet understanding its cause, arranged to have lunch with Gavin at Paultons Square. This was not a comfortable encounter for Gavin, who hated to deal with more than one person at a time, and was in any case in awe of both his in-laws. As the lunch progressed, he did his best to paint a frank portrait of his marriage as he saw it, and of the problems that his own particular personality brought to it. Lavinia's parents were dismayed by what they heard during this 'long Narcissan exegesis' (as Sir Alan was later to describe it), and advised Gavin it would be better if he never saw their daughter again. When they returned home they told Lavinia what they had said. 'After they had gone,' Lavinia recalled, 'Gavin rang me and asked if he could come round and see me – but alone, with no one else there. So he came round, and he was immensely warm and affectionate, and he told me to get better, and then asked me if I would like to write a chapter about the baby otters for his new book, as a way of keeping myself occupied while he was away, which I did.'

A few days later Gavin went abroad. It was to be two months before he set eyes on his wife again.

One reason for Gavin leaving the country was to take some of the heat out of his fevered marriage by removing himself from the scene. Though it would seem Lavinia was the more wounded of the two, Gavin also bore emotional scars from their encounters, and was, as Lavinia acknowledged, 'raw and suffering'.

But there was another no less pressing reason for going – the problem of earning a living, which he had signally failed to do for the last two years. During those two years the royalties from the phenomenal success of *Ring of Bright Water* had continued to pour in – over £25,000 gross in 1961, nearly £30,000 in 1962, a combined total of roughly £650,000 at today's values. But he had not only gained a fortune in those two fallow years, he had also spent one, on cars, boats, travel, high living, improvements at Sandaig and the great expense of keeping such a remote establishment going, and by late 1962 there was little left of the treasure trove that had slipped through his hands. In October Michael Cuddy, running the Gavin Maxwell Enterprises office in Paultons Square, had advised Jimmy Watt at Sandaig: 'We are getting some money through in the next couple of days or so. About £2500. But we must still economise where possible as I have over £5000 in unpaid bills now on the company and personal accounts. So could you please keep spending down to a minimum at Sandaig . . .' A little later Michael Cuddy confided to Jimmy the ominous news: 'For your eyes only – at the present moment we have no, *repeat no*, money in the company account. As of this moment I cannot pay out cash for anything and we have £4200 of unpaid bills on my desk.' Towards Christmas Gavin's American publisher, Jack Macrae III, of Dutton's, warned Mark Longman in London that he had heard Gavin had money problems and might ditch his agent in favour of a high-pressure agent who would force a bigger advance for his next book. At this point Gavin's debit balance at Longman's already stood at over £3500.

It was therefore of desperate importance that Gavin should complete his next book, *The Rocks Remain*, if not by the December deadline, then at least in time for publication in 1963. He had been able to write next to nothing of it during the chaos of the Sandaig summer, and he felt it imperative that he remove himself to some secluded spot abroad where he could write without interruption. He therefore arranged to borrow the house of a friend, Vladimir Daskaloff, who owned a palatial villa on the west coast of Mallorca. Here, in the depths of the Mediterranean winter, he hoped to find peace and quiet in which to enjoy a break from domestic angst and concentrate exclusively on his much-delayed manuscript.

That was the plan; but it was a plan complicated by a tortuous itinerary that ensured he would spend almost as much time in travelling as in sitting at a desk. He intended to drive all the way from the Channel coast of France to Barcelona in his Mercedes roadster; from there he would ship the car to Mallorca, then fly to Algiers for a week before returning to Mallorca to work on his book.

On 19 November Gavin set off in the company of his former Sicilian researcher and translator, Mark Harwood, hurtling through a France prematurely beset by winter storms and snows and Force 11 hurricane winds. 'I've never driven that distance in such appalling weather conditions,' Gavin wrote to Lavinia, now back at her Kensington house. 'From Le Touquet onwards rain, mud, hail, snow, windscreen wipers going night and day.'

At Barcelona docks Gavin delivered the Mercedes in time to be loaded on to the night ferry to Mallorca, and next morning flew to the island to reclaim the car at Palma docks. Entering the outskirts of Palma in the airport coach, however, he was surprised to see his car being driven away from the docks in the opposite direction. Convinced that it had been stolen, he called at the headquarters of the Guardia Civil, where he was informed: 'Your car has had an accident. It is *kaput* – it is not possible to repair it in any way – ever.' This proved to be all too true. While being driven at high speed the car had collided with a concrete pillar in the small village of Campastilla in the east of the island. The force of the impact had bent the chassis into a semi-circle, with the form of the pillar driven into the side of the car to create a gaping space in which two men could stand. Miraculously the driver had escaped without serious injury and after treatment for bruises at a first-aid post he had made his getaway through a toilet window, but was soon recaptured.

The Mercedes roadster had been Gavin's pride and joy, and he was heartbroken at its destruction. But he was also intrigued by the motives and personality of the thief, a nineteen-year-old apprentice third officer from a German cargo ship recently arrived at Palma. Seeing him sitting terrified in handcuffs between his captors in a Spanish police post, Gavin felt a sympathetic rapport with the young man and declined to press charges against him. ('He's a curious chap,' he wrote to Lavinia. 'Aristocratic background, originally East German, father killed in 1944, mother died of cancer when he was fourteen, smokes marijuana, boxes to championship standards, student of Freud and Jung, widely read and knows reams of poetry.') Besides, the incident would provide dramatic material for a chapter in his current book – a chapter in which Gavin's methodical investigation into the cause of the crash was to prove worthy of Hercule Poirot himself.

A few days later Gavin flew to Algiers, now capital of a newly independent nation. 'Margaret Pope was on the tarmac with the Chef de Protocol,' Gavin wrote to Lavinia. 'No customs, no passport formalities, and whisked away in the latter's car. M.P. lives in an *extraordinary* flat which someone had started to build at the beginning of the troubles and then lost heart – the various household offices are scattered quite at random, the shower being in the middle of the kitchen, the wash basin and bidet in the hall, and the loo having only a bead curtain between it and the sitting room. The furniture of the whole house wouldn't raise £5. Taken to the very first session of the new provisional cabinet and sat in the CD gallery between the new Chinese and Yugoslav Ambassadors.'

By early December Gavin was back in Mallorca and installed in Vladimir Daskaloff's villa on the west coast of the island. 'I'm trying to start work again,' he reported, 'and am *determined* to deliver the book by mid-February, when I have vague plans for driving the Land Rover from Casablanca to Cairo.'

Gavin had decided that instead of returning home to spend Christmas with his wife and stepchildren he would have Jimmy Watt over from Scotland for Christmas Day, and his young Sicilian collaborator and protégé Giuseppe for New Year's Eve. Mallorca was not the warm winter refuge he had hoped for, however. The icy weather that had gripped France and frozen the burn and the otter pools at Sandaig had reached the Mediterranean too.

The one great joy was Giuseppe's news. With Gavin's support and encouragement he had become an outstanding medical student and a highly able disciple and lieutenant of Danilo Dolci, the so-called 'Gandhi of Sicily'. 'Giuseppe's full story is much more fantastic than we ever knew,' Gavin reported back to Lavinia. 'God what a struggle and what a fantastic victory.' In two years' time his Sicilian friend would be a qualified doctor and mayor of his town. 'He will become a greater and more significant figure than Dolci in the history of Sicily,' Gavin believed, 'partly because he's a Sicilian and Dolci isn't, but partly because where Dolci has patient wisdom like Gandhi, Giuseppe has a sort of firebrand dedication in which recklessness is tempered with the minimum necessary caution and expediency. Even if he gets himself bumped off now he will have done more for his country than anyone of his age has ever done. But he's thin and worn and looks at least five years older than his age.'

On 9 January 1963, Gavin returned to London, his book still unfinished, to find an unexpected crisis awaiting him. Terry Nutkins, now a tall, good-looking young man in his seventeenth year, had suddenly run off from Sandaig, eloping with a woman some years older than himself, and setting off a chain-reaction of human explosions.

This surprise development had its origins in the previous autumn, when Gavin had been invited for a convivial weekend of good food, conversation and falconry at Spinningdale, the Sutherland home of his friend the actor James Robertson-Justice. Among the other guests were Robertson-Justice's falconer, Phillip Glasier, Eric Linklater and his wife Marjorie, a thirty-year-old American woman called Wendy Stewart, who kept hawks, Prince Philip, Duke of Edinburgh, the President of the World Wildlife Fund, and Prince Charles, the heir to the throne, who Gavin claimed to have taken for a lunatic 90 m.p.h. spin in his Mercedes roadster down the tortuous road to Bonar Bridge – an act of potential regicide, let alone reckless driving.

Not long after the Spinningdale house party, the Duke of Edinburgh sent Gavin an inscribed copy of his recent book, *Birds from Britannia*, and in return Gavin sent a copy of *The Otters' Tale* to Buckingham Palace, inscribed for Prince Philip by Jimmy and Terry as well as himself. Some weeks later, while Gavin was abroad, Wendy Stewart turned up at Sandaig with two falcons and an Indian sparrowhawk; when she left Terry followed her and joined her at her cottage at Spinningdale, just down the road from James Robertson-Justice's house.

'It was not so much an affair as a friendship with a woman, a member of the opposite sex, which I saw as a way out of Sandaig,' Terry commented later. 'Gavin resented it – very much so. He was very bitter about it. When I moved into Wendy's house I had Jimmy Justice knocking on the door exclaiming: "What are you going to do about it, boy, eh?" He and Gavin and the others had rows about it for quite a long time.'

From Paultons Square, a short time after he had arrived back from Mallorca, Gavin sent Lavinia a note (in parts a masterpiece

of disinformation) to await her return from a skiing holiday in
Switzerland:

> 1. I came back to England to find a SITUATION (not for
> the first time as you know).
> 2. Everyone from Spinningdale converged on Paultons
> Square, and as you can imagine the situation did not lack
> strain and what-have-you.
> 3. For some reason everyone looked to me to make a
> decision.
> 4. I was in a v.v. difficult situation, being legal guardian
> of Terry.
> 5. I said, 'When we are adult we make a muck of
> our lives anyway – therefore the youngest person must
> logically be the most important – and in this case it's
> Terry.'
> 6. So I fixed that Terry goes off with Wendy. Hope and
> fear. Terry leaves this week, after going back to Sandaig
> to collect her hawks and his luggage, and is going to spend
> a holiday(?) for 6 weeks with her before starting work as a
> Keeper at London Zoo in March. If things get as bad as I
> fear, he can come back to find refuge at Sandaig.
> 7. As a result of all this I feel worn out . . .
> 8. Jimmy is alone at Sandaig.
> 9. I return there this weekend, for so long as it takes
> me to finish this book, which now seems as if it will
> never be written – but it's the *only* monetary salvation
> possible, and if it fails . . .

After a reunion with Lavinia and a conciliatory meeting with her
parents, Gavin returned on 26 January to a wintry Sandaig, still
frozen hard after more than a month of frost. All but one of the
greylag geese had disappeared in the last few weeks, two of them
falling prey to half-starved wild cats or foxes; and a gigantic female
otter that had recently arrived from Griqualand in south-east Africa
as Teko's mate had been found dead in Teko's bed by Jimmy Watt.
In Gavin's absence Mossy and Monday had become expert escapol-
ogists, and for the first weeks following his return their capture and
recapture became a major preoccupation. Monday, in particular,
seemed to find the call of the wild irresistible. Confine her outdoors

in her stockade and she would shimmy up the sheer five-foot wall of the surrounding palisade or shift stones weighing up to sixty pounds and tunnel her way out through ground frozen as hard as iron; shut her indoors in the bathroom and she would find a way of forcing open the door or gnawing her way through the plaster-board and woodwork. Gavin was to write: 'Monday could climb like a monkey, balance like a tight-rope walker, dig like a badger, move stones that were heavy to a human, jump like a squirrel, make herself thin as an eel or flat as a flounder; no device nor ingenuity of ours could make her once relent her first avowed intent to be a pilgrim. But most of all it was her brain, the systematic application of her many skills and her single-minded pertinacity, that convinced me of the uselessness of the struggle.'

Mossy and Monday had tasted freedom – the sea, the islands, the white sands and the rock pools, the whole wild world that was their natural kingdom – and they would have no more of prison. Fearful that the partly tame otters would be killed by the first human being they approached, Gavin was at first reluctant to release them, and it took three weeks to convince him that their continuing imprison-ment was crueller than any death they might meet in freedom.

So he let them go, and they took up residence under the floor of the new wing, indifferent to the human bedlam above their heads. And there, free to come and go, but reluctant to totally sever their ties with human kind, they remained.

The liberation of Mossy and Monday restored to Camusfeàrna something that had been lost for many months. 'Once again these were wild creatures free without fear of man and choosing to make their homes with him,' Gavin recorded. As if to reinforce the mood, two of the wild geese returned after an absence of seven months, one of them a great gander that on the very day of his arrival came straight up to Gavin to take food from his hands.

In this quiet mood of oneness and benediction, Gavin wrote Lavinia a letter of new-found affection and humility on the eve of their first wedding anniversary:

Lovely Dog,
    The clock's gone round once, and I think the most worth-while thing I can say is THANK YOU from the bottom of my heart for changing, quite suddenly, a sort of despairing grey unreality into purpose and hope again. Until after your return

to London I lived in a weird twilight which, like the haywire winter, was half nightmare because I had lost my bearings and myself; spiritus mundi forgive me, and you must too, if I had produced the same state in you by my shortcomings. God knows they are many, many. The credit for new hope, and for the fact that I have suddenly found myself able to work again is all yours. You are a LOVELY DOG and no matter where the future leads I'll go on thinking that, and wishing that life had seen fit to give you for a husband a less complicated box of tricks than myself.

Thank God neither of us burned boats or pulled up roots in our difficulties. We are going to do our best . . . Bless you, my darling Lavinia, and believe me that I would be a different and a better husband to you if I could be – everything that makes one what one is at the age of forty-eight happened such a terribly long time ago.

My love and admiration.

Lizard

Gavin now devoted himself single-mindedly to completing the book which he hoped was to be his financial salvation. He worked feverishly and for long hours in his study-bedroom amid a thick fug of cigarette smoke, dictating much of the narrative into a tape-recorder for his typist in London to transcribe. The result was a hasty, scruffy, agitated manuscript, part handwritten, part heavily-corrected typed transcripts, the whole spliced together with frequent resort to scissors and tape.

In the middle of February, at the height of this frantic literary activity, I arrived at Sandaig at Gavin's invitation, to be greeted with noisy and ecstatic bonhomie by my old otter friend Teko, now permanently confined behind the palisade of his zoo-like stockade. It was my first visit to Sandaig for nearly two years, and the place had changed greatly since the days of the haywire winter. The way down to the house from the road was no longer by foot along the narrow track that wound over the moorland, but by Jeep along an alarmingly rough and precipitous road that had been blasted out of the hillside above the shore. An entire new wing constructed of sectional wooden frames had been erected since my last visit, and this provided the occupants of the house with the luxury of a flush loo and a hot bath and shower, along with a

workshop and storage lobby. Terry's old room upstairs had been
converted into a proper bedroom for Lavinia, who was also
visiting, and brass-bound portholes (salvaged from the old Royal
Navy battleship HMS *Vanguard* when she was broken up) had been
let into the walls of the upstairs rooms, providing views towards
the burn in one direction and out over the islands and the sea in
the other. The old beachcomber furniture of Sandaig's early years
– the Dakota aeroplane seat and converted whaling barrel – had
been replaced by elegant armchairs, and the tiny kitchen was now
all-electric.

But the new amenities had been acquired at a price, and the
secluded, unworldly charm of the old Camusfeàrna had gone for
ever. In its place sprawled an unsightly pioneer outpost – all
wooden shacks, palisaded enclosures, half-sunken swimming
pools, broken-down Jeeps, discarded tackle, rusting machinery,
upturned boats, churned-up wheeltracks, pylons and cables, mud
and mess. When I commented on the change, Gavin explained:

In the old days at Sandaig I was very much an unknown
writer. I had few commitments, and I could live a simple life
up here. But no simple life is really very simple, is it? In the
days when this was a primitive place to live and I was almost
entirely self-supporting, the practical problems of existence –
drawing water, cutting wood, cooking, foraging, beachcombing and so on – kept me busy from the moment I got up in
the morning to the moment I went to bed at night. But this
kind of life was out of the question as soon as Sandaig became
my full-time home, with otters to be looked after and long
hours of writing to be done now that I was a well-known
writer and in demand. So a sort of spiralling empire-building
process began, and inevitably, as soon as I got married and
acquired two stepchildren, this process escalated. As a general
principle, I think that the moment one ceases to be a nomad
and settles in one place, one is subject to an ambitious and
overwhelming desire to change the face of the place one is
living in in some way.

My visit was not entirely a social one. Gavin had decided to establish a film unit at Sandaig and make films about the Camusfeàrna

story instead of writing books about it. He had already bought a camera and wanted me to give Jimmy Watt a crash course in the art of documentary film-making, so the hours of daylight were entirely devoted to shooting a short training film. Gavin and Lavinia (who had arrived at Sandaig a day or two after me) played the leading roles, Jimmy operated the camera, and walk-on parts were played by Dirk, the giant deerhound, the surviving greylag geese and the half-wild otter cubs, Mossy and Monday. The set was Camusfeàrna, the ice-rimmed ring of the burn, the shell-sand beaches, the cinemascope sunsets flaring crimson over the bay and the whitened hills of Skye. So the days passed happily in purposeful and often hilarious endeavour. The evenings were spent in good cheer with a whisky or two before the roaring fire, and the conversation and laughter flowed about the bewintered house. To me Gavin and Lavinia looked right together, and I never doubted that they would continue to do so.

All went so well that Lavinia stayed on longer at Sandaig than the week or so she had originally intended, taking upon herself once again such care as the otter cubs chose to accept from her. Though they came to take food from her hand in the morning and before dusk, she did not know where they went after dark until one night she followed them. Gavin wrote:

It was a season of bitter cold; the days were for the most part still and bright with winter sunshine, but the nights were arctic, and the burn was frozen right down into its tidal reaches . . . A little before dusk one evening Lavinia, who had been down to the burn to break the ice and draw water, heard them calling to each other at some little distance from the house. Following Monday's small, urgent voice, she came upon them playing in a partly frozen pool, shooting under stretches of ice, and bobbing up where it ended, climbing on to it and rolling upon it, diving back and splashing as they sported together. Fearing that they would resent her intrusion, Lavinia had approached them by stealth, crawling upon all fours; only when they began to move on down the stream did she stand up and call to them, but they found in her presence no cause for any alarm. As they neared the tide she walked beside them, their heads now no more than silhouettes on a sea blanched by sunset colours, until suddenly a curlew rose before them

with its rasping cry of warning, and in a panic they turned
and raced back upstream and into darkness. The next night
again she followed them down the burn in the dusk, and lost
them in the thickening darkness as they swam out towards
the islands.

It was not until 23 February that Lavinia finally left Sandaig, taking
with her the completed manuscript of *The Rocks Remain*, which
Gavin had written in less than a month. He himself came south on 3
March, leaving Jimmy Watt alone and in sole charge of the Sandaig
establishment.

Gavin was due to sail to Morocco on 9 March, and on his last
evening in London he informed Lavinia out of the blue that he did
not wish her to set foot at Sandaig again, except during her sons'
holidays. He said he could not work when she was there, and
wished to live his own life and have his friends there when he liked.
They quarrelled, Gavin cancelled his sailing, then flew to Africa on
13 March. The marriage was to all intents and purposes dead.

Gavin was in Morocco for a month, his marriage seemingly behind
him, and was based mostly at a small country inn run by his French
friend André Deschasseaux and his wife at Asni, an oasis of green-
ery on the slopes of the High Atlas to the south of Marrakesh.
Much of his time was spent in intrigue of one sort or another with
officials of various kinds – the Minister of Defence, the Governor
of Marrakesh, the Glaoui's former secretary, the American Embassy and the American Cultural Mission – partly to further his
researches for his book about the Lords of the Atlas, partly to find
employment for his young Berber friend Ahmed, who had now
returned to Morocco from Europe in circumstances as mysterious
as those in which he had left it. With his marriage apparently over,
Gavin was back in his element, leading a life that suited him in
a land that was sympathetic to him, and driving his new Mercedes
roadster (an identical replacement for the one that had been
destroyed in Mallorca) at fantastic speeds on the Moroccan roads
– up to 145 miles per hour at times, and averaging nearly 98 miles
per hour from Marrakesh to Mogador. Though he was still writing
to Lavinia as if nothing had happened between them, his letters
avoided all reference to their relationship. 'Trouble about running with hares and hunting with hounds,' he wrote excitedly

on 20 March, 'is that one is suspect by all parties. My association with Moroccans and Margaret Pope makes the U.S. think I'm a V.A.R. spy, and my association with French and Americans makes Moroccans think I'm a reactionary colonial spy. Gawd awmighty have I stood the American Embassy attachés some drinks and things today. And Gawd, how well I know that hard marble-eyed look of distrust that comes quite suddenly and chills one just when one thinks trust is established.'

On 5 April Jimmy Watt arrived in Marrakesh to help Gavin drive the Mercedes back to England overland. They arrived in London at Easter and left almost immediately for the north. When Lavinia brought her children up to Sandaig for the Easter holidays, Gavin reiterated his ban on her setting foot in the place, and she left, never to return. Her mother was so outraged that on 28 April she wrote to him: 'I thought your *ukase* to Lavinia that she should not return to Sandaig was quite the most insulting thing I have ever heard. It is the sort of order you might give to a temporary cook, or that an Oriental Pasha might give to his mistress . . . Before I knew you, I had heard that you had the reputation of periodically quarrelling with both friends and neighbours. I wonder if you are inclined to make Lavinia a scapegoat for your own short-comings?'

A week later Gavin and Lavinia had one last violent row at Paultons Square. 'The next morning he vanished,' Lavinia reported, 'and went into hiding (persecution mania – he thinks I pant round London looking for him); I then got messages from various friends whom he'd been in touch with, first to say he wanted a separation, then that he'd been to lawyers, talking about divorce, injunctions and God knows what else.' In fact Gavin was hiding with his friends the pianist Louis Kentner and his wife, a sister of Yehudi Menuhin, who lived nearby. He had also sought help from his psychiatrist, Dr Ellis Stungo, for the death throes of his marriage left him in a state of intense stress.

By this time I was far removed from the scene of the disaster. Travelling through Siberia as a special correspondent for the BBC, I was virtually incommunicado. But in a letter written from Sandaig on 5 May Jimmy Watt provided a brief profile of Gavin's state of mind and point of view at this unhappy time: 'Of Gavin, things are not happy at the moment. He is in London *somewhere*. I wish he was up here where maybe I could help. I feel it is too much for

Gavin and he cannot continue coping with it. Being who he is, he is more susceptible to mental upheaval than others.'

Gavin and Lavinia had been married at this point for one year, three months and six days. During that time they had never spent more than three weeks at a stretch in each other's company.

Towards the end of June both sides made approaches to their lawyers. When Gavin tried to reassure his stepsons that nothing was changed between him and them, in spite of his separation from their mother, Lavinia's father would have none of it. He wanted a total break, as he wrote to Gavin on 15 July:

> You want the best of both worlds. You are determined to rid yourself of your wife, whom you ought never to have married, as Nature didn't intend men of your temperament for matrimony; especially when that temperament is, as in your case, tinctured with genius. The biographies of literary figures afford abundant evidence of this, and of their tendency to exasperate to frenzy the unfortunate individuals of both sexes with whom they have closely associated. You are making against your wife preposterous charges of 'insanity' and 'wanton inhumanity', which, to all who know her (which you don't) suggests doubts of your own sanity.
>
> Simultaneously, you expect to maintain with her two sons a close and intimate relationship. The sooner you get into your head that such a relationship is now impossible and stop pontificating about their present or their future (which are no concern of yours whatsoever) the better. To suggest that either of the boys should go to Sandaig when you have shut the door on their mother seems to me incredible behaviour.

And that was that. When Elias Canetti informed Kathleen Raine that Gavin's marriage was over, she said: 'God is not merciful but he is just.' To an old school friend Gavin wrote bitterly (choosing Italian to render emotions that were too raw for his native tongue): 'Siamo finito la mia moglie ed io. Che confusione, che dolore! E ormai *basta*, ma *basta* per una vita.' ('We are finished, my wife and I. What chaos, what pain! And that's *enough* – but *enough* – for one life!') Ahead there lay nothing but the anguish and bitterness of divorce.

Looking back, there is no doubt that Lavinia had loved Gavin with great respect and devotion, in full knowledge of his complex character, and that she had done all she could to make their strange alliance a valid and lasting one. It is equally clear that Gavin, too, had loved Lavinia in his way, and had tried as best he could to adapt to the unfamiliar and alien habitat of married life. Later he was to ascribe the failure of the marriage to 'incompatibility'. In reality, it failed not because Lavinia was who she was, or even because she was the sex she was, but because she was an adult human being – a species with which Gavin had never been able to associate at close quarters for long. 'He never grew up,' Lavinia was to remark years afterwards. 'Intellectually he was like Sophocles. But emotionally he was like Peter Pan. He had no idea how to cope with the idea of being loved. It was very sad, the destruction of a very real friendship of many years' standing. But I don't regret it, looking back. It was a part – a jolly tough part – of life's rich pattern, and though I was blistered and seared by it, I was able to pick myself up and go on and do things I might not otherwise have done.'

Neither marriage nor any other permanent relationship could in the end have worked for Gavin, no matter the person and no matter their sex. For he was essentially a free spirit, and his world was the boundless, unconfined world of the distant hills and the open sea, the wild swans and the seals' cry, the far horizons of the heart and mind. As Stanley Peters, an old friend of London days, remarked: 'He was like an animal living in the trees quite happily and people were always trying to tempt him down and put him in a cage.' Though he had much love to give, he feared to receive too much in return – for to be loved was for him a threatening, smothering, confining, entrapping thing, from which he instinctively turned as the enemy of the freedom he cherished and the adventurous quest and creative impulse that were the essence of his being. As Lavinia commented at the time: 'In marrying he put his own noose round his own neck – and the roped wild animal fights ten times more strongly and bitterly to get free.' So he was confined to transient and ephemeral forms of love – the love of animals, the love of the young – which by their very nature, and by the simple passage of time, were doomed to end, if not to fail.

If the savagery of the otters had destroyed the myth of Camus-feàrna, the failure of his marriage was the first stage in the destruction of Gavin himself, and other stages were soon to follow.

TWENTY-NINE

A chapter of accidents

I wish we could meet and talk over the many prisons
of life – prisons of stone, prisons of passion, prisons
of intellect, prisons of morality, and all the rest. All
limitations, external or internal, are prisons – and life
is a limitation.

OSCAR WILDE TO R.F. CUNNINGHAM GRAHAM

Emotionally shell-shocked after the trauma of the past year, Gavin
retreated to Sandaig to lick his wounds and replan his future. His
first instinct was to escape even from there. The Pan paperback
edition of *Ring of Bright Water* was published at the end of June,
and Gavin braced himself for a renewed onslaught on his peace and
privacy by a growing army of fans. The press only served to inflame
public curiosity. 'THERE IS PEACE NO LONGER AT CAMUS
FEARNA' read a huge headline in the *Scottish Daily Mail*: 'Because
of these all-too-frequent intrusions he is thinking of leaving his
home. His immediate ambition is to sail round the world in a wind-
jammer.' 'OTTER MAN IS TOURIST OBJECTIVE', proclaimed the
Edinburgh Evening News: 'Maxwell and his pets will have an even
more frustrating summer this year . . . But life at Camusfeàrna
goes on much as before. The colony of terns on the rocks near the
lighthouse is now something like four hundred strong and they fill
the foreground of some of the most breathtaking scenery in the
world.' No wonder fans in their thousands flocked out of the cities,
Camusfeàrna-bound; and no wonder the hounded 'otter man'
informed the *News* reporter he was planning to escape – this time
to Tibet. 'It's the only place in the world I should like to go to,'
he said, adding: 'I am by nature a restless person.' To others Gavin
announced his resolve to lose himself in the Far East somewhere,
or in the Tibesti Mountains of Chad, deep in the Sahara Desert.
When Scottish BBC television journalist W. Gordon Smith came
to Sandaig to interview Gavin for a programme that was eventually

broadcast on Christmas Day, he encountered him at his most melodramatic and conspiratorial:

> Gavin loathed being interviewed on film, but he kept going .
> for a few days and then he began to behave very peculiarly –
> he became very silent and strange. Finally he called me over
> to the house, gave me a dram and told me he couldn't go on
> with the interview as he had business of overwhelming
> urgency to attend to. This was the time of the Christine Keeler
> scandal. John Profumo, the War Minister, had just confessed
> to lying to the House of Commons about his relationship
> with Miss Keeler, and had resigned and gone into hiding. The
> former Minister, Gavin confided to me, was now holed up at
> the house of a friend of his in the neighbourhood – possibly
> he meant Lord Dulverton's shooting lodge at Eilanreach – and
> the press had got wind of it. He, Gavin, had to go and help
> sort it out. And with that he took his Norwegian revolver,
> stuck it in his belt, gave me a confidential look and roared
> away over the hill in his Land Rover.

Fantastical or not, this was Gavin's real world – a world that was
to come into increasing conflict with the forces of ordinary external
reality that had already begun to grind him down. As a temporary
escape he went to Greece to stay with his brother Aymer at his
villa on the Aegean island of Euboea – an excursion that began and
ended with disaster. On the morning of 24 June 1963 he set off
from Tormor in his Land Rover to drive to Inverness and catch
the train to London on the first stage of his journey to Greece. He
had only driven half a mile or so when a stag bounded out of a
heathery knoll on his right and jumped right in front of the vehicle
and down the steep hill-slope to his left. Gavin swerved, and was
just righting the steering wheel when a second stag leaped on to
the road immediately in front of him. There was a dull thud and
the Land Rover somersaulted twice down the hillside, coming to
rest on the driver's side. Gavin found himself pinned in his seat by
a heavy suitcase that had fallen on him from the passenger's seat,
now directly above him. He managed to shove the suitcase off, but
then found that his left foot was trapped between the pedals. Only
by dint of some violent twisting and squirming was he able to free

his foot and haul himself up through the passenger's door above
his head.

Once free of the Land Rover, Gavin lit a cigarette and assessed
the damage. The vehicle seemed unscathed. There was no sign of
the stags and no blood on the bumpers, so it seemed that both
animals had escaped without injury. And so too, apart from a few
bruises and a long graze across the instep of his left foot, had Gavin
himself, or so he thought.

He walked back up the road to Tormor to have one of Mary
MacLeod's restorative cups of tea and telephone for a recovery
vehicle to haul the Land Rover back on to the road. He was still
puzzled by the uncharacteristic behaviour of the stags, which in
summer never normally ran *down* a hill into danger. John Donald
was no less puzzled. 'It's not like the beasts at all,' he agreed,
and chided Gavin: 'You get away with driving that Mercedes at a
hundred and fifty miles an hour and you and the population of
the British Isles survive it, and now you leave the road in a Land
Rover doing less than twenty.'

But Gavin had not got away with it as lightly as he thought.
Five days after the accident he arrived by plane in Athens. As he
walked across the tarmac to the airport building he became aware
of a strange cramping pain in his left foot. Much to his surprise,
the pain became so intense that he had to stop. Only when he stood
still did it recede. Aymer was waiting at the airport with his car,
and after that there was little walking for Gavin to do that day and
he pushed the incident to the back of his mind.

Next morning they set sail from the port of Khalkis in Aymer's
fifty-foot motor yacht, *Lady Delft*. It was a beautiful Aegean summer morning, and as the yacht's white bows thrust through a sea
the colour of lapis lazuli, Gavin's worries slipped away and he began
to feel as free and exhilarated as he had at Sandaig in the old, carefree
days. 'Perhaps,' he thought afterwards, 'the secret of keeping one's
vision was always to be a nomad, never to remain long enough in
one place to allow time for the deadly clouding of sight, the creep-
ing cataract, that is composed of preoccupation with past mistakes
and their present results.'

They came in to Katounia, on the north-west coast of Euboea,
and after unloading Gavin's baggage at his brother's villa, whose
flower-decked, vine-covered terraces looked down on to the sea
immediately below, set off in a small inflatable rubber speedboat,

roaring down the coast to a calm little bay below the towering, three-thousand-foot cliffs of Mount Kantili. It was a heavenly spot. A pair of eagles wheeled in swooping arcs on the wind-sheer above the great cliffs, wild oleanders flowered brilliant and pink at the head of the tiny beach, and the sea beckoned warm and emerald green in the cove. Though Gavin could not swim, he could, with the aid of a snorkel, bob out to the edge of the sea shelf and stare down into the shadowy abyss beyond, but when he returned to the shallows and tried to dive for an angel shell lying open and empty on a rock a few feet down, he experienced a sudden excruciating pain in his left foot.

Now, for the first time, he thought there might be a connection between the pain and his accident. If he walked a hundred yards he had to rest to let the pain wear off; if he was in the sea for more than five minutes he had to come out and warm the foot on a hot rock until the cramp eased.

Gavin had little need to exert his ailing foot for the rest of his holiday, for the next day they embarked on a cruise of the Aegean islands of Skiros, Skiathos and Skopelos, in the Sporades, and the opportunities for walking far were few. But on the fourth day of the voyage another accident occurred which could have been disastrous had it not stopped short at farce.

On the morning of 4 July the *Lady Delft* put out from Trikeri on the south-east corner of the Gulf of Volos and set course for Kamena Voula with Gavin, Aymer and a Greek crew of two on board. Shortly after leaving, the captain reported that the port engine showed no oil pressure, and it was decided to carry on at reduced speed with the starboard engine alone. Towards midday, however, a deafening clattering noise – *gru gru gru gru gru!* – was heard from the area aft of the port engine.

A quarter of an hour later the captain reported that now the starboard engine had no oil pressure either. The engine was stopped and the hatch lifted, to reveal that both engines were under water and the boat was filling fast – in twenty fathoms of water and half a mile from the nearest land. Before long the water was up to the wheelhouse window, and Aymer gave her not much more than twenty minutes before she went down.

Lashing the rubber inflatable to the yacht's starboard side, they drove its outboard motor at full throttle in an effort to nudge the sinking craft towards Euboea's north-eastern shore before she sank.

A hundred yards from the beach the keel grated sickeningly on the stony shallows and the yacht began to keel over. Salvaged belongings, mattresses, cigarettes and wine were ferried to a narrow shingle beach, and Gavin paused to take stock of his new surroundings – the mountain skyline, the field of new harvested corn, the aromatic shrubs and scattered pine, olive and fig trees.

'It was baking hot,' he noted in his diary, 'and cicadas shrilled wherever there was no foliage. All that we did had for me the leisurely, porcelain quality of a Jane Austen picnic.' The whole incident was, he wrote to a friend after the boat had been salvaged, 'thoroughly Robinson Crusoe and much more my cup of tea'. Even in adversity there was nothing Gavin enjoyed more than a good drama.

Gavin returned to Sandaig in July to pick up the threads of his professional career. By now this was all he was fit to do. Without the Greek summer sun to aid the circulation of his foot he was virtually crippled. He could scarcely walk, and when he sat at his desk he had to rest his foot on a hot-water bottle to avoid cramp setting in. Sandaig, he realised, was a wildly unsuitable place for someone in his condition. Now he felt as much a prisoner there as the otters were behind their wooden stockades. All sense of freedom had gone. But he began to perceive, perhaps dimly at first, that something else was going, too – the vision of Camusfeàrna, the spirit of the place and everything it had meant to him and to others.

By turning his one-time sanctuary into a permanent base and developing it into the tiny but complex empire it had now become, he had destroyed all the joy he had once found in its beauty and freedom, and it had become a burden to both his spirit and his pocket, and a drain on every minute of his time and every ounce of his energy. Sandaig had always been a house of crisis, but now it was a treadmill as well. Jimmy Watt, who had now been five years in Gavin's employ, was the practical genius of the establishment, and without his skill and know-how the human, animal and mechanical components of Gavin's world would have ceased to function long ago. But Gavin's little Highland outpost by the sea had expanded to a point where not even Jimmy could cope with all the daily contingencies and periodic emergencies of Sandaig life. Jimmy was responsible not only for the welfare of the otters and the provisioning and day-to-day running of the greatly extended house, but the operation and maintenance of two Jeeps and a Land Rover, six dinghies and their outboard motors, and the *Polar Star* at her ill-sheltered moorings north of the islands. Replacements for the sorely-missed Terry Nutkins came and went at intervals, each leaving behind their own particular trail of disaster and adding to the burden of Sandaig's soaring costs.

Because of its isolation and inconvenience the annual expense of maintaining the Sandaig establishment totalled £5000, and before long the figure was to soar to over £7000 (about £75,000 in today's money). The telephone alone cost £1000 a year. The otters ate over £20-worth of eels a week, despatched live by rail at huge expense from Manze's fish shop in Fulham, London. The nearest laundry was eighty miles away on a Hebridean island. 'I remember working out at one time,' Gavin told me later, 'that if I'd been foolish enough to telephone the general stores in Kyle of Lochalsh and asked for a box of matches to be delivered to me in the usual way – mail-boat from Kyle to Glenelg, mail-car from Glenelg to Tormor, then my own Jeep from Tormor down to Sandaig – that box of matches would have cost three shillings and eight pence by the time it reached me, or well over twenty times what it would have cost in the shop.' The only way Gavin could meet his colossal outgoings was to immure himself in his little study-bedroom and write for long hours every day. He became a prisoner at his desk, not just because he could not walk far from it without suffering agonising cramp, but because he had to work like a literary galley-slave to pay the mounting bills.

The only freedom Gavin could find now was on the *Polar Star*. When the weather was right and he had the time he would take her out to cruise along the winding sea lochs; or down to Mallaig; or out to the beckoning Hebridean island of Eigg that lined Sandaig's southern horizon like a recumbent lion; or to visit his old friend John Lorne-Campbell, the laird of the isle of Canna, now only an hour and three-quarters away at twenty knots on *Polar Star*. 'The glory of summer days on *Polar Star* is with me still,' he was to write,

but perhaps most of all the quiet evenings when we returned her to her moorings at sunset and we would sit for long in the open after-cockpit. We would sit there until the hills had become black silhouettes against an apple-green afterglow, the only sounds the water lapping against the hull and the crying of the seabirds, the colonies of gulls and of Arctic terns on the islands beside us. These moments of peace and stillness at *Polar Star*'s moorings had come to represent to me what the waterfall once had, the waterfall now disfigured by pendant lines of black alkathene piping that carried the water supply to the house and the otters' enclosures. Enclosures: the whole of Camusfeàrna by now seemed to me an enclosure, the sea the only freedom.

That summer Gavin had signed a contract with Longmans (and with Duttons in New York, who paid a handsome advance of $20,000) for an autobiography of his childhood, which was eventually to bear the title *The House of Elrig*. This, he informed me at the time, was to be the first of a planned series of three autobiographical volumes, which in conjunction with the books he had already written (about shark-fishing, Sicily, Iraq and Camusfeàrna) would span his life from birth to the present day. He was already busy contacting friends and contemporaries of years ago to enlist their help. To Anthony Dickins, who had been a friend at Stowe, he wrote: 'I'm writing an autobiography; 1st volume age 1–16, when I left Stowe. I'm looking, hoping to be reminded of things which will start new trains of thought and revive old ones . . . I am looking for *myself* at that age – someone I can remember and relive, but not without all the ways others saw me – their side (so hateful then!) of their assaults at my soi-disant purity.'

Gavin was anxious to explore new themes and to get away from the image with which press and public had saddled him since the publication of *Ring of Bright Water*. 'Because I had written about my pet otters,' he complained,

it seemed that I had become in the public mind an otter man, an animal man, without further scope or interests; I had become type-cast, and the books that I had written about human beings with much greater labour were overshadowed by the massive image of the otters. There is a general unwillingness in the public mind to allow a man to be more than one thing or to have more than one pronounced characteristic, for it is simpler to classify and thus to know, or believe one knows, in which pigeonhole to look for whom. The great mass of human beings is determined that its fellows should conform to a recognisable type; the nonconformist is an implicit threat because one does not know what to expect from him; he makes for insecurity.

Ironically, however, because of the time-lapse between a book's completion and its publication, Gavin's first new book for nearly three years seemed to promote the very otter theme that he now disowned. *The Rocks Remain*, published on 21 October 1963, was the third of a trio of books featuring Camusfeàrna and the otters. It was not a work he was proud of. He saw it as a pot-pourri of unrelated incidentals, and referred to it as 'this silly book'. To a friend he confided: 'You won't like *The Rocks Remain*, I'm afraid. Between you and me it was written in just a month during the worst of my marital crises, and perhaps for that reason it is riddled with doom. Gawd – if I'd added the truth about that to all the other disasters!' Writing to John Guest, the senior editor at Longmans, he asked anxiously: 'Do you *really* enjoy *The Rocks Remain*? I had no confidence in it at all and I do value your opinion a very great deal.' Unfortunately, John Guest shared Gavin's own view, and in his reader's report (for Longman's eyes only) noted tartly:

The new book is a bit of a hotch-potch. One feels that the author has pushed himself at it, at various times and various moods; that he is lacking self-discipline; and that the success of *Ring of Bright Water* has gone to his head a bit, so that he is less self-critical. He is relying on readers to take anything from his pen, just because he *is* Gavin Maxwell . . . About three-fifths of the book deals with Camusfeàrna – though there is a different slant and the story is less idyllic. All this Camusfeàrna material is first-class, vivid, interesting, excellently written – only a shade below *Ring*, and not always below. It is the other two-fifths that are uneven . . .

It is frustrating that a writer so talented as Gavin is so touchy, so unapproachable (conceited), so unamenable to normal friendly discussion of his work. But I believe it is no use expressing anything other than enthusiasm for what he turns in. He may yet become a more stable character.

Robin McEwen, who had done some of the artwork for the book, had similar reservations about it. 'Gavin's book seems a triumph of the publisher's art,' he wrote to Mark Longman after receiving an advance copy, 'though possibly, and with all due reservations, and in *sotto*-est *voce*, not of the writer's.'

Mark Longman had decided on an initial printing of forty thousand copies of *The Rocks Remain*, almost double the first print-run of the bestselling *Ring*. The book sold over thirty-three thousand copies in the first ten days after publication, and by Christmas there were only two hundred copies left and another ten thousand were ordered to be printed; in the United States the sales figures were almost identical. During the same period another hardback edition of *Ring of Bright Water* was printed for its fourth Christmas in succession – despite the fact that the paperback version was selling prodigiously.

Gavin had landed another bestseller. The *Observer* serialised it and commissioned their photographer Colin Jones to illustrate the serialisation. The critics, sharing the opinions of neither the author nor his publishers, reacted as ecstatically as they had to *Ring*.

A lone dissenting voice was that of the author and poet Geoffrey Grigson, who disliked aristocrats almost as much as he disliked animals, and found himself confronted with a hefty dose of both. In his review for the *New Statesman* Grigson derided Gavin's 'defiant conceit' and his 'upper class recourse to evasive, excessive communion with animals', and went so far as to confess: 'I have a tiny sympathy with the minister of the Church of Scotland who shot Mr Maxwell's latest otter cubs' (a misreading of Gavin's text). Gavin felt he understood the motives behind this review. 'In 1950 or 1951 I went to the Nag's Head pub with Roy Campbell,' he wrote to a friend. 'He encountered Grigson, who had written just such a slimy review of some work of Roy's. Roy made him crawl round the pub on all fours while he kicked his backside. Grigson hasn't forgiven my presence on that occasion.' Gavin could not resist reminding Grigson (and the public) of this humiliating incident in a letter of riposte to the *New Statesman*.

Grigson apart, Gavin had notched up another critical success; and much to his delight he was in the money again. This time he was determined not to blow his fortune on personal indulgences and high living – or at any rate, not all of it. He would invest his riches as wisely as he was able. No one knew better than Gavin that he was no businessman – the shark-fishing venture was ample proof of that. But this time his choice of investment struck him as fool-proof – especially as its financial attractions coincided with his personal interests and ambitions. He would buy a lighthouse – in fact, he would buy *two* lighthouses, and whizz from one to the other like a rocket in his high-speed flagship, *Polar Star*.

Three miles from the small lighthouse on the furthest of the Sandaig islands, west-south-west across the Sound of Sleat, lies the much larger lighthouse of Isle Ornsay, off the Isle of Skye. The signal from the Isle Ornsay lighthouse – a double flash every seven seconds – is the only light that can be seen at night from Sandaig. It was this light that had so transfixed me when I first arrived at Sandaig in the breathless darkness of an early spring night five years before, for it lent an infinite perspective to that haunting nightscape, beckoning one on like a will-o'-the-wisp to the very edge of the vast and silent sea. Gavin, too, was drawn to it, and would often stand at the tide's edge in Sandaig bay, lost in silent reverie as he stared across to Isle Ornsay in the gathering dusk, waiting for the stab of light from the distant white tower that marked the frontier of night. The place had an additional significance for Gavin, because it was between Isle Ornsay and the Sandaig Islands that he had encountered his first basking shark nearly twenty years before – an encounter that had led, step by step, to Camusfeàrna. Gavin had never landed at Isle Ornsay lighthouse, but the lighthouse-keeper was an old acquaintance of his who sometimes called at Sandaig on calm evenings when he had been fishing for mackerel, and at dusk one quiet evening in the summer of 1963 he had called again, with news.

'I'm afraid this is the last dram I'll be taking with you,' he told Gavin. 'Ornsay Lighthouse is being made fully automatic, and I'm being transferred to Ardnamurchan. The Northern Lighthouse Board will put it up for sale, no doubt, and it'll be a lucky man who gets it.'

Gavin pricked up his ears at this. He had always been drawn to islands and the encircling moat of water they interposed between him and the rest of the world. He had once been Laird of Soay, and had later tried to buy Temple Island on the Thames at Henley. As he was only too well aware, he was merely a grace-and-favour tenant at Sandaig and at the expiry of his lease he could be homeless – and alternative houses on the coast were simply not available.

'There is virtually nothing left up here,' he once told me when I was searching for a foothold in the Highlands. 'Between Moydart and Torridon, which is a great stretch of coastline, there is nothing. Even if you found a ruin with four walls standing, the landlord wouldn't sell it to you; and even if he did, you wouldn't get planning permission to rebuild it.' Isle Ornsay appeared to Gavin to be an ideal insurance against possible future homelessness. Flat out in the *Polar Star* it was only ten minutes away from Sandaig, and the lighthouse accommodation, consisting of two long back-to-back cottages and a large walled garden, offered great potential for conversion. Gavin made enquiries, and discovered that preference would be given to a purchaser who was prepared to buy not only the Isle Ornsay lighthouse cottages but those of Kyleakin lighthouse, eleven miles from Sandaig by sea, in the Narrows of Skye. Only the cottages were for sale – not the lighthouses themselves, nor the islands on which they stood.

One glorious summer day, then, Gavin set out to inspect the lighthouse properties in *Polar Star* with Jimmy Watt and Alan MacDiarmaid. At Isle Ornsay they anchored a few hundred yards from the lighthouse and rowed ashore in the dinghy. Gavin surveyed the wheeling birds, the sounding seals, the profound peace and immense panorama that spread before the islet, from the distant point of Ardnamurchan to the towering hills of Knoydart and Loch Hourn and the minuscule Sandaig light dwarfed by the vastness of the hills that formed its backcloth. 'It was as though I had found Camusfeàrna once again,' he wrote:

> The same sense of freedom and elation, the same shedding of past mistakes and their perennial repercussions. Here, it seemed to me, where the rocks and the white stone buildings were the only solid things in a limitless bubble of blue water and blue air, one might be able to live in peace again, to recover a true vision long lost by now in the lives of other humans and in the strife of far countries; here one might set back the clock and re-enter Eden . . .
> I did not know, though I was already in middle age, that you cannot buy paradise, for it disintegrates at the touch of money, and it is not composed solely of scenery. It is made of what many of us will never touch in a lifetime, and having touched it once there can be no second spring, no encore after

the curtain falls. This is the core of our condition, that we do not know why nor at what point we squandered our heritage; we only know, too late always, that it cannot be recovered or restored. I did not know it then; this was paradise, and I was going to buy it for hard cash.

If Isle Ornsay lighthouse was like paradise, Kyleakin lighthouse was like home. Unlike Isle Ornsay, which was really a tidal peninsula, Kyleakin Island (also known as Eilean Ban, the White Island*) was a true island, in the middle of a narrow shipping thoroughfare between Skye and the mainland at Kyle of Lochalsh. Dodging between the busy ferry boats, Gavin nudged the *Polar Star* into a small bay on the southern side of the island and dropped anchor clear of the tide's swirling current. Despite its proximity to towns and traffic and the summer tourist trade, Gavin was deeply drawn to the hilly rock and heather of Kyleakin, for it reminded him of his childhood home at Elrig – the house that for long had been his only refuge in a frightening and unfamiliar world. 'At Kyleakin,' he was to write, 'I felt as if I were coming home. It was here, I decided that I would live if ever I left Camusfeàrna.'

Though the lighthouse-keepers' cottages on both islands would cost a good deal to renovate and convert to the standard he required, Gavin was determined to buy them both. One of them, he argued, could provide him with a future home, while the other could pay its way by being let to rich tourists drawn by their wild settings and his own famous name. 'The Kyleakin one I'm going to do up to luxury standards and possibly let to some American millionaire with the charter of a boat. My brother Aymer gets £200 a week for a tiny villa and his boat (seven knots if you're lucky). And I believe just as many Americans visit Skye as visit Greece, so . . .' By the end of September the negotiations for the island cottages were almost complete, along with those for two cottages in Glenelg, one run-down and the other virtually derelict, which in a fit of mental aberration he had bought (as he bought his boats) without ever clapping eyes on them.

I was at Sandaig at that time with my future wife, and one bright

* In fact the correct Gaelic name for Kyleakin Island is not Eilean Ban (White Island) but Eilean na Gillean (Island of Boys). The 1903 ordnance survey confused it with the larger island to the north, properly called Eilean Ban, and the wrong names have stuck to the wrong islands ever since.

autumn day we sped out in the *Polar Star* to inspect the spectacular properties of which Gavin was now the proud owner. But Gavin himself was out of sorts. The injury he had sustained in the Land Rover crash in June still troubled him and he had some difficulty in walking. This seemed to prey on his mind, for he was more than usually tense and moody. 'Gavin is up and down as is his wont,' I wrote home. 'He leads the most disorganised life I know – most of the disasters are avoidable.' It was not just his injury which confined him to his room. A record-player filled the house with the exuberant sounds of a new kind of pop music by a group called The Beatles, and there was now beer and darts in the annexe, both unheard of before. Sandaig was more overrun by human-kind than I had ever seen it, for in addition to Gavin, Jimmy Watt, and Philip Alpin (who had replaced the irreplaceable Terry Nutkins), Gavin's company manager from London, Michael Cuddy, was staying at the house, as well as my fiancée and myself, while a dozen schoolboys from a progressive school in Fife, on a field-study trip under the care of one of their teachers, the mountaineer and writer Hamish Brown, had taken over the croft opposite the main house.

Gavin had first encountered the young and bearded Hamish Brown and his pioneer outward-bound school parties one hot day in early June, when a boy had knocked on his door and asked him, with great composure and in the difficult dialect of Fife, to help identify a fish he had caught in a bucket out at the islands. 'I asked him if he was interested in natural history,' Gavin recorded at the time, 'and he replied, "Well, we've all become a bit keen lately." He said that he came from Braehead Junior Secondary School (mining area, very poor) and that the rest of the party were over at the islands, so I told him to ask them all in for a cup of tea.'

In his diary Hamish Brown recorded: 'A memorable visit. The boys delighted into silence at the house, its owner and animals.' Gavin learned that Hamish Brown had conceived the idea of de-urbanising the boys and enthusing them about the natural world by taking small groups of them on two-week field trips to moun-tainous and roadless areas in the Highlands. 'The result has been that boys of the most unlikely background have developed a phenomenal interest in wildlife of all kinds,' Gavin noted. 'I had some evidence of this interest myself. I took them up to the water-fall to watch the elver migration, and gave them an explanatory talk on the life history of the eel, which was new to them. Most urban boys would be bored stiff by it, but they were actually jostling for position so as not to miss a word. They also displayed themselves most knowledgeable about the various birds and beasts they saw here.'

Gavin was so impressed with what he saw that he was prompted to dash off a note to Peter Scott, now Chairman of the World Wildlife Fund, proposing that children's subscriptions should be used for financing field expeditions like those of Braehead School throughout the British Isles, rather than for saving some endangered species of, say, tortoise, many thousands of miles away. Though Peter Scott himself was open to the idea, and sent a copy of Gavin's letter to Prince Bernhardt of the Netherlands, then President of the World Wildlife Fund, for his consideration, Gavin's scheme did not meet with an enthusiastic response, and the raising of money from children to save endangered animals remained the first priority.

Nevertheless, the radical ideals of Braehead were to have a considerable impact on Gavin's theories about the education of the young. This was a subject to which he was to devote a considerable amount of thought following Hamish Brown's first visit, coinciding as it did with the recollections of his own unsatisfactory education, which he had begun to write down for his new work-in-progress, his autobiography of childhood.

And so, in October, Hamish Brown was back at Sandaig with another party, to whom Raef had lent his long, one-roomed croft as a base. Gavin had installed film and slide projectors in the croft, and one evening he gave a slide show about his Moroccan travels, followed by a screening of films about my ballooning adventures over Africa and pictures of the journey through Siberia and Central Asia from which I had recently returned. The enthusiasm and high spirits of the party were infectious – all the more so for the lonely and dramatic setting in which they found themselves. 'What a place,' Hamish Brown jotted in his log:

Day of a hundred things with a thousand views to ring the changes . . . Force 10 gales in Minch. Wild night and stormy day. Spume flying past the door. Lying in bed watching it through the glass door, with the white boat and beach, grass, bracken, and far stormy hills of Skye all flickering in a million

changing lights. Cuillin edge just visible in moonlight . . .
Down to dinghy and set sail and drifted sedately out into the
Sound. Lost way and gale caught us and we drifted right across
in the darkness on to rocks. Rowing hard took an hour for
the half mile up to the beach. Lights all shining on shore and
glitter in water . . . Days beginning to race away and hard to
know days of the week . . . Timelessness . . . Last full day
and another memorable one. All very sad to be leaving. So
much still to do! Bed at one o'clock with a big moon and a
sky patched with stars and clouds and the bay quiet in the
silver light beyond the ebb tide band of dark shore . . . God,
I love it here.

For the moment Gavin's most urgent preoccupation was with his
half-crippled foot. Now that his Greek suntan had worn off the
true colour of the foot was revealed. It was a cold bluish white,
with a cratered ulcer forming near the base of the big toe. When
Dr Beveridge examined it, she warned Gavin that he ran the risk
of gangrene and amputation of the foot if he did not take urgent
action.

So late in November Gavin went down to London to seek the
opinions of specialists. Their advice was conflicting. One said it
might be possible to replace the damaged blood vessels with artificial ones. Another declared there was no alternative to a major
operation – a lumbar sympathectomy. The blood vessels were too
small to replace, he said, and would be cast off by the body's system
in a year or two. Already the foot was showing the initial symptoms
of necrosis.

From London he returned to Scotland, where he placed himself
in the hands of an acquaintance who was perhaps the greatest surgeon in Scotland at that time. First there was an examination even
more detailed and searching than those he had already had. Then
there was an arteriogram, an agonising examination in which a
substance which appears opaque on X-ray was injected into the
arteries at the groin.

Afterwards it was clear to Gavin that he could not go on as he
was. When he set off to do his Christmas shopping in Glasgow he
found he could hardly walk at all without the help of a stick. Even
without the threat of gangrene and amputation, Gavin was
reconciled to the need to undergo the lumbar sympathectomy

operation, and he was not excessively dejected when he returned to Sandaig.

When photographer Terence Spencer and reporter Timothy Green from *Life* magazine arrived to do a story about the bestselling author and wilderness man of Camusfeàrna, they were surprised to find not the craggy, reclusive St Francis figure they had expected, but a sophisticated gourmet with a zest for life and a passion for fast cars and guns. Tim Green's notes record:

Maxwell is 5'9½" high, weighs 126 pounds, has blue eyes – if you can ever see them – and fair, mouse-coloured hair, slightly receding. His mighty deerhound Dirk weighs 125 pounds and when he stands on his back legs he can reach all of seven feet which makes Maxwell look like a dwarf. 'My great interest in life,' said Maxwell, 'undoubtedly centres around human beings (and then, perhaps, fast cars, pistol shooting and shotguns).' At first hearing this may sound strange from a man who seemingly cuts himself off from the world in a remote home surrounded mainly by animals. But Maxwell believes it is only possible to understand man by having a thorough understanding of animals first. 'Medical students start by studying animals lower than man. The same thing applies with psychology – animal psychology is part of all psychology degree courses, lower animals first, homo sapiens last. So in my case a stage on the way to understanding human beings is an understanding and affection for animals.' Maxwell doesn't let his standards drop and enjoys good food and large quantities of Scotch whisky. Breakfast may consist of caviar and white wine, while for lunch a Maxwell speciality is what he modestly terms canapé of smoked salmon but is much more exotic. He starts by placing lobster or caviar between layers of smoked salmon, adds a little mayonnaise, then sets to work with lots of different things – a dash of sugar, cayenne pepper, lemon juice and smoked shrimps. This is by way of hors d'oeuvre, for Maxwell also fancies himself as a game cook.

It was at this juncture, while waiting for major surgery, that in accordance with the laws then operating in the United Kingdom

Gavin was required to 'provide evidence' of adultery for his forthcoming divorce action. As often as not the 'evidence' in such cases
was totally bogus, and entailed the 'offending' party (usually the
husband) organising a fictitious adulterous encounter with a person
of the opposite sex, and arranging for a friend or private detective
to act as witness and provide evidence as to the pretended adultery
in a divorce court. Gavin first tried to enlist the help of his former
commanding officer in SOE, Colonel Jimmy Young, who ran the
Portsonachon Hotel in Argyll, a convenient venue for an arranged
liaison of the kind the court required. But Young declined to take
part in such a charade, so Gavin prevailed on friends who lived
near Inverness to help him out instead. One evening in mid-
December he arrived at the couple's home in the company of a
woman of the town whom he introduced as his wife, and shortly
afterwards retired with her to an upstairs room, emerging a little
later to ask for a cup of tea. In due course it was arranged that
Gavin and Lavinia would be divorced, on the grounds of adultery,
later in the summer.

That ordeal over, Gavin now faced up to another. After the
Christmas Day broadcast of his television interview at Sandaig, he
was admitted as a private patient to the Bon Secours in Glasgow
on Boxing Day 1963 – the same nursing home in which Terry
Nutkins had been treated for his otter wounds more than two
years before – to undergo a lumbar sympathectomy. The lumbar
sympathetic nerves lie against and on each side of the spine at about
the same level as the kidneys. Part of their function is to control
the supply of blood to the lower limbs, and normally they act like
taps which are permanently half turned on. By removing the left
one entirely the surgeons hoped to provide a full, unregulated flow
of blood to the crushed arteries of Gavin's foot, and in that way
restore it to a normal condition. It was a relatively commonplace
operation, with a high success rate, and if all went well it involved
no more than two weeks in hospital and a month or two of convalescence afterwards.

But all did not go well. When he came round from the anaesthetic
Gavin was aware of an appalling pain in his left side, and within a
day or two he began to feel very ill indeed. He had caught a hospital
staphylococcus, and by the time the surgeon came to see him again
he was vomiting black bile, each retch seeming to tear the wound
wide open. Twice more he was sent back to the operating theatre,

each time returning with drainage tubes protruding from his wound.

The worst was still to come. The handling of the intestinal mass during surgery had brought about a paralysis of the digestive system, a condition known as *ileus*. Gavin's gut had ceased to function and as a result gases began to form in his belly without any means of escape, as happens in a corpse. Gavin lay on his bed like a stranded whale while his belly swelled and swelled till it resembled an inflated set of bagpipes from which the drainage tubes stuck out like the drones and the chanter. The condition was often fatal, and Gavin's surgeon could not disguise his concern. Several drugs were used to try and relieve this grotesquely bloated condition, but without success. Then one night there came sudden relief, as dramatic as any *coup de théâtre*, when Gavin was woken by the most stupendous and prolonged fart he had ever heard and felt his belly deflating like a barrage balloon. They had found the right drug at last.

Gavin made a restless, rebellious patient, all the more so in that he was in the hands of nuns, who to him represented the impersonal authority of organised religion, against which – remembering the numbing constrictions of the Irvingite Church of his boyhood and the iron rule by which the Catholic priests governed the Sicilian poor – he instinctively bridled. Some of the nuns, however, he found saintly and warm-hearted, and one in particular – a strikingly beautiful sixteen-year-old Irish girl who was working in the nursing home as a probationer while she waited to join the Order – he felt particularly drawn to. The orphaned daughter of a fishing family in Connemara, she had worked on her father's small fishing boat since she was ten, and had been rescued by this nursing order of nuns so that she might become a nun herself, renounce all earthly things and forget her past life.

'Forget the sea and the salt wind and the sunshine and the great open sky,' Gavin thought; 'forget the feeling of wet sea sand and weed beneath bare feet, forget the pitching of a boat in the waves; the crying of gulls; the rasp of frayed and ripping rope on childish palms . . .' Such suppression of the joys of human life filled him with a blind anger.

Gavin's conversations with the girl echoed his inner dialogues with himself. While still convalescent in hospital he had resumed work on his autobiography of childhood, and quickly realised that his current state of helplessness and dependence provided him with a unique insight into those boyhood years of long ago, not by remembering them but by actually reliving them, so that the past was recreated as a kind of present, complete with long-lost scenes, conversations, feelings and states of mind.

After four weeks Gavin was discharged from hospital. His brother Aymer came to fetch him, and drove him down to the family home at Monreith, in Wigtownshire – a sad house now, with half its rooms closed and the garden overgrown. There he was to spend the remaining period of his convalescence under the eye of the family's local general practitioner, Dr Gavin Brown, a good friend of many years' standing.

Though the flow of blood to Gavin's left foot had been restored, he still could not walk properly without suffering cramp, and as the surgical wound in his belly had not yet healed he had to carry a drainage tube in it, which felt like a spiked golf ball that bounced at every step he took. When Dr Brown came to dress Gavin's wound the first morning, he told him: 'Well, you've got an awful mess of a belly, Gavin. One thing's certain – that'll never be a hairline scar, and unless you want a cosmetic operation you'll never have a flat stomach again.' A three-inch section of the nine-inch incision still gaped an inch wide, and it was expected to take another six weeks for the wound to close.

But Gavin was not altogether unhappy. Convalescence at Monreith was a kind of escape from the real world and all its worries. After a week Dr Brown tried to persuade him to walk down the half-mile drive to the lodge gate to meet him. But though Gavin stayed on for several weeks at Monreith he never did manage to reach the gates, and when he finally returned to Sandaig late in February 1964 he could not yet walk properly, and was still more or less helpless.

Early in March Gavin wrote to Constance McNab: 'Life has been a series of crises of one sort or another since I came back here ten days ago – as it always is. Another shipwreck (I was ashore) and the loss of the boat for an indefinite period – that would be enough by itself. Jimmy is excellent as always and manages everything practical. I received a very beautiful gift last night – a parcel from a priest containing the vessels of Communion, chalice, cruet and plate – in return, he wrote, for what my books had done for him. An exchange of symbols.'

In spite of the strong sense that time was running out and the place was running down, Sandaig remained the hub of the otter network of the area, and new otters continued to show up there, along with other wild creatures. Anyone with an unwanted otter invariably contacted Gavin, who invariably agreed to care for the waif in question. One of the oddest among the new arrivals was a small, domesticated otter called Tibby that belonged to a crippled bachelor on the isle of Eigg. Anxious to find his pet a permanent home before he became too infirm to look after her, Tibby's owner brought her to Sandaig, and when he left she was put in Teko's enclosure, for Teko had never objected to any otter that had shared his quarters with him. But Tibby proved as compulsive and able an escapologist as Mossy and Monday had been. Instead of heading off for the wilds each time she escaped, Tibby would make for one or other of the villages in the area, where with unerring accuracy she would locate the only man who resembled her late master – a cripple on crutches. 'Perhaps,' Gavin mused after her last sighting, 'if I had never had the operation, and had lost my foot, I should have earned Tibby's allegiance for life.'

By now Mossy and Monday had taken up residence on one of the Sandaig islands where in past years there had always been an otters' holt. The two otters had been seen increasingly rarely, but one day in the summer of 1964, when Gavin was writing in his room, he heard an incredibly penetrating whistling, squeaking sound coming from the direction of the waterfall – the sort of sound a young otter makes when it is trying to find its parents. He limped across the field but all he could see was Mossy, looking lost and hopeless on a rock beside the fall. Then he heard the penetrating call again, low down below his line of vision, and raising his head a little he peered down and saw three very small otter cubs near the foot of the fall, and a small sharp face like Monday's peering round a rock at the top. Monday, it seemed, had climbed the fall, but the three cubs had been unable to follow her, while Mossy, as usual, had been unable to cope with the situation. Gavin hobbled back to the house to fetch his camera, but by the time he got back to the waterfall the young family had gone.

Monday, with all her knowledge of human ways, was evidently determined that she and her cubs should remain free, and it was some years before Gavin was to see her again, though he was comforted by the fact that otters were again breeding at Camusfeàrna, and that Otter Island once more justified its name.

But Sandaig was a strange place for Gavin now. Unable to walk, he acquired an almost sedentary, invalid habit of mind, and seldom left the house, except by boat. He sat at his desk in his lonely room and wrote for increasingly long hours every day, working simultaneously on *The House of Elrig* and the long-overdue *Lords of the Atlas*, and growing increasingly frustrated and ill-tempered as he did so. It was the beginning of a strange metamorphosis in his role at Sandaig and those of the staff who had been holding the fort during his absence – Jimmy Watt, Mike Cuddy and Philip Alpin.

'Their solicitude and their desire to relieve me of every kind of task and responsibility, other than that of writing,' he wrote later, 'worked upon me psychologically to increase my helplessness and dependence; at first I felt myself to be a cypher in my own household, and by degrees that is what I became. They were the young and healthy, really and actually the masters; never had an adolescent rebellion so complete and satisfying a success with so small an expenditure of force.'

THIRTY

A pattern of islands

Be not afear'd; the isle is full of noises,
Sounds, and sweet airs, that give delight, and hurt not.
WILLIAM SHAKESPEARE, *The Tempest*

In July 1964 Gavin celebrated his fiftieth birthday. At almost the
same time he was finally divorced from Lavinia – the end of an
experiment in living.

Gavin was now seriously alone. He was also seriously broke.
His literary agent cum business manager, Peter Janson-Smith, had
warned him: 'I was alarmed to learn that earnings this year are so
far in the region of only £500. A major financial crisis would therefore seem to be in prospect.' Michael Cuddy, who ran Gavin's
London office, confirmed the worst. 'Money-wise we are in the
most critical condition we have ever been,' he wrote to Sandaig.
'We can't pay any accounts at present. Our bills total £3500 and
there will be some pretty hefty legal ones coming. I can't pay
anybody. We must just sit it out until more money comes in and
I have no idea when that will be.' As a desperate measure to raise
immediate cash Gavin sold his rare Maserati racing car and put the
manuscript of *Ring of Bright Water* (which he had given to Peter
Janson-Smith as a gift but then asked to be returned) up for sale at
an auction of valuable autographs and manuscripts at Christie's,
hoping it might reach a reserve price of £1000; but no sale was
forthcoming. The future began to look bleak.

Gavin devoted all his energies to completing the two books
which were now due – his childhood autobiography and his Moroccan history. But his restless and frustrated aspirations were directed
elsewhere. His two lighthouse properties were for him symbols of
the freedom of which he was now so painfully deprived at Sandaig.
He had always been attracted to small islands as the ultimate refuges
from the cares of the world and the menace of human kind, and
he was ambitious to transform the lighthouse cottages on Isle

Ornsay and Eilean Ban into stylish residences which he could let out to rich holiday-makers and perhaps retreat to himself one day. 'Those lighthouses became my chief distraction,' he was to recall, 'because they seemed then to represent something emergent and hopeful in the general muddle of my personal situation.' So the die was cast, and instead of selling them and buying some sensible house with a road to it, he committed himself to spending huge sums which he had not got in pursuit of another romantic dream.

To achieve that dream Gavin enlisted the help of a couple whose acquaintance he had made at Glenelg the preceding spring. Richard and Joan Frere lived in a beautiful old house overlooking Loch Ness, some sixty miles away to the east. Joan was an interior designer and Richard was a mountaineer, an aspiring writer, and a man of many parts who was destined to play a crucial role in Gavin's struggle for survival during the ensuing years. Born in 1922, the son of a country squire and great-nephew of a British Ambassador to Spain, from whom he inherited the title (which he did not use) of Marquis de la Union, Vizconde de la Alianza, he had spent his early boyhood on his father's country estate in Norfolk and the rest of his life in the Scottish Highlands, whose hills, lochs and glens he considered his true home country. Like Gavin, then, he was a Highlander by adoption, and like Gavin too, he was the sworn enemy of the urban and industrial life, and a lifelong devotee of high hills and wild places. Imbued with a dogged determination to remain his own master, he had supported his growing family as best he could by a variety of abortive projects, including mushroom growing, poultry farming and timber extraction; and though these activities had served only to prove that in business terms he possessed what sailors call 'negative buoyancy', this had not dented his relish for an independent and unusual way of life.

Richard had not been impressed by his first brief encounter with the famous author, about whom many wild rumours had been spread in the locality. 'His manner was abrupt and uneasy,' he recorded, 'and consequently touched the edge of rudeness. I felt that here was a man who liked to prepare himself for meetings; chance encounters had no charm for him. Soon he made it clear that he wished to talk no more and stalked away in a kind of outrage, like the offended ghost of Hamlet's father, to take shelter behind his spectacles in a quiet corner of the bar.'

Richard never expected to meet this churlish-seeming writer

again, and felt no great desire to do so. Even when chance brought him and his wife to Sandaig the following autumn he continued to view Gavin with some diffidence. Though he enjoyed the company of Jimmy Watt and Terry Nutkins, who seemed to hold Gavin in great affection and respect, he had grave reservations about Gavin's famous otters, Edal and Teko, whom he regarded as rather slimy and untrustworthy.

It was not until May 1963, when Gavin called at the Freres' home at Drumnadrochit while en route from London to Sandaig, that Richard's impressions changed. Gavin was in one of his ebullient moods. 'How different he seemed from the forbidding character I fleetingly remembered,' Richard recalled, 'or from the sinister recluse of many a wild report . . . so charming, erudite and glittering with sophisticated wit.' The droll tales he told of his adventures abroad had the couple alternately enthralled and doubled up with laughter.

In April 1964 Gavin asked the Freres if they would be willing to undertake the renovation of his lighthouse properties, starting with Isle Ornsay. He could offer no immediate remuneration, he warned them, but by the time they began work on the Kyleakin Island house he was confident things would be different. The Freres saw the work as an exciting challenge. Joan welcomed the chance to engage her talents as an interior designer, while Richard regarded making and building as his greatest creative satisfaction, and in any case loved the Isle of Skye. A small private income from a family trust would tide them over the financial shortfall. So the work began.

Richard first set eyes on the Isle Ornsay property in May. It was not a propitious encounter. The interior smelt of the grave, for the sea-damp was everywhere, the walls black and streaming, the woodwork dotted with a spreading fungus. Simply to paint such saturated walls was a challenge; to turn such a gloomy and rudimentary structure into the luxurious residence Gavin had in mind was a daunting proposition. The problems were not simply those of the builder's and decorator's arts. Isle Ornsay was a remote place on the edge of a wild ocean, and simply to come and go presented a herculean struggle with the elements. At low tide the whole bay was an expanse of sand across which it was possible to walk to the lighthouse rock; but when the tide was flowing a boat was needed to make the crossing, and Richard knew nothing about boats and had no experience of the sea, or any love for it. Gavin arranged for one of the small boats from Sandaig to be left on the Skye shore at Isle Ornsay, but Richard viewed this craft with the greatest suspicion and distaste, and it did not reassure him that it was called a pram and looked better suited to a pond than the margin of one of the world's great oceans.

So his seafaring adventures began – and his lonely days and even lonelier nights on the lighthouse rock. 'The Isle Ornsay lighthouse cottage in the early days was primordial, without a stick of furniture, and no light or fuel. And it was eerie beyond belief,' Richard wrote; 'All around me were new sounds, some known and understood, some as odd and mysterious as the dark shadowed island outside . . . My ears sang for hours with compulsive, nervous listening.'

Soon Gavin's – and Joan's – ambitions for the refurbishment proliferated and soared, and Richard's period of service was extended to accommodate them. By now he had acquired a modest mastery of the sea and progressed by stages to more ambitious voyages – even across the open sea to Sandaig or the Knoydart shore, or down the Skye coast to Kinloch. Such excursions were not without their hazards, which did not always owe their origin to nature and the elements. One hot, still, early evening in June, after being royally entertained in the customary Scots manner at Sandaig in the morning and at Kinloch in the afternoon, Richard fell asleep at the tiller. When he woke, the sun was several degrees lower in the sky and the boat was steering a circular course. A great shout of applause reached his ears as he stirred and sat up. A crowd of people had been observing his wayward progress from the distant shore with tremendous glee. Richard waved and the applause redoubled.

Gavin was not amused when Richard rang him on the newly installed telephone when he finally reached Isle Ornsay. In such moods, Richard noted, Gavin behaved very like his own (Richard's) mother, creating a mood of pained martyrdom if he felt himself overlooked. Why hadn't he telephoned earlier, Gavin asked him?

'I couldn't,' Richard replied. 'I was drunk in charge of a pram.'

By the middle of June the conversion of the Isle Ornsay cottages into a single sumptuous four-bedroomed residence was almost complete. On 17 June a great collection of elegant furnishings was off-loaded on to the lighthouse jetty from the Glenelg ferry, which had been specially chartered for the occasion, and manhandled by a swarm of willing helpers (including Hamish Brown and a fresh party of boys from Braehead School) up the slope and into the cottage. The place now wore an air of opulence and good living. Precious antiques and foreign exotica filled every room, from the Chang Dynasty china bluebirds, Regency settee and 1788 Adam cabinet to the ivory-inlaid Berber musket and powder horn, ancient Sicilian amphora and Tibetan yak horn embossed with stones. Moroccan rugs, antique embroidered Greek waistcoats, a Chinese embroidery peacock, a framed eagle's wing, nineteenth-century whaling harpoons, and paintings and drawings by John Gould, Gerald Wilde, Michael Ayrton and Gavin himself hung on the walls.

The day following the main move, Richard was assigned the tricky task of ferrying one of Gavin's prize possessions across the Sound of Sleat from Sandaig to the lighthouse cottage. This was the 'Admiral's bed', which took up almost the entire length of Gavin's boat (a large, seaworthy new dinghy called the *Eider*), and overlapped the sides by several feet. Though the sea was calm when Richard set out with this precarious cargo, a north-west wind blew up as he approached Skye, and as the boat rolled in the swell the sides of the great bed dipped into the sea and its drawers began to slide out and float away one by one. No sooner had Richard recovered one drawer than another would slip into the water. By the time he reached Isle Ornsay the tide was out and he had to manhaul the contraption all the way to the lighthouse rock and up the slope and into the house. To justify his exertions he decided to spend the night in the bed, only to find (as Lavinia had found before him) that the mattress was as hard and unyielding as a wrestler's mat.

It soon became plain that Richard Frere was almost as chronically accident-prone as his employer. One day he found the luxuriously appointed sitting room full of sheep; the creatures were lying about all over the carpet 'like courtesans after an orgy', amid a litter of wool and droppings. He drove them out of the house with one of Gavin's shark harpoons, but they trampled and smashed the huge sheet of plate glass that was waiting to be installed in the picture window. When Richard tried to ferry a replacement window across to the lighthouse rock he ran into a brisk sea which twisted the outboard engine off the stern of the dinghy, so that it disappeared

'with a despairing gurgle and a stream of bubbles' in thirty fathoms
of water. In the years to come such calamities were to seem trivial
in comparison with those that succeeded them. Richard was a philosophical man with a keen sense of the absurd, and like his employer
he perceived in all mishaps and setbacks at best the obscure work-
ings of Murphy's Law, and at worst the machinations of blind
Fate. Against such unpredictable powers all human planning and
organisation were in vain. At least, as Richard noted with relief,
'With Maxwell spilt milk was *spilt*.'

The first batch of holiday tenants were due in August. The day
before their arrival Gavin and Jimmy Watt made an inventory of
the contents of the cottage. The list seemed endless, for Gavin had
brought with him a huge quantity of personal possessions – mostly
souvenirs from his past life and foreign travels – with which he
proceeded to clutter up Joan Frere's balanced design. Among them
were a number of photographs of young Arabs he had taken in the
Iraq Marshes. Beautiful though they certainly were, Richard felt
that they need not have been so prominently displayed high up on
the bathroom walls, and whenever he had a bath he felt embarrassed
by all those dark, lustful eyes looking down at him through the
geraniums.

It took so long to complete the inventory that Gavin and Jimmy
decided to join the Freres for dinner and stay on overnight. After
the meal Gavin and Richard lingered on at table with a bottle of
whisky. Gavin was cheerful and wide awake, as he usually was in
the late evening, and asked Richard to stay up with him for a while.

'I wonder,' said Gavin, 'if you would be happy to sit down in
the company of a murderer?'

Richard was taken aback, and hoped that he was joking. Of
course, Gavin went on, he was not a murderer. But he was a
homosexual. Did that worry him? Richard replied that it did not,
and that though he was not so inclined himself he felt some sympathy for Gavin in this matter. This annoyed Gavin, who looked
gloomy and hurt. He drained his glass and lit a cigarette.

'You are much too heterosexual to try and understand us,' he
said.

Richard replied that he found homosexuality unnatural. By now
Gavin was in a state of suppressed anger.

'You are a prig,' he retorted, 'and in some ways ignorant. You
do not know Morocco, so I shall tell you that there it is a custom,

an accepted thing, that young men of position spend some years in the houses of elder men as adopted sons. In return for the love and affection that they give, they receive advancement and worldliness. No harm is ever done to the boy who, as a married man or in later life, looks back upon his sponsor with feelings of affection. What is wrong with that?'

'Nothing,' replied Richard, '– in Morocco. Isn't that the point?'

They went on talking for hours, until the bottle was empty and the paraffin lamp had gone out and a grey dawn was peeping through the fog of cigarette smoke. Richard finally rose from the table, leaving Gavin to sit it out alone in the lightening dawn, and later he heard Gavin go outside. 'When he did not immediately return I went to the door to see if all was well with him,' Richard was to write. 'He was standing quite still on a rock above the sea, his eyes apparently fixed on the red dawn flaring over Camusfeàrna.'

Richard Frere had got to know Gavin moderately well during the months he had been working on Isle Ornsay, and had begun to respect him as a brilliantly talented and larger than life man who was always capable of surprises. Gradually he formed a picture of the contradictoriness of Gavin's character and the opposites of which it was composed. Gavin, he perceived, was endowed with a keen intelligence, sharp wit and a powerful memory, yet in practical matters he was a dunce. He quickly lost his temper with the day-to-day irritations of life and the minor foibles of human behaviour, yet displayed almost Christ-like forgiveness when laid low by major catastrophe and colossal human error. He could be full of fun and humour one moment and overwhelmingly black and gloomy the next; generous or mean, compassionate or vindictive, stoic or neurotic, brave or timid. In spite of his apparent self-confidence and urbanity he was essentially a shy person; and in spite of his touching faith in the perfectibility of human nature among the young, he viewed all adults as potentially dangerous and treacherous, and used his power to flatter and charm them quite cynically, even resorting to bribery to buy their loyalty or friendship. Essentially, Richard decided, Gavin was a man of extremes, and uncompromising in all things – especially when he had had a few whiskies.

For all Gavin's flaws, Richard had come to quite like him. But he did not expect to be involved in his affairs again, for he judged that Gavin's finances were in a state of such terminal decline that he would be unable to afford any ambitious new projects in the future. In this he misjudged Gavin's resilience, his imperviousness to the very idea of retrenchment. Early in September Gavin completed his childhood autobiography. 'The MS has, thank God, been very well received,' he wrote to a friend; 'publishers say it's the best thing I've done, which is a boast, because I find any stationary position (not moving forward) intolerable.' Shortly afterwards he collected the balance of the advance due on delivery, which restored his financial equilibrium, if only momentarily, for Gavin had promised his family that the book would not be published during the lifetime of his mother, now an ailing old lady in her late eighties. In the brief interval of illusory solvency that followed he again approached the Freres. Would they, he asked them, consider converting his Kyleakin lighthouse cottages? This time he offered to pay for their services, but the figure he mentioned was so derisory that Joan declined to be involved, leaving Richard to do the conversion alone – this time to Gavin's own design. Richard looked forward to the work. He had already experienced a nostalgic yearning for the solitary island life and the yelp and slap of the sea; besides, he loved a challenge.

The layout of the cottages on Kyleakin Island was much the same as that at Isle Ornsay, but their condition was far worse. The moist salt air had wreaked far greater havoc, some of the wooden floors had rotted away, and rubble and dust lay everywhere. 'It was by far the most depressing place in which I have ever expected to live,' Richard noted. 'It was like going back several stages in evolution.' Unlike Isle Ornsay, Eilean Ban was a true island, exposed to every vagary of wind and sea in the middle of a deep, exposed shipping channel through which the wild ocean tide rushed like a mill race. Coming and going with building materials and supplies in a small, open boat was not something that could be undertaken lightly, and one false step could easily lead to disaster – especially now that winter, with its violent storms and hurricane winds, was fast approaching.

Fortunately Richard was not alone this time, for Terry Nutkins had arrived to lend a hand for a month or two, bringing with him his dog and two wildcats – a male and a female hand-reared from kittenhood by himself and his friend Wendy Stewart. Terry had brought about a reconciliation with Gavin following the fracas of two years before, and though he was no longer part of the Sandaig establishment he was happy to work on Eilean Ban for as long as he was needed. Richard was grateful for the young man's help and company, for he found Terry a tough, amiable and hard-working companion, as well as a handy cook and a first-rate seaman. Not long afterward they were joined by another of Gavin's ex-employees, Philip Alpin, who had left Sandaig and enrolled on an adventure course a short while before and who now sought an opportunity to put the character-forming benefits of this experience to practical effect. As the Atlantic wind roared in and the first snows settled on the encircling mountain peaks, the three men settled down like a marooned polar party to battle with the winter and transform Gavin's dream into reality.

Gavin himself, meanwhile, was much preoccupied elsewhere. He wrote to Constance McNab: 'I finished my book (autobiography of my first seventeen years) *ahead* of schedule, and have now started on a "standpoint" work of philosophy/psychology which I shall continue at the same time as trying to complete the Glaoui over the next year.' To this 'standpoint' work, which was intended as a work of serious and original intellectual research in the field of comparative psychology, Gavin was to give the title *The Heritage of Fear* – a thesis concerning the roots of human and animal behaviour which he was to claim as 'my great discovery' and 'an entirely new idea'. He was to toy with this theme off and on over the next year or two, but for the moment his attention was drawn to the problems of animal behaviour at a more practical and immediate level.

Earlier in the year he had acquired a Pyrenean mountain dog, a magnificent white-coated creature whose original owner had been unable to cope with the animal's aggressive nature. Gavin told Constance: 'It was hubris to take on a dog already classified as dangerous, which is now causing us infinite trouble by menacing humans and killing sheep. In such creatures constant contact is necessary, and even a short absence makes havoc. With infinite regret we are castrating the dog as the only alternative to killing him. I hate the idea of any mutilation, and that one in a glorious male animal revolts me.' To carry out the operation Gavin called on the services of Donald MacLennan, the vet from Skye.

'He had some way-out ideas on a lot of things,' MacLennan recalled, and nobody could dissuade him until he'd proved that they were wrong himself. He had a notion that if he caught the dog in the act of attacking one of the sheep around Sandaig, and wrapped him in the skin of the dead sheep and practically suffocated him in it, it would stop him. So he tried it, but with no success. He tried everything, and eventually he decided the only thing to do was to castrate him. I was hoping and praying that he wouldn't go through with this, but lo and behold, he did.

Anyway, when the appointed day arrived and I came walking down through the wood, loaded with all my bits and pieces, I was absolutely dreading it. I went into the house and the first thing I saw was a tumbler of whisky. So I looked at it and said: 'Is that for me?' And he said: 'Yes, it'll help you tackle the dog.' And I said: 'If I drank half that I'd be seeing two dogs and the good Lord knows one's enough.' So anyway we started and everything went just like clockwork . . . Yes, he had a tremendous way with animals.

Gavin was confronted with a new year as bleak and daunting as any he had ever encountered. He had crashed his Mercedes just before Christmas, three boats had been lost in stormy weather at Sandaig, and he was besieged by Moroccans, for Ahmed was at Sandaig to help with the final stages of the Glaoui book, and Si Mohammed el-Khizzioui, the Glaoui's former secretary, was staying with friends of Gavin's at Stirling, where he seemed to have developed exaggerated expectations of Gavin's personal wealth. These were mere aggravations, however. Far worse was to follow. 'The year 1965 opened with a succession of body-blows so massive,' Gavin was to write, 'that I came very near to being knocked clean out of the ring altogether.'

The cause of this débâcle was one Gianfranco Alliata, Prince of Montereale, a former Monarchist member of the Italian Parliament then living in Rome, who on 13 February 1965 brought an action for libel at the Queen's Bench Division of the High Court of Justice in London against Gavin Maxwell and his publishers, Longmans Green & Co.

The basis of the Prince's complaint lay in certain passages in *God Protect Me from My Friends*, which had been published in Britain nine years previously. In 1958 an Italian court had found Gavin guilty on a charge of criminal libel brought by Italy's former Minister of Posts and Telegraphs, Bernardo Mattarella, and Gavin had been sentenced to eight months in prison (which he never served) and fined £3000 (which he paid). Gavin had believed that that was the end of the matter, but in September 1962 the Prince Alliata, a friend of Mattarella, announced that he too intended to bring a libel action against him, this time in an English court, on the grounds that the book was injurious to his character and reputation (such as it was, for he had already been tried for bigamy in both an Italian and a Brazilian court).

Gavin became anxious as the date of the case drew near. Before the opening hearing he had been given a word of advice by Tony Lincoln, the barrister friend who rented a *pied-à-terre* in Gavin's house in Paultons Square. 'He was terribly wound up the night before the hearing,' Lincoln recalled. 'So much so that at one point he interrupted our conversation, went to the window, pulled back the curtain and looked nervously out. "The Mafia are after me," he said. "They've got men outside." I pleaded with him not to wear his dark glasses in court. The glasses made him look terribly sinister – more like a Sicilian *mafioso* than a reputable Scottish author – but he chose to ignore my advice.'

Prince Alliata was represented in court by Mr Colin Duncan, Q.C. The defamatory passages in *God Protect Me from My Friends*, he contended, were based on testimony given by Salvatore Giuliano's lieutenant, Gaspare Pisciotta, at the trial of Giuliano's followers at Viterbo in 1951. Pisciotta alleged that Prince Alliata had used his political position and influence to aid and abet Giuliano, and had conspired with him to perpetrate a massacre at a 1947 May Day rally of the Communist Party at Portella della Ginestra, in Sicily, in which at least eight people had been shot dead and thirty-three wounded. 'Alliata was the power behind Giuliano's throne,' Gavin had quoted Pisciotta as saying, 'without whom Giuliano never moved, and in whom he had absolute trust.'

. Gavin and his publishers were represented by David Hirst, who denied that the words were defamatory and claimed qualified privilege. No one seemed to doubt that Gavin would win the case, but the process proved complicated and lasted several days. By the second day it was evident that things were not going well for Gavin. 'The whole trial was to me a sort of nightmare,' he wrote afterwards. 'I found it difficult to believe what was happening . . .

I began to suffer an acute sense of unreality, doubting my ability to add up even a number of years that would fit on to the fingers of one hand; this did not increase my own coherence in the witness box . . . And so it dragged on day after day. Soon I felt that I was not enjoying the judge's sympathy and after a while I had lost the jury's too.'

The fact that he had worked on the disputed book so long ago and was no longer master of all the details it contained contributed in part to his incoherent performance in the witness box; it was not that which lost him the sympathy of the court, however, but his dark glasses. They were not just dark, they were black, and totally opaque; they obscured a large part of his face and invariably induced a negative reaction in any person who did not know him. 'As I had predicted,' Anthony Lincoln commented afterwards, 'the glasses completely lost him the trust of the court.'

As he sat there, feeling miserable, indignant and maligned, Gavin must have rued the day ten years before when he ignored the advice of his publisher's libel lawyer to remove the name of Alliata from his manuscript, or overlooked the fact that Alliata's alleged complicity in the May Day massacre had been investigated and dismissed by an Italian court in 1953. Pisciotta had been proved a liar at his trial, the judge pointed out in his summing up on 22 February, and his allegations against Prince Alliata were known to have been unfounded. 'To repeat a libel was to publish a fresh libel,' the judge added. 'Why repeat it if it was a lie in the first instance?' Turning to the evidence Gavin had given in court, the judge had this to say: 'Mr Maxwell went so far as to say to the jury that these statements in *God Protect Me from My Friends* were put in the friendliest spirit . . . If that was the act of a friend, the jury might think that Prince Alliata might well say, "God protect me from my friends"!'

The jury retired, and returned a little under two hours later. In court Prince Alliata had stated that he wished the defendants to be '*severamente puniti*'. But though the jury's verdict was in favour of Alliata, this had not been a criminal case under British law, so there was no question of punishing the guilty parties, only of compensating the plaintiff for his possible loss of reputation in England. As he was not a public figure in that country he was awarded damages of only £400. However, the court decided that Gavin and his publisher were liable for the costs of both sides, which ran into five figures. 'I walked out of the court,' Gavin recalled, 'knowing that it would be years, if ever, before I could pay my share. I hope I shall meet his Lordship in an after life – if we are heading in the same direction.'

Gavin had barely had time to settle back in at Sandaig than more grave news forced him to return to the south again. To a friend, Bruno de Hamel, he reported:

Within a week of the end of the Alliata case my mother (eighty-seven) had another stroke, and sank very gradually until she died on 18 March, having survived six days after the doctors had said she couldn't possibly last more than another twenty-four hours. My sister and I sat with her right round the clock, and when it was over there was not only exhaustion but a mass of business matters and then several hundred letters of condolence to answer. In the end I only got back here yesterday evening [5 April].

The financial crisis is at least temporarily solved. I did not expect to inherit anything from my mother, because when the matter was last discussed three years ago I was so stinking rich that I agreed to waive my inheritance in favour of my brothers and sister – but in the event it turned out that my mother – bless her heart – had chosen to ignore this agreement and left her original will as it stood. Thus averting disaster not at the eleventh hour but, as you might say, at five minutes to twelve.

But Gavin was wrong in believing that disaster had been averted. He unwisely paid a portion of his legacy of £9000 into his ailing company's account, and saw it instantly gobbled up without trace. A terrible financial crisis was gathering like a storm front, and he picked up the threads of daily existence at Sandaig with a feeling of deep foreboding, relieved only by the brief return of the wild geese to Camusfeàrna for the last time.

The geese were the descendants of the small brood of unfledged greylags Gavin had brought to Sandaig from Monreith many years before – birds that were themselves descendants of the greylags he had wing-tipped in Wigtown Bay in the pre-war days when he had been an ardent wildfowler. Every spring after that the geese had returned from their unknown winter feeding grounds to breed on

the reedy little lochan across the road from the MacLeods' house
at Tormor, a mile or so above Sandaig. Their arrival late in April
or May had always been one of the dramatic events in the Sandaig
year, for to Gavin the geese were the very symbol of freedom, of
the vast windswept spaces and the boundless sky, their wild haunting cry – 'like a bugle on a falling cadence . . . a tumbling cascade
of silver trumpets' – the authentic sound of the north.

Now, in the late spring of 1965, he heard the geese again – 'far
away, thin and clear at first, then fainter and buffeted by a stiff
southerly breeze that drove before it big shapeless white clouds
above an ink-dark sea'. There were five of them, heading inland
high over Sandaig in a tiny but perfect V formation. Gavin called
out to them, and they checked their course a moment, as if in
acknowledgment of the fact that they were indeed the Sandaig
geese, then passed on out of sight in the direction of Tormor. Five
minutes later they returned, slanting steeply down on outstretched
wings from the skyline of the hill, to alight on the turf in front of
the house – two ganders and three geese.

One pair left almost immediately to nest inland in one of the
many hill-lochs far above the house and was never seen again. A
solitary unpaired goose stayed alone in the vicinity of the Sandaig
beaches until she was killed by a local wildcat or fox. The remaining
pair nested on the lochan at Tormor, as they had always done. But
Mary and John Donald MacLeod, Gavin's nearest neighbours for
so many years, had recently left the area, and their roadside cottage
lay shuttered and empty. Without their protective presence the birds
were at the mercy of any human who happened to pass along that
lonely road. The female did not even lay, and one day the male
was found floating lifeless among the reeds, shot through the neck
at close range. His mate disappeared soon afterwards, and no wild
goose ever came back to Camusfeàrna again. 'With their absence,'
Gavin recorded, 'something, for me mystic, had gone forever.'

It was probably at this point that Gavin's mind began to turn to
the possibility, inconceivable in the past, that he should one day
leave Sandaig. The place was dying, and he found no more joy in
it, or indeed in anything in his present life. Though he rarely found
himself alone these days, he enjoyed no close or meaningful
relationship, and began to retreat bit by bit from contact with his
former friends and acquaintances. The stream of summer visitors

of former years dried to a trickle, and his once voluminous correspondence was reduced to a few brief and perfunctory notes. All Gavin's available time and energy was now concentrated on writing his books and fighting for survival. Such a dour, single-minded existence inevitably constricted not only his physical movements but his intellectual horizons as well; gone, for the moment, was the infectious fun, the tireless curiosity, the unbounded enthusiasm, the ceaseless quest that marked the positive side of his contrary nature. The one bright beacon in his life was the lighthouse property on Eilean Ban, which was now nearing completion.

All through the brief days of the northern winter, with their storms and winds and frosts, Richard Frere had laboured long and loyally at converting the two run-down cottages on Kyleakin into a single, sumptuous residence along the lines of Gavin's design. It had not been plain sailing. The *Eider*, the dinghy Richard used to come and go from the island, was broken up by a combination of high wind and tide while beached at Kyle; and her replacement, a leaky ex-lifeboat called the *Assunta*, sank at her moorings while laden with coal, sand and cement (though she was salvaged soon after). Nor did Richard's two young assistants last long. Terry Nutkins walked out when Gavin forbade Wendy Stewart from visiting the island to see the wildcats she had helped rear; and once Terry had gone Philip Alpin lost heart and asked to go too. But it was not just Terry's departure which prompted Philip to leave; it was also fear. Quite simply, the island terrified him – as it terrified others who came within range of its restless ghosts and hidden, haunting voices.

Gavin had always in one way or another been associated with the supernatural and the paranormal. John Hillaby had noted his susceptibility to superstition as far back as the sharking days; and Gavin had always half-believed in Kathleen Raine's supposed psychic powers. He was cautiously predisposed to accept that the supernatural formed an imperfectly understood part of the natural phenomena of existence – though he was, as he put it, 'essentially of the faithless generation that waited for a sign.'

Such signs were not lacking. In the course of a week during the previous summer Sandaig had been visited by a poltergeist that had hurled a marmalade pot a full six feet off a shelf in the kitchen parlour (this was witnessed by Jimmy Watt and Richard Frere as well as Gavin himself), propelled a kitchen windowpane five feet into Edal's enclosure outside, projected a pile of gramophone records into a neat pile in the middle of the living-room floor, flipped a baby's bottle in Gavin's face, and tossed a laundry basket half the length of the annexe coat room. The sheer weight of paranormal evidence forced Gavin to abandon his scepticism.

No further supernatural manifestations occurred within Gavin's domain until Philip Alpin set foot on Kyleakin Island. Then, as Richard Frere put it, 'he had come into range of the island's psychic wavelength, and his subconscious mind had been invaded'.

That there was something on the island which could not be explained in ordinary terms had been known to several generations of lighthouse-keepers. The experiences of all who had lived in the house which Gavin now owned on Eilean Ban had a common, unvarying pattern. First there were the sounds. These came from just outside the house, rather than within it, and they were of two kinds – low-pitched, incoherent human voices, muttering in a language that was neither English nor Gaelic, sometimes rising and falling as if in argument; and loud metallic clangs. Such sounds were usually heard in the small hours of the morning, but only in the autumn and winter, and not by everyone – Gavin, it seems, never heard them (and neither did I), but Richard Frere did, though only after Philip Alpin arrived to help him late in 1964.

Alpin was frightened from the outset. At night he could not abide to be left alone in the house, and would follow Richard about like a shadow, even out into the dark when Richard went down to the water's edge to check the boat before turning in for the night. Once Richard found him buried under a huge pile of bedclothes with a large spanner in his hand. 'He had heard many voices,' Richard reported to Gavin, 'and he was very, very frightened.' So frightened that in January he asked to be allowed to leave the island, and was put on the first train home.

Now Richard was alone on Kyleakin. For the first three nights he slept soundly. On the fourth night a strong south-westerly wind was blowing and he slept fitfully. Shortly after 3 a.m., when the wind had dropped and the rain had started to fall, he was awakened by a high-pitched metallic clang. A few minutes later, as the old moon rose over the sea, voices sounded outside, and seemed to move down the north side of the house from west to east. The voices continued for about ten minutes, the clang being repeated two or three times, but strangely the sounds did not unnerve

Richard unduly, for the atmosphere inside the house was a benevolent one, and he felt at ease. In the subsequent weeks he heard the same performance repeated often again, though never in stormy conditions, and by March it was all over.

Richard Frere was an eminently rational and level-headed man, but even he was confounded by the ghostly voices of Eilean Ban. On Isle Ornsay he had been subject to a similar barrage of night noises, but he had been able to trace each to its normal, physical cause. This was not the case on Eilean Ban, for no normal cause was ever found, and he was left with nothing but the local legend by way of explanation. Seven hundred years ago it seemed that King Haco of Norway anchored his invasion fleet in the lee of Eilean Ban on the eve of his last, disastrous attempt to conquer Scotland. From him is derived the name of Kyleakin – the Narrows of Haco – and it is to the ghosts of his time-locked army that the voices on the lighthouse island are popularly attributed in the area.

There were also visual apparitions, which were even more difficult to account for – kilted figures, dancing lights, ships that vanished into thin air. The first of these incidents to take place after Gavin acquired the island occurred in April 1965, shortly after the night voices had ceased, when a number of people in Kyleakin village on Skye saw a lamp burning in the kitchen window of the lighthouse cottage, though electricity had not yet been installed and the house was empty and securely locked at the time. Some weeks later a friend of Richard's, a clear-headed, no-nonsense businessman, saw a stranger come up the path round the house and then, to his complete bafflement, vanish into thin air before his very eyes.

These mysterious events did not hinder Richard Frere's progress towards the completion of his task. The dark, dank, dingy cavern of seven months ago had been transformed into a bright, sumptuous house, with a great vista of Loch Alsh and Loch Duich to the distant peaks of the Five Sisters of Kintail, and a single spectacularly beautiful sitting room all of forty feet in length, with windows looking across to Skye and furnishings which Gavin himself had chosen.

Gavin was not at hand to admire the finished property on Eilean Ban. For some months he had been dreaming up schemes for further exploiting the commercial potential of his two lighthouse properties. Two such schemes won his particular favour – a dolphinarium at Isle Ornsay and a commercial eider-breeding colony (for the production of eider down) on Eilean Ban. The latter, about which he had been thinking in a desultory way for several years, was the more practical project. There had always been a small eider-breeding colony on one of the Sandaig Islands, but Gavin's tenure at Sandaig had been too tenuous and the eider colony too tiny to allow him to develop the breeding site even on an experimental basis. But Kyleakin Island – or more exactly a small uninhabited island immediately adjacent to it – offered a perfect site. Thirty pairs already bred there every summer, and by farming them and increasing their number Gavin hoped he might be able to establish a minor industry in the area.

Within only a week or two of his purchase of the lighthouse properties in October 1963, therefore, he sought the advice of his friend Peter Scott at Slimbridge Wildfowl Trust about raising eider ducklings in the wild. Towards the end of May 1965, when the Kyleakin Island property was nearing completion, Gavin took the matter up again in a more serious way. There was now a cogent extra reason for pursuing the project, for as soon as he finished his interminably delayed book about the Glaoui he planned to begin a new book provisionally entitled *The Two Lighthouses*. Clearly, the story of his struggle to start an eider farm on a West Highland island could form an important part of his new work, and make the project doubly worthwhile.

Gavin discovered that in Iceland eider ducks had been farmed for their down for some eight hundred years, and on Peter Scott's recommendation he got in touch with Iceland's greatest living naturalist, Dr Finnur Gudmundsson, with a view to visiting his country and learning the techniques of eider farming at first hand from local experts. On 11 June, with Jimmy Watt for company, Gavin took a plane from Glasgow to Reykjavic to begin a short fact-finding tour of the eider farms in that remote, sub-Arctic island.

Gavin disliked Iceland's capital town – the natives were hostile, he found, and the cost of whisky astronomical – but enthused enormously about the vast wilderness that occupied most of the interior beyond – a land of fire and lava, ice and glacier. Heading for Dr Gudmundsson's remote fortress island far to the north they passed through an almost empty country of bare hills, iceberg-filled fjords, black lava-sand beaches, snowy mountains, belching geysers and high falls, populated by a myriad of birds, huge herds of wild ponies, gigantic flocks of silent, bizarrely-coloured sheep, and dense, loudly humming clouds of biting black-fly that filled the lower air like an uninhabitable fog.

Some of the eider colonies Gavin visited were surreal places, more like country fairs or gipsy encampments than duck-breeding sites, for the nesting birds were attracted by multicoloured flags, strings of red and white pennants and bunting, and whirring children's windmills stuck in the ground around their nests. His notebook rapidly filled with the facts and figures of the business. Eider down came from the lining of an eider duck's nest once the critical early stage of egg incubation was complete. It was not superior to the down of any other duck, but the eider could be concentrated in greater numbers than other species, which made it far more valuable for commercial farming. Thirty nests yielded a pound of down (worth about £10 in 1965), and in a peak year Iceland produced about 4½ tons of eider down for export (worth about £100,000 at that time). Already Gavin was calculating how many pairs of eiders his own island could hold, and seeing it in his mind's eye fluttering with flags.

When he returned to Sandaig in the last week of June, Gavin felt confident he could establish a commercial eider farm on Kyleakin Island's neighbour (which was to be known henceforth as Eider Island). He quickly assembled his Iceland notes into a report which he circulated to all bodies he thought might be interested in supporting a new industry for the crofting population of the Scottish West Highlands and Islands, where eiders in large numbers already bred in a natural state. Gavin hoped that, using the techniques he had learned in Iceland, he could raise the eider population on Eider Island from thirty to two thousand. But many vicissitudes, both financial and personal, were to intervene before he was in a position to begin the experiment.

At the end of June Gavin made a lightning visit to Eilean Ban, bubbling over with his Iceland adventures. He cast a cursory glance round the cottage, gave Richard his perfunctory thanks for all he had done, and rushed off.

Richard was not amused. Gavin, he knew, was planning to hold a house-warming party on the island for some of his friends in a few days' time, and it was evident that neither he nor Joan, who had worked long and hard to transform the houses on both islands,

would be invited. Richard felt deflated and somewhat bitter. Deject-
edly he finished the few jobs that remained to be done, closed the
house, took the boat back to Kyle for the last time, and went home.
Though he had come to feel some rapport with Gavin, he did not
at this time count himself as one of his friends, and he did not
expect to hear from him again.

The day after Richard left the island Gavin returned to it in *Polar
Star*, bringing with him a working party to help prepare the house
for its first residential occupation. They worked all day, and did
not leave till the twilight afterglow of late evening began to fade.
The tide was running at about eight knots as it raced through the
narrows of the Sound. Gavin, who was at the wheel, brought the
boat round and nudged her in towards the pier at Kylerhea against
the swirling tide; but he was thirty feet too far inshore, and as
Jimmy Watt, the starboard lookout, called out in alarm, Gavin felt
the sickening crunch of keel against rock once again. It was not
until dawn that *Polar Star* was floated off on the returning tide and
towed ignominiously away for another round of repairs to her
long-suffering hull.

This was only the first of a series of accidents and setbacks which
followed in such rapid succession that they seemed like the urgent
harbingers of ill-omen.

A few days after the *Polar Star* ran aground, Gavin's small house-
warming party assembled on Kyleakin Island. Some of the guests
– the Earl and Countess of Dalhousie, and their daughter, Elizabeth,
Countess of Scarborough, and Susan Stirling, the sister-in-law of
Colonel David Stirling – were old friends and relatives. Some –
like former naval officer and retired businessman Bruno de Hamel
and his wife – were almost brand new. 'It was a *very* nice house
party,' Bruno de Hamel recalled, 'and Gavin was very relaxed. At
Sandaig he was a lord in a labourer's cottage, but at this first gathering on Kyleakin Island he was able to dispense hospitality like a
lord in his own right.' Among the many toasts that night was one
proposed by Jimmy Watt, who gave thanks to Richard Frere for
bringing 'the blessings of electric light' to the house. As he stood
to raise his glass Jimmy reached out a hand to steady himself against
one of the light-brackets on the wall, and received such a powerful
electric shock that he was thrown to the floor, where for a brief
moment he lay unconscious.

As if this was not enough, Gavin himself was struck down a

week or two later by a return of his old wartime duodenal ulcer. So excruciating was the pain that he was almost incapable of speech, and the Glenelg doctor – a new arrival by the name of Tony Dunlop – had to give him two injections of morphia before driving him off to hospital in Inverness for tests. On the morning of 4 August the hospital specialist pronounced the results. Gavin's condition was the result of an acute exacerbation of an ulcer of long standing. Three courses of action were possible – an immediate gastrectomy, or two months' hospital treatment without surgery, or an operation in November, if Gavin was prepared to take the risk of waiting that long. Fearful of further abdominal surgery, and overwhelmed by pressing work commitments, Gavin chose the last of the three options.

A few hours later, while he was still in hospital, Gavin received a phone call from London. That morning an emergency meeting of the directors of Gavin Maxwell Enterprises had been held at Paultons Square to discuss the latest deterioration in the company's affairs. Gavin had been due to attend the meeting, but now the phone call gave him the conclusions his directors had reached without him. The news was frankly bleak. GME faced a major, perhaps terminal, crisis. The gap between income and expenditure yawned like a chasm, and unpaid debts soared heavenwards. The directors' recommendations shocked Gavin profoundly: it seemed that all the company's assets, including the two lighthouses, would have to be sold at once, Sandaig closed down and the otters put in a zoo.

THIRTY-ONE

On the rocks

Whither is fled the visionary gleam?
Where is it now, the glory and the dream?
WILLIAM WORDSWORTH, *'Ode:*
Intimations of Immortality'

The crisis had begun to break in the preceding April. 'I was horrified
when I saw the final accountants' breakdown of the previous financial situation,' Gavin had written to Bruno de Hamel. 'My *average*
earned income for the three financial years ending April '64 had
been £22,312.3.6. The only thing I could account for was the 3/6d.
The mess we got into was basically due to letting other people
manage expenditure – which I am not going to allow to happen
again.' Gavin had stood the truth on its head, as Peter Janson-Smith
only too clearly perceived: 'Gavin's financial troubles were due
entirely to his total inability to see reason and stop buying things
for inflated prices whenever he felt like it.' Bruno de Hamel was
soon to find this out for himself the hard way.

A veteran of Dunkirk, de Hamel was well versed in the drama
of the last-ditch stand; but no rearguard action in his experience
was so desperate or vexatious as Gavin Maxwell's ill-conceived
retreat from solvency.

'I liked Gavin in the beginning,' Bruno was to recall. 'The life
he was leading was exceedingly romantic, and I rather admired
this. And he was a rebel – a highly articulate rebel – and I admired
that, too. He was very generous of spirit, but he couldn't afford
to be generous in any other way – he was almost totally broke and
I was never paid a penny for my services.' The dire state of Gavin's
collapsing company had been attributed by the accountants to faulty
internal accounting – what Gavin was to call 'mismanagement of
company affairs'. A scapegoat was required, and the head that
finally rolled was that of the hapless Michael Cuddy, who ran the
London office – a loyal and conscientious young man whose

position had always been untenable, for he was powerless to control Gavin's spending. 'He was very demanding,' Michael Cuddy recalled,

> always wanting things and thinking up new schemes and ideas that cost money. I found it very difficult. I was not part of the Sandaig set-up and I felt isolated. If I'd been a different, stronger personality I might have been able to cope with him. I tried to do what Gavin wanted but this was not necessarily what he needed for his own good. So I was fired. It was a very unpleasant, emotional meeting. Gavin was white with anger. He said the way I had run things had imperilled the company. He was extremely aggressive. It hurt me like a stab in the back. I'd counted him as one of the three close friends I'd had in my life and I loved working for him. My life had changed after I met him. He had given me a tremendous chance and I felt grateful to him and loved him as a friend. But now I felt very bitter.

Gavin's treatment of Michael Cuddy so outraged Raef Payne that it led him to quarrel with his old friend for the first time in years. For the moment Gavin agreed to keep Michael Cuddy on as his private secretary, while appointing Bruno de Hamel as the company's new broom. The picture Bruno presented at the board meeting on 4 August was a depressing one, and his recommendations were painful. The company's debts would have to be liquidated as quickly as possible, a lot of precious possessions would have to be sold, and Gavin's spending would have to submit to the strictest company control. For Gavin, to whom the very idea of retrenchment was anathema, these words were like a match to a powder keg. Bruno de Hamel recalled:

> I think he looked on me as a magician who could do a few tricks and get him out of trouble. But as soon as I had worked out what the problem was and advised him what to do about it, he didn't want to know. Everything stemmed from his blind refusal to face the problems of his own creation. That's why he blamed it on everyone else – he wouldn't face up to his own problems. He was very lofty about money – his spending was completely out of control. He'd earned a great

deal of money in the years before but somehow he'd eaten his way through the lot, leaving a net profit of just £52. Agreed, Sandaig was a rather expensive, impractical place, but it wasn't just that – it was the boats, the cars, the lighthouses, the London flats, the foreign travels (he spent a fortune on Iceland) – a great big ego trip, and a very expensive one, which the otters paid for. It was a bit of the old seigneur coming out – a *folie de grandeur*, really. But it was difficult to get him to see reason. We formed a finance control committee but the moment we tried to exert some control over his spending he became very perverse. He didn't really respect our function at all. One way he showed his disdain was to refer a lot of damn silly little questions to a board meeting, so that you'd have a bunch of busy, responsible professional men – a top literary agent (Peter Janson-Smith), a senior accountant (Ron Parker), a leading barrister (Robin McEwen) and the Master in College at Eton (Raef Payne) – sitting round a table debating whether to authorise the mending of Gavin's dishwasher or the purchase of a deep freeze instead! But the main question of balancing expenditure with income he never addressed to us at all.

It wasn't really a question of getting rid of the otters and closing Sandaig down. He could have kept the Sandaig enclave going, with all its special mystery and mystique. It was the empire building that broke him – that and the awful Alliata case out of the blue. All I was trying to do was point out that his affairs were in a mess but that he could get out of it if he took the proper steps. He was obviously a very successful writer, but I felt that as a writer he shouldn't be burdened with all this. 'It's distracting you,' I told him, 'it's taking all your time and energy. You'll never write properly until you get out of this mess.' But the moment you tried to help him he accused you of running his life. For a while I tried to pull him round but he wouldn't play ball at all, and then he became really quite abusive and most unpleasant. 'You've just been *flirting* with me!' he said, very rudely. That took my breath away – it was quite uncalled for. So I resigned. I never saw or spoke to him again.

Looking back, it's obvious that *Ring of Bright Water* went to his head, blew his mind. He'd had a lean time up to then. He'd lost his shirt on the sharks, never earned any money with his books, and then one of them landed him up in court. So when he struck gold with *Ring* it was a miraculous transformation for him – and it happened to coincide with his aristocratic aspirations, to be able to cut a dash and be a bit of a lad. Riches to rags to riches and back to rags again – that was his story.

So on 4 August Gavin left the hospital in Inverness and returned to Sandaig determined to find his own solution to his financial crisis. He felt bound to reject Bruno de Hamel's proposals because he realised they would have deprived him of his image, his mystique and his ménage. The proposals only made sense from a purely practical point of view. That apart, they would have destroyed him. Above all he was determined to hang on to his lighthouses, for losing them would mean the end of his cherished eider project, and at that time there was nothing in his life to replace it. Taking over the function of managing director himself, he began to take such actions as he thought necessary.

First he set about trying to raise mortgages on the lighthouses. Then he closed down the London end of the business altogether, moving out of Paultons Square (where all but the basement had been taken over by Robin McEwen and Anthony Lincoln) into a small, rented *pied-à-terre* in the basement of Vladimir Daskaloff's large house at 11 The Boltons in Kensington. Next he began to turn his attention to Sandaig, whose running costs now exceeded £7000 a year. But here his pruning was light and desultory, and his own fleet of cars and boats remained intact. To meet the cost of keeping the otters at Sandaig (approaching £20,000 a year in today's money) he proposed launching a public appeal, and persuaded the Scientific Director of the Zoological Society of London (Dr Harrison Matthews) and the Chairman of the World Wildlife Fund (Peter Scott) to act as Trustees.

For twelve hours a day Gavin sat at his desk – half the time devoted to trying to finish *Lords of the Atlas*, half to fighting the paper war against the creditors and the banks. There was no doubting his determination and his energy, but he had ignored the advice of his colleagues at his peril. By attempting to raise mortgages on the lighthouses he was opting to increase his burden of debt rather than reduce it. And the bills continued to roll in – a whole new avalanche of which even his fellow directors had been ignorant at the time of their crisis meeting. After having applied his mother's legacy to his company's debts he had no further private means. Next to nothing had been invested during those heady days when he had been at the peak of his affluence. His literary income, which he had once described as 'indecently large', had been reduced to a trickle, and though his autobiography of childhood, *The House of Elrig*, was published to great acclaim in October, it only slowed the tempo of his accelerating financial decline, for he was in hock to his publishers as he was to everyone else.

It was Gavin's tireless literary agent Peter Janson-Smith who almost single-handedly kept him afloat, now and in the years to come. Handling Gavin's frequent tantrums and often querulous and importunate demands with unruffled patience, Peter ceaselessly sought out and secured commissions for articles, reviews, broadcasts and foreign sales of books – anything that would stem the tide of his client's debt. In the process he became not only a business adviser to whom Gavin could always turn in times of trouble, but a good friend as well.

The House of Elrig was published in Britain on 4 October 1965, and in America not long after. The book was a nakedly honest and compulsively readable evocation of the traumas of a sensitive, dreamy, aristocratic misfit's childhood and adolescence, and of his deeply imprinted passion for the heather and bracken landscape of his desolate native Galloway – the antecedent of the Camusfeàrna of *Ring of Bright Water*.

Gavin's latest literary progeny was received with a united chorus of praise from the critics. 'Never has he written more powerfully,' declared the *Daily Telegraph*; 'He evokes an almost unbearable nostalgia.' The *Daily Mail* described Gavin as 'a seducer with words, demanding an intimacy with the reader which is hard to resist'. Julian Jebb, in the *Sunday Times*, enlarged on the theme of 'intimacy' as the essential clue to Gavin's writing as a whole: 'His otter books enjoyed their immense popularity because of this peculiar intimacy which he can generate between the reader and himself. They had the seductiveness of an enormously long letter from a close friend. But in a sense all his literary work has been preparing for this present book. The interweaving of anecdote, self-analysis and the discoveries of poetic sensibility make this the finest piece of writing Mr Maxwell has yet produced, an intricately conceived, enthralling self-portrait.'

Above: Terry Nutkins with Teko.

Right: Gavin and Teko.

Below: Teko running free in the surf in Sandaig Bay, 1961.

Above: Gavin in heroic Thoreau-esque pose carries a lame sheep down the hill to Sandaig, 1960.

Left: Gavin Maxwell and the Duke of Edinburgh chat at a Spinningdale house party-picnic, Sutherland, autumn 1962.

Below: Camusfeàrna under snow in the severe winter of 1961–2.

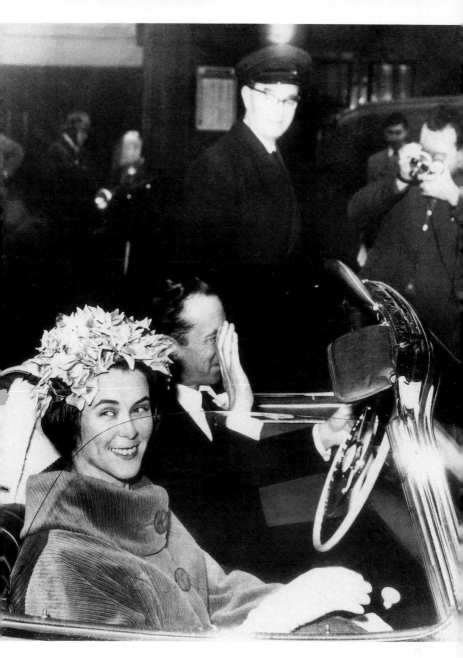

Gavin and Lavinia drive off in the Mercedes roadster after their wedding in Covent Garden in February 1962.

The Kasbah of the Lords of the Atlas at Telouet in the Moroccan High Atlas, where Gavin and Lavinia spent part of their honeymoon.

Gavin tending an injured climber in the High Atlas.

Monday on the day of her arrival.

Mossy and Monday in the early days of their sojourn at Sandaig, February 1962.

PEOPLE AND 'CREECHERS'

Above: Lavinia and Monday.

Left: Gavin and Dirk.

Below: Douglas Botting with Edal

Free at last, Teko surveys Sandaig's wild vistas with Andrew Scot. The spirit of the old Camusfeàrna is reborn, October 1967.

Early on the morning of 21 January 1968, the house at Sandaig still smoulders after the fire that had destroyed it during the night.

Left: Gavin in the long room of his new home, the lighthouse cottage on Kyleakin Island, as described on page 513.

Below: Richard Frere and Owl.

Left: Lisa van Gruisen and fox cub.

Below: Douglas Botting's last view of an ailing man and his ailing otter – Gavin and Malla, November 1968.

but his concentration was distracted by an eagle that swept low above him, driven by the wind, and when he looked for the deer again it had vanished into the murk. Gavin was left soaked and alone on the windswept hill, with the light fading and five miles to walk home in the dusk. But for a few hours he had escaped back into his real world, and he was content.

Miraculously, when Gavin returned to the hospital in Inverness for his dreaded gastrectomy a few weeks later, the X-rays revealed that his duodenal ulcer had vanished. He went back to Sandaig momentarily deluded that the tide had turned – so much so that he felt emboldened to initiate extensive alterations to the lighthouse cottage at Isle Ornsay, so that it could more profitably accommodate twelve paying guests instead of eight as at present. Once again he called on the services of Richard Frere. It was now nearly half a year since Richard had parted company with Gavin on cool terms, and he was so taken aback to hear Gavin's voice on the phone that he agreed to his proposition at once, without even bothering to discuss the details of the work or the contract. Why the instant capitulation, he asked himself afterwards? Had he become such an addict of island life that its call overcame all reason? Or was it Gavin himself? 'In truth he had his good side and his bad,' he reflected, 'and no perceptive man could deny that there was a certain persuasive magic about Maxwell.'

So Richard's wild Hebridean adventures began all over again. It was winter now, and the weather was black and stormy. Again the wind howled and the sea surged, and again Richard's dinghy sank to the bottom – twice, in fact, once with Richard on board. During this inclement time Richard saw nothing of Gavin, besieged in the dark, secluded hell that had once been his paradise. But he spoke to him occasionally on the telephone, and from those distant conversations across the gale-swept water he was able to gauge the progress of his desperate rearguard action. One midnight during a violent storm, when the sea was exploding against the lighthouse rock of Eilean Sionnach and hurling white spume against its dripping tower, Gavin rang again.

'It is a dreadful night, Richard,' he said; 'and a dreadful night for me as well.'

He had just been speaking with one of his more predatory creditors, and the encounter had depressed him. It was not just that,

The publishers were ecstatic. They had printed a first impression of twenty-five thousand copies, and sold more than half of them in the first week. By January the book was second in the bestseller list – above even *The Guinness Book of Records*. *The House of Elrig*, Longmans reminded Gavin, was 'a very important book for your future as a writer'. But he firmly resisted their invitation to write a sequel covering the next decade or so of his life. 'I demur for two reasons,' he wrote to them on 25 October: '(a) the awful libel spectre, and (b) I was such an intolerable young man!'

The new book stemmed, but did not reverse, the tide of debt. Somehow Gavin staggered along. The price of his freedom was servitude – and with it the fading of the vision of the ideal life and the hope for love, beauty, joy and tranquillity. Gavin's struggle was not just against humdrum adversity, but against the death of the spirit, enslaved and oppressed by routine. In October, as a break from the monotony of his desk work, he accepted an invitation to go deer stalking, hoping the tough physical challenge might prove to be the tonic he so sorely needed. It was more than that. It was a reaffirmation, a return to his roots. 'The days that I spent on the hill,' he recorded, 'gave me a feeling of complete and utter release, of a unity with nature that I had long lacked at Camusfeàrna.' One incident especially he remembered as precious manna to his parched spirit. He was standing on the top of a mist-covered hill, visibility down to twenty yards, the only sound the wet wind tearing in great gusts at his face and sodden clothes. He wrote: 'Suddenly, from far away, from the hidden hill-face beyond the gulf, borne thin and clear on the wind, wild and elemental, came the sound that during all the many years I have spent among the red deer of Scotland, in their aloof tempestuous territory of rock and mist, has never lost its fascination for me – the voice of the stag in rut . . . I stirred to that desolate music as I stirred to the whip of the wind and rain . . . This was my world, the cradle of my species, shared with the wild creatures; it was the only world I wanted, and I felt that I had no place at a writing desk.'

Then he heard the same wild voice again only fifty yards away, and it set his heart hammering. Instinctively he dropped to a prone position, and borne on the wind he could smell the strange, elusive, pungent, musky, sour-sweet smell of the rutting stag. He lay with his chin pressed to the ground, teeth chattering, rifle at the ready, though. There was a pause. Then he drew a long, melodramatic breath. 'Now Jimmy wants to leave,' he said, 'and I just can't go on.'

Gavin had been struck at his most vulnerable point. Jimmy Watt had been at Sandaig for eight years, and had proved Gavin's most loyal, trusted and valued friend. 'They were – as I had first and subsequently known them – the heart and soul of Camusfeàrna,' Richard was to record. The two of them were more like father and son, but now the time had come for Jimmy to spread his wings and make his own way in the wider world, beyond Sandaig's isolated ambience and the dominating influence of his possessive if benign guardian. Jimmy's decision hit Gavin hard. It was, he believed, 'the death-knell of the old Camusfeàrna'. It would be more than that. It would mark the end of what he had come to regard as his home and family, the loss of his one true and readily available ally in a hostile world, the one constant and unchanging face to which he could return in a wandering and turbulent life. With Jimmy gone, Gavin himself would be cast adrift, anchorless, rudderless, and desperately alone upon the swirling tide.

And not only that. Jimmy was the practical overseer of the place; it was he who kept this complex, vulnerable establishment, with all its buildings and boats and vehicles and human and animal inhabitants, in running order through every crisis. Jimmy was indispensable to Sandaig, and Gavin used every possible means to persuade him to stay. A protracted emotional tug-of-war ensued that paralleled the financial struggle. When Richard met Gavin a week or two later he seemed to have aged ten years. 'My God, Richard, I'm exhausted,' he said; 'Keeping up this front is hell.'

At the beginning of December Gavin finally delivered the manuscript of *Lords of the Atlas* to his publishers – six years after he had contracted for it. The reader's report was not encouraging. Anyone expecting 'a new Gavin Maxwell', the reader claimed, would be doomed to disappointment. The book was a long one and the story was complicated and confusing:

> I hardly know what to say about this book. I simply couldn't grasp it. Gavin only writes well when he is describing what he has seen and experienced. He has seen and experienced none of this book with the exception of a marvellous first chapter

when he describes the great unfinished Glaoui castle of Telouet
at more than eight thousand feet in the High Atlas. There is,
furthermore, one aspect of the whole thing that really worries
me. Where on earth did he get all this material from? I can't
imagine him ferreting about in French military archives. My
heart sank when I read in the Author's Foreword that Gavin
has borrowed heavily from *Morocco That Was* by the late
Walter Harris (the *Times* correspondent in Morocco before
1900). In point of fact, he has quoted practically *the whole* of
it! For myself, I can hardly detect the tone of Gavin's voice
except in the first chapter.

This was one man's view, and it was wide of the mark. Sublim-
inally, perhaps, Longman's reader was rueing the fact that *Lords of
the Atlas* was not a kind of sub-Saharan *Ring of Bright Water*. But
there were to be many readers who, judging the poetic lyricism of
Ring too rich and cloying for a modern palate, found the leaner,
sparer story-telling virtues of the Moroccan book more to their
taste, and would even vote it Gavin's finest work. For Gavin's
baroque, cruel tale of Moorish despotism handled a complex,
highly arcane saga in such a measured and masterly way that it was
destined to become a classic of its kind, an outstanding account of
the Arab world by a Western writer.

So Christmas approached, and with it a period of still airs and
calm seas. The snow fell on the hills and a kind of peace descended
on that sad, dejected house within the ring of bright water. At home
with his family on New Year's Eve, Richard Frere waited for the
chimes of Big Ben that ushered in 1966, then began to telephone
his greetings to absent friends. His good cheer was quickly dashed
when he came to call Gavin. 'Never,' he was to write, 'had there
been a man to knock the sun out of the sky so quickly.' Gavin, it
seemed, was alone, for Jimmy was out celebrating in the village.
Worse, Gavin was now sure Jimmy would leave Sandaig when he
himself got back from his next winter foray to North Africa. 'I
should not blame him,' he said. 'I suppose he must have a life of
his own.' Perhaps Richard ought to take over the company?

After he put the phone down Gavin made a call to Beryl Borders,
the young woman who had once typed his manuscripts in London
and had been on hand to console him after the death of Mij. For
personal reasons (she was in the middle of a marital break-up),

Beryl was now looking for a temporary asylum for herself and her pets. Gavin told her that in a few days' time he would be leaving Sandaig and going abroad, and invited her to move in at any time after that, for as long as she liked.

Late on that same New Year's Eve, far away in Sicily, Gavin's friend and collaborator Giuseppe sat writing a desperate letter as he waited for the chimes of midnight in his lonely room in Salvatore Giuliano's mountain village of Montelepre. Three months ago their mutual friend and colleague Danilo Dolci had openly accused Bernardo Mattarella, Minister for Foreign Trade in the Italian Government, of being a member of the Sicilian Mafia. This was the same Mattarella who had brought criminal libel charges against Gavin after the same accusation had been made in *God Protect Me from My Friends*. Now Mattarella was bringing Dolci to trial in Palermo on the same charge. As one of Dolci's closest aides in his crusade against poverty and violence in rural Sicily, Giuseppe knew that now he too was at the mercy of 'the friends' of 'The Friend', and he desperately needed to have word from his *padrino* – the one close ally and protector he could trust, who would understand and give him the strength and courage to face his perilous future.

'I've got used to feeling you very close to me in the last few days,' Giuseppe wrote, 'but even though you've always been present in spirit, not to have any word from you is a terrible thing for me . . . I am alone in the house here thinking about you as I never have before. In a few minutes I will drink a glass of wine to you and to destiny . . .

'I'm going to be here day after day waiting for some word from you, because all the rest, believe me *padrino*, doesn't have the slightest importance. Don't forget – I want to hear from you one way or another as soon as possible. I trust you. *Tanti baci.* Your godson.'

To this cry in the dark Giuseppe received no reply from a *padrino* as embattled, impoverished and benighted as he.

'You are doomed to live alone for ever,' a Siamese fortune-teller in Marrakesh had once warned Gavin, 'and like the Wandering Jew to wander and travel until you die.' This dire prediction, coming soon after the end of his honeymoon with Lavinia, had given him pause for thought at the time. Now it seemed the omen was coming true. For during the next two years Gavin was indeed to live a rootless and footloose existence – a nomadic life that was partly the consequence of circumstance and partly of the hopelessness and emptiness that now began to seize his inner being.

For some time Gavin had been planning a trip with his friend Raef Payne to Rewalsar, 150 miles north of the Indian hill town of Simla, where a refugee settlement had been established for Tibetans fleeing the Chinese occupation of their country. Gavin hoped that he might be able to collect material for a new book from interviews with the exiled Tibetans, a sociological study of the alienated and deprived rather along the lines of *The Ten Pains of Death*. When these plans fizzled out – at the end of the year the Tibetans were moved on to another camp further south, and by then Gavin couldn't afford the trip anyway – he decided to cut his losses and return to Morocco, ostensibly to undertake further research, but in reality to escape from the mess of his collapsing life at home.

For two months he wandered about the mountains and the desert south of the country with Raef Payne, his Berber linguist friend Ahmed, and a mule-driver from the Sous by the name of Boujamar. Compared with previous visits Gavin was desperately short of funds. 'Money melts,' he wrote to Jimmy Watt. 'How is the Treasury (may Allah fill it!)? As you see, I'm doing my best NOT TO WORRY – but I do rather dread my return and the bankruptcy proceedings . . . It's an odd feeling not having anything definite to do, and it's difficult to get used to. In a quiet way I fuss about eider islands and lighthouses and debts and mortgages and whether this year will be as awful as the last one, but it all seems a long way away – which, as a matter of fact, it is.'

From time to time Gavin cabled his literary agent, Peter Janson-Smith, for more money. But his friends rallied round, loaned him cash, bought him drinks, laid out a table for him. At a restaurant in Asni in the High Atlas, he wrote, 'Raef and I had an *enormous* meal, frogs and all, plus six bloody Marys and wine and coffee and cognac, and when I asked the waiter for the bill he said his instructions were that we were guests of the house . . . I can't move a muscle without some Englishman whom I haven't seen for twenty years coming up and saying "Gavin!" – it's really very odd. However, Wilfred Thesiger and his fantastic eighty-six-year-old mother arrive at the Hotel Tazi this evening . . .'

Thesiger-style, Gavin travelled with a well-stocked chest of medicines which he dispensed to the sick in the remote mountain villages. 'The drugs in my medicine chest are nothing short of miraculous,' he wrote to Jimmy Watt:

At Telouet the superbly beautiful eleven-year-old daughter of the Mokhazhi [headman] had had a raging fever for fifteen days and seemed to be at the edge of death, but with a course of injections was cured after five days as we proceeded on our philanthropic way. Likewise Ahmed's father, with one ball the size of a goose egg, and René Bertrand's wife, shrunk to the size of a monkey. This same Mokhazhi at Telouet has an indescribably beautiful white Arab stallion, trained to a point at which it can be galloped bareback by a stranger, which he wants to sell because he isn't given enough allowance to feed it as he wants. It used to earn big money hired to film companies and ridden by female film stars who had never been on a horse before. I feel I would pay that money just to look at it. It ought to come to England.

In a fit of mental aberration – or a gesture of defiance or romantic indulgence – Gavin bought the animal, cabling his long-suffering agent Peter Janson-Smith: 'Have bought white Arab stallion. Please send £500.' Gavin couldn't afford it, he could barely justify it – but, in spite of his desperate financial circumstances, he had to have it, and he formed the idea of breeding a race of wonderful white Arab horses at Sandaig. He could see no other way of saving this beautiful animal from the slow death by cruelty and neglect which awaited any creature that had outlived its usefulness in North Africa. He was no horseman, but the horse captivated him; it could rear and dance at command, it loved human beings for their own sake, and he dearly wished to have it in Britain with him. Above all, perhaps, he identified with the stallion, which was for him a potent symbol – a proud animal in exactly the same predicament as he found himself to be. Now the knight errant had his horse, the White Knight had his white charger – even if he had next to nothing else.

THIRTY-TWO

Bitter spring

To eat thy heart through comfortless despairs:
To fawn, to crouch, to wait, to ride, to run,
To spend, to give, to want, to be undone.
EDMUND SPENSER, *'Mother Hubbard's Tale'*

Gavin returned to London and reality in the middle of April 1966. He was not glad to be back. His debts had grown in his absence, and so had the number of creditors. Many of them had run out of patience, and some had resorted to the law. The mortgages on the lighthouse properties, on which he had pinned his hopes of salvation, had failed to materialise, for their island location did not recommend them to mortgagers. Now there seemed no alternative but to send Edal and Teko to a zoo, close down Sandaig, and *in extremis* sell off one (if not both) of the lighthouses. Two employees who were meant to have prepared Eider Island for the eider duck experiment under the nominal direction of Jimmy Watt quit their jobs, leaving the project high and dry. Then on 21 May the surviving old hands, Jimmy Watt and Michael Cuddy, finally set off into the wide world beyond the confining horizon of Gavin's domain.

'I left perfectly amicably,' Jimmy recalled of that decisive moment:

I didn't even want to go. But I felt I couldn't live under his shadow for ever. He had been my guru – my father, if you like – and I owed everything to him, almost. If you needed help there was no finer person to turn to – he gave all his time and energy to what you had to say. He gave a lot of himself – the letters written late at night, the long conversations about everything under the sun, the donations to people and causes in need. He laid himself on the line, took a lot of risks, made himself vulnerable – and some people took advantage of him because of that, made him look a fool. Of course, he wasn't an easy person and there were times when living at Sandaig was very fraught. Gavin could be better than the best of fathers, worse than the worst of dictators. If he was in one of his moods everyone got very jumpy and it was impossible to relax. It was much easier when he wasn't there – one got up earlier, got more done. It was his energy that drew people to him, but some people couldn't cope with a person composed of opposites like Gavin – you never knew which opposite you'd get next.

Gavin wrote a final envoi to Jimmy, whom he regarded as a son, before the young man turned his back on the house and the burn and the sea for the last time as an employee: 'It's 2 a.m., which is the first moment I've had to write to you . . . You've kept this place going for a long time, often in very difficult circumstances. I'm *very* grateful to you for what you've done for this place and for me, over a long time. I think you are a superlative person, and will always think so, because it's true. Bless your heart; and my love to you and my absolute wish for your happiness, no matter what it might be.' Never spend your capital, he advised the departing twenty-one-year-old; never burn your boats; never hesitate to make use of people to help you on your way; and never forget that mutual dependence is the basis of human existence. 'All human relationships are built on sand,' Gavin wearily confided to a friend at this time. Desolate and hurt, he hardened his heart and did his best to forget everything but the bitter struggle to survive.

Gavin stayed on in London in apocalyptic mood, not improved by the news from Sicily. He had finally written to Giuseppe shortly after his return from Morocco, giving him news of his recent setbacks and warning him that he could no longer afford to fund his young protégé's medical studies as he had done up to now (£600 in the last year alone).

'*Finalmente*!!!!!!!!!!! At last!' The young Sicilian was overjoyed to hear from his *padrino* for the first time in a year. He sent news of Dolci, who had begun a week of fasting in Castellammare and wanted Gavin to join him for a few days: 'Dolci said, "But where is Maxwell? Isn't he in England?" and I replied, "Maxwell, Maxwell? I've heard next to nothing for a year!"' Dolci was going to call Giuseppe as a witness in his trial, at which he would speak out publicly against the Mafia in their own heartland. 'I will have to testify,' Giuseppe advised Gavin, 'that when you were in Castellammare in 1954 we found a note with a Mafia death threat in your car. Do you remember? This is important to Dolci. Certainly it may be dangerous for me but I consider it a duty to help him against the Minister. I am definitely under surveillance here – everyone knows I'm working for Dolci, but don't worry, I'm keeping my eyes open.' To complicate life still further, Giuseppe had important exams to sit at the end of the month, and more in June, before he qualified as a doctor in the autumn. Two weeks later he wrote again with further news. Mattarella was no longer a Minister, and a committee of the Italian Parliament was now investigating him. Many of his Mafiosi friends were in prison and Giuseppe had given the names of other Mafia supporters from his area, so now he would probably be summoned for questioning before the Anti-Mafia Commission:

Well, *padrino*, I hope nothing bad happens to me, but I believe in truth and justice and I hope that many will follow my little example – then (who knows?) things may improve in Sicily. Oh how I wish the world knew! I know all this is dangerous, but it is necessary. In the end I learned something from you. I'm afraid of not being strong enough. You are strong, that's for sure – I'd like to have some of your courage, I'd feel safer. If something happens to me now, now you know everything and I hope I am worthy of everything you have done for me.

Greetings from my mother, she always asks after you. I am afraid for her. She doesn't know anything at all, but she is ill and if she knew it would distress her deeply. My fiancée knows and she is very frightened.

In the event, Danilo Dolci was found guilty of libelling Mattarella and sentenced to a long term of imprisonment. In a peculiarly Italian way, however, the sentence was 'cancelled', for it would have been too scandalous for the State to have punished Dolci for saying openly something that everyone knew. Mattarella died four years later.

There was once a time when the reverberations of these urgent struggles in far-off countries would have preoccupied Gavin intensely. Now he felt unable to respond to their distant echoes, for his energies were confined to the arena of his own personal struggle to survive. In his desperate state of mind he felt the same about the places in his life as he did about the people – he wanted to disburden himself of all the sad, dark memories of the past and to walk off over the desert horizon alone.

Gavin's friends were saddened by his situation but did not know how they could help him. 'I have severe financial problems of my own,' Robin McEwen wrote from Marchmont, his stately home in the Scottish Borders, 'which does not prevent my appreciating the depths of the tragedy which requires you to sell the Islands and leave Sandaig. I am truly sorry about it all.' Raef Payne echoed this sentiment: 'When I think back to the delight you used to take in the birds and the shells and the burn and the sea wrack,' he wrote to Gavin, '– well, the loss seems a tragic one.' Constance McNab wrote: 'I do not like to picture you alone in that room. It will be good when you move and make a home again. But never think of yourself alone, do not fear it. As long as I can *creep* you have only to say and I am there, and my home is yours. I'll *feed* you too. In any case we are always alone . . . I would like you to come to a point where you can sit in an empty room "as in the presence of an honoured guest" as one Zen master puts it. Be still . . . You are brave to go on speaking, writing. I dare say one has to. But you are brave all the same.' And a few days later she added: 'You are feeling your way back. But unless you come to greater under-standing, you will break again. Your way back is through new love, through healing the sick, rescuing animals, creating beauty, through not projecting sterile suffering, through accepting yourself. Nothing can be bent out of shape without disaster. There is only metanoia, metamorphosis, new life.'

The pressing question was where to live in the future. It was not just a matter of a roof over his head – it was finding a niche in which he could function, a place where he could sink new roots, and be happy. In Morocco his friends Michael and Cherry Scott had offered him rooms in their own beautiful villa in Tangier. But was living abroad the answer? Was there, indeed, any answer? Why leave Sandaig anyway, Robin McEwen wondered. 'I don't quite understand why you don't regard *Sandaig* as your base, and gradu-ally draw in your horns, financial and otherwise, so that if the worst comes to the worst, you would still be "sitting in your pitch pine parlour" just as at the beginning of *Ring of Bright Water*.'

Gavin did not want to return to Sandaig immediately. With Jimmy gone he felt it would be a sad place. In any case it was full to bursting with new occupants. Beryl Borders, the practical young woman who had typed his early books, and Fionna, her seven-year-old daughter, had moved in at the end of May, bringing with them a whole pantechnicon load of donkeys, ponies, cats, geese and dogs (a dozen of them, ranging from Great Danes to miniature poodles) to add to Gavin's two otters and three deerhounds (Dirk, his recently acquired mate Hazel, and their newly born cub) already in residence. Beryl felt that Edal and Teko had lacked contact and routine care over the last year or two, but they became normal again once they felt comfortable and secure. Richard Frere, who had taken over the running of Gavin's company, soon formed a high opinion of Beryl – who was on crutches after breaking both her knees in a car crash – but was less enthusiastic about her menagerie.

'Beryl is excellent,' he reported to Gavin, 'and excellent for Sandaig. But Beryl's dogs make life at Sandaig a grim trial. In the morning one is woken by the whole range and variety of the voice canine, from the yip-yap of her somewhat obnoxious mongrels to the Baskerville baying of her Great Danes. One gets out of bed and trips over the excremental deposit that some night wanderer has surreptitiously bequeathed for one's enjoyment. All day long one falls over dogs. They lie in wait, in darkness, behind doors. They meet you on the stairs. They breathe on you when you eat. You take your turn in the bath with them. Verily, they are a bit much – and would become a very serious problem if you were trying to write at Sandaig.' Sandaig, Gavin noted, had entered upon a new and more visible phase of its decline; it had become an Animal Farm where the four-legged ruled. 'The casual copulations of this curious community,' he wrote later, 'resulted in a spectacular population explosion. At one moment there were, to say nothing of other species, twenty-six dogs.'

Gavin was in no hurry to return. There was much to preoccupy him in London. First and most pressing was the question of finding a home for the otters. A new zoo shortly to be opened in Aberdeen seemed the most suitable prospect, and after Gavin paid a visit in June it was agreed that the otters should move in when the construction of their enclosures was completed in October.

There was also much neglected literary business to attend to.

The manuscript of *Lords of the Atlas* had roused a hornets' nest of libel problems. Under British law it is not possible to libel the dead. The problem was, who was dead and who was not? Libel lawyer Edward Adeane (later to become Private Secretary to Prince Charles) drily noted: 'Where characters are clearly dead (e.g. Si Hammon who was eaten by a lion and then shot) I have not noted passages defamatory to them. I must however confess that I was alarmed by the author's casual reference to one 106-year-old Moroccan who was apparently in the best of health.' In France the position was trickier still, for under French law it is possible to libel even the dead. As the text stood, *all* the descendants of the Glaoui would' be entitled to bring libel actions, and so would a number of French officers of the old colonial régime, or surviving members of their families. Safer, Gavin's publishers decided, not to tempt fate again – the book would not be sold in France or any other country where a similar libel law prevailed.

Gavin's attention was now distracted by the need to adjudicate a literary prize which bore his name. In 1960, when he was beginning to feel rather rich from the proceeds of *Ring of Bright Water*, he had founded an annual prize – the Gavin Maxwell Prize for English – with the aim of encouraging aspiring young writers at his old school at Stowe. Gavin himself was both judge and donor, and every May he would visit the school to award the £10 cash prize – a large sum by schoolboy standards (worth £100 today) – for the best piece of descriptive writing about a personal experience. Gavin's appearance at the school to award the prize was always a matter of some comment. 'I had expected to meet a hearty bluff northerner in tweeds and a pipe,' recalled Brian Stephan, the master who administered the prize. 'Instead what appeared was a very sleek, very intense and rather neurotic fellow with a big Mercedes sports car and heavy black glasses who looked the exact opposite.' One of Gavin's visits coincided with that of the actor Sir Ralph Richardson, who had a son at Stowe and had agreed to read extracts from two or three of John Donne's sermons in the chapel during the Sunday morning service. As distinguished guests Gavin and Sir Ralph were seated together in a pew adjacent to the pulpit, Gavin looking rather ominous and *mafioso* in his black glasses. Afterwards a small boy was asked whether he had enjoyed the service and Richardson's readings. 'Yes, I thought he was splendid,' replied the boy. 'But I thought his bodyguard was a creep.'

Gavin not only marked the prize essays himself, but wrote full and detailed comments for the guidance of their young authors. Several of the winners of the prize – Charles (Jesse) Graham, for example, and Justin Wintle – were stimulated by Gavin's encouragement and advice to become writers after leaving school. Graham won the prize twice – the second time for a fictitious account of an encounter with a vagrant American guitarist on a beach in Greece. 'Fiction was against the rules,' he recalled: 'But I got away with it – or maybe I didn't. Some months later Gavin came to give a talk to the school literary society and floored me by gaily announcing the most remarkable coincidence. He had been in Greece and met the selfsame folksinger! I didn't know what to say. Except it reminded me of one of his other remarks that always stuck in my head: "All writers are liars. Writers of fiction are merely avowed liars." He was very encouraging to all my dreams of writing, read my scraps, advised, suggested books to read – and gave me practical help when I wrote a novel (at school). He also advised me never to throw anything I'd written away. He wrote me a letter about this:

> Even if you re-read things you've written and think they are poor you will almost inevitably also find particular phrases or images or ideas that you can put to new uses. For example, on page 71 of *Ring of Bright Water* the whole passage about the wild swans – 'All through the night I heard their restless murmur as they floated light as spume upon the peat-dark waves . . .' – was taken from an unsatisfactory poem written five years earlier. I couldn't get the poem into the right shape, and finally abandoned it, but turned back into prose it was exactly what I needed for the book and still had the mood in which it was originally written.

'He listened, said what he thought, never patronised or talked down. I remember one day he gave me a spin down the school avenue in his convertible Mercedes. He took the Oxford bridge at ferocious speed. The car was literally airborne. He chuckled and said, "I've always wanted to do that." He was a celebrated author who happened to be kind and encouraging to a sixteen-year-old aspirant writer. I never saw a dark side. I didn't know him in his whole range. For what he gave me I'll always be grateful.' Graham later became a Hollywood scriptwriter, and Wintle a novelist and travel writer.

No winner of the Gavin Maxwell Prize was more grateful to Gavin or enjoyed a more spectacular take-off to his career as a consequence of his encouragement than Richard Branson, who won the prize in 1966 (having been runner-up the previous year). Gavin came down to Stowe to present the award with Gavin Young, who was on leave from reporting the Vietnam war for the *Observer*. Over lunch Richard announced that he was about to launch a new magazine called *Student*, aimed at a mass readership in schools and universities. The project had snowballed somewhat – the first issue was to be a hundred pages long – and had become almost a full-time job. The dilemma which he put to Gavin was this – should he complete his education at Stowe, where he had a year or two still to go, or should he abandon his education altogether and concentrate on *Student* and the entrepreneurial career which he believed to be his destiny? He could not have asked a more un-typical adult for guidance at such a critical crossroads in his life. Gavin was entirely for giving the young their head and encourag-ing them to achieve their creative aspirations. As a result of his own experiences at school, and the theories of progressive educationists like Bob Mackenzie and Hamish Brown at Braehead, he had become a convinced opponent of the conventional, formal, authoritarian and exam-orientated education system prevalent in Britain at that time. His response to Richard's dilemma was unequivocal – if his magazine was really the most· important thing in the world to him, if running his own business was where his ambitions lay, then he should leave Stowe at once and get on with it.

Later that afternoon the two Gavins drove Richard back to his parental home in Shamley Green, Surrey, and on the way they stopped off at my own home in the nearby village of Compton. The discussion continued, and by the time we sat down to supper Richard announced his decision. He would leave Stowe and bring out his magazine. All three of us – Gavin, Gavin Young and myself – would contribute articles to it, and Gavin would provide useful introductions. At the foot of the little wooded hill on which my house stood lived another of Gavin's old friends – the author and artist Wilfrid Blunt, whose brother Anthony was Surveyor of the Queen's Pictures (and was later exposed as a KGB spy) – who could perhaps contribute a further article.* The sixteen-year-old Richard Branson left to pursue his destiny. Today he runs his own airline, Virgin Atlantic, and with the recent sale of his Virgin Record group – the world's largest independent record company – has become the ninth richest person in Britain (and, incidentally, he keeps otters).

Gavin stayed on at my house after Richard's departure, for we had other business to discuss. He had contracted to write a popular zoological reference work called *Seals of the World*, for publication in 1967, and I had agreed to rewrite and edit the text he had sub-contracted from two able but unliterary young zoologists at the Zoological Society of London. He was also anxious to discuss the details of an expedition we were proposing to make to Mongolia to search for the rare Przewalski's horse, the wild ancestor of the domesticated horse, and to look through my photographic library for pictures with which to illustrate his current project, his 'stand-point work of philosophy/psychology', to which he had given the title *The Heritage of Fear*.

The thesis of *The Heritage of Fear* concerned the roots of human and animal behaviour. 'The most obviously disastrous aspect of man's nature is his enormous aggression,' Gavin argued in the out-line he gave me to read, 'and observation of other animal species led me to begin with the hypothesis that there could be no aggression between members of the same species without this being due to fear in the widest sense.'

There were, he went on, two basic sorts of fear: 'primal' fear (fear of death, fear of pain, fear of loss), which was shared by man and the lower animals alike, and 'secondary' fear, which was peculiar to man alone. 'Secondary' fear could be dated back to the earliest written records of the human race. The commonest noun in the Old Testament, for example, was 'fear' (or words derived from it), with 'smiting' and 'slaying' a close second. 'The Old Testament,' he concluded from this somewhat tenuous analysis, 'is a massive example of the link between fear and aggression.' The New Testament was in striking contrast, however, for the teachings of Christ enjoined mankind *not* to fear. 'It is a terrible tragedy,'

---

* Only Gavin's article – a thoughtful piece about education – got into the first issue, along with contributions by Henry Moore, David Hockney, the Archbishop of Canterbury, John Le Carré and Vanessa Redgrave.

commented Gavin, 'that the Christian Church should, by its vast structure of sanctions, have increased a thousandfold the human heritage of fear its founder sought to dispel . . . In the last analysis, we still act most of the time through motives of fear.'

'Exploring a new idea,' Gavin continued, 'is like beginning a huge jigsaw puzzle . . . When a large chunk suddenly fits together as though by magic one experiences a wonderful moment of discovery.' That 'wonderful moment' had occurred at Sandaig one day when he happened to observe his deerhound, Dirk, defecating in a leisurely way on a favoured patch of grass; while the dog was thus occupied a sheep walked by doing the same thing – but never once stopped walking or browsing. 'It was then that a key portion of the jigsaw suddenly slid together in my mind. The dog and the sheep, though both domestic animals, represented two great mammalian divisions – the beast of prey and the preyed upon. Or, to put it a different way, the feared and the fearful. The fearful, who might be killed and eaten at the first moment they were off guard, simply could not afford to take time off. The feared, like the dog, had no enemy but man, whose arrival on the scene has been so recent that it has not yet produced evolutionary changes in the habits of the predators . . . I felt I was on the edge of a great discovery. It all fitted in.'

Gavin now turned his attention to the sexual behaviour of various species. This, too, appeared to prove his thesis. The sheep took only five to ten seconds to mate, the dog anything between twenty minutes and two hours. The preyed-upon rabbit mated in three to eight seconds, the predatory ferret averaged an hour. Buffaloes, zebras, wild asses and elephants – they all proved the point. 'Therefore it was with great solemnity – almost awe – that I approached the data on the primates and mankind himself,' Gavin wrote. 'I was unprepared for the inherited "fearingness" of the primate body: chimpanzee, ten seconds average; contemporary primitive man, five to twelve seconds; modern civilised man, according to Kinsey, 120 seconds median. Our bodies – in this and many other ways – still hold our heritage of fear, and the more fearful the individual the more obvious it becomes.'

Sadly, Gavin's 'great discovery' did not find much favour. A lucrative £2000 contract for a series of articles for the *Daily Mail* was cancelled when he delivered *The Heritage of Fear* instead of the cuddly stories about his animal pets the newspaper really wanted.

And when he submitted a revamped version of the same material (entitled 'The Sexual Life of the Herbivores') to the pre-eminent scientific journal *Nature*, it was rejected. The reasons are not hard to find. Gavin was a capable field naturalist but not a qualified or rigorously systematic scientific zoologist. His thesis, interesting as far as it went, was largely under-researched and unsubstantiated, and it ignored inconvenient animals that were both predatory and preyed upon, feared and fearful. And though there is no evidence that Gavin had ever read it, Aldous Huxley had aired similar theories on intra-specific aggression in a much more exhaustive fashion in his pre-war book, *Ends and Means*. Much as Gavin would have loved to have achieved distinction as a conceptual thinker, his true métier was that of a brilliant descriptive writer, and it was to this that he was now to return.

Later in the summer he gave his theory another airing when he addressed the Stowe literary society, the Twelve Club, and astonished the headmaster by asking whether he might be permitted to take up residence in one of the many decorative eighteenth-century temples that were dotted about the school's magnificent gardens. His preference, he said, was for the Temple of Venus, a Palladian structure overlooking the lake in the south-west bastion of the ha-ha, containing behind its Ionic portico a single bare, dark, horse-fly infested room. Gavin's curious request was turned down on the grounds that it would establish an unwelcome precedent.

When, later in the year, he travelled to Dublin to lecture to the Royal Dublin Society on 'The Ring of Bright Water', he met the distinguished Irish writer and poet Monk Gibbon backstage after the lecture. Gibbon was almost seventy, and a great admirer of Gavin's book and his way of life, and afterwards he sent him a copy of his masterpiece, *The Seals*. Gavin's letter of thanks was so effusive in its praise of the book – 'a work of art', he called it, 'a work of genius' – that Monk Gibbon kept it among his most treasured possessions for the rest of his life, and used it to persuade his publishers to have the book reprinted.

With nowhere particular to go, Gavin sought refuge in Margaret Pope's apartment in Lausanne, Switzerland, for a few weeks in the summer – air-ferrying his Mercedes over at her expense – ostensibly to enlist her detailed and expert knowledge of Moroccan personalities to help solve some of the many potential libel problems that laced the text of *Lords of the Atlas*. There, in a single period of forty-eight hours, Gavin received news of the cruel deaths of two of his most treasured animals – his Pyrenean mountain dog at Sandaig and his wonderful white stallion in Marrakesh – both in sickening circumstances and both as the direct result of acts of neglect by young employees in whom Gavin had placed his trust.

Gus, the huge Pyrenean dog that had earlier been castrated because of his savage nature, had died after one of the new employees at Sandaig had left him out all night, tied by a chain to a running line; it was a wild night, and in looking for shelter the dog tried to cross a stone dyke at one end of the running wire, but was caught up by his chain and died of strangulation as he hung there.

Titish, the white stallion, had died because he had been treated with stupid neglect by Gavin's Berber friend Ahmed, who had simply pocketed the money Gavin had given him to pay for the horse's feed and upkeep. Hobbled in a filthy, stinking stable with donkeys and cows, without water, oats or proper forage, Titish was in a terrible condition and already ill with tetanus when an officer of the Society for the Protection of Animals in North Africa went to inspect him in Marrakesh at Gavin's request towards the end of June. The horse was finally killed off when Ahmed rode him several miles at full gallop in the blazing mid-morning sun, all but destroying the poor creature there and then and accelerating the course of the tetanus from which he died three days later.

Gavin was sick with horror and anger at the cruel deaths of these fine animals. The youth who had allowed the Pyrenean dog to die at Sandaig was summarily sacked. The monthly allowance which Gavin had been sending to Ahmed's family for several years past was abruptly terminated, and in spite of the young Moroccan's pleas and imprecations Gavin refused to have any more to do with him ever again. Gavin was systematically cutting his links with the past and with what he called his 'lost causes' abroad. Even his twenty-five-year-old Sicilian friend and collaborator Giuseppe, whose progress from barefoot, impoverished street urchin to medical graduate had been almost entirely encouraged and funded by Gavin, felt the icy chill of his *padrino*'s aloof indifference.

'Gavin is a truly remarkable man,' he had written to a mutual friend, Penelope Biggs, 'and though his spirit is like a sea in a storm, his heart and mind are those of a great man; to me he is like a father, and there is nothing in the world that would be sufficient to repay him for even a fraction of the kindness and generosity he has bestowed on me.' But soon Giuseppe was fearful that something had changed: 'I have a feeling that I have lost Gavin – *per sempre*, for ever.' This saddened him profoundly, for Gavin had always represented for him a reality that encompassed a grand and life-enhancing vision. Penelope Biggs, who had taken over the funding of the young man's medical training now that Gavin could no longer afford it, implored Gavin not to desert him now.

'I know you must have many problems on hand, and can guess at much mental anguish and spiritual weariness behind it,' she wrote. 'But *please* Gavin, for your own deepest sake as well as his, don't destroy this relationship. Material help, as you very well know, is only a fraction of what you have given him. He has rested in his faith in you, and what he believed you expected of him has given him the vision and the strength to tackle all that he has achieved. Don't snatch it away from him now that he needs it most. So much of his future depends on you. Do you still believe that the Kingdom of God is within – that we each have a little drop of God in us – that love in the abstract is what every human mammal hungers for? Please Gavin, write to him.'

There was only silence. In vain Gavin's former protégé wrote and cabled his distant godfather, signalling wildly from the Mafia island on which he seemed marooned. He had passed his exams. He was sending some wine from his mother's garden, hoping that 'in drinking it you will taste Sicily and the thought of me will be closer to you'. He was hoping to stay with Penelope Biggs in London at Christmas. He hoped Gavin was managing to live in some way or another. 'I feel your life is bitter,' he wrote. 'Life is hard, I know, but have courage.'

Gavin needed more than courage; it seemed that nothing less than divine intervention could save him now.

THIRTY-THREE

The curse

I find no hint throughout the universe
Of good or ill, of blessing or of curse;
I find alone Necessity Supreme.
              JAMES THOMSON, *'The City of*
                          Dreadful Night'

There was no respite for Gavin from his long succession of afflic-
tions. 'It seemed that fortune could never come my way again,' he
was to write; 'every piece of news from day to day was of delay,
disaster, or death.' In the company of his friends he would put a
brave face on it, wryly and facetiously misquoting *Isaiah* to describe
his present situation: 'A man of sorrows, and not unacquainted
with grief.' What had he done to deserve all this, he wondered;
what was the cause? A few days later he received an explanation
of a kind from a most unexpected quarter.

In the last week of July 1966 Gavin went to stay with his brother
Aymer, who now lived almost permanently at his house in Katounia on the island of Euboea. Looking down on the pantile roof of
Aymer's house was the house of his nearest neighbour, a Cambridge historian, theologian and translator of modern Greek poetry
by the name of Philip Sherrard. As it happened, Sherrard was one
of the oldest and closest friends of Kathleen Raine, and by a fateful
coincidence Kathleen arrived as a guest at this house the day before
Gavin arrived at Aymer's.

Kathleen had met Gavin only once since their final quarrel at
Sandaig six years before, and that was fleetingly – 'for the duration
of a heart-beat' – outside a chemist's shop near Paultons Square a
few months after his marriage. That brief encounter was for her
like a fragment from a world which no longer existed. Gavin's
departure from her life had been more final than anything she had
ever experienced. She hoped for nothing more, wanted nothing.
Her fate, she felt, had run its course.

One day soon after her arrival she returned to the house to find a note: 'My dear Kathleen – Today seems a day when Aymer has no particular plans, so if you are free to lunch with me at the taverna? Say meet about 1.15 there? Scribble assent or dissent below. Gavin.'

'Heaven knows I did not seek him out,' Kathleen wrote later; 'would have avoided him had he so wished.' So at the bottom of Gavin's note she scribbled her apologies: 'Too hot at lunch-time.' But when she got to Aymer's door to return the note she had a change of mind (or heart, perhaps) and crossed out what she had written, substituting: 'Yes, as always. Love Kathleen.'

So they met, under the olive trees outside the little taverna beside the mother-of-pearl sea that looked across to Mount Parnassus. 'He looked as if he too had suffered,' Kathleen remembered; 'as if a dark shadow enveloped him.' They talked all through the heat of noon, and Gavin told her in outline the story of his life during all the years they had been apart, and when at length they rose to leave, Kathleen gave him the manuscript of the autobiography she had come to Euboea to complete – her own version of those times – the story of her heart.

Many times afterwards she would ask herself why she had thought to do such a thing. The book was not intended for publication – at least not while her parents were still alive. And it was not meant to be a mere chronicle of events but an attempt to understand, to somehow make bearable, her life – a life in which Gavin had played such an overwhelming part. 'It is one thing to write such a record,' Kathleen conceded; 'quite another to read it.' Gavin, seated in Aymer's garden overlooking the sea and the mountains, with the sun parching and the cicadas screeching in the fig tree, read it – read it with a mounting sense of anger and dismay. One paragraph in particular leapt from the page – the story of the curse all those years ago.

'She had put her hands upon the trunk of the rowan tree and with all her strength she had cursed me, saying, "Let him suffer here as I am suffering." Then she left, up over the bleak hillside.

'I put down the manuscript and stared at the coarse dark-green grass of the Greek lawn, thinking how exactly the past years had paralleled her blind desire for destruction.'

The murder of Mij, the sudden savagery of Edal and Teko and the end of the Camusfeàrna idyll, the failure of his marriage, his

injury in the motor accident, the financial catastrophe, the departure
of Jimmy Watt and the impending banishment of the otters and
closing down of Sandaig . . . It all made a kind of sense – deep
down he had always believed in Kathleen's strange occult powers.
But what were the limits of the curse, where would it end?

Gavin met Kathleen again in Katounia a few nights later. It was
a night of a brilliant moon and they talked for hours. Only then,
as Kathleen remembered, was the full and awful bitterness of the
truth she had not perceived made known – Gavin's truth.

'Gavin was entirely to disown and deny any participation in a
relationship I had thought mutual,' she related afterwards; '"Outrageous" was the word he used. Canetti had been quite right when
he had so solemnly assured me, "Gavin does not love you, Kathleen. Not in any sense of the word love; not at any time."'

Gavin was bleakly precise, pitiless and unforgiving, and asked
Kathleen to name a single person close to her whom she had not
destroyed. 'What was your love for me but an infatuation?' he
demanded. 'You are a destroyer, Kathleen.'

He had been destroyed, that much he had known before he even
set foot on this Greek island. Now he believed he knew how he
had been destroyed, and why – and by whom. And as the bright
moon rose behind Mount Kantili, he too became a destroyer, and
by the end he had left Kathleen nothing from the past to which to
cling. Her memories of her love had been like fixed stars in the
firmament; but now, she wrote, 'the stars fell from heaven'.

'Parting,' Kathleen recalled, 'the moon cast our shadows on the
spent dust; exhausted by hours of torment given and received, we
kissed, at last, as long ago we would have kissed at parting, and
Gavin said, "write *something* kind about me."'

A day or two later Kathleen pushed a letter through Gavin's door:

Dearest Gavin,

I realise that the most painful thing for you is to be written
about at all; and yet you might on reflection find in what I
wrote some excuse for other thoughts – to have meant so
much to another person is surely some cause for happiness?

I had to write it now, to try to understand what a life is,
to free myself, if you like. You yourself have, after all, been
engaged in the same search for one's lost self in a return to
the past. I thought, in *The House of Elrig*, you had done just

that – rediscovered your essential, radical self, and the soul's radical innocence, in the child you described . . .

As to friendship – yes, Gavin, I remember. I said to you, I know, that our relationship was 'not friendship', and that love cannot be turned into friendship. Very different in kind. I thought it was mutual Platonic, or spiritual, love, of a kind; it seems that I was altogether mistaken in thinking it in any way mutual . . .

If I failed you it was for much deeper reasons; and we must both be judged by the only Judge; who is, as you long ago said to me, Love. Indeed if I were to forget all else you ever said to me I should remember your saying, 'God is love'.

But why go on. I think we must both see that for two elderly and eminent writers to go on as we did the other evening has indeed its comic side.

I hope perhaps to see you before you go –?

With love, Kathleen.

It was not until the end of August that Gavin finally returned to Sandaig, after an absence of nearly nine months. He found the place much changed. Only Beryl Borders and her daughter were there now, and Gavin was the only male. The number of dogs had recently been reduced somewhat, following allegations that some of them had been responsible for a series of depredations among the sheep on the neighbouring hirsels; but after a masterly feat of detective work on Gavin's part the allegations were found to be false, and the dog population at Sandaig was restored to its former level.

It was a strange life – the oddest period, perhaps, in the entire Camusfeàrna saga. Off and on for four months Gavin lived cheek by jowl with Beryl inside the house, rarely going out and only occasionally leaving Sandaig. Not since his early childhood at Elrig, probably, had he lived for such a long unbroken stretch in the company of another human being. And yet, in a curious way, it worked out. Gavin was not averse to the little comforts of life that living with a kindly and undemanding woman could bring, and in spite of the bedlam caused by the hordes of pets with which he was surrounded he found life less stressful at Sandaig than it had been in the recent past. 'I found him really very easy to live with,' Beryl recalled of that period. 'But he used to have blow-outs. Once a week, perhaps because of sexual frustration, he would go round the house complaining about everything. He didn't drink when I was. there – only if a visitor was coming, when he'd drink half a bottle of whisky to help him face up to it.' As for Beryl, she was very fond of Gavin, and held him in great respect and affection. She was only too willing to help him in any way she could, for had he not provided her with a port in a storm?

Meanwhile the menagerie continued to increase. One sunny day in late September Gavin decided to take the *Polar Star* out for a run to the lighthouse islands off Isle Ornsay and Kyleakin, returning later in the day (minus the starboard propeller) with a hundred-weight of mackerel he had caught for the otters, a flightless Fulmar petrel he had rescued from the sea, and a helpless Manx shearwater that had been blown ashore on Sandaig beach in the recent gales. The two birds, housed in the bathroom amid piles of seaweed, added to the general tumult of the Sandaig bestiary, and it began to seem that there were so many creatures in and about the house that it was almost impossible to move. 'Any open door,' wrote Gavin, 'was an automatic invitation to a vast and vocal avalanche of dogs, of all sizes and shapes, but with patently conflicting desires. The fantastic fertility of the household was crystallised for me by the discovery one day, previously unknown to anyone, of a litter of weaned kittens living in the loft above the lobby.'

It was difficult to get down to any useful writing in such a house-hold, and apart from a few reviews for the *Observer* and an occasional American newspaper Gavin did not try. On 24 October 1966 *Lords of the Atlas*, Gavin's long-gestated history of the rise and fall of the cruel and ambitious House of Glaoua – from obscure mountain faction to power-brokers of the nation and back again – was finally published after six years of intermittent, tortuous and extremely expensive labour. In spite of his publisher's suspicions to the contrary, the book was largely a work of original research, its sources – unpublished notes, anonymous verbal communications, fragmentary references, long-buried documents from the early days of the French imperium – so scattered that putting them together as a continuous narrative was (as Gavin put it) 'like collecting and assembling widely dispersed pieces of a jigsaw puzzle'. This was one reason it had taken so long to unravel the full story and had entailed so many visits to Morocco – this and what Gavin called 'the infinite procrastination of Moors'. The time, effort and travel the book had involved far exceeded the advances and royalties ·

Gavin ever received for it – the payments he had made to one informant, the Glaoui's former secretary Si Mohammed el-Khizzioui, alone exceeded the publisher's advance. And delving into such an arcane and secret history in such a closed, medieval and culturally alien society proved even more difficult and time-consuming than primary research does at the best of times. That Gavin achieved his aim is a tribute to his powers of persuasion, his gift for intrigue and arras diplomacy, his stamina and professionalism. The result is a work that is still, a quarter of a century later, required reading for any informed visitor to Morocco.

Longmans congratulated Gavin on the 'blazing press' he received for the book. The reviewers heaped praise on it, making nonsense of the publisher's preliminary report. 'In telling the story of El Glaoui,' Nigel Dennis wrote in the *Sunday Telegraph*, 'Mr Maxwell has written his best book. It is a waste of time to praise it with superlatives . . . the year has not produced a better book. Both subject and writer equally deserve our thanks and attention.' Geoffrey Moorhouse, in his Introduction to a later paperback edition, was no less fulsome. The book, he wrote, 'combined scholarship with a flair for the imaginatively written word. To call it a travel book is as inadequate as calling a camel a quadruped.' But it was not, he felt, exactly a pleasant book. The barbarity of the régime it described was horrific by the standards of any age. Pretenders to power, real or imagined, were thrown to the lions or flayed alive, while T'hami El Glaoui, Pasha of Marrakesh, the most commanding figure in the story, had mounted the severed heads of his enemies outside his gates not long before he attended the Coronation of Queen Elizabeth II. 'Repulsive as much of it is,' wrote Moorhouse, 'the book is only made readable by Gavin Maxwell's narrative skill. Now there's your writer's writer at work: perfectly balanced, rhythmical, concise, feeling.'

Fear of a rash of libel suits had precluded publication of the book in France, and even in Britain it was withdrawn from circulation for a while when it was discovered that Gavin had wrongly called an American Professor of Islamic and North African Studies 'a European Jew', and inadvertently described the wife of a member of the Glaoui family as the daughter of Edward G. Robinson. In Morocco, not surprisingly, the book was banned as being contrary to the public interest, and not even Si Mohammed el-Khizzioui, who had been Gavin's go-between in Marrakesh, ever received a copy. But at least the interminable labour was over, and Gavin was free to turn to something new, though exactly what he did not really know. 'I never want to do another researched book again,' he confided to me at this time, '– *ever*!' At the beginning of November he put a few tentative ideas to Michael Hoare at Longmans – a much more personal book about Morocco (under the title of, say, *Moroccan Journeys*), or a spell with Gavin Young in Vietnam.

But it was his animals that were uppermost in Gavin's mind. The otters' move to Aberdeen Zoo had been put back several times but was now fixed for the end of November. 'After which,' Gavin wrote to Constance McNab, 'God knows what!' Inevitably the press got wind of the news. 'GAVIN MAXWELL SENDING OTTERS TO ZOO' proclaimed a *Daily Telegraph* headline. 'The otters' home, Sandaig island, near Skye, is becoming too expensive to run. Everything including the otters' food, has to be brought long distances. The lease of Sandaig, which is owned by Lord Dulverton and rented for £1 a year, has another seven years to run. Mr Maxwell is also selling, for a total of £27,000, two islands off Skye which he bought three years ago.'

On hearing about Edal's impending departure, her original foster-parents, Malcolm and Paula Macdonald, who more than eight years ago had handed their young Nigerian otter cub over to Gavin after their chance encounter in Kyle of Lochalsh, arrived at Sandaig to ask for their otter back. They had given Edal to Gavin when they had been in no position to look after her; now the position was reversed, and they were anxious she should not have to spend her last years behind bars. But at an emotional meeting Gavin had turned their request down flat, and after some heated words the couple left the house, with Paula in tears and the old friendship in ruins.

This unfortunate confrontation seems to have induced a crisis of conscience in Gavin's mind, for next day Richard Frere, who was at Sandaig on one of his regular business visits, noticed that he was steadily sinking into a mood of depression. He had been drinking most of the day, which didn't help. At length Gavin got up, turned to Richard and said: 'I need some exercise. I shall go for a short walk.' He took his duffel coat from the coat rack in the porch, opened the front door and strode out.

It was a wild day. A Force 9 was roaring in from the southwest and the gulls drifted and banked on the wet wind; the sky was

almost black and the crests of the waves in the sound were short,
white and vicious. Gavin turned towards the burn, crossed the
bridge and began to climb the old foot-track that led steeply up
over the hill and the moor. At a flat patch where the track bent
sharply left he stopped to get his breath back, and turned to stare
the way he had come, over the house to the bay and the scatter of
islands beyond. A small school of whales nosed down the Sound
of Sleat, and a fishing boat butted the chop of the sea in a cloud of
white foam. On Skye the first snows on the hills stood out bleakly
white against the dark grey scurry of the lowering clouds. He
recognised the scene as from long ago, but now it held for him
nothing that he wanted to remember.

'I was looking down upon Camusfeàrna, and I believed I was
saying goodbye to it after eighteen years,' he was to write. 'Suddenly there came a sharp flurry of hail, and I pulled up the hood
of my duffel coat, and crouched back into the steep hillside. It gave
no shelter; there was no shelter from any wind, and I knew it
suddenly and completely.'

As he stood there he tried to remember the place as he had first
seen it – 'a weather-worn cottage within a stone's throw of the sea,
standing unfenced upon a grass green field, only the low marram-
grown dunes between it and the breaking waves. Untenanted,
deserted, waiting . . .'

Much had changed since those heady, joyous days. His nearest
neighbours, the MacLeods, had gone now, like everything and
everyone else, and their little house of green corrugated iron up at
Tormor stood empty, so that there was no human habitation within
five miles of where Gavin lived. The very hills had changed too,
and the rough windswept moorland of rock and peat-bog and
heather was now covered in a low, dark, dripping forest of young
sitkas and larch. As for the house, its simple charm was a thing of
the past – the wrecked Jeeps, the ugly prefabricated extensions, the
posts and wires and palisades, the *Polar Star* high and dry on its
massive steel cradle, had destroyed it for ever. 'Now, as I sat
huddled in my duffel coat, I was surveying what I had done to
Camusfeàrna – what I had done to the animals and what I had done
to myself.'

The recent rains and snows had turned the burn into a racing
torrent and the flood water lay in broad pools all over the flat grass
around the house. One of these pools was in Teko's enclosure, and

it was a curious shape – a perfect figure of eight, marking the pattern of Teko's daily walk, a zoo pattern of behaviour, the consequence of boredom and frustration.

The sun had set now behind the jagged peaks of Skye and the Isle Ornsay light flashed its intermittent gleam across the darkening sound. Gavin stirred himself and began to pick his way back down the steep track towards the house. A full gale drove the rain in from the sea and it slashed at his face as he stumbled downwards; from the bay he could hear the roar and hiss of the breakers as they pounded the shore on the incoming tide. The wild tumult of the approaching night echoed and reinforced the tormented struggle within his own mind. 'The otters were going,' he reminded himself, 'Camusfeàrna would be closed; somewhere I would find a new life . . . It was, after all, the end of an era, and that comes with greater or lesser shock to every human being who ever lived.'

But was it right, he asked himself? Was it right to betray the animals who had put their trust in him and made his home their own, who had been the basis of his own fame and one-time fortune? Was it right to betray that great army of the reading public, the fans of *Ring of Bright Water*, who wrote to him now to share his grief at his impending departure from Camusfeàrna and to protest at his decision to put the otters in a zoo?

Gavin recrossed the rushing burn, skirted the rowan tree and halted outside Teko's enclosure, which adjoined the landward end of the house. For some minutes he stood there in the driving rain. He wanted, obsessively, to say goodbye to Teko one last time. Teko's sleeping quarters were in the little slate-roofed lean-to built on to the end of the house. Gavin opened the door, switched on the light and stooped inside. Teko wasn't there. It was hardly surprising. The little shed was uninhabitable. A gale had dislodged one of the roof-slates and the floor was under an inch of water, the infra-red lamp had fused and Teko's blankets were soaking.

Gavin called Teko's name in the dark, and the otter, which had hardly known human contact for years, came bounding in from his enclosure, wet, cold and disconsolate. 'He greeted me as might a castaway on a desert island greet his rescuing ship,' Gavin wrote. 'All his language . . . he employed in welcome, in rebuke, in renewed hope for the future.' Gavin rushed out, ran to the main house and burst into the kitchen-parlour shouting for dry blankets. To a startled Richard Frere he looked as 'wild as a scarecrow'.

'That otter is not going to any zoo!' he raged at the luckless Richard. 'I don't care if you are bloody angry with me, Richard. That otter stays here!'

Gavin went back to Teko's quarters. He dried Teko with a towel as he used to do when the otter was a cub and lined his lorry tyre with fresh blankets so that he could sleep in comfort – on his back, mouth open, head resting on Gavin's forearm, snoring lightly. Gavin knew now that he could never send Teko to a zoo, and that somehow the otter should be returned to the sea and the burn. Quite how, he did not know, but it had to happen. 'If it did not I would be a betrayer, and a betrayer of animal loyalties becomes a betrayer in human situations too.'

Richard was aghast when he heard Gavin's decision. He was convinced that only by putting the otters in a zoo and closing down Sandaig would it be possible for Gavin to survive financially. If Ornsay wasn't sold in the next few weeks, he told Gavin, Sandaig would be uninhabitable – no electricity, no phone, no food, no money. And then who would look after Teko?

Richard hoped he had played his trump card. But he was wrong. Gavin was looking searchingly at Beryl Borders – and in response Beryl gave him an almost imperceptible nod of the head. Now Richard perceived from what quarter Gavin had received the strength to make his decision. Beryl, he concluded, 'had condemned herself to a hard and lonely winter, happy in the knowledge that she was wanted'.

If Teko was to stay on at Sandaig, there was no overriding reason for Edal, the more self-sufficient of the two otters, to be sent to the zoo either, and in the middle of December, having prevaricated for several weeks, Gavin informed the highly disgruntled zoo to this effect.

Gavin now prepared to leave Sandaig for a six-month stint in North Africa. He had rented a flat in Tangier with the aim of devoting himself exclusively to writing a new book far from the worries and distractions of his beleaguered life at home. This book was to be an account of how his life had come full circle – from the time years ago when he was sitting at Sandaig with one otter and no money and writing *Ring of Bright Water*, which would make him rich and successful, back to the present when he was sitting at Sandaig with two otters and no money . . . Longmans considered the plan 'an absolute winner – if it could be done without libelling everyone that Gavin has met in the last six years, including Longmans'. To keep body and soul together while he wrote it Longmans agreed to pay Gavin an allowance of £1000. The book was his only chance of reducing his debts, for he was now virtually bankrupt – even his indebtedness to his publishers now touched five figures, Prince Alliata libel damages included.

There was only one other iron left in the dying fire – the sale of the Isle Ornsay lighthouse cottage. The actor Alec Guinness had been tempted, but finally thought better of it. 'Greatly regret that my wife and I must decline Isle Ornsay cottage,' he had cabled a disconsolate Gavin. 'We feel it would be too great a responsibility to look after from such a distance.' Now an English lawyer and his wife had expressed an interest in the place, and Gavin pinned his very survival on their decision. He was on the point of boarding the plane to Tangier when Richard Frere gave him the news over the phone. The deal was off. A long, hard, bankrupt winter stretched ahead.

So, late in December Gavin flew away to warmer climes. Of that moment he was later to write: 'I was not saying a true farewell as I had planned and prepared. I was returning, come what might, hell and high water. I felt that by now I was acquainted with both.'

THIRTY-FOUR

The rearguard action

We are all in the gutter, but some of us are looking at the stars.

OSCAR WILDE, *Lady Windermere's Fan*

The expatriate road to Tangier was a well-beaten one; a host of international gamblers, Nazi spies and fugitives from justice of one sort or another had frequented this waterside melting pot in times past, and a bevy of Anglo-Saxon writers, most of them American, had hauled their typewriters out to this extreme tip of Africa long before Gavin set out on their trail. Paul Bowles was the current writer in residence, and it was here that Tennessee Williams, Truman Capote and William Burroughs had also lived, written and extended the parameters of their being by such means as happened to come to hand at the time.

In his apartment at 1 Rue Dante, Gavin unpacked his suitcase, set up his typewriter, arranged his paper and ink and began to write for his life. 'I've settled down here,' he wrote to Jimmy Watt a few weeks after his arrival, 'and found a few really pleasant and interesting friends, and find writing so much easier than amid all the worries at home. I think I shall probably emigrate once the otter problem is finally solved somehow; I seem to have become rootless with the breakup of Sandaig. I find myself dreading spending the whole summer there.'

It was a strange existence, holed up amid the street cries and car horns of a strange city on the northernmost fringe of Arab Africa, scribbling away day after day about life with otters in a tiny patch of wilderness on the edge of the Hebridean Sea. During the working day Gavin's mind was filled with nostalgia for his home in the distant Scottish Highlands; but once the sun had set over the old port another kind of nostalgia took over, a *nostalgie de la boue* that found release among the dockside dives and drinking holes of Tangier's seamy nether world. It was here, perhaps, in an oddly academic sort of way, that Gavin experimented with hashish, which was widely prevalent in North Africa (though theoretically illegal in Morocco at the time). He wrote to me:

I smoked hashish – you know, little hashish pipes – and I got no reaction from it at all except an intense headache. I was mainly interested in my pulse rate. I went up to twenty-five pipes in two and a half hours, which is pretty high, and at the end of this time my pulse rate was 160 and I didn't feel very well. After a while I reached the conclusion that the reason for the popularity of this drug in North Africa is as a means of raising the pulse rate prior to sexual intercourse so as to produce an intensified orgasm. If you read Masters and Johnson, I think, you will find that orgasm rises to a pulse rate of 160 and if it falls much lower than 140 it's liable to be unsatisfactory. Personally, I failed to find anything else in it. I also ate the stuff in 'joint cakes' and I felt as though I'd had about five double whiskies, though I didn't feel particularly happy.

It was possibly under the influence of this unfamiliar substance that Gavin wrote to Jimmy Watt in April regarding the problems of coherent, creative thought in his present surroundings:

After due and undue cogitations, borborborygmi [sic], farts and regurgitations a couple of ideas emerged in the form of smoke rings which are still hanging around the room somewhere if I could spot them. Though possibly the result of hallucinations, halitosis and hashish, they looked like halos when I last saw them . . . I've got them now; one has taken refuge in the fridge, and the other, slightly rhomboid in shape, was very happy in the dregs of a bottle of Pernod. In fact it didn't want to come out again. Anyway, I've got them both cornered now, in a small bottle marked 'Not for human consumption'.

In some respects Gavin's life in Tangier had regressed to something like his hard-up existence as a painter in post-war London twenty years previously. He was poorer than he had been for years. 'Life here is hell,' he wrote to Beryl Borders. 'I am without money and living like a tramp, which is not a happy situation.' The outlook looked even blacker when *Lords of the Atlas* was withdrawn from circulation in the United States because of libel problems. 'Christ, I just can't win!' Gavin lamented. 'It's probably penury again for a long time.'

Wilfred Thesiger, on his way to the Sahara with his formidable mother, was particularly struck by Gavin's strange behaviour at this time. He recalled:

Gavin was very odd about money. In Tangier he hadn't got any – hadn't got a car or anything – so my mother and I would pick him up and take him out to lunch a few times. Just before we left, Gavin said to me, 'I do hope you and your mother can come and have lunch with me. I'd like to return your hospitality and I've invited the Consul General to join us. You'll find him interesting – he was a prisoner for a long time in China.' So we met up at the Rembrandt Hotel for drinks before lunch, and Gavin took me on one side and said, 'Can I have a word with you? As you know, I'm absolutely broke and I can't afford to pay for this lunch. Could you pay for it?' So like a bloody fool I said, 'Yes, all right Gavin.' I thought the least he would do when the Consul General came in would be to say, 'You owe this luncheon to Wilfred – he's insisted on paying for it.' But he didn't. He just said, 'Well, now, pick yourself a very good lunch.' So we had a very expensive lunch at a very expensive restaurant, with wine and liqueurs, and at the end the Consul General said, 'Thank you, Gavin – you've just given me one of the best lunches I've ever had.' And then, when no one was looking, Gavin pushed the bill across to me and I said to myself, 'Well, you've had it, Gavin, I don't really want to see you again.' And I didn't.

In faraway Scotland all was not well. Fighting his desperate rear-guard action against Gavin's increasingly hostile creditors, Richard Frere became as artful as a fox with the hounds on its tail. But even his ingenuity and dedication to his unenviable task could not delay the inevitable for ever, and one by one the most persistent creditors obtained judgements against Gavin Maxwell Enterprises or closed their accounts; the electricity and telephone were in imminent danger of being cut off, which would deprive Sandaig of the means of existence, and before long it was barely possible to pay even for fuel for the Land Rover.

Beryl Borders was holding the fort at Gavin's Highland home, but as winter deepened and life at Sandaig grew harder and more rugged still, her mood began to undergo a sea-change. Richard noticed that little by little she was becoming less boisterous and more withdrawn. Life in the wild weather and long dark nights at the northern sea's edge was unremittingly dour, requiring considerable physical exertion and mental resilience to survive. As well as looking after her own animals Beryl had to care for Gavin's and keep the place in running order come frost or flood. Every night she toiled over the mile and a half of peat-bog and mountainside to meet the mail van at Tormor; every night she stumbled down again with supplies and Gavin's mail in a 50-lb rucksack. Apart from her little daughter Fionna, there was no human company, and no diversions, no transport, no chance of getting away, and precious few perks and rewards. She received no remuneration from Gavin, and only a little over £5 a week to defray expenses.

Until now Beryl's respect and affection for Gavin had been unbounded; but gradually, in the absence of any warmth and encouragement from him in return, the conviction grew in her that he was simply using her – 'like a packhorse' – and disillusionment set in, and with it a mounting list of grievances. She felt Gavin had betrayed her friendship and trust, taken all and given little in return, demeaned her in front of his friends as 'a servant of a very low order' and 'a beggar under his roof'. Worse, she claimed Gavin's company had cheated her over a house in Glenelg and misappropriated her £500 down-payment on it. In fact, Gavin had offered to sell her the house – one of the two he had rashly bought in Glenelg at the same time as his two lighthouse cottages – at the valuation price of £2500, but shortly afterwards accepted a higher offer from someone else, which forced Beryl to raise her own offer to match it. In the autumn of 1966 she handed over a second payment of £2000 which instantly vanished into the maw of Gavin's deeply indebted company – a source of contention that was to grumble on for years. It did not help that one of her beloved Great Danes was caught in the act of savaging some sheep and was promptly shot dead by the outraged shepherd.

Though Mike Cuddy and Richard Frere and his family were able to take over the burden of running Sandaig from Beryl for a few weeks in late winter, the damage had been done. At the end of March Beryl's lawyers demanded that Gavin either hand the Glenelg house over to her or give her £2000 deposit back. 'Gavin, always on the lookout for duplicity in women, stormed in distant Africa,' Richard Frere recorded of this sad episode. Beryl responded with a score of bitter letters accusing him of ingratitude. Though the immediate quarrel was patched up, Beryl's underlying resentment was to survive for many months to come.

In the middle of March Gavin sent the first twenty thousand words of his new book off to his publishers, hoping for some interim reward, for all he had in his pocket was £44 in Moroccan money. He felt cut off from his home country and news from Sandaig was scant. 'Communication with England seems so uncertain as to be practically non-existent,' he wrote to Beryl in April. 'But at least I have got a major part of a book written, which I suppose I couldn't have done anywhere else.' Then on 18 April Gavin was startled to receive a telegram from Beryl which jolted his mind back to Sandaig in times long past, and momentarily helped to lighten the mounting tension between them: 'MONDAY CAME HOME TODAY WITH THE DOGS LET ME KNOW WHAT TO DO.'

It was eighteen months since Gavin had last set eyes on Monday, the semi-wild native otter, with her three cubs near the Sandaig waterfall. By return he sent an excited telegram: 'WONDERFUL NEWS PLEASE FEED AND ENCOURAGE BUT MAKE NO ATTEMPT CONFINE STOP SUGGEST TIBBY NOT MONDAY STOP MACDIARMAID WOULD KNOW.'

But it was indeed Monday that had come home, not Tibby, the otter with a penchant for men on crutches. And it was not just Monday – her timorous mate Mossy had come with her. The extraordinary news was confirmed in Beryl's second telegram: 'FEEDING FEMALE INDOORS PINK SPOTS NOSE INJURED BY TRAP FEEDING MALE UNDER LOBBY ALAN [MACDIARMAID] DOES NOT RECOGNISE CONFINEMENT UNNECESSARY WRITING.'

Bit by bit, with the help of a series of letters from Beryl which arrived out of sequence via the erratic Moroccan mails, Gavin was able to piece together the story of the miraculous return of Mossy and Monday to the Sandaig house after an absence of four years.

On 13 April, it seems, Monday had been caught by her right foreleg in a trap at the edge of the lochan up at Tormor. When she was released she flew at the man who had trapped her, then made off in the direction of Sandaig. Five days later, unable to fend for herself because of her injury, she evidently remembered the house which had once been her home and shelter, and simply walked into it with two of Beryl's dogs. Beryl fed the newcomer, who seemed perfectly tame and at ease in the house, made a bed for her in the bathroom and put antiseptic cream on her suppurating leg. Later that evening Monday's mate, Mossy, turned up at the house and took up residence under the floor of the coatroom.

For the next four days Beryl kept Monday in the bathroom and fed her a regular diet of fish. By the end of that time the otter's condition was much improved, and she began to take an interest in her surroundings (discovering among other things a mirror, in which she saw her own reflected image for the first time). To enable her to come and go as she pleased, Beryl cut a hole in the bathroom wall, and for the next two weeks Monday was out all day with her mate, returning at night to eat and sleep in the house. It was then that Beryl discovered Monday was pregnant. She hoped that the otter might have her cubs in the house, but this was not to be, for when Monday's leg was fully mended she and Mossy left the house where they had sought temporary refuge with human kind, never to return. 'I often see them over at the islands and in the river estuary,' Beryl wrote to Gavin. 'How wonderful it is to see them swimming and playing naturally in the sea and dashing around with each other quite free.'

It was not only the wild otters that had returned to the Sandaig house. 'A poltergeist has come here,' Beryl wrote; 'Yesterday it broke two windows; one while I was sitting on the corner of the sofa, and one in the kitchen while I was washing up.' Beryl's last paragraph caused Gavin the greatest heartache: 'Sandaig is more beautiful than ever now; there are great banks of primroses, blue-bells, violets, and a great profusion of wild flowers everywhere.'

On the same day that Monday returned to Sandaig Richard Frere issued a dire financial report. 'We have reached the end of the road,' he wrote. The latest interest in the lighthouse properties had evaporated. One of the properties in Glenelg was in such a ruinous condition that a demolition order had been issued against it, and Beryl Borders had declined the new asking price for the other house. Richard himself was owed nearly half a year's wages.

Gavin's present penury had finally convinced him that he would, after all, have to find a new home for the otters and close Sandaig down. To put *Polar Star* to more profitable use he proposed using her for tourist outings on Loch Ness. Beyond that he could see nothing. 'The future seems very uncertain,' he wrote to Beryl; 'Until the lighthouses are sold I can't even begin to think about it.' To Jimmy Watt he confided his immediate plans, hoping (in vain) to enlist the young man's help during Sandaig's final stages.

As the weeks passed and Tangier's brief spring began to ease into Mediterranean summer, Gavin's life in the old Arab town began to disintegrate bit by bit. 'He was working very hard and taking pills to go to sleep, wake himself up, keep himself going,' recalled Cherry Scott. 'Tangier was the worst possible place for someone like Gavin – violent, corrupt. It evoked the wrong side of him.' To the alarm of his expatriate friends he became involved in unseemly scrapes with Tangerine low-life, and he was tricked and robbed on every side. Alarmed at this turn of events, his long-standing Australian friend George Greaves, a Falstaffian figure who was the doyen of the foreign press corps, did his best to persuade Gavin to leave Tangier and go home. 'Gavin is getting into trouble,' Greaves warned Margaret Pope. 'You should do something about it. He hasn't got any money.' 'Well, give him some money,' Margaret Pope replied, 'but get him out of Tangier.' The trouble was that Gavin had no real home to go back to any more, and was full of strange presentiments. 'Make a note of this, but don't tell anyone,' he told Michael and Cherry Scott. 'I read my obituary in a dream last night, and I very much wonder if I'm going to survive September 1969.' He hung on, moving from apartment to apartment – from Rue Dante to Rue Goya and on to the Boulevard de Paris – toying with his book and dreading a return to the financial and emotional uproar that awaited him in Britain, until even his own self-imposed deadline had passed by. Not even Beryl's last poignant telegram could budge him: 'JAMES DIED TONIGHT PLEASE COME HOME.'

James Borders was Beryl's estranged husband, a jovial Cockney lawyer thirty years older than her. Though Beryl had left him at a time of marital strain to seek sanctuary with her daughter and her animals at Sandaig, his sudden death from a heart attack left her emotionally shattered. Faced with the funeral and urgent matters to attend to, she had no option but to go south – but how could she leave Sandaig, with its huge population of animal dependents, while Gavin lingered on in Africa? Even now Gavin could not, would not, come home. Once again it was Richard Frere and his family who filled the breach, foraging from the local ecology at Gavin's bidding and collecting more than five hundred herring gull eggs from the nesting colonies on the Sandaig islands to feed (in omelette form) to the otters, including the peripatetic Mossy and Monday. When the Freres returned home Mike Cuddy took their place at Sandaig, not realising it would be two months before Beryl came back, not two weeks, as he had thought.

When Beryl finally returned from her husband's funeral, she was almost immediately given Gavin's *coup de grâce*. He would not return to Sandaig, he informed her, until she had left it and taken her menagerie with her. In the meantime, he had already arranged to replace her with a seventeen-year-old assistant who had volunteered to look after Sandaig until it was closed down at the end of the summer. For Beryl this was a humiliating affront, and from that moment the crumbling relationship plummeted into recrimination and hatred. She would only leave Sandaig, she raged at Gavin, when it suited her, and that meant after her daughter had sat her exams and her donkeys had given birth to their foals and he had returned the money he owed her. 'No wonder you treat me like a fool,' Beryl railed in a letter written on the day of Gavin's departure from Tangier, 'for I have obviously been one. How you must have laughed at my expense . . . Fionna is very excited about your return. She still thinks you're God unfortunately. I am very, very sorry you are not my friend.' For Richard Frere, observing the sad dénouement from the wings, this was a painful dilemma. 'I had now shut my soul to the moral rights and wrongs of this sorry situation,' he was to recall afterwards. Much of his sympathy lay with Beryl, he acknowledged – but she did not employ him. 'It was as bleakly simple as that.'

When Gavin returned to England on 18 June 1967 he had already devised a half-formed plan for the otters' future. A zoo was out of the question; but a safari park (then a recent innovation in Britain) might be just the thing. An acquaintance of his by the name of Michael Alexander (a wartime inmate of and escaper from the notorious German prison-camp at Colditz) ran safari tours round the Duke of Bedford's great park at Woburn, and was enthusiastic about the idea of Edal and Teko finding a home there. When Gavin went down to Woburn a few days later he was greatly encouraged

by what he saw, and particularly impressed by the potential of the
'Chinese Dairy Lake' – a small round lake covered in water-lilies
with a covered oriental-style colonnade on its banks. Here at last
was the otter paradise he had been seeking, and he began at once
to make plans for the islands and fountains and heated sleeping
quarters with which he hoped to improve the site for his otters'
future comfort and enjoyment.

Gavin returned to London, and was almost immediately struck
down by a series of alarming physical disorders. The first hit him
without warning one morning as he sat down at his desk to make
a telephone call. When the number answered he found he had totally
lost his voice and could not even manage a whisper. The next day
he felt distinctly ill with headache and nausea, and began dosing
himself with antibiotics, but after five days without any sign of
improvement he called his doctor. The doctor, however, was less
interested in Gavin's general condition than in the crepitations he
discovered in the base of his left lung. He thought Gavin might
have an early pneumonia, while Gavin himself believed it might
be lung cancer, for which, as a heavy smoker, he was a classic
candidate. So convinced was he that he was doomed that he rang
Richard Frere at Sandaig to tell him so in a conversation of confidential high drama. The X-ray revealed nothing untoward, however, and the mysterious condition soon cleared up, or so it seemed.

But Gavin's state of health was to continue to give cause for
concern. During his latest sojourn abroad he had acquired a very
rare intestinal protozoa by the name of *coccidia isospora belli*. This
infection had first been recorded among Allied troops at Gallipoli
during World War One, and was next observed among Axis troops
in Tunisia and Algeria during World War Two; it had never been
recorded from Morocco before, so Gavin had notched up a medical
first. The symptoms included violent diarrhoea, nausea, vomiting
and acute abdominal pains, and after a fortnight in London Gavin
had lost a stone and a half in weight and was so weak he could
barely drag himself across the room. There was no known cure for
this unpleasant condition, though it was believed to be self-limiting
and to run a course of six to seven weeks. In the meantime the
doctors tried drug after drug in the hope that one of them might
turn out to be a match for the thriving colony of rare *coccidiae* to
which Gavin's luckless guts played host.

In the midst of this debilitating affliction came good news at last;

indeed, coming so soon after the negative cancer diagnosis, Gavin might have been forgiven for believing that the tide had turned and the power of the rowan tree curse was on the wane. First, his agent Peter Janson-Smith advised him that literary income was now coming through again, from miscellaneous royalties and foreign contracts; then, on 15 July – his fifty-third birthday – Isle Ornsay cottage was sold in the space of twenty-four hours, black fungus and rising damp notwithstanding. Both Gavin and the company were, for the moment, solvent again.

Though Gavin was still weak and ailing he decided to head north anyway, for his last summer at Sandaig was dwindling away at an alarming rate. On 1 August he arrived at Richard Frere's front door at Drumnadrochit. The protozoa infection was receding and no longer worried him greatly. 'At least, it's out of the ordinary,' he joked with Richard. 'That appeals to me.' Fresh air and rest and a regimen of large leisurely whiskies at Drumnadrochit completed the cure. But by 4 August Gavin had developed an intense pain in his *right* lung. It was agonising to laugh or to cough, and he could take only the shallowest of breaths. He thought it might be pleurisy, but when he began to spit blood he was not so sure.

Meanwhile he had been invited over to Isle Ornsay to meet the purchasers of the lighthouse cottage, Mr and Mrs Stuart Johnstone, and discuss the cottage's inventory before sealing the sale. So on 8 August he motored across Scotland with Richard, 'doped,' so he said, 'with the maximum amount of pain killers that could be trusted not to kill me as well.' And not just pain killers. Gavin was an extremely shy man, especially in the company of strangers, and often resorted to Dutch courage when required to confront new faces. The combination of antibiotic and Scotch proved a lethal cocktail. He slumped, mumbling incoherently on the sofa at Isle Ornsay, confronting the Johnstones with a celebrated author seemingly ailing in mind as well as body. 'It's the protozoa,' Richard Frere informed his startled hosts as he nodded reassuringly in the direction of his hopelessly befuddled employer. 'He's just back from Africa, you know.'

THIRTY-FIVE

Revived fortunes

But all shall be well, and all shall be well, and all
manner of thing shall be well.
JULIANA OF NORWICH, *Revelations of Divine Love*

From Isle Ornsay Richard drove Gavin on to Sandaig and his first
night in his Highland home for nearly nine months. Sandaig was
vacant now. As a temporary measure Beryl Borders had moved
into the house in Glenelg, promising to vacate it when Gavin paid
her her £2000 back. Now only one white Roman gander, a timid
cat, two donkeys and six poodles were left of the horde of creatures
that had once ruled this animal enclave by the sea. It was a brief
homecoming. By morning Gavin was coughing blood again, this
time in some profusion, and he was fearful he had escaped cancer
only to contract tuberculosis. Richard Frere returned to Sandaig
once more and drove Gavin back to the other side of Scotland,
depositing him at the Culduthel Hospital in Inverness, where he
was incarcerated inside a glass cubicle for tests for suspected
pleurisy.

Within twenty-four hours Gavin was ringing Richard asking to
be rescued. He didn't like the hospital, he said, he couldn't stand
the discipline, he hadn't even got TB. Mysteriously, though the
pain had been in the right lung, the blood seemed to have come
from the left lung – from a blood clot that might be attributable
to the *coccidiae* and in the normal course of events might be expected
to disperse of its own accord. So Gavin discharged himself as an
in-patient and signed on as an out-patient, putting up at the long-
suffering Freres' and travelling to the hospital every three days for
further blood tests. During this enforced convalescence he busied
himself with boyish enthusiasm on building a scale model of one
of the two elaborate otter houses that were to be fitted into the
colonnade around the Chinese Dairy Lake at Woburn.

Summer was nearly over when Gavin finally returned to Sandaig at the end of August 1967. The house was in a sorrier state than at any time during the nineteen years that Gavin had known it. The unusually wild winter and the long occupation by Beryl's animals had wreaked a special kind of havoc. Indoors the woodwork and plasterboard had been clawed, gnawed and holed, the bathroom ceiling had collapsed under the weight of a pack of poodles billeted in the loft above it, windowpanes had been broken by the poltergeist and rugs and carpets fouled by the dogs and cats. Outside the picture was little better. The winter winds had discoloured the once-white exterior walls of the house to decaying shades of fungus-green and dirty grey, and swept away the sand that covered the rubbish pits dug in the dunes, exposing a midden of rusty cans and old bottles. Forty head of cattle had trampled the surrounding turf into a mire of mud and dung, forced their way through the wooden gates, smashed the post-and-rail fence in front of the house and put their hoofs through the planks of the bridge over the burn. Far worse, someone had switched off the largest of the deep freezes, and the stench of eight hundredweight of rotting haddock inside it reminded Gavin of a similar disaster in the pickling tank on Soay during the shark-fishing days.

'Camusfeàrna,' Gavin noted simply after his return, 'was in a mess.'

But a few rays of sun beamed down here and there out of the pall of clouds that lowered over Gavin. Now, suddenly, there were rumours of a film deal in the air, and the prospect of real money coming in hard on the heels of the Isle Ornsay sale raised the prospect of an imminent end to the long financial nightmare.

The cinema industry had shown keen interest in *Ring of Bright Water* even before the book was published. When Michael Powell pulled out, the American producer Joseph Strick took over. For some years Strick had held an option on the book; then, in the early autumn of 1967, he decided to exercise it. The news caused an excited tremor of anticipation at Sandaig, for the money involved was substantial and would solve Gavin's financial problems for some while to come – and might, indeed, obviate the need to close down Sandaig after all. The terms of the draft contract had been agreed by Peter Janson-Smith; all that was required now was for the film's director, Jack Couffer, to come up to Sandaig, meet

Gavin, discuss the script and decide whether the real ring of bright water was suitable as a location for the film.

Gavin and Richard Frere shared the universal preconception of the Hollywood movie director – a fat, tough, sub-literate wheeler-dealer who chewed cigars, dined off silver and lived breathlessly on the verge of imminent cardiac arrest. Gavin decided that, for the significant occasion of Jack Couffer's visit, no expense should be spared. He telephoned Richard's wife Joan and asked her to scour Inverness for the very biggest Havana cigars, the very finest vintage ports, the most exquisite delicacies.

The day came, and Jack Couffer arrived, to everyone's surprise, on his own two legs, having found the way down over the hill by himself. Even more surprising, he was the exact reverse of what they had expected – 'a huge, rugged fellow with the undeniable stamp of outdoor living upon him', Richard Frere recalled. He rejected a whisky, even refused a mighty cigar, but appreciated the venison cooked to perfection by Gavin himself. Jack Couffer, it turned out, was no habitué of Sunset Boulevard but a genuine wilderness man in his own right. As director and cameraman for Walt Disney Wildlife Productions he had tramped many of the world's wild places, and far from being sub-literate had written a book about his adventures, called *Song of Wild Laughter*.

After lunch they got down to business. Jack Couffer produced the script of the film and laid it on the table for Gavin to read. Gavin read the first few pages eagerly, then more haltingly, as if in disbelief at what he saw. When he spoke it was, as Richard reported, 'in a voice of deep hurt'.

'But you can't *mean* it,' he said, ' – this is just not possible. You have depicted me as a middle-class businessman, as a, as a . . .'

His voice trailed away. He was trembling with anger and disappointment. He pushed the script across to Richard. Richard opened it and his eye alighted instantly on a line of dialogue in which Gavin was addressing his greylag geese.

'Scram, you guys!'

Gavin meanwhile had helped himself to a large whisky, and thus fortified returned to the fray. The script, he informed Jack Couffer, was a sham, a prostitution, a crime. It would have to be entirely rewritten. If it were not he would not allow his name to be associated with it and would sue anybody who made use of his book.

'Then I guess,' drawled the unruffled Hollywood director, 'we don't have a deal.'

Richard seized the first opportunity to halt the meeting. While Jack Couffer prowled round the house, Richard took Gavin on one side and bullied him into a compromise. 'Gavin Maxwell' the businessman was to be replaced by 'Graham Merril', a rebellious clerk who had formerly resided among the Marsh Arabs of Iraq. This and a few other minor changes to the script were agreed, and they had a deal. The money would come. The film would be made. Shooting would start early next year and Bill Travers and Virginia McKenna, whose film version of *Born Free* had been a wild box-office success, would be the stars. While Jack Couffer strode up the hill on the first leg of his return to sunny Hollywood, Gavin stayed behind in the Hebridean twilight and from behind his bottle of Johnny Walker contemplated his impending immortality on the silver screen.

In every way, it seemed, Gavin's fortunes were on the mend, and the years of retreat and disaster behind him. Even at Sandaig there was the promise of a return to the peace and stability of an era gone by. Earlier in the year, while still abroad, Gavin had taken on a temporary assistant whom he had neither met nor spoken to in order to help close down Sandaig and move the otters to their new home. The new employee was Andrew Scot, a Kentish youth of seventeen who had just left school. He was a devoted fan of *Ring of Bright Water*, and over the preceding five years had written many letters to Gavin in which he had expressed his passion for the Scottish wilds (this had led him to change his surname to Scot) and his yearning for the Camusfeàrna kind of life.

The employment of such a sturdy and resourceful young man at this time could not have been more fortunate. Far from being downcast by Sandaig's present shambles, Andrew positively relished the challenge. 'It's been such a chain of good fortune,' he told me later, 'more than you could believe would happen to someone. I mean reading the first book and taking part in the second, the true sequel to *Ring*.' The isolation, the primitiveness, the wind and the rain, the hard slog over the hills for mail and supplies, the foraging for firewood along the desolate beaches in all weathers – all this Andrew took in his stride. From the outset Gavin and Richard Frere warmly approved of his enthusiasm, his capacity for unsupervised hard work, his love of animals and his keen appreciation of the beauty of his wild surroundings; and though Richard detected in the young man's nature a touch of shadow and introspection which he feared might react uneasily with Gavin's own complex psyche, he welcomed his arrival as the potential saviour of Sandaig in its final phase.

It was Andrew's encouragement, probably, that spurred Gavin to make the momentous decision to give Edal and Teko a taste of liberty after their years of captivity. Teko was the first to see the half-remembered world beyond the blank confining wall of his wooden palisade. One sunny morning in early September Gavin opened the gate to his paddock and called his name, and with a welcoming chirrup Teko emerged from the dark behind his half-closed door, and a little uncertainly, as if bewildered and lost, walked out into the unconfined world he had not seen for more than four years. When he caught scent of Gavin Teko began to talk as he had in the days when he was free to roam the house – the little joyful, affectionate cries that had not been heard for so long.

Teko greeted Gavin with emotional affection. What, Gavin wondered, had he done to deserve such loyal trust? 'I had confined him for four years,' he wrote; 'I had deprived him of the human society to which as a baby he had been conditioned by no will of his own; I had even at one point determined to send him to a zoo. I had betrayed him.'

Teko was a sick animal. The right-hand side of his face was swollen and his right eye was completely closed. He had an infected tooth and was clearly in pain. On that first short walk in the outside world he had no wish to swim or wander; he would not stray from Gavin's feet and every few yards he would stop for fresh reassurance. Once he was back in his little house his only concern was that Gavin would not leave him alone again. 'What torture the human species inflict upon their "pets",' Gavin reflected.

After a five-day course of antibiotics Teko was restored to health, and on his next venture outside he proved a very different animal. This time he made a dash for his old haunts, and plunged into the burn with all the zest and *joie de vivre* of years gone by, chasing fish and porpoising through the calm reaches of the stream. He emerged at frequent intervals to rush up to Gavin, stand and reach up to him and utter his excited squeaks of joy. Every day from then on Gavin took Teko out to the waterfall and the island beaches.

Some of the spirit and colour of Camusfeàrna was at last restored.

Giving Edal her freedom was a more difficult proposition. She had been the more explosively violent of the two otters, and ever since her attack on Jimmy Watt in early 1962, five and a half years before, no human being had touched her and she had never left her enclosure. Yet Gavin was determined to give it a try, and a plan of campaign was devised. A new gate was inserted into Edal's fence, so that she could go straight out on to the dunes above the sea. Medical supplies – dressings, a surgical needle and thread, cocaine solution and a hypodermic syringe – were on hand in case something went wrong and someone was injured. At last, on 11 September, everything was ready. Andrew was posted to a spot on the hillside from which he could watch all that ensued and warn any casual visitor that a potentially lethal animal was loose in the vicinity; he was to follow Gavin's progress through binoculars, and if Edal attacked he was to run down to the house and telephone the doctor in Glenelg at once. Carrying a pot of pepper for self-defence, Gavin opened the gate to the dunes and uttered the call that used to sound and re-sound so often about the house in those distant days when Edal was a young and gentle and free-roaming member of the Sandaig family.

'*Whee-ee! Ee-eedal! Whee-ee!*'

There was a pattering of paws in the tunnel that led from Edal's sleeping quarters – and there she was, standing beside Gavin, poised at the exit to the sand and the sea and the great rustling, splashing, scenting, breezing broad void of the forbidden world beyond the palisades.

Edal was interested in none of it. She stood at the door of her prison – then proceeded to investigate with studious intensity the lock mechanism of the prison gate! Gavin had half-expected she might make a mad rush for the sea; half-hoped she might have greeted her long-lost human foster-father with rapturous joy; he had forgotten the keenly intelligent curiosity with which she had once explored the world – and that that world had changed for her. All around her were man-made objects – most of them damaged – which she had never before seen. Only a few yards from the gate stood a broken-down Jeep, and for minutes on end she examined its axles and half-shaft, its switches, pedals and steering wheel. So she proceeded, from the Jeep to the upturned, staved-in dinghy, then on to the work-shed that housed the deerhounds and thence to the looming shape of the *Polar Star* on its wheeled cradle. Only then did she turn, with Gavin, in the direction of the great expanse of the open sea, crossing the exposed sands of the ebb tide to chase dabs in the shallows. 'She was plainly happy,' Gavin recalled, 'and I no longer felt afraid of her; nor, I think, did she in any way mistrust me.'

A few days later it was Andrew Scot who took Teko out over the dunes and down to the beach and the mouth of the burn, watched intently by Gavin through a port-hole in an upstairs room of the house. Only four days later, at the end of their third walk, the unbelievable happened. Gavin was sitting at his desk when he looked up and spotted Andrew and Teko coming down the Jeep track. A few moments later he was distracted by the sound of otter laughter. He looked out of the window and saw Andrew and Teko romping on the grass. Teko was free and restored to the world and humankind at last.

A few weeks later Gavin's old relationship with Edal was restored in full. It was a rare and magical autumn day in late September – not a breath of wind, the sea still, the tide far out. Gavin took Edal out to the white shell and coral sands of the island beaches and the marine garden of the shallow bay beyond the island bar. Suddenly it was as though time had never passed, as though both man and otter had set foot in this enchanted world for the first time in their lives, and stood there in wonder and exhilaration at the very beginning of their long adventure together. Released into that brilliant sunlit bubble of seemingly limitless space, Edal gave full rein to her elation and dashed about all over the white sand and porpoised wildly at high speed through the shallow translucent water. For Gavin too it was like a return to an earlier era, and he looked about him not with the jaded, unseeing eyes of the careworn adult he had become but with the bright, unclouded vision of the absorbed child, the enraptured poet-painter he had once been.

So absorbed was Gavin in his rediscovery of Camusfeàrna's half-remembered natural paradise that he momentarily forgot about his gambolling otter. Then he felt a sudden nudge on the back of his leg and turned to see Edal corkscrewing in ecstasy through the water. Remembering a game they used to play, he took her by the tail, and began to swing her round by it faster and faster till she let herself go limp, her face wearing a long-forgotten look of fulfilment. When Gavin let her go she went shooting away in the clear water, and as he watched her he wondered which had restored most to the other. 'To me the sky and sea looked brighter, more real,' he wrote, 'the shallow sea's floor more brilliant than before, for an enduring mist of guilt had been lifted from them all. I was content now to let the future resolve itself, for I knew that I could no longer break the trust of animal friendship . . . High above me, wheeling in taut arcs, two buzzards mewed like kittens, and a single wild goose flew northwards over the Sound – a Pinkfoot, calling continuously, lost, as I had been for so long.'

They began to retrace their steps back towards the house. At a halfway point Edal stopped and sat on a knoll to dry and polish herself on the heather and toboggan down the grassy slope, arms and monkey fingers waving. Her fur, Gavin noted, now had a sheen he had not seen for years, and her eyes were no longer dulled by the sensory deprivation of confinement but bright with new-found life and vigour. He pulled her towards him as he used to when she was a cub, and blew in her fur and rolled her over and tickled her toes and whiskers, and she responded as Teko had done, with little snuffles of affection.

'When we started home Edal and Teko had between them given back to me the land in which I lived, the vision that I had lost . . . In moments of peace such as I experienced that day with Edal there exists some unritual reunion with the rest of creation without which the lives of many are trivial . . . The way back cannot be the same for all of us, but for those like myself it means a descent of the rungs until we stand again amid the other creatures of the earth and share to some small extent their vision of it.'

Gavin had planned to close Sandaig down by the autumn, but autumn came and went, and Christmas fast approached. Though Richard Frere happily sawed and hammered away at the two otter houses he was constructing for the Woburn ottery, there was no longer the same urgency to move the otters there, for the financial pressure which was the underlying motive for the move was now largely a thing of the past. Besides, for the first time for many years peace and contentment now reigned at Sandaig, and with the liberation of the otters life had returned to the routine of the early days. Teko came into the living room each day to romp with his human companions, and Edal was a friend who was feared no more. Gavin still seemed disposed to go through with the move, which had gathered a momentum of its own, but the outcome was not entirely in his hands, and he now felt that it would be no disaster if it did not take place after all.

At Woburn, meanwhile, there were many setbacks and delays in preparing the Chinese Dairy Lake for the otters and their elaborate otter houses, and in the middle of December, exactly a year after the breakdown of negotiations with Aberdeen Zoo, the authorities at Woburn telephoned Gavin to announce that they could not approve the programme.

On 8 January 1968 Gavin and Richard travelled south to view alternative sites at Woburn. But none looked suitable, and Gavin shook his head decisively and strode off through the snow. 'Compromise never suited him,' Richard noted. 'He preferred to scrap an idea rather than modify it.'

They returned to the north. Perhaps, Gavin suggested, they might find a suitable site in Scotland. They came to the conclusion that the best place for a new ottery was Richard Frere's own back garden, where rough woodland gave on to a small stream. Gavin was never happier than when hatching a new idea; he had a passion for making plans, for any creative act that did not entail sitting alone writing a book. 'In his mind's eye,' Richard recorded, 'the Drumnadrochit Wildlife Park was taking shape hourly.'

But Gavin's euphoria did not last long. On the evening of 19 January his mood darkened and he began drinking heavily. By the early hours he was well soused, comical and tiresome by turns, and causing growing concern to his two guests – Jimmy Watt, on a short visit, and Magda Stirling, Gavin's attractive twenty-two-year-old cousin, who was spending a few days' holiday at Sandaig. At three in the morning Gavin was falling about and dropping lighted cigarettes all over the house, and his guests were not sure whether to go to bed and leave him to his own devices, a danger to himself and perhaps to the whole establishment, or to stay up with him and deny themselves sleep. Eventually Jimmy staggered off upstairs, and Magda, left alone with her deeply inebriated uncle, decided that there was nothing to do but put him to bed. On an impulse she tucked up in bed with him, not out of any sexual motivation, but out of the compassion of one who understood what he was going through and loved him dearly. At about five, with Gavin calm and dormant, she finally fell asleep herself, having helped him through his despair to another day.

The next morning, Saturday 20 January, Richard Frere drove over to Sandaig on a working visit. The house was quiet when he arrived. Andrew Scot was deep in a game of chess with Magda. Of Gavin there was no sign – he was still in bed, Richard was told, sleeping off the night before.

The day passed slowly and uneventfully. Gavin emerged from his study-bedroom eventually, looking distinctly the worse for wear, and began to prepare one of his Maxwell's bean feasts for his guests' lunch. Apart from Magda, everyone seemed subdued. Soon the midwinter light began to fade, the lamps were switched on and the curtains pulled. At three the departing guests began to pack, for Jimmy had a train to catch from Inverness and Magda was on her way to see her fiancé in New York. The goodbyes were protracted; Gavin chose this moment to take Richard on one side for a private conversation lasting half an hour or more, and by the time they were finished it was getting late and they had to rush. At the door Richard looked back. Gavin and Andrew were sitting at the chess board on the fish-box sofa beneath the shelves of groceries on the far side of the room. The remains of a bean feast congealed on a plate on the dinner table. In the open hearth, beneath the mantelpiece with its Latin inscription '*Non fatuum huc persecutus ignem*' (It is no will-o'-the-wisp that I have followed here), lay a pair of punctured bellows and a huge piece of driftwood smouldering fiercely.

Richard closed the door, never to open it again.

THIRTY-SIX

Fire and ice

Some say the world will end in fire
And some in ice
From what I've tasted of desire
I hold with those who favour fire
But if I had to perish twice
I think I know enough of hate
To say that ice is also great
And would suffice.

ROBERT FROST, *'Fire and Ice'*

In the small hours of 21 January 1968 Gavin was slowly woken from a deep sleep by a painful choking sensation. For a moment he lay there fearing his lung problem had returned, but when he opened his eyes they smarted dreadfully and he realised the room was full of a strong reek of smoke. He reached out to switch on his bedside lamp, but though there was a click there was no light. Fully awake now, and thoroughly alarmed, he leapt out of bed and began to stamp on the floor and beat on the wooden walls of his room with his fist. Andrew slept in the room above, and Gavin knew the first thing he must do was to wake him.

'Andrew! Andrew!' he yelled. 'This house is on fire!'

There was no response that he could hear. Adrenalin racing, unshod and very nearly unclothed, Gavin groped his way out of the room and began to climb the stairs. Halfway up he collided with Andrew tumbling down, half-blinded by smoke and gasping desperately for breath. Gavin pushed him through the front door out into the open air, then grabbed the fire extinguisher from the lobby wall and burst into the living room, from which he could hear a low, deep, unnerving crackle. A few feet inside he was met by a wall of heat and acrid smoke. Round the fireplace the varnish of the pitch-pine panelling was bubbling furiously, and just below the ceiling flames were advancing on the open beams and planking of the floor above. Gavin directed the fire extinguisher at the hottest part of the room, but the flames subsided only momentarily, then roared back. Unable to hold his breath any longer, he rushed out of the room.

By now Andrew had got his breath back, and with remarkable presence of mind had dashed into Gavin's room, grabbed the manuscript of *Raven Seek Thy Brother* and carried it out to safety. Outside the front door they briefly conferred. The otters had to be rescued first; after that they would salvage what they could from the house. But which otter should they rescue first? It seemed Teko would be in gravest danger, for his little shed was right next to the main wall of the house, and a light south-westerly wind was blowing the flames in his direction and away from Edal's. As they rushed round to Teko's stockaded quarters they were astonished to see that the whole of the roof was on fire and tongues of flame were leaping out between the cracking slates; and as they stood there, transfixed by the sight of this galloping conflagration, a mass of burning debris came crashing down the stairs and sealed off the main entrance to the house.

Through all the smoke and bedlam Teko had been sleeping peacefully. Andrew reached in, snatched the startled otter from his blanket-covered lorry tyre, slung him over his shoulder, rushed across the muddy field to Raef's cottage and threw him in through the door. Teko was safe, but what of Edal? Gavin ran round to the wooden annexe at the other end of the house. Because there was no light other than the guttering flicker of the fire in the main building it was hard to tell whether Edal was still in her quarters or not, but the hatch to her outside paddock was open, so it seemed reasonable to assume she was in no danger.

Gavin returned to the front of the house to find Andrew, who had displayed great courage and foresight throughout this catastrophe, wrestling with the gun case that was bolted to the wall opposite the main entrance. Tug and twist as he might, Andrew could not move the case, so he smashed the glass with his elbow and began to pass the guns out one by one, severely gashing his hand as he did so. Before he had got all the guns out Gavin shouted: 'Andrew, for God's sake come out of there *now*! Look, the ammunition –!'

Over five hundred rounds of ammunition, from small calibre .22 to heavy calibre .350 magnum, had tumbled out of the gun case into the red-hot debris at the foot of the stairs. Andrew took one look and dashed out of the door, leaving behind two barrels, a Winchester rifle and Gavin's Colt pistol from SOE days. Almost immediately the ammunition began to explode, and all around the burning house the sound of gunfire rattled away, as if the place were a hotly fought ambuscade in some remote frontier war. The building was by now far gone. The roof was falling in and flames roaring out of the upstairs windows. The living room was an inferno and the air howled as it rushed in through the door and broken windows to feed the hungry flames.

Andrew cried out to Gavin: 'The long room is on fire!'

'And Edal?'

'I don't know. I just don't *know*.'

Andrew had climbed in through a window, but the room was black with thick, tarry smoke and he couldn't even open his eyes. He tried another window, next to Edal's compartment, but it was too hot to touch.

The fire had burst through the side door and set the annexe alight. The roof-felt was melting and the tar was running down like black treacle to fill the room with thick, poisonous smoke. If Edal was still in that room it was hardly possible she could be alive. Even if she had been alive, she could not have survived the next phase of the remorseless destruction of the house, for suddenly the gas ignited, the long room blew up, the walls fell down and the roof caved in. Sweeping on into the workshop, the flames ignited the paint tins, petrol cans and Calor-gas cylinders stored inside, which detonated like cannon fire as the roof and the upper floor of the house collapsed into the cauldron below. A bright glare momentarily lit up the trees along the burn and on the slopes above the dying house, and two muffled explosions echoed between the islands and the hills like a salute of guns.

It was all over. The house had gone. Its contents, including virtually everything Gavin possessed in the world, had been destroyed. Edal was nowhere to be found. In the bitter cold of the winter night Gavin sat shocked and shivering inside the *Polar Star* on its cradle overlooking the bay. Up on the hill Andrew, shoeless and half-clad, was racing towards Tormor to raise the alarm. The dawn was a long time coming, and by then Camusfeàrna was far beyond help or redemption.

*   *   *

Richard Frere was asleep at home when the telephone woke him at six on the morning of Sunday 21 January. Police Constable Nairne at Glenelg gave him the bleak news. The house at Sandaig had been burned to the ground, he said. Gavin and Andrew were alive but the otter Edal was believed to be dead. Aghast, Richard made a quick check in his office and confirmed the worst. The contents of the house were uninsured – the insurance premiums had not been paid for two years. Grieving and guilt-stricken, Richard set off on the hour-long drive to Sandaig.

A fire-engine, unable to negotiate the rough track down to Sandaig, stood parked and abandoned at Tormor. Richard drove the Land Rover slowly down the treacherous trail towards the house, and at the last bluff overlooking the bay and the field paused to look down at the grim scene below. Smoke still poured out of the gutted house, filling the air with an acrid blue haze that made his eyes water. The house, still glowing, was almost totally destroyed, with only the outside walls standing. Of the wooden annexe that had housed Edal only charred fragments remained. All around the grass had been scorched yellow by the intense heat of the flames.

Richard drove down to the field in front of the burnt-out house. Firemen were prodding about amongst the embers looking for clues to the cause of the fire and for anything that could be salvaged. There was very little evidence of either. The destruction was total. The bedrooms, staircase, study, living room and kitchen no longer existed. A few scorched and buckled household appliances like the cooker and refrigerator still stood amid the debris, along with a jumble of water tanks and cylinders that had fallen through from the upper floor, much of it still red-hot. Everything made of wood or paper had vanished utterly, including not only the furniture and the pitch-pine panelling of the walls, but the whole of Gavin's precious library and that portion of his archives that had been stored in his study, along with the trophies and mementos of a lifetime of travel and adventure.

Richard found Gavin in the *Polar Star*, 'looking,' he wrote later, 'like a plant blasted by frost, black and drooping.' The Glenelg doctor had already given him a heavy sedative, and at first his speech was rambling and incoherent. He asked Richard if he could find it in his heart to bury Edal, and when Richard asked where, Gavin pointed to the rowan tree near the house. 'Later we shall do her some justice,' he muttered in a barely audible voice.

Richard had difficulty finding Edal's body in the burnt-out ruins of her quarters, where she had been trapped and killed by the flames. Her charred little cadaver had been so shrunk by the fire that Richard could carry her in the cups of his hands. He dug a shallow hole beneath the rowan, laid Edal in it and marked the spot with a stone. Then he remembered that this was the same tree upon which Gavin had once been cursed.

Gavin had begun to tremble uncontrollably with the cold and shock, and Richard took him to the Land Rover and ran the engine to warm him up with the heater. With Edal buried, Gavin seemed to accept that Camusfeàrna was gone for ever.

Andrew returned in the dinghy at about this time. His hand was heavily bandaged and he was near to exhaustion, but his thoughts were only for the welfare of Gavin and Teko. Teko was still locked up in Raef's croft, but his quarters had not been damaged – with hindsight it was clear that it was Edal that should have been rescued first – and Andrew was able to return the surviving otter to his old home.

Throughout the morning the press straggled down the hill to report the destruction of Camusfeàrna. For the most part they kept a tactful, considerate distance and were content simply to print the short statement prepared by Gavin. The police were less obliging. Constable Nairne had been a model of kindness, but his superior officer felt duty-bound to thoroughly investigate the disaster and eliminate all suspicious circumstances from his enquiries.

'Mr Maxwell,' he asked Gavin at the conclusion of a plain-speaking interview, 'did you set fire to the house yourself?'

This was too much for Gavin, and too much for Richard too. He took the detective to one side. He was wrong to suspect an insurance swindle, he informed him. The building was not Gavin's and the contents were not insured.

The short grey winter day began to fade. One after the other the reporters, firemen and police began to leave the scene, trudging wearily up the hill. Such was Gavin's state of shock that at first he refused to make use of Raef Payne's croft without Raef's permission, and only consented to do so when Richard managed to contact Raef by telephone and received his whole-hearted assurance that they must 'use anything, everything', for as long as it was wanted. Gavin, Richard and Andrew took refuge in the one-roomed croft. None of them was hungry, but they forced down a basic meal and helped themselves to restorative measures of Raef's Scotch. So long as Sandaig was Teko's home both Gavin and Andrew felt obliged to struggle on there, for after all that had happened it would have been cruel indeed for one to leave the other in solitary wretchedness. Late in the evening Richard decided to return home. He did not wish to intrude on the private grief of the survivors or endure the gloom that would succeed it. Nor could he look Gavin in the face while he was still consumed by guilt over the insurance fiasco.

Richard walked over to the smoking ruin in whose ravaged heart the fire still glowed bright. 'Somewhere away to the north there was a cry like an otter's. Was it Mossy or Monday, perhaps, crying from some holt of their choosing in the dark river's bank? I could see the rowan tree in the glow and I walked over to it, found the stone and rested both my hands upon it, staying there a while until the cold and a sense of desolating loneliness sent me back to the Land Rover and the long road home.'

THIRTY-SEVEN

The White Island

I met my love in Avalon
Beside the bay;
I left my heart in Avalon
And sailed away.
AL JOLSON SONG

The croft was small, dark and rudimentary – a single long room, with a fireplace at one end, two small windows like embrasures in a castle wall, a low door, a few sticks of rudimentary furniture, and an impressive array of sea gear and wet-weather kit hanging from the rafters. In the days when a crofting community had tried to wrest a living from the soil at Sandaig, the croft had been lived in by an old lady, who was driven out by an abnormally high tide. Later it had been the schoolroom, and the initials of those long-dispersed children who had won the dour struggle for literacy in that isolated settlement could still be seen chiselled into the wooden beams and window-surrounds inside. There was no sanitation, no hot water for baths, no privacy, but lots of mice.

The place was not entirely without its virtues. Situated almost on the beach at the southern end of the little bay, but sheltered from all but the worst of the weather by the wooded cliff in whose lee it crouched, it looked out over a marvellous panorama of dunes, islands, sea and mountains, from the alder-arched ring of the burn to the distant profile of Eigg, a slab along the horizon of the Hebridean Sea. Nor was the croft without a modicum of comforts. For some years the local laird had leased the building to Raef Payne as a holiday home, and over a period of time Raef had restored it from its ruinous condition, installed electricity, and generally made it weatherproof and habitable for short stays. Here Gavin and Andrew, in a state of great austerity and simplicity, and with few personal possessions, settled down to brave the winter. A month after the fire, Gavin wrote a letter of sad reflection to Raef's mother, an old friend:

> Thank you so very much for writing. What can one say – what can you say – what can anyone say? A dream has died at the age of 20 – a ripe old age for a dream. I think I am still suffering from shock – I didn't know it could last so long. Perhaps it lasts longer the older one grows and the older the dream was. The charred ruins of the house confront one every time one opens this door. Sometimes they seem negative, sometimes they produce vomiting; one has no warning in advance and the effect doesn't seem to wear off. Morale, I'm afraid, is low for the moment . . .
>
> How long ago everything seems – at the same time how close at hand . . . the ducks and the flapjacks and all the awful understandings and misunderstandings and drunken Bentleys and hawthorn-torn shirts. And deaths, human and animal. And the idea that one was somehow going to influence the world (I suppose I have, in a way).

Gavin told me later: 'It just seemed to me that everything had gone with Sandaig and that I owned literally nothing. Andrew and I started off, I suppose you might say, as beggars. We had escaped from the fire with nothing but a pair of trousers each – we hadn't got shoes or socks, we hadn't got shirts, we hadn't got pullovers. The world seemed a complete dead end. There was nothing more to do – it was over.'

During the week following the fire Richard Frere made several visits with a host of essential items. Then extra succour came from an unexpected quarter. Friends and well-wishers all over the world soon learned of Gavin's plight – I heard the news myself over the BBC World Service while staying on an RAF fighter base in Singapore. Before long they began to send parcels of food, clothing and home comforts, from books, indoor games, a record player and a typewriter to socks, pullovers and balaclavas. The Earl of Dalhousie sent a three-piece Harris tweed suit, Tony Dunlop donated a large pile of blankets, and a five-year-old boy in Cornwall posted a tin of sardines with a note on the lid which read: 'Thes is for Teko case hees hungry.' Gavin's psychiatrist, Dr Ellis Stungo, sent a note: 'I always had a fear you would set yourself alight and

well recall an evening in London when you used your well-filled
wastepaper basket as an ashtray. I was so worried that I phoned
Robin McEwen and asked him to come round to keep an eye on
you.'

The precise cause of the fire was never discovered, though its
epicentre was believed to be in or around the living-room fireplace
or the lobby behind it. When I heard the news of the disaster my
mind went back to the winter I had spent at Sandaig and to the
smoke I used to see seeping out from the pitch-pine panelling on
the adjacent wall whenever there was a good fire burning in the
range. Where smoke could find a way, I had warned Gavin, so
could sparks and even fire, but nothing had been done. Beryl
Borders had voiced a similar suspicion when the police investigated
the case. 'I told them the wiring was bad in the annexes,' she wrote
to Gavin afterwards, 'and the chimney was weak in the living room
and I never had a big fire.' Once a fire had started there could be
no stopping it, for the varnished wooden walls and ceilings were
like a tinder box waiting to be ignited.

It was not until a week or two after the fire that Gavin discovered
none of his possessions had been insured. He heard the news when
he telephoned the insurance company to ask about the position,
and afterwards he rang Richard Frere to pass on the information. He
expressed no anger at Richard's oversight, and attached no blame to
him; he was just grateful, he said, for Richard's help in relieving
him of the burden of life's practical problems so that he could get
on with his work. 'At first I could speak no word in answer,'
Richard wrote later. 'Guilt which stemmed from my carelessness
was added to shame that I had not understood him to be so big a
man. Never again did I doubt his presence among the immortals.'

For the rest of the winter the Sandaig refugees hung on in the
croft, huddling in front of the driftwood fire through the weeks of
frost and howling gales from the sea; then through the spring, with
its primroses and nesting gulls and skeins of migrating geese, and
into the long, blue days of high summer. For six months Gavin
did little work and received few visitors. He played chess now and
then, listened to his favourite comedians (Peter Sellers and Tony
Hancock) on the record player, and read some of the books that
had been donated by well-wishers. He walked the high-tide line
with the irrepressible Teko, talked to Owl, the six-month-old
tawny owl he had acquired from Sir Henry Douglas-Home, the

brother of the former British Prime Minister Lord Home, watched the sunsets flaring behind Isle Ornsay, and thought and dreamed.

He had, he knew, come to the end of an era in his life. Yet he continued to cling to his last foothold at the edge of Sandaig Bay. It was as though he was unable to come to terms with the cataclysmic change in his situation, with his imminent exile from the ring that had made him and his otters famous around the world. 'It has indeed been a difficult disaster to take in one's stride,' he wrote to the headmaster of Stowe, 'because what has gone *was* one's stride, and in one's fifty-fourth year it is difficult to get into a new one.'

It was Teko that jolted him into action. Teko's original owner, who worked in West Africa, had heard about the fire on the radio and telegraphed to ask whether the otter was alive or dead. This reminded Gavin that no matter what had happened he still had responsibilities, and that somehow he had to provide for the remaining otter. There was now no question of Teko being sent to another owner. 'Now he will never let Teko go,' Richard Frere warned Gavin's accountant. At that time it was not clear whether Andrew Scot would want to stay on. He had originally been engaged only on a temporary basis, and after this disaster Gavin thought that he would go. The fact that he wanted to stay on was another factor in Gavin's decision as to where he would live.

Once Gavin attained a state of mind in which he was able to make a decision, the decision made itself. Isle Ornsay had been sold the previous year, and London was out of the question. Gavin had hoped that because Camusfeàrna was famous worldwide it might be rebuilt and devoted to some purpose that conformed to the public's image of it. 'I felt it ought to be a place of pilgrimage,' he wrote, 'not for my sake but for what it had come to represent in people's minds. And when they arrived there they should have facilities for seeing nature, or (shall we say) for being in the same frame of mind in which I wrote *Ring of Bright Water*. But no – it was going to be left a ruin, unbuilt, unrestored . . .'

Gavin's landlord, Lord Dulverton, had no wish to see any phoenix rise from the ashes. 'The fact is,' he explained later, not unreasonably, 'that he really did give me a lot of trouble after I had taken pity on him and gave him a base at Sandaig, whose privacy and charm is now entirely a thing of the past.'

There was only one place left to go – Eilean Ban, the White Island, in the narrows of Skye. To any ordinary mortal it might have seemed the height of folly to envisage permanent residence on a tiny, trackless, rock-bound desert island such as Kyleakin, with no utilities on it and no boat service to it. But Gavin was no ordinary mortal.

'I felt drawn to Kyleakin,' he had written in his latest and as yet unpublished book, 'as I had to few other places in my life . . . At first I thought it might be due to nothing more complex than the fact that Camusfeàrna, with all its echoes of past unhappiness and loss, was out of sight. But I think now that it was a far call back to childhood, for the long, rough heather, the briars and the out-crops of bare rock might have been those surrounding the House of Elrig, where I was born, the house that obsessed my childhood.' It was here, he decided, that he would live if ever he left Camus-feàrna. He loved its situation and he enthused about its potential for development as an eider colony and zoo park, ideas which he now began to pursue with renewed vigour. On the White Island, perhaps, lay his last, his true Avalon.

But the decision could not be implemented straight away. Kyleakin Island had to be made ready for its new occupants. The house had not been lived in for three years, the generator had not been turned over for two. Slates had been blown off the roof and the damp was coming back through the interior walls. More importantly, quarters had to be made ready for Teko, together with an escape-proof paddock or garden; and a radio-telephone had to be installed to provide communication with the outside world. For several weeks in the early spring Richard Frere was busy making the necessary improvements to the Kyleakin establishment.

By May the work was finished, but there was still no telephone. June came and went and still there was no telephone, but Gavin decided he could put off his departure no longer. 16 July was fixed as the date on which he would turn his back on Camusfeàrna for the last time and move his ménage to his new home on the White Island.

Andrew Scot, Teko and Owl, and a few possessions, set off from Sandaig to Kyleakin by fishing boat. Gavin proceeded separately, travelling by road to Kyle of Lochalsh, where he met up with Richard Frere. Together they crossed over to the island in Gavin's small boat, the *Assunta*, a former ship's lifeboat. It was not an easy day for any of them, but especially for Teko. 'You can imagine,'

Gavin told me not long afterwards, 'trying to move a wild animal from the place that has been its home for nine years. We had the most appalling first week. Teko seemed determined to try and return to Sandaig, and escaped day after day.'

On 18 July Teko made his first and most successful escape bid. His absence was not noticed until the evening, when Andrew Scot took him his evening meal and found he had gone. A search of the tiny island revealed no sign of the errant otter, and it was not until Gavin began to scan the sea with his binoculars and spotted a dinghy making straight for the island that the mystery was solved. 'Have a look at *that*!' he said to Richard. Richard took the glasses from him and saw an astonishing sight.

'A man was rowing the dinghy,' he recounted subsequently; 'in the stern were four delighted children; between them, rolling about in ecstatic joy, was an object which was undeniably the missing otter.' The party landed and the man told all he knew; Gavin and Richard filled in the gaps. Teko had been found in the man's house in Kyleakin village on the Isle of Skye. To get there, the otter had broken out of his escape-proof garden on Kyleakin Island, made his way across the island to the water's edge, swum across the strongly flowing steamer channel, landed on Skye, headed into Kyleakin, crossed a busy main road, found a way into the house, discovered the bathroom and clambered into the empty bath. There he had been discovered by a young child, and the two had become instant friends. Realising that the otter must be the property of his famous new neighbour on the island across the water, the child's father had promptly set out to return the creature to his owner. By this time Teko had greatly taken to his young friends. 'It took quite a lot of persuasion to convince him that his home was on the island,' Richard commented, 'and not in the village opposite.'

Though Teko escaped several more times, never again did he swim out to sea. On 20 July he broke out of his quarters a second time and was found in the lobby of the house. Three days later he got into the sitting room and staked out his territory by urinating in a wide circle over the expensive carpet. Richard Frere, who after all these years had never before come into direct contact with this famous but unpredictable animal, took the precaution of standing on the back of the settee out of harm's way. The next day Teko escaped again, returning of his own accord at tea time. Confined to the spare bedroom, he quickly turned the place upside down and inside out. 'Utter devastation,' Gavin noted succinctly in his diary. Removed to the annexe, an outbuilding that had been converted into a self-contained bed-sitting room, he reduced this too to chaos. Finally Teko gave up his vain search for his lost territorial home and settled down to a new life on the island.

For Gavin it really did seem a new beginning. The anguished memories of Sandaig and its long sequence of disasters were now behind him. His period of penury, too, seemed at an end. Money from the film rights to *Ring of Bright Water* and from advances and serial rights for his new book, *Raven Seek Thy Brother*, had at last enabled him to pay off his old debts. Between June and October 1968 just under £13,000 was paid into Gavin's account – a tremendous sum by the standards of the literary profession, and the equivalent of some £150,000 at the present time of writing. During the same period, however, over £12,000 was paid out in settlement of outstanding accounts, the bulk of it to Gavin's bankers. This did not leave much to tide Gavin over the winter, but for the moment he was out of the red, and enjoying an illusory sense of prosperity. 'I shall be very surprised,' he assured me a week or two after he had lashed out on a new de luxe 220 SE Mercedes saloon to supplement his sporty but unreliable 300 SL, 'if I ever get into debt again.'

Gradually he began to settle back into a working mode. It was not easy, for he still had no phone and no secretarial help. Occasionally urgent business from the outside world commanded his attention. Most pressing was the question of libel in *Raven Seek Thy Brother*, which (like most of Gavin's previous books) bristled like a porcupine with defamations and libels of all sorts, arising from his brushes with the medical, legal, academic and zoological professions and with various personal acquaintances during the course of his life and adventures over the last five years.

Closer to Gavin's heart was the future of British otters, a question which had preoccupied him for some years – more so since the death of Edal. Not long after the Sandaig fire Gavin had, at the suggestion of Peter Scott, opened a popular appeal, called the Edal Fund, under the umbrella of the World Wildlife Fund, of which Peter Scott was then Chairman. Both Gavin and the WWF believed that the tragic death of the world's most famous otter should be turned to the advantage of the animal kingdom, in particular the otter. At that time the otter was not on the official list of protected animals, and was still hunted. Many experts believed the otter was facing a severe population decline, though hard facts were scarce. A national campaign for donations to the fund was launched, and the Mammal Society was asked to undertake a survey to determine the status of the British otter and the extent of its decline. But it soon became clear that Gavin and Peter Scott and the WWF did not see eye to eye as to how the money should be spent. Gavin wanted instant action to save as many British otters as possible as quickly as possible, and an immediate end put to the most obvious horrors, such as hunting with otter hounds and trapping for skins; he chafed at the delay that an otter survey would entail. Peter Scott saw things from a broader, more international perspective. From Paris he sent a telegram to Gavin, who was still without a phone, stating his point of view: 'Edal Fund should help all otters not merely British stop principal effort needed against river pollution and fun-fur trade but opposition to hunting and vermin control must also figure stop Mammal Society as objective scientific assessment essential to carry balance of public opinion.'

Gavin began to grow restless. He felt Peter Scott was too busy to give his proper attention to the Edal Fund, and began to feel left out of things, even slighted. By the middle of October he was waxing wrathful. Since his move to the island he had become markedly more quarrelsome, and the targets of his aggravation were increasingly his oldest and closest friends. Now it was Peter Scott's turn. Marooned, incommunicado and increasingly paranoid on his lonely Scottish rock, Gavin felt impelled to pick a fight with the friend he admired and envied perhaps above all others. For Peter Scott was just about everything Gavin had ever wanted to be himself – a war hero, a leading naturalist and ecologist, an enormously successful wildlife painter, the founder and director of one of the world's premier wildfowl sanctuaries and one of the world's leading conservation organisations, a pioneer of natural history programmes for television, *and* a national gliding champion, an Olympic and America's Cup yachtsman, the son of one of Britain's greatest popular heroes, and an eminent international figure in his own right – the list was endless. Feeling ignored and powerless, Gavin got the biggest target he knew in his sights.

First came a long, emotional phone call in which Gavin reproached Scott in a rather hysterical manner – though for what was not entirely clear. Then came a series of petulant postcards. Gavin accused Scott of being too big for his boots, of megalomania and empire-building at the expense of old friendships and small but urgent causes. He was dissatisfied with the way the WWF was handling the Edal Fund, he said, and threatened that if there was no improvement he would pull out and make a public statement giving his reasons. Scott replied on 18 October:

My dear Gavin,

I am much saddened by your cards. We have been friends for rather a long time even if we had our ups and downs, and it seems a pity that we have to have 'showdowns' (or 'showups'?).

I am 'busy' and have been for weeks trying to make a statement about WWF and otters. We have a situation which I don't believe is so terribly complicated and difficult.

In the statement which went out about the Edal Fund we said: 'This scheme would naturally have as its first target the otter species in most danger of extinction, but if there is sufficient response it would be desirable to give all possible assistance to any populations of otters which have suffered depletion or are under pressure.' This would mean help for British otters.

Lord knows I personally detest otter hunting, but I reckon we must see whether that is really the best place to spend Edal Fund money. Restocking ex-polluted rivers in the English Midlands with an undertaking not to hunt them for five years might be much more useful. Otter hunting will be dead in five years anyway. Actually the Manu National Park for the Giant Otter in Peru is probably far more important than anything in Britain.

I'm desperately painting to earn some money for the Scott family which is pretty broke. The Bewicks [swans] will be arriving in a couple of weeks. Couldn't you come and see them one day? And don't let's quarrel because of lack of communications between us. P. Scott is *always* available to talk to G. Maxwell – not for finding out what would be the clever thing to do but what would be the right thing to do – and for just talking to his old friend.

　　Yours
　　Pete

Gavin replied somewhat huffily from Kyleakin a week later:

> The only contact I can make with you personally is after a row, and the complete silence between rows is bound to make for misunderstanding. On such occasions you invariably remind me of our long friendship; I'm sure you will understand that there are occasions on which I feel somewhat aggrieved that there is so little evidence of this friendship on your side. Of all my long-time friends you were literally the only one who, after the fire had left me without any clothing but one pair of blue jeans (no top half, shoes or socks) sent me not so much as a jersey or a message of sympathy.* Of course I feel this to be sad, as anyone would, but it isn't an irritant, as the handling of the Edal Fund has been . . .
>
> To turn to more pleasant subjects, there is nothing I'd like more than to come and see the Bewicks. I wonder whether after the New Year would be any use? Life here has its teething troubles, and is very much of a full-time business – a sort of House that Jack built – what with fuelling the boat that carries the diesel to drive the pumps that pump the diesel to fuel the generator that pumps the water . . . to say nothing of the days when we are cut off from the shore by heavy seas. But it's a marvellous place, as I hope you'll come and see for yourself, and as at Slimbridge there is always something to watch from the windows . . . Do try and pay a visit here when you can.

Sadly, the old friends never met again. Nor did the Edal Fund (later renamed the Gavin Maxwell Otter Fund) ever fulfil its early promise. Most of the money, never substantial, was siphoned off into research, little of which did much to save endangered otters, and it was left to others – notably Philip Wayre of the Otter Trust in Suffolk – to carry out the sort of action Gavin would have liked. It was not through the Edal Fund that Gavin made the greatest impact on public opinion about otters, but through *Ring of Bright Water*, which marked the beginning of a groundswell of worldwide support for otter conservation that has continued to the present day. Gavin's contribution to saving the otter was immeasurable,

---

* Two days later, Gavin made the same accusation against me. In vain I pleaded that I had been in the Far East at the time of the fire and helpless to assist – I was condemned for betraying his friendship and trust.

and was probably the greatest achievement of his life. Today the otter is a protected species, and is making a comeback in many parts of Britain.

The house on the White Island pleased Gavin greatly. 'This is a glorious place,' he wrote to Peter Janson-Smith not long after he had taken up residence in it, 'and you must come and pay me a visit. Next year, when I have some animals on the island and the eider colony is in full swing, I am going to open the house and island to the public – but the interior of the house is so beautiful that one could almost open it now.'

Gavin was proud of his new home, and all through the later summer and autumn he held open house for a steady stream of friends and relatives. The converted lighthouse keeper's cottage on Kyleakin was not only grander than Sandaig but much easier to entertain people in, offering a great deal more comfort and space and a more obviously spectacular setting. Gavin's hospitality was no less spectacular. He boasted a drinks tray which was laden with every kind of spirit and liqueur, and his dining table groaned under many a lavish and lordly spread. Colonel Colin Mackenzie, CMG, who had run SOE Far East during the war, was now Gavin's nearest neighbour, and a good friend. He and his wife Clodagh lived in Kyle House, on a rocky promontory of Skye only three hundred yards across the water. He vividly recalled the hospitality on the White Island: 'When he invited us for lunch he sent a boat over to collect us. His drinks table supported anything up to twelve bottles of different whiskies. Conversation flowed easily – and was necessary, as cooking seldom seemed to start till after 2 p.m. Food was abundant and rich. I remember one lunch which started with lobster and continued with a whole grouse each.'

THIRTY-EIGHT

Opting out

This shadowy desert, unfrequented woods,
I better brook than flourishing peopled towns.
Here can I sit alone, unseen of any,
And to the nightingale's complaining notes
Tune my distresses and record my woes.

WILLIAM SHAKESPEARE,
Two Gentlemen of Verona, 1594

Behind shades in the Hebrides,
To keep your eyes in.

DEBORAH RANDALL, 'Gavin'
(in *The Sin Eater*, 1989)

The old single-track Highland Line train from Inverness to Kyle
meandered slowly through an autumnal Highland landscape as marvellous as I could ever remember it. It was October 1968. Four
years had passed since I had last come north to visit Gavin in his
West Coast home, and I had forgotten how foreign the landscape
was to a southerner like myself, how stark and invigorating, how
lambent and pellucid the quality of light, how shrill the lovely blue
sky of the north, how hushed this lonely world of gorse and
bracken, tarn and sea loch could be. Autumn was more advanced
up here; the woods rusting, the berries blazing, the leaves of the
silver birches flickering like spinning coins; around Kyle the tops
of the mountains were already covered in a light dusting of snow,
the first harbinger of the approaching winter.

Gavin had sent Andrew Scot in a dinghy to pick me up from
the jetty at Kyle and we motored the mile or so to the island.
Gavin's new home was set in a vast amphitheatre of rearing rock
and tossing sea; a landscape of interlocking mountain peaks and
ranges and long, enfiladed sea views. Astern, looking across Loch
Alsh and down Loch Duich, reared the Five Sisters of Kintail, blue

and distant; on the port quarter loomed the Cuillin of Skye, and to starboard the splendid mountain fastness of Applecross; ahead lay the humped shape of Raasay and other smaller islands scattered across the Inner Sound. We passed the White Island's close neighbour, the Eider Island, then pulled into a small bay on the south shore of the main island and landed at a small jetty. The *North West Scottish Pilot* described the area as the most dangerous stretch of the British coast, liable to Force 11 squalls that could spring up in five minutes without warning. I had barely set foot on Eilean Ban when a heavy sea mist suddenly came down and blotted Skye from view. Gavin had chosen his moat well.

I looked about me. On the left rose a seventy-foot-high lighthouse, automatic now, that was connected to the main body of the island by a bridge. A steep path led up from the jetty to the lighthouse cottage, a long, single-storeyed, limewashed building situated below the ridge that formed the highest part of the island. I walked up to the double front door and was ushered into the long reception room that ran most of the length of the house. Gavin was standing waiting to greet me. He now sported an auburn beard which gave him a raffish air, and looked more drawn and aged after the tribulations of recent years, but at the same time he seemed more content and expansive. 'My dear Douglas, what can I give you to drink?' he exclaimed cheerily, waving his hand in the direction of an enormous silver tray crammed with bottles. 'Where would you like to sit? *This*,' proudly indicating a large antique sofa, 'was Sir Walter Scott's settee. Next month they're delivering William Wordsworth's writing desk to me. *Generally* speaking, *by* and large, *all* things considered – a bit different from Sandaig, don't you think?'

Gavin had lived at Sandaig in the homespun, makeshift way that befitted a simple tenant. But he had moved into the lighthouse quarters on Kyleakin Island – two long, narrow, back-to-back cottages that had been stylishly converted into one – in a manner more befitting a laird of the isle, or at least its part proprietor and sole permanent resident. The southern-facing cottage had been knocked into a single forty-foot-long living-room-cum-study from which a picture window looked over the windswept straits to Kyleakin village and the mountains of Skye. The rear-facing cottage, whose view was obscured by the ridge behind, contained three comfortable double bedrooms and a stylishly appointed bathroom. All was sumptuous throughout.

The long room made much use of windows and mirrors to lighten and broaden its corridor-like proportions, and its antique elegance was much more in keeping with Gavin's aristocratic roots than the humble improvised charm of Sandaig had ever been. It had been converted by Richard Frere in accordance with Gavin's design, illustrated with his own watercolour impressions, which may have been influenced, consciously or subconsciously, by the design of the Long Gallery at Syon House, the seventeenth-century home of his uncle, the ninth Duke of Northumberland, by the Thames at Isleworth.

It was a fabulous room, strongly reflecting Gavin's life and interests, and richly furnished in the manner of a stately home in miniature with antiques, objets d'art, natural historical bric-à-brac, the gleanings of a lifetime of exotic travel. A log fire smouldered in the large open hearth and perfumed the room with the sweet aroma of wood smoke. Two long Victorian sofas were ranged against the walls on either side of the fireplace, upholstered in silk brocade and furnished with ancient embroidered silk cushion covers looted by an ancestor from some distant palace in eighteenth-century Imperial China. Above the fireplace hung a huge framed wax-and-fishbone representation of Icarus falling by Michael Ayrton; above a doorway was a framed cast of a fossil *archeopterix*, the primordial proto-bird; around the walls hung a set of sixteen original watercolours of British game birds by James Thorburn, along with an enormous gilt mirror and curved Moroccan daggers with silver sheaths and jewelled hilts.

Oddly at variance with Gavin's image as a popular figure in the new conservation movement were various relics that hailed back to the pursuits of a past generation of sporting naturalists – the era of the collector, stuffer and trophy hunter, in which Gavin himself was brought up. On one wall hung a pair of steel harpoons buckled by their impact with a basking shark's back – souvenirs of Gavin's epic encounters with this giant fish. A pair of stuffed jays stood on the mantelpiece and two mounted birds of prey stared ferociously at each other across the width of the room. A great outstretched fish eagle's wing, framed behind glass, spanned a wall in another room. The sitting-room carpets, in a patterned Indian weave, were scattered here and there with the skins of goats, the fleeces of brown and white sheep, the hides of red and fallow deer, and a hearth-rug made up of the furs of twenty North African fennec foxes.

Though Gavin himself was not entirely oblivious of the paradox, it did not greatly concern him. His entire life and his whole personality had always been made up of opposites. The killer of animals co-existed with the protector of animals, just as the recluse and opter-out co-existed with the upper-crust and establishment man. On a second mantelpiece stood a bevy of invitation cards to exclusive functions, including one from the Duchess of Argyll asking him to a private concert at Inveraray Castle, with a handwritten message appended: 'Do hope you can come and stay.'

Throughout the house the effect was ornate and luxurious; everywhere were discreet touches of old-fashioned aristocratic gracious living. In my bedroom, furnished with Moroccan tapestries, antique brass candlesticks and an enormous gilt mirror, my bedside table proffered a tiny flask of whisky, a carafe of water, and an ornamental Persian box full of cigarettes. 'I have tried to arrange it,' Gavin explained, 'so that wherever you sit you have a box of cigarettes, a lighter and an ashtray next to you.' There were cigarettes everywhere, in Persian boxes and Moroccan jars, silver boxes and pewter cases, on sidetables and sideboards, by the lavatory and by the bath, even on the dining table, where at dinner that evening a little silver ashtray and a silver box of cigarettes bearing the Maxwell family crest was set before each place. Gavin told me he was now smoking up to eighty cigarettes a day, and I noticed that he was often breathless after the slightest exertion. The meal itself was as lavish as the ambience – pâté, tomato salad in a cream and basil sauce, roast pheasant and game chips, raspberries and cream, an enormous Stilton on the sideboard, all washed down with claret, sauterne and Drambuie – real desert island fare.

The weather had taken an appreciable stride towards winter during the night, and next morning a fresh layer of snow covered the tops of the hills and a bitter easterly wind came prying and jabbing down the sound. Over on Skye I could see the long, thin ribbons of the waterfalls plunging sheer from the corries high in the hills and dispersing in mid-air in an explosion of white spray like firework smoke. All day long, and throughout the succeeding days, migrating birds streamed over the island in headlong flight to the south – fieldfares in a constant procession, a squadron of whooper swans, vast galaxies of white-fronted geese in precise V-formations, with greylags trailing behind them in loose, untidy skeins, the air full of their wild and urgent clamour, rising and falling in the wind.

Gavin, I noticed, felt the cold badly and looked pinched and wan inside the hood of his anorak as we explored the tiny bounds of his rough, heathery, ankle-snapping domain. Though the going was rough it did not take long to complete our round of the island. Within the confines of the eight and a half acres of sea-girt volcanic boss on which Gavin had chosen to perch himself there was a surprising variety of habitat, with a rocky, heather-covered top, a cliff or two, a couple of little marshes, a boggy valley full of rushes and cotton-grass, a boulder shore, and all around the wild and teeming ocean waters.

So, after a lifetime of pitching and striking camp, Gavin had come to his final retreat, furnished with all the totems and trappings of his ancestral roots, as if at last he was now anxious to come in from the cold. By any ordinary standards it was a strange place to establish a permanent home, for he was extremely conspicuous on the island, though almost totally incommunicado. But Gavin liked to see people staring at him as they sailed past, unable to turn up at his front door. Now he had the island home he had always wanted, a sanctuary that, for all its comfort and elegance, resembled a prison of rocks and stones, heather and bracken, surrounded by a moat of often violent sea, though from the island's single eminence there was a wonderful unobstructed panorama of mountains, islands, water, wilderness.

Unlike tidal Isle Ornsay, Kyleakin was a real island, and you came and went on the sea's terms, which were harsh and uncompromising. Though the channel was narrow, a strong tide swept through it; and whenever it collided head-on with the prevailing wind from the west or south-west the sea raged. Between spring and autumn there could be paradise days of calm and sun; but white horses, beating surf, flying spray and horizontal rain were the usual order of the worst of winter days. At such times, those who had arrived could never be sure of leaving, and those who had left enjoyed no guarantee of return. Now the easterly was gusting to Force 9, a strong gale, and the tops of the waves in the narrows were breaking in white plumes of blown spindrift. For the six days immediately preceding my arrival, Gavin told me, the sea passage had been so rough that he had been cut off from all communication with the mainland on which he depended for supplies.

And yet he loved it. 'It is better than Sandaig in many ways,' he told me:

> I like to be able to look down on the sea. Living at sea-level at Sandaig was claustrophobic in the end – the horizon was too near, too confining. The sea is much busier here, too, and I am endlessly fascinated by the comings and goings of people and birds and sea creatures. Every tea-time, for example, the island steamer, a kind of miniature *Queen Mary*, passes close by from Kyle. Every evening a large flock of ravens pass over the house on their way from Skye to their roosts in the hills beyond Kyle. Every Friday the ring netters come in from Atlantic coastal waters, followed by vast numbers of gulls feeding on the fish guts the fishermen toss to them. Every spring and autumn there are tremendous flights of migrating birds of all sorts flying over the island or resting on it. Every time I look out over the sea I see something new and strange – a Portuguese man-o'-war floating by, perhaps, or a killer whale blowing, or dolphins leaping, or basking shark cruising about, or a school of rorqual whales moving through the narrows. I've bought a x40 telescope with a tripod and with this I can watch all the toings and froings in the streets of Kyleakin opposite my window – I'm a kind of voyeur of a real-life Hebridean *Under Milk Wood*. I even have a perfect view of the public telephone box, and if ever any of my guests ring me up asking for the dinghy to come over and collect them – not knowing that I have a perfect view of them through my telescope – I like to surprise them by saying, 'Yes, I'll send the boat if you promise to stop picking your nose, or smoking that ghastly pipe!' and so on and so forth.

Gavin had ambitious plans for the White Island, and they were to absorb much of his time and energy in the ensuing months. Close to his heart was the projected commercial eider duck colony on the Eider Island.

It was too late in the season to do much about it for 1968, but he had high hopes for 1969. In the meantime, he kept a careful eye on the birds. They were never far away. During my stay on the island I often saw large flotillas of these solid, ocean-going creatures just offshore. During October the eider population had been steadily increasing, and by the time I left it was up to four or five hundred. Gavin was full of optimism for the project. 'You see those sticks with little blue markers on them?' Gavin remarked to me, pointing towards the Eider Island. 'That's where they nested this summer. We've marked two hundred nests. We've also burnt the undergrowth off so that more of them can nest next year. Unfortunately we've burnt too much off, there probably won't be enough cover for them, so we're going to have to plant thousands of seeds before next summer's breeding season.'

Gavin had also turned his mind to a complementary new project which he outlined to me with great enthusiasm:

What I am going to do here is establish a private zoo park for typically Scottish fauna – a small collection of all the creatures that people want to see – ravens, buzzards, herons, wildcats, hill foxes, native otters and so on, which you couldn't normally see at close quarters in the wild. Everything except deer, because deer could wade across to the Eider Island and trample on all the eider nests. I might even open the house to the public and charge them ten bob a time to look at a famous writer's home and all his pets. If the people pay to come and look at these creatures, I won't have to try and write a book every year, as I do now. This has been a great strain on me for a very long time and I've thought that I could write better books if I was able to take two years to write a book instead of one.

Gavin had recently lost his old world, and he desperately needed to establish stability and security in his new one. On Kyleakin Island he was not only returning to the terrain of his enchanted boyhood; he was also going to populate it with the loved and familiar creatures of his past.

The nucleus of the zoo park – in which the birds and animals would live in a semi-wild state, not in zoo conditions – was already there. For a start, there were the wild seabirds and marine animals that lived on or around the island or passed close by it on their seasonal migrations. Then there was the little group of creatures that Gavin had imported on to the island. Chief among them was Teko, the most famous living otter in the world. Now in his tenth year, Teko was sadly old and toothless and testy, and had, in a sense, been put out to grass to live out his last days in honourable retirement. He inhabited a centrally heated little hut not far from the main house and spent his waking time making holts in his stone-walled, wire-covered garden, which contained a water tank where he could swim. He was seldom seen and was never introduced to strangers.

Then there was Malla, a young female European otter that had been found in some shrubbery in Caithness and brought to the island less than two weeks before my arrival. Malla was only three months old, just fourteen inches long and a little over two pounds in weight. She had only just been weaned and had to be fed every three hours on a special mixture of evaporated milk and water, mixed with the yolk of an egg, two drops of cod liver oil, a pinch of bone flour and a vitamin compound, plus a saucer of finely chopped raw liver once a day. In spite of the painstaking care with which she was looked after, Malla was frail and ailing and her chances of survival seemed small.

Finally there was Owl, 'a ball of fluff the size of a tennis ball when she was found,' Gavin told me. Not until Owl was fully fledged did it become apparent that she was no ordinary tawny owl but a so-called grey-phase tawny owl, a very rare bird in Britain. Owl was a friendly little creature, enjoyed human company, and spent much of her time during my visit perched placidly on the back of an elegant armchair in the sitting room. She had dislocated her left wing when she fell from the nest and was unable to fly. 'Of course, she doesn't know she can't fly,' Gavin assured me, 'she probably thinks all owls are like this. But it means she can't hunt for herself, so I have to feed her – mice, rabbits, gulls, meat, fur, feathers and bone.'

That was the nucleus of the projected zoo park – an ageing otter that was seldom seen, a dying baby one, and an owl that couldn't hunt or fly. Not a promising start, but Gavin was full of enthusiasm, and these were early days.

The ostensible reason for my visit to Kyleakin Island was to interview Gavin for a series of articles I was planning on the subject of 'opters-out'. In the late sixties – the era of the youth revolution and experimental life-styles, of flower power, hippies and back-to-nature self-sufficiency – opting out by the successful and well-heeled was a growing phenomenon in both Britain and America.

It involved quitting the so-called rat-race, turning one's back on middle-class affluence and aspirations, and seeking a more meaningful, and usually more menial or contemplative existence in some remoter, simpler, environment. My subjects were to include an international fashion model who had retreated to an undeveloped islet in the Seychelles, a successful television producer who now tilled the soil as a crofter, a painter who worked as a deckhand on a trawler fishing the Newfoundland Banks, an Englishman who lived in the rainforest of British Honduras – and Gavin Maxwell, who lived with wild animals on a tiny Scottish rock.

My conversation with Gavin on this theme continued over a period of days and often far into the night, and ranged over many subjects – his childhood alienation, his views on education, on sex, drugs, animals, the future of the Highlands, his road to the *Ring*. Gavin spoke shrewdly and eloquently; there was never a dull sentence or a dull moment. But he was not an easy interviewee. He could cling to a train of thought or the logic of an argument like a terrier to a bone or an otter to an ankle. He was impatient with muddled thinking, and could be very tough. When I suggested, for example, that territories might one day be put aside for opters-out in a totalitarian state he retorted: 'I am not prepared to discuss what might happen under a totalitarian state. I would not be there. I should certainly be liquidated for my beliefs and I should not take any part in the proceedings by being martyred. I refuse to discuss this hypothesis.' When, for some unaccountable reason, the conversation got round to God, specifically what I termed an 'objective, God-like perspective on the human condition', Gavin snorted: 'What on earth makes you define the deity in this curious term? Have you ever before thought of God as being objective? And if you haven't, why do you choose this particular moment to speak of God as being objective? In so far as we were brought up to believe in the existence of God at all, we were brought up to believe that he is extremely subjective towards life – certainly not objective.'

Sometimes, if there was a lull in the conversation, or his mind wandered momentarily, or (late at night) the whisky began to do the talking for him, Gavin would come out with some startling non sequitur that gave vent to a passing obsession or momentarily engaged another level of his personality. In the middle of a discussion about the philosophy of escapism, for example, he would suddenly exclaim: 'There ought to be a law against the joining up of sausages!' After propounding the theory that opting to live on a tiny island, where one was surrounded by water, was really a subconscious return to the security of the womb, where one was surrounded by the amniotic fluid, he instantly lurched, disconcertingly and without apparent reason, into a ribald ditty dredged up from his boyhood memory:

> This is Ann of Barking Creek
> Who had her monthlies twice a week;
> Said Maude of Woking,
> 'How provoking –
> Not much poking, so to speak!'

Sometimes he would resort to horseplay and clowning to lighten a long session of earnest discussion. On one occasion he began to squirm on the sofa, wrestling with his right leg. 'Oh, opters-out can do lots of amazing things,' he jested. 'I can bite my toenails, for example, which most people can't do at my age! I'll do it for you now if you like! Normally speaking, I only do it when I'm very, very worked up – I bite my toenails continuously! A very bad habit!'

The ceaseless distractions of daily life on Kyleakin Island caused many interruptions, and the weather and the state of the sea were a constant preoccupation, so Gavin was always leaping up to peer out through the picture window at the straits below. One such occasion produced a bizarre consequence. Gavin had spotted a small boat struggling through rough seas to bring fresh supplies to the island. Fixing it through his telescope, he gave a running commentary as the boat drew near. 'If he's got any sense he'll keel – he'll keep the sea broadside,' he muttered. 'There's not much he can do – he's got the sea on his quarter wherever he goes.' In the silence that ensued a curious sentence – a variation on the famous statement uttered by Nelson at the Battle of Copenhagen as he held his telescope to his blind eye: 'Signal? I see no signal' – came into my head: 'Fruit bats? I see no fruit bats!' This was an odd enough sentence to dream up, but what made it even odder was that a few seconds later Gavin – still peering through his telescope – repeated, loudly and formally, the very same sentence: *'Fruit bats? I see no fruit bats!'* I asked him why he had said it, but he replied he had no idea. When I told him that I had thought it seconds before he said it, he was not at all surprised. 'Happens all the time. All the time.' And it seemed that indeed it did. At about this time Richard Frere, too, noticed a strong increase in what he called 'telepathic empathy' as far as Gavin was concerned – 'a weird gift of being able to pick up a signal consisting of crude emotion from another person'.

Eventually the interview was completed, the batteries of my tape recorder failing as Gavin ended his final soliloquy, his voice slowly fading into a long, electronic silence, as if he himself were receding far into the dark. It was the first interview he had ever given that covered the whole span of his life and a wide spectrum of his thoughts. It was also the last long interview he ever gave. His views were trenchant and perceptive, and help to explain in part how, in his fifty-fifth year, and famous around the world for his idyll of nature in *Ring of Bright Water*, he came to rest at last on a desert rock in the middle of a tidal rip on the edge of the great ocean.

'I'm not sure that I am a typical opter-out at all,' he began:

But it *is* true, as you know, that I've always wanted to live on an island, an oasis apart from the rest of the human race. In that sense, I was an opter-out long before the present trend, and even though I am only a part-time opter-out, I do have some experience of opting out as a way of life, and I understand the forces that push one into it and occasionally pull one back from it.

I believe one of the basic factors about an opter-out is that he refuses to subscribe to the rule of any kind of authority. More than that, he feels himself to be superior to the generality of human beings. Somewhere at heart he feels that he is stronger, larger, more powerful than other people. He feels that the kind of life they are living is not good enough for him, so he protests against it – he's going to try and enlarge his own life. And then, like every other living creature, he finds that the extent to which he *can* enlarge his life is strictly limited, and the first time he touches the confines and finds he can't go any further, the first time he feels the cold of the winter wind, he tries to come back in. But very often he's not allowed back in, or only very tentatively. This makes his position very dubious – is he strong enough to go on being an opter-out, or is he strong enough to admit his weakness to the people he's left and say 'I want to be welcomed back in'?

For most opters-out this is a life-long struggle. For me I'd say it's been a life-long struggle for a long, long time. The mere fact of leaving one's home, leaving one's environment, of travelling widely and being away for months or even longer periods, means your friends are no longer your friends in the same way when you come back. Every time one is away and out of touch it becomes more and more difficult to make contact again, so eventually one's friends, one's home world, fade away. I suppose Ulysses was the archetypal opter-out and when he returned home after years of wandering the only living thing from his past that recognised and welcomed him was his dog.

In my view the main reason people opt out is to find a niche in life. By that I mean a milieu in which the opter-out finds a sufficient feeling of security to function as a human being. This might be a place with no people at all. The niche doesn't have to be a place where you are alone – it could be a place with twenty people, or a hundred, though not, I think, a thousand – but it must contain the essentials for human existence. And the essentials for human existence stem from aggression, because we are an aggressive species, in the same way most other species are. We have territorial demands, for example; we have the need to assert our presence, to do this, achieve that . . . Any community or niche in which you fit yourself, whether it is somewhere populated, like Gauguin's Tahiti or James Hilton's fictitious Shangri-La, or somewhere without human beings where you are merely aggressing against other species, must have this outlet for aggression, this is absolutely essential. I think you must have a sexual life as well but I don't think in the human species there is a necessity to integrate yourself with other members of your species. After all, one of the main reasons for opting out is to put more space between yourself and the mass of human beings. This is perhaps one of the reasons for the great popularity of castaway stories like *The Swiss Family Robinson* and *Robinson Crusoe*. The fact that these two stories had such enormous popular success surely demonstrates that this is a basic desire in people. It is certainly one of *my* main reasons for opting out. Here on

Kyleakin I've given myself half a mile of deep water between me and the nearest human being.

And I'm not the only one. There's been a great influx of English people into the West Highlands this year trying to find a cottage that is at least a quarter of a mile away from anyone else. The demand is becoming fantastic – though of course there is next to nothing to be had because all the land is owned by the big landlords, who will not sell or even let so much as a byre. People have got this feeling that they must find something that has no contact with other human beings. In my view, they are suffering from what I would call an induced hysteria, which is the consequence of intense over-crowding in mass communities. Not long ago an experiment was carried out on rats which produced much the same result. The rats were subject to intense overcrowding under labora-tory conditions and this induced hysteria in the rats and eventually produced a race of delinquent rats – deviant rats, homosexual rats, rats that were homicidal towards each other – or perhaps 'raticidal' would be a better word. I know that I would personally fall victim to this same hysteria if I had to live in the big city for long and this is one of my reasons for opting out.

Recently there was even an article in the *Daily Telegraph* which argued that by the year 2000 the modern State would have to provide special territories – reservations, if you like – for people who wanted to opt out of a civilisation that was characterised by a massive population explosion, increased urbanisation, an advanced technological life-style and a leisure revolution; and the paper proposed that in Britain the West Highlands and northern Scotland should be set aside for such people. Well, I think this is an extraordinary contradiction in terms. You can't have reservations for opters-out. An opter-out does not accept authority. If he's asked to live in a reserve then he's accepting authority. Besides, this scheme sounds a little like the provisions Tsar Nicholas made for *his* opters-out in Russia, don't you think? He sent them all to lovely little holiday homes in the salt mines in Siberia, did he not? And you, Douglas Bot-ting, are the only person I have met in my life who has lived in both places – Siberia and the West Highlands – and you must admit there are certain factors in common!

The dream of opting out is like nostalgia for one's childhood – a time when one had no responsibility. But I think anyone who has a dream of this kind is doomed to failure and doomed to great unhappiness and doomed to change their life completely. If it's an urge – a determination – and not a dream then I think perhaps it can work. But it would not be an ideal life – there are great disadvantages. The people who saw in my book *Ring of Bright Water* an ideal life – a paradise – were extracting the message they wanted to extract, even though I did imply in that book that there were great difficulties in living this sort of life.

The great difficulties posed by everyday life at Sandaig – the logistical and transport problems, the accidents and emergencies, the soaring costs of even the most elementary items – have been described in detail already. Though the White Island was a more sophisticated establishment, the problems caused by its isolation and exposure to the elements were if anything more severe than those at Sandaig. The problems of small island life were not eased by Gavin's total lack of aptitude in practical matters or by his partial lameness in one foot, which made it difficult for him to get about as he used to, especially on an island as rugged and treacherous underfoot as Kyleakin. Gavin may have found a niche and a feeling of security, but it was hardly a place where he could function as a human being without a tremendous amount of help from others. It was clear to me, as it must have been to Gavin himself, that he could not have survived on the White Island for more than a day or two without the active and continuous support of Andrew Scot and Richard Frere. As Kathleen Raine commented to Richard after her first visit to the island: 'I only wish you may succeed where so many have failed in keeping his life within workable limits for him. The search for freedom involves him in such constricting complications!'

In the diary I kept of my visit the entry for the last day of October – Hallowe'en – provides a profile of an average day on Kyleakin Island:

It is appreciably colder. The first really heavy snow of winter has fallen on the Cuillin and the high mountains beyond Kyle. Roads are blocked and gales are beating the coast. The wind

is easterly, bitter and fierce. It knocks down the TV aerial
that was erected only yesterday and after Andrew puts off to
Kyleakin in the dinghy it gets up to Force 9 or so and Gavin
has to ring the Post Office in Kyleakin and leave a message
warning Andrew not to attempt the return crossing till the
wind dies down a bit. Andrew phones back to warn Gavin that
the diesel generator that provides the electricity and pumps up
the water is about to run out of fuel but Gavin can't understand
his instructions about how to fill it. 'I don't even know how
to switch it on or off,' he tells me. 'I don't understand machinery and I don't like it.' The firewood is wet, Gavin has squit-
ters, his sister rings to say that his eldest aunt, aged ninety-six,
has just died, and then Teko is found throwing a fit and is
thought to have pneumonia. Gavin rings the vet but he is out.
He tries to ring him again at 11 but now the radio phone
seems out of order. The way the wind is it will be difficult
for the vet to visit tomorrow anyway; and it looks as though
Andrew will have to stay the night over in Kyleakin. Meanwhile the kitchen piles up ankle deep in dirty plates, the wind
roars and the sea surges. It is a constant battle to keep the
whole thing running smoothly. At 12 we have the first whisky
of the day and Gavin informs me that – to crown it all –
the island is haunted. Loud metallic clangs and low-pitched
mutterings in some strange tongue can be heard at dead of
night – Richard Frere had heard them clearly, apparently, and
so had Mary MacLeod from Tormor, and many lighthouse-
keepers in the past.

Not until my last evening on the island did Gavin's mood, which
had been remarkably sunny and buoyant throughout my visit,
begin to darken. Undoubtedly the whisky, which he imbibed in
heroic measures, was partly to blame; but it seemed as though he
was undergoing something more profound than a simple shift of
mood. Progressively he became argumentative, then aggressive,
then positively paranoid. Hitherto I had admired enormously the
courage and resilience with which he had weathered the terrible
blows that had been dealt him in the last few years. But that last
evening I realised that they – or something – had taken their toll.
Time and again he reverted to the theme of betrayal, treachery
and desertion. Even his friends, myself included, were part of an

imagined web of treachery that he claimed was being woven behind his back by all and sundry.

The next morning, before I left the island to catch the train from Kyle, I took photographs of Gavin as he nursed his sickly otter cub, Malla. Both looked desperately frail, and Gavin seemed to move painfully and with difficulty as he crouched down beside the baby animal to feed it milk from a spoon. At that moment, as I stepped through the door for the last time and made my way down to the waiting dinghy, I feared for them both.

I was never to see either of them again.

THIRTY-NINE

A bright bitter sea

Life is what happens to you while you're busy making
other plans.

JOHN LENNON

On 2 December 1968 *Raven Seek Thy Brother* was published. The
book was billed as the true successor to *Ring of Bright Water*, but
its story was a very different one, and so was its mood, laden with
doom and melancholy, as many reviewers pointed out.

The reviews were mixed, the critics mostly bemused by the long
catalogue of disasters that had beset Gavin during the last five years,
the introspective, confessional tone of the writing, the erratic life
it described, and the deeply troubled, darkly mystical nature of the
author, 'more at ease among ghosts and animals than the human
race'. Some condemned the book's vein of bitterness and self-pity,
others praised it as 'a celebration of courage and compassion' (*Daily
Telegraph*), one saw it as 'a study of the psychology of living with
the weight of the past' (*Times Educational Supplement*). The *New
York Times* ascribed Gavin's troubles to 'neglect or oversight or
arrogance' and deemed Kathleen's curse, which was described in
the book, 'an excuse, not a reason'. In the light of this dark and
brooding final volume of the Camusfeàrna trilogy, *Ring of Bright
Water* was reappraised as 'the author's own desperate flight from
the shadows of the mind'. In the *Chicago Herald-Tribune*, Alan
Pryce-Jones noted: 'His talent is a disturbing one: the gift of happiness eludes him, and though the furies never quite catch up with
him, for much of the time they are in hot pursuit.'

The underlying thesis of *Raven* was that Kathleen Raine's curse
had been the cause of the long series of setbacks Gavin had suffered
during the years covered by the book (1963–68). Though the book
did not say as much, there was implicit in its conclusion a question:
after the fire which had burned down Gavin's house and killed his
otter, was the curse finally spent – and if not, where would it end?

That she should have been cast in the role of a witch in Gavin's book was a terrible blow for Kathleen. 'I was both hurt and angry,' she wrote later, 'that after all my only place in any book of Gavin's was not as a friend who had loved and helped him once but as the woman who had laid a curse on him.' Gavin, for his part, was no less aggrieved that anyone should have laid a curse on him at all, whether it really was the cause of all his suffering or not. Some months were to pass before their mutual grievances were aired in a final stormy confrontation.

Advance orders for the book were promising. The first print run of twenty-five thousand was bought up by the bookshops before publication and another substantial printing had to be put in hand. The book trade put *Raven* in the top twenty bestselling Christmas books, alongside John Updike's *Couples*, Alexander Solzhenitsyn's *The First Circle* and the latest Agatha Christie. 'We can therefore be assured of a good income during the coming year,' Peter Janson-Smith wrote to Richard Frere, 'and I may be able to get big advances for the next book.'

On the day following publication Gavin made one of his rare forays to London. Several important items of business drew him to the metropolis. There were book signings and radio interviews in connection with the new book. There was lunch with his publisher, Mark Longman, to discuss his ideas for his next book – the story of the Kyleakin zoo park and eider colony and other West Highland adventures. And there was the preview of the film of *Ring of Bright Water* at a dubbing studio in Soho Square.

As well as directing the film, Jack Couffer also co-wrote the screenplay with Bill Travers. The leading roles were played by Bill Travers and his wife Virginia McKenna, ardent animal protectionists who had scored a big box-office hit with their film of Joy Adamson's bestselling book *Born Free*. The film version of *Ring* took the basic idea of Gavin's book and totally transformed it into family entertainment. The biggest change was in the persona of Gavin himself, who became a disillusioned insurance agent called Graham Merril. A local West Highland lady doctor was added as love interest, and the cottage at Sandaig was transformed into a single-roomed croft near Oban, far to the south of Sandaig. Though the landscape was relatively lowland, Wolfgang Suschitsky's camerawork was superbly evocative of the magic of the West Coast. The otter scenes, too, were authentic and poignantly reminiscent of the months I had spent looking after Teko in years gone by – so much so that it brought tears to my eyes to watch 'Mij' (played by a clawed Canadian otter) run free along the beach and swim with joyful abandon in the burn. The script was thin but the actors were sympathetic and seemed to enjoy their scenes with the otter, who was clearly the star of the show, everywhere snuffling and grunting his way into mischief.

In short, it was a *nice* film, and it is not difficult to see why Gavin enjoyed it once he had got used to the portrait of himself and the liberties taken with his text. Virtually his only complaint was that the geese used in the film were not wild geese. The scene in which Mij was killed moved him greatly – 'far too near the bone', he said afterwards. As an inveterate film fan he found it rather gratifying to be the real-life model of a motion-picture hero – even if he had to suffer the relative indignity of being metamorphosed into the ingenuous Graham Merril in the process. Once, after it went on general release, Gavin crept into a small Scottish cinema incognito and sat through the film, waiting in trepidation for the loud lamentations of the children in the darkened auditorium as the road-mender's spade once more smashed into Mijbil's skull.

Gavin and I had arranged to meet for lunch during his London visit, but I had to return to Scotland for a short lecture tour and we were unable to meet. I lost contact with him after that. In the New Year I moved house and in the late spring set off on an expedition into the Mato Grosso wilderness of central Brazil. For several crucial months I was far removed from news from home and from the dramatic events that now overtook Gavin's life.

Gavin was back at Kyleakin Island for Christmas. By and large the last few months had been happy ones after the trauma of the fire and its aftermath, and the omens looked good for the coming year. Sadly, the young otter cub Malla did not live to see the New Year, relinquishing her tenuous hold on life despite the love and care that were lavished on her. Irrationally, Gavin blamed Andrew Scot for her death, an unfair charge that marked the beginning of a serious deterioration in their relationship. At about the same time, Gavin's two gigantic deerhounds, Dirk and Hazel, who had been fostered out shortly before the fire at Sandaig, rejoined Gavin on Kyleakin Island. Sprawled in front of the large fireplace in the long room they gave the place an appropriately baronial air.

January, with its long nights of frosts and stars, passed without incident. Visitors continued to come and go and a start was made on the infrastructure of the zoo park by Andrew Scot and Willie McAskill, a Skye handyman from Kyleakin. At the end of the month, finding the tiny island in midwinter an inclement and claustrophobic place to be, Gavin set off on a round of visiting in the outside world. It had long been his custom to spend a few weeks of each year looking up old friends and relatives on a circuit that included some of the grand houses and castles of Scotland – Inverclune, Brechin, Marchmont, Kier, Shennanton, Enterkine, Inveraray and his own family's Galloway home at Monreith – moving from one to the other like some Bedouin prince among the desert encampments of his extended tribe. He was always a welcome and popular guest, for he was not only regarded as an old friend, but a famous and entertaining one as well. He was away for the whole of February, returning to Kyleakin on 3 March. Richard Frere met him in Kyleakin village when he got back, and was a little dismayed by Gavin's appearance. He looked ill and walked hesitantly, breathing heavily. But Gavin was in good spirits. The time away had refreshed him mentally, if nothing else, and he was fired with enthusiasm to get the eider breeding site ready before the nesting season began in May. Richard was sent off to forage for the necessary materials to prepare an eider breeding ground along the lines Gavin had observed in Iceland.

Richard went shopping in Inverness. 'I went to Woolworth's and asked for two hundred children's windmills,' he wrote, 'remarking to a cretinous young assistant with a leer that they were to attract the birds. Another shop wonderingly sold me clusters of tiny bells.' Elsewhere he collected a pile of long thin poles, several hundred canes and quantities of young conifer branches, and Peter Janson-Smith sent 750 yards of gaily-coloured flag bunting from London. 'The island soon became a visual reproduction of an Icelandic colony,' Richard continued. 'The skyline bristled with poles, the air was filled with the tinkle of bells and whirr of tiny windmills, and little green tents of conifer branches appeared all over the charred ground. The coloured bunting was strung between the poles where it flapped gently in the wind, looking for all the world like the washing of a marooned gypsy tribe.'

Gavin and Richard spent a spring day searching for old nests, marking them and putting in windmills at appropriate points. Gavin was in high spirits, and by the last week of March the tiny

Eider Island was en fête with flags and bunting and Gavin had counted some three hundred eider off the shore. All, it seemed, was going to plan. By then John Lister-Kaye had arrived on the island for a preliminary discussion about the zoo park and various other projects. The twenty-three-year-old Lister-Kaye had already helped set up a wildlife park near Bristol, and had made Gavin's acquaintance during a short visit to Sandaig a few years back. In February 1969 Gavin had invited him to work with him as the curator of the projected zoo park and co-author of a newly conceived book on British mammals. Jumping at the chance of leaving his job among the belching steelworks of south Wales, Lister-Kaye headed north for Kyleakin Island.

'Gavin's enthusiasm was boundless and infectious,' he recalled. 'Formidable snags of every shape and description loomed up to limit the extent of the project, but he over-rode each in turn with an exuberant flourish of his hand and the confident assurance "Oh! That's all right, we can manage that somehow or other," so that by the end of my stay I was utterly convinced of the project's potential success and longed to move north and become involved with it.'

But all was not as well as it seemed. By the end of March money was again becoming a source of concern for Gavin and his sorely-tried company. The long-running Beryl Borders affair had come to a head, and Gavin now had to find £2000 to pay her off in return for vacant possession of the house in Glenelg. Early in April, Richard Frere wrote a plea for help to Peter Janson-Smith in a vein that had long become familiar to both of them: 'I am more than a little worried about my inability to damp down – without being a spoilsport – Gavin's flights of financial fancy. We have become far more deeply involved in this zoo business than I anticipated . . . I shall now have to turn my most disapproving gaze on this project . . . One of Gavin's more unattractive habits is to involve himself in some financial adventure to the point of no return, and then tell me about it.'

One such adventure was a sculpting party at Marchmont at which Gavin had ordered five bronze heads – three of his god-daughter, Katie McEwen, and two of himself – from the sculptress Fiore de Henriquez, who had been a friend of Gavin and Robin McEwen for years. These did not come cheap. And there were wages and salaries due and old creditors and new bills to be settled. 'All this amounts to the usual cry for money,' Richard complained, 'of which you must be heartily sick.'

To all intents, Gavin was bust again, with little prospect of a fat cheque from a film company to bale him out a second time. But on 2 April, the day the film version of *Ring of Bright Water* was given its Royal Charity World Première in the presence of the Duke of Edinburgh at the Leicester Square Odeon in London, Gavin was served notice that a great deal more than his solvency might be at risk. The première, in aid of the World Wildlife Fund, was a glittering occasion, with fanfares from the Herald Trumpeters of the Life Guards and heftier blasts from the Band of the Scots Guards, Gavin's old regiment, to play the glitterati in. It should have been Gavin's day of days – but he was not there. At the last moment, unable to face the kind of event that had always been anathema to him, and knowing that he neither felt nor looked his best, he confided to Richard Frere his intention to duck out of the engagement.

Instead of basking in the publicity and the glory that was his due in London, Gavin set off for the town of Keith to obtain capercaillie and blackcock for his zoo from a local breeder. He drove the Mercedes as far as Inverness, then asked Richard Frere to take over the wheel. He had a terrible headache, he said; it was so severe that he could not drive any further. Richard noticed with alarm that Gavin's brow was tightly clenched and that his skin bore an unhealthy grey pallor.

Gavin, it seemed, had had 'a hell of a headache' ever since he had come back to Kyleakin Island from his round of visits in early March. 'Bit of a nuisance,' he had told Richard, 'because it makes concentration difficult. Any ideas?' Richard had already noticed disturbing signs of emotional instability and mental irrationality in his friend's behaviour in recent days, and he had observed for some little while Gavin's paranoiac tendencies, his dark mutterings about plots to have him killed, of mysterious sinister forces at large in Kyleakin across the water. Gavin had begun to fall out with Andrew Scot in a bad way, and the increasing tension between the two led first to acrimony, then to quarrels, scuffles, even fisticuffs – especially in the evening after Gavin had had a dram or two. In the midst of this incipient crack-up Gavin's British publisher, Michael Hoare of Longmans, and his American publisher, Jack Macrae of Duttons, arrived on the island to discuss Gavin's literary future.

But not even the presence of his publishers – in a sense the two most important arbiters of his professional destiny – could keep Gavin calm for long. One night Jack Macrae, having been kept

awake by the uncomfortable lumpiness of a stack of 'girlie' maga-
zines secreted under his mattress, heard a 'terrible racket' outside
his door – almost certainly another violent nocturnal battle between
Gavin and his out-of-favour assistant. Asked at breakfast what had
caused the noise, Gavin calmly explained to his incredulous guests
that his ex-wife, Lavinia, had conjured up a poltergeist and directed
it to fling all his books off their shelves. It was not until the two
publishers came to leave the island that Gavin admitted he had
been suffering from 'exquisite headaches', of a type Michael Hoare
thought suggested a brain tumour.

Only a few days later, on 9 April, Gavin engineered an apocalyptic row with Andrew Scot which raged till three in the morning.
Richard was an appalled witness of this head-on collision, and for
the first time he saw in Gavin a mental turmoil of an altogether
different order. The fracas followed a chance remark, and by the
end there was little left unsaid. Bitterly Gavin upbraided Andrew
for his untidiness, his absences and much else – including again the
death of Malla. Many of the charges were clearly fantastical. In
vain Richard remonstrated with his incensed employer. 'Richard,'
Gavin replied, 'can you not understand? The boy will destroy me.'
By the end Andrew had handed in his notice. He would stay only
as long as it took to find a replacement.

After he had gone, Richard rounded on Gavin. 'Well, there you
are,' he said. 'That's what you wanted, isn't it?'

But of course it wasn't. Without Andrew life on the island would
be impossible in any practical sense. Without Andrew Gavin would
be totally alone, apart from intermittent visitors. Without Andrew
he would be utterly lost – even destroyed, as he had predicted. And
it was he who had driven Andrew away. 'It did not surprise me,'
Richard concluded, 'to see that he was crying openly.'

Richard was now deeply alarmed about Gavin's health. After the
incident on the road to Keith he began to wonder whether he was
suffering from a tumour on the brain, and he was insistent that
Gavin should have a thorough medical examination. On 17 April
Gavin checked into the Royal Northern Infirmary in Inverness for
a week of tests to find the cause of his continuous headaches and
underlying malaise. Just as in 1967, no cause was found, and Gavin
returned to Kyleakin Island puzzled but greatly relieved at being
given a clean bill of health.

April passed in desultory fashion. Gavin's headaches improved somewhat and he pottered about the island as spring advanced towards summer. A few small animals arrived for the zoo park but the eider colony seemed to have failed for that season, with only a few birds nesting. Andrew Scot still clung on, but Gavin's quarrels with him raged as violently as ever. On 30 April Richard Frere noted in his diary: 'Nastiest day I've ever spent on Kyleakin. Constant contention between Gavin and Andrew.' The flow of visitors continued unstaunched. Though Gavin's public image was that of a recluse and a loner, in reality he could stand only a day or two of his own company before he grew restless and morose; and he had, besides, a practical need to dilute with outside company his stormy and inescapable contiguity with Andrew.

On 2 May 1969 Kathleen Raine returned for a second visit. Her arrival coincided with an escalation of the pain of Gavin's headaches and a fresh outbreak of hauntings and other inexplicable paranormal phenomena. Simon MacLean, the lighthouse man, twice saw a strange light which moved about outside the house and around the bay and the lighthouse at midnight, and Gavin himself heard doors opening and closing in unoccupied rooms, and footsteps when there was no one there. Rarely, if ever, had such hauntings been observed on the island so late in the year.

Kathleen's visit was not only haunted but volcanic. The trouble began when Gavin played her a record of the theme tune from the film of *Ring*, with lyrics by the pop musician Val Doonican:

> Where sun and wind play
> On a ring of bright water –
> That's where my heartland will be . . .

Not unnaturally, Kathleen resented the fact that nowhere was there any mention that she had played any part in the story, or any acknowledgement of her contribution both to the title of the film and the lyrics of the song. 'I hoped he might have understood,' she was to write, 'that his *Ring of Bright Water*, because it was written in his heart's blood, was written in my heart's blood also.' But he did not, and they quarrelled furiously. At one point she exclaimed: '*My* work will be remembered when yours is forgotten.' 'That,' Gavin replied, 'may very well be true.'

Inevitably the subject got round to the way Gavin had portrayed her – publicly pilloried her – in his new book. When she first read his version of the curse incident in the manuscript of *Raven Seek Thy Brother* she was dumbfounded, and her father wanted her to sue Gavin for libel. What Gavin had written, she felt, was a falsified version of part of their story. At first she had even thought that Gavin had described the curse simply because it made a good story, and for no other reason. It seemed a bitter return for all she had tried to do for him. 'But now,' she confided to Richard Frere afterwards, 'I am prepared to believe that he did believe himself under my curse and that that may indeed have influenced his thought and behaviour, giving a reality of a kind to a state of fear or worse, and in that way brought that last illness upon him.'

What Kathleen was really objecting to was the wording of her curse in Gavin's draft manuscript of the book: 'Let him, and the house and all that have to do with it suffer here as I am suffering, for as long as he shall live.' Kathleen claimed this was an elaboration and falsification of what she had really said. According to her own book, *The Lion's Mouth*, her actual words had been: 'Let Gavin suffer, in this place, as I am suffering now.' At Kathleen's insistence Gavin amended his version of the curse before publication to 'Let him suffer here as I am suffering.'

'I only wanted him to see, to understand, how much he had hurt – could hurt – by asking so much and then dismissing so lightly,' Kathleen continued:

I would have thought none knew better than Gavin that words spoken in anger are very different from prolonged ill-will. Everyone who knows me knows that I do not ever harbour resentment – sometimes pain but never resentment . . . Probably the truth is that in his last years he saw many things in an embittered and distorted manner – in part because of his unrecognised illness, in part from the collapse of his life in so many ways. Aymer said to me: 'Gavin is lucky to have you to blame, isn't he?' But perhaps Gavin's mother – intelligent, charming, upright, and possessive – was the real witch . . . Gavin and I fell into one of the great human myths, and enacted a part of an archetypal story. You could not kill, or even modify, so basic a myth, by any appeal to mere fact. But that I failed him I cannot deny. And Mij . . .

So on her last night on the island they quarrelled, as Gavin had quarrelled with many of his friends in recent months. 'He was surely more ill than he knew or we realised,' Kathleen wrote to me later. 'But Gavin I think quarrelled only with those whom he knew were irremovably his friends, and whom he knew would know that quarrels made no difference to the relationship. The things that meant most to him were the music of the wind and the rain and the heat that came from the heart of friendship.' At the core of their quarrel and of his anger and tumult in those last months, she felt, was his sense of total inner despair.

He had got himself into some awful tangles – personal, financial. He had tried everything and it hadn't worked out. Looking back, I think Gavin's life was a tragedy – but not such a tragedy as the lives of people who have not lived their lives, have not enacted who they are. We are all *something*, we are all, good or bad, a life which has to flower in this life – and a great many don't. But Gavin lived his life, he didn't sleep through it. Coleridge said that every poet is a man of action manqué, and you might say that every man of action is a poet manqué. For Gavin the action was the poetry. I think, for that reason, it was not innately inappropriate that Gavin appeared to choose me as someone he would have in his life – it was very much the same vision, but he lived it and I wrote it.

I have never again sought or desired any relationship of the kind I had with Gavin. That was that. That was my story. Being alone without being lonely has a lot to recommend it. Because the only Beloved, as the Indian teachers know, is God. There is only the one Being, and we seek the divine in the people we fall in love with, in nature, in a thousand things. And that is the great deception – attributing the divine to something or someone else. But I did see in Gavin that which was truly his true spirit – which was very beautiful. He *was* very beautiful, you know. Everyone is if you see them in that light.

On Iona a fortnight or so after bidding Gavin farewell, Kathleen wrote a poem, 'Message for Gavin', whose concluding lines suggested she would never see him again:

Since not again can I be with you life with life
I would be with you as star with distant star,
As drop of water in the one bright bitter sea.

On 13 May Fiore de Henriquez arrived on the island bringing her
bronze busts of Gavin and his god-daughter, Katie McEwen. Gavin
was delighted with Katie's likeness and sent her a postcard: 'Fiore's
bust of you is the nicest thing in the whole of this house – it's
almost as beautiful as the subject, though I suppose it's a poor
substitute. Bless you.' At the beginning Fiore's visit proved one of
the jollier occasions on Kyleakin Island that summer, and as the
whisky flowed the long room resounded to the rousing lilt of Italian
songs. But Fiore was soon aware that all was not well. 'Gavin was
a very Nordic, delicate, beautiful kind of man, full of bravura. But
his eyes were horrendous,' she recalled. 'They were red and burning
from the inside. Something was very wrong.' At night Gavin and
Andrew would fight in the kitchen, sometimes with kitchen knives,
with Gavin wildly drunk and totally out of his mind. 'I wanted to
stay,' Fiore recalled. 'I thought I could help. But the situation was
hopeless.' After three days she left.

It was the visit of another woman that was to cause the greatest
and most cataclysmic explosion in the Maxwell household. Lisa
van Gruisen arrived on Kyleakin Island from Edinburgh in June.
She was delivering a young fox for Gavin's zoo park, which by
now covered much of the island with a complex of aviaries and
enclosures and a network of scaffolding containing a growing population of native animals and birds, including herons, magpies, car-
rion crows, ravens, buzzards, and a golden eagle with one leg that
had been caught in a horrible gin-trap. A devoted fan of Gavin's
books, Lisa was in a state of considerable trepidation and excitement
at the prospect of meeting such a famous writer, a guru for many of
her generation, about whom she had heard many strange rumours –
that he was a weird and complex eccentric, a homosexual, a bigam-
ist with up to three wives and a bastard child in Kent, and much
else. Such rumours added a zest to the reputation of a man she
admired immensely for 'the power and beauty of his writing'.

She was not disappointed. Physically she found Gavin unprepos-
sessing, cadaverous and ill-looking. But he had 'terrific style' and
'a tremendous guru-like presence', and his voice, his words, the
brilliance and intensity of his conversation and sense of humour

held her in thrall. 'I had never heard anyone speak as he spoke,' she was to say later. 'He spoke as he wrote and he wrote as he spoke – utterly beautifully.' Gavin, for his part, was enchanted with Lisa. He gave, her a signed copy of every one of his books. He whisked her around Skye in his powerful Mercedes. He took her into his confidence and asked her to do the same for him. Before she knew where she was the eighteen-year-old girl had, to all intents and purposes, fallen in love with her fifty-four-year-old host.

All might have been well had not Lisa missed the train from Kyle the following evening and been obliged to put up in the hotel in Kyleakin for the night. Next morning Andrew Scot, wearing a home-made sealskin waistcoat, came to fetch her, but instead of taking her back to the island he took her for a morning's drive-about, first to Isle Ornsay and then to Sandaig. There, in the legend-ary Camusfeàrna, he declared that he had fallen in love with her. This was confusing enough for Lisa, for though she was not unaware of Andrew's 'rugged and romantic appearance' (as she put it in her diary), it was not of him but of Gavin that her mind was full that morning. Greater confusion was to follow. When they returned to Kyleakin Island in the early afternoon they found Gavin in a towering huff – brooding, jealous, angry and a little the worse for whisky. A terrible, oppressive atmosphere enveloped the house. Gavin was abominably rude. Before they knew it they were all screaming and raging at each other. Many of the details of what was said are lost to memory, but Lisa was later to recall that Gavin accused her of ruining his life by taking Andrew, his lifeline, off with her, then suggested she should become Andrew's mistress, and capped this by proposing that he (Gavin) should marry her himself. Lisa did not know what to do or where to turn. Andrew wanted to leave with her, she wanted to stay with Gavin, Gavin wanted first one thing and then another. She felt pulled in all directions.

The drama was reaching its crisis when Lisa abruptly left to catch her train. Richard Frere came to ferry her back across to Kyle and with a sense of profound relief put her on the train to Inverness. As she climbed on board, she turned and said: 'They're very pecu-liar people, aren't they?' Then she was gone. 'Her complex impact upon the occupants of Eilean Ban,' Richard noted, 'innocently set the final seal of dissolution upon that small society.'

What happened in the wake of Lisa's departure was summed up

by Gavin in a single word in his diary for Friday, 13 June: 'Débâcle'. When she got home Lisa wrote to Gavin: 'I can only say I have paid very dearly for what were three of the most beautiful and happy days I can remember. I think I will always be grateful to you for them and am only sorry that their effect was so drastic and so miserable. I have forgiven *you* – please forgive *me*.'

In reply Gavin wrote an account of his version of events in a letter sealed with wax stamped with the Maxwell family crest. After Lisa had left, he wrote, Andrew had been inconsolable and had reproached Gavin long and bitterly for trying to keep them apart:

> Well, that awful night, when you left, well . . . He told me he would kill me before morning. Perhaps wrongly, I took this seriously and telephoned the police, saying that I was alone on the island with someone whom I believed to be insane. (He had a knife.) They wanted details, and I referred them to the doctor, who said he couldn't discuss a patient on the telephone . and referred them back to me. I said I couldn't give a name, and the next day I told them that it had been a stranger who had now left, so it was no longer of any importance. (There were some rather awful and unseemly struggles during that time – well, you can imagine it.)
>
> I think you've been most sweet and kind to everyone, and I should like to count you among my friends if I may.

Richard Frere was largely dismissive of these and other allegations made by Gavin against Andrew. In Richard's view, Gavin's letter was intended to deter Lisa from renewed contact with Andrew – and given that a real or imagined grudge existed in Gavin's mind, there was no limit, he felt, to his powers of invention.

Some days later, after receiving Gavin's letter, Lisa wrote to him again: 'I have the strangest and most disturbing feeling that I must say something desperately urgent to you – like one of those terrible dreams when all the forces within you are driving you in desperate pursuit of you know not what . . .'

On 9 July, the day Andrew Scot finally left Gavin's employ and went out into the wide world (as a deckhand, it was said, on an ocean-going fishing trawler out of Grimsby), Gavin wrote again to Lisa, who was now in Paris doing a summer course at the Sorbonne and the Louvre and working as a part-time *chauffeuse* for

Gavin's old and eccentric cousin, the Duke of Argyll, who had an apartment in the city: 'Yes, I too had that curious feeling of urgency, and I think I know exactly the feeling you describe, but I'm not sure I understand the cause. I don't think it's basically sexual (though perhaps partly) but more the sudden touching of two lives that seem to have something to do with each other in some way, even if one doesn't know what. When you arrived I felt "this isn't just an attractive girl bringing a fox – something is *happening*," and like you I didn't know whether it had to do with Andrew or you or me or what . . . Well, Lisa, I do very actively look forward to seeing you again. Bless you.'

Before leaving the island Lisa had written the date on which she intended to return in Gavin's appointments diary – 14 September. When she began to doubt whether she could afford the fare for the journey from Paris to the West Highlands, Gavin wrote a five-page letter to reassure her and urge her to come back to see him:

> I don't think you should let money stand in the way of your paying a visit here and perhaps laying a few ghosts – unless, that is, you are too proud to accept the fare from me. So? Don't get wrong ideas – I'm not asking for bed, and am not even sure I want it, but I know I do want to see you again without classifying the relationship.
>
> Love, of whatever kind.
> Gavin

'In retrospect,' Lisa felt, 'I don't think either of us knew what we were doing. We just wanted to lay the ghost – the love or obsession or whatever it was, the extraordinary sense of urgency about wanting to get to know each other, that had made our first meeting so terribly urgent and meaningful. His proposal to marry me may have been a chess move in a game to outmanoeuvre Andrew, and I may just have been a catalyst in a chemical reaction, but at the same time it is clear there was something else. I don't know what other word you can use but "love". Reading the letters it looks as though we were heading flat out for a disastrous affair. Remarkable really, considering how much older he was than me, and how ill. Even at the end he was still questing.'

FORTY

No coming back

'But man is not made for defeat,' he said. 'A man can
be destroyed, but not defeated.'
ERNEST HEMINGWAY, *The Old Man and the Sea*

Whatever hopes Gavin may have had for the future, the storm
clouds were gathering now, thick and black. A temporary replacement for Andrew Scot, David Wright from Peterhead, had already
taken over, and an assistant curator for the zoo park, Donald Mitchell, arrived the day Andrew left. But with Andrew's departure
from the island Gavin had become like a castaway, marooned,
abandoned, rootless. In a thank-you note to his London housekeeper, Mrs Lamm, who had sent him a card for his fifty-fifth
birthday on 14 July, he wrote: 'I don't feel myself to belong anywhere special, things change so quickly, don't they?'

But there were still a few moments of peace and happiness to be
snatched in Gavin's embattled life. Towards the end of May he had
made a nostalgic return to the land of his boyhood in Galloway in
the company of Richard Frere, partly to introduce a showing of
the film of *Ring of Bright Water* in Newton Stewart and make a
collection for the Edal Fund, partly to obtain fox cubs and wild
birds for the zoo park, and partly to look into the possibility of
acquiring from his brother Sir Aymer, who lived abroad, the decaying family mansion at Monreith and thereby re-rooting himself in
the country of his birth – a forlorn dream. Richard remembered
those few carefree sunlit days picnicking and birdnesting around
Elrig, Monreith and Wigtown Bay as the happiest he had ever spent
in Gavin's company. But the interlude was soon over; and when
Gavin returned to Kyleakin Island the storm clouds were still there,
but darker and closer than before.

During June Gavin's health had declined steeply. The headaches
returned – 'a plateau of discomfort,' as Richard put it, 'interrupted
by peaks of more severe pain.' Gavin bore this unremitting assault

without complaint; only the tight furrow across his brow gave any hint of the torment within. So it continued for a week or two, until one morning early in July Gavin's undiagnosed affliction made another, more terrifying leap, attacking a completely different part of his ailing frame without a moment's warning. Richard recalled: 'He was speaking to me on the telephone at some length when he suddenly halted in the midst of a sentence and cried "Oh, my God!" with a sharp intake of breath. I said urgently: "What is it, Gavin?" He could not answer, being speechless with pain.' Jimmy Watt was visiting Gavin at the time, and saw him turn deathly white as he half-turned in his chair, clutching his left thigh with both hands. Deep in his thigh he had suddenly felt a pain of a totally new order of ferocity – 'as though a six-inch nail had been hammered into the bone' – and though it subsided he still could not walk properly next day.

Thenceforth his thigh bone ached continuously, like his head, and he began to cough at nights, a deep, dry, hacking cough, and to suffer repeated thromboses. He went to the hospital in Broadford on Skye for more tests and X-rays, but again the doctors could find nothing wrong with him. This was no comfort to Gavin, who felt so desperately ill that he sought solace from any source that came his way. From a faith healer in Nairn he bought a herbal cure called Exultation of Flowers that was supposed to cure anything from colds to cancer; and when the Skye vet, Donald MacLennan, came to the island, Gavin asked him: 'If I went down on all fours and you examined me, do you think you could find out what is wrong with me?'

Gavin faced his illness with immense courage and dignity. He rarely if ever complained to anyone. He continued to oversee the work on the zoo park, write his book reviews for the *Observer*, entertain his friends and colleagues and fulfil his engagements. In the middle of July he travelled south to open Stuart Johnstone's new wildlife park at Mole Hall in Essex, stopping over in his London flat in the Boltons. Next morning, when Mrs Lamm came to tidy, she was shocked by his appearance.

'I can never forget that day,' she recollected. 'I knew there was something wrong but I didn't know what. "Will you be all right?" I asked him, and he replied, "Yes, don't you worry, I'll be all right." Then he said: "Is there anything you'd like to take from here? Take whatever you'd like to take." Why did he say that, I wondered? "Well, goodbye," he said, and I began to cry. "Now, now," he said, "don't worry, I'll be all right. I'm going somewhere and I'll be coming back. I'll see you tomorrow in the morning." But he didn't come back and I never saw him again.'

By the time Gavin returned to Kyleakin Island he was in dreadful shape. But two weeks later, though he was not in a fit condition to travel anywhere, he bravely insisted on fulfilling an engagement in Clydebank, where he was to introduce the film of *Ring of Bright Water* at the opening of a new cinema and leisure complex. It was the kind of occasion he would normally have avoided, but it had been agreed that a substantial part of the proceeds should be donated to the Edal Fund, and he was determined to fulfil his engagement even though he was wracked with pain. To the businessmen, city dignitaries and movie starlets among whom he uneasily mingled Gavin must have appeared an improbable, if not shocking apparition. He looked dreadfully weak and ill; and with his black glasses and trimmed, pasha-like beard, his white tie and tails, his gold and enamel Persian charm hanging from his neck on a long gold chain, and a rigid smile fixed on his face as if by plastic surgery, he looked more like an ambassador from some obscure oil-rich enclave in the Persian Gulf than the simple back-to-nature drop-out and otter man of *Ring*; none guessed the pain and the courage it cost him to be there.

Richard Frere met him in Kyleakin when he returned on the evening of 1 August, and was shocked at the sight of him. He could hardly walk and the effort to get out of the car made him cough and tremble. His face was grey, his eyes clouded by pain, and his forehead shining with sweat.

They went into the King's Arms Hotel and, seated in an inconspicuous corner of the bar, Gavin told Richard that he was now certain he had cancer. He brushed aside his friend's well-meaning protestations and reassurances. This was a very different matter from his previous cancer scare, he insisted. He was a dying man and he wanted Richard to accept the fact and help him make decisions here and now about the disposal of his property and the future of the island and the zoo park project. Richard, shocked and tearful, suggested nobody could be sure.

'Don't be stupid, Richard,' Gavin told him with a look of affection. 'That remark does your undoubted intelligence less than justice. We are *both* perfectly sure.'

★   ★   ★

Even now, Gavin continued to behave to the world at large as if all were normal. His unselfishness and lack of self-pity in these dark days were the hallmarks of a very strong and a brave man. On 4 August his secretary Jacky Hone, who had typed his last three books and answered all his fan mail for him, came for a few days' holiday on the island. 'He gave no indication whatsoever of how he must have been feeling,' she recalled. 'He was the perfect host and did everything to make me feel welcome. In the evenings he cooked dinner, refused to let me help in any way whatever, and was marvellously entertaining company. I remember Richard Frere came one evening and he was *so* funny and we all laughed and laughed till we cried. And the whole time he was *very* kind, considerate and affectionate. It was, for me, a perfectly idyllic few days and it is terrible to think, in retrospect, how ill he must have been, and that I didn't know.'

On 11 August Richard drove Gavin slowly and carefully to the hospital in Inverness. The tests were more probing than before, but for the first few days yielded no more information than all the previous examinations. Then, on the seventh day, the doctors finally arrived at a diagnosis. Gavin rang Richard from the public pay-phone in the hospital.

'You'd better come along as soon as you can,' he said, speaking in a very hoarse voice. 'The last blood test has confirmed my belief.'

At the hospital entrance Richard encountered Jimmy Watt, who had called in to ask after Gavin. He was 'white and shaken and quite broken up' by the news. They found Gavin in his room looking amazingly unconcerned, all things considered. He had cancer, he said, and didn't expect to recover. Jimmy had agreed to carry out his plans for the island and would also be his heir.

Richard left to go shopping for a few comforts for the patient. When he returned he found Gavin sitting up in bed, looking drawn and pale and impassive. Gavin asked him to pour out a couple of drinks. He had turned to brandy now after a lifetime of Scotch – the cancer had affected his tastebuds. Seeing that Richard was ill at ease, Gavin told him: 'Please don't let my situation embarrass you . . . I promise not to afflict you with unnecessary sentiment. Displayed emotion has always been considered bad taste in my family as I expect it has in yours. We don't cry easily or make a fuss over the inevitable.'

The doctors had told him that in six months he would be living on borrowed time, he said. He had a primary cancer in the lung and a secondary one in the femur, which accounted for the tremendous pain he had felt in his thigh. Radiation treatment might cure the femur, but there was nothing that could be done about the lung – the general condition, which had probably started with the first scare on his return from Tangier in 1967, was too far gone. Why previous X-rays had not revealed such an established and extensive cancer was a mystery, as were the headache and the thromboses.

'That's probably another death sentence,' Gavin said to Richard, 'to run concurrently with the first.' He fell silent and stared blankly in front of him. Richard detected a small hint of fear in his eyes. It would take a little while for a full comprehension of his situation to sink in. 'I hated to think what his thoughts would be on waking,' Richard was to write later.

During the next two days, while Gavin languished in his hospital bed, Richard was busy making contact with Gavin's family and friends to give them the grim news. The news became even grimmer when the specialist, urged by Gavin to give a completely full and frank prognosis of his condition, spelled out blow by dreadful blow the likely course the disease would take in the ensuing months – how the cancer would run rampant round the rest of his body, how eventually he would die either from total exhaustion or from massive internal haemorrhaging.

Gavin listened impassively to this catalogue of horrors. 'Charming!' he remarked when the doctor had finished. This sang-froid belied his inner feelings. In reality he was, as Richard noted in his diary, 'very sick at heart and afraid'.

Not long after the diagnosis Gavin asked if he could go home, just for a week, to tidy up his affairs. The doctors agreed readily enough – there was not much the hospital could do for him in his advanced state of disintegration anyway – and on 21 August he was out of bed and back in his Mercedes with Richard at the wheel, bound for his island home on the other side of Scotland.

It was, not surprisingly, an agonising homecoming. Sitting upright in the car made Gavin's neck and chest hurt abominably, and he felt every turn and bump in the road. They drove along Loch Ness, through glorious Highland landscapes now tinged with the rust and golds of early autumn, to Cluanie and Glenshiel. By this time Gavin was in great discomfort and fidgeting abominably.

He felt 'bloody awful', he told Richard, and asked if he could take over the wheel for a bit – a little light activity might do him some good, he reckoned, if Richard's nerves could stand it. It was his last chance to indulge in one of his greatest pleasures – never again would he be able to drive a car very fast among his beloved hills. In spite of his suffering he drove the big green Mercedes as fast and as skilfully as ever, overtaking a few tourist cars with all his usual squealing of tyres. But at the end of the glen he was pale and shaking and told Richard he'd had enough. Richard took the car on to the Dulverton house at Eilanreach, and they continued to the island next morning.

Jimmy Watt was there and helped him through his last, brief sojourn on the island for which he had had so many plans and dreams. No guests came to stay, and Gavin used the respite to try and clear his thoughts about his all too finite future. Sitting at Wordsworth's desk he toyed as best he could with his last professional task as a writer – a review of Alan Moorehead's *Darwin and the Beagle* for the *New York Times*. To various close friends he wrote announcing or confirming his terminal condition. One of the letters he received in reply was from a favourite cousin, Wendy Campbell-Purdy. It gave him much delight, for she had written simply: 'Hard cheese, Gavin.'

Though his headaches made prolonged concentration difficult, and he was obliged to sit for long periods without moving or even speaking, he wrote with great dignity and clarity of mind. To Lisa van Gruisen he wrote a letter (which she did not see until after his death) on 21 August:

Dearest Lisa,
    This is the most difficult letter I've ever had to write . . .
Since I last wrote I have been in hospital. The diagnosis and prognosis are blunt and unequivocal – I have an inoperable cancer, and a matter of months rather than years to live. I don't know where I shall be during the time that remains, but probably not much at Kyle Akin . . . Please don't feel bound to see me – I shall understand *completely* if you'd rather not.
    I wonder if this was some component of the urgency we both felt at Kyle Akin?
    My love and blessings.
    Gavin

To Kathleen Raine he wrote: 'I am asking you to accompany me in spirit.' He received in return not just a letter of sympathy but a moving expression of a love that had never died.

My dearest Gavin,

I will not say 'the doctors may be wrong' – though they may be – for death must come, however long delayed, and the marvel is that we are able to forget that time is so short at best. Suddenly all the truisms are truths – this world is only a moment, and home is elsewhere. But you and I, here, have seen the beauty of eternity, such beauty and such glimpses of joy . . .

I have never been able to say how much I love you – but surely you know. And at any time, anywhere, you have only to send a telegram and I will come. And at any time, any- where, you have only to think of me, and you will find me with you in thought and love.

Dear Gavin, I have tried for many years to put you from my mind, because you did not want me in your life; but I shall do so no longer – I will always be beside you, and you must never feel alone. Of course, it is only in the arms of God that we ever really are; but the people we love *are* the faces and disguises of God. So you have been for me always – whether for sorrow or for joy. And in the end, these things are not measured by pleasure or pain but by something else. Love, I suppose. There really is no other word . . .

I don't think it was ever as a 'lover' I desired your love. Something else – a more than brother. Anyway, I am here now for whatever you may ask of me or need.

Kathleen

Gavin's last letter to Kathleen gave vent to some of the bitterness he inwardly felt at the fate that had befallen him and the imminence of his premature extinction. He asked for some of her poems from past days, and perhaps some charm or talisman that might allay his fate or assist his passage through the pain of his remaining life. As well as sending him the poems she had already written, Kathleen wrote a new one – 'In Answer to a Letter Asking me for Volumes of my Early Poems' – one of the most beautiful and moving of all the poems that Gavin had inspired in her. It began:

> You ask for those poems of Paradise
> I wrote in heart's blood for your sake,
> Yet this, your ultimate request,
> Is made to me in bitterness.
> If hate were love, if love were hate
> It could not make our tale untold,
> It could not make our blood unshed . . .

The poem ended with an image that almost burned on the paper
– could stand, indeed, as a permanent memorial to the very spirit,
the life-stance of her doomed friend and loved one:

> Where Sandaig burn runs to the shore,
> Where tern and eider nest secure
> On their far island salt and bare
> Beyond our world of guilt and time,
> Yonder I have seen you stand,
> Innocent of all you bear:
> What can I say but 'you are there
> And I, and all, did we but know,
> Who weep and mourn in exile here.'

'I held up a mirror to Gavin through my poetry,' Kathleen told
me. 'He saw himself in the mirror of my poetry. And that finally
is what I have given Gavin, I suppose – immortality. I think "On
a Deserted Shore" [the long poetic sequence she was to write after
Gavin's death], to my sorrow, is the only poem I've written which
I'm absolutely sure has a life of its own, which will endure. So just
as he has given joy to others through his own sacrifice, so have I.
But look what it came out of – out of Gavin's death, my bereave-
ment, my guilt, remorse, everything – you see? What was suffering
to him has given happiness to others, and what was suffering for
me has raised the human spirit for others. It's such a mystery.'

As best he was able in his troubled circumstances, Gavin turned
his mind to the future of his estate and that of the handful of
people he regarded, in the absence of a family of his own, as his
dependants. John Lister-Kaye was due to arrive in a few days' time
to take up his duties as the permanent curator of the zoo park, and
Gavin hoped that he could still make it a going concern, though

he was aware that (as he wrote to a friend) 'the unfortunate fellow has given up a good job to take on something which now looks a bit precarious'. But Gavin's main task was to try to make things shipshape before his death – above all to sort out his finances so that he could settle his debts with honour and pass on a worthwhile inheritance to his heir, Jimmy Watt. This would not be easy. Money troubles had returned to haunt him, and there was no prospect of any large literary earnings coming in in the immediate future. His book about the White Island, the sequel to *Raven Seek Thy Brother*, would obviously never be written now. The real snag was that, as a bestselling author, he was his own capital – 'one's death is just the same as burning stocks and shares which yield £10 –15,000 per annum', he wrote to a friend. What could he do? Where, at this eleventh hour, could he turn?

He could think of only one solution to the problem. On 23 August he sent a long telegram, in Richard Frere's name, to his elder brother Aymer on the Greek island of Euboea, informing him of his illness and begging him to bail him out financially one last time.

It so happened that Aymer himself was lying at death's door when he received Gavin's letter, having suffered a cerebral thrombosis only a few minutes before the letter arrived. The news that his brother, like himself, was gravely ill distressed Aymer enormously. But it was some days before he could be transported from his Aegean island to a hospital in Athens, and some weeks before his doctors would allow him to worry about business matters. In the meantime Aymer's lawyer, Nassos Tzartzanos, sent an interim telegram: 'Of course will give all help required. All love and thoughts to Gavin. Doctor says no possibility of travelling in near future.'

On receipt of the telegram Gavin wrote a lengthy letter to Mr Tzartzanos, again in Richard Frere's name, outlining in greater detail the kind of financial help he had in mind from Aymer. The sum he was looking for, representing two years' outgoings, was £20,000 – over £150,000 in today's money. A precious week passed by before a second telegram arrived from Aymer's lawyer. The sum Gavin had in mind was impossible, he said, for it would involve the liquidation of all Aymer's company assets. 'After having discussed his brother's problems with me he suffered relapse which forced doctors forbid any business before you hear from me. Please give

Sir Aymer's love to his brother and assurance he will do all he can when he can.'

There was no magic solution to Gavin's problems. The best Richard Frere could do was to lie to him about the state of his bank account and give him the impression that he was better off than he really was, for there was next to nothing to bequeath.

As for his own future movements, these were inevitably shrouded in uncertainty. His neighbours across the water, Colin Mackenzie and his wife, had offered to make the two-roomed wing of their home at Kyle House available to him, with one room for a nurse and the other for him, so that he might spend his dying days in care and comfort. Gavin himself, however, spoke of eventually transferring to the London Clinic 'for greater ease of communication'. The only certain thing was that he had to return to the hospital in Inverness on 27 August for about ten days for chemotherapy and other treatment.

Richard Frere again drove him to the hospital. In the week since he had last seen him Gavin's decline had become so marked that he greatly doubted he would live for anything like six months. Even supported by cushions in the back of the car he experienced intense pain for most of the ride, as Richard could see when he looked in the rear-view mirror. 'I realised that he knew beyond any doubt,' Richard wrote afterwards, 'that this was his last sight of the wild country which he had loved and understood so well.' There would be no coming back.

FORTY-ONE

The tunnel

Get rags, get rags, all angels, all
Laws, all principles, all deities,
Get rags, come down and suffocate
The orphan in its flaming cradle,
Snuff the game and the candle, for our state
– insufferable among mysteries –
Makes the worms weep. Abate, abate
Your justice. Execute us with mercies!

GEORGE BARKER, *The True Confession of
George Barker* (1950)

Gavin had a room in the small private ward of the hospital. He was able to sit up and usually wore a bright red polo-necked pullover. Propped up in bed, a hawk-like and cadaverous figure, with his black glasses and his raddled lungs he resembled nothing so much as an uncanny incarnation of the hawk that bore his name.

His mind was still active and he managed to read a little now and then. On his bedside table he kept two of his favourite books of poetry – both by friends, both with gorgeous jackets of Moroccan gilt-tooled leather. One was the *Collected Poems* of Roy Campbell, the other *The Hollow Hill* by Kathleen Raine. As best he could he also continued to fill in his appointments diary. The entries record the major medical incidents and the comings and goings of close friends and relatives and those who had urgent business with him. They reflect his determination, in spite of everything, to fulfil his responsibilities and maintain some sense of order and purpose in his life – not to give up, not to let go. 'It was very typical of Gavin,' Peter Janson-Smith was to recall, 'that he had, in all the years I had known him, become hysterical, childish and totally unreasonable at every minor disaster that had befallen him, but accepted the final doctors' verdict with total calm and dignity.' Gavin's diary also provides a measure of his progressive decline – each day the pressure on the ballpoint pen grows feebler, the marks on the paper fainter, finally becoming no more than pale, spidery traces, after which the pages fall blank.

On his first day back in hospital, 27 August, Gavin recorded that 3.5 litres of fluid was removed from his right lung. The next day he noted the arrival in Inverness of John Lister-Kaye and spent an hour with him enthusiastically going over the plans for the zoo park, and covering sheets of paper with sketches of the animal enclosures and skilful caricatures of the animals that were to inhabit them. Later his old SOE friend, Hamish Pelham-Burn, arrived, followed by his Stowe chum Anthony Dickins, who was moved to tears by Gavin's courage and good cheer. When Dickins asked what he thought was the greatest achievement of his life, Gavin replied: 'Having a new species of otter, Lutrogale perspicillata maxwelli, named after me.' On 29 August Gavin's infinitely steadfast and resourceful literary agent, Peter Janson-Smith, arrived from London to discuss the literary prognosis and worked out a scheme by which Gavin would, if he had the strength and the time, start work on a final book, the autobiography of a man dying of cancer, to be called *The Tunnel* – a title based on a waking vision to which he had been subjected in the past few days. If he did not live to complete the task, Richard Frere would finish it to the best of his ability. In the event, the book was never even started; all that can be gleaned about Gavin's last creative concept is encapsulated in what he was able to impart to Richard about it from his hospital bed. Recently, he said, he had had a recurring vision. He was walking down a long, dark tunnel with openings here and there in its side. At first he saw shadowy figures in the openings, whom he thought he recognised, but the further he travelled down the tunnel the less real was the world he glimpsed outside, till eventually he barely gave it a glance, but stared ahead into the distance where the tunnel, now oddly secure and comforting for him, seemed to terminate in velvety dark.

Had Gavin been granted the time to write this book it might, perhaps, have been his finest work, the one his true admirers had been waiting for. Freed from commercial restraints and the need to conform to the expectations of his audience and the conventions of society, and with the experiences of his life intensely heightened by the imminence of his death, he might have written as he had sometimes spoken in the late hours over a dram with his friends –

passionately, brilliantly, his intellect and emotion fused in a burning celebration of his interior vision.

But it was not to be. The ceaseless struggle against devouring death was all. His diary continued the bald record of the progress of the battle. 'Pain moved to left lung,' he reported on 30 August; 'Very bad night.' On 2 September he recorded his continuing descent into Purgatory: 'More veins – 1 ltr – unable walk.'

It was now a matter of great urgency for Gavin to finalise his will. Raef Payne, who was to be his executor and joint literary executor (with Peter Janson-Smith), flew up to see his old friend immediately on his return from a holiday abroad, while John Butters, Gavin's Edinburgh solicitor, came to the hospital to draw up the document. To Jimmy Watt he bequeathed all his personal possessions (with certain named exceptions) 'wherever they may be – and with the hope that he may wear my signet ring and the stone I wear as a neck pendant'. Three antique stone and ivory figurines and a rock crystal cross were bequeathed to his much-loved god-daughter Katie McEwen; the Order of the Garter tiepin, which had been given to his uncle, Lord James Percy, by his uncle's grandparents, went to Kathleen Raine; Richard Frere received the Mercedes saloon; Andrew Scot the 12-bore Cogswell & Harrison shotgun and a Parker fountain pen 'to remind him that he can write'; Dr Tony Dunlop received a miniature Indian silver Communion set; and Mrs Lamm's motherly care as Gavin's London housekeeper was rewarded with a gift of £500. After various other smaller bequests Raef Payne, Gavin's greatly trusted and respected friend of many years, was given the choice of any objects of personal property not listed elsewhere in the will.

Gavin added various codicils. One concerned the future of the zoo park on Eilean Ban, which was so close to his heart. 'I should like the collection to be known as the Gavin Maxwell Scottish Wildlife Park,' he decreed, 'of which James Watt will be the owner and John Lister-Kaye the Curator for as long as he chooses to remain.' Another codicil concerned the manner of his interment. 'I wish my body to be cremated,' he stated, 'and my ashes to be buried on the site of Sandaig house (now being razed). A large boulder to be placed over the ashes, inscribed either by letter-cutting or by insertion of a bronze plate, "Beneath this stone, the site of Camusfeàrna, are buried the ashes of Gavin Maxwell, b. 15th July 1914, d. – ." The landlord of the ground has already given his permission, and as a forestry road is now being constructed to Sandaig the transport of a large boulder should present no problems.'

So it was done. It seemed that the only thing left unresolved was the last of the two dates on the bronze plate. But Gavin's friends could not let him slip away without exploring all last avenues of succour and hope. John Lister-Kaye arranged for Stuart Lennox, one of Britain's leading chest specialists, to come to Inverness to examine Gavin. In the short period of waiting before Lennox's arrival, with all important business tied up and little left to occupy his still alert and active mind, Gavin relaxed somewhat. He still hoped to be able to leave hospital and move in to Kyle House on 8 September, perhaps even go rabbit shooting on nearby Pabay Island with John Lister-Kaye if he was up to it.

On 3 September he was buoyant enough to pen his last written work. It was not a serious work, but under the circumstances it is miraculous that he was able to write it at all. Though the cancer was eating into his skull it had evidently not affected his brain, which was as creative as ever. This last offering, called 'Rabbits', was a hastily scribbled fragment of verse which represents, if nothing else, a defiant two-finger gesture directed against fate and the blind and hostile heavens – and also, perhaps, through the medium of the hyperactive creatures, the 'symbol of fertility and inexhaustible virility' that are the poem's subject, an affirmation of the author's belief in life and love. From the jaws of death Gavin's wit and sense of fun bubble resolutely through.

> Rabbits
> Have 2 habits,
> Breeding
> And feeding
> (The purpose of the 2nd
> Is just to keep them fecund
> And is not meant to interrupt
> The tupping and the being tupped).
> The feeding is clean,
> The breeding obscene –
> In précis
> It is mécis;
> The doe is in an interesting condition

The same day as her parturition,
For passing the buck
Is an unknown habit
In the female rabbit;
And so is any undertaking
To make an honest buck
– They need no making.

Now rabbit is a curious word
Whose origin I've lately heard;
Robert, as a human name,
Is the origin of same
(Just why I don't pretend to know;
The dictionary tells me so):
The archetypal randy man
(Casanova also ran)
A symbol of fertility
And inexhaustible virility
(See things like Playboy Bunnies' legs
And rabbitry in Easter Eggs).
One thing is sure, we share with Bobby
The only really worthwhile hobby.

Next day Stuart Lennox arrived from London, examined Gavin
and his clinical records, and pronounced his second opinion. It was
every bit as bleak as the first had been. The cancer was rabid and
ravaging every part of Gavin's body. Before long he would go
blind and then lose the use of his legs. He might last at the most
three months under sedation. There was nothing that could be done
to effect a cure. There was no hope. From that moment forward
Gavin knew that his life had no value, and that the sooner it ended
the better. He pinned his hopes on his circulatory system, which was
in tatters. There seemed a reasonable prospect that a cerebral or cor-
onary thrombosis might bring a quick and painless end to his suffering before the disease progressed to its ultimate horrific conclusion.
A likely candidate for the killer role soon presented itself – an enormously distended blood vessel, a thick, raised ridge, which pulsated
violently like some throbbing reptile in his groin.

  'This might finish me, mightn't it?' Gavin asked Richard Frere
hopefully in a hoarse voice. Richard had seen his own father die of

something similar and told Gavin so. Gavin gave an audible sigh of relief.

On Saturday 6 September, Gavin was wheeled into the theatre for an operation to drain his lungs. It proved a difficult business and it caused him much pain. Afterwards Richard visited him. He found Gavin sitting up in bed with a tube connecting his chest to a half-filled bucket of bloody fluid on the floor.

Detecting Richard's feeling of revulsion, Gavin muttered in a gurgling voice: 'Isn't this awful? I could have done without this.' It was too late for meaningful contact, and after ten minutes of silence Gavin suggested that Richard come back the next day – the doctors thought he might be a little better then. 'When I shook his cold limp hand,' Richard recalled, 'I was pretty sure it was for the last time.'

'He has the mark of death upon him,' Richard wrote in his diary for that day. 'I do not think we can hope for better things now, except perhaps mercy.'

That night, when the nurse bade Gavin goodnight, he said to her: 'It's not goodnight, nurse, it's goodbye.' And in the early hours of Sunday morning, 7 September 1969, that brave, frail, wayward heart stopped still. He was only fifty-five. Icarus had not fallen to earth but burned up in space.

People reacted in different ways to the news. For Richard, who had been closest to him at the end, there was the feeling of guilt and remorse that is normal among those who have attended a dying loved one. Sir Aymer Maxwell was still in hospital in Athens when he heard the news, and was greatly shaken by it. Too ill to travel home, he sent a telegram: 'Deeply grieved and worried because unable be near beloved brother.' Kathleen Raine received the news in Dublin. But she knew before she heard. 'Over my head on the evening before he died, a V-shaped flight of curlew had flown low, reminding me of Gavin's beloved greylag geese . . . And as that formation of curlew flew low over me, I had thought, "Gavin!"' Kathleen's natural response took a poetic form. Within hours of Gavin departing this earth she had written this simple and deeply felt elegy (from 'On a Deserted Shore'):

> The faint stars said,
> 'Our distances of night,

These wastes of space,
Sight can in an instant cross,

But who has passed
On soul's dark flight
Journeys beyond
The flash of our light.'

I said, 'Whence he is travelling
Let no heart's grief of mine
Draw back a thought
To these dim skies,

Nor human tears
Drench those wings that pass,
Freed from earth's weight
And the wheel of stars.'

On the morning that Gavin died Terry Nutkins, who was camping at Sandaig with his young wife, was looking down from a hill as a bulldozer levelled the burnt-out shell of Gavin's house. That same morning Jimmy Watt was driving to Wales when he experienced a sudden splitting headache such as he had never experienced before or since – a pain so severe that he had to ask his fiancée to take the wheel. Later a friend rang to say that Gavin had died. 'I felt then that I had been left alone in a desolate world,' he recalled afterwards. 'Gavin had been better than the best of fathers. But with his death I felt as though he had abandoned me. I was in the middle of the mourning process for a long time after.'

John Lister-Kaye, newly arrived at Kyleakin Island, was just beginning to get to grips with his duties when the news came that his employer and mentor was dead. He noted in his diary: 'After breakfast Richard Frere phoned to say that at 4.30 this morning Gavin died under heavy sedation in Inverness hospital. Indeed a sad moment.' All day the phone never stopped ringing. The BBC and the national newspapers telephoned for confirmation of the news. So did the local police, who had been receiving a stream of enquiries from well-wishers in the neighbouring towns and villages. From far and wide telegrams and phone calls of sympathy and commiseration poured into the tiny island, a great many of them from Gavin's readers. 'We must continue here as best we can,' John noted at the end of a nightmare day. 'Gannet very lively and strong and feeding well . . .'

Lisa van Gruisen arrived in London from Paris for her pre-arranged rendezvous with Gavin on Kyleakin Island and was stunned to learn that she had arrived too late. 'I was knocked sideways by his death,' she recalled. 'It was as though a lover had died. For months afterwards I couldn't go into a bookshop in case I saw one of his books on the shelves.' Mrs Lamm was at Paultons Square when she heard the news. Anthony Lincoln came down the stairs and said to her: 'You knew Mr Maxwell, didn't you? Well – he's dead.' Mrs Lamm was speechless; then she burst into tears. 'I cried and cried,' she said. 'It was so sad. He was still so young to die.'

I was in France, and was shocked and saddened to hear of Gavin's death on the BBC morning news. I had always regarded him as a great man, in his idiosyncratic and sometimes contrary way; quite the most remarkable person I had ever met. But though he had died before his time, I was glad that at least he had been spared the anguish of encroaching old age, of loneliness and insecurity, the final defeated retreat from a remote and rugged island home that failing powers would have one day forced him to abandon. I rang Peter Janson-Smith, and he confirmed the details. He was puzzled, as many people were, that death had come so soon – though having watched Gavin drink most of a bottle of brandy and smoke most of a packet of cigarettes in the hour he was with him in hospital, Peter could see he was not going to do anything to prolong his life. Gavin had died within three weeks of being told he had six months to live. There was a hint, a faint whiff in the air, that his death had not been entirely natural. John Lister-Kaye, for example, felt inclined to wonder whether Gavin had jumped, perhaps, or been gently helped over the edge. It was a reasonable question, given the circumstances. John Lister-Kaye recalls having a conversation with Gavin the day before he died in which Gavin discussed with him various ways of ending it all, including injecting air into his veins and tying a tourniquet.

The autopsy did not entirely dispel the doubts, though it did confirm the extraordinary extent of the cancer. In addition to the original primary in the lungs there was a second primary in one of the kidneys, together with five secondaries throughout the body which had deeply pitted the skull – hence the headaches – and all but eaten up the cervical vertebrae, so much so that it was just hanging by a thread. If Gavin had had the strength to turn his head sharply sideways he would in all probability have broken his neck.

However, the likelihood of euthanasia being secretly administered to any patient in a hospital in Presbyterian Scotland during the period in which Gavin died is extremely remote; and Richard Frere, the last visitor to see Gavin alive, is convinced that suicide was no less unlikely. He wrote to me:

> I am disinclined to believe it was suicide. My own belief is that Gavin was prepared to stick it out despite his educated guess at what was in store for him. Both Eustace [Maxwell] and I saw the death certificate and Eustace took it with him. Neither of us were in the least surprised at its conclusions [that Gavin had died of a massive coronary thrombosis]; for my part I had seen the bulging blood vessel in the groin, which I took to be a main artery as it inflated with each heartbeat like a bicycle tube being pumped up. I am satisfied that Gavin saw this as a likely cause of his early death, and had no intention of expediting it . . . You may take it from me, if you wish, as one who had a daily and concentrated dose of the man for over three years, that Gavin Maxwell died of natural causes.*

The obituaries were extensive. The *Daily Telegraph*, while acknowledging that Gavin was a greatly accomplished writer, rued the success of *Ring of Bright Water* – if it had been less successful 'perhaps Gavin Maxwell would have written more and better travel books'. The *Scotsman*, in a lengthy tribute ('Master of prose who lost his sanctuary'), came closest to an in-depth appraisal:

> With Gavin Maxwell die many unattained ideals, many unfulfilled projects, and no one knows how many unwritten books

---

* To the question of whether Gavin's death was due to suicide, euthanasia or natural causes was later added (in circumstances which would undoubtedly have given Gavin himself cause for prolonged laughter) a fourth possibility. In September 1991 the police on Skye received an allegation, emanating from California, to the effect that Gavin had been murdered by a blow on the head. It was only when Richard Frere presented conclusive evidence to the contrary that the police abandoned the difficult plan of exhuming Gavin's cremated remains for forensic tests.

. . . The carefree existence his vast public imagined him to enjoy sent hundreds of people searching the Highlands for cottages like Camusfeàrna. Even without the benefit of otters, the remote and primitive life became an ideal, almost a mystique, which struck a chord in thousands of people trapped in an urban rat-race . . . Gavin Maxwell is dead, and the final chapter will never be told – not, at least, in his own words. His best-known books tell of his own life, and yet he gave away very little of his inner self. He managed, somehow, to conceal behind his impeccable prose much that might have thrown light on a mysterious and elusive personality. Yet he managed, without the aid of sensationalism, to beguile thousands of non-readers into sitting down and reading a book. And that's no mean achievement.

Gavin's publishers issued a statement which spoke of 'the warmth of his response to animals and to the beauty of the natural world', and his corresponding aversion to the modern world and urban preoccupations, science and technology. 'Brave, humorous and loved for his vulnerability by his closest friends, he turned his sensitivity to best advantage: his books gave, and will continue to give, pleasure to countless readers.'

Looking back over all those years it seems to me that perhaps Gavin's greatest achievement was to make out of his own life an amazing drama, a theatrical *pièce de résistance*, in which he was the protagonist on a stage of his own making, playing a part he improvised as he went along. If he came to a dull bit he would wind it up and create another extraordinary scene, which could literally be a scene – a quarrel – or an adventure like the wrecking of the *Polar Star*. Whereas a playwright or a novelist would simply write this down on paper, Gavin had to act it out and *then* write it down. So his life was a succession of dramatic crises, and when in the end the drama turned to tragedy it took a classically Greek form: a hero who was an aristocrat and a nearly-great man (but flawed in some crucial regard) was struck down by the gods for the sin of hubris – and the hubris in Gavin's case was the work which had brought him fame and fortune, *Ring of Bright Water*.

On Thursday 18 September 1969, Gavin Maxwell's ashes were brought to Sandaig in a small wooden cask stowed in the boot of his green Mercedes driven by Richard Frere – three weeks almost to the day since Gavin had taken the wheel of that same car for the last time and driven down Glenshiel like a bat out of hell. Sandaig that September morning was at its finest – a clear, singing sky, a dry east wind, purple heather abounding, the trees just touched with autumn gold, the Skye hills still green across the dancing waters of the Sound. The house which had been Gavin's home, the hub of the *Ring of Bright Water* legend, had gone utterly, bulldozed flat, the fire-blackened rubble buried out of sight in a great covered pit in the dunes. Amongst the wind-bent marram grass on a ridge of the dunes, staring out across the sea into the round void of the shining sky, stood Kathleen Raine, who had arrived from Canna by sea on the boat of Gavin's ex-sharking skipper, Bruce Watt. Around the disturbed ground where the house had once stood a small assembly of friends and relatives gathered to pay their last respects. The sky was eggshell blue, the waterfall roaring in full voice. 'I was quite overcome by the beauty and grief of it,' Richard recalled, 'and moved closer to my wife and little daughter, sure anchors against a perverse desire to shout for joy in this place of graves.'

The open-air service ended when Jimmy Watt laid the casket containing Gavin's ashes in the grave and Kathleen Raine placed a bunch of rowan berries from the tree upon it; then a tapestry of flowers designed by Terry Nutkins – a mass of pinks surrounding the image of an otter picked out in white carnations – was set down over the place where Gavin's ashes had been laid to rest, the exact spot where the desk on which he had written *Ring of Bright Water* had once stood. The day ended, as Gavin would have wished, with a few companionable drams in Raef's croft at the sea's edge; and not until the sun began to set across the Sound did the assembly begin slowly to drift away.

'The sky had turned apricot at the edges and royal blue overhead,' Richard Frere wrote, 'and the twilight fell like dew upon Camusfeàrna and its ghosts. I gave but one backward glance at the darkening field ringed by the flat white sea and thought still of my dear and worthy friend as my feet stumbled on the rough track which led back to the uncaring world.'

> Sleeper beneath the rowan-tree,
> You have become your dream,
> Sky, shore, and silver sea.

I returned to London in time for a memorial service arranged by
Raef Payne and Peter Janson-Smith and held on 23 September
before a much larger gathering of Gavin's friends and relatives in
the Church of St Paul in Covent Garden. The programme spoke
of Gavin's 'love of beauty, especially the beauty of the natural world
and all its creatures; his gift of sharing this love with others through
the artistry of his words; his courage, his humour, his friendship'.
At the end of the service, conducted by the Eton Chaplain, a
soprano sang the 'Pie Jesu' from Fauré's *Requiem*, her voice ringing
out in the silence, and then fading, leaving only the silence.

Only Teko was now left of the denizens of the Camusfeàrna
idyll. Of this lone animal's fate Donald Mitchell, who was John
Lister-Kaye's assistant at the Kyleakin Island zoo park, later wrote:

> The night after I heard of Gavin's death, while I was attending
> to Teko, I realised that there was now little future for the otter
> – the man who loved him had died, and the animal's future
> was bleak. That night, standing on top of the island looking
> up at the multitude of stars, I made a silent prayer to Gavin
> to take Teko – I felt strongly it would be right. Only a few days
> after Gavin's ashes had been laid to rest in the ground, and
> exactly two weeks after his death, Teko disappeared and was
> later found dead at the bottom of his pool. It was presumed at
> the time that he had drowned after suffering an epileptic seizure
> while swimming. I felt this was very odd – an *otter* drowning?
> Ever since then I've had a strange feeling that Gavin's 'spirit' did
> return to take Teko with him. Who knows?

Teko was buried at the foot of a great boulder on the top of the
White Island and his name was carved into the face of the rock above
his grave: 'TEKO 1959—69'. A lonely but appropriate memorial,
surrounded by sea on all sides, to the last of the *Ring of Bright Water*
otters.

And so it was ended. In the short space of twenty months everything had vanished, swept away as if it had never been: the man,
the otters, the house, the vision of Camusfeàrna. Only the ring
remained, the waterfall ceaselessly tumbling, the burn winding
round to the sea.

Avalon was lost. Or was it, then, truly gained at last?

The Watcher at the Door

All through the night I watched the ruined door,
Intent, as gamblers watch the fall of dice;
Awaiting verdict, prisoner at the bar.
Shadows crossed it, once I heard a voice.

At dawn a mountain hind emerged alone,
Quick step and sure as with some purpose known,
Some will that animated the unmarrowed bone,
For through her ribs I saw the lichened stone.

At noon a naked form was there;
A watcher, indistinct, began
To follow as it turned and ran
Seaward over the shore.

At dusk a broken wheel appeared
Held by a hand I could not see,
And I knew that someone whom I feared
Had discovered an empty room in me.

GAVIN MAXWELL, 1951

EPILOGUE

What infinitely precious thing
Did we seek along the shore?
What signature,
Promise in pearly shell, wisdom in stone?
What dead king's golden crown, tide-worn,
What lost imperishable star?

KATHLEEN RAINE, from
'On a Deserted Shore'

In the spring following Gavin's death I set off on a six-thousand-mile circumnavigation of the coastline of Britain as a member of a conservation project called Operation Seashore. The weather had been unkind at the start, and we sailed northwards along the east coast in blizzards and icy rain all through April and into May. Only when we had reached our most northerly position and passed through the much-feared tide rips of the Pentland Firth – the so-called 'Merry Men of May' where the North Sea meets the Atlantic – did the weather at last turn benign.

For a month we nosed along the north coast of Scotland and down through the Hebridean Sea beyond Cape Wrath. The sun beat down on us, daylight hardly ended, and we turned as brown as buccaneers. We had three tenders with us on our motor yacht – a small dinghy and two inflatables; with these we periodically abandoned our mother-ship and scurried off to explore the scatter of rocks and islands beyond our bow. Throughout the long hours of daylight we motored and rowed to hidden coves and rock-guarded islets looking for bird colonies and sea caves and whatever we could find, the boat's bow butting the swell of the plankton-green sea, the gulls in our wake screaming above the bubbling of the outboard's exhaust. Rocks and islets, shimmering in the sun, appeared insubstantial, atomised. Dark torpedo shapes nosed through the crystal water towards the weedless rocks – salmon, maybe, or sea trout.

So we nosed our way south towards the Isle of Skye, past the clamorous cliff-face bird slums, the seals basking on the rocks, the buzzards wheeling on stiffened wings between the basalt crags, the ocean swell exploding in the sea caves with a gunshot boom, and finally, on Midsummer Day, the last day of the halcyon spell of anticyclonic calm that had blessed our voyage through the Hebridean Sea, we crept between Scalpay and the Crowlin Islands and entered the Narrows of Skye at Kyle Akin. And there stood the White Island just as I had remembered it, the stubby lighthouse proud on its rock, and the house huddling close under the low, rocky ridge.

I lowered a boat and paddled ashore, and walked up to the house. Three young men who were strangers to me were dismantling that grand interior where Gavin and I had once talked of the past and the future, of hopes and dreams, long into the small hours. The Icarus stood against the mantelpiece waiting to be crated up. Wordsworth's desk had already gone, and Sir Walter Scott's settee, too. I had the feeling that I had stumbled on to the set of a play that had ended its run; the actors had departed and now the props were being bundled up and carried away. The two deerhounds, Dirk and Hazel, looking listless and decrepit, staggered to their feet and stared at me blankly. Owl, I gathered, had found a foster home in Devon and her wing had mended. Most of the other birds and animals had long gone, together with their keepers. A young drama teacher by the name of Ian Alexander, who had met Gavin the previous summer and stayed at Sandaig while he repaired the *Polar Star*, had bought Kyleakin Island not long after Gavin's death, hoping against the odds that he could keep alive the concept of the Gavin Maxwell Wildlife Park. But the White Island that day struck me as chill and forlorn; even the ghosts had gone, and I was glad to row back to the yacht and raise anchor and sail on until, with a sharp turn south into Kyle Rhea, the island was lost to view and to memory.

The sky that day was of the purest royal blue – not a cloud, not a hint of rain, the barometer as steady as a rock, the air pungent with the warm land smells of bog myrtle and young fern. A kind of festive spirit overtook us. For me, it was as if I were entering the region of a half-forgotten dream; for as we advanced down the

Sound of Sleat towards the open sea the component parts of the landscape began to resolve themselves into a once-familiar scene. Ahead lay the Isle of Eigg, and craggy headlands sliding into the position in which I had remembered them. On the port bow rose a small white lighthouse on a little island of rock and moss where wild sea otters used to have their holts. Perhaps they did still. I searched the sea through field glasses, but saw only the shearwaters scurrying low over the water, angling their wings to the crests and hollows of the waves as they followed the contours of the ocean.

We turned past the promontory of the furthest island and entered the bay. I recognised it, of course; I remembered every rock and tree of it. It was Camusfeàrna. Someone put out an anchor and it sank through the translucent water and threw up a puff of sand as it hit the bottom. We dropped an inflatable over the side and I climbed down into it with our Australian skipper. The frothy white line of our wake led to a tiny bay and a beach of dazzling white sand. As I leaped ashore, the skipper said: 'Nice little old spot.'

'Yes,' I replied, and added: 'I've been here before, you know.'

It was here that for one long winter I had held fort against the storms, with two otters for company and driftwood for fire. Now it was hot and still, yellow flag iris blazed in a patch of damp bog, bright orange lichen glowed on the grey rocks; the burn was almost dry after a month of drought, the waterfall only a whisper of its former torrential self. The place was more beautiful than I had remembered it, but it had changed beyond recall.

The house had gone, obliterated so completely that there was little indication it had ever existed. Not a brick or a tile was left; just a square patch of fine rubble and sand on which the grass and nettles were already spreading. I drew my foot through the rubble but no fragment of the past came back to me. A large block of unhewn stone marked the spot where Gavin's ashes had been laid to rest. Near the burn stood a small stone cairn where Edal was buried, surmounted by a brass plaque with words inscribed by Gavin in commemoration of her: 'Whatever joy she gave to you, give back to nature.'

I crossed the burn and walked up the steep track down which I used to carry potatoes, fuel and other supplies, lurching into the wind on fitful black nights. It was still a hard climb up the first stretch and I paused to get my breath back at a kind of natural platform where the track bent sharply left. I looked down. The boat rode quietly at anchor in the bay; sounds of laughter drifted up to me – a radio playing, a splash as someone dived off the stern. I turned to climb higher and, as I did so, I caught sight of something curious and yet oddly familiar. In the very centre of a flat, grey rock, for all the world like some kind of votive offering or portent, lay a black animal dropping, still fresh in that hot sun. I looked at it and at once recognised the ground-up fishbone texture. An otter had preceded me up this track. It must have scampered ahead of me only a few minutes before, paused at the same spot as I had and left this memento on the rock.

I was suddenly immensely glad. I called out in the silence, uttering my poor imitation of a range of otter cries, but no grey-brown shape came bounding through the bracken towards me, I saw no furry round muzzle peering quizzically over the long grass, heard no chirruping response. I had hardly expected to. But I was grateful for that simple assurance of the continuity of life at Camusfeàrna. Years before, the wild sea otters in the bay had used the house as a place where they could drop by for an egg or an eel on hunting trips away from home. And now, in spite of everything that had subsequently happened here, it was clear that otters still roamed the shores and hills of Camusfeàrna, that in the end nothing had changed, the wilderness prevailed, only time had happened. It was an affirmation.

I turned back and with a lighter heart retraced my steps towards the sea and the westering sun.

ACKNOWLEDGEMENTS

Janet Adam-Smith (Mrs Carlton); Ian Alexander; Michael Alexander; A.G. Archer; Colonel James M. Ashton; Penelope Biggs; Colin Booty; Beryl Borders; Michael Bott and the University of Reading Archives Department; Ion Braby; Richard Branson; Patrick Brodie; Hamish Brown; Rupert Bruce-Mitford; Charles and Brigid Burney; Lieutenant-Colonel The Lord Burnham, JP, DL; John and Viv Burton; John Butters; Mrs Cameron-Head; Archie Campbell CMG; Elias Canetti; Mrs Capel-Cure; Suzanne and André Charisse; George Clarke; David Cobham; Mark Cocker; Dominic Cooper; Alan Cormack; Rupert Corry; David Cox; Dr Peter Crowcroft; Michael Cuddy; Marie Curry; Richard Curtis; The Right Honourable Earl of Dalhousie, Kt, GCVO, CBE, MC, LL.D; The Countess of Dalhousie; Natalie Davenport; Gwenda David; John Davies OBE; Del and Mary Davin; Lady Patricia Dean; Anthony Dickins; R.Q. Drayson, DSC; Lord Dulverton, CBE, TD, DL; Dr Tony Dunlop; Dr Bob Earll; Hetta Empson; Rede Fitzgerald-Moore; Joan and Richard Frere; David Gascoyne; Tex Geddes; Monk Gibbon; Morag Gillies; Phillip Glasier; Lady Hersey Goring; Jesse Graham; Carol and Francis Graham-Harrison; Colonel Iain Grant; Lady Tulla Gubbins; Philippa Gugen; Dr Christopher L. Hall; Michael Halpert; Bruno de Hamel; Lady Elizabeth, Duchess of Hamilton; Dr Walter Hamilton; Lavinia and David Hankinson; Audrey Harris; Duff Hart-Davis; Sir Rupert L. Hart-Davis; Dr Havard; John K. Hay; Fiore de Henriquez; Hertford Society, Hertford College, Oxford; Andrew and Margaret Hewson; John Hillaby; Professor Matthew Hodgart; Stanley Hodgkinson; Jacky Hone; Patrick Howarth; Patrick G. Hunter; Elspeth Huxley; Major Ronald Ingleby-Mackenzie, JP; Dr Hamish Ireland; Margaret Jackson; Peter Janson-Smith; Colin Jones; Oliver Graham Jones; Peter Kemp, DSO; John Frere Kerr; Tony Kilmartin; Raymond Knight; Gavin Lambert; Reginald and Mrs Lamm; T.A. Landry; R.D. Lea; Derek Leach; Patrick Leigh-Fermor; Sir Anthony Lincoln, QC; Marjorie Linklater; Magnus Linklater; Sir John Lister-Kaye; Longmans, Green & Co.; Dr John Lorne Campbell; Alastair Macdonald; Dr James L. McDougal; Lady Brigid McEwen; John McEwen; Colin Mackenzie, CMG; John MacLaughlin; Donald John MacLennan, MBE; Constance McNab; Jack Macrae; Lady Marjorie Marling; Barbara

Mattheson; Dr Harrison Matthews, FRS; Sir Michael Maxwell, Bart; Donald Mitchell; Robert F. Mole; W.G. Morison; Giuseppe Moro; Annabelle Morton; John Mowat; Michael Murray; Pat Nash (née Bachelor); Dr John Nesfield; Daphne Neville; Philip Ninds; Terry Nutkins; Ron Parker; David Tree Parsons; Raef Payne; Hamish Pelham-Burn; Stanley Peters; Margaret Pope; Michael Powell; Kathleen Raine; Katie Rigge; Chris Riley; Lady Elizabeth, Countess of Scarborough; Scots Guards Records Office; Michael and Cherry Scott; Sir Peter and Lady Philippa Scott; Barrie and Pat Shaw; Vera Shaw Stewart; S.J.H. Sherrard; Colonel Cuthbert Skilbeck; Anthony Smith; W. Gordon Smith; Special Forces Club; Terence Spencer; Brian Stephan; Irene Stirling; Magda Stirling; John Stockwell; Stowe School and Old Stoic Society; Eddie Strutt; Lady Joan Stuart-Smith; Wilfred Thesiger, CBE, DSO; Dr Chris Tidyman; Christopher Turner (Headmaster, Stowe School); Lisa van Gruisen; Graham Watson; Jimmy Watt; Philip Wayre; Sir Peter Wilkinson, OBE, DSO; Jane Williams; Richard and Anne Williamson; John Winter; Justin Wintle; Christopher M. Woods (SOE Advisor, Foreign and Commonwealth Office); Gavin Young; Professor Christopher Zeeman, FRS, Principal of Hertford College, Oxford.

BIBLIOGRAPHY

BOOKS BY GAVIN MAXWELL
Harpoon at a Venture (US title *Harpoon Venture*), 1952
God Protect Me from My Friends (US title *Bandit*), 1956
A Reed Shaken by the Wind (US title *People of the Reeds*), 1957
The Ten Pains of Death, 1959
Ring of Bright Water, 1960
The Otters' Tale, 1962
The Rocks Remain, 1963
The House of Elrig, 1965
Lords of the Atlas, 1966
Seals of the World, 1967
Raven Seek Thy Brother, 1968

BOOKS REFERRING TO GAVIN MAXWELL
Adams, Richard, *The Adventures of Gavin Maxwell*, n.d.
Alexander, Michael, *The Reluctant Legionnaire*, 1956
Blakey, Joseph, *Coles Notes: Ring of Bright Water*, 1972
Botting, Douglas, *Wilderness Europe*, 1976
— *Wild Britain*, 1988
Brown, Mick, *Richard Branson: The Inside Story*, 1992
Channon, Paul, *The Natural History of Otters*, 1985
Cocker, Mark, *Loneliness and Time: British Travel Writing in the Twentieth Century*, 1992
Frere, Richard, *Maxwell's Ghost*, 1976
Geddes, Tex, *Hebridean Sharker*, 1960
Hamilton-Hill, Gordon, *SOE Assignment*, 1973
Knighton, C.S., *Kyleakin Lighthouse: A Short History*, 1982
Lister-Kaye, John, *The White Island*, 1972
Mackenzie, R.F., *Escape from the Classroom*, n.d.
Milne, Alasdair, *The Memoirs of a British Broadcaster*, 1988
O'Connor, P. Fitzgerald, *Shark-O!*, 1953
Powell, Michael, *Million-Dollar Movie*, 1992
Raine, Kathleen, *The Lion's Mouth*, 1977
— *Collected Poems 1935–80*, 1981

Randall, Deborah, *The Sin Eater*, 1989
Scott, Peter, *The Eye of the Wind*, 1961
Thesiger, Wilfred, *The Marsh Arabs*, 1964
— *Desert, Marsh and Mountain: The World of a Nomad*, 1979
Tomkies, Mike, *Between Earth and Paradise*, 1976
Watkins, Anthony, *The Sea my Hunting Ground*, 1954
Watson, Graham, *Book Society*, 1980
West, Nigel, *Secret War: The Story of SOE*, 1992
Young, Gavin, *Return to the Marshes*, 1977

ARTICLES – SELECT LIST

Anderson, Marshall, 'Camusfeàrna Revisited', *Glasgow Herald*,
   10 February 1990
Botting, Douglas, 'The Man who Wrote *Ring of Bright Water*', *Sunday
   Telegraph*, September 1985
Crumley, James, 'Deep Waters: The Story of Gavin Maxwell' *Scotland.
   on Sunday*, 26 May 1991
Dickins, Anthony, 'Gavin Maxwell: A Postscript', *London Magazine*,
   September 1976
Frere, Richard, 'Ring of Bright Memory', *Scotsman*, 8 April 1989
MacLeod, John, 'The Ring that Became a Vicious Circle', *Scotsman*,
   2 June 1990
Rogers, Byron, 'Back to Paradise', *Radio Times*, 8 September 1979

SOURCE NOTES

CHAPTER 1
The House of Elrig
Correspondence and interviews: Gavin
  Maxwell (Kyleakin 1968); Sir John
  Lister-Kaye; Sir Michael Maxwell,
  Bt.; Lady Mary Maxwell (via
  Lavinia Hankinson); Elizabeth,
  Duchess of Hamilton; Cherry Scott;
  Dick Curtis (letter to Cdr Burney)

CHAPTER 2
The House of Elrig
Correspondence and interviews: Gavin
  Maxwell op.cit.; Anthony Dickins;
  John Nesfield; John Hay; Ion Braby;
  Col. James M. Ashton; Patrick
  Brodie; A. G. Archer; Christopher
  Turner

CHAPTER 3
The House of Elrig
Stowe School archives
Correspondence and interviews: Gavin
  Maxwell; Anthony Dickins; John
  Hay

CHAPTER 4
Ring of Bright Water
Raven Seek Thy Brother
Gavin Maxwell 'Game Book 1932–5'
Gavin Maxwell interview 1968
Anthony Dickins diary 1935
Evelyn Waugh, *A Little Learning*
Correspondence and interviews:
  Patrick Brodie, John Hay, Col.
  James M. Ashton; Raymond
  Knight; R. F. Mole; Archie
  Campbell CMG; W. G. Morison;
  John Frere Kerr; Rede Fitzgerald

Moore; John Mowat; David Cox;
  Rupert Bruce-Mitford; Prof. Sir
  E. C. Zeeman, FRS

CHAPTER 5
Raven Seek Thy Brother
Gavin Maxwell interview 1968
Stowe School archives
Scots Guards archives
Evelyn Waugh, *Diaries*
Gavin Maxwell–Peter Scott
  correspondence

CHAPTER 6
Harpoon at a Venture
Raven Seek Thy Brother
Scots Guards archives
SOE archives
W. E. Fairbairn, *All-In-Fighting*, 1942
SOE (Canada) Training Lectures
Gavin Maxwell SOE lecture notes
Gavin Maxwell 1968 interview
Gavin Maxwell–Peter Scott
  correspondence
Correspondence and interviews: Prof.
  Matthew Hodgart; Dr James
  MacDougall; Dr Hamish Ireland;
  Tex Geddes; Hamish Pelham-Burn;
  Derek Leach; Peter Kemp; Suzannne
  Charisse; Vera Shaw Stewart; Sir
  Peter Wilkinson; Col. Cuthbert
  Skilbeck; John McEwen; Chris
  Woods, BBC TV; Mrs
  Cameron-Head

CHAPTER 7
Harpoon at a Venture
Interviews: John Hillaby; John Winter;
  Kathleen Raine; Irene Stirling

John Hillaby, 'Highland Jaunts' (Folio
    Society)
Anthony Watkins, *The Sea My
    Hunting Ground*, 1952

CHAPTER 8
Harpoon at a Venture
Peter Scott, *The Eye of the Wind*
John Hillaby, 'Shark Hunting', *Picture
    Post*, 21 Sept 1946
Interviews: Tex Geddes; Dr Harrison
    Matthews; John Burton; Dr
    Havard; Dr Bob Earll, Marine
    Conservation Society: 'The Basking
    Shark: Its Fishery and Conservation'
Nicholas Russell: 'The Mantle of the
    Monster', *Independent*, 31 July 1989

CHAPTER 9
Ring of Bright Water
Gavin Maxwell–Raef Payne
    correspondence
Correspondence and interviews: Raef
    Payne; Magda Stirling; Hamish
    Pelham-Burn

CHAPTER 10
Kathleen Raine, *The Lion's Mouth*,
    1977
— *The Year One*, 1952
Julian Maclaren Ross, *Memoirs of the
    Forties*
Dan Davin, *Closing Time*
Anthony Dickins, 'Gavin Maxwell: A
    Postscript', *London Magazine*, Sept
    1976
— 'Tambimuttu and *Poetry London*,
    London Magazine, Dec 1965
— 'Fitzrovia 1934–56' (lecture notes,
    n.d.)
Gavin Maxwell–Raef Payne
    correspondence
Correspondence and interviews:
    Anthony Dickins; Kathleen Raine;
    Lavinia Hankinson; Natalie
    Davenport; Tomas; Elias Canetti;
    Jane Williams

CHAPTER 11
Ring of Bright Water

Kathleen Raine, *The Lion's Mouth*,
    1977
— *The Year One*, 1952
Gavin Maxwell–Raef Payne
    correspondence
Gavin Maxwell correspondence: Lady
    Mary Maxwell; Sir Aymer Maxwell
Gavin Maxwell interview 1968
Correspondence and interviews: Raef
    Payne; Lavinia Hankinson; Sir
    Michael Maxwell

CHAPTER 12
God Protect Me from my Friends
Gavin Maxwell interview 1968
Gavin Maxwell–Raef Payne
    correspondence
Gavin Maxwell, 'I was Spurred by
    Publisher's "No"', *Smith's Trade
    Circular*, 24 May 1952
New Statesman, 1950–52
Interviews: Janet Adam–Smith; Earl
    of Dalhousie; Kathleen Raine; Tex
    Geddes; Gwenda David; Beryl
    Borders; Sir Rupert Hart–Davis;
    BBC Archives ('The Critics')

CHAPTER 13
God Protect Me from my Friends
A Reed Shaken by the Wind
Wilfred Thesiger, 'The Marshmen
    of Southern Iraq', *Journal of the
    Royal Geographical Society*, Sept
    1954
Mark Longman correspondence
    (Longman archives)
Gavin Maxwell–Raef Payne
    correspondence
Interviews: Graham Watson; Lady
    Brigid McEwen; Wilfred Thesiger;
    Tomas

CHAPTER 14
Wilfred Thesiger, *The Marsh Arabs*,
    1964
— *Desert, Marsh and Mountain*,
    1979
— 'Marsh Dwellers of Southern Iraq',
    National Geographic Magazine, Feb
    1958

Gavin Maxwell–Raef Payne
correspondence
Interview: Wilfred Thesiger

CHAPTER 15
A Reed Shaken by the Wind
Gavin Young, *Return to the Marshes*,
1977
Gavin Maxwell–Raef Payne
correspondence
Interviews: Wilfred Thesiger; Gavin
Young

CHAPTER 16
Ring of Bright Water
Gavin Maxwell, 'Technique of Travel
Books', National Book League, 6
Dec 1960
Richard Meinertzhagen, Diary
Mark Longman correspondence
(Longman archives)
Interviews: Gavin Young; John Burton
Press reports on Iraq marshes:
Independent on Sunday, 16 June 1991;
Sunday Times, 16 June 1991;
Observer, 28 Feb 1993, 7 March 1993

CHAPTER 17
Ring of Bright Water
Kathleen Raine, *The Lion's Mouth*, 1977
Gavin Maxwell interview 1968
Gavin Maxwell–Raef Payne
correspondence
Douglas Botting correspondence
Interviews: Raef Payne; Kathleen
Raine

CHAPTER 18
Ring of Bright Water
Kathleen Raine, *The Lion's Mouth*,
1977
Gavin Maxwell–Mark Longman
correspondence (Longman
archives)
Interviews: Beryl Borders; Raef Payne;
Kathleen Raine

CHAPTER 19
The Rocks Remain
Ring of Bright Water

Kathleen Raine, *The Lion's Mouth*,
1977
Graham Watson, *Book Society*, 1980
Gavin Maxwell, Wilfred Thesiger,
Mark Longman correspondence
(Longman archives)
Douglas Botting–Gavin Maxwell
correspondence
Mrs V. Lamm, 'Can you cook
sausages?'
Interviews: Kathleen Raine; Anthony
Dickins; Sir Anthony Lincoln QC;
Graham Watson; Peter
Janson-Smith;
Daily Express, 5 March 1958

CHAPTER 20
Ring of Bright Water
Raven Seek Thy Brother
Douglas Botting, *Wilderness Europe*,
1976
Gavin Maxwell interview 1968
Douglas Botting correspondence
Timothy Green, notes for *Life*
magazine interview 1963
Correspondence and interviews: Raef
Payne; John McEwen; Jimmy Watt
Gavin Maxwell–George Hardinge
correspondence (Longman archives)

CHAPTER 21
Lords of the Atlas
The Rocks Remain
Gavin Maxwell, 'Lords of the Atlas'
synopsis (Longman archives)
Douglas Botting, 'La Mission
Maxwell au Soudan', 1959
Gavin Maxwell correspondence with
Douglas Botting, Marjorie
Linklater, Raef Payne, Jimmy Watt,
Mark Longman
Timothy Green, *Life* interview,
op.cit.
Correspondence and interviews:
Margaret Pope, Gavin Young

CHAPTER 22
The Rocks Remain
Kathleen Raine, *The Lion's Mouth*, 1977
— 'Envoi' (*The Hollow Hill*, 1964)

Alasdair Milne, *Memoirs of a British Broadcaster*, 1988
Gavin Maxwell, Sandaig diary 1960
Gavin Maxwell correspondence:
Oliver Jones; Mary Davin;
Constance McNab; Kathleen Raine
Correspondence and interviews:
Donald MacLennan; Marjorie
Linklater; Mary McLeod; Constance
McNab

CHAPTER 23
Ring of Bright Water
Michael Powell, *Million-Dollar Movie*, 1992
Timothy Green, op.cit.
Gavin Maxwell fan mail files
Gavin Maxwell correspondence:
George Hardinge; Mark Longman;
Vera Canetti; Constance McNab
Correspondence and interviews: Gavin
Maxwell 1968; Michael Powell;
Anne Williamson; Mike Tomkies;
Dr Peter Crowcroft; Margaret Pope

CHAPTER 24
The Rocks Remain
Gavin Maxwell, 'FLN Report' (Algeria, 1961)
— Moroccan Notebook, 1961
Gavin Maxwell correspondence: Paula
MacDonald; Jimmy Watt;
Constance McNab
Douglas Botting, *Wilderness Europe*, 1976
Correspondence and interviews: Gavin
Maxwell; Margaret Pope; Oliver
Jones

CHAPTER 25
The Rocks Remain
Interviews: Peter Janson-Smith;
Michael Cuddy; Terry Nutkins;
Jimmy Watt
Jimmy Watt correspondence: Douglas
Botting; Constance McNab
'Shooting incident in Sandaig Bay' (Longman archives)

CHAPTER 26
The Rocks Remain

Kathleen Raine, *The Lion's Mouth*, 1977
Interviews: Lavinia Hankinson;
Kathleen Raine; Peter Janson-Smith;
John Hillaby
Lavinia Hankinson, personal archive
Gavin Maxwell correspondence:
Lavinia Renton (Hankinson); Raef
Payne; Jimmy Watt
Daily Mail, November 1961, 2 Feb 1962

CHAPTER 27
The Rocks Remain
Gavin Maxwell correspondence:
Lavinia Renton; Nicholas Renton
Lavinia Hankinson, personal archive
Douglas Botting, personal archive
Correspondence and interviews:
Lavinia Hankinson; Marjorie
Linklater
Home magazine

CHAPTER 28
The Rocks Remain
Lavinia Hankinson, personal archive
Correspondence and interviews: Gavin
Maxwell 1968; Lavinia Hankinson;
Terry Nutkins; Stanley Peters;
Kathleen Raine
Longman archives
Gavin Maxwell correspondence:
Anthony Dickins; Lavinia Renton;
Sir Alan and Lady Lascelles
Michael Cuddy (GME archive)
Jimmy Watt–Constance McNab
correspondence

CHAPTER 29
Raven Seek Thy Brother
Gavin Maxwell, 'Report on sinking of
Lady Delfi' (typescript 1963)
— 'An author's life' (typescript 1963)
Gavin Maxwell correspondence:
Anthony Dickins; Constance
McNab; Bruno de Hamel; John
Guest; *New Statesman*
Timothy Green, op.cit.
Correspondence and interviews: Gavin

Maxwell 1968; Ian Alexander;
Hamish Brown; Lavinia Hankinson
Hamish Brown, Sandaig diary 1964

CHAPTER 30
Raven Seek Thy Brother
Richard Frere, *Maxwell's Ghost*, 1976
Correspondence and interviews:
W. Gordon Smith; Donald
MacLennan; Sir Anthony Lincoln
QC; Bruno de Hamel; Richard Frere
Gavin Maxwell correspondence: Peter
Janson-Smith; Michael Cuddy;
Bruno de Hamel; Constance
McNab
The Times, 'Report on Alliata Case',
February 1965
The Times, 'She will not Cease from
Mental Fight' (Kathleen Raine
interview), 18 April 1992
The Oldie, Kathleen Raine interview,
March 1993
Kyleakin Lighthouse Cottage
Inventory

CHAPTER 31
Raven Seek Thy Brother
Richard Frere, *Maxwell's Ghost*, 1976
Gavin Maxwell correspondence:
Bruno de Hamel; Jimmy Watt;
Giuseppe M.
Correspondence and interviews: Peter
Janson-Smith; Bruno de Hamel;
Michael Cuddy; Richard Frere; Raef
Payne
Bruno de Hamel, GME finance file
Longman archives
Julian Jebb, 'Natural Introvert', *Sunday
Times*, 3 Oct 1965

CHAPTER 32
Raven Seek Thy Brother
Gavin Maxwell, 'The Heritage of Fear'
(typescript)
Gavin Maxwell correspondence:
Jimmy Watt; Bruno de Hamel;
Giuseppe M.; Robin McEwen;
Constance McNab; Penelope Biggs
Richard Frere: *Maxwell's Ghost*, 1976
— GME files

Correspondence and interviews: Jimmy
Watt; Brian Stephan; Charles (Jesse)
Graham; Justin Wintle; Richard
Branson; John Burton; Monk
Gibbon; Margaret Pope
Longman archives
Mick Brown, *Richard Branson: The
Inside Story*, 1992
RSPCA (North Africa), 'Report on
Titish'

CHAPTER 33
Raven Seek Thy Brother
Kathleen Raine, *The Lion's Mouth*,
1977
Richard Frere, *Maxwell's Ghost*, 1976
Geoffrey Moorhouse, Introduction to
Lords of the Atlas, Century
paperback, 1983
Longman archives
Gavin Maxwell/GME
correspondence: Kathleen Raine;
Alec Guinness
Correspondence and interviews:
Kathleen Raine; Beryl Borders

CHAPTER 34
Raven Seek Thy Brother
Richard Frere, *Maxwell's Ghost*, 1976
— GME files
Gavin Maxwell correspondence:
Jimmy Watt; Beryl Borders
Interviews: Wilfred Thesiger; Beryl
Borders; Richard Frere

CHAPTER 35
Raven Seek Thy Brother
Richard Frere, *Maxwell's Ghost*, 1976
Interviews: Andrew Scot; Magda
Stirling

CHAPTER 36
Richard Frere, *Maxwell's Ghost*, 1976
Gavin Maxwell interview 1968
Dr Tony Dunlop interview

CHAPTER 37
Raven Seek Thy Brother
Richard Frere, *Maxwell's Ghost*, 1976
— GME files

Gavin Maxwell 1968 diary
Gavin Maxwell interview 1968
Gavin Maxwell correspondence: Mrs
   Payne; Dr Ellis Stungo; Beryl
   Borders; Peter Scott; Peter
   Janson-Smith; Brian Stephan
Correspondence and interviews: Raef
   Payne; Col. Colin Mackenzie; John
   Burton; Lord Dulverton
GME accounts

CHAPTER 38
Douglas Botting, Kyleakin tapes,
   notes and diary 1968
Gavin Maxwell interview 1968

CHAPTER 39
Richard Frere, *Maxwell's Ghost*, 1976
— 1969 diary
— GME files
Kathleen Raine, *The Lion's Mouth*,
   1977
— 'Message to Gavin' (*The Lost
   Country*, 1972)
John Lister-Kaye, *The White Island*,
   1972
Gavin Maxwell 1969 diary
Gavin Maxwell correspondence: Katie
   McEwen; Lisa van Gruisen
Correspondence and interviews:
   Kathleen Raine; Richard Frere; Sir
   John Lister-Kaye; Jack Macrae III;
   Fiore de Henriquez; Lisa van Gruisen

CHAPTER 40
Richard Frere, *Maxwell's Ghost*, 1976
Kathleen Raine, 'In answer to a letter
   asking me for volumes of my early
   poems' (*The Lost Country*, 1972)
Gavin Maxwell correspondence: Mrs
   V. Lamm; Lisa van Gruisen;
   Kathleen Raine; Sir Aymer Maxwell
Correspondence and interviews: Mrs
   V. Lamm; Donald MacLennan;
   Jacky Hone; Kathleen Raine

CHAPTER 41
Richard Frere, *Maxwell's Ghost*, 1976
John Lister-Kaye, *The White Island*,
   1972
Kathleen Raine, 'On a Deserted
   Shore', 1973
— 'Northumbrian Sequence' (*The
   Year One*, 1973)
Gavin Maxwell 1969 diary
— Will and Codicil
Correspondence and interviews:
   Richard Frere; Peter Janson-Smith;
   Anthony Dickins; Dr Tony Dunlop;
   Jimmy Watt; Lisa van Gruisen; Mrs
   V. Lamm; Raef Payne; Donald
   Mitchell; Sir John Lister-Kaye
Longman archives
Scotsman, 10 Sept 1969

EPILOGUE
Douglas Botting, *Wilderness Europe*,
   1976

INDEX